R. MacGregor Dawson, Professor of Political Economy at the University of Toronto, undertook the preparation of this biography in 1950, on the request of the Literary Executors of the late Prime Minister. Dr. Dawson had already written a classic of Canadian scholarly and general literature in his *The Government of Canada*, and had twice won the Governor-General's Award for academic non-fiction. He was given a completely free hand by the Executors in writing the book; they did "not desire a purely laudatory work, but a truthful account as written and interpreted by one who is in general sympathy with Mr. King and his work and career."

Dr. Dawson was given access to the enormous Mackenzie King archive, roughly estimated to comprise two million pages of material, including correspondence, state papers and records, drafts and documents, Christmas cards, dinner-seating arrangements, notes jotted on odd scraps of paper, the King family letters, and an extensive personal diary, maintained for fifty-seven years. This diary has never been opened to the public, and, indeed, Mr. King directed that it be destroyed on completion of the biography. The sorting and filing of papers and the transcription of the diary occupied a skilled research staff for seven years. Large grants from the Rockefeller Foundation have been used to meet the expense of this work.

The death of Dr. Dawson occurred suddenly in the summer of 1958, after he had completed his reading of the proofs of Volume I, but before it had gone to press. In addition to the work of organization and research, he had already written large portions of the second volume, and arrangements have been made for the completion of the great work to which he had devoted seven years of major achievement.

WILLIAM LYON MACKENZIE KING

A Political Biography

William Lyon Mackenzie King, 1900

William Lyon

MACKENZIE KING

A Political Biography

*

1874-1923

R. MacGregor Dawson

UNIVERSITY OF TORONTO PRESS

TO MY WIFE

without whose courage and devotion I could not have completed this book

PREFACE

LATE IN 1950, the Literary Executors of the late Mr. Mackenzie King, W. Kaye Lamb, F. A. McGregor, J. W. Pickersgill and Norman A. Robertson, decided to make his papers available for the preparation of a biography. This was intended to take the place to some degree of the memoirs which he had himself contemplated but on which for various reasons he had made virtually no progress whatever. Accordingly, funds which had originally been given by the Rockefeller Foundation to Mr. King to aid him in the preparation of the memoirs were transferred to the Literary Executors to be used by them in meeting the necessary expenses arising from the biography. This re-grant was later increased by the generosity of the Foundation.

When I was asked to write Mr. King's life, I was given free access to the enormous collection of papers which had been entrusted to the Literary Executors under the terms of his will. The research and writing which were involved in the assignment proved to be much heavier than they or I had expected, and hence only now is the first volume in print. Much preliminary work, however, has been completed, and other volumes are expected to follow in due course.

The conditions of writing the book which were accepted by both of us have made my task as author a very pleasant one. The Literary Executors at the outset expressed the hope that so far as possible Mr. Mackenzie King might be allowed to tell his own story. An effort was therefore made to lend both colour and a sense of reality to the narrative by using liberal excerpts from the diary and the correspondence, both of which present much material which has not hitherto been accessible. The Literary Executors and I also agreed that I should have a "completely free hand in writing the book," though they were to be able at any time to make whatever representations to me they might wish, on the understanding that these were in no sense to be construed as directions. They did "not desire a purely laudatory work, but a truthful account as written and interpreted by one who is in general sympathy with Mr. King and his work and career." These are my own words which I used in an attempt to express our interchange of views; and they give a fair summary of the preliminary conversations. I am pleased to add that the understanding has been faithfully observed by the Literary Executors in spirit and letter at all times; nor can I recall a single "representation" being offered.

The book is to a large extent a co-operative effort. The Mackenzie King archive has been roughly estimated to comprise a million and three-quarters to two million pages of material, most of which is in the files. It is naturally made up of documents of all kinds, but its volume and variety are unusually great, caused in large measure by Mr. King's saving and painstaking habits. It includes, for example, correspondence, both in and out; state papers, records, and memoranda; important drafts and documents; and even such trivial things as Christmas cards, dinner seating arrangements, and notes jotted down on odd scraps of paper. To these must be added, of course, the official debates and papers; and the King family letters, which present a cross-section of social history probably unrivalled in Canada. Most valuable of all is the Mackenzie King diary, which exists with varying degrees of detail for fifty-seven years. The early records are brief and sketchy; the later ones may run to as much as 1,200 or 1,300 pages of typescript a year. The use of the diary is subject to certain restrictions on purely personal matters under the terms of Mr. Mackenzie King's will, but except for these, which are generally quite unimportant, I have been allowed to take free and uncensored extracts. Mr. King incidentally was an excellent diarist in most respects—very reliable as to facts, though inclined when expressing opinions and analysing motives (his own or others) to be swayed by prejudice and wishful thinking. For the most part, however, his factual material is exceptionally accurate, recorded fully, and set out with restraint and an occasional touch of drama. For major events, therefore, these records almost attain the status of state papers, and they open many chapters hitherto generally closed in Canadian public life.

The greatest preliminary step taken by the Literary Executors was unquestionably to put the diary in readable form, and this was especially necessary when applied to those years when the diary was written by Mr. King's own hand. Much of the diary is handwritten, but growing volume and increased pressure on time eventually forced Mr. King to dictate his diary from day to day.

The preparation of a biography made the arrangement of material an unavoidable and urgent task; for its bulk and variety and lack of system inevitably restricted its usefulness. In June, 1954, the Literary Executors (following a suggestion in Mr. King's will) signed an agreement with the Government of Canada under the terms of which the King papers were placed immediately in the custody of the Dominion Archivist: they are to become the property of the Crown on the twenty-fifth anniversary of Mr. King's death (July 22, 1975). The diary, again in accordance with Mr. King's wishes, was not included in the transferred material. My gratitude to the staff of the Archives for the filing and sorting of the papers is obviously enormous, and it is even greater to those research students who have been working with me more directly to promote the writing of the book. These have lightened my labours beyond measure by supplying me with extensive memoranda and comments on certain topics in Mr. Mackenzie King's life and on numerous political, social, and economic trends which have exerted powerful influences upon it. It is the simple truth to say that without such able assistance this book could not have been written nor could so generous a use of the unique material at hand have been at all possible.

Adequate thanks to all my helpers cannot be contained in a preface, but some acknowledgment of their very extensive labours must be attempted. The papers generally were filed and catalogued under the supervision of Professor F. W. Gibson, who was directly responsible for originating the system, and he was assisted throughout by Miss Jacqueline Côté. The dreary task of deciphering the written diary and supervising the transfer of its extensive contents to typescript was undertaken by Mr. Fred A. McGregor. It was a most trying assignment, carefully and painstakingly performed.

The preparation of memoranda, from which a large part of the text was prepared, was entrusted to a number of research students for varying periods of time. The one whose contribution was the greatest, whose memoranda ranged over the widest field, and whose part in the preparation of the manuscript was the most extensive was again Professor Gibson, whose exceptional knowledge, energy, and ability were always at my service. He also ransacked the Borden papers and diary, the Dafoe papers, the Laurier papers, the Sifton papers, the Fielding papers, the Foster diary and other similar sources for possible material which might augment that in the King archive, and I am grateful not only to him but to the trustees of those documents who have made them available to us, and have given permission to use them here. Dr. James Eayrs contributed comprehensive memoranda on Canadian external and Imperial relations; Mr. F. A. McGregor others on Mackenzie King's relations with labour, the Rockefeller family, and the Foundation; Mr. Alec Lane on Mackenzie King's financial and fiscal policies; Miss Jacqueline Côté and Mr. Harry Walker on King's work in the Department of Labour.

I have also held numerous interviews in Canada, Great Britain, and the United States with many people who had immediate contact with Mr. Mackenzie King, and who were consequently able to add material of a somewhat different and more personal kind.

My secretaries, first Miss Lillian Breen and later Mrs. Helen Hodgson, have each made their own special contributions. Miss Breen was associated from the beginning with the project of a King biography, and she had collected a substantial amount of preparatory data even before I had undertaken the book. She has supplemented secretarial qualities of a high order with a particular knowledge derived in large measure from her own experience as secretary to the late Mr. King. Mrs. Hodgson joined the staff in the book's later stages. She has checked the innumerable quotations and references, and has done much of the general preparation of the manuscript for the press, a kind of work for which she was specially qualified.

I should like to mention also the services of Miss Francess Halpenny who, in addition to her normal duties as Editor of the University of Toronto Press, has taken on the textual revision and criticism as a special assignment.

I am pleased to acknowledge my debt to the Parliamentary Library and the Canadian Archives, who have been invariably courteous and responsive to all the demands which have been made on them from time to time.

Finally, I must express my gratitude to my wife and to Miss Eileen Burns for their assistance in reading proof. This acknowledgment is obviously a most inadequate reward for what must always be a tedious and uninteresting task.

My opening sentence regarding a co-operative venture was therefore not lightly made; and I take this opportunity of thanking everyone for their part in helping to bring the book to the point of publication. I hope that as I am in a sense the spokesman for all these people, I have been able to make adequate use of the material they have been good enough to place at my disposal. One cannot forget, of course, how recent is the life of the man whose biography is being attempted, and with it the contemporary character of the material available for the book's preparation. This alone renders impartial appraisal almost impossible, and the securing of full evidence equally so. But it is only fair to add that at the same time the King diary and correspondence are extensive and illuminating, and this mitigates some of the severity of the problem of dealing with very recent events. I must plead the same excuse as that advanced some years ago by the late J. W. Dafoe of the *Winnipeg Free Press* in his appreciation of Laurier. The aptness of the quotation has, if anything, grown with the years:

> Ne'er of the living can the living judge,
> Too blind the affection or too fresh the grudge.

ROBERT MacGREGOR DAWSON

May, 1958

ACKNOWLEDGMENTS

THE LITERARY EXECUTORS wish to acknowledge the kindness of the many persons who have given permission for quotations from unpublished correspondence.

Manuscript materials referred to are held in the King Papers unless so noted.

Acknowledgment is also made of courteous permission for quotation of passages from: *Theodore Roosevelt and the Japanese-American Crisis* by Thomas A. Bailey (Stanford University Press); *Reminiscences* by the Marchioness Curzon of Kedleston (Hutchinson & Co. (Publishers) Ltd.; Nelson, Foster & Scott Limited); *John D. Rockefeller, Jr.* by Raymond B. Fosdick (Harper & Brothers); *Colony to Nation* by A. R. M. Lower (Longmans, Green & Company, Toronto); *Unrevised and Unrepented* by Arthur Meighen (Clarke, Irwin & Company Limited); *An Autobiography and Other Essays* by G. M. Trevelyan (Longmans, Green & Co. Limited, London).

CONTENTS

CONTENTS

WILLIAM LYON MACKENZIE KING

A Political Biography

CHAPTER ONE

EARLY LIFE

WILLIAM LYON MACKENZIE KING was born in Ontario, at Berlin, now known as Kitchener, on December 17, 1874. His four grand-parents had been born in Scotland and had come to Canada within the period 1820–34, forming a part of the great surge of immigration which was to last until the middle of the century. All belonged to the same sturdy, industrious, Presbyterian stock, and in one of them, at least, the intellectual vigour and independence characteristic of the Scot had begun to assert themselves. The notable contribution made by Scotland to Canada is in no way disparaged by the reflection that this little group of four and their issue have probably left a deeper imprint on Canadian life than any similar group in her history.

Mackenzie King's paternal grandfather, John King, was the son of an Englishman who had married a Scottish girl of some substance and come to live near Fraserburgh, Aberdeenshire. Here John King was born in April, 1814. At the age of 19 he enlisted as a gunner in the Royal Artillery and in 1834, following a period of training at Woolwich, he was sent to Canada. He was stationed at Kingston at the time of the 1837 Rebellion, and after some years was made a bombardier and placed in charge of a small detachment at Prescott. He was later moved to Grosse Isle, Quebec. In 1840 he became en-gaged to Christina Macdougall, who had come from Scotland with her family ten years earlier. Her father and especially her brother were opposed to her marriage with a soldier despite the fact that he bore an excellent reputation certified by his minister and his com-manding officer. Two letters written by John to Alexander Macdougall asking for the hand of his daughter show not only a good education but also both firmness and dignity and suggest that the suitor was by no means a poor match. The marriage was performed in April, 1841, at

3

Prescott. In less than two years John King died of consumption, aged 29, and was buried in the Military Cemetery at Quebec. His son of the same name, the father of Mackenzie King, was born four months later on September 15, 1843.

The most remarkable of Mackenzie King's immediate forbears was his maternal grandfather and namesake, William Lyon Mackenzie, born at Springfield, Dundee, on March 12, 1795. Mackenzie's ancestry was pure Highland; both his grandfathers had fought at Culloden, and one of them had shared Charles Stuart's exile for some years.[1] Daniel, the father of William Lyon Mackenzie, was a weaver by trade, and had married Elizabeth, also a Mackenzie from Glen Shee, in 1794. He died when William Lyon was less than four weeks old. As the boy grew up, he proved to be a good student at school and a voracious reader, but early occupations as clerk and in a business of his own gave little scope for his energy and his literary gifts. At the age of 25 he emigrated to Upper Canada. Here he went into business, but after four years he took up printing and began the publication of a newspaper, the *Colonial Advocate*, first in Queenston, and then a few months later in York, now Toronto. In 1822 he married Isabel Baxter, who was also a native of Dundee. They had thirteen children, the last of whom, Isabel Grace, was the mother of Mackenzie King.

From the time Mackenzie began to publish his newspaper his life was a perpetual struggle, for he was a born reformer and he found the Upper Canada of his day was badly in need of reform. The situation in the colony is well known to every student of Canadian history. The executive government, the legislature, the judiciary, business, society, the church, were in large measure under the control of a select few, the so-called Family Compact, who used their position, power, and patronage to advance their own interests and those of their friends. Mackenzie lost no time choosing his side: indeed, his natural sympathy for the unfortunate, his passion for freedom and justice, his hatred of privilege, and his furious resentment at the selfishness and intransigence of the ruling group left him no genuine alternative. He threw himself into the fight without restraint and drew generously upon his ample powers of eloquence and invective. He found many to support him, yet his lack of moderation did much to weaken his cause, for he not only drove his natural enemies into a frenzy, but also antagonized many of the reformers as well. In 1828 he was elected to the Legislative Assembly from the County of York; this was the first of seven successful contests, a number of which were rendered necessary by his repeated expulsion from the Assembly because of alleged libels on that body. In 1834 Toronto elected him as its first mayor.

For years Mackenzie fought for reform in and out of the House with an energy and a conviction which bordered on fanaticism. But his natural impatience and his repeated failure to make any substantial impression on the strongly entrenched positions of the enemy drove him to seek more extreme measures. Eventually when active rebellion broke out in Lower Canada in the latter part of 1837 and the insurgents there appealed to the Upper Canadians for help, Mackenzie decided to strike a blow in their support. He collected a few hundred partially armed men and attempted to march on Toronto with the double purpose of seizing military supplies and replacing the oppressive government with one more amenable to popular control. After one small skirmish, his force was dispersed and the revolt collapsed.

Mackenzie became a fugitive, but although a reward of £1,000 was offered for his apprehension, he succeeded in reaching the United States. There he helped to organize an invasion of Canada which also proved to be a fiasco. In 1839 an American court found him guilty of a breach of the neutrality laws of the United States, and he was fined and sentenced to eighteen months' imprisonment. He served over one-half of his term in a Rochester gaol before he was released, only to enter upon a life of poverty and hardship. His health was impaired by his prison experience, his occupation was gone, and he frequently was unable to provide his family with adequate food and fuel. He succeeded, however, in making a meagre living in various ways, his writing being his chief support.

The life of Mackenzie the reformer, turbulent yet exciting, had had its rewards, for he had been a recognized leader called upon to play a conspicuous and even romantic part in a great popular movement. But the life of Mackenzie the exile was thoroughly unhappy, marked by tragedy and misfortune, and unrelieved by any compensations. He was forced to spend the prime of his life in the United States: twelve years of penury and eclipse, of physical hardship for his family, of bitter frustration for Mackenzie himself. The denial of even a small portion of material success made life grim and distressing, but the

5

real humiliation for a proud man—and Mackenzie had more than his share of the sensitive pride of the Highlander—was that of the mind and of the spirit. For one of his imagination, energy, and past achievement to see his worth unrecognized, to have his abilities rust with disuse, to be ignored by an indifferent public, to sink from a position of leadership to one of obscurity and impotence—this was a bleak and bitter fate indeed. Even the crown of martyrdom was denied him, for after a few years he began to doubt the wisdom of his rash action and on several occasions expressed his regret for his part in the Rebellion. Eventually the period of exile came to an end. A general amnesty was issued in 1849 covering all offences arising out of the Rebellion, and in May of the following year Mackenzie and his family came back to Canada.

Mackenzie's return to the scene of his earlier struggle was also filled with disappointments, for the failure and frustration of exile were continued in large measure in Toronto. He was unable to recapture his old position and prestige. Some of his friends, it is true, gave him a house as a mark of esteem and in recognition of his many public services, but he remained a poor man with no dependable source of income. He was twice offered a government position, but he refused it lest acceptance should endanger his cherished independence.

His political reputation with the people, however, remained high and a year after his return he was elected from Haldimand, which he represented in the Assembly until his retirement in 1858. But he soon discovered that in his absence the changes had been so extensive that those twelve years were the equivalent of a lifetime. His political aims had in large measure been achieved and the country had become accustomed to look to others for guidance. The Rebellion, though a failure in one sense, had done much to promote reform. The British Government had at last realized the serious nature of the situation; Lord Durham had been sent to British North America to investigate and report; and the way had been gradually cleared for the introduction of responsible cabinet government in 1848. Many of Mackenzie's old grievances had therefore been met, and the remedy for others was now placed in the hands of the legislature. Here, however, he showed some of his old quality, and as chairman of a select committee he wielded a decisive influence in making more effective the legislature's control over finance. But the Assembly itself had undergone great changes in Mackenzie's absence. The union of Upper and Lower Canada in 1840 had brought many new problems and introduced a host of new members, party lines had become confused and uncertain, and the old leader found himself almost a stranger in a scene where he had been a dominant figure for many years. His voice continued to be heard in the House, characteristically in support of the minority rather than the Government, but the leading man was now forced to play one of the minor parts. Poor, disappointed, embittered, Mackenzie died in August, 1861.

It is not necessary to attempt here any assessment of William Lyon Mackenzie, but the following will indicate the position accorded him by one of Canada's ablest historians, A. R. M. Lower:

William Lyon Mackenzie, ill-starred leader of an ill-starred revolt, may yet not be lightly dismissed. Fanatic though he was, he was also something more. Although he cannot be hoisted into the position of the impeccable hero, on the plane of other rebels who have had better luck, it is also impossible to dissociate him from the cause of Canada. He stood for the plain man, for the many against the few, for democracy against privilege. He had the wit to discern what was wrong with his province and the courage to battle against it. Canada has had few men of rash courage and inflexible principle, and those few have each cut a wide swath. Mackenzie was one of these, a man whose many faults are lost in an essential integrity, a crusader for what he deemed the right and for what subsequent generations have approved as the right, and therefore a man to whom Canada owes much. . . . Without Mackenzie, Upper Canada would have continued locked in its dreary provincial prison, but after he had brought it to the point of revolt, that was no longer possible: self-government was on the horizon, and just beyond it national life.[2]

Mackenzie King's parents, John King and Isabel Grace Mackenzie, were married at Toronto on December 12, 1872, when both were in their thirtieth year. John King's father having died before the son's birth, the widow and child had lived with her brother, Dougall Macdougall. Macdougall was a newspaper editor and publisher who lived in several places in Ontario, but finally settled in Berlin in Waterloo County. John King studied at the University of Toronto, and after an excellent record became a bachelor of arts in 1864, and a master of arts in 1865. He edited the Berlin *Telegraph* for a short time, and then entered Osgoode Hall, being admitted to the bar in 1869. During one session of the Ontario legislature he acted as Assistant Law Clerk, and he was asked to take over the law clerkship as a permanent position. This he declined, and he moved to Berlin in December, 1869, to begin the practice of law.

Isabel Grace Mackenzie was born in the city of New York, on February 6, 1843, when her father was in exile, and was only seven years old when the family came back to Canada. She grew up therefore under straitened circumstances, and these were made more difficult by the depressing atmosphere which hung over the household of the former rebel in his declining and less colourful years. She was over eighteen at the time of her father's death; and she and her sisters helped her mother make a scanty living by giving music and dancing lessons to young ladies from more fortunate families in Toronto. Happily, adversity seems to have had little effect on her spirits or disposition, and one of her friends remembered her at this period as "a sprightly girl, taken with the lighter things of life. She had blue eyes and light hair, . . . [was] slight in build, and not tall, but was pretty and a pet of the family."[3] She met and became engaged to John King while he was studying law, and five years later when he had become established in Berlin they were married.

Mackenzie King was very fond of recalling how two conflicting strains had been brought together by his parents' marriage, for though both his grandfathers had been engaged in the Rebellion of 1837–8 they had fought on opposite sides. William Lyon Mackenzie was obviously in the thick of the revolt, while John King was stationed with the artillery at Kingston and had actually fired on a small force which had invaded Canada from the United States. The dramatic possibilities of this incident in the family history, however, could not be fully exploited, inasmuch as Mackenzie was not among the invaders even in spirit, but was by this time in New York and was unaware that the hostile expedition had set forth.* It was nevertheless typical of Mackenzie King that in his later years he would seize on and magnify this personal coincidence and draw from it a highly contrived parable which embodied a reconciliation of moral and political principles of the first magnitude. Speaking in Aberdeen, Scotland, in 1937[4] he said:

Each [of my grandfathers] was serving as he thought best and right the traditions and the ideals that were dearest to his heart. John King had

---

*Legend has done the best it could to fill the gap, and it is said that at the time Mackenzie was *thought* by the defenders to have been a member of the invading force.

8

his natural inclinations strongly associated with the Crown; William Lyon Mackenzie's associations at the time were more closely with the people and their struggles for political freedom.

But each of these men was seeking to do his part to preserve what he believed to be best both in the Crown and in popular institutions; and the story of the development of the British Empire has been the keeping of these two together in such a way that instead of there being discord between them there is perfect harmony.*

The Kings had four children: Isabel Christina Grace (Bella) born November 15, 1873; William Lyon Mackenzie (Willie) born December 17, 1874; Janet Lindsey (Jennie) born August 27, 1876; and Dougall Macdougall (Max) born November 11, 1878.

The family lived in three houses in the first fourteen years of their life in Berlin. Mackenzie King was born in the first of these on Benton Street, which was later demolished to make way for another building. In 1886 they moved to their fourth home, Woodside, situated about a mile out of town, where they lived until they left Berlin seven years later. Woodside was regarded by all the Kings as their real home, and the children, who spent the most active and happy part of their youth there, were especially attached to it. "Old Woodside," wrote Willie as an undergraduate, "how I love that place," and fifty-five years after the family had moved away he still experienced a touch of nostalgia when he thought of his boyhood there.[5]

Despite the high place which Woodside held in their affections the Kings were never its owners. The house and grounds had been constructed by a Scot who had attempted to reproduce an Old Country estate on a small scale. Nature had supplied many native trees and wild flowers, and the owner had added a small orchard, lawns, a lily pond, and an extensive flower garden. Behind the house was a steep knoll where in winter the children built snow forts and in summer pitched the tent in which the boys frequently spent the night. The establishment included chickens, pigs, a cow, and a horse. All the children could ride and all could milk, but the milking was normally done by one of the two servants, who were as a rule a man of all work

*Mackenzie King's file contained a reference to a similar idea expressed by G. M. Trevelyan in An Autobiography and Other Essays (London, 1949), p. 158: "It is often remarked that some of our London statues are oddly chosen or curiously placed.... But [those of] Charles I and Cromwell are 'just right.' There they both are, in the heart of our capital, each statue symbolizing aspects of England's life once in mortal conflict, now reconciled, and making up together the best part of what we now are. What is less good in us to-day is neither Roundhead nor Cavalier."

9

and his wife. The Kings exhibited the same tenderness of heart which is often found in those to whom the soil is a hobby and not a livelihood: they sold their pigs, and bought their pork elsewhere. Willie was much more of a gardener than the others, and the fondness for cutting trees and similar activities which he later displayed at Kingsmere originated in Woodside. At the age of thirteen and a half Willie wrote his father and described some of his daily duties:

We have got both the dining room & the hall stoves down. Percy & Thomas took them down. I cleaned the lawn in front of the door and around at the side. We then cleaned out all the orchard and made a terrible large fire of all the limbs and old rubbish in the yard and will use the ashes for to manure the garden. Mr. Coleman never came over to plough to-day and Percy went over tonight and gave him a blowing up and told him that he would make a corpse of him and would . . . him if he did not come over. . . . means one of Percy's long words that he got most likely from Aunt Lybbie he then said that he would be sure to come early next morning   Thomas says that he needs my help all week so as to get all the seeds in. I am quite sure you will not know the place when you get home.[6]

The house was set back a short distance from the highway, and its simple lines and the soft colours of the brick showed to great advantage among the trees. Although it could not be called a large house for that time, the rooms, especially the living room, dining room, and library, were of generous size, and even today the house has an atmosphere which suggests both charm and comfort.* Two features were of special concern to the King children. One was the unfortunate alignment of the piano with the doors downstairs which permitted Mrs. King though three rooms distant to see that the girls kept faithfully to their music; the other was the convenient position of the window of the upstairs sewing room which opened on the roof of the ell so that inconspicuous egress and ingress were possible at all hours. Willie and Jennie appear to have made the most frequent use of these opportunities.

The fact that Woodside was in the country meant that in their younger days the King children were isolated and forced to draw upon themselves for companionship. Bella and Willie tended to pair off together and Jennie and Max, but as only five years separated the

---

*The house fell eventually into a state of disrepair and admirers of Mackenzie King in Kitchener bought the property and had the house rebuilt as it had been before, paying careful attention to details and using many of the materials from the original house.

oldest and youngest, they frequently pooled their interests and resources. As they grew older, other children were able to come to
Woodside more easily and Mr. and Mrs. King were unusually hos-
pitable hosts. Plays—with liberal improvisations—were a favourite
recreation, and Willie's discovery after some time at collegiate that he
could make coloured smoke greatly enhanced the dramatic effects.
All members of the family were fond of music. Although Mrs. King
had taught music before her marriage and had thereby earned enough
money to pay for her piano, she never considered herself to be a good
teacher and did not attempt to instruct the children. Yet they were
all given piano lessons at some time in their early years, and at one
period a governess stayed at Woodside and taught the children music
and German. The family especially enjoyed singing as a group around
the piano in the evening. Mrs. King or one of the girls played the
piano, Mr. King the castanets, and the others provided a vigorous
chorus, whether popular airs, Varsity songs, or, on Sundays, hymns
from the Presbyterian *Book of Praise*. In later years Mackenzie King
continued to derive extraordinary pleasure from such informal singing
of hymns, a fondness which he shared with one of his great contemporaries, David Lloyd George.

The children were expected to perform the usual minor tasks about
the house and garden, and they would sometimes be paid a small
amount for the work. It was understood, however, that this was a
normal part of their duty and hence would as a rule go unrewarded.
They received no allowance or pocket money. Before Christmas each
child was given $2.50 with which to buy gifts for the other five
members of the family, and very extensive consideration was given to
the selection of each present. "I can recall," wrote Mackenzie King
in 1949, "buying little Christmas presents for members of the family.
I remember the anxiety occasioned in these expenditures. I recall
securing for my mother a card case covered with diamond-shaped
'mother-of-pearl' at Fox's jewelry store. I can see the interest Mr. Fox
took in my making the purchase. I was only about the height of the
counter. I thought I had secured something fine."[7]

Birthdays in the King household were major events. Presents on a
modest scale were always forthcoming, and parties at Woodside enjoyed a high reputation. Mackenzie King never lost this habit of his
childhood and always treated birthdays with exceptional respect and

punctiliousness, as deserving not only suitable gifts, but eloquent letters of congratulation, reviews of the past, and anticipations of the future. It also became a well-known idiosyncrasy in his later years for him to try to sign public documents on anniversaries or family birthdays, and he thus derived uncommon pleasure from the fact that on Jennie's birthday he signed the Kellogg Pact and on Bella's birthday the Washington Declaration on Atomic Energy.

Mackenzie King once described his early years as those "of an average, normal boy who took part in all activities which younger men enjoy." It was an accurate summary. His health in his boyhood was unusually good and his interests were wide. He was an excellent swimmer, and played cricket and football enthusiastically, though according to his contemporaries he was clumsy on his feet and never developed great proficiency in any sport. He learned to speak in public at the Berlin High School, and in 1891 (his senior year) he was made president of the Literary Society. He spoke easily and fluently without any display of nervousness, and his skill as a debater soon far exceeded that of any of his classmates. He took part in amateur theatricals. When a spokesman was needed for any special occasion, such as a presentation to the principal or to the physical training instructor, Willie King was the one usually chosen to read the accompanying address.

His appearance was unimpressive, with heavy features, a large mouth, unruly hair, and a thick-set rugged physique. But he was very friendly and approachable, willing to talk freely, and quick to respond with a smile and a twinkle in his blue eyes. He was a good mixer and generally liked. He was fond of girls, although he showed no special preference for any one, finding it better or safer to play the field. They, in turn, liked him, and he was a high favourite with Jennie and Isabel's friends.

He was a natural mischief maker, and his teachers at school soon learned to turn to Willie King when they were at a loss to find the cause of any major disturbance. A number of stories are still remembered by Willie's schoolmates. One autumn day he and another boy (who later did penance for his misdemeanour by becoming a missionary) were caught stealing apples from an orchard near the school. J. W. Connor, the principal, promptly expelled them; but they waylaid him after school and made a moving appeal. "Billie did the talking, and I did the blubbing," said his fellow culprit and the combination proved so effective that reinstatement followed.

On another occasion Willie was the chief actor in a practical joke played on the biggest boy in the school. He contrived to place several bad eggs in the boy's pockets, and then proceeded with a number of other students to "hustle" him. The desired result ensued. The victim with a sure instinct turned on Willie and tried to catch him in the general skirmish, but Willie took to his heels and escaped, though in his haste he ran through the middle of a glass cold frame in a neighbouring garden. Willie King's early reputation for ragging and breaking the scholastic peace was clearly well founded.

From his earliest years Willie lived in a political atmosphere, for William Lyon Mackenzie and the Liberal tradition were integral parts of the family environment. Moreover, John King was an ardent politician, who, while he lived in Berlin, was very active in electioneering and had been asked on several occasions to run as a Liberal candidate. Mrs. King, however, objected to any election contests in the family on the ground that her father's experience had given her all the politics she wanted in her lifetime. Willie's initiation came when as a child he attended a meeting addressed by Sir John A. Macdonald:

The first general election I recall was in 1882. I was seven. Sir John came to Berlin (now Kitchener) where, at the time, my father was practising law. All who have had an opportunity of knowing and seeing Sir John are today grateful for having had that opportunity. I remember best not the political argument but that Sir John was presented with some flowers by a pretty young lady whom he thanked with an embrace. I could do nothing but envy him, and decided then that politics had its rewards.[8]

Apparently Willie soon learned to recall "the political argument" as well as the more pleasing phases of politics. Some years later his father took him away from high school to go to another meeting and when he came back on the following day he was asked to give a report to his fellow students. He did so, but in such detail and reproducing the speeches at such length that the principal was compelled to intervene to permit a fascinated school to return to work.

Even at an early age Willie took his duties as the older brother in the family very seriously. This was especially evident in the absence of his father, for Willie would usually take over the law office and assume as well a heavy responsibility for what went on at home. The following extract is from a lengthy letter written before he was fourteen to both parents who were away on a trip. It had already dealt with the poisoning of the family dog:

I guess you would find it a hard job to get another faithful little dog as faithful as she was   All of us seemed to turn a little Christian-like that day and Max seemed to think that he was the worst sinner of the lot of us   We have a pretty hard job to keep Max & Jenny out of mischief as they are all the time getting into it. Bella is also very fond of having visitors out and going out visiting herself and so is Jenny. . . .

Mr. Wedd showed me how to make out the first notice [of protest at the office] and I showed him the others he said they were all right   there were 7 notices to make out all together so you made $2.50 while you were away anyhow and that is deducting postage ec. . . .

We are getting along first rate and if you feel like staying a little longer why then do so but let us know   I think it would do you both good   I am sure that no person could have kept the office more faithfully than I have.[9]

As he got older, Willie did not lose this superior and mildly censorious attitude to the other children and he enjoyed delivering lectures on deportment, studies, health, and other subjects. The girls took this all in good part, nicknamed him "little old grandpa," and apparently did just what they pleased. Nevertheless they were genuinely proud of Willie and were delighted with his success as a student. They mended his socks and sent him boxes of food for his birthday, but as sisters they were quite aware of his limitations and considered it a duty to remind him that he, too, was mortal. Even Max managed to trim Willie's wings now and then. But Willie was never able to shed his feeling of responsibility towards the erring ones; and as he moved on from school to university and then to other pursuits his enlarged knowledge and experience tended, if anything, to increase his complacency and reinforce the conviction that his judgment was apt to be the best.

Yet the other children gave no reason to suppose that Willie's paternalism was needed, for they were a singularly well behaved and attractive group. Bella, the eldest, was an extremely fine girl, unselfish to a fault, serious in purpose and utterly dependable, and given, as she grew older, to piety and good works. Outside the family, her major concern lay in the church, the Sunday school, and various congregational organizations, but she had many other general interests and

14

was by no means lacking in the more social graces. She also possessed a full share of the sense of humour which was a priceless asset of the King family. Jennie was the most lovable of the children. She was natural in manner, full of fun and life, sharing Willie's sense of mischief, frank in speech, generous and impetuous in disposition, impatient of pretence or subterfuge. All the Kings enjoyed gaiety and a good time, but Jennie derived the fullest appreciation from the dances, the occasional plays, the church, the lectures, and the family life.

Max was the youngest, and as a child naturally tended to be pushed into fourth position. His greatest handicap was the existence of a more capable brother, for the glow of Max's not inconsiderable talents was continually dimmed by Willie's brighter light. Max was not a natural student, and at times he found the grind discouraging. There is no evidence that the family ever drew comparisons between the boys, but the younger one was very much aware of the contrast, and his letters often carried a wistful note as he described some of his difficulties. "You are certainly distinguishing yourself marvellously," he wrote Willie in 1897. "Oh! what it must be to be good, or rather excellent, all around. Several accounts about your running, which have been in the Toronto papers, & that article of yours, which appeared in The Globe, are causing a great deal of interest here. Not a few people have been speaking to father & mother about them."[10] Under such circumstances Willie's homilies, though well meant, were not apt to prove helpful. As Max matured, however, he was more able to escape from this oppressive atmosphere and assert his personality. Once he stood on his own achievement, he developed a marked degree of independence of both mind and character.

The letters which were exchanged after Willie went to the University of Toronto in 1891 naturally give a great deal of information about the King family. They cover a wide range. Those from Willie describe his studies, and other activities at university; those from home discuss sermons, church affairs, clothes, servants, parties, dances, food, and all the other minutiae which might be of interest. The output was enormous. Willie wrote regularly every week, and while the letters were sometimes brief, more often they were full and detailed. For years the flow from the King home averaged about three long letters a week. The girls rarely missed writing every Sunday, Mr. King wrote at some time during the week, and Mrs. King and Max sent the occasional short letter. One of the more unusual features of this correspondence was the affection which welled up in it. The members of the family loved one another, and they did not hesitate to say so to a degree that would be found embarrassing in many families no less devoted. To the Kings such a lack of reticence came naturally, and it gives an additional charm to the correspondence.

A glimpse into the King home with the affection, pride, and frank appraisal which appeared in the children's relations with one another is afforded by a few extracts from letters written to Willie by his sisters while he was at university in Toronto and later Chicago:

I must . . . tell you how delighted we all were to hear of your being elected President [of the class at the University]. You know if your *"big sister"* did not write & congratulate you on your success the class of '95 & its President would *utterly collapse*. . . . Jennie was just about asleep when we heard about it, but she managed to say, "It beats me how that *little kid* is so lucky." That is *her* way of putting it. . . . The *whole* of Woodside send their congratulations. You seem such a young boy to be made a President but I hope in every way the position you have attained will bring much pleasure to all about you & that you will act in a way becoming the grandson of the late William Lyon Mackenzie. Is not that a speech? [Bella to Willie, Oct. 25, 1892]

I with the others must thank you for the picture. . . . To tell the truth I think you look like *distress*. Why in the world don't you brush your hair, it looks as if you had just rolled out of bed, it is so untidy, you talk about *my* hair & the part in the middle, but you can't even boast of that much, only a *cowlick*. . . . All the other boys have on their *night-caps*. Where is yours? I think Jennie & I will have to knit you a cap, only we don't know the size of your head or brain as it will have grown considerably during the past months. [Bella to Willie, March 2, 1893]

Whenever a letter comes we get together & listen while father reads it aloud & you wouldn't believe the joy it brings us, these are times that we will all look back to as well as you. You seem to grow dearer to us, if that could be so, for you have been so faithful all through & deserve so much praise. How it pleases father, to speak of none of us, I am sure you have no idea. He talks about you & your work half the time. I do hope & pray that, if you are spared, a bright & useful future may be in store for you, for as the Minister said yesterday, should it not be our greatest aim to do good. [Bella to Willie, May 22, 1893]

Father has just commenced to read aloud out of the "Presbyterian" & dear knows when he will *let up*. It is decidedly awkward to try to write to you while this performance is going on. . . . Thank Heaven! Father has "let up" at last. It is lovely to hear him read but not when you are trying to write. . . . Father is *going it* again. [Jennie to Willie, Aug. 8, 1895]

Have you been watching the mails for a letter from your beloved home? Well we imagined as much and decided not to let you be unhappy any longer. Isabel is warbling "Somebody loves me" and is no doubt thinking of you. Father, who got home yesterday, is preparing for a [University] Senate meeting, Mother is looking up bargains, and Max is studying. Most characteristic occupations! . . . We are almost finished housecleaning. All the carpets are down again and the dining room curtains are up. . . . It has been a grand performance, but we've got through it remarkably well without scraps or anything unpleasant. [Jennie to Willie, Sept. 14, 1896]

Well, Billy boy, I am, as I said before, half asleep, I wish you could peep in and see the three faithful females seated around the dining room table writing to their absent loved laddie. [Jennie to Willie, Oct. 18, 1896]

To think of dear old *grandpa* 22 & *Bates* [Bella]—23—& *ma & pa* 24 yrs married. We'll soon all be up among the ancients. . . . Such a golden future as we all feel there is in store for you, not in the way of outward reward but in the blessings & joy you may be privileged to shed into the lives of your fellowmen. [Bella to Willie, Dec. 13, 1896]

An important aspect of the life of the members of the King family was their concern with the church. They were strongly Presbyterian. All were regular in their attendance at the church services; the children went to Sunday school as a matter of course, and when they grew older became communicants. Each member was interested in some of the many activities of the church, whether these related to the selection of a new minister, the choir, a church supper, or the content of a sermon. Neither Mr. nor Mrs. King appears to have shown much interest in what later became known as social work, but all four children at some time or other took an active part in organizations designed primarily to help the poor and underprivileged.

Education was regarded by the Kings with all the respect and some of the passion of the Scot, and though they could in one sense ill afford it, none questioned the need or desirability of money spent for this purpose. The children were given as good an education as Berlin could provide, a governess was engaged for some time at Woodside, and Bella was sent to a girls' school in Toronto. Willie went to university for his arts course and Max for medicine, although these imposed heavy hardships on those at home, who were already finding it none too easy to meet even their own expenses. So far as the boys could assist, they did so, and after Willie began advanced work he gradually became self-supporting.

Not the least valuable part of the home environment was the social poise and competence which the children unconsciously acquired from the more frivolous side of their parents' lives. The Kings were one of the leading families in Berlin, and the youth, attractiveness, gaiety, and natural friendliness of Mr. and Mrs. King made them popular hosts and desired guests at the dances and other entertainments given in the town. A brief account of one of their functions appeared under "Social Gossip" in the Berlin *Telegraph* in September, 1892:

On Thursday evening, the 18th ult., Mrs. John King gave an At Home at her cosy residence, "Woodside." The warm weather precluded much dancing, but that did not in the least mar the pleasure of the evening, so a most sociable time was spent, everyone seeming in high spirits after the refreshing rambles of the summer holidays. The grounds were beautifully illuminated and the winding walks lined with Chinese lanterns made a very inviting promenade of which I noticed a number of the young people availed themselves. Most of the society people of the sister towns were there and also a number of visitors, among whom I noticed: Mrs. Chalcraft of Toronto, Miss MacBeth of London, Miss Thom of Toronto, Mr. Campbell of Guelph, Mr. Holmes-Orr of Montreal, and Messrs. Johnson and Buckingham of Stratford.

When the Kings moved to Toronto in the summer of 1893 they found the social demands much more trying. They were on intimate terms with a number of the prominent families there, but they lacked the money to enable them to live up to the standards of many of their friends. Fortunately this does not seem to have affected their social acceptability, but Mrs. King and the girls were nevertheless engaged in a continuous effort to make their scanty resources yield the maximum return. They sought out bargains in the stores, did much of their own sewing, adapted clothes to meet the vagaries of fashion, and joined in enthusiastic praises of the final result. "We have been busy sewing," wrote Jennie in 1899, "and when you see mother's dress I am sure you will think we are wonders. It is lovely & Mother is a little picture in it. Isabel too is to be quite fine but her dress is not quite finished."[11] A few months later the winter wardrobe engaged Jennie's attention: "All last week we were busy sewing at Isabel's dress and it is such a success that it quite repays us. It is the most becoming thing she has had for a long time and it fits her beautifully. Isabel can wear crimson well as she is so slight and tall."[12]

The girls were 20 and 17 years old when they moved to Toronto and were therefore at an age when forced economies on such matters must have been very hard to bear, yet they accepted these frugalities without complaint. One other illustration must suffice. "The grand St. Andrew's Ball," wrote Jennie in the autumn of 1896, "is to be held in the pavilion and we have not decided whether we will go or not. I have the first Highland schottische with Charlie & the first Reel of Tulloch with Mr. Ogilvy Watson—if I go. If Father gets a ticket other than by paying out hard cash we will go but if not we will bide tae hame."[13] A week later she reported: "Last Monday was St. Andrew's Ball but as no tickets came we stayed at home. Father & I were sadly disappointed but George Macdonnell came up & we spent a very pleasant evening at home."[14] Willie, of course, suffered from the same general stringency though clothes were for him not a major concern. What might have become a problem was settled satisfactorily on his eighteenth birthday when he was presented with his father's old dress suit cut down to fit its new owner.

It is evident that the King family life was an unusually happy one. Although the deep affection of the members for one another was chiefly responsible, they possessed many other auxiliary virtues which conspired to produce the same result. The sympathetic understanding, the sense of humour and indulgence in good-natured banter, the outspoken praise of one another's virtues and the tolerance of one another's faults, the constant encouragement of effort and the unqualified appreciation of the performance—these the Kings possessed and practised. They formed a social unit in a very real sense, highly integrated and with tremendous internal loyalties. They stood staunchly together, fought one another's battles, gave support when and where it was needed, rejoiced in victories and extended consolation in defeat. In the development and fostering of these characteristics, all members of the family must have had a share, but it is clear that little would have been possible without the constant vigilance of the parents who furnished both the inspiration and the example.

The father was a tall man, dignified in bearing, with blue eyes and an Edwardian beard. He had a kindly disposition and a friendly manner which consorted well with an easy-going nature. He was very

19

fond of children, and his own were a constant source of both interest and pleasure: for them he would take unlimited trouble and make any sacrifice in his power. "I am much affected by his intense love for me," wrote Willie in 1897, "he seems more interested in my welfare than in his own."[15] The children, for their part, regarded their father with great affection, unmarred even in their youngest days with any vestige of reserve or fear. He had had a distinguished academic career at the University, and these scholarly interests he retained to the end of his life. He therefore welcomed the opportunity to join in the education of the children, and he endeavoured with some success to guide them in their studies and develop in them a sense of literary appreciation. He followed Willie's university career and later achievements with intense pride and kept in constant touch with him, for even in that family he could hold his own as a frequent and voluminous correspondent. Like Lord Chesterfield, he wanted his son to get ahead in the world, and his letters, therefore, abound in advice on all kinds of topics, from the choice of a rooming house to the wisdom of Willie's conciliating his late enemies after a successful university election.

I hope you will continue to make friends of the leaders of the Faculty. They can do everything to advance your interests, & when they find you are enthusiastic in your work, they will, I am sure, do all they can to assist you and to push you forward. There is everything in starting right—getting into the best "set" & cultivating the friendship and goodwill of the intellectual, refined & cultured in the University and elsewhere in your new home.[16]

John King was a speaker and writer of distinction. His love of English literature and natural gifts of expression made him much in demand as an after-dinner and extempore speaker and he was equally effective on the public platform. As an author he was both able and industrious; he possessed a felicitous style and writing apparently came easily to him. He had won a graduate prize at the University for an M.A. essay which was later published in the *Canadian Monthly*.[17] He also wrote for *The Week* and in later life contributed many articles of a quasi-literary nature to the Toronto *Globe*. In 1886 he entered the lists on behalf of his father-in-law, William Lyon Mackenzie, with a brochure called *The Other Side of the Story*, a critical review of T. C. Dent's *The Story of the Upper*

Canada Rebellion. In 1914 he brought together biographical essays which he had previously written on three prominent figures in the history of the University of Toronto, and he published them under the singularly uninviting title of *McCaul: Croft: Forneri.*

His competence as a lawyer was more evident on the scholarly than on the practical side of his profession. In 1893 he was offered a part-time lectureship in the Law School of Upper Canada (Osgoode Hall) in Toronto. He accepted the position, moved from Berlin, and with his teaching salary as a basic income, endeavoured to build up a Toronto practice. His experience at Osgoode Hall was on the whole a very happy one and he held the lectureship for twenty-two years. The work was most congenial, and he placed a high value—higher, it must be confessed, than did his contemporaries—on the prestige attached to the position. He was a good teacher: the students liked him and not infrequently showed their appreciation by making a gift at the end of term. This "was an event of joy tinged with a bit of sorrow," wrote an old student, "because he would generally break down and cry a little either during the presentation or in his remarks expressing his thanks."[18]

His interests as a teacher of law and an author led him to write at length on his special field, the law of defamation, a propensity quite conceivably influenced by the extensive experience of William Lyon Mackenzie in that field. His first effort was a paper (later published) given before the Canadian Press Association in 1889 on criminal libel, and this was followed by a number of papers and articles in professional journals. In 1907 his first book appeared, *The Law of Defamation in Canada,* and it was followed in 1912 by *The Law of Criminal Libel.*

While John King derived great pleasure from his scholarly activities, they were pursued in large measure because of his inability to make a success of the practice of law. He had had, it is true, a fair practice in Berlin, including some criminal prosecutions as Queen's Counsel, but this had yielded an inadequate living. A number of his country clients paid in kind rather than in cash, the family was apparently spending too freely, and the available funds were not enough to meet expenses. The opportunity to go to Toronto therefore had looked attractive, Mackenzie King recalled in 1949, for the children "were now grown up, there would be better advantages for us in a larger centre; also . . .

he [father] and mother would find more interest in living in Toronto than in the old Berlin community where he had not the chance of associations that he expected to have in a larger city."[19]

The move turned out to be a mistake, for the new practice never became as large or as profitable as the one in Berlin. Mr. King's hope, expressed to his elder son in 1899, that the position at Osgoode would serve as "a recommendation and guarantee of fitness for a higher and more lucrative place" in the profession[20] went unfulfilled. His knowledge of his specialty, libel and slander, was unrivalled in Canada, but the narrowness of the field restricted his opportunities to turn this to account. Basically, he was handicapped by the fact that his interest in law was primarily that of a theorist, and his whole nature resented the routine and drudgery which were the necessary accompaniment of any office practice. He lacked the toughness of fibre, the aggressiveness and pertinacity which are useful to any lawyer and were essential to one who in middle life came from a small community to Toronto to set up a practice. John King was quite aware of these limitations, though not, perhaps, sufficiently determined to overcome them:

No one is more conscious than myself of my own infirmities, & no doubt I could have done better in some things; but a man's nature works on his fortune and his fortune on his nature. That has been my case to a very large degree. I came into this world with a highly sensitive nature, & I cannot get rid of it. Extreme sensitiveness will mar anyone's success in life, and I know it has marred mine. If I had had coarser feelings and a harder nature, careless of riding rough shod over everybody and everything, I would have been better off to-day.[21]

Even the greater social amenities of Toronto as compared with Berlin were far from being an unmixed blessing to the King family, for life in the city not only made more demands on time, it was also more expensive and the necessity of keeping up appearances was much greater. In 1894 Max had a long and serious attack of typhoid which led to additional expenditures the family could ill afford, and they ended that year with a substantial debt and a chattel mortgage on the furniture on which for a time they paid 12 per cent interest. John King was also compelled on several occasions to borrow on his life insurance. These debts hung on for many years and caused him untold worry. He was not extravagant by any ordinary standards and he was quite unselfish and made no demands for himself, but he was much concerned at his inability to provide many comforts and small pleasures for the family. "Oh! how I wish I were comfortably enough off to do what money alone can do for all of you," he wrote Willie in 1898.

It is often a great pain to me that I can't do in that way what I would like to. If I had to live my life over again I would do very differently. I would commence to save at the very outset & lay up a store for the future. Say or think what you like, money prevents a lot of friction in life & conduces to one's happiness to an infinite degree. It helps a man in a thousand ways, and gives him advantages personally & socially which nothing else can give. . . . The world is very considerate & tender with a man when it knows that he is independent of its smiles or its frowns.[22]

Yet John King's obligations, though relatively heavy, were far from overpowering had he possessed any sense of finance. He had virtually none. His resources were few, he worried endlessly about his financial troubles, but he failed to take the simplest steps to protect himself or to make the best of the meagre assets he possessed. From the time he went to Toronto, he was always living on the margin of solvency. He had, however, one characteristic which helped him through many trials. He was an unfailing optimist, sure that his affairs would somehow improve in the future. The storms might be violent today, but for John King the barometer was always rising.

The sense of failure, however, was never far away, and he was in constant need of reassurance and a new stimulus. To that end he sought and found many indications that his worth had been given some recognition. He was touchingly proud of his position as an alumni representative on the Senate of the University of Toronto, an office which he held for an unbroken term of thirty-five years, and as each election came around he became much concerned lest he should suffer defeat. A large part of his literary work and particularly his two substantial volumes on defamation, although in part designed to earn money, represented also a determined effort to make the world recognize his merit. He wrung nourishment from the driest husks: a short chat on the street corner with a justice of the Supreme Court, the successful outcome of a case, a word of commendation from a colleague, and the applause given by his students at the last lecture of a course. He was not a vain man; he badly needed help and comfort in circumstances which offered all too few signs of appreciation.

Willie did his best to help, and exerted himself times without number to bolster up his father's morale. Birthdays provided the ideal occasion, and Willie would then review John King's achievements for the past year and draw from them fresh inspiration and encouragement for the future—a habit, incidentally, which he must have inherited, for his father did the same for him when his birthday came around. Both seemed to derive profit and pleasure from the exercise.

It was his mother, however, who left the deepest impression on Mackenzie King. She was rather short, slender, pretty, with deep blue eyes and fair curly hair. A photograph taken when she was forty-two shows her to have been a most attractive woman possessing a great deal of character. It is a strong face—a fairly large nose, a good firm chin, the head well set on the shoulders, and a glint of humour in the generous mouth and the wide-set level eyes. Age did not impair her charm. J. W. L. Forster, who painted her portrait on two occasions, wrote: "Mrs. King retained a beauty of spirit and of person to advanced age, possessing delicate, but deeply modelled features, and bright, responsive eyes in a face set in a corona of silver, wavy hair. Costumed always in original yet exquisite taste, Mrs. King was a welcome test to the ambitions and power of any artist."[23]

Her natural vivacity and sense of fun made her the life of the family. She played games and romped with the children in their early years, and as they grew older she remained essentially the companion rather than the parent. She had poise and dignity, yet given the proper occasion could discard them in a moment and become a lively, frolicsome girl even younger at times than her daughters. Her appreciation of the ridiculous was irrepressible and at times caused her some embarrassment, for more than once her letters stated that she was in disgrace because of her inability to behave with proper gravity during the church service. She was at the same time subject to recurring periods of nervous exhaustion. Her high-strung temperament would cause her to do everything at top speed until she wore herself out, and then the reaction, accompanied by nervous indigestion, would set in. For a few weeks she would be forced to rest, but no sooner had she picked up than the tempo would begin to rise and the cycle would be resumed once more. Although she was a conscientious reader, at heart she was no student, and appeared to derive very little genuine profit from her reading. She was a poor and infrequent correspondent, and her letters contain little of the spirit and zest which she felt but which the other members of the family were able to record with so much less effort. In expression of affection, however, only Willie could surpass her. Thus when Willie was successful in his oral examination at Harvard in 1899, she wrote:

It is something we have looked forward too [to?] and though in our hearts we were sure of your success our trembling fears made us wish it was all over. As I bent my head in prayer on this Good Friday morning I thought how good God had been to me in answering my *earnest* desire for both my boys. . . . Billie you have been a good boy and greater love than even Father or Mother's will be yours. You have laid a foundation that cannot easily be upset. I love you with all my heart for it.[24]

Mrs. King's lovely appearance was greatly enhanced by her fastidiousness and good taste in dress, and to ensure that she was well attired at all times was a major occupation—almost an obsession—of the family. Her attractiveness produced unstinted admiration on all occasions, but the King family were disposed to interpret this as representing not only a personal tribute to her but also a partial recognition of the family's worth. New gowns and hats were sparingly bought at times, but, as already indicated, the chief source of supply was the old wardrobe which was re-made and re-furbished by clever and willing hands. The letters to Willie are filled with references to these home-made transformations which made mother look the finest and the fairest lady at any gathering. Jennie described one of these occasions for him in June of 1898:

Mother and I went to the garden party at Government House yesterday and enjoyed it very much. As usual we worked till the very last moment but the result was all that could be desired and Mother looked a perfect little picture. She wore her black and white silk made over & trimmed with lace, and her little bonnet was sweet. . . . Sir Oliver [Mowat] spoke so nicely to Mother going in and said he was so glad she had come and going out he had another little word with her.[25]

Willie and his father were no less ready with their appreciation and praise. "Your Mother," wrote John King to his son in 1898, "is all right again & looked as pretty as a picture on Sunday with her new dress & her lovely little bonnet."[26] A few months earlier Willie had written his mother on her birthday and after a eulogy of her virtues extending over two pages added:

I enclose a little scrap of paper torn from the corner of my first scholarship earnings at Harvard with explicit directions that it is to go towards having a photograph taken of you *without your hat on*. You must show just as much of your face as you possibly can and let the beautiful curls cluster about it, that future generations may know that there was given to you on earth the crown of glory which is but the divine assurance of the happiness which is to be hereafter.[27]

To her general attractiveness Mrs. King added a gentle manner and a sensitive nature, and her eyes would fill with tears when anyone was rude or unkind. But she was far from spineless or meek. She could show plenty of courage; she usually knew what she wanted, and she had the will and energy to achieve it. Tears might spring from love and sympathy, but they could also be put to a more positive use. She was the one who kept the family accounts, and later she was entrusted with the allowance which Willie sent for the upkeep of the house. The children not only adored her, they waited on her, ran errands for her, and took care to see that she was always the centre of attraction. The affection of all the children for their home was unusually strong, and it was their mother who gave the home its life and character.

The King children grew up under the William Lyon Mackenzie tradition. His name might still be a by-word with some of the continuing Tories in Toronto—one of the neighbours in the city would not speak to them for years because of Mackenzie—but both parents encouraged the children to regard their grandfather as a national hero. John King became a special guardian of the reputation of his father-in-law as his pamphlet in Mackenzie's defence attested. Mrs. King would tell the children anecdotes about her father, his love of his family, his patriotism, and the hardships he endured for the cause, although her own recollection of the period of exile in the United States was naturally slight. She felt no resentment for these events, though she must have thought the country ungrateful in its treatment of her father and been determined at all costs to avoid any repetition of the hardships which had marked her early life. Mackenzie King's copy of Lindsey's *Life and Times of Wm. Lyon Mackenzie* contains the following note (undated) written in his own hand: "Mackenzie King has never forgotten that his own mother was born during the years her father was a political exile, and as a child shared the privations which all of the family were called upon to endure." One grandchild, at least, carried some scars.

It is evident, therefore, that Mrs. King had more reason than most parents to be ambitious for her children. There was a score to be settled; not in any vindictive sense, but as a kind of compensation for misunderstanding and lack of appreciation: to right a wrong, to re-establish a reputation not universally acclaimed, to vindicate for the benefit of all sceptics the name of her father and her family. She herself harboured no doubts of Mackenzie. She knew his character, his aims, his frustration, his efforts, his achievement, and she was unreservedly proud of him; but to many he and the family were still under a cloud of disloyalty and obloquy. She was apparently convinced that this should at all costs be dissolved and the family name and fortune be re-established. She was unable to do anything directly to bring this about, and her husband, whatever expectations she may have entertained at one time, was clearly not the aggressive type who would make his mark in the world and thereby furnish the demonstration she desired. Her hopes therefore rested on the children, and of these Willie early displayed the gifts and the personality which marked him for success. The community which had done so little for William Lyon Mackenzie who had done so much for it would be able to make belated amends by acknowledging the worth of his grandchild and namesake. Who could deny that even the name might have been prophetic? And would that circumstance in itself not add to the effectiveness of the atonement? At all events, Willie was the one to carry out the mission, and he would be assured of all the means and encouragement which a fond mother could bring to his assistance. She wrote Willie at Harvard in 1898:

I will have a few quiet minutes with my boy whose success has given me untold of [sic] pleasure. . . . Far and near people are speaking of your cleverness and *goodness*. Surely there is no greater gift I could wish for than good and clever children. . . . How strange it was that you hit on that particular article of Prof. Ashley's and that he should forget and that you should be right. Oh! you are a lucky cub Willie.[28]

It would be unfair to both Mr. and Mrs. King to assert that Willie was the favourite child. They loved their children all equally and never, except for urgent reasons, gave to one what they denied to the others. But there is no doubt whatever that Willie was the one who

27

was expected to lead the family out of their relative obscurity, to ensure their social and financial future, to show the world that the Kings had the qualities which win distinction and success, and this view was shared by both parents and children. Sacrifices were therefore cheerfully made for him; encouragement was his at all times; they bore with patience Willie's attitude of superiority and wisdom; and if they thought, as they did on at least one occasion, that he was in danger of losing sight of the main objectives and of endangering his career, they made a concerted effort to bring him back into line. Willie was thus not so much the favourite as the elect: he became the family's hostage to fortune, a joint venture on which the hopes and ambitions of all were staked.

Mrs. King did not attempt to plan Willie's future in any definite sense: her desire was rather a vague product of an aspiration and a resolve unaccompanied by any clear idea of its nature or the manner in which it was to be realized. The achievement must be noteworthy and Willie's happiness in it substantial; the remainder was secondary. Similarly she had little comprehension of what Willie's years at the university involved, although they were presumably a preparation for the life which was to follow. Politics, of course, were on the face of it the most suitable and tempting career to bring about a realization of her hopes: this coincided with his grandfather's major interest, and whatever success was there attained would be both conspicuous and unequivocal. But there is no evidence to indicate that Mrs. King wanted him to enter politics. Her father's experience had prejudiced her against them, and she was reluctant to see another member of her family enter so thankless and uncertain a life. Later, she accepted with a good grace what the fates provided, but the choice of a political career was Willie's and not hers. The decision once made, she had little difficulty in imagining Willie at the very top. In 1905 Forster painted the well-known picture of Mrs. King seated before the fireplace at Kingsmere with an open book in her lap. Only Willie and his mother knew the full significance of the book. It was the second volume of Morley's *Life of Gladstone* and it lay open at the chapter "The Prime Minister."

CHAPTER TWO

UNIVERSITY OF TORONTO

IN THE AUTUMN of 1891 Mackenzie King enrolled in the Faculty of Arts at University College in the University of Toronto. He was not yet seventeen. A year later he entered the honour course in political science, and was awarded a Blake scholarship in political science and history. For the next three years his studies were mainly in politics, economics, constitutional history, and law, in most of which he stood at or near the top of his class. He graduated in 1895 with first-class honours. In 1896 he received the degree of bachelor of laws at Toronto.

King's undergraduate years corresponded with a period of unusual activity at the University. It was just beginning to feel the stimulating effects of rapid growth encouraged by the federation of colleges brought about in 1887, the success of which had been virtually assured by the inclusion of Victoria University three years later. The University of Toronto now offered arts, medicine, engineering, and a little law, and its affiliated institutions provided professional training in other fields. Student registration rose from 1,091 in 1891–2 to 2,135 in 1903–4, and the teaching staff increased from 82 to 177 in the same period. The arts faculty contained a number of outstanding men. W. J. (later Sir William) Ashley occupied the chair of political science until 1892, when he left for Harvard and was succeeded by James Mavor.* Maurice Hutton taught Greek; William Dale, Latin; W. J. Alexander, English; J. G. Hume, philosophy. George M. Wrong became lecturer in history in 1892, and professor two years later. King's main contacts were with Mavor and Wrong. None of his

---

*Ashley, a graduate of Oxford, was a professor successively at Toronto (1888–92), Harvard (1892–1901), and Birmingham (1901–25); he organized the first university school of commerce in England.

professors, however, succeeded in arousing his enthusiasm or strongly influenced his future career. His personal relations were much closer with the Rev. William Clark, professor of mental and moral philosophy at Trinity College, an outstanding and probably the most brilliant member of its faculty.[1] King was not one of Dr. Clark's students, but he formed while at the University a warm friendship with him and his wife which was to endure for many years.

But the first impact of the enterprising young student from Berlin was not on his professors. A few days after Willie appeared on the campus, the *Varsity*, the student paper, reported a conversation between someone referred to as "Rex" and another student, in which the naive freshman had introduced himself as the son of "Senator Rex" of Berlin.[2] The incident, which had apparently been somewhat distorted in the telling, is obviously of little consequence save to indicate the impression King made on his fellow students and his extraordinary ability to attract attention and to make the most of his opportunities. For he brought the matter before a meeting of his class (1895)—presumably on a plea of parliamentary privilege—and, he said, "explained the whole affair to [them] who listened without one interruption for about 8 minutes. I was not a bit nervous and I think kind of surprised some of them. I asked them in closing that I hoped they would not believe any such report and thanked them for their kind attention. Then when I sat down they cheered for about five minutes and called out, 'What is the matter with King, he's all right.' The president and lots of the others congratulated me after the meeting." The nickname of Rex remained, however, and he shrewdly added to the account he gave his parents the comment that if the whole affair "has done anything, it has done me good because now I know nearly every man in the college, or rather they all know me."[3]

He found to his delight that the boyish pranks of the high school were reproduced on a grander scale at Toronto, and his first letters home tell of the "great time" he had had at the Autumn Convocation and at the Opera House. Fifty chairs were smashed on the first occasion, and the police were compelled to interfere on the second, which ended up with the usual serenade in front of one of the girls' schools. This sportive trait persisted for years. In 1893 Rex and five others appeared before the University Council on a charge of tearing down an old shed on the campus on Hallowe'en. They were fined $15 each, an act which led to an indignation meeting, a Glee Club parody in their honour,* and a student subscription to discharge the fine. On the next Hallowe'en King was chosen by a mass meeting of students to take charge of all arrangements for a theatre night and he quite lived up to the best university traditions in such matters. He reserved "the gods" for the use of the student body, obtained advertising for the programme and helped compose the parodies for the songs, had a piano taken up to the gallery, and assisted with the decorations. On the night of the performance Rex presented the bouquets to the actresses. His perquisites included a lower box at the theatre, photographs of all the actresses, an afternoon stroll uptown with the leading lady, and the honour of giving her—at the students' expense—a supper after the show.

King was an enthusiastic participant in many student activities. He still enjoyed public speaking, and he appeared in debates before the Literary Society and was in some demand as an after-dinner speaker. But on the whole these occasions were infrequent, and he took little or no part in the mock parliament. This restraint was, of course, in marked contrast to his high school record, and may have been due in part to a realization that he could no longer hope to excel in this highly competitive field. The chief reason, however, was probably lack of time, for his energies were so widely diffused that he necessarily was forced to limit his commitments. He was elected president of his class in its second year, did some work for the Y.M.C.A., and was fairly active in university politics. He became a member of the Kappa Alpha fraternity in October, 1893. His ability as a singer was not of sufficiently high standard to allow him to become a regular member of the University Glee Club, but he occasionally sang with them, and sometimes accompanied the Club on tour in the role of treasurer. Although he was very fond of singing and could play the piano in a desultory fashion, his performance was marked by enthusiasm rather than polish. His post with the Glee Club allowed him to take in the entertainments and to send a report of the trip to the *Globe*. He enjoyed all plays and some operas, but lack of funds was always a serious handicap. To the resourceful student, however, this was only a challenge. "The gods" supplied, of course, the most frequent answer;

*The lyrics ran:
> "I had fifteen dollars in my inside pocket
> Sing song sitty won't you kimeo;
> But I tore down a shed and now I haven't got it,
> Sing song sitty and a kimeo."

but King was sometimes able to gain admission as a member of the press, and would on other occasions secure a minor part on the stage as a supernumerary where he could see the play as the guest of the company.

He wrote with exceptional ease, though his style was marred by an innate tendency to verbosity. This fault his professors tried to cure, and won at least temporary success.* For two years he was an assistant editor of the *Varsity*, and as such was responsible for certain regular features as well as occasional special reports and articles.[4] The alleged rejection of an early poem of King's is the theme of one of Stephen Leacock's brighter comments:

There was, I recollect, a young freshman named William Lyon Mackenzie King who sent us in a poem. The boy's name somehow has stuck in my mind all these years. He sent us in a poem called, *Why I like the Winter* or *The Futility of Human Greatness*. I remember that Doc McLay said it was one of the worst poems we had received that week. We sent it back to King with a smart rebuke as a warning. Perhaps we were wrong. Without our rebuke King might be an established poet today. As it was he abandoned literature. Nor did I ever hear that he had any career beyond a little temporary employment at Ottawa.[5]

It is, perhaps, of small moment to note that Leacock must have invented the whole incident, for he had left the staff of the *Varsity* some months before King came to Toronto as an undergraduate. Leacock's retort would probably have been that the story could easily have been true and that later verses by King (which appeared in the *Varsity* on February 1, 1895) supplied only too clearly the evidence to support his contention. These published verses would have justified the "smartest" of rebukes, and not even the most kindly editor would have experienced any doubt or remorse for having dealt firmly with so mawkish an effort.

> A little thought, a little word,
> A little deed of kindness,
> A little love, a little trust,
> These are the things that bind us.
>
> A little tear, a little prayer,
> A faith that faileth never,
> A little closing of the eyes
> And we are His forever.

*A number of his second year essays, corrected by Professor Alexander, are in the King Papers.

In athletics Rex's record was much the same as it had been in high school: he strove valiantly but rarely progressed beyond the spare man on the second team. His competitive sports were rugby, cricket, and track, but he also rode horseback, boxed, and swam, and appeared conscientiously at the gymnasium. He was always anxious to be considered an athlete and he liked to associate with those who were, even though this meant no more than acting as an announcer at the annual games or following the harriers in a four-in-hand. Such activity was in large measure simply an expression of natural energy and enthusiasm, but it was given an additional impetus by his strong desire to excel in all things and to become one of the leaders.

A new and dramatic opportunity appeared in his senior year when the antagonism between the students and the university authorities became so acute that it culminated in a "strike" or boycott of lectures in February, 1895. The story of the dispute is both complex and controversial,[6] for a part of it was the result of a rivalry between the Vice-Chancellor on one side and the Chancellor and the President on the other, which was aided in some measure by political influences arising from the close association of the Ontario Government with university affairs. Placing these complications to one side, however, the students were able from their own experience to produce against the university authorities an impressive list of grievances, which included inefficient teaching, alleged nepotism in making appointments, control over the choice of two outside radical speakers to address student meetings,* interference with the expression of opinion in the Varsity (which had led to the suspension of the editor from lectures), and, finally, the act which brought matters to a head, the dismissal of Professor Dale, who had written an injudicious letter to the press attacking the administration and questioning the qualifications of a number of his colleagues. It is a well-known fact that student bodies crave a little excitement from time to time to relieve the monotony of study, and the most welcome of all disputes is a clash on a matter of principle with the administrative authorities. This element was not absent from the Toronto affair; but what made the affair unique was the conscientious endeavour of the administration to provide the students with timely grievances. Some of the students' complaints may have been excessive in degree if not objectionable in

*One of these was Phillips Thompson. See infra, p. 101.

33

kind, but the basic faults were there: a stiff-necked and tactless President, supported by an intolerant administration which was determined to allow the students little freedom either in voicing their own opinions or in controlling their own affairs.

Three students emerged at the head of the revolt. T. Hamar Greenwood (later Viscount Greenwood) was unquestionably the leader, and the two others were James A. Tucker, the suspended editor and eventually a martyr to the cause, and W. L. M. King. The students had no representative body to speak for them, and decisions were therefore made in mass meetings called for the purpose. King seems to have been in his element on these occasions. He was a ready and effective speaker, for he responded quickly to the stimulus of a large audience and he felt a strong emotional compulsion to uphold freedom of discussion and to denounce any exercise of arbitrary authority. "If there's anything that makes my blood boil, it's tyranny," he exclaimed in denouncing the actions of the President before one of the many indignation meetings,[7] and his audience agreed with him to a man. Tucker wrote well but spoke badly, and it was therefore left to Greenwood and King to take the initiative in promoting many of the resolutions and directing the discussion at different stages of the dispute.

The dismissal of Professor Dale was announced on Friday, February 15, 1895, and it was followed by the voluntary resignation of his assistant, F. B. R. Hellems. Attendance at lectures virtually ceased as the students gathered on the campus and discussed this new development. King wrote in his diary:

At 12 Max brought the news that Prof. Dale has been dismissed & Hellems resigned. I was that excited that I could not keep still, my blood fairly boiled. I scarcely ate any lunch, hurried up to the college, called on Prof. Dale, DeLury & others, went to see Tucker. At 3 was held the largest Mass Meeting I have ever seen, in Wardell's hall, Spadina Ave. I moved the resolution "to strike" until we were granted an investigation. [It was seconded by Greenwood.] Carried unanimously (except 4). The meeting was very enthusiastic.[8]

Several other resolutions were passed, the chief of which was one stating that the boycott would be continued until Professor Dale's dismissal was reconsidered or until the investigation was granted.[9]

Monday was the first day to test the efficacy of the boycott. Only five students attended lectures. On Tuesday and Wednesday the results were substantially the same. On Wednesday, however, President Loudon let it be known that he was willing to meet a representative committee of students to discuss the relations between the University and University College Councils and the student body, and another mass meeting was called that afternoon to decide on a course of action. It was attended by some 800 students. The offer of the President was accepted, and a committee for this purpose, composed of Greenwood, King, and fourteen others, was appointed. On motion of Greenwood and King and after a long and vehement discussion it was decided to suspend the boycott pending negotiations. Many students thought that they had given in too easily and wished to maintain the boycott until Professor Dale was reinstated, but Greenwood's influence turned the scale. A trace of the same discontent was evident at the Conversazione two nights later, when one of the student cartoons represented King as the King of Clubs, calling out on one side, "Let us boycott lectures," and on the other, "Let us return to lectures." Had the caricature been preserved for posterity, King's political opponents would, no doubt, have been only too happy to adapt it for other purposes in later years.

The students' committee met the university authorities several times in the next few weeks, and King and Greenwood again did a large part of the talking. The committee accomplished little. Professor Dale's reinstatement could scarcely have been expected, but the University might well have shown some magnanimity in its treatment of Tucker. As it was, he was refused admission to the examinations, and his suspension was not removed until September. In the meantime the students had collected a substantial sum to help pay his expenses elsewhere, and he graduated from Leland Stanford the following year.

The boycott had nevertheless had its effect. It helped to convince the Ontario Government that an investigation of university affairs was imperative, and acting on the request of President Loudon (not, the Government was careful to point out, on the students' resolution) a Royal Commission was appointed for this purpose, the Chief Justice of Manitoba acting as chairman. It sat for two weeks and heard evidence from students, faculty, and a few others. King was one of those examined; and though his evidence was relatively unimportant, it provided one of the few gay moments of the investigation. He was challenged by the counsel for the University to state if he personally had any complaint against President Loudon, and somewhat unnerved by the glowering barrister, hastily confessed that he had no such complaint and that the President "had always treated him with great respect."[10] In later years King confessed that this was probably the worst slip of the tongue he had ever made.

The report of the Commission[11] made no concession to the students except to admit the obvious that the authorities had on several occasions shown a want of tact. The findings rested largely on the extent of the University's legal powers rather than on how these powers might have been tempered and adjusted to meet the demands of the students. The kindest thing to say about the effort of the commissioners is that they had little conception of how a university should be conducted, that they were alarmed at the students' assertion of their rights, and they were therefore determined to gloss over what must have appeared even to them as the shortcomings of the administration.

A very important side of King's life in these years, as before and later, was concerned with spiritual matters. This concern had its origin in the Christian beliefs and principles of his home. His deeply religious nature had thrived in this environment, and a few months after his seventeenth birthday he and his sister Bella had joined St. Andrew's Presbyterian Church in Berlin. To the end of King's life the emotional and even sentimental side of his personality remained extraordinarily responsive to the spiritual appeal of sermons, prayers, the reading of Scripture, and the singing of hymns. It was not uncommon, for example, for him to burst into tears at a church service when some hymn or prayer touched a sensitive chord, and this emotion would occasionally become so strong that he would be compelled to leave. "Hymns have a great effect on me," he wrote in his diary while still an undergraduate, "and I trust they always will have tender associations, [I] will always cling to them."[12] He was from early days a sermon-taster, and many pages in his diary as well as a substantial part of the letters which passed between him and his family are devoted to discussions of the most recent sermons they had heard. "There is nothing in the world I like better than a good sermon," he wrote in 1894, "nothing I hate more than a bad one,"[13] and his regular church attendance for the next fifty-six years bore witness to both his piety and his optimism.

His spiritual experience in all its manifestations was always in-

36

tensely vivid and intensely personal, and he felt a deep concern for individual salvation which seems to have been shared by many students at that time. He was abnormally conscious of his own sinfulness and he would be tortured by a conviction of his many inadequacies; nothing less than perfection was his goal, and the effort towards such a goal was therefore bound to be discouraging and the pursuit unending. These thoughts, feelings of guilt, and thwarted aspirations were always extremely real, they haunted him continually, and gave him no permanent peace. His diary abounds in confessions and regrets for misdemeanours, both major and minor, and times without number he expressed the hope that his many failings would be forgiven and that his life might be dedicated more completely to the service of Christ. He also displayed the zeal and ambition of a missionary. If he thought a fellow student would be at all receptive, he tried to reform him. His manner of approach was adapted to the person, for at times it would consist of a theoretical discussion of life and eternity, while on other occasions it might be very personal and become an emotional exhortation to repent and begin a new life.

King's constant concern for things of the spirit and his propensity for discussing these matters determined in large measure his choice of friends. He was well liked at the University and his circle of friends and particularly of acquaintances was very wide. It included a number of fairly distinct groups: those whom he had known at school in Berlin; those who were also friends of his family; those with whom he was associated in student activities, such as the *Varsity*, his own graduating class, and others. Although there were a large number of men at the University of Toronto at this time who later made a name for themselves,* Rex was on intimate terms with only a few of them during his student days: Charles W. Cross (later Attorney-General of Alberta); Rev. E. A. Wicher (later professor at San Francisco Theological Seminary); Rev. J. G. Inkster (later a Presbyterian minis-

*The following names might be mentioned: B. K. Sandwell, Arthur Stringer, Harvey O'Higgins, Hector Charlesworth, James A. Tucker, Norman Duncan, in journalism and literature; Malcolm W. Wallace, James T. Shotwell, Pelham Edgar, W. A. Kirkwood, D. Bruce Macdonald, in education; Arthur Meighen, G. S. Henry, C. W. Cross, W. E. N. Sinclair, T. Hamar (later Viscount) Greenwood, in politics; E. A. Wicher, Thomas Eakin, J. G. Inkster, in the church; R. H. Coats, S. J. McLean, O. M. Biggar, in government service; R. F. McWilliams, A. C. Hardy, in law; H. A. Bruce in medicine; Edward W. (later Sir Edward) Beatty, J. S. McLean in industry.

ter in Toronto); and James A. Tucker (later editor of Toronto *Saturday Night*).* He tended to seek his friends chiefly, though not exclusively, among those whose ruling purpose in life was self-improvement and the moral and spiritual uplift of mankind. Wicher, Inkster, and Tucker fell in this category, as did Henry Albert Harper, who was later to go to Ottawa and work with King there. They were all very serious, very altruistic, and given to long semi-philosophic discussions on ethical and allied problems. It is to be feared that they also tended to be priggish, but no one can doubt their inherent sincerity or the excellence (they would have used the word "nobility") of their high purpose. A letter written by King to Harper after a short reunion with Tucker in the spring of 1896 suggests the idealism and affection which bound them together.

Jim Tucker was in the city yesterday & I had a little chat with him. We were speaking of you and for the moment my heart yearned that the three of us might be together only for a little while. All of us have much in common and all I believe are firm and lasting friends. Jim is looking the same as ever and *is* the same as ever—kindly, sympathetic, generous, firm in principle and staunch at heart. I have always liked him and his familiar face & genial company while they were present rekindled the flame of love which burns in my heart for him. It was natural that having had the pleasure of a half hour's talk with him I should long for a word from you. I say it again I wish we had been together we three, & the thought has left its influence for since I have reflected on what we *might* have done while opportunity presented itself. Had each learned the hidden secrets & longings of the other's heart while at College we might combined have been a power which would have left its influence on many lives. But why regret the Past! Let us rather hope that our divided or separate efforts were not without some good reward.[14]

King showed, moreover, an eagerness to put his Christian principles into practice in a way and to a degree which is uncommon in a student and almost startling in one who was so actively interested in the lighter side of university life. A few weeks after he went to Toronto he began to visit patients at the Sick Children's Hospital. He did this virtually every Sunday afternoon throughout the college term for four and a half years, and for a time he also attended a church service there on Sunday morning. Occasionally he would take others with him; but usually he would go alone to his special ward of about

*Tucker died in 1904 at the age of 32 after a most promising career as a journalist. A volume of his poetry was published posthumously.

twenty children, read and talk to them and tell them stories, and present twenty-five cents to any so fortunate as to have a birthday. From time to time King turned his attention to the task of reforming prostitutes and getting them back into their own homes or securing their admission to institutions dedicated to their rehabilitation. He kept in touch with these girls in the ensuing weeks, would try to strengthen their resolve by reasoning and prayer, and if, as happened not infrequently, they slipped back into the old life, he was disconsolate for days afterwards. In 1894 he helped to found a newsboys' association in Toronto, and gave it thereafter his steady support. A year or so later he became greatly interested in a men's club in one of the city's poorer districts. Here he spent many enjoyable evenings, chatting with the members, singing songs and hymns, giving occasional informal talks, and joining in the debates.

This reforming zeal was not confined to the poor and the unfortunate. His desire for self-improvement was so absorbing that he tended to overlook the fact that others were not equally concerned to remedy their deficiencies, and his family and his friends were the chief sufferers. He was constantly giving unsought advice to his brother and sisters, and as he grew older his suggestions extended to his mother and father as well. He showed particular anxiety for the intellectual development of the family, and "little old grandpa" would advise his mother and sisters on their reading and, when home, would make doubly sure by reading aloud such authors as Toynbee, Longfellow, Oliver Wendell Holmes, Zola, Meredith, and De Quincey.

The same tendency appeared in his relations with his friends and with the many girls of his acquaintance. He continued as a university student to be very susceptible to girls and always found a large number of them extremely attractive. They, in turn, liked him; for his affable manner and pleasant smile were accompanied by a talent for organizing social activities and a willingness to throw himself enthusiastically into any new venture. He had his own method of approach which seems, for a time at least, to have been quite effective, consisting in large measure of a flattering desire to discuss with them the more momentous issues of life. Thus he reported that in one comprehensive discussion of two and a half hours they "spoke . . . of God, Eternity, Immortality, Life, &c. Both [of us] were confidential & earnest."[15] It was his habit on such occasions to indulge in his fondness for reading aloud some of the classics of English literature, and one can only marvel at his temerity in trying to entertain a charming high-spirited girl on holiday in Muskoka by spending hour after hour in reading massive extracts from Gibbon's *Decline and Fall* and Ruskin's *Stones of Venice*. In an undated letter from Muskoka to Bert Harper in the summer of 1896 he wrote:

This weary & distorted old brain has been having a most delightful rest. Nay more than that. I have been increasing its weight in a manner analogous to that of the body described. . . . I have been reading a little of Ruskin and a little of our old friend "Dave" Ricardo. I have had moreover as a delightful audience, two bright intellectual and beautiful young ladies who swing in hammocks or sit at my side as I read aloud. I will hear their silvery voices in a moment or two telling me that they are ready for more, an interruption having occurred to enable them to have the regular afternoon bathe. I think their hair is about dry by this time.

But more seriously, I never felt so deeply impressed with the all pervading presence of an infinite God who inhabits Eternity than in this delightful spot, Nature in all its purity and beauty proclaims on every side the magnificence of His handiwork and my soul enjoys a communion with His world about not to be expressed in words. But of this more fully when I see you. The silvery voice of which I told you has just called out "Will, are you ready?" and of course I answered "always." So I must close.

Unfortunately the result of many of these pleasing encounters was apt to be mutual disillusionment. King was disturbed to find after a brief experience that the girls did not have all the "noble attributes" he had imagined and did not share to an equal degree his concern for the things of the intellect and of the spirit. It is but fair to assume that his companions made the simultaneous discovery that association on so high a plane could become after a few hours extremely fatiguing, and that Willie King, despite an engaging personality, and a becoming earnestness, could be—all too frequently—a bore.

King's social graces were nevertheless highly developed, and he began as a student to show an uncanny talent for making contacts with people, and especially people who mattered, a talent which was to become even more noticeable as he grew older. Many illustrations might be given. Thus when Lord and Lady Aberdeen visited the University in 1894, King acted as a footman when their sleigh was being pulled through the streets by admiring students. "I showed them into their carriage then I ran along side it & talked to the Governor General and Lady Aberdeen all the way to Victoria College.

I enjoyed the conversation with them very much."[16] When he was appearing as a super in *The Merchant of Venice* with Irving and Ellen Terry he found occasion to have a pleasant little talk with Miss Terry in one of the intervals. On his way to Muskoka he fell in with the Bishop of Algoma and engaged him in conversation. And so it went on. A day at Niagara in August of 1896 produced even more opportunities than usual:

After breakfast I had a little talk with Miss Lizzie Lamport & with Miss Palin (an artist) with whom I spent most of the morning. I also had a lovely chat with Mrs. Root wife of an American Consul in Buffalo. I had lunch with Miss Palin. Afterwards I met a great many ladies, especially pleasant was a talk I had with Mrs. Root & Mrs. Hoyt of Buffalo to whom Mr. Vanerst[?] of Chicago Univ. is related. Father came over for the afternoon. I met a number of others whom I knew. Mrs. Aylesworth of Toronto was very pleasant & going back on the boat I had a most delightful conversation with Miss Fitzgerald of Hartford, Conn. whose brother (I think) is French Consul there. We had a very delightful talk together & she is exceeding pretty, tho' much older than I am. Miss Ramsay & the Travers were also on board & other ladies & gentlemen whom I knew. When we got home Josie Downey was here I had a pleasant talk with her. I have enjoyed the 2 days' outing exceedingly.[17]

King's undergraduate scholastic record, as already indicated, was excellent. In addition to his scholarship in the second year, he won first-class honours in his third year, and was ranked second with first-class honours in his final year. It is nevertheless impossible to indicate any specific benefit or inspiration which he derived from these studies. The most that can be said is that he found his greatest enjoyment in economics and politics and that these courses prepared the way for what was soon to become his chief concern, social economics and welfare. Even so, the drive behind this choice was primarily emotional rather than intellectual.

He was a conscientious worker, and his rugged constitution enabled him to participate in a great many student affairs without serious neglect of his studies. Achievement rested on work rather than on native talent or brilliance, and he studied hard and systematically. He was a great believer in condensing his material, and formed the habit of placing the written result on his bedpost and memorizing it as he dressed and undressed each morning and night. He had also the ability to display his goods to advantage in the examination shop-window—a kind of proficiency not unconnected with his synopsis system—although occasionally fatigue would cause him to falter. He possessed one characteristic of most good students: he was able after the examination was written to form a shrewd estimate of his mark on each paper.

His relations with Professor Mavor, while at first satisfactory, deteriorated in later years. Mavor clearly considered that Mackenzie King was unfit to do graduate work, and did his best, both in conversation and in his refusal to support his application for a graduate fellowship at Toronto, to dissuade him from going on. Both King and his father were convinced that Mavor and others had played favourites, and in the University Senate John King attacked the system under which fellowships were awarded. John King, however, was always very ready to detect real or imaginary conspiracies, and his son was at times not above making similar charges. The evidence is far from conclusive, but one receives a strong impression that influence was by no means negligible in determining the awards, and that the real complaint may have been that the King influence was not weighty enough to bring home the prize. Willie felt terribly hurt that his Alma Mater did not give him the postgraduate recognition he was confident he deserved, and he vowed that he would prove the authorities to be wrong. His pleasure in later successes was in no way lessened by the reflection that Toronto had thereby received an unequivocal demonstration of its failure to recognize his capacity.

The question of King's future career was constantly before him throughout his years at Toronto. He entered the University with leanings towards law and the Christian ministry,[18] being encouraged in the one by his father, and in the other by his own religious convictions. As time went on, law steadily lost ground. By the fall of 1893 his mind was apparently made up, and his repeated confessions of his many shortcomings seemed only to strengthen his determination to devote his life to the church. Nevertheless doubts and uncertainties continued to plague him, and the mere arriving at a decision would set in motion more misgivings as to the wisdom of the course he had chosen. Thus the last entry in his diary for 1893 was that he had "decided . . . to become a Minister of the Gospel of Christ"; but only two weeks later he wrote that though the ministry was still his choice "yet I have a very great desire to go into politics."[19]

There is, indeed, little doubt that a political career had never been entirely absent from his mind as a remote possibility. It bore a strong emotional appeal although it seemed to him to have little hope of realization. His family environment, his natural bent, his love of public speaking, his few experiences in Berlin with electoral campaigns, had all developed a general interest in political life. Nor could he escape being influenced by the career of William Lyon Mackenzie, though during his first few years at the University this tradition was more latent than active, a matter of pride rather than of emulation. It was sufficiently strong, however, to lead him and several friends to the cemetery a few days after his arrival in Toronto in 1891 as an undergraduate. "There was no one to show us the way around," he wrote home, "but I thought I remembered the place where grandfather's grave was, and as if led by instinct I very soon found it. It made me feel proud to see it with all the boys around, although there is no great monument to mark the spot, after all what is a great monument but a cold piece of stone it speaketh not as much as Nature's beautiful green turf and the few white stones that adorn its countenance."[20]

In the early part of 1894 politics seem for a short time to have stepped into the favoured position. It was then he wrote the passage in the diary quoted above, expressing a longing for a political career. The next day he attended a debate on the resolution that "the rebellion of '37–'38 was justifiable." Professor Wrong presided, and King joined in the discussion from the floor, apparently taking exception to some of Wrong's remarks on Mackenzie.[21] Within a fortnight he was engaged in reading John King's pamphlet on Mackenzie, *The Other Side of the Story*, which, he said, he "enjoyed very much."[22] Even so, politics still remained, at least consciously, no more than a theoretical possibility, rising at times to unsettle his plans for the future. Thus when he heard Laurier address a meeting in Toronto, he was again filled with a momentary political ambition; but his usual attitude was fairly summarized by another later entry in the diary: "I have a grt. longing for politics, but do not think I may go in it."[23] Here, as elsewhere, he gave no reason for his rejection of politics, though it may be inferred that inadequate means provided a sufficient discouragement at this time.*

---

*An interesting postscript is furnished by the development in Mackenzie King's signature from childhood to maturity. The first letter of his which is available was

43

A new and powerful impulse was now about to come into King's life in the form of an increased social consciousness and the challenge which it presented in suggesting yet another possible career. While to some extent this new interest flowed naturally from his own basic feelings and beliefs, it was also the product of the general response which his generation was making to the evils which had appeared in the train of the industrial revolution. The factory system and the expansion and congestion of city populations had accentuated, if not in large measure created, many grave social and economic problems, and humanitarians were devoting themselves to the improvement of conditions which were generally recognized as intolerable. There was "a growing uneasiness, amounting to conviction," wrote Beatrice Webb, "that the industrial organization which had yielded rent, interest and profits on a stupendous scale, had failed to provide a decent livelihood and tolerable conditions for a majority of the inhabitants of Great Britain."[24]

The movement towards social reform began in Great Britain in the late eighteenth century, and it was still in full swing a hundred years later. Howard, Shaftesbury, and Chadwick had their successors in Kingsley, Maurice, and Ludlow, the founders of Christian Socialism, and in Octavia Hill and her followers in the Charity Organization Society. The Fabian Society was organized in 1884, and in the 1890's entered what was perhaps its most vigorous and productive period with a membership which included Sidney and Beatrice Webb, George Bernard Shaw, Sydney Olivier, and Graham Wallas. William Morris had just described his utopia in News from Nowhere. In 1889 Charles Booth began the publication of his monumental survey of London Life and Labour which by 1903 was to run to seventeen volumes. A similar reform movement arose in the United States, although it was slower in getting under way and tended to be more diffused and specialized in its manifestations.

---

written when he was almost nine years of age and is signed "Willie King." The next letter extant is dated May 1, 1888 (age thirteen and a half) and although it is written to his father, bears the full signature of "William Lyon Mackenzie King," an alteration which might well have been due to his growing consciousness of being the grandson of the patriot. This was still being used when he went to the University, but a little later in that year (November 22, 1891) the letters to his father and mother begin to be signed "W. L. M. King." Owing to gaps in the files the exact date for the adoption of the next and final form cannot be determined, but after the summer of 1896, he signed consistently "W. L. Mackenzie King."

A number of these reformers had some influence on Mackenzie King; he was later to meet the Webbs, the foremost authorities of their generation on trade unionism and British local government. But the first and deepest impression was made by Arnold Toynbee, a brilliant young economist and writer who died in 1883 at the age of 31. Toynbee's approach to both economics and religion had been intensely practical. The theory of economics, he thought, must be brought nearer to the facts, and religious truths served little purpose unless they could "be clothed with flesh and blood, and brought into some relation with actual life."[25] His strong sympathy with the life of the labouring classes gave him a missionary's fervour and sense of dedication, and he devoted a large part of his life to improving the lot of the poor. In this labour he became associated with the Rev. S. A. Barnett whose parish was in one of the slum districts of London and who first instituted the "settlement" as an agency of social reform.

Barnett and Toynbee held the same ideas on social responsibility, and believed that any useful work among the poor and underprivileged must go far beyond the mere relief of economic needs. Education, a broadening of interests, sympathy, religious belief, and a desire for self-improvement were all factors in restoring dignity and happiness to the victims of contemporary society. To establish effective contact with these people it was necessary to go to them as a friend, and Barnett (and Toynbee for a time) lived among those they were trying to help. Barnett's idea of a settlement took tangible form when in 1884, following the death of Toynbee, Toynbee Hall was founded as a memorial to the young reformer. Barnett became its first warden. The settlement furnished a permanent nucleus for community work; it had its own staff, who by identifying themselves with the local area and its problems were able to promote a spirit of neighbourliness and mutual understanding. Clubs, lectures, study groups, concerts, and other educational, cultural, and recreational facilities were not only aids in creating the right atmosphere, they also made in themselves a most valuable contribution to the life of the community.

On July 11, 1894, King wrote in his diary: "Tonight I read . . . some notes & jottings by Arnold Toynbee. I was simply enraptured by his writings and believe I have at last found a model for my future work in life." A few days later he followed this up by reading Toynbee's *Industrial Revolution.* King's own mind and heart responded eagerly to the forces which had dominated Toynbee's life: his interest in economics, his religious bias, his humanitarianism. King's desire for a purely personal salvation had been already partially transmuted into a desire to help the unfortunate, and his social welfare work in Toronto had given him a new satisfaction. He accepted Toynbee as his mentor and guide, one who had worked along substantially the same lines though in a wider sphere and inspired by a carefully formulated philosophy. His first encounter with Toynbee, moreover, came just at the time when he was studying economics and political science and was becoming more and more attracted to them. His academic training could in this new venture be given a most practical application and could be turned to the solution of some of man's most desperate needs. Here was the promise of a career that would combine an intellectual discipline which he enjoyed with a cause to which he was emotionally responsive: he could be in the forefront of a reform movement that offered many opportunities to an earnest and intelligent young man. So deep an impression did this experience make that after an interval of forty-five years King could recall it vividly. He wrote on December 2, 1939:

> Out walking, I thought of Arnold Toynbee and of how, when I had read his *Industrial Revolution*, I was so overcome with emotion at finding my ideal of a man and the purpose of life in the kind of work which he had set for himself, that I recall kneeling down and praying very earnestly that I might be like him.[26]

Toynbee's influence remained a potent factor in King's life for many years. He read and re-read Toynbee's writings and also returned time and again to the biographical material on his hero. He carried two of the books to Muskoka in 1895, read them there, and on his way back read part of the *Life* to his friend Harper. In the same summer he began to develop friendly relations with the Socialist Labour party, a group of Toronto radicals with a decided Marxist bent. King attended some of their meetings and had many talks with their leaders. But he was in no danger of becoming a socialist. In December, 1895, he spoke at a working men's club against socialism and argued that it was not then feasible and would in any event be unable to cure all wrongs. Education, the enlightenment of the masses, and religion would accomplish more permanent good.[27] This was, of course, pure Toynbee doctrine. So intimately, indeed, had he by this time identified himself with Toynbee that on one occasion when the latter's name was mentioned in a public lecture the reference "brought all the blood to my face in a rush. I felt it almost as a personal reference."[28]

The kind of work to which Barnett and Toynbee had given a substantial part of their lives was also being given a trial in the United States by Miss Jane Addams. In 1891 she had begun in Chicago the settlement known as Hull House which had taken Toynbee Hall as its model. King's interest in settlement work as an aid in coping with social problems was further stimulated by hearing and meeting Miss Addams when she spoke in Toronto in 1895:

This morning I went to the Pavillion to hear Miss Addams of Chicago deliver an address on "The Settlement Idea." I never listened to an address which I more thoroughly enjoyed. I sat at the reporters' table . . . and took full notes for my own pleasure. . . . After the luncheon I met Miss Addams and [later] I had a pleasant talk with her. . . . [The next day] Miss Addams spoke on her work in Hull House. The history of the movement, taking it back to the influence & practical work of Arnold Toynbee was more than delightful to me. I love Toynbee and I love Miss Addams. I love the work in which the one was and the other is & which I hope soon to be engaged in.[29]

In this summer also his interest in his grandfather was revived by reading (apparently for the first time) Lindsey's *Life and Times of Wm. Lyon Mackenzie*. Mackenzie's example may have tended to turn the mind of his grandson to politics, but it was likewise exerting a strong pressure in the direction of social studies and welfare work. Politically, King admired Mackenzie for his part in securing a more democratic form of government for Canada; but as a budding social reformer or professor of social science he felt a deep respect and affection for his grandfather because of Mackenzie's hatred of entrenched privilege and his concern for the lot of the poor and oppressed. "Well may I love the poor," Mackenzie had written, "greatly may I esteem the humble and the lowly, for poverty and adversity were my nurses, and in youth were want and misery my familiar friends; even now it yields a sweet satisfaction to my soul, that I can claim kindred with the obscure cottar, and the humble laborer, of my native, ever honored, ever loved Scotland."[30] King was moved by the beauty and sincerity of the passage, and when reading it, he said he imagined that he could feel his grandfather's blood "coursing through my veins."[31] Two days later he was so moved by what he read in the biography that he could not get to sleep after he went to bed.[32] A few days later again he wrote in his diary:

> I never remember a week when I have experienced such inward desires, ambitions, hopes, &c. as this past one. Reading the life of my dear grandfather I have become a greater admirer of his than ever, prouder of my own mother and the race from which I am sprung. Many of his principles I pray I have inherited. I feel I have. I understand perfectly the feeling that prompted his actions. I can feel his inner life in myself. I have greater desire to carry on the work he endeavoured to perform, to better the condition of the poor, denounce corruption, the tyranny of abused power, and uphold right and honourable principles. I have also felt a closer relationship to my own father & a greater desire to make his cares & pleasures my cares & pleasures. I pray earnestly we may struggle together to the betterment of each & all.[33]

It is evident that the life of his grandfather gave King both inspiration and confidence, though the exact road he was to follow was still in doubt. And if he found there much to stir his pride and ambition, he was also able to draw from it a sense of destiny. He was impressed with the hazards Mackenzie had encountered and especially with the many times he had narrowly escaped death. Yet despite all these perils, his life had been preserved; his youngest child, the last of thirteen, was born in exile; and she had lived to bear a son, one who now carried the grandfather's name. "Surely," King reflected, "I have some great work to accomplish before I die!"[34] Six weeks later, in the middle of his summer vacation, he wrote down the same thought, although it was here coupled with a more explicit avowal of his uncertainty as to where his fate would lead.

> I might as well record here thoughts that are constantly flooding my mind. I feel that I have a great work to do in this life. I believe that in some sphere I shall rise to be influential and helpful. As yet I do not know where it is to be. I believe it may be a professor of Political Economy, an earnest student of social questions. Or it may be in public life, parliament perhaps—what if [it] might be both? Here is my ambition, if it is right, if it is going to make my life good and useful, if it make me helpful to others and a faithful servant of my great Master, may it be granted. If it is to take me a step farther from Heaven than I am today, may it be blighted as cursed, e'er [sic] the desire unfolds itself.[35]

Accurate indeed was the comment given many years later by B. K. Sandwell, one of King's fellow students at Toronto:

There were several much more brilliant personages than King in the student body at the time [of the student strike]. About King however there hung already a sort of aura of destiny, which to me was inexplicable by anything in his personality or performance, and which probably emanated from his own absolute conviction that he had what in religious circles is designated a "call."[36]

Mackenzie King graduated in the spring of 1895 with his future still unsettled. He had applied to the University of Chicago for a fellowship in economics and was offered one of $320 which after long hesitation and some misgiving he declined. It was an astonishing decision in view of his expressed wish to go on in economics and social welfare, and must be ascribed for the most part to excessive filial piety. His mother was very reluctant to have him leave Toronto and his father was equally reluctant to have him abandon law. When the actual decision had to be made, he veered away from economics, decided he should try to get his degree in law in the coming year as a preparatory step to the profession, and persuaded himself that he had a fair chance of securing a fellowship at Toronto. The day after he refused Chicago, he became articled to his father as a student in law. Two weeks later he applied for a fellowship at Toronto in political science, an award which would also have allowed him to pursue his legal course if he so desired. In exactly ten weeks from the time he took out his articles, however, he decided to give up law, apparently because he disliked the office work and saw little future in the profession. Social economics and politics became the favourites once more. He was not far from the truth when he wrote his friend Harper on July 24, 1895: "I am a most peculiar compound. I do wish the quantities were not so evenly mixed. I think that the Pol. Science element is beginning to come to the top. What would you think of me devoting my time to this work—becoming some day if possible a professor!?!?!?! of Economics????!!!!"

His refusal of the Chicago offer was also caused in some measure by his father's inability to give him any substantial aid in meeting his expenses. He had felt the pinch throughout his university course. The money came from home in driblets, and occasionally he would be forced to borrow from other students until the next instalment arrived. Laundry made a recurring demand on his small reserves, and a board bill might precipitate a major crisis. When his family moved to

Toronto, his direct demands on them naturally became less, but at the same time the funds available for his education also diminished. After his graduation, Rex set himself the immediate task of trying to straighten out his father's finances. He did a little work in the law office; induced his father to abandon an unprofitable partnership; secured retainers for his services from the city newspapers; persuaded him to sell some of his law books to secure some needed cash; and moved him into a new office. These expedients helped to meet the general problem, but they obviously could do little to meet his immediate need of money to pay for his postgraduate course.

At the end of the summer of 1895 King learned that the Toronto fellowship had been bestowed elsewhere, and he decided to practise journalism until the way was clear to continue academic work. He began as a reporter on the *News* at $5 a week, and in ten days' time he shifted to the *Globe* at $2 a week more. Two days later at a students' supper he responded to the toast to "The Press."

His regular work was to report on the police court proceedings, and he was also given special assignments of a varied nature. One unusually full day in March, 1896, he described as follows:

I had a zigzag route to follow today, and the extremes seemed far apart. This morning I was at the police court, recording lists of drunks, vagrants, burglars, orders of prot'n, cases of non-support, & the like. This kept me busy till nearly noon. I then wrote a little advance notice of a funeral & went to the Cathedral & reported a beautiful sermon by Canon Dumolin on the prodigal's return. His reference to Ian MacLaren's book was very touching. After dinner I attended the funeral of Mr. Vickers & had to go from there to the Toronto Opera House & report a special matinee given by all the Co's in Toronto. Peter Mackenzie came with me. I wrote up acct. of funeral, then of theatre. Got home about 7.30, studied Corporations from 9–11. I fear my life is too much like the course I have recorded; I fly from good to bad, & bad to good, always loving the good, but not having the strength at times to resist the evil.[37]

Although the assignments were often dull and the strain exhausting, King enjoyed his newspaper work. Following a practice which later became chronic, he made a virtue of necessity, and even persuaded himself that this interlude was exactly what he needed to prepare him for a career in social economics. "I will find this a good plan," he wrote with determination in November, 1895, "to see the shadowy side of life. . . . I will derive great benefit for my after work. I fully intend to make academic work my profession and am taking Journalism as an extra year of practical experience in the great school of life."[38] Nine days later he wrote: "Look at this for the phases of life I have seen today—criminal & pauper—political—religious—death—academic—theatrical, [I] have been in 5 different worlds, what a training for a student of Social Science."[39]

Although he had taken on a full time job with the newspaper, King stuck to his earlier purpose to read for the bachelor of law examinations in his spare time. In view of his abandonment of law, this was an extraordinary step, although he may have wished to convince his father that he was willing to give law a full trial before switching to social economics. "I am getting just sufficient law at present," he wrote to Harper in the summer of 1895, "to disgust me with it. I want to stay with it till I become so thoroughly sickened of the business that I may never regret the day I have gone against my father's desires and abandoned a profession which I admire much in some respects but which I have tried to steer clear of."[40]

The reading course in law, it must be admitted, could not have been a very stiff one; but even so, the programme King undertook was by no means easy. He naturally had little opportunity to do any studying during the day, and he and another student, Charles Cross, worked away several hours a night during the winter months. He could not have succeeded except for his sturdy constitution and his capacity to endure hard and continuous labour, though even with those assets he found that he was often too tired to do a satisfactory evening's work. But he persisted, wrote his examinations, and came fourth on the honours list, missing a first class by only a few marks. Of the three ahead of him, two were to become barristers that year, and the other was in the third year of the law school. On June 12, 1896, King received his LL.B. degree.

Early in 1896 King applied to a number of American universities for a fellowship. Chicago was the only one to make him an offer, again a fellowship worth $320, which he accepted. He at once began to search for ways to add to his capital. The *Globe* treated him very well and not only provided a little extra remunerative work but secured him a railway pass to Chicago. He was also able to obtain some employment as a tutor in French and in military law, the latter being a subject about which he knew nothing and which he had to prepare as he went along. At the end of the summer he had laid aside almost $200.

A few weeks after he had accepted the Chicago fellowship, however, he began to question the wisdom of his decision and consider the advisability of applying to Toronto for a fellowship in constitutional history. Eventually he filed an application with Toronto, only to withdraw it two days later. His vacillation and the arguments pro and con were carefully written out by him in mid-June in a lengthy memorandum. He gave as his chief reason for remaining in Toronto the strong desire of his father and mother to have him stay at home and his own reluctance to leave them. The fellowship at Toronto would also give him an opportunity to realize a long felt desire to write a constitutional history of Canada. Moreover, an income of $500 a year (probably for three years) would allow him, if he lived at home, to save a substantial amount which could be used later to defray expenses incurred in studying abroad. If he went to Chicago the financial problem would be serious; his expenses would be far greater, and his means less adequate. Finally, there would be the advantage in Toronto of being with his old friends, at his own university, and in his own country.

On the other hand, he believed that his studies at Toronto would in many ways prove unsatisfactory. He had little admiration or respect for many of the staff, and work with Mavor was not likely to be congenial. While two or three years in constitutional history were attractive, he would be drawn further away from economics, which was the subject he really preferred and the one which would allow him to give his best to his fellow man. The memorandum continued:

Lastly, what is the meaning of this silent voice which has given me no rest, which says: Go to Chicago, go to Chicago. You are wanted there, you will succeed there, above all you will become more earnest there, you will think more seriously of man & life, you will be drawn closer to the living God. Ah, this voice it is which has made me make the decision I have arrived at. I wrote my letter [withdrawing the Toronto application] this afternoon at its command, I mailed it tonight at its silent mandate. It has wrestled with me before. It has been wrestling hard of late. When I declined against my father's wishes to proceed with the study of Law it prompted me—I have felt more satisfied every day that it did so. Now that I have again been forced to wound that father's heart, God grant that in the end he may see that "He who guideth & knoweth all things does for us what is best." I believe that in Chicago my love for the masses will deepen, I will be thrown more on myself, character will develop more, my real hidden nature will reveal itself better, I can get out of old ruts & break off from old & indifferent habits and become more zealous. I believe I can be drawn closer to God there. . . .

It was in church . . . that I finally said definitely to myself: "wait no longer." There under the influence the most for good, I took the step I have, there the voice spoke to me most clearly. Was it not the voice of God?[41]

The decision taken, King's misgivings as to his future largely vanished, though he had an occasional qualm about giving up the ministry. Even the Dominion general election on June 23 and the overthrow of the Conservative Government after eighteen years in office did not raise any fresh ambitions, though he was naturally excited on election night and "proud and happy" the next day. Weeks later he could still write: "I cannot tell what pleasure the Liberal victory in Can. has given me."[42] But the spell of Chicago was still dominant:

I think daily of my work in Chicago. It will be such a release to get into a higher plane of thought & action in, I hope, a more spiritual life. I hope the settlement idea will prove what I imagine it to be. Even should it mean bare floor & walls I would gladly welcome it, if it develops character and makes me useful to others, less a slave to self.[43]

To the cynic, Chicago would appear to be an odd place to expect to find either a more spiritual life or a higher plane of thought and action. It was time for King to come down to earth, and this realistic touch was supplied by Inspector Stephen (one of his pupils in French) who apparently had no illusions about conditions in Chicago. His farewell gift—which he suggested King should take with him—was a service revolver.

CHAPTER THREE

UNIVERSITIES OF CHICAGO AND HARVARD

ALTHOUGH the chief reason which took Mackenzie King to the University of Chicago in the autumn of 1896 was participation in settlement work, his first lodgings were with Dr. William Hill, an instructor in economics, who proved to be both a congenial and a helpful companion. After a brief hesitation, King elected to do the major part of his graduate work in sociology, which lay closer to his chosen field than economics, and he took as the subject for his thesis the International Typographical Union. His first term's programme included courses on tariffs, money, general sociology, the family, and a seminar on social institutions, most of his instruction being under C. R. Henderson in sociology and J. Laurence Laughlin in public finance. To this normal schedule he added conferences with social workers, meetings with labour leaders, and welfare projects of various kinds. In two years' time he could complete the work for the degree of doctor of philosophy.

He settled into his new environment with his usual zeal and confidence in himself. The confidence was not entirely unjustified. Three days after his arrival in Chicago he had so impressed the head of one department that he was promised a fellowship for next year of $520 if he would elect to take that year's work entirely in sociology. At a reception given for all the Fellows he decided that he must be the youngest of the lot, but he told his family that he was not afraid of holding his own with the best of them. "Wherever I go," he wrote naively to Jennie: "I seem to feel at home. . . . I have no doubt that my newspaper work is responsible for that. . . . If I go to a place it seems as though it were part of my business to be there & I take in everything as a matter of course. I meet many people & it seems my

54

business to meet them. I ask a great many questions & I learn a good deal. I think it is a good thing to be use[d] to meeting people."[1]

Shortly after his arrival in the city he visited Hull House and was shown around the buildings by Miss Jane Addams, who remembered their meeting in Toronto. Hull House, as mentioned in the previous chapter, had been founded seven years earlier in imitation of Toynbee Hall, and already it had acquired an international reputation. The settlement was in the middle of the nineteenth ward, where crowded tenements fought for living space with stockyards, railroads, and factories. The ward's people were mostly unskilled immigrants, struggling under adverse conditions accentuated by low wages and irregular employment, a large number of them being not only poor but destitute. "The district is situate almost in the heart of the city," King wrote to Albert Harper in December, "[it] is the most crowded & undoubtedly the filthiest. Around this strange conglomeration is a literal barricade of brothels with their unfortunate daughters of unhappiness and scattered through it more thickly than anything else are saloons & gambling hells of every sort & description. Misery & wretchedness, vice & degradation, abomination & filthiness are the characteristic features on all sides."[2] In 1896 over 2,000 were being helped weekly by Hull House through its creche, kindergarten, library, studio, lectures, clubs for all ages and groups, and many other forms of social service. Miss Addams furnished the drive behind these activities and she was assisted by a corps of voluntary and paid workers, a number of whom lived at Hull House. "Miss Addams . . . is a most inspiring woman," King told his family. "She is a wonderful organizer, everything passes under her review & with it all she works steadily & unceasingly in many different ways. . . . Little children, boys & girls, grown men & women all love & respect her, and yet to be with her and to judge from what she says you would hardly know that she was more than the humblest worker."[3]

Some weeks after King's arrival he attended a representative meeting of all the settlements in Chicago and came away with a renewed appreciation of their usefulness. "The settlement work, take it altogether," he wrote to Jennie on October 18, "is about the best thing I have yet seen. I can enter into it with heart & soul." Although he had made tentative arrangements to go to the University Settlement he found his quarters there and his prospective room-mate unattractive, and he began to look elsewhere. A few days later (October 31) he became, on Miss Addams' invitation, a resident member of Hull House. He was overjoyed at his good fortune in being given the opportunity to participate in the work on which he had set his heart.

Let me tell you [his parents] that at no time in my life did I feel the genuine happiness which I experience daily. There may be many reasons for it. Doubtless the very congenial work & surroundings have much to do with it. . . . I am glad to feel that my life is actually counting for something. My work in the settlement makes me a factor (though a very tiny one) in human progress, I feel I am aiding in a movement which is leading to uplift & better society.[4]

Although his parents must have been prepared for a move of this sort, they received it coldly. Such plans played no part in their conception of a successful career. The original arrangement, John King wrote, was "a most favourable one for your work & for your professional & social advancement . . . conducive to your immediate and prospective benefit in every way. You were living in an academic atmosphere in a position to form ties & friendships with the Faculty that could not fail to be helpful. . . . Hull House no doubt has some attractions & advantages, but are they of the solid, substantial character on which to build for the future?"[5] Mackenzie King answered fully and in great detail, asserting that it was cheaper to stay at Hull House and that he was especially happy to be given this opportunity to follow Toynbee's example in living amongst the poor. Having also pointed out that the University of Chicago urged students to work in a settlement as a part of their education, he then turned to the *argumentum ad hominem*. The staff at Hull House were cultured and refined, and his social and professional contacts there were bound to prove useful in the future. He even produced for his father's benefit several millionaires who were contributing dollars and sometimes daughters to the work of the settlement.[6] John King was apparently impressed by the "solid, substantial character" of such an environment, and raised no further objection.

It is difficult at this time in King's career to form a true conception of his state of mind. Although his letters from Chicago and Hull House are cheerful and enthusiastic, the entries in his diary frequently show discouragement and uncertainty. Two days before he went to

56

Hull House he was prepared to forswear economics as "a paltry thing beside the eternal & real principles of life" and to wonder whether he had not made a mistake in giving up the ministry. The day after he entered the settlement he heard Dr. John Watson (Ian Maclaren, the author of *Beside the Bonnie Brier Bush*) preach, and even the very practical Christianity of Hull House seemed powerless to reassure him that he was moving in the right direction. A month later he wrote: "Daily I am being forced into the Church. I see what is needed. I see the false antagonisms being aided by foolish efforts to do Christ's work without mentioning the name of Christ." He thought at one time that he would drop his studies; again that he would earn money to enable him to go to Oxford next year; and finally that he might have a mission chapel of his own and pay his way by university teaching.

The major cause of this turmoil in King's mind seems to have been a basic conflict between a genuine desire to make an unselfish use of his talents and an egotistical determination, no less strong, to make a name for himself in whatever field he might select. This conflict would often take shape as a choice between one of those careers which were obviously and primarily for the higher good of mankind, such as the church and social work, and one of those which had less lofty pretensions, such as the university and politics; but this distinction might break down, for, as noted above, his entrance into Hull House did not quiet inward reproaches that he was forsaking the church. At other times, his ambition might thrust itself more boldly forward, and he would be forced into attempting some reconciliation between his desires for service and for personal success. This was done largely by his persuading himself that the higher the position which he could reach the greater would be the opportunity for service, thus making ambition merely incidental to the main purpose and inherently worthy because of its association with a noble object. The two motives of ambition and public service became in this way unconsciously blended in his mind, and, in fact, remained that way all his life.

This combination of motives is found in the concluding entry in King's diary for 1896, and the same paragraph states in the plainest terms that he not only wanted to lead but was quite confident that he would be able to take a prominent place once the choice of a profession had been made.

As yet I know not into what channels my life energy will be directed, this possibly the coming year will solve. There are three worthy ambitions which spread themselves before me, a leading position in political life—life of the state—a leading position in University life—and a leading position in the Church. Which of the three if any I am fitted for if any [sic] I leave to the future with the earnest prayer that God will direct me into the one in which my service can be best given to His cause, and with the prayer that if any of these or other causes may take me away from Him that my life be blighted e'er [sic] that time come.[7]

It was part of the same need for reassurance that he always tried to express his decisions in morally acceptable terms so that they should stand before the world pure and unchallengeable. He was also always unduly anxious to avoid any criticism or any possible misconstruction of motives. His decision to move to Hull House was recorded in his diary accompanied by the thought that "when I contrast conditions there with my present surroundings here, my motives cannot be considered selfish."[8] His idea of having his own chapel was followed by the reflection: "All work done for poor &c to be done free of charge, then there could be no doubt as to my sincerity or earnestness."[9] And later: "Men cannot mistrust my motives or claim that I am [would be?] in the church for a living."[10] Such anxiety or sense of guilt is not a natural accompaniment to decisions whose primary purpose is found in a desire to serve one's fellow man.

Although Hull House had promised well, it brought King no more than a temporary peace of mind. For while his mission to help the unfortunate kept him at the settlement (with occasional qualms for neglecting the church) his ambition constantly pulled him towards the university and the possibilities which might open up beyond. Success, as he envisaged it, was not apt to be obtained in the dirt and obscurity of the nineteenth ward. Conditions in the slums might well constitute a tremendous challenge to any reformer, but they were not likely to give a young man like King an opportunity to show his mettle to those people who could not only recognize the worth of his efforts but also accord him the advancement he desired. The university, on the other hand, with its emphasis on competition and its facilities for registering and rewarding successful effort was ideal for his purpose; there intensive effort coupled with native ability could be counted on to bring immediate recognition of a fairly tangible kind.

His work at Hull House, moreover, proved to be disappointing. It consisted for the most part of helping to conduct some of the many clubs in the settlement, speaking at meetings, participating in conferences, and doing a small amount of visiting in the slums. He felt that he was not making any notable contribution, and, what was probably much more important, discovered that he did not like the work in the slums when he encountered it at close quarters. Settlements ceased to be the ideal social experiment which he had read about in Toynbee's life and had heard Jane Addams talk about in Toronto. The work was mean, dirty, and repulsive, and it yielded drab and meagre results. King was too fastidious and too sensitive to his environment to endure the squalor which he encountered daily. "Now I see," he wrote later to his parents, "what a terrible tax the sight of so much distress and poverty must have been, also the continual noise, the long journey and other things not forgetting the smoke, dirt & often the unhealthy odors. One could stand all this if they have their whole time for it but it [is] too much when one has hard intellectual work to do as well."[11] It was once said of Lord Rosebery that he desired "the palm without the dust" and King showed a similar attitude towards the more disagreeable kinds of social work. It was not, however, a habitual failing, for in other spheres King did not spare himself, though the dust was often plentiful and the palm uncertain.

For some time he endeavoured to meet the demands of both settlement and university. The effort was not successful. He was attending more than the normal number of classes, he was working on a thesis which demanded extensive reading and many personal interviews, and at least half his evenings were taken up with some phase of settlement work. The University and Hull House were six miles apart, and two hours a day were consumed in travelling. No graduate student could do himself justice under such handicaps. Under this heavy mental and physical strain, King's interest and enthusiasm in all his activities waned, and he became nervous and worried. Fearing a breakdown he consulted a doctor, but was reassured to find that physically he was in good shape. He realized, however, that this duality of interests had to be broken up, and he decided to discontinue settlement work and confine himself in the immediate future to the university. Miss Addams was reluctant to lose him and offered him temporary employment at a small salary which would have enabled him to stay at Hull House, but he declined it. He left the settlement early in January, 1897, after a total residence of less than two months.

It was typical of him that he should try to convince himself that this drastic reversal in his plans was accomplished "without thrusting aside a single high ideal that I have ever entertained."[12] True, he had been forced to recognize that his supply of time and energy was not unlimited, but there was also the inescapable fact that he had had two alternatives before him, and that he had chosen the university in preference to the settlement. He had, in other words, followed the course which self-interest suggested, rather than the other, but he hoped by reiterating his high resolves to quiet the pangs of conscience which kept reminding him of his earlier unselfish motives in coming to Chicago. The step he had now taken implied a weakening if not a relinquishment of plans which he had cherished for years, a turning away from the Toynbee way of life, an abandonment, at least temporarily, of his mission, expressed in an earlier letter to Harper, to find "a home among the poor & downtrodden, the outcasts if you will, with 'the pariahs of this world' as De Quincey speaks of them. . . . I will live with them and share with them what powers for good have been bestowed on me."[13]

King may also have made (although there is no evidence of it) the eminently sensible reconciliation between duty and ambition, namely, that he would devote himself exclusively to the university in order to fit himself better for settlement work at a later period. Certainly by the time he went to Harvard that autumn he had accepted this view in regard to the competing claims of the university and public service as a whole, though it might be noted in a memorandum of that time that even then he derived little happiness from having resolved his problem and come to a firm decision of where his duty lay:

What is my duty is the great question. It seems to me as tho' I wd. have to devote almost my entire time to my studies this year, (1) my future success in life depends on my immediate success here, & now I have a chance which may not come again. I have had to work hard to earn it & not to avail myself of its opportunities to the full wd. be a mistake. (2) I will develop more systematic thought & get a better grasp of my subject. (3) I must look at life as a whole, my usefulness in the long run will I believe be greater by waiting patiently for my work in public & meanwhile fortifying myself with a reserve of knowledge which can be called into use when there is little time for preparation. My scholarship [at Harvard] makes it a duty for me to do good work & I believe by concentrating for a year or so, hard as it will be, my enthusiasm will not slacken. . . . I carry a consciousness that I ought to be doing for others, but if God spares me to use this knowledge I am now gaining at a future time will it after all not have been working for others even now. It is a real deprivat'n to devote almost all my time to my own work & yet my doing so is not from selfish motives. Oh God, Crush every such motive as rises [sic] solely for & from self.[14]

Even after leaving Hull House, he remained unsettled and restless, although this was not caused by any yearning to return to the slums. He seemed to suffer a revulsion from settlement work, for his interest in it vanished almost completely. He moved away from sociology towards economic theory, perhaps in unconscious reaction from his experience in the applied field, and he became increasingly bored with his thesis on the International Typographical Union as it neared completion. His opinion of his professors, originally favourable, became much more critical, though he developed a strong admiration for Thorstein Veblen, an original and stimulating thinker on the social and economic organization of society, from whom he took a class on socialism in the spring term. Veblen's critical and satirical attitude to many of the basic assumptions of capitalist society evidently appealed to King and he described him as "the best lecturer I have as yet listened to." King at this time read widely in Henry George, John Stuart Mill, Lassalle, Sidney Webb, Marx, Engels, and others. His comments on these men are few and not very revealing; those on Marx (that he was abstract, obscure, unconvincing, and—later—"very logical") leave one with the feeling that he had not begun to appreciate Marx's power, and the records show no sense of severe shock at Marx's materialism. King was impressed by Henry George. "I daily become more convinced," he wrote, "that land shld. belong to state also that [?] R.R. [railways?] &c. I see much to admire & much of truth in Socialism."[15] He was nevertheless sceptical of the soundness of its plans and leaders. He attended a meeting which was held to consider the founding of a socialist colony and he heard Eugene Debs and others speak on the subject; but he dismissed their efforts as "largely all demagoguery" and insincerity. His mixed views on socialism had largely an emotional basis, composed for the most part of his distrust of the rich and his desire to aid the working classes, with a strong moderating element from his low opinion of many of the leaders in the labour movement. His attitude on monopolies and the concentration of wealth reflected the same general influence, although the expression of his opinion to his family in May suggests not deliberate conviction so much as the most recent university lecture he had heard on that subject:

The trend of thought is rapidly going against private monopolies of all sorts and this is an age when economic opinion is rapidly formed. Chicago is in an uproar over the attempt of the Street Railway Corporations to get a franchise of the roads for 50 years. . . . A few more years and these terrific gains of corporations made at the expense of the community will go into the proper box—the people's fund. This is an age of reform along social & industrial lines. it is above all the "economic era," and the battles for the next generat^n & many other will be fought out over economic principles and along economic lines. I am glad that from all appearances I am to have a hand in the fight. It is a good cause, and I doubt not that our family has a right to uphold *the cause*.[16]

John King's reply made no attempt to answer this outburst, but he was probably disturbed by his son's aspersions on the people of standing and influence in the community. An entry in King's diary after his return to Toronto four months later reads: "Prof. Baker was here tonight & sided with me in my discuss'n vs. father & mother in posit'n relating to wking. class. They think I am too democratic—Never."[17]

King's withdrawal from Hull House also gave him more time to devote to the gymnasium, and he was gratified at being asked to train for the spring term sports under the direction of the famous Chicago coach, Alonzo Stagg. A Chicago paper referred to him on January 14 as "a promising track candidate" and said: "King has a long stride and seems to have lots of endurance. In the two quarter-mile runs which Stagg gave the squad he appeared to run easily and to have a strong sprint on the end."[18] King ran in several races, and finished second in one of them. He found the track work, however, a heavy physical strain, and after some months he decided to drop it.

He was also able to find time to continue to indulge his fondness for public speaking, for which Hull House had provided many opportunities. His audiences included men's and women's clubs, church groups, and an occasional labour organization, and once at least (in the summer vacation) he preached in a Presbyterian church in Ontario. In January, 1897, he heard of a debate which was to take place between the Universities of Chicago and Michigan, and he resolved to try for the team. The subject was the cabinet system of government. He debated in the two preliminary contests, and was chosen to lead the Chicago team in the main event. Unfortunately he became ill and was forced to withdraw. He usually spoke with fluency and had little need for notes, though in his first debate he confessed that he got "a little rattled" at one stage. His own comment on one of his speeches on Toynbee was: "I talked for over half an hour without a single note, was delighted to find that thoughts came readily to me. I was deep [sic] in earnest & had no difficulty in giving forth the convictions of my heart."[19]

Such writing as he did at this time was undertaken in most instances to pay his expenses, though this period also saw two serious articles on economics. John (later Sir John) Willison, the editor of the Toronto *Globe*, was a friend of the King family and he was always willing to help both Mackenzie King and his father earn a few extra dollars. He agreed to take an article on Hull House which Mackenzie King wrote in due course.[20] * Two articles appeared in the *Journal of Political Economy* in 1897: one on "Trade Union Organization in the United States"; the other on "The International Typographical Union."[21] The first was little more than a skilful presentation of general material. The second embodied careful research in a difficult field, and showed a balanced judgment and liberal attitude applied to trade union problems. King submitted his thesis on "The International Typographical Union" (about double the size of the published article) to the University of Toronto in the spring and was granted the degree of master of arts.

In March, 1897, King's work at Chicago suffered a serious interruption, for he contracted a mild form of typhoid and spent almost three weeks in bed. His sojourn in the hospital, however, was by no means unpleasant. He became strongly attracted to one of the nurses, and the relationship continued for some time after he had left the city.

Once King's close association with settlement work was broken, he evidently felt no need to remain in Chicago. His change of attitude is not easy to understand, particularly in view of his growing interest in the nurse which should have produced the opposite effect, at least as long as she remained in the city. It is possible that he may have

---

*Another article on the same subject, "The Story of Hull House," appeared in the *Westminster* (Toronto), Nov. 6, 1897.

regarded his Hull House experience as a failure and hence wished to avoid further contact with it; or he may have thought that the University had little more to offer him; or it may have been a recurrence of his desire to return to Toronto. In any event, he decided to leave, and he began casting about for a fellowship. Aid of some kind was imperative. His father could contribute little or nothing to his support, and his own earning power in vacations was clearly limited, so that even with the greatest frugality there was a substantial gap to be filled. His expenditures were, indeed, incredibly small, and they are all recorded in accounts which he kept in great detail. Thus in 1896 (when he was working on the newspaper for eight months out of the twelve) his total income (up to December 16) was only $430.75 and his expenses $410.20—a delicacy of balance which seems to have been typical of his budgetary practice.*

His hope was to obtain a fellowship at the University of Toronto, for he missed his family and he was confident that he could help them, perhaps financially, and certainly by contributing to their happiness and morale. He might, he thought, obtain the first Ph.D. degree that Toronto would confer in economics, and it could turn out to be "one step nearer the presidency of that University which I think is a rightful ambition to have, & which I can attain to if I will."[22] Professor Mavor, however, whether from prejudice or genuine disbelief in King's ability, did not support his candidature, and the two fellowships available went to other students. Mackenzie King was both angry and disappointed at the outcome, but it spurred him on to try to secure help elsewhere. He had unfortunately already withdrawn his application for what appeared to be a sure fellowship at the University of Pennsylvania and he firmly refused to go back to Chicago where a renewal could have been secured for the asking. After several unsuccessful attempts elsewhere in the United States, he followed the strong urging of two of his Chicago professors to try

*The income for this year was made up of newspaper salary and earnings of $275.75; tutoring, $75.00; fellowship at Chicago, $80.00. His expenditures were, of course, affected by the fact that he lived at home for three-quarters of the year. They ranged from university fees (for one term) of $40 to very minor items such as the following, selected from his accounts as typical: Lunch downtown .25; pair of tan boots (Dack's) guaranteed for 9 mos. $5.00; licorice .05; carfare .10; poor old woman who was picking up scraps .10; church collection .05; concert .15; LL.B. exam & degree $22.00; lost .05; lunch with Tucker .50; peaches .05; postage .15; candies for A—— D—— .60; shade which I broke at Trinity .25; little girl to go home in car out of rain .10; laundry $1.40.

Harvard. This attempt was at first equally barren. "I am greatly worried over what to do next year," he wrote on June 22. "I wd. like to go to Harvard, but can hardly risk the venture of [if] no money. I dread remaining in Toronto without some suitable remunerative employment. The disappointment of Toronto has been greater than I at first realized. . . . I am making myself sick with worry."[23] Three weeks later, however, he was overjoyed to hear that Harvard had awarded him a scholarship of $250 for the coming session—one of several reserved for needy students:

My whole life was filled with happiness. I could see a Divine Providence guiding me most lovingly. This will determine my course largely thro' life. I am determined to make it the beginning of an honourable career. I intend to go on now ever upward if God so wills. . . . My whole being is filled with noble ambition. I have to secure more funds, but more faith & work will accomplish that. I will work to show my worth, & Mavor and Toronto will regret its [sic] action.[24]

The summer of 1897 yielded little in revenue but it did produce one outstanding experience and opportunity. Jobs were difficult to find in Toronto, though secretarial work at two conferences, tutoring in French, and the writing of several articles produced meagre rewards. Early in September King secured a position on the *Mail and Empire*, and after a few days' reporting, persuaded the editor to allow him to prepare a series of special articles on social problems in Toronto. Four long unsigned articles, published a week apart, were the result: they dealt chiefly with crowded housing, foreign colonies, and the sweating system.[25]

It is difficult to realize how scanty were the aids available sixty years ago for an investigation of this kind, and King showed great resourcefulness and imagination in digging up his material. He assembled his data on foreign colonies, for example, from such diverse sources as the census; the rabbis, priests, ministers, and Salvation Army workers in the poorer areas; the compilers of the city directory; police headquarters; rescue homes; employers; the leaders of different nationalities in many occupations; a public school inspector; the city hall (for statistics on applications for relief and for pedlars' licences); the post office (for the use by foreigners of the savings bank); the "McMillan" ticket office (for those who made arrangements to bring their families to Canada).[26]

The facts regarding the sweat shops he obtained almost entirely first hand. The basic conditions were the same as in other countries and tended to be associated with the clothing industry. The manufacture of the garments was let out to contractors, who either undertook the work under their supervision in their own factory or in the workers' homes or sub-let to others who did the same. There was virtually no effective outside supervision, and the uncontrolled competition depressed prices and wages to the limit of human endurance. King gave many illustrations of what he had seen and had been told. In one home a sick woman was being assisted in her work by two daughters: one, sixteen years of age, had worked for the past eight years at a rate for most of the time of two dollars a week; the second, nine years of age, was sewing at her own machine. A third daughter was employed in a factory making buttonholes at three dollars a week. Their piecework rewards were 12½ to 15 cents apiece for men's trousers; and 5 cents each for boys' knickerbockers, but they had to supply the thread themselves. One shop was engaged in making buttonholes: large ones at a dollar a hundred, others for 50, 60, or 75 cents a hundred, according to size. Another contractor who paid more than the average wages gave his women employees three to five dollars a week, his men about double. Another plant nearby paid girls one dollar a week, after they had served a month's apprenticeship free. A good girl might get six dollars a week in some places, but this was exceptional. Many other examples were given. Light, air, and sanitary conditions varied, but in most instances were very bad and unhealthy. King also visited a union shop where he found that working conditions and rates of remuneration were far superior to those where there was no such protection.

The investigation and the writing of the four articles took but twelve days and were accomplished therefore under great pressure. Although much of the writing had to be done in the early morning hours, the results showed no sign of haste. The articles were, indeed, journalism of a high order. They were well written and readable; the facts were stated clearly and unemotionally; contrasting systems and practices were outlined; and the reader was left in no doubt of the abuses or of the possible legal remedies which might be applied.

Although King had had a general idea of the existing conditions, his sympathies made a passionate response to the poverty and misery which he encountered. "What a day I have had to-day," he wrote in his diary on September 18 after a tour of the Toronto sweat shops, "& how have I witnessed the oppression of man over his fellows"; and the entry closed: "What a story of Hell. My mind all ablaze."[27] The following day was Sunday, and he wrote again in like vein:

Went to church & heard one of the finest sermons I have ever listened to. . . . I could not keep the tears back, & in the singing of the hymns which followed "Work for the night" etc I cried outright. It was the whole ambition of my life expressed so grandly   Surely one cannot accuse me of being an idler   I am striving to occupy every hour to *work work work* for my fellow men. The thoughts of yesterday hang about me. Oh such work & no pay, no reward—I felt in church as though I were worshipping with parasites, so much need outside in the sweat shop. May accomplish something yet.

With this preparation and in this shocked and combative mood he called that afternoon with his father on the Kings' friend, Hon. (later Sir) William Mulock, then the Postmaster General.* King's diary gives a straightforward account of what followed.

I had a talk with him [Mulock] on economic questions & particularly the sweating system. I left with father & then went back to speak of the manffr [manufacture] of clothing for militia etc & told him I was going to protest against old methods. We then had a long talk & he offered to put in force any practical remedy I would suggest. Later he sd. he would appoint me to conduct an investigat'n in past abuses & frame measures of reform—$200, $100 for expenses $100 for report. He was deeply interested in the quest'n. He dictated a letter to be sent on at Harvard & gave me verbal instruct'n then. Thus already something has been accomplished for the workers. I believe here [is] the line of reform which should lead to great relief. Mr. Mulock was very kind, he urged upon me to think more of making provision for myself. He is anxious to effect reform. Told me what he had done so far re contracts & what he wd. do in consequence of our conversat'n. He wd. not have thought of the matter but for our talk. This work will involve my coming home at Xmas, spending a week in Montreal & one in Hamilton. It was [means ?] that I make a definite stand on the side of labor, as it involves the showing up of corrupt'n & robbery by wealthy men. I will have only the *truth* no matter what the cost. . . . This has been a happy day & some good accomplished.[28]

The sweating system was no new phenomenon in Canada; two federal investigations—one a Royal Commission on the Relations of

*He was soon to be the first Minister of Labour in the Laurier Government (1900–5) and later became Chief Justice of the High Court of Ontario (1905–23) and Chief Justice of Ontario (1923–36).

Labor and Capital, the other an inquiry into the system itself[29]—had already called attention to its evils. But nothing had been done, presumably because of an apathetic public opinion (with the exception of the infant labour movement) and because no political leader had been willing to risk the radical interference with freedom of contract which the abolition of these evils would necessarily entail. On this occasion, however, the report of conditions, informal and scanty though it was, found a sympathetic Minister, who was willing to listen and eager to reform. Thus while Mulock commissioned King to broaden his investigations, he was so convinced of the necessity for some immediate action (spurred on, it may be, by a pending by-election in industrial Toronto)* that he decided to apply a remedy in the Post Office Department without waiting for further information. In consultation with King he drafted an amended contract form which ensured that henceforth mail bags, postal uniforms, etc. would be manufactured on the premises of the contractor and according to government regulation regarding hours of labour, fair wages, and sanitary conditions. This was immediately put into effect for new contracts in the Post Office Department.[30] A week later Sir Wilfrid Laurier announced that similar steps would be taken throughout the government service.[31] The change was applauded by reformers throughout Canada, it received newspaper support in the large cities, and its far reaching consequences were indicated by the enthusiastic approval of the labour organizations which saw in it hope of more humane working conditions.

King might well look back on that Sunday in September when he talked with Mulock as a "happy day," for few young men could point to so substantial an achievement before they were twenty-three years of age. The day proved, indeed, to be one of the most decisive in his life. The investigation then launched was to take him into the federal civil service and eventually to open the door to a political career. King was quick to anticipate the possible political rewards of championing the cause of the poor, to realize how his desire to serve humanity could be united with his desire to promote his own future. Thus in November when the Government's anti-sweating measures were

*D. J. O'Donoghue, Secretary of the Parliamentary Committee of the Trades and Labor Council of Toronto, wrote King on October 28, 1897: "The Govt. made the stroke of a life-time through the wise, tactical and courageous action of Hon. Wm. Mulock."

freely discussed in the by-election in Toronto he wrote to his parents:

Surely I have the right to feel for once in my life that strange and magnificent conception of being in a degree the "power behind the throne"—this is not claiming too much I hope. This has turned out to be the first influential part I have played in the history of Canadian politics. It is particularly interesting because of the class on whose behalf the measure has been taken. . . . Now that a contest is being fought out in large measure on an issue which will be typical of the great majority for coming years, I have thoughts again of an old ambition—one I used to feel as a very little child—that Canadian politics was a splendid field for work. I sometimes hope that in future years I may be able [to] represent a cause which I love as none other, an upholder of the rights of the many against the privileges of the few. . . . The average politician lives on the surface of things, he is but the crest on the wave, the real strong force is often hidden and never known. I intend to be a politician at least to this extent, that where I can exert a force for good I intend to do it, and if the men of the hour are delighted with the spray which is soon dispersed, I gain infinite satisfaction from knowing the force which put the whole in motion. . . . It is better to be a power, though you be never known, than to be a dancing puppet, a mere sounding brass or a tinkling cymbal. . . . This it seems to me is where the economist plays his part. He must if he be honest . . . get nearer to the truth & know better the plan of action than those who carry it out.[32]

King was not publicly identified, of course, with these reforms in their early stages. Even his newspaper article on the sweating system had been unsigned, and it was not published until October 9, three days after Laurier had committed the Government to follow the lead of the Post Office. But King was not to remain long in obscurity. He worked on the subject at Harvard that autumn, and during the Christmas vacation he visited Montreal and Hamilton to extend his study of "the methods adopted in the carrying out of the government clothing contracts." In January, 1898, he submitted his formal report to the Postmaster General—comprehensive yet concise; general in its indictment of the sweating system, yet specific and detailed in its illustrations. It gave the oppressive methods used in carrying out clothing contracts through the system of sub-letting and the resulting homework; it described the wretched conditions under which the work was done, the long hours, the starvation wages; and it demonstrated beyond a doubt the need for stringent government regulation. The report amply confirmed the findings of the original newspaper article three months earlier and it discovered the same general conditions in

Montreal and Hamilton that had been found to exist in Toronto. When printed,[33] the report was very well received, and another printing was made the following year. In the meantime, King's name came before the public in two signed articles on the subject in the Montreal *Herald*,[34] and these gained him a wide and favourable publicity. An unsigned article by him also appeared in the *Globe* in November, 1898.[35] When to his Canadian investigations are added his study at Harvard on the subject and a potboiler research project for the Consumers' League of Massachusetts on working conditions in Boston,[36] it is evident that by the end of 1898 King had acquired both a thorough knowledge and an impressive reputation in this field.

Two years later, in July, 1900, the House of Commons on the motion of the Postmaster General passed a Fair Wages Resolution, which declared that in all government contracts and in all contracts for works aided by federal funds conditions should be imposed which would prevent abuses from sub-letting, and that every effort should also be made to secure the payment of such wages as were generally accepted as current in each trade.[37] It was an obvious corollary to the anti-sweating measures.* Considerable credit for its adoption should therefore be given to the earlier contribution of Mackenzie King, who nevertheless had some doubts regarding the Government's sincerity in introducing a resolution rather than a bill: "I will seek to prepare such a report on returning," he wrote to his family, "as will not leave them a loophole of escape. . . . You needn't say so to Mulock, but he as well as the rest need watching in this, and if he is wise he will not flinch from the stand he has taken but push it to the close."[38] D. J. O'Donoghue, the veteran labour leader who had been very helpful in the sweating inquiry, was appointed as the first "Fair Wages" officer to enforce the government regulations.

Mackenzie King had left for Harvard in early autumn, 1897, between the publication of his second and third newspaper articles in the *Mail and Empire*. On his arrival he at once sought out Professor Ashley. King had not actually met Ashley in Toronto before the latter's departure from the University, but he had written him several letters a year or so before he himself arrived at Harvard. To Ashley

---

*The Ontario legislature had passed a similar resolution April 4, 1900 (*Labour Gazette*, Sept., 1900, pp. 25–6).

he presented a letter of introduction from Goldwin Smith,* one of the most distinguished of John King's friends in Toronto. Ashley was extremely kind and was able to secure an unfurnished room for King in Lawrence Hall, an Episcopalian theological seminary. But the high costs King encountered on all sides appalled him, especially as fees, room, board, and furnishings demanded immediate outlays which threatened to destroy his small capital. Ashley wished to see him work in pleasant academic surroundings and to this end agreed to stand as his guarantor for the lease of his room. This kindness, however, did little to lessen King's worries, for he was determined to pay his way, and was embarrassed at being placed under any obligations to one of his professors. Yet he was averse to living in boarding-house discomfort; not only did he dislike poor quarters, but he realized that in such an environment he could not do good work and that it was most important to associate with congenial people. He was intelligent enough to appreciate that this year at Harvard was his great opportunity and that success now would in large measure shape his future. He wrote home at the end of September:

I feel terribly discouraged and certainly cannot undertake serious work with such a [financial] strain. I am thinking of letting the college go for a year & taking a position as factory inspector in Boston . . . which at the end of the year might enable me to go thro' here all right. I can see this place has much to offer. To my mind it is almost ideal. . . .

If I had known what I know now I would never have come without being better secured. . . . I go to bed with a heavy heart, my first days at Cambridge have been the most trying of my life.[39]

The next morning he was more cheerful, and his postscript ended: "I am here to win & win I can and will." But he still needed $100 at once, and as he knew he could not get it from home, he appealed to his father to suggest someone who would be willing to make a loan to tide him over the next few months. After several days of frantic worry and uncertainty (one night at Lawrence Hall he slept on the floor with only two overcoats and borrowed blankets for a bed) he

*Goldwin Smith, who had been professor of history at Oxford and at Cornell, had retired in 1871 to Toronto where he took an active part in Canadian journalism, notably in the *Canadian Monthly, The Week,* and the *Farmers' Sun.* He was an advocate of a commercial union of Canada and the United States and thought political union of the two countries inevitable. Of his many books on history, politics, and literature, *Canada and the Canadian Question* (1891) was probably the best known in Canada.

decided not to leave the University; but he gave up his room at the seminary to cut down expenses and took a furnished one in a private house a few blocks from Harvard Yard. At once his feelings changed, and he declared that he was now "the happiest man in Cambridge," and was enjoying "the most delightful and comfortable quarters." "I have begun to share in Cambridge life and to feel its inspiration . . . even my most highly colored imaginings have been surpassed by the beauty and strength of this place. The University life is what I have often thought of in imagination but did not believe could really exist."[40]

His decision to change his room had been made before he had heard from home. John King's reply, when it came, was most comforting: it displayed the affection and sympathy which could always be relied upon, but it also disclosed financial reserves which were as unexpected as they were gratifying. He sent $10 in the first letter, $20 two days later, and then the welcome news that he had seen the Postmaster General, told him of his son's worries, and had secured $100 advance on the sweat shop investigation. John King added with characteristic optimism:

> You must never undergo such a strain again, because you can rely with perfect confidence on my seeing you through safely. . . . In future, dear Willie, please state your wants financially & otherwise, fully & without the slightest hesitation. . . . I am *determined* that they shall be met & I can meet them without difficulty. . . . Now will that [$100] be enough? Will you require another $100, & if so when? We must look ahead, you know, & I will be glad if you will tell me exactly, because I have some more strings to my bow.[41]

King was quick to sense Harvard's unique character and charm. "This feeling [of inspiration] is ever present with you," he wrote after five days in Cambridge. "As you walk beneath the magnificent elms, or sit in the lecture halls, or look at the Charles River, wherever you go, whatever you do there is with you a spirit of reverence and inspiration."[42] A visit to Mount Auburn cemetery deepened this impression. He had "never seen anything of its kind so beautiful," and he was much moved by the simple stones marking the graves of New England's illustrious dead: Longfellow, Lowell, Parkman, Artemus Ward, Agassiz, Edwin Booth, Charles Sumner, and Phillips Brooks. The university courses he found completely satisfactory; but he felt (as he had also felt at Chicago) "the sad loss of not being properly grounded" in his earlier work. "Get your grounding as thorough as you can," he wrote Max. "One only realizes how absolutely uncertain his foundat'n is when he begins to put something substantial on top of it."[43]

His professors at Harvard, unlike those at Toronto and Chicago, fully measured up to his needs and expectations. "For the first time," he wrote home early in 1898, "I have felt that true admiration and respect for my professors that I always longed to have. I feel I am gaining from them daily. Their example is a noble one, their inspiration is real."[44] His lectures in his first year included foreign exchange from Professor Dunbar; the history and literature of political economy from Professor Ashley; taxation and economic theory from Professor Frank William Taussig. In his second year, though he wished to take some political science (particularly under A. Lawrence Lowell, later President of Harvard) his choice was affected by the requirements of the general examination for the Ph.D. degree, and he elected to devote most of his time to economics. He continued, therefore, to do work with Dunbar and Taussig, as well as with several others, notably with Edward Cummings who taught labour relations, which King, following his early interest, had decided to make his special field.

Professor Dunbar was the head of the department of political economy, "a great and able man" in King's opinion, modest, unassuming, and a lecturer of unusual clarity and effectiveness. But although King admired Dunbar, he quite lost his heart to Taussig, who remained his favourite professor, an opinion in which many generations of students shared. Probably the leading economist of his day in the United States, Taussig was a Harvard graduate and did all his teaching at that university, his special fields being the tariff and the history of economic theory. He was, King wrote, "a *splendid* man"; "I simply love the man & admire him intensely"; "Taussig is a great teacher. I never was under his equal before." Taussig's benign manner, his fatherly interest in the young Canadian's progress, his Socratic method of teaching and forcing his students to think, his keen mind and mastery of his subject won his students' unreserved admiration and affection. To Taussig must be given the credit for confirming and consolidating King's belief in the theory of free trade, although King admitted that theory might have to be shaded by practice. After

73

listening to Taussig lecture and reading Cairnes on protection he wrote: "I feel more convinced than ever. In fact convinced for the first time of the truth of the theory of free trade. We must have regard for conditions in practice. I see the side against protect'n more clearly than ever. This has been a day, if not of political convers'n, at least of conviction."[45] Taussig, for his part, soon began to appreciate his new student's qualities and this good opinion steadily mounted with time. He encouraged King's efforts, rewarded him with high marks and fellowships, and at the end of his course assured him that he could count on a post at Harvard.

King was also greatly indebted to two professors from England who were at Harvard in his time. Each took a warm personal interest in his welfare. His first contact with Professor Ashley has been already noted, and he continued to see him frequently. He found Ashley very kind, but somewhat cold and cynical at first, and disinclined to encourage his enthusiasms, a manifest advantage (though King did not think so) when he came seeking advice. Ashley evidently entertained some doubts of King's ability, for although on the first test he gave him the only A— in the class, he added this shrewd comment: "This paper reproduces the lectures very intelligently, but there is hardly as much evidence of independent thinking as I should like to see. *Your facility in writing is a little dangerous.* I gave an A against my rule never to mark *unoriginal* work, because the reproduct'n is *so* intelligent. But I do so with hesitation."[46] He had other misgivings also, though these were evidently overcome six months later after King in an evening's discussion had outlined his hopes for a life of public service. "He said: King we do not understand each other, I believe you have lots of good stuff in you. I think I know you better now. Your manner is not the outcome of conceit."[47]

Professor William Cunningham who taught economic history at the universities of Cambridge and London, lectured at Harvard in 1899. He was impressed with King's capacity and idealism; and King, while ranking Taussig first as a teacher, considered Cunningham the finest lecturer he had heard. They shared an admiration for Arnold Toynbee, whom Cunningham had known intimately. Cunningham must have been greatly taken with the young student, for at the end of term he asked for his photograph, and sent his own photograph to King together with a copy of one of his books.

74

Mackenzie King had been at Harvard only a few weeks when he presented a letter of introduction from Goldwin Smith to Charles Eliot Norton, cousin of Charles W. Eliot, the University's president, and himself professor of the history of art and probably the most distinguished American scholar of his day. Norton, now seventy years of age, had been a member of the literary coterie in New England which included Longfellow, James Russell Lowell, Hawthorne, Oliver Wendell Holmes, Whittier, and Emerson. He had also close associations with many outstanding Englishmen, notably Carlyle and Ruskin, and foreign scholars visiting the United States often called at "Shady Hill," his home in Cambridge, to pay their respects. Norton "had a rare genius for friendship," wrote a contemporary, "and it mattered nothing whether its object were Ruskin or Lowell, or a college undergraduate in whom he discovered signs of promise."[48] King was so fortunate as to be included in this circle, and as Norton's frequent guest he met many interesting people with whom normally he would have had no point of contact. In the summer of 1898 King and a young journalist lived at Shady Hill while the Norton family was in the country, a rare privilege for a susceptible youth who was anxious to develop his appreciation of art and literature. King wrote home enthusiastically describing his delight at being able to live in this "home of greatest culture on this continent" with its walls hung with paintings by Tintoretto, Veronese, and Turner, its library containing the Ruskin diary and books once owned by Gray and Coleridge, its dining room where Dickens and many other literary figures had once been entertained.[49]

King was unquestionably fond of Dr. Norton, who was so sincere in his interest and so genuine in his hospitality. But he could not—if he was to be true to his nature—be unmindful of the substantial advantages to be derived from the connection. "His friendship will be invaluable,"[50] he wrote home even before he had met Norton; and six weeks later after a Thanksgiving dinner at Shady Hill he added exultantly: "I stood on the pinnacle of Cambridge, and Cambridge you know stands on a high elevation."[51] In subsequent months he strengthened his position by attending the teas, dinners, and musicales at the Nortons as well as squiring the three Norton daughters on many occasions. He joined the Cambridge Musical Society (paying a five-dollar fee which he could ill afford) because it gave him an opportunity to meet some of "the nicest people in Cambridge" and because its programme included a session at the Longfellow house. John King was, of course, not the one to discourage his son in this realistic approach. He wrote:

A man's success very much depends on his social qualities—especially in a place like Cambridge. All that you have told us about Prof. Norton, his home, family, & friends has given us no end of pleasure. He is certainly a man to cultivate, & you should not neglect any opportunity of doing so. And the same may be said as to all the other professors over there. They are all men of influence & their good opinion of a man is simply invaluable, & will bring to him inestimable advantages in a thousand ways.[52]

King's appreciation of the advantages of Dr. Norton's friendship does not tell the whole story, however. He liked older people, not only because they could help him but because he was genuinely pleased to meet those who had done important things—and he was fully aware that few students were privileged to dine with such distinguished figures as William James, Josiah Royce, Jane Addams, Taussig, Cunningham, and the President of Bowdoin College. Moreover, older people in return liked him. He had a good family background, his manner was courteous and ingratiating, and he made, according to Ashley, "a pleasant impression upon those with whom he comes in contact."[53] His ability was unquestioned, and he was obviously a young man with a future. He had earnestness, he had enthusiasm, and he proved the seriousness of his purpose by the effort he was willing to make to reach his goal. These were qualities which older people appreciated and if he occasionally showed some conceit of his powers, this was likely to be forgiven because of his youth and undoubted merits.

But most of his contemporaries did not regard him with the same tolerance. His academic performance may have made no enemies among the students but it gained few friends, and many traits combined to give him the appearance of affected superiority—which was, of course, not entirely groundless. His very seriousness, his singleness of purpose, his sense of dedication, his ingrained priggishness, his determination to live alone so that he could better control his time and methods of study conveyed this impression. His constant desire to meet the right people and especially the phenomenal success of his efforts were apt to cause amusement or irritation among the students, and in either case he did not improve matters by talking freely of his distinguished friends. King was quite conscious of this and he tried—though with little effect—to stop himself. "I yielded to an old fault of talking about myself. What have I done! Nothing as yet and I seeking to be a man—humility & self-denial must be the first step."[54]

On the other hand, King's friendliness, his enthusiasm, and his sense of fun overcame many of these handicaps, while his earnestness of purpose was an attraction and not a deterrent to those of a serious type. At Chicago his only close friend was Professor Hill though the attentions he received from other students while in hospital would indicate that he was on the whole well liked. At Harvard, however, despite the fact that lack of money kept him from living in a university residence, he had a fairly large group of intimates. The chief of these were J. E. George, C. E. Seaman, D. F. Grass, Walter Gillespie, W. P. Cohoe, and N. M. Trenholme. He also kept in contact with his old Toronto friends, Wicher and Harper, and he was invariably interested in hearing from or about any others from his undergraduate days.

Mackenzie King's two years of residence at Harvard (1897–9) were years of hard work accompanied by gratifying results. His regimen (which he outlined in a long letter to Max[55]) was composed of concentrated, systematic effort, seasoned by a moderate amount of exercise and relaxation. At times his resolution would weaken and he would renew his determination to succeed by inserting at the head of a day's entry in his diary such reminders as "Work every hour," "Don't miss a moment," "Watch this week," "I must come out head in February." Yet he went to the gymnasium regularly for fencing, running, and basketball;* he did not neglect the theatre; he spent a good deal of time in discussions in his rooms and on walks with other students; and he was usually available for social engagements.

King also contrived to do a little welfare work in boys' clubs and in hospitals and to address the occasional trade union meeting. Very early in his course Professor Ashley had tried to persuade him that this kind of activity, worthy though it might be, could come later, but

---

*Mackenzie King derived great satisfaction in 1898 from the fact that in the "strength test" he was given a rating of 836 points, the result of an elaborate computation which included the chest, arms, legs, and back. Members of the university crew and football teams required 700 points. In his enthusiasm King hoped to bring his aggregate up to 900, when he would be "in the group with the first 50 strongest men at Harvard. Group A is, however, splendid. This has given me immense pleasure. It means a lot of strength." W.L.M.K. to Mr. and Mrs. King, Nov. 5, 1898.

these arguments were at first only partly successful. As the doctorate examination approached, however, King became more convinced of the wisdom of the advice and he resolved to cut out all outside work which might compete with his studies. "I can do more for the working classes in the end," he wrote, "by establishing my position first, gaining knowledge, influence & authority. This is what they need most on their side."[56] As in Chicago conscience and ambition were again reconciled.

His academic record at Harvard was exceptionally good and marked him as one of the outstanding graduate students in the social sciences. In June, 1898, after his first year in Cambridge, he received the master's degree, and in March, 1899, he passed the "general" oral examination for the degree of doctor of philosophy.* His thesis, yet to be completed, was designed to fit in with his major interest and accomplishment: a study of the clothing industry with special attention to the sweat-shop problem.

His success as a student was reflected in his improved economic position. The scholarship, the remuneration for his report on the sweating system, and a few dollars from occasional newspaper articles carried him to the end of his first year at Harvard; and henceforward finances, while always a worry, ceased to be an acute problem. In May, 1898, he began to tutor a few weak students, and for the rest of his time at Harvard this produced an average income of about $100 a month. That summer and autumn he investigated, as already noted, working conditions in the Boston stores on behalf of the Consumers' League, and this both broadened his knowledge and helped to replenish his pocket book. Best of all, he was awarded for the academic year 1898–9 the Henry Lee Fellowship of $450.

King was very fortunate in the students he tutored. The chief of them were Peter and Robert Gerry, who not only were likeable boys but were backed by almost unlimited resources.† In the summer of 1899 King spent six weeks with the Gerrys at their magnificent home at Newport, Rhode Island, where he acted as both companion and

*His first year showed in three full courses and three half-courses five A's and one B. No marks were given for the doctorate examination.

†The boys' father was Elbridge T. Gerry, a grandson of Elbridge Gerry, who was a Governor of Massachusetts, a signer of the Declaration of Independence, the fifth Vice-President of the United States, and one of the early exponents of the art of "gerrymandering." Mackenzie King's pupil, Peter Gerry, eventually was elected to the United States House of Representatives, 1913–15, and to the Senate (from Rhode Island), 1917–29, 1935–47.

tutor. He enjoyed the dinners, races, dances, bathing, and other recreations of Newport; he tried his first jumping on horseback and had his first fall; he drank his first champagne. But he was disgusted at the extravagance and dissipation of the rich, and his existing bias against great wealth was confirmed and hardened by this experience. Nevertheless his liking for the two Gerry boys remained undiminished, and he also began at Newport a friendship with Miss Julia Grant (grand-daughter of General U. S. Grant, eighteenth president of the United States) who was shortly to become by marriage the Princess Cantacuzene. These friendships remained unbroken until King's death.

King's affection for the nurse in Chicago continued to increase during his first year at Harvard; and although the two never became formally engaged, they were at one time very close to it. He felt strongly drawn to her because of her fine character and personal charm, but he also believed that her influence on him would be beneficial, that she would bring back, as he expressed it, the Toynbee ideals into his life. He felt that he was becoming more selfish, more self-satisfied, more intent on intellectual ease and enjoyment. He must be more faithful to the memory of William Lyon Mackenzie, he told his diary. "His mantle has fallen upon me, and it shall be taken up and worn. I never felt it could be done before. I see it now. With Miss ——— by my side I can stand out against all the world and stand I will. His voice, his words, shall be heard in Canada again and the cause he so nobly fought shall be carried on."[57]

But this happy relationship took no account of his family; and Mackenzie King was in this respect pathetically immature and inclined to give exceptional weight to their wishes. The attitude of the King family towards any immediate matrimonial engagement, indeed, revealed unmistakably the role which they had assigned in their minds to the brilliant son. They accused him of selfishness, of imprudence, of undue haste, of being willing for a passing fancy to sacrifice his whole career just as it was opening before him. The suggestion that he should tie himself down to this Chicago girl—and one who belonged to the socially unacceptable nursing profession at that—was utterly out of the question. They knew best what was in his interests and for his happiness, and they were even more sure, although this was not so strongly stressed, that many of the hopes which they had centred on the promising student would be utterly destroyed if he were allowed

79

to plunge prematurely into marriage. Even Jennie reproached him with ingratitude to those at home. "What we all did hope and believe," she wrote, "was that you would make a name for yourself that would help us all. You will never know the sacrifices that have been made for you."[58] His father elaborated the same theme in greater detail:

I can conceive of scarcely anything that would be more prejudicial to yourself and those whom you love . . . than your contracting any such alliance. . . . You have a position and prospects now that, if wisely used, will make your future, but otherwise not. If you do what you think of doing you will simply blast your prospects and all the hopes we have so fondly cherished. . . . I had confidently counted on your giving me very valuable assistance in [providing for the family]; no one can do as much for sisters as a brother, and especially one who has your opportunities. Say and think & feel what you like, your striking out on your own account in the way you have spoken of means an end to all such hopes & expectations. . . . I think your first duty is to those at home; it is a duty that should outweigh every other consideration.[59]

But it was King's mother who applied the whip without mercy:

The struggles have been long and hard at home and I hope you will not think me selfish when I say I had counted on you to help to lift the cloud. Things are looking brighter than they were but no matter *which way* we turn it must take time to lift the burden off our shoulders. . . .

I have built castles without number for you. Are all these dreams but to end in dreams? I am getting old now Willie and disappointment wearies and the heart grows sick. Sometimes when I hear you talk so much what you would do for those that suffer I think charity begins at home and as you do so shall it be done unto you. I am not grasping for myself but I do feel for your sisters and I know you who have such a big heart will not forsake me.[60]

This assault completely unsettled Mackenzie King. He found himself torn by a conflict of loyalties, pulled in one direction by the steel bands of family affection and duty, and in the other by the silken cords of his love for the girl. It was an unequal struggle. Nevertheless for months he was bewildered and undecided, and his emotional disturbance was so great that at one time, as he himself said, he was not far removed from a complete breakdown. The girl also developed misgivings, caused, it may well be, by King's unpredictable attitude and the frantic and almost incoherent letters which descended on her in torrents. At last in September, 1898, the two agreed to separate, and two years later the nurse was married.

King's disagreement with his family and his later conviction that they had been right and that he had treated them shabbily brought forth fervid protests of his affection for them and a desire to make amends for the worry he had caused. He felt that he had been neglectful and decided that he (and the others also) should do more "to build up a happier home"—a view which he developed in considerable detail in five letters involving some 21,000 words. An important side of King's endeavour was the maintenance of mutual sympathy and common effort made richer by the development of a wide cultural life. In truth none of the family seemed "to have learned how to live, how to read & take care of soul & body & mind,"* he reflected, and this sentiment was the basis of his own counterattack. So successfully, however, did he make his point that the unfortunate Bella, who had begun despite John King's objections to train for a nurse in Boston, was badgered into returning to Toronto to cultivate her mind and to brighten the family circle. The urge to dominate proved at least to have a reciprocal side! For some time the family sent reports on their reading, music, and study to Harvard, and even his father wrote that he was going to make better progress with his book on libel. Mrs. King seems to have acquiesced in this cultural revival, but her sense of humour would not allow her to take it very seriously. "I have started the second part of Pendennis," she wrote. "Isabel is becoming more cultured every day. She practises, walks, reads, darns stockings and in fact is so active I cannot commence to relate all her accomplishments to say nothing of her valuable qualities."[61]

It was during the next year or two, doubtless as a consequence of his frustrated love affair, that King's relations with one member of his family began to show a new intensity. Hitherto he had made no conscious distinction between his father and mother, "two parents," he quoted, "each one dearer than the other," but now he began to single out his mother for special attention and praise. His affection for John King remained, though he became increasingly critical of his father's easy-going nature, his procrastination, his dilettantism, his

---

*Diary, Nov. 19, 1898. Precisely a year later he was to write to his mother: "This is enough preaching, I suppose. Poor old grandpa, he has to worry a little, and when he seeks to reform himself, he wants to reform the world at the same time. But he does get a lot of pleasure out of seeing you read." W.L.M.K. to Mrs. King, Nov. 19, 1899.

81

social prejudices. Father, he confided to his diary, "spends too much time on newspapers & small talk, lives as tho' he were a gentleman of leisure, when he is in debt [and] irregularity is present in all the household management. Meanwhile little Mother suffers & her life is not made full & beautiful as it should be."[62] The family debt was slowly being paid off, but its presence for years cast a shadow over the entire household.* It had limited the assistance which could be given to the boys for their education, it had led Bella to take up training as a nurse, and it had induced Jennie to join the Mulock household for some months as a companion. Little could be done immediately to improve the situation, but Mackenzie King confidently looked to the time when he could help liquidate the debt and put his father's confused finances in order.

As Mrs. King began to rise even higher in her elder son's estimation and become the embodiment of all that he loved and cherished, his letters, which had never lacked in affection, now became excessive in their praise. His diary references, too, which had always displayed tenderness and appreciation beyond the practice of most children, now were burdened with the most florid encomiums. Where he had previously been a devoted son and admirer, he now worshipped at a shrine, endowing his mother with all the virtues and finer attributes of womanhood. "Mother is like a little girl," he wrote in January, 1899. "I do love her so much. She is so bright, cheerful, good, happy & lovely. She has so much grit and courage in her. I have met no woman so true & lovely a woman [sic] in every way as my mother."[63] And this led—with his recent experience fresh in his memory—to the almost inevitable addition some months later: "If I can only win such a wife as I have such a mother, how infinitely happy!"[64] Early in 1900 he wrote to his mother from London:

I have no less than five photographs of you in my room,† three on the mantle [sic] over the grate, one hanging in a frame, and one in the cedar

*In 1896, for example, John King put a chattel mortgage for $300 on the pictures in the King home although there was already a mortgage on the furniture. The mortgage on the pictures came due four years later when John King had characteristically forgotten to attend to it. A man arrived at the house to seize the pictures, but a frantic effort effected an adjustment at the last moment. Jennie King to W.L.M.K., Feb. 14, 1900.

†He undoubtedly had a wide choice, for one of the remarkable extravagances of the King family was its tendency to be photographed on the slightest pretext. Thus John King had his photograph taken in 1898, Mrs. King in 1899, and Mackenzie

The four King children, 1881: Max seated in chair with Willie beside him;
Bella in front on the left, Jennie on the right

The King family, about 1888: Bella is seated in front of her mother;
Willie is standing in the rear

of Lebanon frame. One I often take down & put on my table as I have it now, and when I read Margaret Ogilvie [sic] I had it in my hand most of the time. But these pictures are less often before me than the image of you I have constantly in my mind. Trenholm [sic] said to me one night, "There is no mistaking who your sweetheart is!"[65]

One other example from the diary eight months later must suffice:

I felt very sorry to see her [Mother] go and have felt a sad loneliness each time I have thought of her since which has been very often. She is, I think, the purest and sweetest soul that God ever made. She is all tenderness & love, all devotion, knows nothing of selfishness and thinks only of others. Her heart has explained to me the mystery of God's creation and she lives in the light of His love. It is like coming near to an angel to be with her, and where she has been there a holy calm and purity seems to remain when she has gone. The more I think & see of her the more I love her and the greater do I believe her to be. She is as young too in heart & feeling as a girl of 15, in beauty she is wonderfully fair. Everyone looks with admiration on her.[66]

In the spring of 1899 Harvard renewed King's fellowship for another year with the privilege of using it for study abroad. King accordingly left for England in September, taking with him for reading on the boat Lindsey's *Life and Times of Wm. Lyon Mackenzie* and Toynbee's *Industrial Revolution*. His description to his parents of his feelings as he set forth is typical of his romantic nature, his earnest purpose, his egotism, and his love for self-dramatization:

I go away not without many feelings of saddness [sic] at the thought of a long separation in time & space, yet with a heart filled with courageous hope and gladness, a mind newly fired with earnest determination and a body reinvigorated by rest and recreation. I have no fears, but many hopes, and go out as did the knights in search of the Holy Grail, as with the conviction of one who is doing the right and is seeking a treasure which is worthy of any search. For I go to learn, to search for Truth, to gain in understanding and to fit myself for a life of greater service to my fellows, & better satisfaction to myself. . . . I go with a firmer belief that God rules in His Heaven and has His plans for the children of men and that the Hand which has guided thus far will guide still and care for and protect you all while I am gone.[67]

King followed Professor Ashley's advice and stayed in London at the Passmore Edwards Settlement in Bloomsbury. He found it very

King in London in the same year. In the spring of 1900, in Germany, King had paintings made from photographs of both his mother and father. "I think that now I shall retire from the photo business," he wrote Max on December 16, 1899. "It has taken up so much of my time or thought during the year about to close."

different from Hull House in its pleasant surroundings and the people it served, who were for the most part working men and girls from shops and factories. All that was required of him was attendance at a few dances and club meetings and delivery of a number of public lectures. He gave a course on current industrial questions, some lectures on Canada with lantern slides, and selected readings from Longfellow and Oliver Wendell Holmes. He often joined in the open discussion at other meetings. "There is nothing in this world that I like better than public speaking if I have a subject I know and can feel," he wrote,[68] and all he needed was an outline and a little time to go over the points in his mind. He was especially effective in a debate, and his account for Jennie of one of these, though not entirely unbiassed, is nevertheless convincing:

> In opening the debate I spoke for nearly three-quarters of an hour really without looking at my notes save once. . . . There was not an interruption, but that splendid attention which is the greatest of all inspirations. They gave me a splendid reception at the close. . . . [In rebuttal] I spoke for about a quarter of an hour & was intensely in earnest. The audience gave me continuous applause, and interruptions of "hear hear" came in from many sides. . . . This was an audience of working men to whom the subject was the most vital. . . . I know I made an effective speech. . . . When I sat down there was a very loud applause. . . . It does delight me to feel & know that I can hold and influence an audience and especially an audience of this kind.[69]

He admitted several times, however, that he had lost much of his interest in settlement work. This may help to explain why he did not visit Toynbee Hall until he had been in London for more than four months and the fact that he apparently never met the Warden, Canon Barnett. Such neglect would have been unthinkable two or three years earlier, and was, no doubt, the result of a major shift in interest to university work.

His academic life was centred on the London School of Economics and Political Science. He went there on his second day in London; he paid the School five pounds; he attended some of its lectures; and he made use of its excellent collection of material on labour problems.[70] Sweat shops were still a major concern; not only did they form a part of his thesis, but Mr. Mulock had promised him another $200 for a supplementary report on sweating in England. Professor Ashley had given him a letter to Sidney and Beatrice Webb, whose *Industrial*

Democracy he had studied at Harvard and found "splendid reading."* He found the Webbs "exceedingly cordial." They entertained him and offered their help through letters of introduction, pamphlets, and a reference list on King's subject. Sidney Webb also described the methods he had found useful in pursuing his own researches. King attended some of Mrs. Webb's lectures, and though he thought they were excellent, they were unable to break down his prejudice against women as public speakers. Mrs. Ramsay MacDonald, whom he had met with her husband in Toronto and Boston in 1897, also helped him with manuscript material on factory inspection and put him in touch with various people who could supply information he needed.

For one whose paramount desire was to help the working man, King still proved singularly impervious to the appeal of socialist arguments directed to the same end. Marx was to him only one of a number of writers who had made an analysis of capitalistic society and had advocated socialism as the remedy, and if King gave any thought to the class struggle, it does not appear to have made any great impression on him. He was critical of the economic and social effects of socialism and disliked the materialism which was embodied in most socialistic thinking. He was, in short, a fairly typical liberal of his time, and as such distrusted all schemes which threatened to abolish private property and curb individual initiative and freedom by repressive measures. "Under a regime of social[ism]," he wrote in July, 1899, "the secret of present indust'l greatness wd. be taken away,—viz. private property as a stimulus to exertion, & the socialist alleged motives cld. avail little with man as he now is—& man does not change in a day."[71] "I find myself becoming ever stronger against govt. action except for making restrictions, regulat'ns etc. chiefly because of the deteriorating effect it tends to have on human character."[72] "While my love is mostly for the wkg. classes," he wrote again in his diary six months later, "I am inclined to believe that it is better for public bodies to leave the matter of ownership etc. alone—I am on the whole opposed to 'Socialistic Schemes.'"[73] At London he gave a lecture on "State and Labour" in which he dealt with the "Object'n to Scientific Socialism, as being destructive of forces which have made for progress in the

---

*"I think Webb perhaps idealizes trade unions, still there is much in what he says I believe in. I find the book appeals strongly to me. What would I not give to write just such a book—a history of labor in the United States or America." Diary, Oct. 14, 1898.

past, self initiative, self reliance, independence, the impracticability from management pt. of view, and the destruction, by increase of popl'n [population], if once people allowed to look to state for a living."[74]

It is evident that King believed in the existing system of private ownership with state regulation introduced as a check on its worst abuses. He was fond of reviewing the past and pointing out how much the lot of the working man had improved over the last fifty years.[75] But he showed no impatience with the slowness of this development, nor did he seem to consider its possible acceleration through state enterprise. His perception of the conflicts and trends in contemporary industrial society was, in fact, cloudy and confused, and his thinking was still further obscured by his belief in vaguely applicable Christian principles as guides to social reform. The following extract is the most coherent part of a resumé of a lecture he gave in February, 1900, on "Christianity and Labour":

Pointed out that the former [Socialism] looked to change in external condit'ns, that Xtianity regarded these as due to indiv. action [?] & only permanent good by changing source of this, human heart & motives. In diagnosis of world, Christianity saw the greatest law broken. The unhappiness etc. were evidences of this they shewed a want of harmony with the purpose of the world, which was love. God is love therefore in remedy[?] it looked not to change in condit'ns, but change in causes wh. brought them about, heart of man, & fulfilment of the law of love. Pointed out how social changes without this wd. fail, with this social condit'ns wd. soon adjust themselves. Then spoke of Xtianity as a motive power in social reform. Action responding to ideal & [word illegible] the [word illegible] & of Xtianity as satisfying the heart, indept. of all external condit'ns, being a discipline of life etc. etc.[76]

Both the Webbs and the MacDonalds were members of the Fabian Society. With this aggressive and exceptionally able and well-informed group who advocated the gradual extension of state and municipal ownership as the means of establishing the socialist state, King found himself quite out of sympathy. Although this is easy to excuse, the same cannot be said for his verdict on the Fabians themselves. His diary records his feeling that they were "rather on the edge of things," well meaning, "but as a class they seem to be people with hardly education enough to see deeply, hardly manners enough to be refined, and hardly enough of this world's goods to want other than a change in the social order. There is a sort of 'soreheadedness' among a good many of this sort . . . arising from some misfortune in their own lot or because others have failed to sufficiently recognize them—perhaps this is too wholesale."[77] One can at least be thankful for this final qualification. No doubt the Fabians had their share of cranks and crack-pots, it would be odd if they had not, but to dismiss the Webbs and MacDonalds (all of whom he knew), George Bernard Shaw (whom he had heard speak), Sydney Olivier, Graham Wallas, and others with the above appraisal does little credit to King's perspicacity. His opinion may have been influenced by the Fabians' lack of appreciation of himself, or by the feeling that he was being "patronized,"[78] or even— so strong was his prejudice in these matters—by his dislike of the social habits of some of the Fabians. Of one of their gatherings he wrote: "Two of the women smoked, some of the men stayed near to the wine & whiskey, others talked. I did not care for the crowd at all."[79] King was always prone to judge causes by his impressions of the people who sponsored them.

One Englishman who impressed King very favourably was John Burns, the member of Parliament and the leader of the great dockers' strike of 1889.* His diary describes a visit to Burns' home in late January, 1900:

This morning I was [up] about 8, & after breakfast went by bus & train & street car to John Burns' house in Lavender Hill Battersea. Met Burns near the door & he took me into his study. I spent a very pleasant morning with him, he shewed me his collection of materials on fair wages & sweating & I was pleased to find that almost without exception I had already become possessed of the papers & reports he had. He has a very good library, so far as the arrangement of papers & reports go. His books are the best known ones dealing with labour questions. . . . He took me around thro' his constituency. I have seldom been more pleased at the appearance of any place. The streets were scrupulously clean & all about the houses, they were cottages in rows like terraces, put up by the Artisans Dwelling Co. as a result of the Earl of Shaftsbury's [sic] work & street presented the same clean, thrifty, comfortable & home-like appearance. He took me round to the works department, where the same splendid cleanliness was evident. The vestry does its own street cleaning & paving. The sidewalks are made of a compound from the burned refuse & garbage. The Polytechnic Institute & schools were fine buildings & the beautiful park stretching along the side of the Thames made the whole an almost ideal workingman's

*Burns entered the Liberal (Campbell-Bannerman) Cabinet in 1905 as a Labour representative, and served there as President of the Local Government Board.

87

town. Street after street no sign of public house or pawn shop. After going over all Burns said "now you have seen the man, & his works," he had too much this pardonable folly of conscious self achievement. I could not help admiring him & certainly got the impress'n that he was a man of ability, certainly of honesty and a worthy representative of his class.[80]

King's admiration for the co-operative movement was a logical accompaniment of his distrust of socialism and his desire to encourage the working man to be independent. He attended one of their large delegate meetings and was "delighted with the whole spirit & tone of the place & discussion":

I could see that the effect of cooperat'n had been to make them take a wider view of business life, to look at the capitalists' as well as workers' side of a quest'n & to consider the larger & human problems. I was astonished to hear what many of the societies are doing, in Woolich [*sic*] they are building extensively. The problem they have is what to do with Surplus capital. The sight was one of the most inspiring I have seen. Cooperat'n has in it all the virtues claimed for Socialism, without its defects, it is individualistic, all self help, self initiative, & self dependence, no govt. protect'n. I am greatly taken with the movement as the best thing seen yet to put the working classes on a high level, to make them good citizens & men, & to raise them above the plane of industrial strife which destroys & enslaves.[81]

The circle of King's acquaintances grew wider during his stay in England and was by no means confined to the Fabians and labour leaders. The most distinguished of these he met while visiting Dr. Cunningham, who was now back in Cambridge, and they included Alfred Marshall, Lord Acton, J. N. Keynes (father of Lord Keynes), Henry Sidgwick, and G. M. Trevelyan. Marshall was particularly kind to him, and King was "charmed with him & delighted with the inspiration of his words, but more or less overcome with the sense of my own unworthiness."[82] King later added to his academic collection the names of three economists, H. S. Foxwell, F. Y. Edgeworth, and James Bonar, and on a trip to Oxford he met the heads of three colleges, Edward Caird of Balliol, Charles B. Heberden of Brasenose, and Rev. Walter Lock of Keble. The Oxford experience, however, was not nearly so inspiring as that at Cambridge. He had no Cunningham as host who could introduce him to men of the calibre of Marshall or Acton. King's friendship with Charles Eliot Norton gave him an invaluable *cachet*, for Norton's reputation stood high, and there were those, such as Lord Acton, who had met Norton and had corresponded with him.

Mackenzie King's predilection for famous people did not stop with the living, but extended to their surviving relatives. He was especially delighted to talk to the sister, brother, and widow of Arnold Toynbee and to increase thereby his detailed knowledge of Toynbee's life and work. He met also the son of Thomas Huxley, the daughter of R. H. I. Palgrave, the widow of J. R. Green, the nieces of Walter Bagehot and Charles Kingsley, and even the grand-daughter and four great grandchildren of David Ricardo. While they might conceivably be useful for name-dropping, even the most hardened cynic could scarcely suggest that King hoped to use the influence of these people to his advantage. He was at least a generation too late for that. Not entirely, perhaps, for another in the same category was Mrs. Humphry Ward, who was a grand-daughter of Thomas Arnold of Rugby and a niece of Matthew Arnold, in addition to being a novelist in her own right. Mrs. Ward took a liking to the young Canadian, saw him from time to time at the Settlement, and entertained him at her country home at Tring—where, incidentally, he met Hon. Alfred Lyttelton, M.P., Mrs. Lyttelton, and several others. There is small cause for wonder that all members of the King family were impressed with the reception that their representative was receiving in England: "You are far beyond your years in many things," wrote even the unworldly Bella. "Most men 10 years on would be content to have gained & accomplished what you have. . . . You have had opportunities & have used them well. . . . Your letters with the account of your doings are simply marvels to us—We live in a great deal of your happiness & success. Our lives are made better for it all."[83]

The Boer War broke out shortly after King arrived in England, and he was there during the "Black Week" in December, 1899, and the much more cheerful period of Cronje's surrender and the relief of Kimberley and Ladysmith. King was unequivocally against war. "The Love of God & War," he wrote in the diary, "cannot be reconciled by any philosophy under Heaven, it is to fetter men's intellects & to insult them to ask them to accept it."[84] He had no doubt of the correctness of Dr. Norton's condemnation of the recent American war with Spain, and he believed that the Boer War could have been averted had greater care and patience been exercised. "I fear that even yet we know too little of foreign parts and their real grievance. Whether knowing the conditions of Canada in '37 has made me partial or not I don't know, but certainly it seems to me that before war comes, something else might have been done. I cannot imagine even the Boers being over unreasonable if every effort possible had been made to conciliate them."[85] Like many of his contemporaries, however, he admitted that once the decisive commitment had been made, there was no choice but to see the war through to the end. He was greatly moved when he stood on the streets of London and saw the Coldstream and Grenadier Guards leave for South Africa. The British had something that Canadians could scarcely know, "something of pride & glory, something which makes a people one . . . common heirs to the enjoyment of its liberties, its historic past and its present greatness. This sense of national life . . . seems to permeate everywhere, it is the great *mortmain* of the past which holds the present & future generations in its grasp. . . . Everything is history, nothing dates from today. . . . There is no break with the Past and the Future is directed by it."[86]

The rallying of the Empire in a common cause and the Canadian participation also appealed to King's imagination and emotions. The war, he thought, would continue to develop that Empire sentiment which had been given so great an impetus by the Queen's Jubilee. He could scarcely restrain his feelings as he "read of the liberality & grt. enthusiasm of our people at home. If England knew as much of & cared as much for Canada as Canada does for her there wd. be a strong sentiment. Yet I feel the feeling for Canada strong wherever I go, & Englishmen seem glad to welcome me as a Canadian."[87] His enthusiasm was such that he found himself looking ahead twenty-five years and contemplating in a manner strangely unbecoming to a young Canadian Liberal some sort of Imperial federation in which all parts of the Empire would be represented.

In March, 1900, King left England for the Continent. He stopped a few days in Paris and Brussels, and then moved on to Berlin. He was soon made to feel at home and was brought in touch with the English-speaking community (including the United States Ambassador) through the kindness of Rev. J. F. Dickie and his wife. Mr. Dickie was an old friend of John King: he had assisted at the latter's marriage, and had baptized Mackenzie King in Berlin, Ontario. King did not find either the University or the professors as helpful as he had hoped, and the results of his two months' stay were not very satisfactory. He translated some "uninteresting books," and obtained information which would be useful for comparative purposes. But his progress in the language was slow. He could understand "a certain amount," but spoke, he said, "most frightful German & have not mastered the language at all."[88]

King's money was by this time running low, but a loan of $100 from his father allowed him to go on to Switzerland and Italy, where he spent an enjoyable five weeks devoted in large measure to mountain scenery, cathedrals, and art galleries. On the Italian tour he was accompanied by Trenholme, his friend from Harvard, who had also been a frequent companion in London. He left Trenholme in France, and returned to England on July 5.

It was in Rome on June 26, 1900, that Mackenzie King received the offer from the Postmaster General which was to affect his whole life. It read: "Will you accept the editorship and management of new Government Labor Gazette, Ottawa? Begin duties early in July Salary fifteen hundred dollars. May increase. If yes, come. Wm. Mulock."[89] King's thoughts on receiving the message were confused and uncertain, and he wrote in his diary:

This was a great surprise but I experienced little elation because of it. I was disappointed in not getting any word from Harvard without which it is impossible for me to arrive at a decision. All day I have been reflecting on this offer and confess that I am unable to see my way clear to an acceptance of it. What holds me back is the breaking away from an academic career. I have consciously set this before me for years past, and now, just at the moment when it is likely to begin comes an offer which takes me into another field altogether. I am much distressed in mind about the matter for it is a crisis, and on it turns the future of my life in large part. What distresses me most is the thought that I am unable to sift my own reasons & motives aright, to assure myself that in rejecting the govt. offer it may not be drawing away from duty, and in clinging to the University life, seeing a path which is selfish & pleasant rather than one that is strenuous & hard. . . . The University salary will probably not be more than a third of this, but wealth is not in money. In short, I am asking myself which course of life will have the greatest influence on character, if I am to be of real service, character must be strong. Will it not be stronger fashioned for a few years more amid such influences as those which Harvard promises, rather than at the seat of government, with its policies ambitions & passions. When I try to imagine myself separated from the University I cannot abide the thought, it makes me almost ill, and yet I see noble opportunities in this other work. I can arrive at no immediate decision.[90]

His letter written home on the same day gave some of his thoughts in greater detail:

It is a hard problem to decide. The government's offer is a quite exceptional one. It means having the control of the labor organ of the Dominion and laying the foundations of a government department of Labor with all the significance that this may have. It is a position giving exceptional power, and opportunity for splendid work, for work that may be of lasting service to the country at large. To me personally it would mean an opportunity to carry on the work which grandfather began before, and this with my love for the country for which he lived and died and in which we have all been born, as well as my desire to be of service to the classes in the community whom I believe to be often little thought of, these things make me prepared to go to Ottawa at once. But it means, too, a life along a different path than the one I have been choosing. I have tasted some of the fruits of a life of scholarship and I must confess I am loath to leave them.[91]

At this moment, of course, Mackenzie King really had no choice before him. That rested with Harvard. King had written Taussig some months earlier stating that he would take a Harvard opening at any sacrifice, but he had as yet received no reply. He therefore decided to mark time, and he cabled Mr. Mulock the next day that as negotiations with Harvard were pending he could not give an immediate acceptance. His diary (June 27) noted: "I feel more inclined to hold to Harvard than ever"; but on the following day: "I almost decided that unless a letter [comes] from Harvard, or some news awaited me on return to Rome, I would cable acceptance to Govt offer." The day after this entry (June 29) he received a letter from Taussig offering him an instructorship at $400,* with outside work which would give him an additional $200. He decided forthwith to accept the Harvard offer, though he refrained from cabling Ottawa immediately—"why I don't know. My intention was certainly to refuse & I was very happy in the thought of being at Harvard."[92]

So the matter rested for six days without any further communication from Mr. Mulock. In the meantime John King was bestirring himself in Canada. He wrote Taussig informing him of the offer (of which he

*King pointed out in a letter home (June 29, 1900) that this post was higher than an assistantship, which must have been very low indeed in the hierarchy. It was, however, a part-time job, and would have left him time to complete his thesis.

had indirectly heard through Mulock) and adding that he did not know what arrangements were contemplated at Harvard. What would Taussig advise his son to do?[93] Taussig replied that Harvard had offered Mackenzie King a position, but there was no assurance of permanence and he thought that King should take the government post. Taussig wrote:

I am confident he would do the work thoroughly well, and it is work which—however troubled at times by politics—is worth doing. . . . It is a matter of regret for me that I shall not have his services next year, for I had looked forward with confidence to having his aid in the conduct of our large course. But in his own interest I should advise him to avail himself of this opportunity. And the Canadian Government is to be congratulated on making so good an appointment. . . . As his record here shows, your son has won a high place in my regard and in that of my colleagues.[94]

Thus when King arrived in London on July 5 he found awaiting him a cable from his father saying that Taussig had advised him to accept the Government's offer. "This has given me the whole problem to go over again," King wrote in his diary. "I cannot bring my mind to an acceptance, and my present intention is to wait till I return home."[95] However, after giving the question a little more thought and discussing it with Dr. Cunningham and several others, he made his decision. On July 9 he cabled his acceptance to the Postmaster General, and five days later he sailed for home.

CHAPTER FOUR

CIVIL SERVANT

MACKENZIE KING landed at New York on July 21, 1900, and went directly to Toronto to see his family and confer with William Mulock, the Postmaster General and his Minister. One of his first acts was to go to a barber and get rid of his moustache; the beard which he had also cultivated during his trip on the Continent had disappeared before he left England. Unhappily no photograph exists to record the result of this experiment which was never repeated. After a day and a half in Toronto, he left for Ottawa to take up his new duties.

Some uncertainty about his future work lingered in his mind, but he was well aware that great opportunities were now opening before him. His sense of mission was still strong, and his anxiety to be worthy of the task had in no way diminished. Shortly after his arrival in Ottawa he wrote in his diary:

It is just exactly a year ago today since I left Toronto for Newport & later for the Old World. What a lot has transpired in a year, and how much I have to be thankful for. I have seen more & had more of success than I could have imagined it possible to have. . . . It reads like a fairy tale—yet it is true—& I am not satisfied. What vanity that we should ever seek & yet it is not that I have not all I want, it is that in some ways I have too much. I seek rather the silence, the rest, the peace—and a corner of the world away from man. But has not God been kind and has a Divine Providence not in truth been leading me. I am, I think, more satisfied in heart & rested in mind than when I went away. . . .

The thought comes to me of the grand opportunities of the year which lies before me now. If so much can & has been accomplished with all the ground to cover that has been, surely better things can be done in the year now to begin. Bending to the task before me, watching each hour that it may be a useful one, seeking to achieve the right I can work & wait & what is best will come. This I must & will do. I will seek to see more of

94

the opportunities that are at hand, & to be shifting around less in thought for the changes of the future. I believe that God has led me thro' the mist and is bringing me into a clearer day. That He has His hand upon [me] to achieve this work, and that He has brought me to an end. "Lighten our darkness we beseech thee, O Lord" is the great prayer of the human heart seeking as I am for the way, to the truth & the light.[1]

Assuredly there was plenty of work awaiting him, for the labour movement in Canada was entering an interesting and dynamic stage. Industrial development was only now getting well under way, and there was as yet little appreciation of the fact that labour was entitled to special protection against the abuses of the new era. This protection was not easy to provide. Diffusion of responsibility between Dominion and provincial authorities inevitably made legislative and administrative controls more difficult than they would have been under a single government, and the effect was either no action at all or hesitant and often dilatory action. If the provincial powers were clearly involved, further difficulties arose, for the remedial action then rested with a number of independent legislatures. Identical problems might be ignored in some provinces and met by quite different solutions in others. This haphazardness was in itself unsatisfactory, and so too usually were its results as these became manifest in interprovincial trade relations.

Speaking generally, the British North America Act gave the provinces the greater part of the jurisdiction over labour questions. But up to 1900 the provinces had shown little desire to use their power. Ontario had passed Canada's first Factory Act in 1884, and it had been followed by similar statutes in some of the other provinces. These acts had a limited scope, and were designed chiefly to protect the health, safety, hours of labour, and employment of women and children. The Royal Commission on the Relations of Labor and Capital in Canada had reported in 1889, after the Factory Acts had operated for five years in Ontario and four in Quebec, that their results had been negligible: "While acts bearing upon this subject . . . if properly enforced, would remedy many of the evils of factory life, . . . it is notorious that they have so far accomplished little or no good."[2]

The male worker did not receive even this casual attention from the provinces. The same Royal Commission had revealed "excrescences upon the system for which individuals are altogether responsible," and there is no reason to believe that by 1900 conditions had materially improved. The report had called attention to cases of brute force exercised by employers against their labourers; long hours often exceeding the prevailing ten-hour day; lack of means of escape in the event of fire; absence of guards on machinery; failure to use suction fans for dust removal; payment by the "truck" system; unfair regulations regarding discipline and conduct.[3] If an employee was injured at his work, he was compelled in his claim for compensation to prove the employer's negligence. If he was guilty of a minor mistake or a misdemeanour, he could be penalized for a violation of his contract. If he wished to leave his employment, he could not do so without giving notice or forfeiting his wages; but, on the other hand, if his employer wished to get rid of him, he could be discharged without notice. Trade unions were generally unrecognized, and were regarded by many employers with the deepest hostility; thus the major instrument which could be used to overcome these evils was rarely available.

The provinces had made a modest beginning in facilitating the settlement of industrial disputes. Ontario and British Columbia had statutes providing for voluntary conciliation, and Nova Scotia had provided for compulsory arbitration in the coal mines. Little use, however, was made of any of these statutes. Yet the strikes were often violent, and there were occasions when the militia was called out to suppress disorder. The day after King came to Ottawa the press carried the following report:

The Militia has been called out to maintain order at the fishing village of Steveston [B.C.], . . . where 1,500 fishermen, attached to 47 canneries, are on strike preventing 4,000 Japanese and Indians from fishing. . . . Colonel Woarsh, Officer Commanding, announced that his men had not come there for amusement, but for business; that each man had four rounds of ball cartridge and at the first sign of interference they would fire and the work would be short but quick.[4]

In the Dominion's jurisdiction the statutory provisions were even more scanty. The Trade Unions Act of 1872 and its amendments had legalized unions and made them immune from prosecution as promoting conspiracies in restraint of trade. This protection was, of course, largely negative and did little to break down the hostility of employers and induce them to deal with the unions. Nevertheless the labour organizations advanced slowly, aided by a number of American unions and by personnel with union experience from Great Britain. The unions were based almost entirely on separate crafts and not on the whole industry in which the workers were engaged. The total union membership in 1900 is not known with exactness, but it was in the vicinity of 20,000. About 8,000 of these members were affiliated with the Canadian Trades and Labor Congress, and the balance were in large measure associated with international organizations of which the American Federation of Labor was the chief.

The Canadian Parliament had passed two other statutes regarding labour. The first was the Mechanics Lien Act of 1873, which made the worker's wage a direct lien on the work performed. The other, the Alien Labour Act, was passed in 1897 and amended a year later. It was primarily a retaliatory measure aimed at the United States which had been deporting Canadians who had sought employment across the border. The Canadian Act forbade aliens to enter the country under contract if their immigration had been assisted by the prepayment of transportation or by other means. The common remedy was deportation.

To these enactments must be added the efforts of the Dominion to set a good example in a field where it had no jurisdiction to enact laws. The federal Government had an undoubted right to interest itself in conditions of labour as the purchaser of supplies or as the primary contractor who could insist on its own terms being followed in any contracts in which it was concerned. In these capacities it intervened by the anti-sweating measures and the Fair Wages Resolution; one the direct, the other the indirect result of Mackenzie King's earlier efforts.* The Department of Public Works had begun to apply the terms of the Resolution in March, 1900, before it had received the formal approval of the House of Commons, and the Ontario legislature had picked up the idea and adopted a similar resolution in April of the same year.

The Laurier Government took another step forward in labour relations in 1900 by securing the passage of the Conciliation Act.[5] The Royal Commission on the Relations of Labor and Capital in 1889 had endorsed the use of boards of conciliation and arbitration,†

*Supra, pp. 67–70.
†The terms "conciliation" and "arbitration" are frequently used in these early years with imprecision. "Conciliation," however, usually denotes a deliberate effort to secure agreement in an industrial dispute through some kind of negotiation or

and had also recommended that a Labour Bureau under a Minister should be established within one of the existing departments. Through this Bureau statistics might be collected, "information disseminated, and working people find readier means of making their needs and their desires known to the Government."[6] (Provision had been made in 1890 for a "bureau of labour statistics," but the statute was never put into effect.[7]) The Conciliation Act made provision for the establishment of *ad hoc* voluntary conciliation boards (to be discussed later), and also authorized a Department of Labour. There was no intention of creating a separate department under its own special Minister at this juncture, and the organization was therefore placed under the Postmaster General as the Minister who had hitherto been most concerned with labour questions.

William Mulock lost no time in getting under way, and he even offered the editorship of the *Labour Gazette* (which was to act as the collecting and transmitting agent for labour information) to Mackenzie King before the bill had passed the House of Commons. On July 6 when the question of an editor was raised in the House, he could reply quite truthfully: "I have someone in view, and if we are fortunate enough to get him, I think he will be entirely *persona grata* to all classes—the labouring class as well as the employers of labour."[8] Three days later King cabled his acceptance from London.

King arrived in Ottawa on July 24, 1900. "The first glimpse of the city was from the lately fire swept district," he wrote, "and it was gloomy enough. The business part of the town is small & like that of a provincial town, not interesting but tiresome. . . . I will miss greatly the University society and the pleasant surroundings of Cambridge. Ottawa is not a pretty place save about the prlmt. bldgs."[9] In view of the European cities which he had recently visited, this response was not surprising. The population of Ottawa was only 55,000, and it still bore the marks of its frontier origin as a lumber town and a terminus

---

exchange of views which is facilitated by an outside disinterested party. It is thus simply a device to enable collective bargaining to function more readily, and as collective bargaining becomes more common in any industry the need for special machinery of conciliation in that industry tends to disappear. "Arbitration" implies the intervention of one or more outside arbitrators or judges who issue a pronouncement or decision after each party to the dispute has presented its side. The arbitration may be compulsory or voluntary at two stages. The process may be forced on the parties or accepted by them without pressure, or the decision may or may not be made binding. The use of arbitration is normally a confession that collective bargaining has broken down.

of the Rideau Canal. Just the year before a beginning had been made to add to the attractiveness of the city by the creation of the Ottawa Improvement Commission, a body which proceeded to show how the city's natural advantages could be greatly enhanced by intelligent, though modest, expenditures. Many years later King was to take the initiative in a much more ambitious effort of civic planning designed to make Ottawa one of the loveliest cities in North America.

King was not yet 26 when he became editor of the *Labour Gazette*. Queen Victoria's reign was now only six months from its close; it had opened in the same year that William Lyon Mackenzie had led the Rebellion in Upper Canada. Laurier was completing his first term of office, and getting ready for a general election in November. Four days before King came to Ottawa Winston Churchill landed in England from South Africa where he had been serving as a combatant and war correspondent. Six weeks later Churchill, the popular hero, was elected from Oldham, and took the first step in his long parliamentary career. The South African War had become a series of forays and minor engagements with Boer commandos, one of which was led by a lawyer, philosopher, and geologist named Jan Christiaan Smuts. The two John D. Rockefellers, father and son, were just beginning to form the vast philanthropic and research organizations which have since been associated with their names. Franklin D. Roosevelt had finished his schooling at Groton that spring, and was to enter Harvard in the autumn of 1900. Two years earlier Ernest Lapointe had graduated from Laval, and he was at this time practising law in Rivière du Loup.

"I don't believe Mr. Mulock thought he was organizing a new Govt. deprtmt.," wrote King in his diary on his first day in Ottawa. "He undoubtedly knew it, but not the significance of it. I find myself at present the whole thing, department, Editor of Gazette, staff & all, and have to begin at the base with the finding of suitable quarters."[10] Fortunately the Minister was still in Toronto, so King was able to use his office in the Langevin Block until his return. Eventually he found quarters on Metcalfe Street which he thought might serve. His time during these early days was fully occupied. He had long talks with E. H. Laschinger, the Minister's Secretary, and Dr. R. M. Coulter, the Deputy Postmaster General; he met the Parliamentary Librarian and his staff; he settled on the official letter-head and the format of the *Labour Gazette*; he began an article on "Conciliation" for the first number of that journal. In short, he made the normal tentative efforts to familiarize himself with his new environment. He found a number of old acquaintances from Toronto, but he deplored their lack of serious purpose and their inclination to think of nothing but their own amusement. He was delighted to find that his old friend, Bert Harper, was now working in Ottawa as the correspondent for the Montreal *Herald*. The two thought alike on many questions, and asked nothing better than to go on long walks together or to sit around the fireside reading aloud and exchanging views on ethics, religion, politics, literature, and other less serious topics. In October they were able to secure two bedrooms and a common sitting room in a house on Maria Street, now Laurier Avenue West.

All these new experiences, however, were unsettling. King felt out of his element and began to regret his move to Ottawa. Nor was he reassured by conversations with two senior civil servants who advised him not to regard the service as a permanent career. "I feel very much distressed and most unhappy," he wrote in his diary. "I feel I have made a great mistake in accepting this Government offer, that I have been untrue to my best in interest and development. When I think of Harvard and the opportunities & inspirations there my heart sickens at the thought that it is closed to me. My work here can only be a tiding over of another year. Then I will return to Harvard if they will have me."[11] It was only a momentary outburst. The mood of depression soon passed, although the dream of going back to university life still remained strong.

Ten days after his arrival he was writing a political speech for his Minister:

> I feel I can do the working classes much good by committing the Government to a certain line of policy, by the expressions of a Minister in public in regard to that. Mr. Mulock will give the speech about verbatim as I have it. I will get him for example to state that the "government should be a model employer" to insist on justice of fair wage clause, & following [?] public funds into hands of workers,—closing avenues of corruption in award of contracts, etc. etc. I have given him a good speech, It is good politics for him. It is good for the working classes. Here my greatest power will like [lie ?] & I can be a power behind the throne. What matter the credit so long as the end is achieved?[12]

When he gave Mulock an outline of the speech the Minister "seemed much pleased with it." Mulock was very conscious of the political advantage to be derived from labour reforms, and had told King in their first interview in July that the Government was looking for votes on the *Labour Gazette* venture. Mulock was, in fact, a tough politician, whose approach to the problems before him was governed by an unsleeping determination to strengthen his own party and discredit the Opposition.

King soon discovered how this bias was going to affect his own work. On August 5 he wrote in his diary:

Today I had a pretty good revelation as to the attitude of politicians towards govt. work. Mr. Mulock went thro' my articles & everything wh. in any way cld. count for a Conservative he scored out. He wd. not have even a reference to reports begun by them, e.g. statistical year book, tho' mentioned only as a source of information. When I spoke of publishing legal decisions he was opposed to this because in a recent decision made in favor of labor, the judge had been a Conservative. A C.P.R. strike is on, & he wd. give it full attent'n because most of those interested [are] Conservatives. He has no other guide or criterion, that [than ?] how is this going to affect the party? He wants to have the first issue [of the *Labour Gazette*] really a campaign document filled with references to past doings of gov't. I am trying to impress on him the fact that this not only is wrong but bad politics, for thro' the latter medium alone will I be able to reach him. Tell him that the work must contain unbiased statistical material. He told me of appointing Philipps Thompson [*sic*]* as Toronto correspondent, sd. that all the apptmts. wd. have to be political, & that the govt. wd. have to make them. I will not have a say. This has all made me terribly indignant & I have with difficulty restrained myself. But for leaving the Govt. in a bad way I wd. feel like resigning, but I hold on hoping to see if it is possible to affect [*sic*] my way in the end.

We came down to Toronto together & he drove me first to Toronto Club & then to Falconbridge's where I left him. I was scarcely able to talk all the way.

On the way back I called to see Gurofsky,† whom I spoke with a few minutes. M. hinted tho' he did not ask me directly to say a good word for the party. But I will ask nor suggest to no man to vote for this or any party, & will take no part in politics at all. If I find it impossible to be independent I will step out.

King did not step out. But he tried at once to counteract the effect

*Phillips Thompson was one of the two radical speakers who, by order of the authorities of the University of Toronto, were not allowed to address the student meeting before the "strike" of 1895. *Supra*, p. 33.

†Louis Gurofsky, a labouring man and a reformer, was one of King's great admirers. He had given assistance to King in his sweat-shop investigation and had helped him to make contacts with labouring men elsewhere.

of this first appointment. He looked up Phillips Thompson the same day, "& being full of indignation I impressed on him the need of being independent & standing against party influence. I was much pleased with his appearance & manner & nature   he will be a good man."[13] The next day King saw Thompson again. "I shewed him my plan for the Gazette which he thought right in every way. He promised to back me up in the effort to make the Gazette an independent journal, dealing with such points as the workingmen cared for most. He gave me a copy of his book 'Labor & Politics,' last night. I like the old man."[14] Three days later King had a talk with Dr. Coulter, the Deputy Postmaster General. Coulter confessed that he was often dissatisfied with his work, and that he was frequently sickened by the way in which politics permeated every activity. "He thought Mr. Mulock a 'humanitarian' at heart, & anxious to do for the wkg. classes. He was a shrewd politician, but used politics to effect reform as much as reform to help on politics. . . . I told him of my intention to hold this office only temporarily & we both agreed this was best, & that whatever came it wd. have been a good & profitable experience."[15]

Appointments to the new branch were nevertheless a continuing worry. Mulock made no secret of his desire to obtain men who would help the party politically; and King was naturally moved to wonder about his own appointment: "Was it partly gratitude on the part of Mr. Mulock for the fair wage suggestion," King asked in his diary, "or was it because of likely [?] merit, & because the apptmt. would be satisfactory!"[16] He left the question unanswered. Patronage therefore governed the appointment of Gazette correspondents in outside centres, and some of those in the Ottawa office. King thoroughly disapproved, but perforce accepted it. He managed, however, to get some men of his own choice appointed to the better positions, which was simply patronage of another kind, though one much more likely to add to the Department's efficiency. In October King had Harper appointed to the staff and later made Assistant Editor of the Gazette. After Harper's death in 1901 he secured R. H. Coats (eventually to become the first Dominion Statistician) for the same post.

Mackenzie King lost no time in building up the importance of his Department on the foundation of the Labour Gazette and its contribution to labour problems. On August 17 he took his plans to the

Minister, with the remark that "we must make a genuine department of this,"[17] and asked at once for one or two men to help with the *Gazette* and the compilation of the statistical tables. He suggested, and Mulock agreed, that he should himself take charge of the conciliation work, which was, of course, also a new departure. The application of the "fair wages" and anti-sweating standards to work done under federal government contracts and the investigation of charges under the Alien Labour Act* were naturally placed under King. The "fair wages" work necessitated the drafting of detailed wage schedules which were attached to the government contracts, and this in turn often involved a trip to the area to determine the prevalent wages. King set up an extensive reference library, and began to stock it with labour publications from different countries. A list of labour bureaux in the United States was compiled and a system of exchanging publications on labour matters was instituted. Correspondents were appointed in different cities to report regularly on labour conditions. The *Labour Gazette* published court decisions affecting labour and tables of strikes and lockouts throughout the Dominion. A clipping system was begun based primarily on Canadian newspapers, and an attempt was made to keep in touch with all phases of labour movements within the Dominion. This project, King thought, could be made one of the most useful features of the whole affair.

While discussing the plans for the future on August 17 Mulock first mentioned his desire that "in a short time" King should be given the rank of Deputy Minister. King raised no objection to the suggestion. Apparently Mulock had no immediate intention of assuming the title of Minister of Labour in addition to that of Postmaster General, though it was reasonable to suppose that if he did so, King's chances of becoming a deputy would be greatly increased. In any event, King thought it was worth a try. That same afternoon in another interview[18] King suggested that Mulock should "come out in a labor speech as Minister of Labor. That he should assume that title, use it & make a speech as labor Minister. I told him I would write out a speech . . . outlining the policy of the Gov't etc."

Mulock, a wealthy man, was at first a little diffident at posing as a representative of labour, but King was able to overcome his objections.

---

*Prosecutions under the Alien Labour Act were vested in the Attorney General.

He said they will make fun of me if I come out as the champion of Labor. I told him I did not see how they could, that his actions had not so far as I knew contradicted the statement. Then he said with a touch of real pathos, I can reply to them that I have known what it means to work hard for my bread, to use the spade, to dig & to plough. Then he said had I better say that, and I told him by all means to do so,—but not in his first speech—to wait till attacked & to use this in reply, that if he got opportunity to do this before an audience of workingmen they would carry him out the house—& so I believe they would. I proposed to him to have paper printed with office of Minister of Labor on, & he said to go ahead with it at once. I asked if Order in Council were necessary to assure the use of title, but we see by statute that he is entitled to use it. . . . I honestly believe he never knew how great a thing he was undertaking as when he had the Conciliat'n Bill passed. The Fair Wages business started it.

Mackenzie King's mind was certainly ranging far in advance of his Minister. Exactly seven weeks after he came to Ottawa he told Dr. Coulter that he would rather be Minister of Labour than hold any other Cabinet position. "Perhaps," he added in his diary, "if the Govt. win this election they will 5 years from now make a separate portfolio for Minister of Labor, and I might have opportunity to get the position."[19] One thing, at least, was certain: King was on his way. On September 15, 1900, he was made Deputy Minister of Labour, although he did not receive a deputy's salary until January, 1902.*

The first issue of the *Labour Gazette* appeared in the middle of September, 1900. The editorial set forth its purpose:

The *Labour Gazette* . . . is published with a view to the dissemination of accurate statistical and other information relating to labour conditions and kindred subjects. . . .

The *Gazette* will not be concerned with mere questions of opinion, nor will it be the medium for the expression of individual views. It is an official publication, and as such will seek to record only such statements of fact, and such collections of statistics, as are believed to be trustworthy. In the selection and publication of these, care will be taken to have the information as complete and impartial as possible, and so to arrange it that, while furnishing from month to month facts and figures of current interest, these may at intervals be classified and compiled in such a manner as to show, over periods of time, the trend and development of the subjects dealt with. The work thus undertaken will, it is hoped, establish a basis for the formation of sound opinions, and for the drawing of correct deductions,

*The initial salary that King was promised on appointment was $1,500, but he was given $1,750. Five months later it was raised to $2,250, and after another twelve months the Cabinet decided to give him a deputy's statutory salary of $3,200.

but these, in themselves, are tasks which lie beyond the scope and purpose of the *Gazette*, and are ends it will seek to serve, not to meet.*

The Laurier Government with an eye on the coming election was anxious to capitalize on its efforts in the labour interest. The Trades and Labor Congress met in Ottawa in September, and the delegates were welcomed by Sir Wilfrid Laurier. The Minister of Labour also spoke, reviewing some of the measures which the Government had recently introduced and calling for suggestions from the Congress. He presented Ralph Smith, a member of the British Columbia legislature and the President of the Congress, with the first copy of the *Labour Gazette*. The Congress, while very appreciative of the recent efforts of the federal Government, nevertheless did not rise to its opportunities and passed a resolution favouring independent political action.

The Government's labour policy seems to have been of moderate interest during the campaign, but King wrote that "with the exception of Mr. Mulock, most of the Cabinet seem to be afraid of touching it."[20] The election returns were a disappointment to Mulock, for the Liberals lost ground in Ontario. "He said of the labour business that it had had a steadying influence & had worked well in certain places."[21] The Government, however, was re-elected with a majority of fifty seats.

King soon discovered that a large part of his time would be devoted to conciliation work. The Conciliation Act of 1900, which was copied in large measure from a successful British statute on the subject, had for its object the prevention and settlement of industrial disputes. The Act was based on voluntary action in that either party was free to invoke or accept conciliation or both could agree on arbitration.† There was no obligation to accept any judgment or finding except as freely assumed by the parties. The great emphasis was thus placed upon friendly intervention, the bringing together of the parties and their views for discussion, and the focussing of public opinion on the questions in dispute. With many industries where the union was completely unrecognized as a negotiating body this meeting around

*Fifty years later in its special commemorative issue (September, 1950) the *Labour Gazette* printed a facsimile of this page, and added that this "statement of editorial policy is still adhered to as the *Labour Gazette* reaches its fiftieth anniversary."

†Another part of the Act dealt with the registration of conciliation boards organized on the initiative of employers and employees.

the conference table would not be feasible, and the mediator would in such an event form a liaison between the parties and attempt to find a common ground by holding separate interviews with each in turn. Any attempt to apply compulsion on the parties involved was considered to be beyond the powers of the federal Parliament.

Although the Act had been passed before King came to Ottawa, he was in complete sympathy with it and especially with its emphasis on voluntary action. Early in 1901 he discussed the general question with Smith Curtis, a former Minister of Mines in British Columbia and later a member of Parliament, who favoured compulsory arbitration in the public utilities. King expressed his own view in his diary:

It were better to leave industry more alone, save in laying down rules & restrictions against unfair play, & also subjecting it to the influence of public opinion where this could be focussed thro' a Department or other means as e.g. in Conciliation. . . .

I think . . . he is mistaken in regarding compulsory arbit'n as a great panacea. Most men who consider & advise it, see only the seeming immediate effect upon stoppage of strikes, they fail to see that a strike may after all bring greater good than its prevention. I cannot believe it [in ?] the compulsory adjustment of wages schedules. No judge unless he be an economic divinity could regulate rightly wages in any trade of importance for 1 year.[22]

King and the new Conciliation Act met their first test in October, 1900, in a strike in Valleyfield, Quebec. Labourers engaged in excavation work for a new factory for the Montreal Cotton Company struck for higher wages, which were refused. The Company then brought the dispute to a close by discontinuing the work for the year. Several disturbances occurred, however, when the strikers interfered with the workers in the factory, and the militia was called in at the mayor's request to restore order. The mill operatives then struck as a protest against the use of troops.*

On the following day the Minister of Labour (acting at King's suggestion) offered the services of the Department to settle the dispute between the company and the operatives. The imminence of the general election made it difficult for Mulock to go to Valleyfield

*The *Labour Gazette* is necessarily the chief source of information on most of these disputes. Its neutrality, however, was ensured by the fact that any bias would be quickly detected and resented by the parties involved and its value in providing a reliable medium of information destroyed.

himself, though he offered to do so; but he suggested that his visit be postponed and that in the meantime the strike should be suspended. Without waiting for a reply, he sent Mackenzie King to the scene to see what could be done. As soon as the Government's communication was made known, a large number of the operatives returned to work, but some 300 were still on strike when King arrived. He gave a detailed account of his efforts in a November letter to his parents:

My visit to Valleyfield was as you have seen quite a happy one. It was quietly made, and the end successfully achieved. . . . I got into Montreal shortly after 8, & went on immediately to Valleyfield where I arrived about 10. I saw a number of the strikers hanging around the locks, and sent for one, the Secretary of the Union, to whom I made myself known. After having a shave in a barber's nearby and breakfast, I went over to the locks and had a talk with some of the men, in order to get their point of view. Later on I went to see the Mayor, who gave me his version, and in the afternoon I saw Greenshields and Dunn [?] the Co's solicitors who had come to Valleyfield from Montreal and were staying at the Manager's House. I saw from the talk I had with them that the Co did not desire to have me professedly as a conciliator but that I could nevertheless force them to. I pointed out my position, maintaining that so long as troops were in the city they had no right to claim that the matter was one of concern to the Co. alone. I tried to discover their attitude, and after showing them what I considered the weak points in it, gave them to feel that I was anxious to have the matter settled satisfactorily for them as well as the men.

I made arrangements then [to] call a mass meeting of the strikers in the town hall, and just an hour or two before the meeting I drove again to the Manager's house, to try and secure from them the sort of terms of agreement which would be acceptable; as I pointed out, if they showed a disposition to be reasonable, I could practically have the men dictate terms which would not embarrass them, and at the same time be acceptable to both parties. I pointed out the greater trouble which wd. ensue from a refusal to meet some demands, and sought again to have the Co. inform me as to what it wd. be prepared to do. I saw that a compromise was possible on the troop question, and that further dismissals could be prevented,* and that some arrangement might be made for taking back men already dismissed, at the same time not weakening the Co's position, on the matter of discipline & authority, but also giving to the men the satisfaction of having their demands realized. I drove then to the meeting and by putting leading questions to the meeting got the men to accept the plan of settlement I deemed wisest, and to make it appear to them as if it were their own proposal. They were extremely orderly and quiet and cheered me heartily when the meeting was over. I spoke to them at first in

*These dismissals had occurred when some of the striking mill operatives had attempted to return to work.

French—tho rather briefly, simply to the effect that I regretted not being able to speak French fluently and judged it better in order that there might be no misunderstanding, that I speak in English and have one of their number translate. So I made a speech sentence by sentence, each sentence being translated, and answered. I got the men to agree to go back next morning on condition of the troops returning before night, no further dismissals, and a reconsideration by the Co. of the cases of those already dismissed.

I then drove to see the Co's Solrs, also Mr. Stevenson, the Montreal Director & the Manager, & conveyed to them the nature of the agreement. We went over together to the barracks (the Company store rooms were so filled up) where I had a talk with the colonel, and was shown some attention by the officers, returned later & had a good talk & laugh with Mr. Stevenson, Mr. Greenshields & others. We discussed the laughable side of the question, and especially the position of the unhappy mayor, who has been made a butt of by both sides.

Next day I went in the morning to see Mr. Greenshields & he told me they had given instructions for the troops to be removed, that there wd. be no further dismissals, and a fixing up in one way or another of those already dismissed. Mr. Stevenson told the Manager, Mr. Lacey to take me thru the mills, which he did beginning at the first stages & showing me the different stages in the mffr. of cotton. The Co. have splendid mills & employ about 3000 hands. I enjoyed the visit to the mills exceedingly. In the afternoon Mr. Stevenson drove down to the hotel to see me and invited me to come up & spend the evening with the few Hussars who might be compelled to wait over, because of cars not yet on hand for the horses. Mr. Greenshields told me confidentially that he considered I had won a great victory, that the Co. were a strong Conservative corporation, and at this time did not want any capital made out of them by this Government, but that I had made it impossible for them to do other than deal with & settle the matter. Mr. Stevenson said when I was talking with him that I was a good advocate, and that Mr. Mulock could not have chosen a better man to give efficiency to his Act.

There is no doubt that this was a victory. . . . I wired Mr. Mulock on Monday night that I thought I could effect a settlement & was acting as conciliator. He wired me next morning "greatly pleased to learn that you are acting as conciliator, use best endeavours to bring about settlement, continue your effort long as any chance of succeeding." By Tuesday noon, I was able to wire him that settlement had been effected, all men back at work & troops withdrawn etc. That night he wired "My heartiest congratulations on successful settlement of Valleyfield strike." I know Mr. Mulock will be much delighted. This is a great triumph for the Conciliation Act and all the better because of the attacks that have been made upon it. I am doubly pleased inasmuch as I practically took the law into my own hands, in telegraphing him to act in the first place, and then coming up to Toronto to see him personally in the second. There could not have been a more fortunate happening or result for the Government at this particular time. It vindicates every section of its labor legislation, and is a special triumph for that which most regarded as the weakest part of it. . . .

I think this strike & the settlement of it will help the Liberals very much in this election, especially in Quebec. I would like to see Bergeron, the Conservative candidate beaten. Mr. Loy is the Liberal against him. If Loy wins I will be extremely happy. Bergeron is the man who attacked so bitterly my report on sweating. I found that it was pretty well known in that district also. The Ministers have begun sending in requests for more Gazettes, & copies of the Conciliation Act. Labor is gaining in importance as an issue every day.[23]

King had thus not only proposed conciliation in the Valleyfield strike, but had been responsible for the settlement. The first strike did not, of course, enter the picture at all. It had been declared and lost before the Minister had offered his help, and the interest of the mill workers in the first strike was confined to its sequel of calling in the troops. Incidentally, one may note that even Mulock had not expected King to act as conciliator, though he was naturally delighted to find that his young deputy had been such a success in that capacity.

Several personal factors contributed to King's success. His first great qualification for this work was his friendly manner and exceptional charm. He met the contestants without delay or ceremony, inspired their confidence, and created the impression that he understood and to some degree, at least, sympathized with the position each had adopted. Most people found difficulty in resisting his courtesy, his patience, and his genuine interest in their problems. "By his tact and good management," wrote the Mayor of Oshawa, Fred L. Fowke, to William Mulock in December, 1900, "Mr. King appears to have brought about an understanding between the Malleable Iron Co. and their employees which we hope will create bonds of unity not easily to be broken in the future. . . . Mr. King seems to have quieted their [the stockholders'] nerves and quite won their respect and confidence, while at the same time he captured the hearts of the strikers."[24]

But successful conciliation required more than good intentions aided by a kindly and sympathetic nature. King also brought to the task a perceptive mind, which was unusually quick and adaptable. He grasped the essentials of the cases which were being submitted, sorted

109

out the parts on which agreement could be expected, and then used these as a rough draft of the main settlement. At the same time he was advancing other points to reinforce this position or to be used as expendable issues which could be conceded when the final stages of the bargain were reached. The useful gift of finding a measure of common consent and building an understanding on this foundation was later to become one of his most valuable political techniques as a party leader. He was also astute enough not to reveal what he had in mind as a tentative solution; indeed, as the above extract suggests, he might try to induce the parties themselves to put forward suggestions which he wished to have embodied in the agreement. Personal character and skill lay at the root of his success in conciliation work.

What was King's idea of the function of a conciliator in an industrial dispute? He answered the question in the first issue of the *Labour Gazette*:

It is the duty of the conciliator to enquire into the causes and circumstances of the difference by communication with the parties; to seek to promote conditions favourable to a settlement by endeavouring to allay distrust, remove causes of friction, promote good feeling, restore confidence, and do what he can to encourage the parties to come together and themselves effect a settlement. He must also seek to promote agreement between employers and employees, with a view to the submission of differences to conciliation or arbitration before resort is made to strikes or lockouts.[25]

It was thus, in King's opinion, no normal part of his function to take sides in a dispute. He was the neutral outsider whose main effort was to use his position of detachment to nourish friendly relations between employer and employed and, when necessary, to try to effect a settlement of differences. But such a conception glossed over the more serious difficulties in the situation. The mediator is unable, it is true, to favour one side against the other; but he can be of little use unless he can make his own assessment of the strength or weakness of each case and act on his opinion. After a certain point in the negotiations is reached, to add his support to what is obviously a shaky or indefensible plea would simply prolong the tension and make any satisfactory agreement impossible. Thus in the above account of the Valleyfield strike King said that he reached a point in the negotiations where he "got the men to accept the plan of settlement I deemed wisest," that is, the point where he became an advocate, openly or otherwise, for what he believed would be a compromise acceptable to both sides. In another case in 1901 King found the union's position weak and the employers resolute, and he based his efforts on these inescapable facts. He was able to produce a compromise to which both speedily agreed.

In some disputes, however, it may be quite impossible for the mediator to keep his detachment and hence to remain entirely unaffected by the circumstances; where, for example, the living conditions of employees are far below what he thinks bearable or justifiable. Even so he cannot weigh in heavily against the employer without imperilling his usefulness. His primary effort must always be to achieve not the ideal, but the practicable. Nevertheless the negotiations will probably enable him to do much within the proper limits of his neutrality. If the working conditions are shockingly bad, they become by that fact eminently proper reasons to be pressed against the employer to induce him to make concessions—if not on moral or social grounds, at least to avert public indignation when the conditions become more generally known. Finally, there would be those rare cases where one side might adopt so extreme a position or might so misconduct itself that the conciliator had no real alternative but to come out flatly against that side. Conciliation would in such an event be quite impossible, and the mediator would simply be recognizing the existence of a divergence of views which he was powerless to remedy.

Successful though King had been at Valleyfield, he was still inexperienced. His own account reveals that after the settlement he had become somewhat familiar with the employers, an obvious indiscretion of which he would not have been guilty in later years. This seems to have passed unnoticed. The imminence of the general election, however, made the Opposition wary of any activity by government officials in that area, and distrust was not quieted when Loy, the Liberal, was elected over Bergeron, the Conservative sitting member. At the next session of the House, in the spring of 1901, F. D. Monk, Q.C., the member for Jacques Cartier, charged that "an employee connected with the labour bureau, a Mr. King" had gone to Valleyfield as a conciliator and had grossly abused his position in order to advance the interests of the Liberal candidate. The union there, he said, was really a Liberal organization, its chief officers were Liberals, and those who joined the union had to swear that they would also join the Liberal

111

party. King "became a political agent" and had told the people of Valleyfield that "the government were prepared to do a great deal for the success of this strike but it was all-important that they should support Mr. Loy."[26] These statements could not, of course, be substantiated, though they naturally caused considerable furore and King filed an affidavit denying the charges. He had, however, made one slip. On his way to the station as he was leaving Valleyfield, he had stopped in front of the Liberal committee rooms and the Liberal candidate had come out to his carriage and talked with him. It was a pitiful survivor of so damning a list of charges, but it taught King how careful he would have to be when engaged in this kind of work.

The incident also revealed the suspicion with which many Conservatives regarded the work of the Department of Labour. The Liberals were beginning to shake off their early cautious approval and praise its efforts, thereby inciting the Conservatives to belittle and discredit them. There was a well-founded suspicion that the Government had hoped to capture the labour vote by creating the new Department, but there seems to have been no grounds for a further suspicion that the Department was using its powers in a partisan manner. While King, for example, was a strong Liberal, he showed no party prejudice in his work. Yet he was not at all indifferent to the political results of the settlement, which had possibly won votes for the Liberal candidate. King's hopes that he may indirectly have struck a good blow for Liberalism appeared not only in the long letter quoted above but also in a later one in which he sent his father the detailed results of the election in Beauharnois of which Valleyfield was a part. After indicating the Liberal majority in Valleyfield, he added with obvious relish: "So you see that Valleyfield won the day."[27]

The attack in the House and its complete collapse added to King's reputation. He certainly suffered no injury in Laurier's eyes and probably none in those of R. L. Borden, the Leader of the Opposition. He sent home a report in May:

The day after the last attack, when Loy brought up the matter, I received an invitation to Mrs. Borden's reception. . . . I had a short talk with Mr. Borden there. I have seen him several times since and he has been most pleasant with me. After the last debate he smiled at me in the lobby in an understanding way. I like Mr. Borden very much. I think he is a gentleman and an honorable man, and a most desirable sort of person to have in the House. He respects himself, and others respect him and that is why he is leader of the Conservative party. Sir Wilfrid put his arm around my shoulders coming out of the House, and said to me that I got the best of him (meaning Monk) he said he thought I deserved every word said in my favour, when I told him I thought the Gov't had been most kind in the matter. All of the Members who have spoken of the attack are of the one opinion, and as far as I can learn, the Opposition share it.[28]

King had met Laurier on other occasions, and he had been greatly attracted by the Prime Minister's presence and manner. Laurier had been tactful enough to mention King's relationship to William Lyon Mackenzie and to comment on his grandfather's achievements. He had discussed the Valleyfield affair with King on two occasions, and had defended him against Monk's attack. In February King had had the privilege of hearing Laurier pay his tribute to Queen Victoria in the House of Commons, and noted his impressions, and his hopes for himself, in his diary:

It was a beautiful oration. The language chosen with care to a word, the thought pure and deep, the theme sustained throughout, eulogy with profusion, deserved praise without fulsome flattery. He spoke without a note & really without hesitation. He did not speak very loudly however, & to a degree seemed to have exhausted a little of his spontaneous force beforehand. I watched him before he began to speak & while calm in manner as he always is he was nevertheless, like a warhorse pawing the turf for a start, he was putting things in order, & taking a mouth full [sic] of water. I was greatly charmed with his reference to the rebellion which I fully expected was coming. As I hung over the barrier from the upper gallery & listened to him I felt the keenest ambition to be beside him on the floor of the House. As I see the "calibre" of other men there, I have no fears as to my abilities if opportunity presented to serve this country well in parliament. For Grandfather's sake I should like to lead, for his sake & the sake of the principles he stood for.[29]

Seven months later, in September, he was even more explicit on the subject of his future. Travelling from Kingsmere with his mother after they had received word of the death of Mrs. King's sister, King was conscious of the "strength and beauty" of her face and her resemblance to her father, and thought of Mackenzie touring the countryside.

Partly because of the association, partly to comfort Mother, partly to express my own ambition & partly because my soul was large, my spirit strong & resolve great, I whispered to Mother that I believed, that if opportunity came in the future I might become the Premier of this country. She pressed my hand & said nothing, then said that perhaps I might.[30]

113

About a year after the Valleyfield strike King sustained a defeat as mediator at Rossland, B.C., where he encountered not only stubborn employers but also aggressive and unscrupulous union leadership. The employers, as in very many Canadian industries of that time, had primitive ideas concerning trade unions and labour relations, and especially in regard to recognition and the conduct of negotiations with the men. The union was a part of the Western Federation of Miners which had a shocking record in the United States for lawlessness and violence and even murder, and which in 1905 was to give birth to the revolutionary Industrial Workers of the World or I.W.W. Five of the six districts of the W.F.M. were in the United States which also provided the leaders. The existing strike of metal miners at Rossland had been called in sympathy with strikers in the United States who were employed by the same company. Local grievances had been added to strengthen the men's claims, the chief of which was company discrimination against union members. The strike was four months old when the union (acting at the instigation of the Dominion Government) applied for the intervention of the Department of Labour.

King went to Rossland in the autumn of 1901 believing the men to be the injured party.* He soon began to change his mind. He found that the local union was completely dominated by the American districts, that the union's constitution had been manipulated by the executive for its own purposes, and that he could get no semblance of co-operation from the union officials. It was obvious that the conciliator had been invited merely as a face-saving expedient. The strike was already lost, for the employers had succeeded in their refusal to recognize the union, and a number of the mines were again operating at full strength. King struggled for over a week without success, and eventually left Rossland without a settlement. His report to his Minister (dated September 2, 1902) was cautiously worded, but although he by no means approved the action of the employers, he found that the evidence placed the unions in an even more unfavourable light. "It is the first time," he wrote in his diary in January, "I have had to come

*The Alien Labour Act (supra, p. 97) was indirectly involved in the dispute through its effect on the supply of immigrant labour. Although King considered the Act to be economically unsound and administratively almost unworkable, he felt the men were receiving inadequate protection against the employers who were bringing in American labourers as strikebreakers. See also Can. H. of C. Debates, April 2, 1901, pp. 2456–92.

114

Mrs. John King, 1885

Mackenzie King, 1891, at the age of 16, while an undergraduate at the University of Toronto

Mackenzie King (on the right) as a university student outside the house on Wellesley St. at which he boarded; on the left is Shannon Bowlby, a fellow-student and fellow-roomer from Berlin, Ont.

"The most delightful and comfortable quarters"—Mackenzie King's room in Cambridge, while a student at Harvard, 1897–8

out openly against the workingmen and it pained me to do it, but if their cause is to prosper, honesty must characterize it."[31]

King's experience at Rossland was not wasted. It opened his eyes, he told his father, to "the possible tyranny of labour organizations through biased and interested leaders."[32] It also showed, as he pointed out in his report, the need to get at the facts in a dispute if the interested parties and the nation were to understand the issues. "On every side there appeared to be a misunderstanding as to the exact state of affairs. Not only was it impossible for the general public to arrive at a proper or just conclusion, in consequence of the many conflicting reports which had been circulated since the initiation of the strike, but even among some of the strikers themselves there appeared to be a good deal of misapprehension as to the real situation."[33]

In April, 1901, King had made a brief trip to Cambridge to pack some of his belongings and to settle his mind "as to the continuing with academic work by seeing what openings there are & viewing again the college life & work on the spot." He saw Professor Taussig, Dr. Norton, and other friends and members of the Harvard staff. All who were in a position to advise him thought he would be wise to remain at Ottawa for at least a year or two. Taussig even suggested that he might go into public life if the opportunity arose, although he assured King that he would be glad to offer him the first vacancy at Harvard or to recommend him for a post at McGill which was then open. While in Cambridge King received word of Monk's attack regarding the Valleyfield affair, which not only annoyed him but hardened his resolve to follow the advice he was being given and stay in the service. "The talks with the professors, my observations of the men, opportunities & all here lead me to feel that I wd. crave the larger life later & wd. be foolish to abandon my present work now."[34] "I am beginning to regard the University," he wrote somewhat sadly in his diary the day he left, "as a place that has played its part & in part a chapter of life & influence closed,—the best chapter doubtless that will be known, tho' it was shot thro' with pain & disappointment."[35]

King's earlier desire to get back to the university had been influenced by his dislike for certain aspects of the life and work of the civil servant. He did not easily accept the vows of silence and obedience which the civil service imposed, though it is evident from his experience in the Valleyfield strike that there was no third vow of anonymity to be observed, or, at least, none that could be enforced. He stated in his diary his dislike for "the avoiding issues" and "the smoothing out of phrases into nothingness to suit a Minister's wishes, or rather command." He deplored also "the whole matter of business detail . . . viewing abilities from the point of view of comparative cost, the answering & fyling of letters, making clippings, managing subscription lists, reading proof & Heaven knows what. . . . Besides all this is the belief which is waxing stronger in me that progress is not to be made thro' governments but by private initiative and self-reliance, that an extension of gov't control in many lines means death."[36]

King spent a large part of the summer of 1901 at Kingsmere, a rural district in the province of Quebec some twelve miles from Ottawa.* He and Harper had cycled there the preceding Thanksgiving—the time of year when the whole country was aflame with the red, copper, and yellow of the hardwoods standing in relief against the darker shades of the evergreens. The two friends were delighted with what they saw, especially with King Mountain, Kingsmere Lake, and the unspoiled natural forest which covered the whole area. They ate their lunch of cold chicken and grapes on the top of the mountain, and their appreciation of the magnificent view was apparently enhanced by readings from Mabie's *Essays in Nature and Culture*.[37] A few cottages had already been built near the lake, and the two enthusiasts decided to come out the following summer and stay at a house where their friends, Dr. and Mrs. W. T. Herridge,† were accustomed to bring their children.

The plan was carried out. Mrs. Herridge, her children and sister, King's mother, Harper, and King formed a happy and congenial party. Except for their summer holidays (when both were away), King and Harper spent almost every week-end in the country, and would frequently go out during the week as well. The railway station was four miles from the cottage where they stayed, but they walked (rising at six to do so) or cycled, or, if time pressed, took the coach; they would arrive at the office at nine. In the afternoon, there was a rush for the

---

*The origin of the name "Kingsmere" is unknown. It had no connection whatever with Mackenzie King, nor with Dr. W. F. King (1854–1916) of the geodetic survey who did some work in the same area.

†Dr. W. T. Herridge was the minister in charge of St. Andrew's Presbyterian Church, Ottawa. His son, W. D. Herridge, later became the Canadian Minister (1931–5) at Washington.

train at five, a four-mile walk, and a good supper awaiting them at the end. The recreations were simple. The party, led by King and Harper, held endless discussions; and they read aloud long extracts from Keats and Matthew Arnold. They climbed the mountain, swam in the lake and explored the surrounding country. "Then came the evenings," wrote Mackenzie King, "with their glorious sunsets, and the walks and talks in the twilight, and then night with its unbroken panoply of star-lit sky."[38] Good companions, beautiful surroundings, a pleasing mixture of work and play, freedom from any very serious worries and responsibilities—why should the summer not have been a happy one? By September, 1901, King had decided to make Kingsmere his summer home. That November the Herridges acquired a site for a house (which King eventually was to buy and christen "Moorside"), and in September, 1903, King bought a part of a small wooded hillside sloping towards Kingsmere Lake.

The following year he built a little cottage on the brow of this hill. It contained a large living room in which he usually slept and several small rooms, with a verandah on the front and on one side. The cottage's chief distinction was a fireplace (copied from one in Shakespeare's home at Stratford-on-Avon), and King decided to use this special feature for an opening ceremony to which he had invited a few friends. A passage from Matthew Arnold was read by Mrs. Herridge, King dedicated the fireplace to Harper's memory (he had been drowned in 1901), and the fire was lit—only to drive all the guests choking from the room when it was discovered that despite the Shakespearean model, the fireplace refused to draw.

This first cottage gave King a permanent foothold in Kingsmere which he never ceased to cherish. He quickly developed the habit of spending all his available time there in the summer rather than seek the charms of the sea shore or inland resorts. Kingsmere was the first and only love of his mature years, and he was unwavering and uncritical in his devotion. In May, 1904, he worked away at painting the new cottage "on the Sabbath" (as his mother remarked reproachfully), and later in the summer Mr. and Mrs. King and Jennie joined him for a month. "This is an ideal spot for a house," wrote Jennie, "and the house itself is as quaint as it can be. I don't think it at all tiny and [it] is certainly awfully pretty. He [Billy] has shown remarkably good taste in his curtains etc. & I only wish you could see it too. All his doors, windows etc. are painted white and it makes the place so fresh. I sleep in the big room and we use the other bed room for a dining room   It is all lovely & Billy is so happy."[39]

King was very jealous of anything which threatened to disturb or limit these periods of retreat to the countryside—yet another symptom of his wider discontent with civil service restrictions. To anyone who knew King in later life and especially to those who suffered under the inconsiderate demands which he constantly made on the time of those who worked for him, his early attitude on office hours can be received only with a sympathetic hilarity. In March, 1901, William Mulock left for Australia and was gone for almost five months. Shortly after his return in August, he saw King once, and later sent word that he wished to see him again at three o'clock Saturday afternoon. King was furious at this attempted infringement of his rights. On Saturday morning he developed a severe headache:

I think that it is, in part, a consciousness of Mr. M. being back and expecting me to wait on his pleasure. This I will not do. I will do my work faithfully, and give it my best energy, thought & abilities, but I will not *serve* any man, nor will I allow my own private personal life to be crushed or crowded. I am going to make a stand now firmly on this point, and guard life in its largeness, quite as much as in the details of work & service. I let him know my train went out at 1.30. He said I could see him at 3, which would mean losing this afternoon which I need so much. Office hours end at one, so I simply declined to remain over & left at one. I will do what is reasonable, but not serve another's selfishness to my own prejudice, be he minister or King.[40]

When the inevitable explosion occurred, King justified his conduct in almost the exact words used above. He survived; but this he probably owed to his friendship with Mulock. It was, after all, a little unusual to have a Minister address his deputy as "Willy, my boy," or to have the Minister, when asked what should be done during a contemplated six months' absence, reply: "Nothing, Willie, only push along that Department as you have been doing."[41]

But although Mackenzie King owed much to Mulock's assistance, no one could doubt that when Mulock chose his deputy he had drawn a winning horse in the sweepstakes. King had on his own merits been doing exceptionally well, especially in the conciliation work where success continued to reward his efforts. From October, 1900, to June, 1902, he brought about a settlement in eleven out of the fifteen strikes and lockouts in which he had been asked to intervene. In the other four, where no settlement was found possible, his opportunities had been limited because he was called in too late—presumably as the last resort of the losing side. In all of these cases, he wrote, "the employers claimed either to have replaced the strikers with other hands or to be no longer embarrassed by the strike."[42] But his results were even more impressive when judged by the speed with which they were attained. In seven of the above cases, a settlement was reached within twenty-four hours of King's appearance on the scene as a conciliator.

Although these results were primarily due to King's personal qualities, he was fortunate in the conditions which he encountered. There was a genuine need for mediation at this particular time. Most of the trade unions were ill organized, badly led, and quick to spring into action. Most employers resented the unions and were anxious to fight and discredit them. Disputes on minor questions would often remain unsettled because the parties were unwilling to meet and discuss or even formally state their differences. King's patience sometimes wore thin under these circumstances. "A stupid blunder of a stupid man dealing with stupid men," was his unaccustomed acid comment on one dispute.[43] Another factor which helped to solve possible deadlocks was that employers found it increasingly impracticable to maintain low wages and other unsatisfactory conditions when the facts were exposed to this new publicity. The greater the national reputation of the young deputy minister, the greater became the pressure on the employer to make a speedy and equitable settlement.

King was never one to conceal his merits: but no matter how much he might have tried to avoid the limelight, his repeated successes could not possibly have allowed him to remain in obscurity. Strikes and lockouts—real or threatened—had news value, and publicity lurked in the background even when the negotiations were most scrupulously guarded. "Again the Conciliation Act," "Mr. King Exonerated" (in the Valleyfield affair), "Triumph for Conciliation," "Call in Mr. King," "Deputy Minister King is Coming," were typical headlines in the press. Nor was King above giving the record a little additional help. "Rex and I have been getting some cheap newspaper notoriety," wrote Harper. "The information is I think pretty much as Rex dictated it. . . . For myself I don't think it proper nor even wise for young men to keep blowing their trumpets too loudly. Vanity is Rex's great weak-

119

ness however and will I fear remain an alloy in his character to the close."*

Few young men of twenty-six could remain unaffected by such success. Within a few months of taking up his work in the Department of Labour King had acquired a national reputation. In the years that followed his reputation was materially enlarged. With it came a variety of honours and awards at least one of which was unexpected, not to say amusing. On a July day in 1904 while he was representing the Dominion Government in an industrial dispute at Sydney, Nova Scotia, King was invited to dine on the French cruiser *Troude*. He stepped aboard to the greeting of an eleven-gun salute.[44]

One of King's reasons for going to Ottawa was to be in a position to pay off the debts which had handicapped his family ever since their days in Berlin. In the first eighteen months he gave his father about $1,200, most of which was by taking over (at his father's request) an existing chattel mortgage on the King household effects. The above amount represented at this time a large proportion of his salary, but he had been careful and had earned an extra $100 during his summer vacation in 1901 by tutoring Peter Gerry in law. "This year & especially the paying off of the mtge.," he wrote in August, "has broken the back of all the debts, but it has been an awful curse & long dragged over the heads of us all."[45] Mackenzie King celebrated his achievement by indulging one of his few extravagances: he ordered a number of pieces of mahogany and rosewood furniture for his library. When his conscience reproached him for such self-indulgence, he rationalized the purchase to such a degree that it became a bargain and a wise investment for the future: "tho' the prices would have frightened me completely before I felt my library was to be my work-room for life & what I get now would become filled with associations & be a daily companion & so it was well to get the best. . . . I will do more work, & it will be helpful to nobler & better living for which no price is too much. I feel greatly elated because of this purchase."[46]

---

*Diary of H. A. Harper, March 31, 1901. King's diary confirmed both Harper's conviction that the article had been a mistake and his pronouncement on its putative father. "I think the write up etc. a mistake and I am sorry it has been done. It will only help to stir up adverse comment & criticism in the ranks of labour, the Opposition & even among friends, & besides it is vanity of the worst sort." The entry, however, concluded with this sentence: "I bought 50 copies of the paper, why I do not know." Diary, March 30, 1901.

Despite King's assistance to those at home, he was still able to save a little and lay the foundation of what eventually became a substantial estate. He had always been frugal, and this tendency was strengthened by the sight of his father's financial troubles and their crippling effect on the family's happiness. "The only way to do," he wrote in 1901, "is to be clear of all obligations, keep deposits of savings, & then live so as to always save a little. I must get my life insured before this year is out if possible."[47] The next day he added: "I cannot understand the incurring of debt where one has a competence, it is inexplicable, with true manhood."[48] Yet his innate love of small luxuries came to the surface in such forms as his purchase of the library furniture, and this inevitably involved the very extravagance which he was anxious to avoid. William Mulock's occasional lectures on the necessity of saving money were therefore timely and King was grateful to Mulock for offering to advise him on financial matters. He wrote in his diary:

He is entirely right, a man shd. save while opportunity is present, lay up not only for middle life, but old age, & now is the time for me. It is well too to cultivate inexpensive habits of living. . . . In any event I do not regret the furniture purchases & think them still good investments. But Mr. Mulock's words have not come too soon for I have been very remiss of late, and have been tempted to go repeatedly beyond the mark. I must begin to save, begin first to overtake many obligations I have outstanding, & lay down a rule, to purchase nothing I can get along without, till I have the amt. on hand to make immediate payment.* Be just before I am generous.[49]

King's resolve to save was powerfully reinforced by the reflection that money in the bank would make him independent and enable him to change his position in the future should a move appear to be desirable. If he was to become Minister of Labour (which he thought possible and even, perhaps, likely) he must be able to afford the accompanying risk and uncertainty of politics. "If I can save enough to draw an income from saving I may be able to take the step into active public life for which my whole nature & ambition longs. God has his own plans. He is defining His way very plainly now. He will do so in the future. Live well & faithfully day by day, believing in God & in His purpose in our lives, this is to achieve our end, and to be led in the paths of 'pleasantness and peace.' "[50]

*He had bought the furniture on instalment payments, and had partly committed himself to buy a lot at Kingsmere.

121

It was not enough, however, for Mackenzie King to remove the load of the family's past indebtedness. He was continually lending or giving money to his father to meet current expenses: to pay the office rent, to pay the house rent, to buy coal, to meet moving expenses when they changed houses, or, to use John King's convenient phrase, for "the settling up of some things."[51] He also sent money to his mother for small luxuries, such as the theatre, and he paid for various studies which the girls took in music, household science, and other subjects. The one inescapable fact was that John King was simply not making a living. By far the greatest part of his income came from his lectureship at Osgoode Hall, which paid only $1,650 a year. His practice at this time had almost vanished. In 1903 he secured a commission to write articles for a legal encyclopaedia, and he was able to earn a few additional dollars by writing editorials for the Toronto *News*. Even under more favourable circumstances he would have been in difficulties, for he never seemed to know what his obligations were at any particular time. Bills, which he had forgotten or just ignored, were continually arising to confound him, and a frantic scramble for money ensued. Even his annual fee for a certificate to practise law caught him unprepared, and a hasty letter to Ottawa secured a loan of the necessary seventeen dollars. His favourite device to tide him over financial difficulties was a bank draft, and when Mackenzie King objected to this procedure he was given a lecture on how a large part of the world was financed. "I never could have brought up my family without the assistance of the banks that way," his father wrote. "And there is nothing in it to make any one ashamed or worried, so long as one feels that he can meet the bill or note when it comes due."[52] The sting of this reflection was in the tail.

It is not surprising that John King was desperately anxious to secure a university professorship in law or a judgeship, either of which would have guaranteed him a living and supplied the prestige which his soul craved. The university appointment could have occurred only once, but the judicial vacancies were a recurring torment. He had no hesitation in exerting all the influence he could muster to secure the prize— not direct influence, he was careful to point out, which was unbecoming, but that which could be exerted through his friends, relatives, and supporters.[53] When these hopes were shattered, he became bitter and vindictive, accusing the authorities of "black ingratitude" and alleging that he was "done with the Liberals forever" and would resent the slight in "every way possible." Mrs. King was more philosophical. "You must keep up courage," she wrote her husband during one of the crises, "and if the good luck comes our way the happiness will be great but if disappointment follows we must have brave hearts and just go on thinking how much better off we are than we were a year ago. As I look round I do not see that those who have got more are much happier."[54] When the suggestion was made by Mrs. King (and indirectly by her husband) that her son should approach one of the Ministers in John King's behalf, Mackenzie King declined to act.[55] He doubtless realized that he would damage his own position and that, as Mulock said some time later, the federal Government had bestowed one good job on the King family, and another could scarcely be expected.

All the children wished to help with the family finances, yet no one but Mackenzie King was in a position to do so. Max had paid most of his way through medical school, spending some time as a medical assistant in stamping out a smallpox epidemic near Sudbury, and going to South Africa in 1902 as a corporal in a medical unit. In 1903 he went to Denver, Colorado, to practise, then to Arizona, and in 1905 to Ottawa. His chief worry during most of this period was to meet his own obligations. The two girls were very anxious to do their part, but in those days genteel employment was difficult to find. Jennie announced in 1902 that she was going to the United States to earn money as a nurse or a companion, but she was apparently dissuaded from making the attempt. A suggestion by John King that Jennie might "do a stroke of business for herself" as an editor in charge of a social column in the Toronto *News* was viewed with acute distaste by both Mackenzie King and Jennie. Nor was it thought possible in those days that the three King women could unaided take care of a house for themselves and one man. People who had any social pretensions—and the Kings had many—simply could not afford to dispense with domestic help. A letter of Mrs. King's to her son in 1902 is most enlightening on a number of points:

I have got my money so that I can pay cash for what we eat and wear be it little or much. My grocer and butcher's bills had got ahead of me but now I do not care what happens. I am going to pay cash for what I get consequently I will have to ask you to let me have the money I have paid for the coal as I used Ada's wages to pay for what we got. After I get the expenses connected with our moving paid I can save ten dollars a month and pay you back after the New Year. I was dumbfounded when I saw father had to have fifty dollars paid for him. He simply will not tell me what he has to pay. He gives me all the money but every now and again there is some thing cropping up that I know nothing about. This money wears the life out of me and I am sick of heart having to speak to you about it. We got a ton of coal about a month ago and when that was due I just took Ada's wages and paid for that and another ton.[56]

It was a peculiar household. The whole family agreed that whatever happened to such matters as coal or Ada's wages, appearances had to be maintained, with Mrs. King as its willing representative at social functions. "It seems mean, Billie," she wrote in 1903, "when you have been so good, to speak of these things, but we cannot get on without clothes." She need not have worried unduly, for Billie was always at hand willing to pamper his mother. She received, no doubt, much less than her vanity desired, but more than the family finances warranted. She had had a new black silk and a new red dress the year before the above was written; a mauve dress in 1903—made from material which had been given Bella for a birthday present, but which Mrs. King was induced to accept—and a grey voile (marked down from fifty to thirty dollars) in the next year. "I have not had one good dress for many a year except the black silk Jennie gave me," she wrote on March 17, 1904, "and a woman of my time of life feels a shrinkingness to go among others unsuitably dressed and as you wished me to get what I liked best I spoke out frankly." These dresses were, of course, usually gifts from Mackenzie King; but few mothers with two marriageable daughters in the family would have sacrificed their needs to her own. Yet such was her finesse that daughters, as well as husband and sons, not only acquiesced but rejoiced in the thraldom which she imposed. "Your mother," wrote John King, still glowing with reflected glory, "was the belle of the wedding beyond all question. . . . She was a picture & attracted a great deal of attention & admiration also. . . . Lady Gay told me that she surely was the belle, & old Mr. Cawthra . . . was equally complimentary. Mr. Howland told me that Lord Minto was so impressed . . . that he asked to be introduced to her." And then the afterthought: "Jennie looked very well also & enjoyed the affair very much."[57]

The same peculiarity of the King family was displayed in another direction. In 1901 Mackenzie King commissioned J. W. L. Forster to paint his mother's portrait.* Mrs. King, her husband wrote, was at once thrown into "a state of great flutter and expectancy." What size should the portrait be? What dress should she wear? The alternatives were apparently bewildering. Black silk evening dress, jet trimming, lace, and pearls? Black silk reception dress with chiffon cape collar? Green velvet walking costume with Gainsborough hat in hand? The donor insisted on a life-size head; and both donor and artist agreed on the "artistic sweep" of the walking costume.[58] The King home was in a flurry for weeks. Later the portrait was hung in the Royal Canadian Academy "in a fine place, and was the subject of a great deal of remark and attention." The *Globe* mentioned it very favourably. Mr. and Mrs. King and Bella went to the opening in full dress and basked in the congratulations which descended on them. What a perfect instrument to achieve the recognition which the Kings were continually seeking! "Your mother's portrait," wrote John King, "is the portrait of a high-toned aristocratic-looking lady, & you will be proud of it."[59] Mackenzie King replied:

Mother's painting continues to delight me. The reference to it in the Globe of Friday is just the sort I expected and has pleased me greatly. That issue of the Globe is a rather significant one for our family. It is the first time that Mother has appeared with the rest of us as a distinguished public personage in print, tho' to those who know her, her distinction must ever be greater than any of ours can ever be, and what we may ever have of such will be mostly due to her.[60]

The painting of portraits proved contagious. In the following year, Forster offered to paint one of John King as a gift, and the offer was gratefully accepted.† When Mackenzie King saw the completed portrait, he resolved to have one of himself.‡ "It seemed to me there was much to justify it tho' it has the appearance of infinite conceit. As a matter of fact it is not such. I am young now, I have done a certain amount at this time. Life has not yet begun to put its mark too heavily upon my features & if God spares me, it may be interesting to see in later days how these lines come."[61]

*This portrait hangs at present (1958) in the dining room at Laurier House.
†This is hung as a companion portrait to that of Mrs. King in the dining room of Laurier House.
‡This portrait is also in Laurier House.

The story of the three King portraits cannot be abandoned without adding as a postscript Bella's delightful comment on the painting of the portrait of John King:

Yes! the portrait is a great affair—in fact, though varied has been our programme for the past week—the portrait is the prominent feature. I am sure before the winter is over our knowledge of art will be remarkable until we will almost exclaim with the English Church Litany "Good Lord deliver us." I am not meaning that unkindly but even with Mother's picture there were times we would be glad of subsiding on the subject. About your note—I was pleased that amidst all the hurry & busy time you are having that you would even take time to think of my accompanying father to the studio. I have not forgotten your advice as to my furthering acquaintances with the artist—it's your first attempt in the matchmaking line—for once you are interested in other than "Labor Unions" & to foster such plans or ideas is more than I would have believed you capable of—this is the pained feeling however much & all as I may be a sort of "unappropriated blessing" & would willingly have me disposed of. I fear it is a case of "matter triumphing over mind" & can't promise to attend regularly the sittings—you know it was just in the way you suggest that Rembrandt fell in love—oh! Billy you are *foxy*. This I must tell you that Saturday after finishing the ginger-snaps & doing some things in this house I had to retire to bed with a headache, & who do you think came to spend the evening— little Forster. Is not that a blow to you? I was sorry too—Today father was sent for & has been *posing*—Mr. Forster thinks the left side of his face the better—why I don't know.[62]

King's career in Ottawa in no way hampered his social instincts or his weakness for female society, and he showed few signs of developing greater discrimination in his tastes. The women were all lovely. "One of the prettiest and most entertaining girls I ever met," he exclaimed in his diary, and he found equally attractive ones wherever he turned. One had "a beautiful face, full of refinement. I think her the finest looking girl I have seen in Ottawa." Another, a guest at Rideau Hall, was "a great beauty"; another was "very pretty and very bright and natural"; another, from Hamilton, was "a pretty girl, with a beautiful dimple, sweet and natural manner." The list knew no end—a dream of fair women passing before him in endless procession.

But his earlier experience had taught him a little caution in such matters. There was a girl in Cambridge, for example, who in 1901 held a high rating and to whom he wrote frequently. "I found it hard **not** to be serious [in writing to her]," his diary relates, "and very much so. It is my nature* and I wish to see how she will respond to this chord in it. The letter is long, but I think safely guarded." Later when he visited Cambridge in April he was disillusioned. He found her sitting before the fire with a male companion reading a book. The intimacy of the scene was too much for the intruder. "I made up my mind in an instant as to her. Did not propose the matinee to-morrow as I had thought I might, & stayed only a short time." His original impression was confirmed two days later when he called again. She "is not as good looking as she was, she has grown stouter, & seems to have less style & grace. I was not much attracted by her, & not being so was doubly disappointed." One or two more serious affairs also developed during this period, but they, too, proved in the end to be transitory.

Ottawa did not offer any discouragements to one with King's partiality for attractive girls. Mothers with marriageable daughters hastened to cultivate the young man with so promising a future, and political society found many opportunities to entertain the youngest deputy minister in Ottawa. Invitations showered on him. Harper wrote, in February, 1901, "Rex and I have come to the conclusion that if we are to do good work we must check the effort to draw us into the social whirl."[63] The day following this resolve King noted that he had refused six invitations. "This last week was like the ragged edge of Hell with its fringe of wasted nights. I will have no more of it."[64]

But it was not easy, especially when one enjoyed it, and was quite convinced that these contacts would be very helpful in the future. John King, of course, gave him every encouragement. "Going to lunch with His Excellency's daughters & seeing them home was a fine stroke. Nothing like it. The social recreation, too, was all right. You need that, even a little small talk also. No man can get through the world properly without being able to command at will a certain amount of small talk."[65] This was too much for Mackenzie King, exasperated as he was by self-reproaches for the past and determined to strive for austerity in the future.

[I cannot regard] the mastery of small talk as a good thing, or other than worse than wasted effort, and along the same line, the going to church and

*Harper wrote of Rex's "proneness to talk to girls with an earnestness to which they are unaccustomed." Diary of H. A. Harper, Feb. 17, 1901.

home with the Minto children—saving the fact that they were bright and natural, rather a species of flunkeyism than a thing to be admired. With the whole "society" world and its ideals I fall entirely foul and am at variance in my best nature. The aims and ideals are false, petty, vain, and belittling to one of intelligence and strength. It is the hot-bed of dilletant-ism [sic], the destroyer of truth and reality, and a thing to [be] shunned rather than courted or envied.[66]

His "best nature," however, was not always strong enough and he would be lured again by the siren song. Two years later, in February of 1903, he was complaining of the same waste of time derived from precisely the same cause: Monday night a small dinner party at Colonel Toller's; Tuesday night a large dinner party at Sir Louis Davies'; Wednesday night a dinner at the Club given by Dr. Minnes for King and two others; Thursday night a dinner at Hon. Sydney Fisher's; Saturday night a dance at the Siftons' home. "This is a terrible record & has got to stop. If for no other reason because I am sick of eating. But truly it is folly of the worst kind. I don't know how many teas & other invitations I refused, about sixteen I think, since last week."[67]

There were special reasons why King found it hard to carry through his resolution to avoid social distractions. To a man with his peculiar background there was a sense in which the endless dinners, teas, and balls were not really a distraction at all, but a fulfilment, partial but significant, of a central purpose. The shower of social invitations carried with it a badge of acceptability, a recognition of individual and family merit for which the Kings had developed a compelling need. It all went back to William Lyon Mackenzie and the ill-starred rebellion which had reduced him to penury and impotence and which had left on his family the stigma of disloyalty and unacceptability. Doors which were open to the orthodox and the respectable were closed to them on that account, or so they felt. Beneath all the enterprises of the John King family there lay a powerful concern, indefatigably nourished by the youngest daughter of the "Little Rebel," to repair the damage and recover the ground which had been lost. Mackenzie King's social and professional conquests in the citadel of Ottawa respectability, like the attention which his mother and her portrait won in Toronto, were proof positive that the sins of the fathers had been, or were at long last being, expunged. King's diary for January 9, 1902, contains a most revealing passage. After mentioning Max's trip to South Africa in the medical corps and his own success as a civil servant, he adds: "Surely the blot of rebellion can be read now in its true light, if blot it was!"

In December, 1901, King suffered the loss of his closest friend. Albert Harper was drowned in the Ottawa River in an endeavour to save the life of Miss Bessie Blair. Miss Blair and a companion had skated into an open bit of swift water, and although Harper realized that rescue was well-nigh hopeless, he plunged into the river to make the attempt. Miss Blair's companion was saved, but both Harper and Miss Blair perished.

The place which Harper held in King's affections was never again filled. Their friendship since university days had become even closer in Ottawa; for they were drawn together not only by their work in the Department but by many shared ideals and sympathies. Their approach to most questions was therefore broadly the same, though there was usually a sufficient area of disagreement to nourish their combative instincts and encourage long and grave discussions. Despite an intense seriousness, however, Harper and King did not neglect the social and frivolous side of their lives, and here too they tended to be thrown together through common friends and a fondness for the same forms of recreation and leisure.

Harper and King were very much given to introspection, and rather enjoyed a recital of their personal unworthiness accompanied, as it generally was, by many resolutions to lead a better life. They quite honestly desired to do good in the world and to serve humanity, and they accepted as an inescapable preparation for their task a life of study and unremitting endeavour. The Department of Labour provided the opportunity. In this sphere they could realize their purpose and at the same time make a visible contribution to the social and industrial progress of Canada. This was, however, not enough for King, whose restless and ambitious nature was not satisfied by the mere consciousness of well-doing, but demanded also a substantial portion of personal recognition. His position as the leader of the two, derived in large measure from his rank in the service and his wider education and experience, was thus materially strengthened by those aggressive personal characteristics which were always driving him into ever greater activity. Harper, on the other hand, was more self-effacing and he was apparently able to find sufficient personal satisfaction in the certainty of good accomplished. He fitted easily into the role of lieutenant and faithful though not uncritical supporter. King's sorrow over Harper's untimely death was thus a composite emotion: the realization of the loss of a close personal friend augmented by a further realization that he had lost a loyal assistant and helpmate whom he could ill afford to spare.

A panegyric of Harper is out of place in this volume, but one or two words need to be said. King undoubtedly did much in subsequent years to cultivate what may be called the Harper legend: the noble, unselfish, idealistic young man who was cut off just as he was entering upon a life of great promise; but King's tributes were sincere, and the object of them worthy. Of that there can be no doubt. "Without many professions," King wrote, "he strove silently for the attainment of a character which would make him, among men, not unworthy of the ideal which he cherished in his heart."[68]

Mackenzie King's grief for Harper was poignant and deep-seated but he kept it well hidden beneath a display of Christian fortitude. His letters home, for example, show a serenity which, however admirable, appears unnatural in so close a friend: it is as though he were consciously using Harper's death to demonstrate the strength of his own belief. "I am really happy," he wrote on December 12, six days after Harper's death, "there is so much of triumph in everything." Three days later he continued:

You may wonder at my saying that despite its trials and anxieties the past week has been one of profound peace and real happiness. Whether it is that the sense of loss is more than swallowed up in the knowledge of gain, the triumph of victory so complete over all the obstacles of life and death, or the closer companionship which can come to souls unfettered by the limitations of this mortal existence I know not, but that all three have been real to me I know. Though it may seem strange to other ears, I feel the loss but little, so much do I feel the gain. . . . There is truly unspeakable joy in my heart, and only where it springs from a selfish thought or impulse, a tinge of pain. There is a great calm, a holy peace, and golden glow, a something like the breaking of dawn across the sea.[69]

His diary told a different story. The work at the office, the return each night to the old lodgings, the packing up of Harper's books and papers, and a multitude of trivial incidents shattered the calm and evoked the more normal responses. There was no triumph here, but only a growing awareness of the extent of his personal loss.

Harper's death made a deep impression in Ottawa. A few days after the tragedy a public meeting decided to erect a monument in his memory, and this took the form of a bronze "Sir Galahad" on Wellington Street. It was unveiled in 1905 by Earl Grey, the Governor-General, and accepted by Sir Wilfrid Laurier on behalf of the Government of Canada.

In 1906 Mackenzie King published a little volume called *The Secret of Heroism*, an appreciation of Harper's life and character, illuminated by extensive extracts from Harper's diary and correspondence. It displayed King's literary talent at its best: great simplicity, careful and even fastidious expression, and a deep and sympathetic understanding of Harper as an idealist, student, and friend. King's purpose, however, was not alone to pay a tribute to Harper's memory, but also to present a study in character which might afford the same kind of inspiration which he as a student had derived from the character of Arnold Toynbee. "I believed," he wrote thirteen years later to B. K. Sandwell, "that the revelations of his [Harper's] spirit through letters and papers in my possession might serve as a like inspiration to younger men, especially as his heroic sacrifice of self had appealed so strongly to the public imagination. This was my motive in writing the book. It is perhaps as much an expression of my own convictions on some of the fundamental things of life as it is of Harper's character and aims."[70]

CHAPTER FIVE

DEPUTY MINISTER

MACKENZIE KING became a deputy minister only a short time after he entered the civil service, and his duties changed greatly as his experience increased. The later record fully confirmed the promise of his early days. The Department of Labour (still under the Postmaster General as Minister: Sir William Mulock until October, 1905; A. B., later Sir Allen, Aylesworth until June, 1906; and Rodolphe Lemieux to August, 1911) expanded rapidly under King's guidance and its position in the nation's economy became firmly established. Nor was King's activity confined solely to departmental work. He showed a noticeable willingness to step beyond the purely routine functions of a deputy minister and he welcomed any additional tasks which the Government might ask him to undertake. His gifts were even better displayed here, perhaps, than in the Department; and the success which followed these other efforts enhanced his reputation, not with the public alone, but also with the Prime Minister and others with whom he was associated. King could not, if he would, remain indifferent to this recognition. His political ambitions, as indicated in earlier pages, were already strong; and every new success as Deputy Minister, as a Royal Commissioner, as a representative on a quasi-diplomatic mission, encouraged him to look ahead to the time when he would be able to enter the halls of Parliament or even the Council chamber itself.

Little need be added to the account given above of his conciliation work, which continued to achieve remarkable success. Many disputes arose, of course, where the Department was powerless because no request for its intervention was made, but nevertheless forty-one interventions under the Conciliation Act occurred from 1900 to 1907.[1] In all but one or two of these cases (occasionally it is difficult to speak with certainty) a settlement was effected through King's good offices.

It is true that in some of these years a buoyant economy with increasing employment, accompanied by rising wages and prices,* helped to prepare the ground and induce the employers to make concessions;† nevertheless, King's personal contribution proved to be a major factor in securing an amicable agreement. He possessed the invaluable gift of leaving both parties to the controversy fairly well satisfied with the result and grateful to the Department and the official who had helped to bring about the restoration of normal conditions. "We cannot speak too highly of the work done by Mr. King when here," wrote an employer in 1903 after one of King's efforts,[2] and the union's comment on the same event was: "On behalf of the weavers and the citizens of the Towns of Milltown and Saint Stephen, I beg leave to express to you, as Minister of Labour, our appreciation of the services of Mr. King, of whose ability, fairness and unfailing tact, we have formed a high opinion."[3]

Mackenzie King as Deputy Minister took a leading part also in preparing new legislation on labour questions. One measure stood out above all others: the Industrial Disputes Investigation Act of 1907. It was precipitated by a prolonged coal strike at Lethbridge in southern Alberta. The strike began in March, 1906, and dragged on into late November, when parts of the prairie were covered with snow. Widespread hardship ensued. In some areas the farmers were forced to burn lumber, grain, and twisted straw to keep out the cold. Schools were closed because of lack of fuel. If the strike had been allowed to continue, settlers, many of whom were living under rather primitive conditions, would probably have frozen to death in their homes. Telegrams and letters poured into Ottawa, and the Premier of Saskatchewan sent a special appeal for intervention. Mackenzie King, who had just returned from a mission in Europe (see *infra*, p. 147), was sent west to act as conciliator. He found that the original issues in dispute—union recognition, wage increases, check-off, reduced hours—had been pushed into the background, and the two parties, grown

---

*"For some time past [1910] and especially since the beginning of the present century, one of the most important features of the general economic situation in Canada has been a rapid and continuous advance in prices and the cost of living"; R. H. Coats, *Wholesale Prices in Canada, 1890–1909* (Canada, Department of Labour, 1910), p. 1. Cf. also *ibid.*, pp. 1–10; Canada, *Report of the Board of Inquiry into the Cost of Living* (1915), I, 130–1; II, 1031–71.

†The same conditions, of course, affected the situation in other ways; for example, many demands were quickly met and never reached the stage where a strike or lockout became a serious possibility.

stubborn, had stalled on such questions as whether any meeting whatever between the parties would imply a recognition of the union. Bitterness and prejudice had obscured reason and made even simple discussion impossible.

King's persistence and patience, heavily supported by public indignation across Canada, eventually brought about a settlement. The utter folly of the situation was evident to any impartial observer. King's report to his Minister did not mince words, and it deserves to be placed beside his angry articles on the abuses of the sweating system:

The calamity which threatened the country and the possible recurrence from similar causes of a like condition are . . . a sufficient justification for not passing over the whole matter in silence. In looking at a situation, so much depends on the point from which it is viewed as to the estimate likely to be placed upon it. . . . I cannot but feel that a little more tact and a disposition to understand aright the position of the other by each of the parties might have averted the whole trouble. Certainly, had the parties been prepared to view their actions with the same regard to the interests of the public that they finally came to view them, the strike would never have continued so long. In the settlement which was reached, both parties, I believe, made concessions in view of the great public emergency, which they would not have made had they not been moved by humanitarian considerations. Up to this point, however, the struggle, so far as third parties were concerned, appears to have been purely selfish. Until brought face to face with the serious situation which the long continuance of the dispute had produced, the public does not seem to have come in for any consideration whatever.

When it is remembered that organized society alone makes possible the operation of mines to the mutual benefit of those engaged in the work of production, a recognition of the obligations due society by the parties is something which the State is justified in compelling if the parties themselves are unwilling to concede it. In any civilized community private rights should cease when they become public wrongs. Clearly, there is nothing in the rights of parties to a dispute to justify the inhabitants of a province being brought face to face with a fuel famine amid winter conditions, so long as there is coal in the ground, and men and capital at hand to mine it. Either the disputants must be prepared to leave the differences which they are unable to amicably settle to the arbitrament of such authority as the State may determine most expedient, or make way for others who are prepared to do so.[4]

These lines well reflect King's state of mind when he returned to Ottawa after the settlement. He reported to his own Minister, Rodolphe Lemieux, and to Sir Wilfrid Laurier, and on their instructions he proceeded to draft a law designed to avoid another crisis of this kind.[5] His natural approach was through an earlier statute, the Railway Labour Disputes Act of 1903,[6] which he himself had drafted. This had provided for the compulsory investigation of labour disputes in the railways, augmented, if at all possible, by conciliatory action. It had been invoked only once, but had worked well on that occasion. Moreover, a wider use of the Act had always been considered a possibility; for when the Minister (Mulock at this time) had placed the bill before Parliament in 1903, he stated that if it proved to be satisfactory in its operation the same principle might be extended to disputes in other industries.[7] The time to widen the Act's range appeared to have arrived. But might not the occasion be used also to improve the system itself? King thought it might; particularly by the insertion of a compulsory "cooling-off" period before either a strike or a lockout could legally take place. This he had originally advised Sir William to incorporate in the Act of 1903, but Mulock had been "unwilling to take both steps at once, and preferred not to go farther than securing the adoption of the principle of investigation and publicity with respect to railway disputes."*

King devoted his Christmas vacation of 1906 to the task of putting this improvement in legal form. A curious feature in the bill's preparation was that it was not seen by any member of the Cabinet at this time or even much later, although a general idea of its provisions had been given to Parliament and it had received its first reading as early as December 17, 1906. Lemieux even wished to show King's draft of the bill to R. L. Borden, the Leader of the Opposition, before he had seen it himself and, of course, before the Cabinet had approved it. King objected, and eventually the bill, together with some of Lemieux's speech which King had prepared, was sent to Quebec so that the Minister might read them there. On January 9, 1907, King placed a final revise of the bill in the hands of the Clerk of the House of Commons, and prepared a statement for the press.[8] King and Lemieux, however, did not "work over" the provisions of the bill until that evening, though the Minister had already given the House a general account of the measure in the afternoon.[9]

The bill had a smooth passage through the House, and received the royal assent on March 22, 1907. It was popularly called for brevity's

---

*This statement is made in the course of a long letter about the circumstances and history of the Act which King wrote on October 23, 1916, to Charles W. Eliot, President of Harvard, in reply to an inquiry from Eliot about its origin.

sake "The Lemieux Act." King never became reconciled to the linking of Lemieux's name with a statute to which the Minister had made no contribution whatsoever and which had so unquestioned a right to be known as King's special child. But Canada has always respected this aspect of ministerial responsibility, and the country has not yet come to the point where statutes are identified by the names of civil servants.

The Industrial Disputes Investigation Act provided that no strike or lockout could be legally declared in a public utility or mine until the differences which had arisen had first been referred to a three-man board of conciliation representing the employer, the men, and the public. The two original parties were each to choose one member of the board, and then agree on the third member, who was to be the chairman. Failing such agreement, the chairman was to be named by the Minister of Labour. The board, in discharging its function, could subpoena witnesses, compel the production of documents, and take evidence under oath. Its aim was to achieve a settlement by conciliation if possible, but if this failed, its report would give in detail the questions at issue and the basic facts, and indicate a possible settlement. If members disagreed, majority and minority reports were to be submitted. The two parties to the dispute were under no legal obligation whatever to accept the recommendation, and they were thenceforward free to take any action they might see fit. The right to strike or lock out, in short, remained unimpaired except for the necessity of delaying action while the inquiry was being held and a report prepared. Herein lay the Act's greatest merit. Compulsion was applied at the point where those with clean hands would have little, if anything, to fear; and an informed public opinion would be able to add its pressure to bring about a settlement. King later set out his views on the merits of investigation as a method of terminating industrial disputes:

Investigation is a letting in of light. It does not attempt to award punishments or to affix blame; it aims simply at disclosing facts. . . . Its use is a high tribute to human nature, for it assumes that collective opinion will approve the right, and condemn the wrong. Willingness to investigate is *prima facie* evidence of a consciousness of right. In the absence of good and sufficient reasons, refusal to permit investigation is equally *prima facie* evidence of weakness or wrong. . . . The statutory right to investigate disputes . . . has been found sufficient to influence parties to industrial differences to settle their controversies both voluntarily and speedily.[10]

136

In later years the Act was amended a number of times, but it remained on the statute book until it was repealed in 1948. Initially it had a great success, and was widely discussed and copied in other countries. Canada became recognized in a few months as a leader in this type of labour legislation. The Act, however, met with one severe reverse in 1925 over a question of jurisdiction.[11] Moreover, its effectiveness gradually diminished as a result of changed conditions. Other and speedier ways were developed to deal with many of the modern disputes of a technical nature, and many unions tended to lose confidence in it because they considered it weakened their position in collective bargaining. Yet although the new statute, the Industrial Relations and Disputes Investigation Act, 1948,[12] is probably better fitted to meet modern needs, it bears many traces of its predecessor, including, above all, the principle of compulsory investigation.

How much of the Industrial Disputes Investigation Act was an original contribution by Mackenzie King? This is a difficult question to answer with exactness. It is very probable that King, steeped for years in the literature and legislation on the subject—to say nothing of his almost continuous practical contact with it—could not be sure himself of the true origin of some of his ideas, though he could be much more certain of his use of related legislation from other countries which had yielded what promised to be helpful material.[13] The obvious connection between the 1903 Act dealing with labour disputes on railways and the Industrial Disputes Investigation Act has already been indicated. Inasmuch as King was also the author of the 1903 Act, he was really adapting and extending his own measure along the lines he had originally desired. Indeed, the greater part of the Act in one way or another can be regarded as the outcome of King's experience as a conciliator and his other work as Deputy Minister. The most accurate statement about the Act's provenance was perhaps that given by King in a speech in Cincinnati in 1913:[14]

The Chairman of the Evening has generously said that this Act is the work of one person; let me rather say, by way of telling the exact truth, that this law in many of its sections is based upon legislation in existence in this country, in Great Britain, in Australia and New Zealand, and in other countries.* It was drawn to conform as nearly as possible to the requirements of the situation as it then existed in Canada, but only in one

*He might have specified the states of New York and Massachusetts.

137

or two particulars is it wholly original. One feature that distinguishes it from other measures is the requirement of an investigation before a strike or lockout takes place. There may be, too, some originality in the methods by which this investigation is obtained and carried out.*

Two illustrations of the influences from experience may be mentioned. Several years earlier King had discovered in his conciliation work that the greatest obstacles to industrial peace were the difficulty of bringing the parties together and the difficulty of unearthing the facts around which the dispute raged. In his report (1902) to his Minister on the Rossland strike of 1901 he mentioned that both the public and the actual participants in the strike lacked information and misunderstood the real situation.[15] This ignorance he found to be a common occurrence. "It seems to me," he exclaimed in September, 1903, "that a fearless exposition of facts and conditions as they are is more needed than any other single thing in dealing with present-day problems."[16] It was but a short step from here to a forced investigation which would bring these facts and conditions to light.

The second illustration is furnished by his role in the special investigation of the chaotic labour situation in British Columbia in the summer of 1903. This was conducted by a Royal Commission (the Hunter Commission), composed of Chief Justice Gordon Hunter of British Columbia as chairman, and Rev. E. S. Rowe. King was the secretary of the Commission; King wrote most of the report; and King made no secret of the fact that he, as Deputy Minister of Labour, had a decided interest in the proceedings. On one occasion, when he thought the Commission was showing a bias in favour of the employers, he intervened with decision:

I went & told him [Rowe] I came not as Secretary of the Commn. but as Deputy of the Department, to speak in its interests. I wanted this report or at least the method of securing evidence to commend itself to wkgmen of the sensible kind. I feared proceedings like today wd. render it worthless thro' bias. . . . I told him I wd feel it necessary to wire Ottawa, unless there was a change. I then spoke of the Dept., its creation & purpose & the part I wanted this Commn's report to play in its development.[17]

At this same time the Railway Labour Disputes bill was before Parliament, and both Royal Commission and bill were simultaneously

*For a similar statement, made in the same year, see W.L.M.K., "How Canada Prevents Strikes," *World's Work*, Aug., 1913, p. 438.

making their contribution to King's—and the Government's—labour policy. "I think," King wrote again in the diary, "the report of this Commn. will be an excellent addition to the literature of the subject & a most valuable document historically & for legislative purposes."[18] His prophecy proved accurate. A better spirit between employer and employed; the acceptance of collective bargaining as a normal procedure; the outlawing of sympathetic strikes, intimidation, and illegal picketing: these and other policies were advocated by the Commission and helped to create the background which King desired and which he hoped would encourage more enlightened labour relations. Other recommendations such as those on "compelling publicity at the earliest stage of the trouble," "the giving at least 30-days' notice" under certain conditions for a strike or lockout, the following of specified standard procedures in disputes, and the overriding interest of the community in maintaining operations in industries of major importance, not only disclosed some of King's thoughts but also expressly foreshadowed provisions of the Industrial Disputes Investigation Act.*

Even some of King's uncertainties were introduced in the Commission's report, made an apologetic bow, and then retired in some confusion. Thus the Royal Commission supported compulsory investigation "sometimes," and (under stated conditions) a modified form of compulsory arbitration in public utilities and special industries, such as mines. "Conciliation," King had written in his diary at the time of the inquiry, "compulsory investigation, and then compulsory arbitration seem the steps absolutely necessary, in view of the interdependence & interrelation of industries & public welfare."[19] But he always accepted this last step with the greatest reluctance, and it never became more than a tentative possibility which he soon abandoned.

To these sources, the product of King's personal experience, must be added the writings and speeches of a number of authorities on labour relations. The Postmaster General in speaking on the Industrial Disputes bill in 1907, for example, referred to Richard T. Ely and several others in the field as having furnished useful information when the bill was being drafted.[20] But the person who left the strongest imprint on King's mind was Charles Francis Adams, an expert of

*Canada, Department of Labour, *Report of the Royal Commission on Industrial Disputes in the Province of British Columbia* (1903), pp. 63–77. The concluding section of the report, however, embodying general recommendations and conclusions, was not written by King alone, but in collaboration with the Chief Justice.

long experience with American railroads, who, in a speech on December 8, 1902, had vigorously argued that compulsory investigation and publicity were far superior to compulsory arbitration in promoting industrial peace.* Adams had even added a draft bill to illustrate his idea.[21] This speech gave the essence of the Investigation Act save for one thing: it made no mention of delay or a "cooling-off" period. The omission, however, was rectified in 1906 by an article in the *Outlook* by Everett P. Wheeler (a lawyer interested in public affairs and a frequent writer on law, history, and economics), who endorsed the Adams suggestion, but with a significant improvement: "One additional clause should be added. . . . A strike pending an investigation by such a Commission should be illegal."[22] This sentence made the outline of the Canadian Act complete in all its essentials. Adams and Wheeler, in short, had arrived at precisely the same solution suggested by King in 1903, when the principles of the Railway Labour Disputes Act were being determined.[23]

Whatever uncertainty may exist concerning the exact origin of some of the ideas of the Investigation Act there is no doubt that the Canadian Parliament was the first body to enact a law of this kind. King could legitimately claim a large share of this distinction. His influence was constantly in the background. The Cabinet had great confidence in his ability and in the policies which he had developed in the Department of Labour; he was generally trusted by both employer and employee,† and his advocacy of conciliatory rather than harsh measures in industrial disputes was well known. Even the Opposition could usually be depended on for a friendly word. When the Investigation bill was before the House, R. L. Borden suggested that King's personal efforts had been the chief explanation for the Department's successful conciliation work in the past and he repudiated the suggestion that he had in any way criticized "Mr. Mackenzie King's efforts."[24] Praise from Sir Hubert was praise indeed! King's proposals could usually be sure of receiving at least a fair consideration;

*Both Mulock in 1903 and Lemieux in 1907 mentioned the Adams suggestion in the House. *Can. H. of C. Debates*, May 6, 1903, p. 2542; Feb. 14, 1907, p. 3026.

†He made, according to his own later account, at least one bargain with labour to secure its support for the passage of the Investigation bill, an unusual procedure for a civil servant to adopt in such a matter (United States, Senate, *Final Report . . . by the Commission on Industrial Relations*, Washington, 1916, I, 716; for King's appearance before this Commission, see p. 236). The railway unions preferred the 1903 Act, so they and their employers were allowed to invoke either it or the new Act.

and they were likely to start with the odds in their favour. "So far as my own work is concerned," King was to write President Eliot of Harvard in 1916, "any contribution of mine has been that solely of assisting in making certain ideas prevail by gaining acceptance for them and their embodiment in legislation, a step which has been made possible by such knowledge of conditions and men as I have had and the opportunities at hand."[25]

King was a realist who for years had been in the midst of industrial disputes, and he was in search of a solution which would bring some measure of peace and satisfy both the state and the major contestants in those disputes. He stood without a rival in Canada in his knowledge and experience of the subject. He was able to bring unique qualities to the drafting of the bill. He adopted ideas from other authorities and procedures from other statutes and worked them successfully into a scheme which would meet Canadian conditions. His credit for the Act therefore really rests on his eclecticism and skilful adaptations and the years of preparatory effort which had left his imprint on the Government's labour policy. He had come into the field at a time of ruthless exploitation of labour (of which the sweating system was a conspicuous example), and he had done his utmost both before and after his entrance to the Department of Labour to remove some of the bitterness in labour relations, to introduce (in his own words) more humanity into industry. The pronouncements of the Hunter Commission sound trite today; but they were not so when they were made, and the facts proved they were badly needed at that time.

One of the results of the spread of unionism throughout the various trades has been to put the workman in a better position to make terms with his employer; to preserve his independence of character; he is now able to drive a bargain and does not have to accept a dole. Formerly, employers were too often in the habit of regarding their men as so many machines or units of labour, and those of them who felt humane instincts thought they fulfilled their whole obligation if they gave an occasional extra remuneration or bonus, or conferred some benefit which they regarded as a gratuity. But the workman of modern times demands as his due a fair day's pay for a fair day's work, and that he shall get a reasonable share of the product of his toil; what he seeks is honourable employment, not slavery; he wants fair dealing and justice, and not charity or patronage.
It is necessary, then, in their own interest, and in that of the community generally, that employers bear in mind that they are no longer dealing with submissive and unquestioning units of labour, but with sentient beings

who have, equally with themselves, senses, affections, desires, doubts and fears.[26]

These words reflect a humanitarianism which had been evident from King's earliest days as a social worker. He believed that human beings must take priority over the institutions with which they were connected. He was becoming increasingly convinced of the importance of people's emotional needs, and he was learning through his work as conciliator that no institution, no law, and no agreement which neglected these could expect to enjoy more than a limited success. Again in January, 1903, when engaged in drafting the Railway Labour Disputes bill, he wrote in his diary:

Read over an article by Miss MacMurchy on The Labour Problem, the best points in it are those in which *stress is laid on the personal equation, and the matter of personality. It lies at the root of all.* This being so, talk of the "solution" of the Labour problem, apart from the "solution" of "restoring humanity," is to speak of an impossible thing. . . .

Worked for a while on . . . some form of arbitration. . . . My present feelings are against the apptmt. of a Permanent Board, as increasing machinery which at the [sic] stage is not necessary. . . . *I wd rather make the whole an addition to Conciliation, thereby strengthening the power of the former & minimizing the need of arbitration. Machinery is nothing, personality everything.*[27] [Italics added]

And the next day he wrote:

I worked almost the entire time on the bill for the Settlement of Labour Disputes. *I think a measure of this kind should be brief, and with as little machinery about it as possible,* its aim should be to afford a means of the public getting an intelligent view of the facts of the situation and of bringing an enlighted [sic] public opinion to bear. In this connection, I would like to make the *Labour Gazette* give greater service.[28] [Italics added]

The Industrial Disputes Investigation Act put King's beliefs into practical form. The clause that each party could pick a representative on the board, that no one was to be bound in advance by any finding, that either party was free to submit grievances for the fullest inquiry—such clauses were based on a clear understanding of how people would respond to these provisions. The prevention of precipitate action, the presentation of ascertainable facts to the contestants, and the approaches to conciliation were shrewdly designed to give the parties an opportunity to get together and to understand one another, to realize how all interests would be advanced by compromise and agreement.

The same insight into human personality made King suspicious of compulsory arbitration. It increased rigidities and formalities. It was too wooden, too unyielding and impersonal. There was always a threat in the background to be applied according to a formula, and the atmosphere was charged with menace. King's insistence that the "other party to industry," the community, should also be given a chance to use its influence was an attempt to tone down the acerbity and stubbornness of the two contestants. It was just not possible to argue about conditions in the Alberta coal mines and ignore the unheated homes and schools and churches, and eventually these considerations became decisive. But, as King said in his report on the Lethbridge strike, "a little more tact and a disposition to understand aright the position of the other . . . might have averted the whole trouble."[29] One purpose of the Industrial Disputes Investigation Act was to provide an opportunity for these benign influences to make themselves felt in disputes which by their nature always tended to become excessively selfish.

This conviction of the overwhelming importance of the human being formed a major part of King's political philosophy. It necessarily implied that a person should not be subjected to avoidable compulsions. He must be convinced that a particular policy was genuinely desirable. The available records confirm that when King was engaged in negotiations one of his great assets was his gentle approach through reasoned argument. Earl Grey said he had a "nice persuasive way of talking," and a Governor-General and a mechanic alike felt the force of logic so winningly presented. He could urge a case and yet never forget for a moment how he himself would have felt in the other's position, and he always showed a proper deference (which he may or may not have felt) to the expression of a dissenting opinion. King believed implicitly that, whenever possible, forced solutions were to be avoided, for they rarely represented a real union of minds. They were likely to prove impermanent, and they tended to leave a residue of resentment as a result of the pressure which had brought them about. There should be a genuine not a nominal acquiescence behind a settlement; a personal conviction which sprang from the mind and heart, not a superimposed verdict. King, the conciliator, like King, the future Prime Minister, worked consistently on this principle. He always stressed the points of agreement, the things that united, and played down the things that divided, so that some understanding was always in sight and some avenue of compromise was always open. All, he argued, are apt to be losers in a quarrel, so why not submerge the differences and come to an amicable settlement or compromise on the points where a solution is readily accepted by all parties?

"We call him the peacemaker" was Earl Grey's introduction on one occasion, and although this description referred to King's work in labour relations, it might have been pushed much further. For King believed that his principles of conciliation could be applied universally because they were based on a great psychological truth. He later wrote *Industry and Humanity* primarily to elaborate his ideas as they affected the field of labour relations, but he thought it was equally feasible to build bridges of understanding between nations in the same way. The principles applicable to the settlement of industrial disputes could, in his opinion, be carried over into the international field. In 1914 he expressed this opinion in a speech given at Detroit:

> There is a relation, a psychological relation between efforts made in one direction and similar efforts made in another. Accustom men's minds in the industrial world to remedy industrial wrongs by appealing to reason rather than by appealing to force, and you have helped to create a sentiment which will also play its part in a much larger way in international affairs. If there is one thing above another that working men have everything to gain from, it is the establishment in the community in which they live of a belief in reason rather than in force in industrial and international affairs.[30]

In 1907, four years after his experience with the Royal Commission on Industrial Disputes in British Columbia, Mackenzie King was made the chairman of a two-man Royal Commission (the other member being His Honour John Winchester, Senior Judge in the York County Court) to inquire into the hours of employment of telephone operators in Toronto. The Bell Telephone Company had proposed to increase the shift of the operators from five to eight hours, and before the Department, which had been asked to intervene by the Mayor, could confer with the parties, a strike had begun. The Commission's report was blunt and devastating. The change in wage and hour schedules "was made, we believe, from motives of cost and service pure and simple, and without any real consideration for the health and well being of those whom it was most to affect." "To offset the increase in cost occasioned by the increase in wages, the hours of service were lengthened." "The company sought to bring about the change on the shortest possible notice, and in a manner which affords grounds for believing that it hoped to enforce the new schedule by taking advantage of the necessities of its employees, and the fact that as young women, many of whom were self-supporting, a threat of dismissal would be sufficient to prevent any general or prolonged resistance."[31]

The Commission laid particular emphasis on the strain which was imposed on the physical and nervous system of the telephone operators, and King's sympathetic imagination lent both colour and force to the findings. The long hours spent in one position, the possibility of electric shocks, the abuse of impatient subscribers, the irritation caused by the intermittent flashing of lights, the occasional buzzing and snapping of instruments in the ear, "the sense of crowding where work accumulates, the inevitable anxiety occasioned by seeking to make the necessary connections whenever a rush takes place, all combine to accentuate the strain upon an operator, and they are all factors more or less absent from other callings in which women are engaged."[32] Everything conspired, the report went on, to bring the health and well-being of the operators into direct conflict with the motive of gain:

It would appear that from the manner in which the Bell Telephone Company carried on operations during the past three years at the main exchange in Toronto, where this conflict between so-called business and health became apparent, in many cases, not only was the question of health a matter of small consideration, but the management knowingly permitted the work to be continued under conditions and in a manner absolutely detrimental to the health of the operators. We believe that where it is a question between the money-making devices of a large corporation and the health of young girls and women, business cupidity should be compelled to make way. The evidence given before us, and the facts of experience, as cited, go to prove that this is a matter which . . . calls for legislative interference on the part of the State.[33] *

King was nevertheless frankly worried about possible political re-

*King wrote in his diary for August 4, 1907, in even harsher terms: "I feel at times as though I would sail without mercy into the Co., so hideously inhuman and selfish its whole policy seems to have been. The imagine [image] is constantly before me of some hideous octopus feeding upon the life blood of young women and girls, the more I go into the evidence, the more astounded I am at the revelations it unfolds." Judge Winchester's share in the report, incidentally, seems to have been confined to inserting apt references from the evidence (Diary, Aug. 1, 1907).

percussions from this plain talk. He wrote home about the labour and the "mental anxiety" involved in writing the report, and the possibility of arousing the ill-will of corporate and other interests,[34] which might be directed against him or the Government. "Yet it is necessary," he had stated in his diary, "to be fearless, and enmities must come sooner or later to the man you [who ?] seeks reform, so that one has to find one's reward in the sense of justice & fair play in one's own conscience."[35] And a few days earlier: "While it may mean personal unpleasantness, it will mean a gain for workingmen & women. I venture to say it is one of the strongest indictments yet made of any single corporation."[36] The report did result, in fact, in substantial improvements in the working conditions of the telephone industry.[37] It does not appear, however, that either King or the Government suffered any ill effects.

In September, 1907, riots broke out in Vancouver as protests against Oriental labour and Oriental immigration into British Columbia. These riots were the occasion for King's being put in charge of a number of other investigations. He was appointed a Royal Commissioner to assess and pay the losses to Japanese residents which had arisen out of the riots, and some months later he was asked to determine the losses to the Chinese in the same outbreak. Again in the same year he was asked as Royal Commissioner to inquire into the methods by which labourers had been induced to come to Canada from India, China, and Japan. King displayed great initiative and determination in these last investigations. He was able—through personal interviews and by threatening to issue a subpoena—to compel the production of a number of confidential documents;[38] these revealed that the Japanese Government had been privy to the evasion of the understanding which it had with the Canadian Government on the control of Japanese immigrants.* The question was later to enter into his discussions with both the President of the United States and the British Foreign Secretary, and was to be a major factor in sending the Lemieux mission from Canada to Japan.

*This odd condition arose from the desire to save the pride of the Japanese, who were important allies of Britain, by avoiding open exclusion. The Japanese had acquired a right under a treaty to enter Canada freely, but this right was restricted by written and verbal assurances given by the Consul-General of Japan in Canada that his Government would by its own action drastically curb the number of immigrants. (*Report by the Honourable Rodolphe Lemieux, K.C., Minister of Labour, of his Mission to Japan on the Subject of the Influx of Oriental Labourers into the*

In 1908 King served as a Royal Commissioner on the conditions of cotton operatives in the province of Quebec, and his report was followed by stricter laws in Quebec on child labour.[39]

He also participated in a number of other investigations. In 1904 he conducted a special inquiry into fraudulent methods which had been used to encourage the immigration of Italian labourers. The resulting disclosures led to further inquiries by Judge Winchester and to the passage of legislation (drafted by King) in 1905 designed to stop false representations being made in Canada to induce or deter immigration.[40] The law, however, could not punish fraud which might be perpetrated outside Canada, and in 1905 King conducted another inquiry regarding false statements which had been made in England to induce printers to come to Winnipeg to act unwittingly as strike-breakers. His report on this incident later formed the basis for a request to the British Government for legislation which would discourage all such practices.[41]

When assessing the losses in the riots in Vancouver in 1907, King was shocked to find two claims presented for losses sustained by Chinese opium manufacturers. He decided to follow up the matter on his own initiative, and in doing so, displayed once again his strong preference for knowledge obtained through direct personal contact. He went through opium factories, visited opium dens, witnessed sales of opium being made in a Chinese shop, and himself purchased a package of opium over the counter. The outcome was yet another report in 1908: this one on the need for suppression of the opium traffic in Canada.[42] He drafted a brief bill to deal with the problem, and it was in due course enacted by Parliament.*

The year 1908 therefore made extraordinary demands on King's energies. In addition to his departmental duties, he submitted reports on no less than five investigations which he had been conducting by his own direct efforts, and in March and April he undertook a special

Province of British Columbia, 1908, pp. 10–14.) These assurances were not observed. In the ten months ending October 31, 1907, over 8,000 Japanese arrived at Canadian ports on the Pacific, although almost one-half went eventually to the United States. Of those remaining in Canada, however, over 62 per cent came from Hawaii and their movements could not, of course, be controlled by the Japanese Government. (*Report of the Royal Commission Appointed to Inquire into the Methods by which Oriental Labourers have been Induced to Come to Canada*, 1908, pp. 15, 24.)

*Can. Statutes, 7–8 Edw. VII, c. 50. This was replaced and greatly strengthened three years later on Mackenzie King's initiative as Minister of Labour by 1–2 Geo. V, c. 17.

mission to England.[43] In October he ran in his first election for Parliament, and in December he began a trip around the world, during which he represented the Canadian Government at a number of conferences.[44] "For the first time in my life," he wrote in his diary on the last day of the year, "I begin to feel as though some tax had been made upon my physical energies, and that I have not the same buoyancy either of spirit or frame which I had in former years."

Why was Mackenzie King singled out for so many divergent assignments? The answer is probably twofold: his recognized energy and ability, and the scarcity of suitable personnel. His unusually wide interests* were well supported by superior intelligence, confidence, forcefulness, native shrewdness, and a knack of producing results. Moreover, his knowledge extended to topics familiar to very few in the civil service, which underwent its first genuine reform only in 1908, all offices hitherto having been filled largely through patronage. The earlier system had produced occasional good appointments (King's selection by Mulock had been of this kind), but it had also led to many poor ones. The number of well-trained men was consequently small, and specialists could be found in only a few fields. Thus when Laurier wrote King in November of 1908 regarding his attendance at the international opium conference (see p. 192) he alluded to the fact that King had "made a special study of the opium problem in this country, and of other questions arising out of our relations with the Far East,"[45] though even the most charitable could never have described King as an expert. The truth was that the Canadian service did not contain anyone qualified to challenge King's knowledge, such as it was, on the subject of opium, although doubtless there were a number of immigration officials who had some familiarity with Far Eastern relations. In the country of the blind, the one-eyed man was king.

*King's wider interests are evident in his correspondence which reveals that while Deputy Minister he was exchanging views on subjects that lay far beyond the normal scope of his department. For example, in 1907 he wrote L. S. Amery a long letter on Imperial relations in which he made a typical contribution: "The one great danger that I see in the Imperialism movement, if such it may be termed, is the possibility of the creation of Imperialist and anti-Imperialist parties either in Great Britain itself or in the other countries of the Empire. If such an unfortunate condition ever developed, it would be the beginning of a disruption from within. The Empire must *grow*, not be manufactured, if it is to be the living entity which will make it a reality. This view I know you share. It is how best to further that growth which is the problem." W.L.M.K. to L. S. Amery, April 2, 1907. See also W.L.M.K. to Richard Jebb, Dec. 30, 1907.

King's ventures into diplomatic and quasi-diplomatic circles made what was probably the most important contribution to his political education and brought him into contact with a number of the leading figures in Great Britain and the United States. His first mission was in the autumn of 1906 when he made a trip to England following his inquiry into fraudulent immigration practices. The purpose of his visit was to urge the British Government to pass legislation similar to that of Canada on the subject, so that the offenders could be prosecuted in Britain before anyone was able to act on misrepresentations which might have been made. John King accompanied his son on the trip.

King's visit was in one way unsatisfactory, for few Ministers were in London in October and his contacts were largely confined to civil servants who could promise very little on their own responsibility. Lord Elgin, the Colonial Secretary, returned from Scotland only a day or so before King left London, and King also lunched once with Winston Churchill, the Parliamentary Under-Secretary, when immigration was presumably also discussed. He saw Lord Strathcona, the Canadian High Commissioner, frequently, and one of his major tasks was to soothe the old man and avoid any suggestion that the latter was being superseded, while at the same time retaining his assistance in approaching the British Ministers and officials. "I also wished to frame the letter [to Lord Elgin]," King wrote in his diary, "in such a way that Lord Strathcona would be drawn into the matter of the negotiations, though, at the same time, keeping their control in my own hands. I thought I would read the letter over to him, and appear to consult him as to the advisability of proceeding in that way, although I was quite determined to see that the above purposes should all be secured."[46]

King was successful in his major effort. He impressed the British Government with the desire of Canada for immediate legislative action and made it difficult, if not impossible, for the matter to be thrust aside or postponed. He failed, however, in an attempt to have the legislation put through in the shape of a separate statute, which in some way he thought would confer on it a "special Imperial significance in giving an opportunity to Mr. Churchill and Lord Elgin to speak directly on matters affecting the colony."[47] All the officials whom he interviewed assured him that a separate act would be a formidable undertaking and Lord Elgin thought passage in that form would be bound to be delayed.[48] This part of the proposal was therefore abandoned. King was able to return home, however, with an assurance from the British Cabinet that the desired clause would be submitted to Parliament during the current session, and in due course it was passed as an amendment to the Merchant Shipping Act.[49]

In 1907 as a result of his earlier work on the subject, King was very nearly chosen to discuss immigration with the Japanese Government and the British Ambassador at Tokyo. Laurier wished, if possible, to make the existing arrangement between Japan and Canada really effective, so that Japan would curb its own emigration to Canada and relieve the Canadian authorities from the invidious task of specifically refusing admission to Japanese as such. When King's advice was sought, he suggested that either Rodolphe Lemieux (Postmaster General) or Sydney Fisher (Minister of Agriculture) would be suitable as a Commissioner to conduct the negotiations. The House being then in session, Sir Wilfrid was reluctant to send a Minister, and King himself became a possibility. His hopes of advancement were much gratified:

Sir W[ilfrid] said he wd be glad to have Lemieux go, if it were the end of the session, but that he could not be spared now. He saw no one in sight but myself, & he wished very much that I would go. . . . I thanked him for the mark of confidence, said I had not thought of it myself, that it might be well to have two Commissioners. . . . As I think everything over it seems to me it would be unwise not to seize this opportunity whatever else it may mean. It is a great mission, a mark of the strongest endorsation on the part of the Govt., and in an understanding of this problem lies much [of] a man's strength & usefulness for the future of this country. . . . I can see that it is the one thing to do. Being missed a little may help too to make a necessity of the cabinet position. If I go and am successful, it means I come back a public man.[50]

Lemieux was anxious to accompany King, but Laurier, after considerable hesitation, refused to let them both leave Ottawa, and selected Lemieux. King was naturally disappointed. Lemieux, however, made an excellent representative and was able to secure a definite understanding with Japan.*

*Report of the Honourable Rodolphe Lemieux . . . of his Mission to Japan, 1908. The understanding was not made public for some time. Briefly, merchants, travellers, and students would be allowed to enter Canada freely, but virtually all labourers were to be excluded, except domestic servants of Japanese already in the country and

Mackenzie King's next mission was of much greater delicacy and made heavy demands on his skill as a diplomat. It also arose from his earlier dealings with Oriental immigration and the British and American interest in the subject. For a young man who had just reached the age of thirty-four, it was a remarkable opportunity, and it gave an indication of how rapidly his reputation for both skill and reliability was being recognized. "You will find Mackenzie King," wrote Earl Grey to Lord Elgin, in March, 1908, "a satisfactory person to talk to. He is level-headed and well-informed, and absolutely straight."[51] And a month earlier, after Theodore Roosevelt had met King and had two talks with him, the President wrote to an English friend, Arthur Lee, M.P.: "King struck me as a very capable, resolute fellow, and his decision of character, coupled with his official position, had enabled him to get hold of a number of Japanese documents such as we on this side of the line had never seen. . . . King . . . is a gentleman and made a very favorable impression on me."[52]

Early in January, 1908, King received a letter from his friend, Colonel J. J. McCook of New York,[53] asking if he would like to come to Washington and have lunch with the President. Theodore Roosevelt had heard of King's conciliation work and his study of Oriental immigration and he had expressed a desire to meet him and discuss informally and unofficially "matters of common interest." McCook said that he could also arrange for King to be invited to the annual dinner of the Gridiron Club, the organization of newspaper men stationed in Washington.[54] After discussing with Sir Wilfrid Laurier the propriety of a civil servant moving in such high circles, King wrote McCook that he would be delighted to accept both invitations. He arrived in Washington on January 25.

President Roosevelt received him with marked courtesy. He placed him on his right at lunch, had him remain afterwards for a short talk, and also called in Elihu Root, the Secretary of State, to discuss further with King the question of Japanese immigration. The President's purpose was soon disclosed. He wished to use King as a channel of

---

a limited number of agricultural labourers to work on lands already owned by Japanese. It was expected that the total of these workers would not exceed 400 a year. Finally, contract labourers would be admitted if the Dominion Government had previously given its assent.

King had a poor opinion of the Lemieux agreement, chiefly on the ground that it offered no certainty that Japan would observe its terms. As it turned out, the agreement was observed carefully by that country.

communication between the American and British Governments to facilitate a settlement of the question of Japanese immigration which in the United States, as in Canada, was creating many economic and other problems. Mackenzie King reported Roosevelt's remarks fully in his diary:

"I will speak to you very frankly, Mr. King, I would speak to you and to Sir Edward Grey, the Grey in Eng. I mean because I think he is a man of large views—not the Grey at Ottawa. If you were going to England I would give you some strong messages to take to Sir Edward Grey. I would have you tell him that in the present situation he could do much for the cause of peace, not that we want to ask the help of the British, but the Japanese must learn that they will have to keep their people in their own country. Britain is her ally, a word thro' her ambassador, spoken in a friendly way to an ally, assuring her of the feeling might go far. I cannot write," he added, "for that would be misunderstood. . . . England's interests and ours are one in this matter. She cannot more allow the Japanese on this side that [than] we can." I made no reply to the reference to going to England, except to say that I thought the Japanese Gov't. already understood . . . that [it] must restrict the numbers of their people coming to this side.[55]

Roosevelt was alarmed at the mounting numbers of Japanese who were coming to the United States directly and by way of British Columbia and Hawaii. Japan had given many assurances that the flow would be checked,* but she had repeatedly gone back on her word:

"I will tell you, Mr. King, we have been doing some pretty plain talking the last few days. We have allowed these people to go too far thro' being too polite to them. I made up my mind that they were simply taking advantage of our politeness. I thought they had done this, and I decided to send the fleet into the Pacific; it may help them to understand that we want a definite arrangement. They have been telling us right along that they will restrict, they have not done so, the numbers have been increasing. Now they tell us they cannot control their people, or prevent them emigrating. On this we will demand a positive guaranty."[56]

The President considered that the Pacific coast of the United States and Canada had identical views and interests regarding Oriental

*In 1907–8 the United States and Japan by an exchange of a series of diplomatic notes made a "gentlemen's agreement" whereby Japan undertook to restrict emigration to the United States by confining the issue of passports to certain classes of her citizens, and the United States in return agreed not to exclude Japanese immigrants. The principle (and motive) was the same as that embodied in the Lemieux understanding negotiated in 1907. S. F. Bemis, A Diplomatic History of the United States (New York, 1950), pp. 671–5.

immigration, and therefore it was also to the interests of the British Government to promote a settlement. Unfortunately, he said, the British did not seem to appreciate the importance and urgency of the question. If the eastern United States were to remain indifferent to the opinion of the western states and Great Britain were to remain indifferent to popular feeling in British Columbia, Roosevelt suggested that the whole area west of the Rockies might conceivably unite and form a new Pacific republic to safeguard its interests against the results of eastern neglect. Although he himself was well aware of this and other dangers lurking in the Japanese issue, he believed the British Government was inclined to consider that American-Japanese tension was now over. That was by no means true. The tension was still there.

Clearly Roosevelt had little confidence in the ability of James Bryce, the British Ambassador at Washington, whose duty it was to convey the point of view of the United States to his Government. "Mr. Bryce," said Roosevelt some days later, "is a fine old boy; he is getting up in years now and is, perhaps, fonder of books than he is of active politics. I would sound him a little on this [Japanese] question the other day, but he seems to view it more as an academic question. It is necessary that the British statesmen should feel that it is a practical and immediate question."[57] Roosevelt apparently chose Mackenzie King rather than Bryce to approach the British Government because he was confident that King's knowledge of the problem and his appreciation of its seriousness would enable him to convince the Foreign Office that the aims of the United States should receive support. This approach through King, moreover, had the further advantage of informality and was less open to the interpretation that the United States was asking for British assistance in dealing with Japan.

President Roosevelt also made his intentions plain in a speech that same night (January 25) at the Gridiron dinner. King wrote that he was "more than amazed" with the tone of the President's address. Roosevelt pleaded guilty to the charge of advocating "a big stick" policy, but said that he wished to rephrase it as one to "deal politely, be conciliatory, but carry a big stick." Politeness was all right up to a certain point, but if advantage was taken of your attitude, then the time had arrived to send your fleet to the Pacific. The United States did not propose to be caught unprepared. Elihu Root also spoke at the dinner. He asked for restraint in press comment on foreign relations, but clearly suggested that war was possible. King had no doubt of the way events were moving.

I see this country [the United States] on the very verge of war. The whole tone of the President's talk with me today was we must have absolutely what we are demanding or war. His speech tonight was be prepared for war, & be ready for it on a moment's notice. . . . It was plain to me, following the lines of his [Root's] talk today, that he [also] fears the possibility of war in the immediate future. There will be war for sure if the Japanese do not see what this country wishes done and do it quickly.[58]

King returned at once to Ottawa and told both Sir Wilfrid Laurier and Earl Grey what he had heard in Washington. Laurier's experience of dealing with Roosevelt, especially in the Alaska Boundary dispute, had left him with a deep-rooted suspicion of the motives and methods of the American President, and, indeed, of Americans generally, whom he regarded, according to King, "as selfish, self-seeking and as caring only for Canada in so far as it may serve their own purpose to be friendly."[59] He was not inclined at first to take Roosevelt's speech seriously, calling it, as Grey reported to Bryce, "all flam."[60] However, Laurier recognized a common interest in the immigration issue, and he felt he could not ignore Roosevelt's implied request for a Canadian emissary to the British Foreign Office. He therefore sent King back to Washington with a message that if he as Prime Minister could render any assistance to the United States he would be glad to do so.

Roosevelt was very pleased by this friendly reply. He proceeded to give King the American position in greater detail, which added little, however, to what had already been said. He had decided from several incidents that Japan had been trifling with the United States on the immigration problem. He did not wish, he stated, to hurt the pride of the Japanese and he was willing to allow them to find their own solution of the problem; but this flow of immigrants from Japan must be stopped—if not by one method, then by another. Japanese students, merchants, travellers, and others were welcome, but the door to Japanese labourers and settlers was forever and unalterably closed. Roosevelt would try to avoid any popular provocation or "incidents": the moving of the American fleet had been necessary to show Japan that the United States was serious and wanted an immediate decision. Mackenzie King's part in all this would be to help Japan to realize—

through her ally, Great Britain—that she must keep her promises regarding the restriction of emigrants, that the United States was not anxious to have any trouble if it could be avoided, but that the decision here rested with Japan. Roosevelt did not want to send a formal communication on this subject to Britain and he wished nothing of this mission to be among the state papers, presumably because it looked too much as though he were asking for British assistance.

Laurier's suspicion of Roosevelt was confirmed when the President, following King's second trip to Washington, wrote Laurier concerning the proposed mission to England.[61] In this letter of February 1, Roosevelt made it appear that the initiative for the proposed mission to the British Government had come from Canada and not from the United States, and that the State Department, acting on the request of the British Ambassador, had shown King the documents covering American negotiations with Japan. These statements were not true,* and the letter contained other inaccuracies as well. Mackenzie King, who up to this point had been favourably impressed with Roosevelt, felt badly let down, for the letter revealed a side of Roosevelt's character which was entirely new to him.† "Every sentence in the letter had the twist of a smart politician, who asks questions with a view of receiving an affirmative reply, and then twists the statement as though it had been offered in the first instance by the person to whom it had been addressed."[62]

The fact that Roosevelt's letter to Laurier had not been marked "private and confidential" led to King's making a third visit to Washington. He carried with him Laurier's reply to the President's letter, and he also obtained a statement from Roosevelt that his letter had

---

*The origin of the idea of a mission to England has been given. The suggestion that King should be shown the documents came from Roosevelt himself. "The President . . . asked Mr. Bryce if he thought it would be well for me to see some of the figures on the subject of immigration, and the papers which contained the correspondence with Japan, and Mr. Bryce said he thought this might be of advantage, and the President directed Mr. Bacon to give me this information later in the afternoon." In the event, King was shown only a part of the papers and was given little time to study them. Diary, Feb. 1, 1908.

Roosevelt repeated the erroneous account of the origin of the mission in the letter to his friend Arthur Lee in England, mentioned above; Theodore Roosevelt to Arthur Lee (later Lord Lee of Fareham), Feb. 2, 1908. *The Letters of Theodore Roosevelt*, ed. E. E. Morison, *et al.* (Cambridge, Mass., 1951–4), VI, 918–21.

†King had written only three days prior to the receipt of Roosevelt's letter that the President "is a man of strong impulses, but they are true impulses. . . . I must say I like his impulses." Diary, Feb. 4, 1908.

been intended to be confidential although it was not so designated. The correspondence and interviews were thus rendered secure from possible parliamentary scrutiny in the future.

Laurier's reply (dated February 20) ignored the President's misrepresentations completely.[63] King had actually drafted a skilful reply for Laurier to send "which set forth exactly what Sir Wilfrid's message to the President had been, and which was intended as a means of placing on record the truth as an answer to the President's statement that Sir Wilfrid *proposed* sending me to England." This was, however, not used by Laurier; as he told King, the correspondence might be published, and "it should not appear that I [King] was going on a mission for the United States, that that might create a bad impression through the country. I said that the President had distinctly understood that, and I was, therefore, the more surprised that he had written as he did, because he knew that if I went to England at all it would be on another mission, and as a means of furthering peace between the United States and Japan in accordance with his wishes."[64]

Laurier's failure to correct Roosevelt's distortions has caused the misleading account to be generally accepted as true.* King's story, however, is in itself so circumstantial and given with such precision and detachment that it carries its own conviction. Roosevelt's attitude was a curious one. He showed a great desire to have his version accepted though in another letter supporting it he also professed to regard the incident as of no consequence. "I do not care a rap about their saying I took the initiative in the matter," he wrote in March to the American ambassador in London, Whitelaw Reid, "for I think it the sign of a small mind to be meticulous on such points. But it is just as well that the facts should be on record."[65]

Earl Grey's account to Lord Elgin, based as it was on King's story,

---

*For example, Thomas A. Bailey in *Theodore Roosevelt and the Japanese-American Crisis* (Stanford Univ., Calif., 1934) wrote (pp. 270-2): "Early in February, 1908, Roosevelt received some disquieting news relating to the failure of the Gentleman's Agreement [with Japan] to operate satisfactorily, when MacKenzie [*sic*] King, the Canadian commissioner of labor and immigration [*sic*], visited him. . . . It is interesting to note that the Canadians, deeply disturbed over the situation, were looking to the United States for support in their anti-Japanese policy, for, wrote Roosevelt, King 'thanked me very earnestly for having sent our fleet to the Pacific' [T. R. to Arthur Lee, Feb. 2, 1908]."

Another misleading account was given by P. C. Jessup in *Elihu Root* (New York, 1938), II, 31-2. A much more accurate version appeared in J. M. Callahan, *American Foreign Policy in Canadian Relations* (New York, 1937), pp. 497-8.

afforded little confirmation of Roosevelt's version; and it revealed the suspicion with which the British Government regarded Roosevelt's manoeuvre:

I have to report that Sir Wilfrid Laurier has received a letter from the President in which the President endeavours to saddle the responsibility of opening these negotiations, upon Canada. Sir Wilfrid has suggested that I should postpone sending you a copy of the President's letter until he has decided upon the terms of his reply.

I have already told you Mackenzie King was lured down to Washington, I believe, at the instance of the President, in order to give the President an opportunity of delivering his views on the relations which, in his opinion, should exist between the North American Continent and Japan, with the object of having them repeated to Sir Wilfrid Laurier. . . .

Mackenzie King returned from Washington with a message from the President that he was about to write a letter to Sir Wilfrid. Two or three days having passed without the receipt of any such letter Sir Wilfrid informed me that he had never attached any importance to the President's indiscretions, and that he regarded the whole incident as closed. Then up comes a letter in which the President tells Sir Wilfrid that he will be glad to come to the assistance of Canada! The whole story would be laughable if it were not an interesting illustration of American methods.

I regard the President's action as evidence of his desire to pull Canada into his quarrel with Japan. Sir Wilfrid thoroughly realizes this and may be relied upon to word his reply in a way which without giving offence to the President, will safeguard Imperial and Canadian interests.[66]

Laurier's letter, which King bore to Roosevelt, was therefore chiefly concerned with the immigration problem. It fully accepted Roosevelt's view of a common American and Canadian interest on Oriental immigration. This acceptance constituted in King's opinion "a virtual endorsement of the Monroe doctrine on the part of Canada so far as a silent invasion of the Oriental peoples is concerned. What is no less significant, and what may ultimately be far more [more far?] reaching is the acknowledgment of the community of interests of the English-speaking peoples in this matter."[67] Roosevelt, too, showed that he had an eye for the future. Even before King left for England, the Japanese Government was proving more co-operative on the immigration question, and Roosevelt suggested a possible widening of the scope of King's mission. "What I would like to accomplish," he told King, "is not merely an understanding for to-day, but some kind of a convention between the English-speaking peoples, whereby, in regard to this question it would be understood on all sides that the Asiatic peoples were not to come to the English-speaking countries to settle, and that our people were not to go to theirs."[68] The immediate occasion for this remark had been a request from Alfred Deakin, the Australian Prime Minister, that the American fleet should pay a visit to Australia, an obvious attempt to demonstrate the solidarity of the two countries on the "yellow peril": "The President then turning quickly to me said: 'Would you like our fleet to visit Vancouver and Victoria?' to which I replied: 'I am not a responsible Minister, and have no authority to speak on any such matter. You understand, Mr. President, that only a member of the Government could express an opinion one way or other in regard to such a matter.' The President then said: 'Whatever you would like, we would do.' "[69]

King's summary of Roosevelt's position after this final visit was given on his return in a conversation he had with Earl Grey on February 27:

It seemed to me that the President was determined on one thing, namely, that this question of the Pacific should be determined once and for all; that [if] he could determine it by bringing about a convention between the English-speaking peoples and so maintain peace, that would be what he would most desire. It would be a great achievement and would serve his end. If it could not be brought about in that way, he was prepared to bring it about by war if necessary.[70]

But Laurier was not at all happy about being led into these deep waters of international policy by one he did not trust. On the other hand, he could scarcely refuse to agree to the President's apparently simple request of allowing King to act as a kind of special envoy. Roosevelt's very misleading letter of February 1 dealing with King's mission had naturally made the Canadian Cabinet even more suspicious of what was afoot, and Laurier had described the letter as "a smart Yankee trick."[71] On February 17 also he had remarked to King that he was not entirely sure of the wisdom of King's going to England at all, and that two of his colleagues, when consulted, thought he should not go.[72] King's comment that it might now be too late to back out had not been reassuring. "It might appear to the President," King had said, "as though there had been bad faith inasmuch as he had revealed his whole hand to me on the understanding that I would be going." Laurier had replied that "the more he looked into the matter, the more it seemed to him to be a deep-laid plot, that he was sorry we had got drawn into it at all."[73]

One element in Laurier's uncertainty was his astonishment that Canada, and King in particular, had been requested to give any help whatever. King's account of Laurier's remarks when he came back from his second visit to Washington is most instructive:

> I am glad [Laurier said] that you saw Bryce [in Washington]. I told His Excellency [Earl Grey] what you have told me, and he was a little sensitive in regard to Bryce. . . . I said to him: "Can this thing really be— is it possible that in a great question of this kind they should send for little" (and here the Premier hesitated just for a second. I feel quite confident that the word he had on his lips was "King." He quickly added:) "our little Canada to be of service in this great question. I could hardly believe it,* and I was waiting to see, but it appears now that it is the fact."[74]

King, too, was somewhat overwhelmed at being chosen to fill so important a role, and on several occasions sought guidance and approval from those with whom he was dealing. Thus he asked Bryce on at least two occasions whether he thought he had adopted the right course and acted discreetly, and said he would be grateful for suggestions. "I was not a diplomat," King added, "but a very young man for an important and delicate mission of this kind." Bryce replied that "he thought I had managed everything as well as it could possibly be managed. He thought the Government were very fortunate in having one who could handle a matter of this kind so well as myself, that as far as he could see I had done entirely what was right."[75] Certainly King's own account of the negotiations indicates that he repeatedly displayed great astuteness in his reticence and in his constant awareness of the restrictions which were imposed on him by his office as a civil servant. His position in regard to Bryce, whom in a sense he was supplanting, was one of extraordinary delicacy. Whatever Bryce may have thought, it said much for his urbanity and magnanimity that he showed not the slightest animus against the youth who had suddenly been selected by Roosevelt to approach Bryce's home Government.†

*See Earl Grey's letter to Lord Elgin, *supra*, p. 157.

†"Mackenzie King's action [on the trip to Washington] was quite correct, and he seemed to me to have conducted the whole of a somewhat delicate affair with propriety and tact. He is a man of real ability who will, I predict, be valuable as well as successful in the public service. We all liked him very much." Grey Papers, James Bryce to Earl Grey, Feb. 1, 1908. But Bryce showed signs of being a little upset; Grey Papers, James Bryce to Earl Grey, Feb. 12, 1908.

The Canadian Cabinet could not possibly announce that King was going to England at Roosevelt's request, and an ostensible reason for the trip had therefore to be found. The Canadian order-in-council which appointed Mackenzie King stated that inasmuch as the Deputy Minister of Labour was very familiar with the problem of Asiatic immigration and as this involved relations with both foreign powers and fellow British subjects in India, he was being sent to England to discuss various aspects of the matter with the Government of the United Kingdom. A week before King left, an event occurred which made the mission a most timely one, for the Government received word that a ship had left India carrying a number of Indian immigrants. These had hitherto been kept out of Canada by an order-in-council of general application which required all Asiatic immigrants to come to Canada by direct voyage from the point of origin, and as no ships sailed directly from India to Canada the barrier had proved quite effective. If this ship were to attempt to land her Indian passengers, however, there was a real danger that rioting would break out in Vancouver. An order-in-council was being held in suspense which would impose a $200 tax on each Indian immigrant, but the Canadian Government was averse to doing this if it could possibly be avoided. Clearly, however, the time had arrived to take some positive action. Laurier instructed King to tell the British Government that this immigration must be stopped. If Britain did not arrange to keep the Indians out of Canada, Canada would be forced to do it herself.

The Deakin invitation to the American fleet to pay a visit to Australia and Roosevelt's openly expressed desire for it to call also at Vancouver and Victoria had raised in King's mind the whole future of Canadian naval policy. Canada, he thought, should be careful not to issue any such invitation. It would simply encourage dependence on the United States and also strengthen annexationist sentiment in the Canadian West. He wrote in his diary on his return from his third visit to Washington:

The situation reveals to me, too, so far as Canada is concerned, the necessity of our doing something in the way of our having a navy of our own. We must admit that in the present situation we are absolutely dependent upon the naval power of Great Britain for the protection of our own country against Asiatic invasion. We might as well face this squarely and meet the situation by contributions to the British Government or by the beginning of a navy of our own, which as a Canadian, would be the preferable course. In speaking of a navy of our own, I do not mean that we would act independently in any way of the British. An arrangement could be effected whereby a complete unity of action could be effected. I think, however, that it would be better for us in voting money to control expenditure and it is well to accompany any imperial sentiment by a healthy Canadian national spirit as well.[76]

King arrived in London the middle of March, and lost no time in carrying out his double mission. Although he stayed only a little more than a month, he managed to meet an amazingly large number of interesting people. These included on the official side Sir Edward Grey (Foreign Secretary), Lord Elgin (Colonial Secretary), Lord Morley (Secretary of State for India),* and a number of top civil servants: Sir Charles Hardinge, Sir Charles Lucas, Sir Francis Hopwood. He also met Whitelaw Reid, the American Ambassador, and such public figures as Winston Churchill, L. S. Amery, Lord Cromer, Austen Chamberlain, A. J. Balfour, and Lord Lansdowne. He renewed old and pleasant contacts with the social reformers: Gertrude Toynbee, John Burns, Ramsay and Mrs. MacDonald, Sidney and Beatrice Webb. Dinners, luncheons, and various other social engagements added a great many names to King's list of acquaintances. He called on Lady Aberdeen and reminded her of the days when he and other Toronto students pulled the Aberdeens around the campus and received some forget-me-nots for their efforts. He had a pleasant talk with Bonar Law, during which each dipped into the future and saw the other as destined for the Prime Ministership. Indeed, Bonar Law carried his prophecy to Balfour with the remark: "You will welcome Mr. King some day as the Prime Minister of Canada"—to which Balfour gave the courteous reply that he hoped so. "I have no doubt," King commented, "he [Balfour] thought that some things were easily done in Canada, but he also doubtless appreciates that Prime Ministers are not in this category. A more pleasant personality, charming, affable —it would be hard to find."[77]

Of all these, Edward Grey, Balfour, and Milner made the most favourable impression. Winston Churchill, whom King had seen on his previous visit, he quite clearly regarded with mixed feelings. "One cannot talk with him," he wrote in his diary, "without being impressed

*Just before King's return, H. H. Asquith became Prime Minister following the resignation of Sir Henry Campbell-Bannerman, and some of the Cabinet personnel were changed as a result.

161

at the nibbleness [nimbleness] of his mind, his quickness of perception and his undoubted ability. He seems to have lost a good deal of the egotism, at least so far as his manner is concerned, though one feels that even yet it is Churchill rather than the movement with which he is identified that is the mainspring of his conduct." One remark of Churchill's that King recorded as "rather characteristic and perhaps no less true" occurred in a discussion of the movement of peoples and the possibilities of war. "On large questions of this kind," the young Churchill concluded, "I have a true instinct and seldom err."[78]

King was especially pleased at the opportunity to see more of Violet Markham,* and these fresh contacts revealed that they shared more ideals and sympathies than either had hitherto realized. Miss Markham, King wrote, was a strong liberal, exceptionally well-informed on all public questions with "a keen perception and great understanding."[79] He also began what was to be a life-long friendship with the Earl of Stanhope, his junior by a few years. Stanhope, who was related to the Pitt family, was about to leave the army and enter public life. Such a move strongly appealed to King, who also admired Stanhope's sincerity, his warm friendliness, and his unassuming nature. Before King left England, Stanhope drove him down to Chevening, his beautiful country home in Kent, where King took keen delight in the unusually fine family portraits, the extensive libraries, and the manuscripts and mementos which had been preserved by the Stanhope family.

The British Ministers were greatly interested in King's account of both the Canadian immigration problem and American-Japanese relations. The India and Colonial Offices agreed that immigration from India must be discouraged, but were naturally anxious to treat Indians with exceptional care because of their status as British subjects. King stressed the fact that the Indians arriving in Canada had been induced to come largely through the activities of the transportation companies whose primary motive was to make a profit from their passage. These immigrants were usually ill-equipped for life in the Dominion; they suffered greatly from lack of funds and from the climate which most

*King had first met Miss Markham in 1905 when she was staying at Government House in Ottawa (cf. *infra*, p. 171). Today a Companion of Honour, she has been a leading English liberal and social reformer and a member of a number of administrative and advisory boards. In 1915 she married James Carruthers, but continued to be known chiefly by her maiden name. Of her several books, the two most recent are *Return Passage* (1953) and *Friendship's Harvest* (1956).

of them found cold and forbidding. Like other Asiatics, they created both economic and racial problems, and their presence was usually resented by the local population. British Columbia had passed many restrictive laws which the Canadian Government (at the risk of losing a number of parliamentary seats) had disallowed. King pointed out that unless the flow of immigrants could be stopped, the Government would be forced to take more extreme measures.

King also developed Roosevelt's thesis regarding the people on the Pacific coast, though with a somewhat different bias which leaned heavily to the British rather than the American side. He told John Morley, the Secretary of State for India:

The proximity of the United States to Canada added an element which complicated the situation. I thought the President and a large number of American citizens were only too glad to develop the opinion that the interests of the Canadian and American West were identical, and that the United States was the proper protector of the peoples on that shore. I added that I thought the President had this in mind in sending his fleet into the Pacific, and mentioned that when I had met him in Washington he had asked me if we would wish to have his fleet in British Columbia. . . .

There were people in British Columbia only too interested in creating the impression that because of the distance, the public men at Ottawa did not appreciate the situation on the Pacific coast and were indifferent to it. . . . There were other persons who were interested in pointing out that there was no use of the people of British Columbia looking to Ottawa for help, that the Anglo-Japanese alliance made it impossible for them to take any action in the matter of Japanese, and that British connection made it impossible to do anything on account of the Hindus. . . . Nothing would suit the purpose of the Americans better at this moment than that some trouble should break out in Vancouver at the time that the American fleet reached San Francisco. . . . It would demonstrate . . . that the whole problem of Oriental immigration was one in which the interests of the two countries was the same.

That there was no doubt in the world that the interests of the Pacific slope, north and south of the boundary line were the same; at the same time I did not think it was necessary for us to demonstrate that to the world, and that we might, in the interests of the Empire, go ahead and make our arrangements between ourselves. That Sir Wilfrid Laurier recognized the obligations and responsibilities of Empire, as well as its advantages, and that he was the first one to take the view that all being of one household, we should endeavour to quietly settle our differences among ourselves, and make our arrangement such that the outsider need not have anything whatever to do with it. . . .

After mentioning one or two other points Mr. Morley said "I think your case is very reasonable and defensible." I immediately interjected (after the manner of President Roosevelt) "I am glad to know that you think so, Mr. Morley."[80]

Morley (with King's assistance) drafted a cable to Lord Minto, now Viceroy of India, regarding the feasibility of restraining Indian emigration to Canada. The Indian authorities replied that while they were unwilling to institute a permit system (which would require legislation), they had already issued warnings calculated to dissuade the Indians from going to Canada to settle. At King's suggestion Morley also had his advisers examine the Indian Emigration Act, and they reported that under its provisions it was unlawful for any Indian to leave the country under contract to work in Canada. This prohibition, hitherto unenforced, removed one of the great dangers in the Canadian labour situation, for few Indians were likely to leave their homes without some assurance that work would be available in the new country. The more venturesome emigrants could be discouraged in other ways, and the most important of these was in process of being settled before King left England for home. On March 27 he received word from Sir Wilfrid Laurier that the Government were negotiating with the Canadian Pacific, and that there was every likelihood that that company would agree to discourage any immigration from India in its ships. Finally, so far as Canadian reluctance to legislate against the immigration of British subjects was concerned, the British Government assured King that neither it nor the Government of India would take the slightest exception to any measures which the Canadian Government might see fit to use in order to discourage immigration from India.*

King's report on the Roosevelt conversations could, in the nature of things, scarcely be attended with an equal degree of success. The British Ministers, however, were most anxious to hear his account, and there is no sign that any of them dismissed his story, as Lord Elgin had done a month earlier, as of little consequence.† One official in the

---

*King's formal report on "Immigration to Canada from the Orient" appeared in *Can. Sessional Papers* (1907–8), No. 36a. It was accompanied by a confidential Memorandum (dated May 2, 1908) on the same subject.

†"The report of Mackenzie King's interview with the President," Elgin had written to Earl Grey on February 19, 1908, "was alarming, but the latest intelligence seems to give reason to hope that all that was said need not be taken seriously." Grey, in a reply dated March 3, entered a strong objection to this summary dismissal of King's account of the seriousness of the situation. (Grey Papers.)

Foreign Office, Charles Lyell, said that King's memorandum on these conversations was important and useful in the information it contained and "had been a surprise to him and others"; another, Sir Charles Hardinge, added that it "had been of distinct service."[81] But Sir Edward Grey, the Foreign Secretary, did not believe that Japan had any desire to place its people on the American continent. Nor did Japan want war with the United States, though it was obviously anxious to get a grip on Korea and Manchuria. Japan had no funds with which to prosecute a war, and she and the United States were so far apart that neither could with impunity venture near the other's coast. Although Japan was Britain's ally, any aggression from Japan against the United States would inevitably arouse British sympathy for the latter. This opinion was shared by everyone with whom King came in contact.

The general impression among the Ministers and officials whom King met was that Roosevelt was too bellicose, and that he might precipitate trouble which might otherwise have been avoided. They agreed substantially with the terse summary which Bryce had given King in February: "I think [the situation] may become serious, I think in the President's mind it is serious, and I think that he would have it serious, but I cannot see that Japan is in any way anxious for war."[82]

Events, in truth, were fast treading on King's heels. The relations of Japan and the United States, which had already changed for the better before King left for England, continued to improve, and King's efforts doubtless played a small part in accelerating this trend. Sir Edward Grey promised King on two occasions that the British Government would see that Japan observed the undertaking which she had given Canada (through Lemieux) regarding emigration,[83] and it is reasonable to assume that Grey would seek the same assurance from Japan regarding its obligations under her "gentleman's agreement" with the United States.[84] Certainly the flow of Japanese into the United States fell off rapidly during 1908.[85] The dispatch of the American naval force to the Pacific in December, 1907, had also not been without its effect, and when the fleet, accepting the invitation of Japan, moved into Japanese waters, it was received with "an unparalleled exuberance."[86] The great improvement in Japanese-American relations in 1908 may be dated from these events, and it found its climax for that year in November in the conclusion of the Root-

Takahira Agreement which settled a number of troublesome questions in the Pacific.[87] Japanese immigration gradually ceased to be a problem, and the question remained dormant for almost twenty years.*

A personal by-product of King's mission was its effect on his own impressions of English politics and public affairs. The more frequent his contacts, the more he was struck with the way in which the two major parties were divided by their concepts of Empire relations, though both contained so-called Imperialist groups. The Chamberlain "Imperialists" and tariff reformers, who were a dominating force in the Unionist party, favoured a closer and more centralized Empire relationship than that then in existence. The Liberal "Imperialists," a relatively less influential group among the Liberals, also believed in the British Empire as a wholesome force in the world but contemplated future development along the lines of a progressively increasing local autonomy for the Dominions.

King used the term "Imperialist" to describe almost exclusively one of the Chamberlain or centralizing school. Time and time again he found himself defending Laurier and Laurier's refusal to make commitments at the last Imperial Conference, and the hostile critics were invariably Unionists. Deakin of Australia was their hero. The Chamberlain Imperialists had looked with distrust on the evident sympathy between Laurier and Botha, and they were dismayed at Laurier's reluctance to give strong support to proposals of Empire preference. To these remarks King had a ready answer. Laurier was willing to be judged by his acts. He had given an actual preference, while Deakin had raised the tariff; he had disallowed laws aimed at excluding British subjects and British allies, while Deakin had helped to frame them; he had refused to invite the American fleet for a visit, while Deakin had hastened to send an invitation for it to come to Australia.† Laurier had

---

*The records indicate that King made no report to President Roosevelt of his mission, other than that tabled in the Canadian Parliament. Roosevelt had apparently lost interest. W. Loeb, Jr. (Secretary to President Roosevelt) to W.L.M.K., May 11, 1908. Grey Papers, James Bryce to Earl Grey, June 5, 1908.

†The effect of the American fleet on Empire relations worried the Foreign and Colonial Offices. The British Government told King that it had not authorized Deakin's invitation to the American fleet, that it did not approve of it, and that it had asked Canada not to follow the Australian example. A few weeks later, however, the British Government changed its mind, at least so far as the visit to Vancouver was concerned, and the Canadian Government—yielding in all likelihood to increased pressure from British Columbia—thereupon issued the invitation. Diary, March 19, April 3, 8, 1908.

consistently shown that he accepted the obligations of the Imperial connection. Moreover, King contended, it was surely a great mistake for one section of the Empire to dictate or advocate a party policy within the boundaries of another section. He found that Bonar Law appeared to be the only Unionist who accepted Laurier's attitude in good part; but a Liberal like Sir Edward Grey gave it his unreserved approval. King was also interested in Grey's realistic answer to the question of what Canada should do for Imperial defence. Grey said he had no suggestions, but that whatever Canada did would be welcomed in Great Britain. He continued:

"You really have had no need of any defence. So far as the United States is concerned there has been no friction between you, and there have been no other countries to worry you, why should you go to great expense for purpose of defence?" I pointed out that our policy had been to develop the country and get in people, and he agreed that this was entirely the best policy in the interests of the Empire itself. . . . He did not think we need fear anything from Japan. . . . Moreover, he said, that before Japan could invade Canada, the President of the United States would invoke the Monroe doctrine, and apart from any assistance from Britain she would not be allowed a footing on our continent.[88]

The fact was that whatever Mackenzie King might think of the Unionists personally, he distrusted their political views, and he especially disliked their brand of Imperialism, with its corollary of central control. These Imperialists, he believed, were in danger of "breaking down the very structure they were trying to create through the hastening of imperial organization."[89] They lacked perspective and understanding, and they failed completely to grasp the strength of national feeling within the Dominions.

A good example of this short-sightedness was afforded by the Quebec Tercentenary which was to be celebrated later in 1908. It was Earl Grey's special project, and one of its central features was to make the Plains of Abraham into a memorial park, the cost of which was to be met by contributions from all parts of the Empire. The Governor-General and others who thought like him on Empire matters were so carried away by their enthusiasm for the scheme that they could not see some of its objectionable implications. He had urged King to give the plan every encouragement when on his trip, and to a degree King did so; but his heart was not in it. On one occasion King told L. S. Amery that he was unable to see how South Africa's love for the

Empire would be increased by asking Botha and the Boers to help erect a memorial to the defeat of another race by the British.[90] King also felt that this idea of a birthday present was too much in accord with the traditional English attitude to the colonies:

It is the parent doing something for the child. It is work from above down. The more one studies the structure of the classes, the more one feels that all these things are in large measure but the price paid by a self-seeking landed, monied or titled aristocracy to maintain its position of eminence and above all of power.

And in a more prophetic vein he also wrote on the same day:

There is in England a real *Governing* class, in the sense that it seeks to control and actually does control and guide the national interests both in England and in the Dominions beyond. The English mind has been so long trained to this way of looking at the world that I can see wherein it will be many years before it will ever come to fully appreciate what self-government means.[91]

King's thinking on these matters was sharpened by his experience at a dinner of the Patriots Club which he attended as the guest of Lord Stanhope. About one hundred and fifty guests were present "including many of the leading Imperialists in England." Amery gave an address on South Africa, and he was followed by a number of speakers of whom Lord Milner was the chief.* Another was Sothern Holland, who in the course of his remarks cited recent events concerning Canada as evidence of growing independence and Imperial disruption. King did not speak, but he became progressively more irritated at what he heard. Later in his diary (April 3, 1908) he gave vent to his thoughts, which, had they been voiced, would have added materially to the interest of the meeting:

I found it very difficult to refrain from speaking, and in fact had Lord Milner not risen to reply at the moment he did, I would certainly have spoken. Had I done so, I would have pointed out, looking at Canada's action simply in the light of Empire building, had Canada negotiated her

---

*King disagreed with Milner, but did not dislike him. "I could see his strength as he spoke, and became conscious that it was the strength of one who believed he had been born to rule. His motives are, I think, above question. He would be guided by a sense of justice in everything, but believes, with the inherent belief that many Englishmen have, that British power is the only means of asserting that justice." Diary, April 3, 1908. There was also a link between the two men through Arnold Toynbee, "my dear and never to be forgotten friend," as Milner called him in a letter to King, Oct. 17, 1906.

own treaties a larger portion of the North American continent would probably have been British territory today; that Mr. Lemieux in returning from Japan, had told the Canadian people that it was the assistance of the British Ambassador and the British connection which had enabled him to negotiate terms with that country, which had helped to solve the Japanese immigration problem so far as Canada was concerned. That he had pointed out that while the United States, a larger country, was still waiting for this situation, we, because of the British connection, had been able to begin later in the day and end more quickly; that words like this, coming from a French-Canadian, instead of breaking a link, were forging one of the strongest links of Empire which it was possible to conceive. Also, that it might be worth noting where she [Canada] had seen imperial interests affected, [she] had also sent an envoy to Great Britain to confer with the British authorities before taking any action of their own accord which might be prejudicial to imperial interests.

That to argue that the Empire was going to pieces because of the withdrawal of parts of the British army and navy from these parts [of Canada] was equivalent to saying that Canada's loyalty depended on might, that we were not a free people, but held by ball and chain; that if dismemberment of the Empire were sought a better argument than this could not be put forth to bring it about; that I saw in the withdrawal of the British army and navy from these parts a means of lessening the imperial burden and providing the necessary first step towards having the Canadian people recognize the necessity of the defence of their shores and territory, and a consequent willingness to meet the expenditure necessary to this end. That so long as a British squadron or barracks remained, to that extent the country was inclined to rest in a sense of security which in the last resort retarded healthy self-reliance.

He would also, he said, have pointed out that Laurier had begun the Imperial preference, and that his lukewarm attitude to certain policies at the Imperial Conference was in part a reluctance to interfere in British political controversies. Laurier's actions as an Imperial statesman could safely be left to the verdict of history. King went on:

I would have concluded by saying that however we might differ in method, it could hardly be necessary at this day to assure the British public that in the fusion of imperial unity we were one in name. I would probably not have spoken in as broad terms as this, but the substance of what was said would have been unmistakeable. Perhaps it is just as well in the long run that the remarks were not made, although I felt the reflection so keenly, and have been little by little becoming more exasperated at the misunderstanding of Canadian motives by the imperialist group, that I have come to feel that a silence on these matters may lead to misunderstanding. I felt this so strongly that I allowed my judgment to outweigh

169

the consciousness that as a Civil Servant it was not advisable to talk on these questions, and being in England on a confidential mission it was well not to be drawn into arguments or controversy. . . .

I am inclined to think that in the Tory camp are those who incline towards rule—in the Liberal camp those who have faith in the many and believe in them. Each camp is actuated in its best men with ideas of service. If imperialism is to succeed service will have to be substituted for rule. What was borne in upon me particularly in listening to Lord Milner and the speeches of others was that it was not so much the welfare of human happiness [sic] irrespective of their race or creed, as the furtherance of the power and strength of the British race that constitutes the main purpose in their programme. Adam Smith, in his doctrine of laissez faire believed that man's self-love was God's providence—so the Englishman believes that in British rule the working out of God's will may come about. The purpose in its motive may be good, the mistake lies in believe [sic] that God's will does not work out as well as and sometimes better in other ways. . . .

Tonight's gathering has impressed me more than any event in connection with this present trip. I feel that it has added a permanent something to such political capital as I may possess.

CHAPTER SIX

THE SHIFT TO POLITICS

MANIFOLD DUTIES as a civil servant by no means prevented Mackenzie King from participating in many outside activities, some of which helped to enhance his reputation still further. In 1903, for example, he was one of the founders of the Ottawa Canadian Club. This organization was national in scope and once a fortnight invited some prominent man to luncheon or dinner, following which he addressed the Club on a political or literary subject. King became the Club's First Vice-President, and in the following year he was elected its President. "It is," he reflected, "an important office, especially this year [1904], & may prove a valuable asset & [sic] testing one's fitness for public life, & aiding towards an entrance. As such I think one owes it to one's self not to be too hesitant & backward, in allowing men of coarser grain & less lofty ideals to seize the reins of power, no matter where they are exercised."[1]

King's liking for Ottawa society continued unabated. There was a noticeable tendency for him to devote more and more attention to those near the top; he still retained his old fondness for meeting important people and he had in no way abandoned his policy of cultivating those who could be useful to him—behaviour which lent itself to an imputation of snobbishness, although this he did not deserve. King also continued to stand high among Ottawa's available young men, and a large number of invitations sought him without any action on his part. There is no doubt whatever that the Mintos and later, even more, the Greys, found him a most useful and attractive person to fill a gap at a dinner party or to act as an escort for British guests who were staying at Rideau Hall. It was here that he met Violet Markham in 1905, and some hint of King's social graces may be obtained from the entry in

171

Miss Markham's diary at the time: "a most charming and able young man, full of the right ideals."[2] But there is also no denying that King showed a persistent tendency to aim high in extending his circle of acquaintances: the years had simply resulted in his raising his sights. One of his associates in the Department of Labour still remembers the occasion when King asked him if he would like to have tea with Madame Nordica (the famous opera singer), an offer which he accepted with some scepticism. Yet after a few minutes on the telephone King had managed to secure an invitation for them both. Evidently King had not forgotten all the wiles or shed all the audacity of the newspaper reporter. The following social notes must have convinced even his ambitious parents that their son was fast coming within sight of the top. The first extract is from the daily press:

The torchlight march, which was the principal event of the evening, was led by Their Excellencies; Lady Eileen Elliot came next with Hon. George Grosvenor, and Lady Violet with Mr. McKenzie [sic] King; and then followed a long procession of skaters each bearing a lighted torch, which formed a picturesque sight as they went through the intricate figures of the march. . . . In the log house deliciously hot coffee, mulled claret and other refreshments were served.[3]

And to his parents he wrote:

I think I told you I was at dinner at Gov't House not long ago and took in Mrs. Hanbury-Williams [the wife of the Governor-General's private secretary]. I was also at dinner at Sir Louis Davies' [Judge of the Supreme Court of Canada] with Sir Wilfrid & Lady Laurier & others and at a luncheon at the Golf Club given by Mr. Fisher [the Minister of Agriculture], sat next to Lady Laurier. Mrs. Willard (wife of the Govr of Virginia) was another guest, about 10 altogether. Was at dinner at Mr. Hyman's [Minister of Public Works] a night or two ago.[4]

Nor did King seem to be in any danger of being forgotten outside Ottawa. In 1906 he could have had a full professorship at Harvard to teach economic history and labour problems. He would have ranked next to Taussig in the department. But Laurier strongly advised against acceptance, and knew well the most convincing arguments to use:

Sir Wilfrid told me [King reported home] not to think of it, that a man with the blood I had in my veins, my talents, etc. had a great future in this country and that I would be lost as a professor, even if I did write books. He has given me assurances enough to justify me in refusing the offer, but

172

it certainly was gratifying to know that the door is open at Harvard if I ever wish to join the Faculty there.*

A year later his name was put forward as a possible Leader of the Opposition in the Ontario Legislative Assembly, but provincial politics did not appeal to him nor, apparently, would this offering have satisfied his mother's ambition.[5] His name was suggested by Sir William Mulock for the presidency of the University of Toronto; and in 1907 he was extremely pleased to represent Harvard at the inauguration of Dr. (later Sir) Robert Falconer in that position. Several odd posts were offered to him, among them the Commissionership of the National Metal Trades Association (in New York), and the Superintendency of the Toronto General Hospital.

In 1906 His Majesty the King made him a C.M.G., a Commander of the Order of St. Michael and St. George. The conferring of this honour caused great resentment, and even anger, in official Ottawa; for many civil servants who had toiled faithfully but without distinction for fifteen or twenty years were furious that a comparative newcomer—and a young one at that—should be given so signal a reward while their long service was apparently forgotten. It was an open secret that the honour had been obtained on the personal initiative of Earl Grey and not of the Canadian Government, which might well have looked askance at singling out a junior deputy minister for preferred treatment. Dinners at Rideau Hall, it was popularly believed, had paid off. Yet the worst criticism that could properly be raised against the Governor-General's choice was that the move was a little premature. If at that time any question as to King's right to recognition could legitimately have been entertained, it must have been silenced by the quality of his achievement during the next few years.

The C.M.G. was but one of many ways in which he profited from the kindly offices of the Governor-General. King's personal qualities were indispensable factors in securing his advancement, but the rapidity of that advance was caused in no small measure from his close relations with two powerful men: Earl Grey and Sir Wilfrid Laurier. "Of all the honours and events of my life," he wrote home in 1910, "I think I prize most the friendship of Sir Wilfrid and Earl Grey. . . .

---

*W.L.M.K. to Mr. and Mrs. King, April 23, 1906. In 1908 Harvard approached Mackenzie King with an offer of a professorship in the new Graduate School of Business Administration. He declined.

When I reflected that it was to their confidence that I owed my present opportunity I could not but feel both very proud and deeply moved."[6]

Lord Minto had, of course, preceded Earl Grey at Rideau Hall; and King, mindful of his father's advice, had gone out of his way to cultivate the Governor-General. But although King's social life progressed as a result, his youth and inexperience were severe limitations, and Lord Minto held somewhat aloof. King's relations with Earl Grey were closer and genuinely sympathetic, inasmuch as they were based in large part on a similarity of outlook and broad humanitarianism. Grey, like King, looked on public service as the highest form of endeavour, and he was eager to give every encouragement to any promising young man whose eye was fixed on a political career. "How fortunate you are," he exclaimed to King, "to be a young man in such times as these, and to be dealing with these questions."[7]

Grey, too, had derived inspiration from Arnold Toynbee, though the Italian patriot, Mazzini, had made an even stronger impression. Mazzini's treatise, *The Rule of Life*, had long been Grey's constant guide.[8] "Love Humanity," wrote Mazzini. "Ask yourselves, as to every act you commit within the circle of family or country: *If what I now do were done by and for all men, would it be* beneficial or injurious to Humanity? and if your conscience tell you it would be injurious, desist." This was a favourite quotation of Grey's and one which was no less in accord with King's concept of public duty. Grey soon recognized this vein of idealism in King, and on his first Christmas in Canada he presented the younger man with a complete set of Mazzini's works.

Grey was a kind and friendly man of great charm and strong enthusiasms. He was a natural reformer, though he was too much inclined to support his causes with an undiscriminating judgment. The nature of his office in Canada, however, limited his freedom of action and often compelled him, as he said, "to walk the tight-rope of platitudinous generalities"; yet his influence behind the scenes was by no means inconsiderable. He was, indeed, a frequent cause of annoyance to the Government, the more so, perhaps, because he was high-minded and his efforts were rooted in a desire to improve the lot of the individual citizen or to advance the general welfare. On one occasion (1909) when Grey's enthusiasm for proportional representation threatened to become embarrassing, Laurier "wished Earl Grey would mind his own business," and King in his diary added: "The truth is His Ex. is getting into too many things."[9] Grey was a faddist. He had an excessive confidence in the results which could be obtained from education, from proportional representation, from co-operation and co-partnership, from town-planning and from assisted housing for the labouring class. Spurred on by his friendship with Cecil Rhodes, he became a fervid Imperialist who wanted to set up a federal Parliament for the whole Empire. To him the British Empire was the noblest political system the world had yet seen. He "loved beauty with all his heart and mind," said one of his friends. "He loved a beautiful woman: he loved a beautiful horse. But there was never beautiful woman nor beautiful horse in all this wide world [which] could compare in his eyes with the beauty of the British Empire. It was to him the magic beauty of the world. He never had any jingo feeling about it. . . . He just loved it as the most beautiful thing under heaven."[10]

This romanticism should not obscure the fact that His Excellency was a pretty sound fellow with his heart in the right place. He was fond of King, respected his industry and ability, and found him all too rare a type in Ottawa, where the entrance of highly trained university graduates into the civil service had received little encouragement. King for his part admired Grey and fully appreciated the advantages to be gained from a friend at court. He became a very frequent visitor at Rideau Hall. He helped draft a syllabus of lectures which Lady Evelyn Grey was planning for the education of the young girls of Ottawa. He gave the Governor *The Secret of Heroism*, and the latter obligingly said he would "send copies with letters for favourable reviews to London Times, Spectator, Outlook—& one to Carnegie, asking him to get out an edition for his libraries."[11] Dinner parties at Government House were not only agreeable, they sometimes developed in a most unexpected direction. It was in this way that King met Colonel McCook, the friend of Theodore Roosevelt, and the encounter eventually led to King's mission to England on behalf of the American President.

It was a fortunate circumstance for King that Earl Grey's tenure of office (1904–11) coincided with the period when King's abilities were rapidly maturing. For Grey was able to give him assistance of inestimable value: he helped to provide King with many of the opportunities which were essential if he was to prove his worth. Grey had no fear of youth or inexperience, and took the long view that responsibility must come early in a career if the full potentialities of talent were to be realized. He therefore went out of his way to push King forward whenever he thought the Government was not making sufficient use of this promising young man. In 1908 he urged Laurier not only to have Canada represented at international gatherings as a general principle but to send King as the Canadian representative on the International Opium Commission at Shanghai. Having secured this attendance, he next succeeded in having King's mission extended to India, and saw to it that he was given a secretary and an allowance for entertaining, which the Government had at first refused. "No one could be a better representative," Grey said to Laurier; King, as his diary reports, "had come to be indispensable."[12] Sir William Mulock's reception of the news of King's selection for another mission only a year earlier, also reported in the diary, had been an explosive "Great God!"[13] but then no man can expect to be a hero to one who has stood *in loco parentis*.

Earl Grey, having no disconcerting recollections of King's adolescence, was able to view the same rapid progress with much greater equanimity. Indeed, it was what he expected and desired. His dominant feeling was pride not astonishment. But he was nevertheless very conscious of possible dangers ahead. He kept a careful eye on King's progress, giving him sound advice and encouragement from time to time, and adding paternal warnings whenever they seemed necessary. A letter from Grey to Laurier,[14] written in 1908 just before King left on the "Roosevelt mission" to England, reveals Grey's confidence in King and his willingness to intervene if by so doing he could be of some help.

I share his [James Bryce's] favourable opinion of McKenzie [sic] King & his belief that a career of growing usefulness & distinction awaits him if he keeps both his health & his modesty—I note that Bryce takes it for granted that McKenzie King will go to London—These visits to Washington & to London are, I am inclined to think, good both for Canada & McKenzie King. They enlarge his experience & increase his efficiency—I hope they won't make him conceited. I know him well enough to give him a word of caution on this point—& if you send him to London shall take the liberty of speaking to him, as a father—I hope he did not tell the President that he had discovered at Vancouver documentary evidence of the complicity of the Govt of Japan in the evasion of their emigration assurances. This is just one of the points where the difference between the trained & amateur diplomat shows itself.*

Occasionally Grey expected, or at least hoped, that King would give support to one or other of his schemes and especially, perhaps, if the endorsation of the Government were desirable. King was usually able to comply, but on a matter like Imperialism, he felt compelled to dissent. Thus after King entered the Cabinet he noted, in November, 1909, that Grey's "manner was not as enthusiastic towards me as usual & I cannot but feel that he is disappointed in my not coming out more strongly for imperialism. He has had hopes I would be an advocate, & has doubtless learned that I find it impossible to do so & be truth [true ?] to my oath as adviser."[15] A few days later Grey tried to get King's help in supporting another idealistic proposal which he had placed before Laurier and which was aimed at preventing war through the application of economic sanctions. King wrote in his diary:

[Grey] spoke to me about a matter he wished kept confidential, he had talked it over with Sir W[ilfrid] again. He wd. like me to think over Sir Wilfrid taking the lead in introducing a resolution making it a crime for any men or companies to lend money to any country for purposes of war till after the matter had been referred to arbitration in a process similar to our Industrial Disputes Investigation Act. If Sir W. wd. introduce this it could be taken up in Eng. & other parts of the Empire, & the Br. Empire lead in the most effective means of securing peace. He wished me to be thinking over arguments in this connect'n to prepare Sir W.[16]

The next month Grey was still advocating his scheme:

Lord Grey has a wonderful imagination. He spoke of the project to get Sir Wilfrid to move at the next Colonial Conference to have Canada take the lead in declaring individuals etc. shld. be boycotted who loaned money for war purposes before question first submitted to Hague. He said he had talked it over with Fisher, & hoped Lemieux & he & I wd. get together & draft a letter for Sir Wilfrid to send to Asquith.[17]

The letter was drafted but there is nothing to indicate that the proposal went any further.[18] The general idea, however, may well have found a lodging in King's mind at this time. Certainly the outbreak of war in 1914 was to find him fascinated as Grey had been by the possibility of invoking economic measures to maintain peace or to force the abandonment of war.

*If this test is to be accepted as of any significance, King's amateur status was confirmed. He had told Roosevelt. Diary, Jan. 25, Feb. 18, 1908.

Grey's high opinion of King and his anxiety to see him enter politics made it inevitable that he should be one of a growing number who saw him destined for the Prime Ministership. King, as has been seen, had repeatedly had the same thought. The Earl of Stanhope came to visit Canada in September, 1908, at the same time that King announced to his friends his decision to enter politics. One day when the two friends were talking together, Stanhope recalled to King many years later, King remarked that if each carried out his intention to enter British and Canadian politics, respectively, Stanhope might become Governor-General and King the Prime Minister of Canada.[19] In 1933 Lord Stanhope was asked if he would consider appointment to the Canadian Governor-Generalship; but he refused because his future in English politics was at that time looking very promising.[*] Had he accepted the office, King's prophecy would have come true on both counts in 1935.

Although Earl Grey's support could be very useful in advancing the career of a rising young official, no one could be as helpful as the Prime Minister. How much more was this so when the young official had political ambitions! For Mackenzie King, of course, was not content to remain even a successful civil servant. When he measured success he was thinking on a quite different plane. He looked on his many achievements as desirable ends in themselves, but he realized that they could also be made to serve as stepping stones to his ultimate objective, and that this objective—the Prime Ministership—could be attained only by following the parliamentary route.

The design took shape as King's recognition in the civil service grew, and from 1905 to 1908 his mind increasingly turned to plans for getting into Parliament and thence into the Cabinet. He was fond of referring to the part destiny was playing in this design and to the working of what he called "the Unseen Hand," but one can discern more normal influences unremittingly at work: King's record of accomplishment, the reputation which he had been able to establish, the many contacts he had made, and his persistent effort to prepare the

[*]Lord Stanhope had been Parliamentary Secretary to the War Office (1918), and, later, Civil Lord of the Admiralty (1924–9), Under-Secretary of State for War (1931–4), Parliamentary Under-Secretary of State for Foreign Affairs (1934–6). He was to serve in a number of other ministerial and cabinet posts, among them being President of the Board of Education (1937–8), First Lord of the Admiralty (1938–9), Lord President of the Council (1939–40), Leader of the House of Lords (1938–40).

way for the transition. For King was not willing to risk any slip by the Unseen Hand, however well disposed. He might be eager to exchange the sheltered life of the civil servant for the uncertain and adventurous life of the politician, but he nevertheless made every effort to ensure that the transfer from the one to the other should be accomplished with the minimum of risk. He had a natural disinclination to be caught midway between the two careers.

In October, 1905, Sir William Mulock resigned as Postmaster General (and Minister of Labour) and went to the High Court of Ontario. He was succeeded as Postmaster General by A. B. (later Sir Allen) Aylesworth. King thereupon sought out Sir Wilfrid Laurier and informed him that he contemplated leaving the civil service after a short interval. Although he had several alternatives before him, the one he most favoured was politics, and two members of the Government, Sir Frederick Borden and L. P. Brodeur, had encouraged him to look in that direction. He told Laurier, his diary for November 4 records, that he was especially desirous of carrying on the work of his grandfather on behalf of the common people, and that from the beginning of his career he had kept this aim constantly before him. He had "remained unmarried, was young and free, had saved one or two thousand dollars,* and . . . if I was to take any risks or chances now was the time, that after 35 or 40, it was difficult for a man to alter the main trend of his work."[20]

Laurier expressed a sympathetic interest in his problem, and inquired if King had made any plans. King replied that he had talked over one or two plans with Sir William Mulock, but he hesitated to mention them lest they should seem too presumptuous or ambitious. He did well to hesitate, and probably would have done even better had he retired from the interview forthwith. For he rightly described his proposals as presumptuous, especially when it is remembered that they were put forward by a young civil servant to a veteran Prime Minister, and had as their primary purpose the provision of a place for himself in the Cabinet. He suggested to the Prime Minister, the diary reports, that the Government might come out with a statement of regret for the loss of Sir William Mulock, and announce its determination to press on more strongly than ever with the work Sir William had

*Two years later King listed his "cash savings" at $7,000, with $1,500 more, secured by mortgage, in loans to his father. Diary, Sept. 10, 1907.

initiated on behalf of labour. As part of this effort the Government would be prepared to make Labour a separate department with its own Minister, and to expand its activities in certain other directions such as the census and statistics. If the Prime Minister did not desire to increase the number of Ministers, Trade and Commerce and Customs could be combined under one man. It could not be denied, King continued, that a radical change in the group of Ontario Ministers was overdue, for most of the present members were both old and weak. The young Liberals were dissatisfied with the way the older men held on to office. "Sir Richard Cartwright & Hon. Mr. Scott had been splendid men, & doubtless were still, they had served their generation well, but their generation was past." Others were reviewed in turn and also found wanting. King does not mention whether he put his own name forward at this juncture, but if he did not, the inference was obvious.

Laurier apparently listened attentively to this incredible recital and expressed a general agreement, though he said his greatest problem was not so much with Ontario as with the western provinces which were beginning to assert themselves and demand Cabinet representation. King thereupon produced another scheme centring about British Columbia which involved making a Cabinet member a Lieutenant-Governor, placing a member of Parliament, Ralph Smith, in the Senate,* and giving King the resulting vacancy in the House. After a little more discussion of this kind, King took his leave. Laurier thanked him for letting him know his plans and expressed his pleasure at hearing of his desire to enter public life. "He said the Cabinet would be where he would want me, and that that would be the purpose of my entering Parliament."

Mackenzie King was delighted with the result of the interview. He hastened to his office and wrote a jubilant letter home—"strictly confidential." "The interview was all that you or I could wish for, and

*Ralph Smith had for years been closely identified with the labour movement and had been President of the Trades and Labor Congress in 1900. He sat as a Liberal from British Columbia in the House of Commons from 1900 to 1911, and he was a member of the British Columbia Assembly 1898–1900 and 1916–17. At the time of his death in 1917 he was Minister of Finance for that province. He had an extremely able wife who succeeded her husband in the legislature after his death, the first woman in the world to do so. Smith might easily have been a possible rival to King as Minister of Labour, for Laurier had a high opinion of him, but he preferred to await a seat in the Senate. In the result, he ran again in the general election of 1908 and was elected.

beyond our best hopes. I will tell you all when I see you. Suffice it to say at present that from this hour I begin *my political career*."[21]

Such news naturally caused what John King called in a magnificent understatement "a very pleasurable sensation at home." All the family (except Max who was now practising medicine in Ottawa) wrote their congratulations, and all were eager to know what was implied in the last three words of the announcement. John King "hazarded some guesses," the chief of which was a portfolio. He obviously thought Laurier was lucky to gain such a colleague, and even assumed a blatantly condescending attitude. Laurier, he said, "is not perfect politically; no politician or statesman is. He has made one or two political mistakes—who in public life has not? but take him for all in all, he is a splendid type of public man, and one whom no young man need feel ashamed to follow & support, with earnestness & enthusiasm."[22] But Mrs. King went unerringly to the heart of the matter.

I cannot but feel that you are going on with a work that your grandfather strove hard to throw the best part of his life into, and now you will have the advantage of a more enlightened people to deal with.

"My political career" has a ring about it that rouses all my nature and I send you all good wishes and trust I may be spared to see [you?] gain the love and confidence of all your followers, and in fact see you a regular Gladstone.[23]

King did not stop with this opening move, and was quite willing to risk Laurier's displeasure by his persistence in urging his case. Two months later he had some reason to believe that the British Columbia portfolio was under discussion, and he sought another interview with Laurier at which he placed other suggestions before him with the same end in view as in their earlier talk. Laurier gave a non-committal, but not discouraging, reply. King reminded himself in his diary on January 2, 1906:

My feelings as a result of this interview are that I must watch matters, deliberately get to work to secure this end by legitimate means, not trust to Destiny tho' it may be on my side. To remember that nothing is certain by [but?] a certainty. Work and Watch. Sir Wilfrid may not be forgetful & is not indifferent, but has men pressing him on all sides. By keeping before him in the right way my chances will be improved. I believe public life is to be my lot. I believe that God's purpose in my life is to help to work out His will in the world in this way. I must seek to realize the greatness of the task, the service to be rendered such a Master.[24]

In a few weeks, the British Columbia vacancy in the Cabinet was filled, and that approach to a seat in the House, at least for a time, was closed. "It is beginning to look," wrote King, "as tho' only a Destiny could determine the end, and this I seem to feel will be so."[25] He was becoming bored with his work. He felt that he was only marking time and that he needed a more active life and new fields of activity. The trip to England in the autumn to secure legislation to suppress fraudulent immigration practices was a help, but in the nature of things it was an inadequate substitute. He continued to produce plans for his political advancement, one of which he laid before Laurier, but nothing came of them. The Prime Minister, however, remained sympathetic, and when the Harvard offer was made in 1906, he renewed his assurances regarding King's future in public service.[26]

Laurier frequently expressed misgivings about Mackenzie King's entering politics without financial reserves of his own. "In public life," he said in their first interview in 1905 on the subject of King's plans, "some independence was essential, if one had to worry over a livelihood it was difficult to do one's best."[27] The "one or two thousand dollars" which to King looked fairly substantial he did not find very reassuring, and he suggested that King might enter journalism for a time to build up his resources. But King was apparently afraid of being side-tracked, and the suggestion was dropped.

In the summer of 1907 Sir Wilfrid tried another plan and endeavoured to interest the intending politician in an eligible widow twenty-four years of age. When he asked King why he did not get married, King replied that he had set his mind on a public career and had kept himself free from obligations which might make the course difficult. " 'On the contrary,' said Sir Wilfrid, 'The right person would be a great help to you in public life, and in securing a foothold. . . . Why do you not think of that young girl whom you met at our house on Sunday. She is a fine girl, I know of no girl of whom I think more, she is good, clever, kind, capable,' and, raising his hand, 'she will have a fortune.' " King expressed a moderate interest and Sir Wilfrid added: " 'Why do you not call at my house to-morrow afternoon and invite Lady Laurier and her to the theatre in the evening? There is the door opened for a beginning.' I thanked him and said I would be delighted to."[28]

The "skirmishing expedition"—as King called it with some amusement—came off, but the divine spark was lacking. Of course, King's specifications were exacting in the extreme. "I am prepared to play fair," he wrote in his diary that day, "give myself and any reasonable project a fair chance, but I will never be controlled save by my heart. . . . Unless she can surpass in my judgment any woman I have yet seen as the one with whose nature my nature could best blend, I will not allow wealth, position or aught else to tempt me."[29] Five weeks later Laurier again brought up the subject, and intimated that King would be a welcome visitor to his house so far as the young widow was concerned. But this very practical approach shocked King's romantic sense, and he told Sir Wilfrid that all this "fore knowledge was a barrier," and that "with me the heart must bind itself alone."[30]

King had entered 1907 with the determination to seek an Ontario constituency and a by-election at the earliest opportunity. (This was the year, too, of the Industrial Disputes Investigation Act, the Royal Commission on the hours of telephone operators in Toronto, and various investigations of Oriental immigration into Canada.*) He had made some progress in the direction of securing the nomination from North Oxford, a safe federal riding which had never failed to return a Liberal since Confederation, when he ran into unexpected difficulties. A friendly reporter wrote an article in the Toronto News in June with the evident purpose of helping King in his entrance into politics. Unfortunately the article not only praised King, it also criticized the members of the Government. It said that the Cabinet Ministers were becoming old and shop-worn, and those from Ontario were especially in need of renewal. Mr. Aylesworth, who had been regarded as one of the few possibilities for the future, had shown himself lacking in the essential qualities of good leadership, and Laurier would be forced to seek someone else from Ontario who could rejuvenate the party there. Parliament did not appear to be able to provide the man who was needed. But "the public service at Ottawa contains the very man who should fit the situation," and the News correspondent begged "to nominate the grandson of William Lyon Mackenzie as a most suitable recruit for Ontario Federal Liberalism."[31] The article reviewed King's career, and made the most generous references to his popular sympathies and his work in the Labour Department.

King knew, weeks before its publication, that the article had been

*Supra, pp. 133 ff., 144 ff., 146.

written and he had at least a general idea of its content.[32] The reporter (C. F. Hamilton), however, had agreed to shelve it until Laurier's return from England where he was attending a meeting of the Imperial Conference. But rumours of King's move to politics and his possible entrance to the Cabinet had already begun to appear; and Hamilton, after trying to get in touch with King, who was not in Ottawa, "resolved to take the responsibility of letting it out."[33] Thus while King had nothing to do with the article's publication at that time, he knew its general tenor and especially the comparisons it drew between some members of the Cabinet and himself.

King, on reading the article, deplored the comparisons, but on the whole was pleased with the remainder. "I like especially its references to my interest in the welfare of the plain people, my knowledge of the problems of the industrial classes, my sympathies with the oppressed and the references to grandfather & the inspiration of his life." He realized that some Liberals might be irritated and a suitable constituency might have become more difficult to obtain; but the article was "generous & wholehearted to a degree, & is a fine introduction to the public."[34] He wrote Laurier at once, however, to explain the circumstances of the article's publication.[35] King's hat was now in the ring, even though it had been tossed there, somewhat precipitately, by someone else.

The party response was immediate and on the whole unfavourable. Although many members of Parliament were not surprised at King's venture, they nevertheless resented an outsider with so little experience and preliminary political effort being considered for high office. Was King willing, one member asked him, to get his coat off and "get down among the boys and work"; and King's assurance that he was prepared to do so, seemed to be received with some scepticism. Opposition inevitably arose from those Cabinet Ministers who had been the subject of attack in the article, who were irritated by King's pretensions, or who were jealous of King's ability and aggressiveness. Earl Grey was notoriously his friend, and Sir Wilfrid was known to be partial to him. Sir William Mulock for his part approved of the new candidate and promptly offered him $1,000 to help defray his election expenses. Aylesworth (now Minister of Justice) could not but feel hurt at the criticisms of the article; but King assured him that he regretted the comparisons which had been made and succeeded in large measure in pacifying him.[36]

Laurier, for his part, was very much annoyed at the incident, and King's most humble regrets offered on his return did little to appease him.

He said it [the article] was most unfortunate, that its statement that there was no material in the House out of which to construct a cabinet was the worst feature. Comparisons were also unpleasant & harmful. It would raise a rebellion in the House if he took me into the Cabinet just now. I then said to him that I saw the position clearly, that I wished him to know I was not seeking a cabinet position till I could demonstrate my fitness for it, that what I had thought was that at the next session it might be well to make the Dept. of Labour a separate Dept. & that if it were I would like to be the Minister.* That this I thought would be fair in view of what I had done, also in the interests of the party. . . . Sir Wilfrid then interrupted & said, Without intending to say anything against the idea of a separate Dept., that for the moment it could be said that one would find many opportunities through the session for bringing this out, there [were] many chances for speaking in debate, that in the House of Commons it did not take a man very long to find his level, he was either up or down very soon after the start, that unless I belied all that he expected & my friends believed of me, & my past record I wd. come to the front rapidly. . . . Whether Labour was made a separate portfolio or not, if taken into the Govt. at any time it wd. probably fall to me.[37]

Laurier's comment to King on the Toronto *News* story had been apt: "This is a case where one may well say: 'Save me from my friends.'"[38] King's ambitions had received a severe temporary check, and any hope he may have entertained to run before the general election was necessarily abandoned. His earlier complacency quickly vanished:

The more I consider [the *News* article] the more harmful I feel it to be. It has created a feeling of hostility towards me on behalf of those on whose support I have to rely—it is this more than any disappointment over lack of certainty in the way of preferment . . . jealousies have been started, which I have in now [no?] way given occasion for, undercurrents already at work against me,—my whole career is prejudiced in advance. . . . God is too good to me His providence too sure to chide or distrust Him. It is a lack of faith that is all. My best course is certainly not to have preferment till I have demonstrated my worth, till I can get it without the asking and till men in fact will ask of me to accept it. . . . It would be folly in other ways to go into the Cabinet even if a chance offered at once. I know very little about general politics. I have not followed even the

---

*This apparent contradiction came from a curious idea King had already put forward: that he would be made the head of a new Labour Department but "without portfolio." He apparently meant that he would be a Minister, but would not, at first, be in the Cabinet, a common occurrence in England and not entirely unknown in Canada.

newspapers as I should. I know nothing about procedure in the House. I am freer as a member to speak my mind, without considering the necessary restraints of the Ministry. I am not the object of such bitter attack, I can have more leisure . . . time to read, to reflect, to prepare, I can become acquainted with the members of the House, and be master of my time & opportunities as I never could otherwise. Altogether I have reason to thank the Providence which removes the temptation of office. Were it present it might—probably would—be seized as a prize, against my own better judgment. . . .

. . . Lastly there is the purpose of God in all, the realization of the dream of my life, the page unfolds as by the hand of Destiny. From a child I have looked forward to this hour as that which should lead me into my life's work. I have believed my life's work lies there, and now I am lead [led?] to the threshold by the Invisible Hand. One step after the other I have been led up to this height. College, settlement life, post graduate study, the sweating investigation, the Department, the settlement of strike after strike, last year's Bill, the recognition from the Crown, all come without the asking all as if Fate or Destiny or the direction of a living and guiding God. . . . Now if the voice of the people of Oxford* is to be heard, if they call me to come as their champion in the fight for a greater liberty, I will hearken to it as the voice of the living God, and with belief in the good accomplished in the past in the purpose of the future, I will bow my head in the presence of this voice and will answer with the words

"Oh! God of Bethel by whose Hand
Thy people still are fed
Who through the weary pilgrimage
Hath all our fathers led.
Our vows our prayers we now present
Before Thy throne of grace
God of our fathers, be the God
Of their succeeding race."[39]

The postponement of King's immediate hopes was naturally disheartening, but his response to the reverse was typical. His worries in such circumstances rarely lasted very long. He did not question the divinely ordered plan, but rather sought further enlightenment on what the future might hold. Although in dwelling on the possible compensating advantages of the set-back, he was in part obeying a natural human impulse to draw the utmost consolation from adverse circumstances, he was also reasserting his belief in his mission. His uniqueness lay not so much in his reliance on divine guidance as in the depth and certainty of that reliance. He believed that he was being

*The constituency where he was hoping to run as a candidate.

186

led irresistibly step by step to a predetermined goal, and this conviction made him sure that eventually he would be successful. The belief was to prove a tower of strength to him all his life. It consoled him in adversity; it came to his aid when he was in need of encouragement. It provided an effective armour against his enemies, and enabled him to throw off misfortune and defeat and face the next encounter with undiminished confidence. "If God be for us, who can be against us?" Who, indeed?

Another aspect of the same belief was that he should never allow himself to be discouraged although God's purpose might be obscured by unlikely and even hostile events. The wise man, he thought, would simply regard these barriers as tests and opportunities for self-development, and he would endeavour to turn any disasters to his advantage. When the appointed moment arrived, he would then be in a much better position to act effectively. How quickly did King begin his search for benefits which might lie hidden in the destruction of his hopes for an immediate seat in Parliament! His optimism had probably been premature. His political education was inadequate. His character and mind needed tempering. But nothing was to be considered final: all opened new and wider doors to the future.

> Then, welcome each rebuff
> That turns earth's smoothness rough,
> Each sting that bids nor sit nor stand but go!
> Be our joys three-parts pain!
> Strive, and hold cheap the strain;
> Learn, nor account the pang, dare, never grudge
>   the throe!

One can be reasonably sure, although King does not mention it, that one of the greatest lessons he drew from the incident of the *News* article was to observe the way in which Laurier tried to smooth over the party dissension which that article was likely to cause. The Prime Minister's position was not an easy one. He had told King that he wanted him as long ago as 1905, but to gain King and to antagonize thereby a large section of his following could do the party nothing but harm. Laurier had to maintain party unity and morale and make every member feel that his service would be appreciated and fairly rewarded. Direct and decisive action on Cabinet reorganization might have to yield, for a time at least, to temporizing action without firm commitments. The leader would often find it necessary to give recognition to provincial jealousies and rivalries, to pursue one policy towards Quebec and another towards Ontario, to avoid taking a step in one direction without a compensating step in another. And ever and always, he must be able to appeal to the loyalty which the members owed to the party and to himself. Loyalty is the great reconciling factor, the final tie, the indispensable foundation, on which the party's solidarity will depend in the last resort.

To put the problem in more specific terms, the unfortunate article had cast a stigma on all Ontario Liberals in the House. At the same time, the remedy suggested by the Toronto *News* correspondent had been the dangerous one of going to the civil service and finding a substitute—a man who, contrary to all precedent in such an office, had his name constantly before the public, had stirred up many political jealousies, and had in all probability caused unhappy comparisons to be made between his talents and those of some of the Ministers. What would be the feelings of those faithful members of Parliament who had been hoping for a portfolio as a final reward for a lifetime of political service? Laurier did not exaggerate when he said that to take King into the Cabinet at this particular time would "raise a rebellion in the House." Nor could the appointment of King as a Cabinet Minister fail to be ill received also by his prospective colleagues who had been singled out for criticism and whose qualities had been unfavourably compared to those of this interloper.

Laurier was not to be hurried into precipitate action on King's claims, but neither could he afford to dally with the general problem. He cut off any possibility of King's immediate entrance to the Cabinet and he set doubting minds at rest (though in doing so he confirmed in part the criticism regarding the dearth of Cabinet material among the federal members from Ontario) by appointing George P. Graham, the leader of the Liberal Opposition in Ontario, as Minister of Railways and Canals. Youth and ability from Ontario were thus introduced where they were badly needed, though not in the way suggested, and Graham became the young Liberal hope from that province. On the other hand Laurier privately encouraged Mackenzie King to seek election, and he appealed to his vanity and ambition by suggesting that he would have many opportunities to display his qualities on the floor of the House. The Prime Minister had confidence in King's capacity

and he had little doubt of the outcome; but the wisest way was to allow
the members themselves to be convinced that this man was fitted to
be a Minister, and could, without coddling, debate and take care of
himself in Parliament.

But though King grasped some of Laurier's worries, his own personal interests were so deeply involved that he was blind to many
other difficulties. He considered, of course, that his own candidacy
was of supreme importance to Canada; and not only did he believe
that his talents were exceptional, but he felt that he was giving up
many benefits and assuming many risks by going into politics. The
Prime Minister seemed to agree with him on these points, yet he was
reluctant to give King anything savouring of preferred treatment—
which King said he did not desire, but which he nevertheless clearly
expected. The mission to Great Britain in March 1908 which had
been set in motion by the negotiations over the preceding two months
with President Roosevelt (see pp. 151 ff.) must have greatly occupied
King's attention for a time but certainly shaped itself in such a way as
to encourage rather than divert his ambition. Laurier had of course
many other more important problems than King's advancement to
contend with, and he remained discouragingly unmoved by King's
worries. King longed for a safe seat (so that, as he liked to put it,
"I could get out and help the party"), but Laurier was not willing to
interfere in an Ontario constituency in order to get one for him. King
wanted Labour to be made a separate department, a move which
would at one stroke enhance his prestige and provide recognition for
his past efforts in the Department, but Laurier was afraid that such
a move might start an agitation to have the portfolio of Labour reserved for labour candidates.[40] King would have liked to have been
made a Minister at once (though he did not ask for it), but Laurier
would not appoint him before the election for that would cause ill-
feeling and disappointment among the other aspirants at a most
awkward time.

King did not appreciate this waiting game, and he found it difficult
to curb his impatience. He said that he saw the necessity of the Prime
Minister keeping those about him satisfied, but he was clearly bewildered by Laurier's "entirely passive attitude" towards his own problem
and complained in May of 1908 that "he does not seek to impose his
own will in the direction of reform as he might."[41] As the time of the

election drew nearer and he still had no constituency, he confessed: "Sir Wilfrid I cannot quite make out. He is personally very friendly, but what his motive is, I don't know. I cannot tell whether he is playing me along to keep me where I am, or not."[42]

In King's own record of the efforts he made to induce Laurier to give him recognition there is naturally little said of Laurier's attitude to what would strike any observer as King's amazing importunity and of Laurier's equally amazing forbearance. Only once King mentions that at the beginning of an interview Laurier glanced at the clock as though he wished to cut the conversation short. For Laurier did not wish to antagonize this impatient young man with the overweening ambition. To encourage him, to bring him along, to season him, and then to have him available at the right time with the acquiescence, if not full approval, of most of his followers—this was Laurier's plan, and it called for tact and caution at every turn.

How different it was when Earl Grey tried to give King a helping hand: an opening to be mentioned here, a recommendation to be made there, a word of advice in season. Grey's objective was both simple and limited—to give a promising young man a useful opportunity to exhibit his wares—and the responsibility for what might happen rested almost entirely on other shoulders. Grey was playing jack-straws, while Laurier was engaged in a complicated game of chess. Laurier's moves were all interdependent and their consequences could never be fully determinate. He had constantly to consider many factors, not the least of which were influences which might endanger the party of which he was the head and consequently the fate of the Government itself, if not at the moment, perhaps two or three years in the future.

Despite some distortion of King's vision on matters which concerned his own immediate problem, is it at all likely that Laurier's skill in dealing with these many imponderables passed unnoticed by this bright young man? At no stage in King's history could it be suggested that lack of observation was one of his failings, and later, when he became a party leader himself, this sensitivity to the complex demands made on him in that capacity was deemed to be one of his outstanding gifts. Was this experience in 1908, therefore, not one of his important lessons? King's frustrations and disappointments at this time may indeed have worked out to his great advantage in the long run. The Unseen Hand, in truth, may have led as well as chastised.

The approach of the election forced Mackenzie King to make a decision on a constituency. He had looked into a number of possibilities, and finally settled on North Waterloo as being on the whole the most promising. Berlin was the county town; and at a public reception and dinner given to Lemieux and King in July, 1907, it had shown great pride in the local boy who was making a distinguished record in the public service. Unfortunately, North Waterloo was Conservative, though 306, the majority at the last election, was not, even in those days, considered large. On September 9, 1908, Laurier and King reached an understanding:

I then said   Well Sir Wilfrid if you will agree to make the Department a separate Dept., & announce it during the campaign, I will run in North Waterloo against Joe Seagram [the sitting member] or any one else. Sir Wilfrid said "Very good." I replied All right I will run in North Waterloo. Sir Wilfrid got up off his chair & struck his knee with his hand & say [said] "I am delighted." . . . He came over to me & stood above me looking straight down into my eyes. He looked long & steadfastly, and his face was lighted with his smile. I looked steadfastly at him, through it all he looked so worn and feeble. There was great spirit & fire there, but there seemed to be no constitution on which it could thrive. . . . He shook hands with me a second time, & I told him I would bring him back that riding, that I would try to win, that I would win.[43]

A few days later Laurier indulged in prophecy: "You will come to the front at once, you will take a great part from the start, you have the instinct for politics: I know what I am saying."[44] He did not have to wait long for a partial fulfilment of his statement. On October 26, 1908,* while the Liberal Government was being returned by 133 to 88 seats, King carried North Waterloo by a majority of 263 votes.

Four days after the election, King obtained a confirmation from Laurier that in the first session a separate Department of Labour would be set up and that he would "have to do with the new Department." He at once put in a claim for other activities which would enhance its importance, and mentioned expressly the census, statistics, and the publication of the Canada Year Book, all of which Laurier thought would be desirable. King also showed considerable interest in more local matters. As the representative of a constituency with a large German population, he helped to secure a senator for this particular group, and he also busied himself with problems of patronage. Earl

*Mackenzie King resigned as Deputy Minister of Labour on September 21, 1908.

191

Grey had been no more than accurate in September when he had remarked: "You are going to be as bad as the rest of them, give public buildings before elections, etc."[45]

But the young member was not to be allowed to rest on his laurels very long. An immediate question to settle was that of representation at the anti-opium congress in Shanghai for which King had been tentatively chosen (at the suggestion of the United States)[46] before the election. It was decided that he would attend as a member of the British delegation. Following the general election Earl Grey pressed to have the trip include stops in Great Britain and India[47] (China was eventually added) to discuss several questions, the chief of which was immigration. Laurier after some little hesitation became converted to this extension of the purpose of the mission, and he agreed with Grey that for this also Mackenzie King was the man best fitted to take on the additional duties.

But now that King was a member of Parliament—and not yet a Minister—he began to have doubts whether he should go. Was it wise to leave Ottawa at this particular time? "Be not troublesome to him, lest thou be put back," says Ecclesiasticus, "and keep not far from him, lest thou be forgotten." King was not at all sure about the first part of the warning, but he had no doubts at all about the second: he liked to keep himself constantly before the Prime Minister when decisions affecting himself were being made. At any rate, here was an opportunity to apply a little pressure to the Prime Minister by deciding to stay in Ottawa unless he were made at least a Minister without portfolio before setting out on the mission. But Laurier was not to be intimidated. He adhered to his early determination not to take King into the Ministry in any capacity until he had actually entered the House, though he gave King an assurance that he would be made Minister of Labour shortly after his return. On this understanding, King decided to take on the assignment.*

What was expected of King on this world trip seems to have been somewhat vaguely formulated by his principals, Grey and Laurier, and for this vagueness it owes something, no doubt, to its rather casual origin. King was, of course, to go to Shanghai, and discuss there the

---

*An account of the world trip and conferences is fully (742 pages) set out in King's diary for the period, covering October 30, 1908, to May 7, 1909. Exact references have, on the whole, been omitted in the following pages.

world opium problem with the representatives of ten or twelve other nations. Earl Grey wanted him to go to India in order to establish friendly relations with the Indians themselves and remove some of the unfortunate impressions caused by the hostility of British Columbia.* "King's sympathies with the Sikhs & Hindus," Grey wrote in December, 1908, "his appreciation of Canada's imperial obligation to render every assistance in her power to the Govt. of India, and his nice persuasive way of talking, might be turned to useful account."[48]

To this plan Grey added his pet scheme for coping with the whole stubborn racial problem: to keep, as he said, "each colour to its own zone." It was basically the same immigration policy that King had noted earlier that year at the time of his mission to Washington and had as its corollary a common North American ban on the immigration of Asiatic labour. "Because I recognize my neighbour as a brother," said Elihu Root, "I am not thereby obliged to allow him to come into my yard and do what he wishes with my property, to plant his seeds in my garden and take what he can out of my soil."[49] (See supra, pp. 157–8.) With this general idea Laurier was in full sympathy, though he was naturally concerned primarily with its application to Canada. The optimistic Grey favoured calling a world conference to work out a permanent understanding between the white and Asiatic powers on the migration of the labouring class from all countries. Laurier preferred to go more slowly and negotiate direct and separate agreements.[50] He would like, he said, if it were possible, to "make joint cause with the United States on this question and have the Monroe doctrine idea followed out between the two countries, and the sooner this was done the better."[51]

King's assignment was thus broadened to include Earl Grey's conference idea, while at the same time he was to explore the question of immigration from India and China. At the moment, of course, the Canadian control of Asiatic immigrants was not at all consistent, for it rested on a number of special arrangements. The question of the Japanese had been settled by the Lemieux agreement; that of the Chinese by legislation imposing a $500 head tax on all Chinese immigrants; that of the Indians by a number of administrative devices,

---

*The irritating manifestations were chiefly violent propaganda against immigration and prohibitive laws, nine of which were disallowed by the Dominion Government from 1897 to 1901.

such as the discouragement by shipping companies, the rule demanding a continuous voyage from the place of birth, general legislation and discouraging publicity by the Government of India. The combination of these policies was so effective, however, in reducing Oriental immigration (especially from Japan and India) that the annual report of the Deputy Minister of Labour in 1909 was able to state that "the inflamed state of public feeling [in British Columbia] noticeable a year ago, appears to have wholly disappeared."[52] Laurier thought the methods might still be improved. He wished, following the example of the Lemieux agreement with Japan, to induce India or China to accept the idea of the voluntary restriction of their own emigrants to Canada. If Canada could get an agreement along these lines with China, for example, the United States would probably follow the Canadian example, and this in turn might lead to a common continental policy on immigration.

Mackenzie King left Ottawa on December 14, 1908, for England. His plans called for conversations with several members of the British Cabinet in London; others with some of the leading officials of the Government of India at Calcutta; and then the International Opium Commission at Shanghai. He would return home by way of China where he would meet representatives of its Government. This schedule was followed, with side trips and other stops being made when they appeared desirable. He returned to Ottawa on May 9, 1909.

King was in England only ten days, but the time was pleasantly and profitably spent. He had long interviews with senior civil servants on India, immigration, and opium, and he was well entertained, including a Christmas dinner with Lord and Lady Morley in Wimbledon, and a day with Sir Edward Grey at Falloden. King found no support in England for the idea of a great international conference on immigration.[53] The feeling was that the time for such a gathering had not arrived, that any result from it would be apt to be temporary, and that a strict zoning policy would not work when applied to certain of the crown colonies. He discussed with Sir Edward Grey the possibility of a permanent Canadian representative attached to the British embassy in some countries, especially the United States, Japan, and China. He found that the Foreign Secretary quite approved of the idea and thought "it would do much good."

In India (where King's old friend, Lord Minto, was now, of course,

Viceroy) King's visit became largely a goodwill mission, as Earl Grey had intended it should be. For this purpose King made many contacts with Indians and British officials. Again he found no supporters for Grey's international conference on immigration. There was, indeed, a general reluctance to re-open the subject at all, and a disposition to regard it as settled. Indian emigration to Canada had ceased, and the Indians showed no dissatisfaction with existing conditions.[54] The Indian Government had sufficient worries already and it did not want to regulate its own emigration beyond the restrictions already imposed. In this cold atmosphere even Laurier's moderate proposal met with no response. King's sympathies responded to the Indian desire for self-government. He believed, however, that any far-reaching proposals were premature, and regarded the Morley-Minto reforms as an encouraging step in the right direction. What shocked him were the cases of racial discrimination which he frequently observed. The Indian question might be complex and, at the moment, insoluble; but he could see no justification for many of these affronts to Indian feeling. He wrote in his diary:

We had an example at dinner tonight of the kind of thing which I believe works most injury. The Indian gentlemen who had been showing us about, and who had been unfailing in their courtesies, were neither of them present at dinner with us, though the elder of the two sat through the whole of the dinner on a chair apart, looking on at the guests enjoying themselves. Later in the evening, when the dance was taking place, he was not seated within the circle but moved about explaining the different dances. There is no excuse for this thing in India. Where men are refined, educated and noble in purpose there should be no distinctions between them. To do so is to place a badge of inferiority by the one on the other.[55]

King was one of five British delegates at the Shanghai opium conference. It had been called at the instance of the United States to promote general reform and to supply additional help to China for the suppression of the opium traffic. Inevitably very different attitudes were represented by different delegations. The Chinese were seriously concerned with overcoming a major evil; the American approach was a combination of reform and philanthropy; the British favoured abolition, but realized more acutely than the Americans the financial and administrative difficulties in the way; many other countries wished to move no further than was absolutely necessary. The delegates included an American bishop, reformers, civil servants, and diplomatic officials

195

from a number of countries, and a Persian who was by occupation an opium merchant! Significant results could not be expected, and compromise was implicit in every aspect of the problem.

In this atmosphere King, though a newcomer, felt quite at home. He found his most valuable function was the familiar one of reconciling conflicting views, especially those of the United States and Great Britain, and he frequently made a suggestion or moved a qualifying clause which enabled the two delegations to come together. After some three weeks the conference brought its sittings to a close by passing a number of broad and general resolutions. It is difficult to regard the work of the International Opium Commission as marking any great advance, though it was no doubt encouraging that the trend of all its resolutions was towards measures for suppression of the traffic. Even the Chairman did no more than claim for the conference that it had "not wholly failed in carrying the problem a stage nearer its final solution."[56] Lord Morley was more frank: the work, he was quoted as saying, had not "amounted to much."[57]

At Shanghai King participated in his first international conference, and despite his meagre knowledge of the opium trade, he had proved to be a useful member. But he came away with no illusions about the value of large international meetings as a means of transacting important affairs—an amusing and unexpected conclusion for one who was, in a sense, looking for support for Earl Grey's grandiose plan for a world conference on immigration. "What I have seen of the procedure and the difficulties with which a gathering of the kind is beset," he wrote, "makes me feel that the experiment of international conferences is a very doubtful one. Other things being equal, I should be inclined to decide against it in regard to most, if not all problems, and adopt a policy of each nation negotiating its own settlements and arrangements with countries concerned."[58] Laurier's preference for negotiations limited to two countries had made a new convert.

King moved on to Peking, where the British Ambassador, Sir John Jordan, had made arrangements for him to discuss immigration with Liang Tun-yen, the head of the Chinese Foreign Office. Four long interviews took place. It appeared that China was willing through the issue of passports to control its own emigration to Canada and restrict it to such numbers as might be mutually agreed upon, and Canada indicated that in such an event she was prepared to abolish the head tax on Chinese immigrants. The final steps, however, were postponed awaiting further discussions.

Making full allowance for the fact that the record of these negotiations with the Chinese Government was kept by King himself, it is impossible to escape the conclusion that the Canadian representative presented his case with skill and resource. Nor should the absence of any definite arrangement at the conclusion of the interviews be allowed to obscure the truth of Sir John Jordan's observations: *

Mr. Mackenzie King's visit has produced an excellent effect by putting the immigration question in a far better position than it previously occupied. The Chinese Government are now fully aware of Canada's difficulties, of her anxiety to meet them in the way least calculated to offend Chinese susceptibilities. . . . Apart from the immediate object he had in view, Mr. Mackenzie King has done good work in placing Canada for the first time in direct official communication with China, and I cannot conclude this despatch without recording my belief that both the Imperial Government and the Government of the Dominion were fortunate in having such an able and sympathetic representative to perform the task.[59]

On his return to Ottawa Mackenzie King found Parliament in session. He took his seat immediately and was sworn on May 10, 1909; prorogation occurred only nine days later. Although there were some signs of welcome by both members and Ministers, he was very conscious that many regarded him as a favoured child of fortune and were jealous of his rapid rise and immediate prospects. Laurier's earlier demand that before promotion to Cabinet rank, King should make a few speeches in the House and should endeavour to placate his enemies was thus proved to be no more than a reasonable precaution.[60] King wrote in his diary a few days after he took his seat: "I feel quite at home. In fact I never felt more at home in my life than in going about as a member, with a member's rights and privileges."[61] When on May 19 he witnessed the Governor-General give his assent to the bill creating a separate Department of Labour with its own Minister, he saw one period in his life come to a gratifying close.

We say that this is a commonplace world, that visions have departed and men have lost faith. Oh that I could without undue self-assertiveness let men look into this achievement, look in & see the working out into reality of a dream of youth, of boyhood, a purpose accomplished, an ideal become

---

*Sir John Jordan was in an excellent position to judge: he was present at all King's interviews with Liang Tun-yen.

a reality, against all odds, against the prejudice of men in what is the bitterest of strifes—wealth & greed in the conflict of capital vs. labour,—against Youth, against privilege, & without influence in the form of wealth or position.[62]

The formal accolade came a few weeks later. On June 2, 1909, Mackenzie King became a member of the Privy Council and Minister of Labour.

Almost simultaneously, another and quite different period of his life reached a climax. Although King had turned his back fairly decisively on academic work, his desire to obtain the degree of doctor of philosophy from Harvard remained strong. It will be recalled that he had passed his "general" examination in 1899 and had yet to submit a thesis and pass an oral examination in the special field to which his thesis belonged. "Would to Heaven I could get my thesis off," he wrote in 1901. "This hangs over me like a cloud." In the following year he spent his entire summer holiday in an attempt to bring the matter to a conclusion. He made moderate progress on "The Sweating System and the Fair Wages Movement," but on the whole the results were discouraging. In 1906 he was still talking about the thesis, and still doing very little.

Finally in 1909 he decided to try to realize on some of his departmental work since entering the government service. He therefore wrote President Eliot in January, from Bombay, expressing the hope that Harvard would "look at the spirit of the requirement rather than the letter" and would accept as a thesis "a bound set of the special reports which I have written on industrial and economic questions."[63] The University was non-committal and suggested that he submit his writings, though it emphasized the need for a specific piece of work, or related pieces of work which would be an approximation to the usual doctor's thesis. King sent in what must have been a unique contribution. It included six annual departmental reports, the report of his 1908 mission to England, and many other reports dealing with such diverse subjects as the Lethbridge strike, the conciliation and investigation of disputes, the opium traffic, the hours of telephone operators, industrial disputes in the mines in British Columbia and the cotton industry in Quebec, and Oriental immigration. All these King managed by great ingenuity to combine in one grand synthesis under the heading of "Publicity and Public Opinion as Factors in the Solution of Industrial Problems in Canada."

The Harvard Graduate School must have been stunned by King's audacity, but it remained co-operative. It agreed to accept one topic from the collection, entitled "Oriental Immigration to Canada," as the necessary thesis, though King was, of course, required to present himself for the special examination. This final ordeal he passed to the satisfaction of the examiners, though not, he said, to his own. It was in the midst of these academic events that King was taken into the Cabinet, and this elevation compelled him legally to seek confirmation through a by-election in his constituency. Happily he was spared this last burden, for he was returned by acclamation on June 21. On June 30 he attended the Harvard Commencement and received the degree of Doctor of Philosophy.

Yet another recognition of King's translation to politics remained to be made. Parliament opened for the autumn session on November 11 and Mackenzie King took his seat as a Minister of the Crown for the first time. His introduction, necessitated by his return in the by-election in North Waterloo, was carried out by Sir Wilfrid Laurier and George P. Graham. Mr. and Mrs. John King were in the galleries; and special mention was made in the press of Mackenzie King's white-haired mother whose features, it was alleged, bore a striking resemblance to those of William Lyon Mackenzie.[64] * "It seems almost like a dream to me," she wrote her son, "but part, I mean where you entered the Chamber with Sir W. and Mr. Graham, will never leave my mind. It was indeed a great day for me."[65] Mackenzie King was more articulate on the significance of the event:

After the House adjourned, I joined Mother & Father and took them to the Speaker's apartments in the Commons were [where] mother talked happily with everyone and seemed as delighted as she could be, people literally crowded about to look at her, and several asked me for an introduction, they all remarked on her beauty & said "how distinguished." It was a delight to me to hear all these things. Surely there is reward in this for her as well as me, reward for the sacrifices her father made, & for what she has had to make in consequence. If her father could only have been present too, I would have asked for nothing more. He would have felt a recompense for all his struggle. His life, his work are all kept alive in this way, and that I feel to be my chiefest part.

Laurier in introducing me, gave the name in full "William Lyon Mackenzie King" and in my ears it seemed to fill the entire room.[66]

*It is interesting to note that L. J. Papineau, a grandson of the other rebel, Louis Joseph Papineau, had also been elected in 1908 a member of the same Parliament.

CHAPTER SEVEN

MINISTER OF LABOUR

EVENTS in the Department of Labour after Mackenzie King became Minister differed little from those when he was the Deputy—evidence, no doubt, of his dominant influence over its policies in the preceding years. There was, however, an increase in the Department's general prestige, of which the change in its legal status was the open acknowledgment. By placing the Department under its own special Minister the Government had recognized the importance of the work the Department was doing and shown that it was conscious of owing a special obligation to the working man and his problems. "In the Department of Labour," Mackenzie King told the Commons in 1911, "we have taken as one of the objects before us, as part of the work which I trust it will be possible to carry on through the years to come, this important question of the preservation of health, the conservation of human life, the protection of the working people the great mass of the people of this country from occupational or other diseases which help to undermine the strength of the nation."[1]

Despite many difficulties, King endeavoured to discharge this obligation during his twenty-eight months as Minister. The measures which arose for consideration were varied, but most of them were clearly designed to improve the health, knowledge, or economic position of the working man: the creation of a Royal Commission on Technical Education; the provision of better statistical information, especially on industrial accidents and on wholesale and retail prices; a proposed eight-hour day in public works; a scheme of workmen's compensation, and laws to prevent phosphorus necrosis, an industrial disease of the match industry.

These were not all initiated by Mackenzie King, but they had his warm support. The proposals regarding the Royal Commission on Technical Education and the eight-hour day in public works had been struggling to obtain parliamentary approval before King became Minister, and in both cases the private members who had originated them were encouraged to bring forward their favourite measures again, which were then backed by the Government.* In this way the Government thought to evade some of the unpopularity which it considered might be associated with these proposals, because of either provincial feeling or popular indifference and hostility. That King's position was far from being passive may be illustrated by his actions in regard to the Royal Commission on Technical Education. He had wanted it while Deputy Minister, and had worked behind the scenes to secure the support of Laurier and of his own Minister, Lemieux.[2] In 1909, after he had entered the Cabinet and had become the Minister most concerned with the work of the proposed Commission, he wrote in his diary: "I am pressing hard [in Cabinet] for the Comm'n and see the need for it more & more strongly as I read up the matter, see what other countries have done & how far we are behind."[3] He supported it vigorously in the House and endeavoured, he said, "to make a speech which would compel the Government to do something."[4] In this he was successful. It fell to King to write all the provincial governments to make sure that they would not construe the Commissioners' investigation as a threat to their powers over education, and the replies being all favourable, the Royal Commission on Industrial Training and Technical Education was appointed. After two years' inquiry in Canada, the United States, and Europe, the Commission presented its report to the Borden Government.[5]

The uncertainty of jurisdiction was one of the Department's greatest obstacles in its promotion of measures which touched on the social and economic welfare of the workers. The more it attempted to deal with such problems the more apt it was to run foul of the powers of the provinces. It irked King to have questions which were clearly of national concern blocked by provincial inertia or hostility, and he had several ways of dealing with the difficulty. One, as with the Commission on Technical Education, was direct action with steps being taken beforehand to secure provincial acquiescence. Or he might resort to an indirect method such as had been invoked so successfully years before in the case of sweated labour. On this occasion, it will be

---

*Hugh Guthrie had moved for a Royal Commission on Technical Education in 1908; Alphonse Verville had introduced bills embodying the principle of the eight-hour day in 1906, 1908, and 1909.

recalled, the federal government, acting as employer, or contractor, introduced the desired reform, and by its example was able to exert great pressure on the provincial governments to follow suit in a matter which was, after all, primarily under their jurisdiction. The proposed bill to introduce the eight-hour day was another case in point. It was to apply to federal public works which the Dominion Government as the employer or contractor could legitimately control, but it was designed also to stimulate provincial action. The bill passed the Commons, but died in committee in the Senate.*

King was strongly behind the proposal for the eight-hour day, and was chairman of the Select Committee of the Commons which reported favourably on it. He believed, as he said in the House in December, 1909, that its major effect would be the education of the public and the stimulation of the provincial legislatures to take action in the desired direction:

This question of shortening the hours of labour is primarily for the consideration of the provincial legislatures . . . but, the discussion of the subject in this parliament is bound to be reflected in future legislation by the provinces and the general expression of opinion in this chamber that the shortening of the hours of labour is a good thing in itself will, we may hope, bear fruit. . . . So far as this question has a bearing upon ameliorating the ordinary everyday life of the working people, I submit that we should in this parliament, so far as we have the power—and we have certain powers in regard to contracts let by the government—we should do all that we can to further that end.[6]

But King was not always so cautious, and his attitude on workmen's compensation suggests that there were times when he favoured a frontal attack on forbidden constitutional territory. Some provincial governments had already adopted a scheme of compensation, and King was anxious to have the federal government at least share the field. The Department of Justice had advised him that his Department had undoubted power to apply a scheme of workmen's compensation to railways, telegraph and telephone companies, and certain other enterprises; but that any federal scheme to cover all industries in Canada would be *ultra vires*.[7] †

*A similar statute was eventually enacted in 1930.
†King favoured some adaptation of the "German system" which was based on "contributions from employers, from workmen, and from the State, making three parties to the agreement"; F. A. Acland (Deputy Minister of Labour), Memorandum to W.L.M.K., re a deputation of representatives of railway organizations, Feb. 17, 1911.

King either was not satisfied to accept this limitation on federal powers or was determined to air the whole question for its educative effect. When a resolution was moved in the House on February 20, 1911, concerning railway accidents with a view to giving better protection to the railwaymen, King took the opportunity to forecast the possibility of future federal legislation which would provide a comprehensive scheme. The question, he said, really went far beyond railways. He thought the resolution should have covered all industrial accidents, and he proceeded to cite the statistics which his Department had compiled on the subject during the preceding seven years. It would be worth considering, he said, whether industry could not be made to bear part of the cost of such accidents without the worker or his heirs having to sue the employers for compensation. This speech was plainly intended to be the opening shot of a campaign which King hoped to continue the following year. The next day he wrote a letter to Stewart Lyon, the associate editor of the Toronto *Globe*, in which he outlined his plans for the future:

My purpose in making these observations at all was to get the general idea before the public with a view of seeing how it would be taken up and creating not only a public opinion but a demand for legislation of the kind.

Knowing your interest in this kind of legislation and the power of the Globe, I would be glad for many reasons to see it lead in an agitation for some legislation of the kind. You might, I think, if you care to do so, go the length of saying that apparently from his remarks the Minister of Labour has legislation of the kind in prospect. I mention this only because I would like, should I introduce a bill next session, which I hope to obtain the consent of my colleagues to do, to be able to point to the fact that the Government's policy had been foreshadowed at the present session, and that the question, therefore, did not come as an entirely new one to members of the House, but that I had expressly suggested to them the necessity of turning over this subject carefully in their minds. . . .

What, frankly, I would like to do is to begin to prepare actively in cooperation with yourself for this legislation. If the Globe could champion the idea just as the Star did the necessity for legislation in regard to combines, I think it would not only help along the enactment of the measure, but would also be of very great service to the Liberal party.[8]

In view of the increasing attention which was being given to the reciprocity question, Lyon suggested (and King agreed) that as a matter of tactics they should not attempt to make an issue of workmen's compensation for at least a few months.[9] Later, of course, King was out of office, and was in no position to carry out his plan.

King's warfare against the menace of phosphorus necrosis displayed again his predilection for getting his facts by personal observation. "Phossy jaw," as it was called, was a loathsome and sometimes fatal disease which attacked the teeth and jaws of workers in match factories using white phosphorus. King inspected a match factory in Hull, visited the homes of some of the sufferers, and even, so he told the House, brought the jawbone of one of the victims to his office as an exhibit. He introduced a bill in 1911 which prohibited the manufacture and importation of phosphorus matches; but it was held up by the unexpected dissolution, and the change was eventually made in 1914 by the new Parliament.[10] His bill to tighten control over the use of opium and other narcotics met with a better fate, and became law in 1911.[11]

The Combines Investigation Act, passed in 1910, was an attempt to cope with some of the abuses which had followed from the rapid growth of large industrial consolidations. These combines were daily becoming more powerful and potentially more dangerous, and the current rise in prices was popularly being laid at their door. The increase in the cost of living and the danger of the Conservative party's taking up the combines issue provided the immediate stimulus to government action,[12] and legislation was promised in the Speech from the Throne on November 11, 1909.*

The bill which was introduced exemplified King's conception of the role of government in a competitive economy. He accepted large aggregations of capital as an inescapable phenomenon in modern society, and he considered that on the whole the movements towards greater combinations might be beneficial. But the aggressive tendencies of large wealthy interests needed to be curbed in the interests of the community, and the obvious economies effected by the combines should in some measure be passed on to the public and not be turned to the combine's sole advantage in higher prices.†

The Combines Investigation bill was in all respects King's own

---

*Chief reliance in dealing with combines had been placed hitherto on those parts of the criminal law and common law dealing with restraint of trade, and on a section of the Customs Tariff Act which authorized the Governor-in-Council to reduce tariff protection to an industry if it were proved in a judicial inquiry initiated by the Governor-in-Council that combines in that industry had been the cause of unduly enhancing prices.

†King did not labour the price argument, rather he admitted that the rise in prices was caused by many factors of which the combines were but one.

measure. He produced and developed the basic idea; he drafted the bill; he persuaded a divided Cabinet to accept it; and he introduced and guided the measure through the House. His ideas were, of course, influenced by what had been done in other countries, especially by the unfortunate experience under the Sherman Anti-Trust Act in the United States. The Sherman Act had assumed that all combines were necessarily bad, and its provisions had therefore failed to distinguish between their harmful activities and those which were innocuous or even beneficial—all were considered to be equally undesirable, and it was left to the administration to draw the line between a good and a bad trust.[13] King's aim was to draft a law that would possess sufficient flexibility in its own provisions to enable this distinction to be made and yet at the same time contain sufficient strength to deal with possible abuses which always constituted an element of danger where tremendous economic power was concentrated in the hands of a few.

Mackenzie King considered that he had found his answer in an adaptation of the Industrial Disputes Investigation Act to the combines problem. He would provide machinery at the public expense to get at the facts, he would discourage trivial complaints, and he would punish only those methods and practices which were clearly shown to be contrary to the general welfare. His bill made this possible in three steps: a complaint presented by six persons reciting the abuses attributed to an alleged combine; a judicial review to ascertain if there were *prima facie* grounds for the complaint; and finally the establishment of a special Board to investigate and report. If the Board found that the combine had operated contrary to the public interest by indulging in such activities as unfairly enhancing prices or unduly restricting trade, fines or other penalties could be imposed by the special Board or by the Governor-in-Council according to the nature of the offence. Most important in King's eyes, however, was the influence of public opinion: the combine would suffer in both reputation and profits by having its business transactions thrown open to the cleansing process of public examination and censure.

The Act was passed;[14] but it was invoked only once in nine years. No permanent agency had been created to enforce it, the machinery was expensive and cumbersome, and the penalties were on the whole too light.[15] The Conservative Government thought little of it, and eventually repealed it and substituted a measure of its own which the courts declared *ultra vires*. King was not discouraged. In 1923, during his first administration, he secured the passage of a new Combines Act—an improved version with much heavier penalties, though constructed on the same general principles as its predecessor.[16]

This is not at first glance a very impressive legislative result for two years' work, even though they were admittedly years of apprenticeship for the young Minister. What were the concrete results? King had helped secure a Royal Commission on Technical Education, he had obtained an amendment to the Opium Act, and he was the moving spirit in placing the Combines Investigation Act on the statute books. Action on the report on technical education and the legislation to prevent phosphorus necrosis had been of necessity held over for his successor. Vital questions, such as the eight-hour day and workmen's compensation, had come to naught.

King, however, was badly handicapped by lukewarm support and a general lack of interest in his field. He was head of a department which was of limited scope and of secondary importance in an undeveloped economy devoted primarily to the extractive industries and commerce. Manufacturing existed only on a small scale. Labour was relatively unorganized, and labour questions could rarely count on a sympathetic hearing. Projects of social reform could muster few advocates in the House. The Cabinet was often uncertain and divided, and little enthusiasm or firm support on these subjects could be expected there. King's lack of assurance which sprang from his youth and inexperience was accentuated by the conviction, held rightly or wrongly, that some Ministers were still jealous of his rapid rise and therefore had little confidence in him or his proposals.* He also suffered severely at the hands of the Opposition. So long as he had been a civil servant, the Conservatives had shown him little hostility and had even thrown the occasional compliment in his direction; but now that the Government was attempting to cash in on his record by making him a Minister, King received his share, and perhaps more than his share, of their attacks. One can accept the Toronto *Globe* on party topics only with great reserve; but its account of King's treatment in Parliament probably contains a good deal of truth, while shedding at the same time an interesting light on King's early deportment in the House:

*"I have enjoyed the work [of the session] though in a quiet way I have suffered keenly at times from a feeling that older men sometimes begrudge the recognition I have received." W.L.M.K. to Violet Markham, May 16, 1910.

Some members of the House of Commons and some Conservative journals have to all appearance conspired to persecute the Minister of Labor, with a view to driving him out of public life, by incessant and senseless attacks upon him and his Department. Such treatment of a Minister of the Crown is not usual in these days, and it is difficult to find in recent times either a precedent or a parallel for it. Mr. King has not invited such attacks by his own demeanor, any more than Mr. Graham has in the Department of Railways and Canals; but Mr. Graham gets off scot free, while no opportunity to belittle Mr. King is allowed to go unutilized. . . .

If the truth must be told, Mr. King's unpardonable offences in the eyes of his assailants are two: he won from their party what has long been regarded as a safe Conservative constituency, and he has disappointed their confident anticipations that he would prove a failure as an administrator. He has ample ability to take care of himself and his Department in the ordinary run of Parliamentary criticism, to which he never objects. He is a model of Parliamentary courtesy and an expert in Parliamentary procedure. He does not feel any need to ask for quarter, and he never complains of unfair treatment.[17]

King's most stubborn obstacle, however, was the constitutional one, which placed virtually all labour legislation in the hands of the provinces. His desire to advance with the times on this topic was continually blocked by the stone walls of jurisdiction, and a large part of his time was taken up with plans to circumvent them. Here, too, lack of strong Cabinet support held him back, and popular ignorance of the field was so great that the Minister was also forced to assume a heavy educational task to convince the public that something could and should be done. King's endorsement of the principle of the eight-hour day and his efforts to foster a federal workmen's compensation act, already noted, showed the direction in which his mind was moving. He was also considering a measure which would extend in some unformulated way his Department's power "to conduct inquiries on subjects affecting the welfare of the working classes" and a power of inspection to prevent industrial accidents, with suitable legislation to follow.[18] Later, he began to work on a scheme which would join the existing facilities for a government annuity to a plan of insurance covering sickness and accident.[19] Clearly King was not prepared to accept the fetters of jurisdiction without a struggle, though he probably did not expect to achieve any permanent solution in this way. Writing Hamar (later Lord) Greenwood in 1910 on the general question of jurisdiction, he admitted that the problem "will have to be squarely faced, and I do not see that it can be ultimately determined satisfactorily by any method other than the one you suggest, namely, an amendment of the B.N.A. Act."[20] In any event, his efforts at this time were soon cut short by dissolution.

The evidence of the statute book thus gives a most incomplete account of the Minister's activity, which was in large measure of an exploratory and preparatory nature. King brought both imagination and initiative to the task. He was well aware of the world trend on these questions, and he recognized that in a competitive age, the prosperity of Canada depended on her capacity to keep abreast of efforts used in other countries to ensure an industrial population highly efficient and intelligently organized. He looked beyond the immediate problem to its wider implications. Technical education, for example, was not simply a means to increase certain skills among workmen and make them more efficient. Its effects were far-reaching. It was a means of increasing industrial efficiency throughout the nation; it would raise the workers' general standard of life; it might even prove to be a major weapon in combatting the "yellow peril" which, King contended, would ultimately cease to be considered a question of immigration and resolve itself into a war of industrial competition.[21]

King regarded himself—not unnaturally so, in view of his past history—as a pioneer in labour matters in Canada. He was not indifferent to day-to-day reforms, but he was also seeking a means of legislative action on some of the fundamental problems with which labour was confronted. Reforms had an important economic side: the improvement in working conditions and the elevation of the workers' standard of life; but they went much further. The test in the last resort was the effect that such reforms would have on human happiness. "I believe," King told the Commons, speaking on the eight-hour day, "that a man should have not merely an opportunity to live but that he should have an opportunity to live happily; and that he cannot have if he is oppressed by excessive hours of labour."[22]

King possessed in his training and experience the ability to pick up the challenge which faced him. The effect of this training as he came to grips with his problems was very noticeable: it was essentially an academic approach based on research. He was a great believer in utilizing the knowledge, experience, and resourcefulness of others. The Industrial Disputes Investigation Act, as he constantly pointed out, was a combination of ideas and practices from many sources, and his study of accident compensation took him to the insurance schemes and methods in use in other countries. Similarly, in 1910 he went to Europe and attended a number of international conferences on labour questions: at The Hague one on social insurance; at Brussels one on higher technical education, and another on occupational diseases and industrial accidents; at Paris one on unemployment; and at Lugano one on labour legislation. These conferences helped in some measure to broaden his knowledge, but they were chiefly valuable in bringing him in touch with others who shared his interests in these fields. The application of King's knowledge, moreover, was tempered by his own practical experience and natural restraint. He was a strong believer in a policy of gradualness. His policy was to take whatever was immediately available, and never to imperil the whole effort by trying to seize more than the occasion warranted. He may have disliked Fabians in the flesh, but he did not disdain to adopt their cardinal principle as his own; this he enunciated to the House in 1910:

The one consideration that has to be kept in mind is this—that you can begin a reform in two ways. You can start with the broad end of the wedge, or you can start with the thin end. You can hold out for too much and achieve nothing, or you can assert a principle and give it force and power even though you limit its application at first.[23]

In 1910 Mackenzie King and Sir Frederick Borden, the Minister of Militia, became involved as mediators in a strike between the Grand Trunk Railway and the unions of conductors and trainmen. The issue was whether the base to be used in calculating wages was to be time or mileage; and the strike followed a refusal by the Grand Trunk to agree to the latter as base, although it had been accepted by every major railroad on the continent. After the strike had gone on for a week, the main question in dispute was conceded to the men, and final settlement awaited agreement on a number of relatively minor points. The unions were conciliatory and anxious to bring the discussion to a close, but C. M. Hays, the President of the Grand Trunk, thought differently. Moved by a desire to preserve appearances, or to save his pride, or to punish the strikers, he began to put forward a number of outrageous claims which could do little but exasperate his opponents (and the mediators) or even cause a complete rupture in the negotiations. So extreme was his attitude that at one time two of his vice-presidents admitted to King and Borden that Hays's conduct was inexplicable except on the ground that he "was not himself,"* a statement which, though a little ambiguous, could scarcely be construed as flattering.

In this atmosphere King and Borden (and especially King) worked unceasingly to bring about a settlement, and eventually succeeded. King's ability as a conciliator was once more acclaimed throughout Canada. The unions were especially vocal in their praise,[24] and their leaders† gave unreserved credit to King for his part in making agreement possible.‡

To King the settlement was much more than a mere victory in an important industrial dispute. In King's mind, as the negotiations developed, Hays became the Prince of Darkness in the Canadian industrial world; he found in Hays the same ruthlessness and stony-faced hostility to the other side which the strikers at Rossland had shown nine years earlier. To Mackenzie King it was an outrage that anyone should completely divest himself of all sense of social obligation and that anyone should be so indifferent to the welfare and happiness of his employees. In the account of the strike which he sent to Laurier on August 4, he gave vent to the indignation which had been building up during his experience of the preceding two weeks:

You may ask me why I feel so sure on this point. My answer is that railroading in the United States§ is a business which with a certain school of men is run on certain principles. One is that human life, to say nothing of human feelings, is not to be considered, either as respects its loss through accident or its massacre as a means to an end. The end is the power of money as against all other powers in the world. To admit the solidarity of labour in any industrial struggle is to admit something more powerful than money, and that must not be done, no matter how great or how tremendous the cost. Mr. Hays has seen himself in this struggle as the chief

*W.L.M.K. to Sir W. Laurier, Aug. 4, 1910, p. 17. This 38-page letter gives the negotiations in great detail.

†The Vice-President of the Railroad Trainmen, James Murdock, though not a Liberal, gave King his active support in the election of 1911. Ten years later King made him Minister of Labour in his first Cabinet.

‡In 1910 Mackenzie King received a somewhat unusual recognition. His old friend, Mrs. Humphry Ward, wrote a novel called *Lady Merton, Colonist.* King was popularly supposed to have furnished the model for her hero, an engineer and budding public figure, whose entry into Parliament was greatly aided by his success in settling labour disputes. Mrs. Ward, not having the gift of prophecy, did not attempt to carry the parallel into the future.

§C. M. Hays was an American.

representative of that school. He knows full well that to win on this one point, and this one point alone, would mean, even if all else were destroyed in the effort, his receiving tomorrow the offer of the Presidency of a dozen different roads. He would be the one man known to labour as the unyielder in any future industrial battle, and that is the asset for which the seekers of dividends on some of the railroads on this continent are prepared to pay any price.

A letter of King's to a close friend, R. A. Daly, a few days after the strike was concluded showed even more plainly that the men and the Government had virtually become one party to the dispute, the railway the other. "The Grand Trunk struggle," he wrote, "was a firsthand fight with a big corporation prepared to be as unscrupulous as corporations can be. I was bound the Government would win, and I am happy to say I think I have succeeded. After the first week, it was not so much a fight between capital and labour, as between a railway corporation and the Government."[25]

The Grand Trunk strike remained a living issue for many years. Although the railway was committed to take back all strikers to their former positions within three months, it did not do so. King was untiring in his efforts to have the railway fulfil its obligations, but could make little progress against the implacable Hays.[26] Even the refusal of the Laurier Government to give any financial aid to the Grand Trunk did not succeed in forcing Hays's hand, and his railway lost millions of dollars through his stubbornness.[27] The strike rapidly entered politics. A comprehensive attack was made in Parliament criticizing the Government for having "wholly failed to make any intelligent effort" to avert the strike, to terminate it, or to compel the Grand Trunk to abide by the agreement, for which, it was asserted, the Government, though not a party, had some responsibility.[28] Unemployed union members attacked both their own leaders and the Government for not forcing Hays to take them back. In 1911 the question became a minor election issue in some parts of the Dominion. When the Borden Government came into office it encountered the same problem of compelling the reinstatement of the strikers. Its efforts were eventually successful, but not until it had refused to pass legislation which the Grand Trunk urgently desired.[29]

Immediately the strike of 1910 was over Hays cancelled all the accumulated pension rights of the strikers on the pretext that they had broken the continuity of their employment. This injustice stood for twelve years, until King became Prime Minister. In 1922, in response to Government pressure, the Grand Trunk saw the light; pension and seniority rights were restored and compensation paid in approximately 1,200 cases.[30]

The period when Mackenzie King was Minister of Labour saw the emergence of a Canadian naval policy, but for fairly obvious reasons his influence on its formulation was slight. His youth and inexperience, his diffidence in placing his views before a Council some of whose members were, he felt, inclined to be jealous of him, his frequent absences from Ottawa, the lack of points of contact between a naval programme and the Department of Labour: all these factors tended to keep him in the background. But questions which involved the Imperial relationship had always held an unusual interest for him; and this interest had been stimulated by his postgraduate studies in England, his later missions there, and his meetings with British political leaders.

Defence—and for Great Britain this had always meant primarily naval defence—had by 1909 entered a new phase as a result of Germany's enlarged programme of naval construction and its undisguised challenge to British supremacy. The Admiralty was gravely concerned for the future, and it naturally turned with renewed hope to the possibility of securing some assistance from the major colonies. Attempts had been made at the Imperial Conferences of 1902 and 1907 to induce the colonies to commit themselves to some plan of military and naval contributions, but these efforts had met with only moderate success. Laurier had been the most unco-operative of all the overseas premiers. He had done little more than admit a general responsibility for defence, while repeating in 1907 what he had said at the former meeting that Canada was "contemplating the establishment of a local naval force" in Canadian waters. Between the two Conferences, Canada had taken over the control and maintenance of the naval stations at Halifax and Esquimalt, but no effort was made to implement this carefully guarded commitment until the tense situation in Europe made some more substantial demonstration almost inescapable.

The truth was that Canadian opinion on the naval question was still diffuse and unformulated, and neither Laurier nor anyone else could tell whether the Canadian people wished to contribute to the British navy, maintain their own separate naval establishment, or do nothing at all. But interest was slowly growing. A resolution passed by the House of Commons in 1909 gave a promise of unity by committing both political parties to the common policy that Canada should proceed without delay to develop her own naval service in close co-operation with the British authorities. The same resolution pronounced against "regular and periodical contributions" to the British navy, but did not rule out the possibility of a special or emergency contribution.

Mackenzie King was not yet a Cabinet Minister when this resolution passed, nor was he even in Ottawa: he was away for the Shanghai conference on opium and his trip around the world. There is no reason whatever to suppose that his opinions at this time had any effect on government policy. His own views on the naval question, however, had been taking shape for some years. He was strongly British in sympathy, but at the same time suspicious of the purity of British motives in urging closer forms of centralization. Canadian contributions to the British navy were therefore to be regarded as doubtful ventures. On the other hand, he was fully alive to the danger of Canada's becoming dependent on the navy of the United States, and he had been quick to take alarm and to realize the possible stimulus to annexationist sentiment when Theodore Roosevelt had suggested to him in 1908 that the American navy might pay a friendly call at Vancouver (*supra*, p. 160). Thus King believed that if Canada was to resist centralization from Great Britain on the one hand and to avoid dependence on the United States on the other, she was virtually compelled to do something towards setting up her own navy, one which would be independent of Great Britain, but which would act in close co-operation with the British forces.

This was a substantial modification of King's natural desires, which leaned heavily in the other direction. He, like many other liberals in North America and Europe, felt a profound aversion to war, and he feared that the existence of a navy might draw Canada into some remote struggle which she could otherwise escape. To men of this essentially pacifist and isolationist outlook the existing naval race was likely to precipitate the very war it professed to prevent. Nor could any realistic Canadian politician be blind to the general unpopularity of spending money for armaments rather than for productive purposes, which in a new country were always in need of assistance. Charles

Murphy, the Secretary of State, returning from a tour of Western Canada in 1909, gave forcible expression to this feeling when he reported that "what the West wants is box-cars and not battleships."[31]

King was less free than most members of Parliament to urge Canadian naval expenditure, even if he had wished to do so. The main justification for a navy at that particular time was not an abstract need for Canadian or Imperial defence, but the very real naval threat from Germany. Two-thirds of the people of North Waterloo, his constituency, were of German descent, and many were Mennonites and therefore pacifists.* King could scarcely expect constituents with these antecedents to look with favour on any expenditure for naval purposes. At any rate he worked with special vigour to secure local public works, and urged on at least one of his fellow Ministers, Lemieux, that these were necessary to counteract any impression that the interests of his constituency were being neglected because of the competing demands of defence.[32]

King also took pains to identify himself with those who were working diligently to preserve peace. When in June, 1909, he received the Ph.D. degree, he was selected to address the Harvard Commencement on behalf of the graduates. He took as his theme the need to settle international disputes by peaceful agencies, "to enthrone," as he said, "Reason above Force." The address was illustrated by references to Canadian-American relations, and it contained a proposal that in 1915 the two nations should jointly commemorate one hundred years of peace.[33] This was one of the earliest suggestions for a centennial celebration, and thenceforward King took a prominent part in both countries in obtaining support for the idea.[34]

A few weeks after the Harvard Commencement King wrote to Lord Stanhope on matters of defence, stressing the need for less warlike policies as "safeguards of peace." He decried especially the European tendency to arouse "war enthusiasm," and suggested that the idea of the centenary celebration might well be extended so as to include not only Canada and the United States, but Great Britain and France as well.[35] Stanhope, as a strong Imperialist, was very restive under Canada's passive naval policy, and he had written King earlier that year expressing his distrust of Laurier's caution and what he looked

---

*The 1911 Census gave the population of North Waterloo as 33,619, of whom 25,352 (66.5%) were of German origin. There were 4,006 Mennonites.

upon as Laurier's unqualified opportunism.[36] King proceeded in this same letter of July 23 to offer a defence of Laurier which gives some indication of how Laurier's great gifts for reconciliation and compromise had impressed the junior Minister.

You do Sir Wilfrid Laurier an injustice in regarding him as an opportunist. He is other than that. He understands the problem of self government within the Empire as few men before him or living to-day have done, and his support from the people comes from that fact. We have had no man in Canada who has done as much to reconcile differences of race and creed and to make of the people one nation. If he hesitates to go the length that some desire, it is because he does not wish disruption and believes that a united progressive Canada is a more valuable asset to the Empire, and will be so through time, than a Canada divided in opinion, or professing an obligation it is not in a position to meet.

King had obviously absorbed one useful political lesson which he was never to lose sight of in his later career. Unity—or at least popular acquiescence in a policy—was rarely obtained or aided by haste or by anything but the lightest of pressures. To proceed deliberately and with the most careful consideration of each of the factors in the situation was usually the quickest and often the only way to make progress. Canada bristled with internal conflicts, and hence, galling though it might be, both domestic and external policies must be kept flexible and be adjusted realistically from time to time whenever circumstances indicated that such adjustment was advisable. If Imperial relations were involved, the problem was simply widened, both for Canada and for the other parts of the Empire. The same kind of adjustment had to be made by each part: compromises within itself to reconcile its own special diversities, and a wide acceptance of those special interests which occurred throughout the whole area. An attempt at integration of separate policies into one comprehensive Empire policy by any sort of persuasion save enlightened self-interest was doomed to fail, and it would be apt to damage irreparably the future of Empire relations. Such, at least, was Laurier's firm belief, and he had acquired a loyal disciple in Mackenzie King.

The apparent unity which might be discerned in the Commons' 1909 resolution soon melted away as different views began to assert themselves. A large number of people wished action of some kind, and preferably the creation of a Canadian navy; some wanted to give one or two dreadnoughts to the British navy, either as Canada's sole contribution or in addition to the local naval unit; still others—Ontario farmers, certain labour bodies, and Quebec—were against any action whatever.[37] These views influenced and were influenced by the stand taken by the political parties, which tried hard to keep their supporters together on an unfamiliar issue and found the resolution to be both a help and a hindrance. The Conservatives were in the worst plight, for they were deeply divided. Many prominent Conservatives from the English-speaking provinces were strongly in favour of a generous contribution to the British navy; while the French-Canadian wing of the party adopted an increasingly nationalist stand which would have nothing to do with gifts, and little, indeed, to do with even a local naval force, on the ground that either policy would jeopardize Canadian isolation and neutrality. This, of course, was broadly the attitude of the nationalists under Bourassa, who were also clamouring for a plebiscite on the question. Another federal Conservative group adhered to the terms of the parliamentary resolution. Borden, after a valiant effort to hold to its terms, was forced to relinquish it and he began to emphasize the greater desirability of a contribution, especially one of an emergency nature with the postponement of a permanent plan for future investigation.

Eventually the great majority of Liberals in the country fell in line with the idea of a Canadian navy, and the Government felt it could safely go ahead. A meeting of the Imperial Defence Conference in London in 1909 had given the proposal of a local navy its blessing, and had thereby confirmed the stand Laurier had taken at the Imperial Conference of 1902. The Naval Service bill of 1910* thus provided for a Canadian naval unit with reserve and volunteer personnel, and placed the force under the control of the Canadian Government, which could, if it were deemed advisable in an emergency, place it under the British Admiralty. At the invitation of the Canadian Government, the Admiralty had already presented two plans for possible units, and the Government, Laurier announced, had chosen the larger one.

The Prime Minister's policy was essentially a moderating and tolerant one. This was at least partially attested by the nationalists (or

---

*An Act Respecting the Naval Service of Canada (Naval Service Act), *Can. Statutes*, 9–12 Edw. VII, c. 43.

"negative extremists" as Laurier called them) saying that he had sacrificed Canadian rights and many English-speaking Conservatives (the "positive extremists") accusing him of disloyalty to the Crown. On the naval issue, as with others involving the British connection, the Government stood for a temperate expression of Canadian national identity within the Empire, a stand which King obviously endorsed, and was to live to uphold on many future occasions.

The Government had insisted that Canada should retain control of its navy when war threatened or occurred, though the method of exercising that control was left to the future. It thus favoured decentralization within the Empire further, with the building up of Canada and Canadian autonomy as a primary endeavour, to be attended by the development of the Empire itself as an inevitable result.

Laurier and King were even able to quote the British Imperialist Lord Milner in their defence of the Canadian policy, although Milner was to be found in a totally different political camp. Milner had happily made the statement a little earlier that to strengthen the Empire defences was "not a question of shifting burdens, but of developing fresh centres of strength."[38] This statement was seized on by both Laurier and King and was adopted as the cornerstone of their policy. To strengthen Canada, in short, was the best means of defending the Empire. Establish new centres of strength, and the whole becomes strong. Increase the responsibility and autonomy of the Dominions, and the Empire will thrive as a result. Laurier believed not only that when Great Britain was at war, Canada was at war; but also that Canada should choose whether she would abstain from or participate in the hostilities. He pointed out that in this belief he was simply expressing fundamental principles of self-government and tolerance which underlay the respect and co-operation of the two Canadian racial strains. To the Imperialist who was fond of speaking of the duty of the people of the Dominions to "think Imperially," King had a ready and convincing answer. Those who lived in countries the size of Australia and Canada were being asked to grow up too quickly. Such thinking might be possible; but it could not occur, he remarked to Lord Stanhope early in 1911, until the people first "have really grasped the significance of their own countries and developed a true national patriotism. Statesmen must [try] to do this and must shape their policies accordingly."[39]

The importance of the naval dispute at this stage of King's life is thus apparent. It helped to set the main lines of his thought on the controversial topic of Imperial relations whether these concerned naval or other arrangements. To accept the idea of separate navies and Milner's "centres of strength" as a keystone of Empire policies made it almost inevitable that sooner or later foreign policy would undergo a similar transformation. There would have to be foreign policies for each part of the Empire; for if the centres of strength were what they professed to be, nothing less would satisfy them. Even a brief dip in the past will disclose that responsible government has never been content with the boundaries assigned to it. If the Dominions were to be responsible for the acts of their navies, they would eventually demand the right to determine all the decisions which affected those navies, and the formation of the concomitant foreign policy would move from London in short order. It is a fair deduction that the seeds of Empire decentralization in all its aspects and with all its difficulties and complications lay hidden in these policies of Laurier and Mackenzie King.

In the naval question King perceived another demonstration of the method of political gradualism, which he was later to use with such good effect in his approach to many Empire problems. Naturally inclined to assume in the naval controversy the general attitude of Sir Wilfrid Laurier, he was thus to solidify the Liberal tradition and make it continuous. This conception of the Empire became more than ever a middle and tolerant policy, one which would cater to Canadian national ambitions while at the same time fostering co-operation within the Empire. These ideas on Imperial questions were simultaneously developed and hardened by the voluminous correspondence which King conducted with his many English friends, of whom L. S. Amery and Lord Stanhope were the chief. Its theme was frequently the old one which most Englishmen were hesitant to accept, namely, that Laurier was performing the highest service to the Empire by refusing to be drawn into plans of Imperial consolidation—the reverse side of Lord Milner's conception. "If the Prime Minister," King said at Hamilton in 1910, "had wished to sever the tie which binds us to Britain he could not have done it a surer way [sic] to accomplish that end than to have started to give the money of the people of this country to another part of the Empire for the construction of Dreadnoughts."[40]

Finally, Mackenzie King gained the conviction from his experience that the evolution of the new Empire would not be planned; as he put it, developments would be "more unconscious than determined." They would be "adjusted to circumstances" and would be applied practically by the governments of the Empire as events like the naval issue afforded them an opportunity. What would be more likely? Did not the history of the Empire suggest it? What could be more suitable for nations which derived their institutions and traditions from Britain, the home of pragmatic politics? A letter to Amery in 1910 expressed this conviction strongly, and at the same time was extraordinarily prophetic of future developments:

I have felt that that will be the most lasting which comes about in the natural order of things, *events* rather than definitely framed methods of procedure being the determining factors. Economic and political necessities will evolve a constitution, but the evolution will be more unconscious than determined. . . . What I fear from the conscious programme . . . is that it is likely . . . to provoke reaction in England against the amount of "giving up" involved, and in the Dominions, alarm at the unknown possibilities. The gradual admission of the self-governing Dominions to a share in the diplomatic, consular and civil service of the Empire under the framework at present existing, would I believe do more to demonstrate the necessity for a change, and the best kind of a change to effect, than the shaping of constitutional framework one way or the other.[41]

An international issue which was to have for King decidedly unpleasant personal consequences a year later was reciprocity with the United States, for it caused his defeat in the general election of 1911. Reciprocity was the name given to a trade agreement which the Liberal Government had entered into whereby many Canadian agricultural products were to enter the United States free or under a low tariff in return for concessions to American manufactures entering Canada. This was not a treaty, but an agreement which was to become operative through joint legislation in the two countries. When the Canadian bill came to Parliament, however, it was opposed and even obstructed by the Conservative Opposition, and an exceptionally prolonged discussion, in which King took no part, ensued. As a result of the Conservative stand, however, the Government chose to drop the measure and call a general election for September 21, 1911. In this contest, the Government was overthrown. Many factors contributed to the result. The Conservatives argued that the agreement was economically a great mistake, and they repeated and magnified reckless statements by various Americans who referred to Canada as almost fated to be annexed to the United States. The Government was defeated by an over-all majority of 45 seats, and Mackenzie King by 315 votes in his constituency.

The upset in North Waterloo was not entirely unexpected, for King had received many warnings from his party workers there that the outlook was at least doubtful. He had tried to stem the tide by careful correspondence and interviews with individuals and by frequent public pronouncements on the main issues. He had never been a warm advocate of reciprocity, foreseeing that North Waterloo, which was active in many lines of manufacturing, was likely to be critical of the proposals. As the junior Minister, however, his influence with the Government was limited. In the Cabinet discussions he had been able to protect to a degree the interests in his constituency, and he had succeeded in tempering some of the objectionable clauses in the pact where they bore most hardly on the manufacturers in Waterloo County. But he seems to have been able to do little more, and some of his colleagues apparently thought they were in no need of any lessons from him regarding the importance of fostering Canadian industry.

King, although he was in private inclined to admit that it was a pity to disturb such favourable economic conditions as those then existing,[42] followed in his campaign speeches a fairly stereotyped Liberal pattern. He defended (as every Minister was bound to do) the terms of the agreement. He stressed especially the expected stimulus it would give to the Western farmers and their growing importance as a market for Eastern manufactures; reciprocity was bound to add greatly to the farmers' purchasing power, and hence benefit the commercial, industrial, and transportation interests. He gave little attention to the purely political arguments, although disturbing predictions in regard to relations with both the United States and Britain were being extravagantly alleged in the press. He preferred to devote himself to such aspects as the cost of living, the effects of industry, and other probable economic consequences of the proposals.

King's defeat in North Waterloo can probably be explained in large part by the reckless way in which he spent his energies in addressing public meetings in constituencies other than his own. He spoke effectively, though with a leaning towards dullness, and Laurier reported at this time that he was "improving steadily."* The Prime Minister was advised by one supporter at least to keep King "on the stump" as much as possible during the campaign,[43] and this must have been done, for King's opportunities were frequent. His efforts, however, seem to have received less than justice. He certainly allowed his own interests to be neglected while he endeavoured to promote those of many of his fellow candidates. He did not go outside Ontario (though he was invited to do so), but he held nineteen meetings outside North Waterloo, and spoke in seventeen other ridings as well. In return, he did not receive in his own riding any assistance whatever on the platform either from his Cabinet colleagues or from any Liberal member of Parliament.

The Liberals had been defeated, and the immediate duty facing the old Cabinet† was to pick up a few of the remaining pieces. When it met for the first time, September 26, the opening order of business, ironically enough, was to fix a date for Thanksgiving Day. Though the Ministers could not be expected to be in the appropriate mood, they considered that under the circumstances their successors would scarcely take exception to a decision on this point.[44] Several days later, the Cabinet held its final meeting, and King's account in his diary has a certain subdued drama in its description of Laurier "looking as dignified and splendid as ever" at this end of an era:

At about 1.30, after telling us that he had arranged to see His Excellency at three that it might be as well to be in our offices in case anything wd. come up which wd. require further action, he said while leaning on the back of the chair, raising himself erect & without looking at anyone in particular "Well gentlemen that is all". The last three words were less audible than the first two, he turned & walked quickly head erect and like one victorious to the little door which goes into the anteroom, and without further ceremony he had parted with his colleagues for ever.[45]

*Laurier Papers, Sir W. Laurier to J. F. Mackay (editor of the Toronto *Globe*), March 7, 1911. Laurier was sparing, however, in his praise. On one occasion, for example, when King sent him a newspaper reporting a meeting, Laurier replied: "I am sorry that I have not yet had time to read it. I am quite sure, however, that it is worthy of yourself. I am glad to say that I have just received from our friend Mackay of the *Globe* a most glowing account of it." Laurier Papers, Sir W. Laurier to W.L.M.K., March 7, 1911.

†It was, incidentally, old and tired. King records in his diary many occasions when he discovered a number of his Cabinet colleagues sound asleep during a meeting.

CHAPTER EIGHT

CASUAL EMPLOYMENT

THE THREE YEARS following the defeat of the Laurier Government on September 21, 1911, saw Mackenzie King at loose ends: he had involuntarily joined the number of those who take work where it happens to be available. Even a position as an ordinary member of Parliament was denied him. He had committed himself to politics; he had enjoyed rapid and phenomenal success; and now he was to experience the uncertainties which always attend the life of an ex-Cabinet Minister. He also had to earn a living.

The great difficulty, of course, was that he had few genuine interests elsewhere which he could rely upon and turn to useful account. He dismissed peremptorily the possibility of making connections with a business corporation. "Business," he wrote Violet Markham on December 17, 1911, "is mere money-making, and to this I do not propose to devote my talents even if I starve." He turned down an editorial post on the Toronto *Star* at $3,000 a year; but entered into an arrangement to write occasional articles for the New York *Outlook* and other magazines. These, for some unknown reason, came to very little. For a time he considered writing a biography of Sir Wilfrid Laurier, and secured for this Sir Wilfrid's agreement and even encouragement.[1] After a little work, however, his enthusiasm petered out, and this project also was gradually abandoned.* Academic work was potentially

---

*King liked to consider himself as an author, and he was fond of noting the subjects of possible books he might undertake to write. In his college days, for example, he was contemplating an economic history of Canada, an account of the development of the Canadian labour movement, and allied ventures in social economics. In 1909 (to take a later period) he spoke of the possibility of his writing in the future a life of his grandfather (W.L.M.K. to Violet Markham, July 4, 1909), and was to an indefinite degree committed to a "book on the Opium traffic" (George H. Doran to W.L.M.K., Feb. 18, 1909). All the King men—John, Max, and W.L.M.— wrote books.

another alternative. It came to nothing owing to a diminution in King's interest, and to the fact that there seemed to be no promising openings.

In public he sounded an optimistic note, which was the more remarkable when one recalls his ambition and that defeat had come just when the outlook seemed most promising. However, the Government had gone out with a good record and on a defensible principle, and King made his exit in company with six other Ministers who also failed to be elected. Speaking at a banquet given in his honour at this time, King intimated that politics in Canada would continue to receive his utmost attention:

I intend to devote myself to mastering, as far as I can, some of the many questions and problems which confront the future of the Dominion; the relation of the east to the west, of the western farmer to the eastern manufacturer, the Oriental question, and, more than all, the way in which the British Empire is shaping itself in different parts of the world and Canada's relation thereto.[2]

But to continue cheerful in adversity occasionally proved too difficult, and he would for a while be unable to maintain a detached outlook on his plight. His native optimism would sometimes become tinged with sadness. He could write in his diary six weeks after the election that he felt God had singled him out as a future Prime Minister,[3] yet a few months later he was plainly fighting discouragement:

I thought . . . how odd in a way it was that with the kind of ability I have & service I might be rendering I should in a sense be walking the streets. This rest, exercise & withdrawal from the world to a degree are doing me good & gradually restoring a normal condition. Work will come soon yet.[4]

His diary in itself reflected his excessive leisure, for though he had plenty of time to write, little happened that he considered important enough to set down.* In June of 1913 doubts came out again in a letter to Violet Markham:

I try to be strong and brave and not shew to others the depression I often feel, and I try to carry the load [of family responsibilities] that is upon me, but I sometimes wonder if I should not give up further thought of public life.[5]

*The diary contains only one entry from March 18, 1912, to the end of the year; only two entries in 1913; and for the first half of 1914, records for only two brief periods.

223

The question of personal finances was never far from his thoughts. His savings were now giving him a return of about $1,600 a year, and he was able to supplement this by an income from speeches, articles, and party hack work. The most heart-warming assistance came from Violet Markham, who combined affection with a strong sense of King's importance in the political future of Canada. She had already contributed to his election expenses; she had sent him on his defeat £200 just to give him the "sense of freedom" he needed at that time; but she feared that he might be drawn away from his profession as a public man because of lack of funds and opportunity. On December 30, 1911, she wrote and offered further assistance, which King was glad to accept. She pointed out that he had had a very special training for public office; and looking at the question from the most practical standpoint, an abandonment of this advantage would be most uneconomic. The mere fact that he had encountered a temporary, though admittedly severe, check should not be allowed to deflect the main course of his life. His primary goal was to become Prime Minister of Canada.

Now my dear friend into this crisis & into this breach, you must let me step. You are a poor man, a poverty most honourable to yourself. I am a rich woman & because my wants are few, relatively a very rich woman. The whole problem of riches is a most difficult one to me. In this world of great injustices & miseries the possession of personal wealth seems to me a most difficult one. . . .

The simple fact is that I want to help you at this crisis, for Canada's sake as fully as your own. For the next three years I want you to take from me £300 a year so that your hands may be free & your independence assured through this time of crisis. There is nothing in such a gift which may not be offered by me & accepted by you in most perfect simplicity. . . . Any obligation to one of your fellow countrymen might tie your hands in some way. With me the word obligation could never arise—there is no obligation between us save that of a deep & enduring affection. So dear Rex for three years feel you are free to work & to *rest*, to lie fallow & study & read & think, without your life being obsessed by the harassing cares of daily bread.*

Amid these uncertainties King managed to keep his eye fixed on the

*Miss Markham also gave some help in later years when serious family illnesses greatly increased King's burden. Even at the time of King's retirement and death, she, in ignorance of his true financial circumstances, was endeavouring to arrange for further gifts in order to add, as she thought, to the necessary amenities of his declining years.

indispensable requisite of a seat in Parliament. Without a seat, he knew, he could not expect to recover the status in politics which he had once enjoyed as a Cabinet Minister. Without a seat, he could not hope, indeed, to have a political future at all, for as a defeated Minister he would be little better than a spectator, living in the past rather than looking towards the future, rejected by the people before he was able to get well into the fray. King's ambition had not changed one iota. His ultimate objective remained the same; his defeat had simply given a greater urgency to the production of some tangible sign that his political star was still riding high. "I shall rest for a time," he wrote to a friend, James Bonar, just after the election, "and see what opportunities present themselves, but that I shall come back again into Canadian public life, I do not doubt for one minute. It may be that present interests will postpone the time somewhat."[6]

In spite of King's decision to "rest and see" he embarked at once on a series of moves which were designed to lend a little helpful support to any favourable possibilities which might appear. He did not mind remaining out of Parliament for a short time, but his instinct, he told Laurier, was to get back as soon as possible. Unfortunately, the other defeated Ministers also had claims to preference for a seat which were at least as substantial as King's: Graham from Ontario, Fielding and Fisher from other provinces. Would any of these be the future leader and the successor to Laurier? On September 26, 1911, Laurier went so far as to say in Council that he would like to have his old colleagues once again at his side in the House, and he mentioned four by name: King, Fisher, Graham, and Fielding. To become Laurier's choice would, of course, be a tremendous advantage to a candidate, but King somehow did not count on this for he did not consider that he was likely to be the favoured one.[7] This feeling in no way slowed up his efforts, but rather sent him on to utilize fully all the means at his disposal for improving his position: to try to impress and cultivate Laurier by writing his biography; to look into the chances in special constituencies from Saskatchewan to Nova Scotia which might be made available by grace of the sitting member or other prominent Liberals; to make many public speeches and appearances especially with leading men in the party; to interview such people as Atkinson of the Toronto *Star* and Willison of the Toronto *News*; and to approach, whenever possible, party organizers and other party members.

King also played an increasingly noticeable part in Ontario politics, although he considered this would be of only limited assistance. He was approached by several outstanding provincial Liberals to take the leadership of the party in Ontario: Laurier approved, but he was also pleased when King told him that he wished to remain in the federal field.[8] King's major interest had been shifting in recent years from labour to national and international questions, and these, of course, consorted best with his ambition. The leadership of the Ontario Liberal party, he told Violet Markham in December, 1911, "might have meant the premiership of Ontario in four years, but what after all is that. . . . I resolutely refused, and at last the party secured Mr. N. K. [sic] Rowell."[9] He nevertheless agreed to be president of the General Reform Association of Ontario, and as such took an active part in the ensuing provincial election of December 11, 1911. The Liberals, however, though they made slight gains, were again defeated.

In the latter part of 1912 Mackenzie King slipped gradually into the task of speaking and writing in the cause of Liberalism, and he was placed in charge of the federal Liberal Information Office.[10] The position paid him a scanty living of $2,500. Speech making, conferences on party organization, discussions on policy with the federal leaders, and the preparation of political pamphlets and briefs occupied most of his attention for over two more years. He edited and wrote most of the *Canadian Liberal Monthly* (a party commentary on questions of the day) from September, 1913, until the following September. He usually had a heavy programme of speeches and lectures in Canada and the United States, some of them purely political, others on such topics as the prevention of strikes or one hundred years of peace between the two countries. But it was bound to prove little better than uninspiring drudgery for one who had been so unusually busy and always on the alert for new forms of activity.

Subsequent events indicated that despite his feelings just after the 1911 election Laurier was not disposed to exert himself to secure King a seat. He was obviously determined that King should represent an Ontario constituency because the gesture might influence the future of the Liberal party, but he confessed that these constituencies were closed corporations so far as securing nominations for outsiders was concerned. Several members of Parliament had offered to resign in King's favour, but the Liberal seats in Ontario were scarce and their

226

majorities were small, so that to open any one of them unnecessarily was likely to prove risky. Mackenzie King nevertheless felt hurt because he believed Laurier had not been active enough on his behalf, and he even used this as a partial excuse to himself for postponing his work on the projected Laurier biography.

At last, however, the tide changed, and King's return to Parliament in a general election became at least possible. He was given the Liberal nomination for North York on March 8, 1913, in large measure, apparently, for his excellent showing in the recent provincial campaign. The great attraction of the offer in King's eyes lay in the history of the constituency: its early representative had been William Lyon Mackenzie. The circumstance that North York was at the moment a Conservative seat was of little account when offset by the family associations of the past.

Relief from financial tension had meanwhile come in June, 1914, when King was invited by Jerome D. Greene, Secretary of the Rockefeller Foundation,* to hold a discussion with Greene's colleagues in that organization.[11] King's original supposition was that the talk had been proposed so that the Rockefeller people might secure information from him on Canadian labour legislation; but this was speedily altered when President Eliot sent a telegram saying that the opportunity before him was "immense" and "well worth a temporary abandonment of Canadian prospects."[12] A further message from Greene was more explicit. He stated that the Foundation was planning economic and social studies bearing on labour problems and industrial relations, and that it was particularly concerned about the lessons which might be drawn from a study of the existing severe strike in Colorado. Was King available for consultation?[13]

The Colorado strike was to play a vital part in King's subsequent history. It had begun in September, 1913, and continued for fifteen months; involved were questions of union recognition, hours, housing, wages, company paternalism, and autocratic company rule in many forms. The bitterness, which had resulted in open warfare and death at one stage,† made the strike an object of public controversy, and feeling ran strongly against the employers. The Rockefellers, who were

---

*King had met Greene a few years earlier when the latter had been secretary to President Eliot of Harvard. Greene had apparently suggested King's name to Rockefeller; Diary, Oct. 10, 1914.

†See infra, p. 233.

227

large shareholders in the major concern, the Colorado Fuel and Iron Company, placed their confidence throughout in the company's officers at the scene of action, but these had been proved hopelessly reactionary in their dealings with labour. In any discussion of the strike by the strikers and the press the Rockefeller family was constantly used as an example of the evil effects of immense wealth coupled with absentee ownership; and other firms, at least equally blameworthy, tended to be passed over because of the greater publicity value of the Rockefeller name.

Mackenzie King's proposed meeting with the representatives of the Rockefeller Foundation took place in New York on June 6; present were King and John D. Rockefeller, Jr. (hereafter frequently called John D., Jr.), Jerome D. Greene, and Starr J. Murphy, a Rockefeller solicitor and adviser. The conversation centred on the topics mentioned in Greene's letter, though the Colorado strike seems to have occupied a relatively minor position. Nevertheless the strike could not be forgotten and the outbursts of violence which had occurred that spring and the unfavourable publicity which had resulted gave urgency to the consideration of labour problems. The strike had not only made John D., Jr. willing and even anxious to tackle the basic difficulties of industrial relations but had also strengthened the appeal which the whole study project made to King. Could King, Rockefeller inquired, suggest any plan to secure better relations between capital and labour, or could he, perhaps, name some person who would be available for such work? King did his best to answer both questions. He displayed a decided liking for representative boards of capital and labour as bodies which might anticipate and solve points of disagreement, and he gave the names of at least seven people in Great Britain and the United States who might be suitable to carry out the work desired.* "It was my intention to ask King to suggest an expert adviser," Rockefeller is quoted as saying,[14] "but his ability, fairness, and energy so impressed me that I requested him to undertake the task."† In King he had found one who not only had ideals, but possessed the wide

---

*Typewritten Diary, June 1–Dec. 31, 1914, pp. 9–11. This is to be distinguished from the Diary in this period, which is the normal record. The Typewritten Diary runs from June 1, 1914, to Nov. 21, 1915 (776 pages) and was not written each day.

†John D., Jr. thought King had been invited to take the position, but King did not so understand it. Typewritten Diary, June 1–Dec. 31, 1914, p. 15.

practical experience as a conciliator necessary to establish better industrial relations and to produce a plan for these of broad application. Colorado might be only an incident, but it could become a very important incident indeed. The present might well be turned to future advantage: the special case might show the way to the general scheme.

In a few days' time John D., Jr. and his associates made the definite proposal to King that he should tie his future efforts to the work of the Rockefeller Foundation.[15] Further talks followed. King was much intrigued by the offer, which naturally lost none of its attractiveness from his unfortunate experiences of the preceding years. He wrote in his diary that "everything combined seemed to make this new opportunity a Heaven-sent deliverance."[16] But there were doubts. Was the proposal as providential as it at first appeared? For one thing, the political outlook, for so long depressing, had just begun to clear. An Ontario election was being held at the end of June which involved many additional duties for King as head of the Reform Association. Laurier had also invited him recently to join his entourage on political trips which would range from the Maritime Provinces to Western Canada—a wonderful opportunity for a young ex-Minister to demonstrate his worth.[17] Moreover, King had some misgivings about Heaven being on the side of the Rockefellers; and, furthermore, what was to become of his destiny as the eventual head of the government of Canada? If alliance with the Rockefellers should involve separation from Laurier, he was inclined to reject the alliance, although the inclination sometimes became a little shaky, and he was occasionally prepared to consider the relinquishment of a political future. But this may have been no more than a sign of his usual hesitation.

After a number of consultations with his friends,* Mackenzie King made up his mind. He liked what he had seen of John D., Jr. and was convinced of his sincerity. He knew that President Eliot, a trustee of the Rockefeller Foundation, shared his high opinion. "Indeed," he wrote in his diary, "without Dr. Eliot's strongly endorsed opinion, the prejudice against the Rockefellers in which up to the time of meeting Mr. Rockefeller I shared, would probably have caused me to dismiss from my mind altogether any thought of associating myself with any

---

*Laurier was reluctant to advise him on so personal a matter, but said that he was sure King would not think of giving up politics for any consideration short of "dire necessity." Typewritten Diary, p. 24.

work carried on by Rockefeller funds."[18] * King was also much attracted by the very magnitude of the project and the opportunity it offered for useful work in the labour field. Finally, he felt it might even be possible to close with the offer and yet keep a way open for a return to politics. Nevertheless the argument against entering the employ of "the interests" continued to worry both him and others,[19] and he realized the political dangers which such a connection would inevitably bring. "Once associated in any way with the Rockefeller concern," he wrote in his diary, "my future in politics would be jeopardized. Had the offer been to enter the service of one of the Rockefeller corporations other than the Foundation, I should not have accepted it."[20] Torn by these conflicting forces, he nevertheless decided to take the job.

By the formal appointment, made on August 13, 1914, King was to conduct his own research under the auspices of the Rockefeller Foundation. He was to be the head of its Department of Industrial Relations, a new departure for the organization. An essential feature of the arrangement was that King was to be quite independent in his work. He had been asked if he wished to have a committee or board to use for consultation, but he rejected the offer and said that he preferred to accept the sole responsibility for the department's research. On this attitude John D. Rockefeller, Sr., who had taken a lively interest in the project, commented: "You are quite right in that; do not have a board."[21]

The salary was to be $12,000 a year.† He was to remain a Canadian citizen, and be free to participate in Canadian politics. If elected to Parliament, he could have leave without pay for the necessary four or five months a year.[22] His residence was to remain in Ottawa, though Rockefeller anticipated an eventual move to New York. In fact, no change of residence ever took place, but Mackenzie King's work often necessitated his leaving Ottawa for weeks and sometimes months at a time. The term of appointment was left, at King's request, for one year only. King knew, of course, that every year from Canadian politics made his return that much more difficult. Voters had no love for expatriates.

Substantial changes in King's activities were inescapable, and even

---

*The funds of the Foundation at this time were over $100,000,000.
†King was told he could have up to $15,000 if he desired it.

welcome. He relinquished the Liberal Information Office, the editorship of the *Liberal Monthly*, and the presidency of the Ontario Reform Association. The Foundation agreed with him that he must fulfil his promise and go on tour with Sir Wilfrid, but the war (which had broken out on August 4, 1914) eventually caused the cancellation of the proposed trip. He was as determined as ever to keep politics well in the foreground and he was therefore very anxious to retain North York as a possible port of entry to Parliament. "To North York I still cling," he wrote in his diary.[23] "I must carry that riding for grandfather's sake, then the future must determine its own destiny which will be as God intends and as I may measure up to the great opportunities that are mine." He had informed the Liberal Association there of his new position and had emphasized the freedom of the executive to choose another candidate if it so desired. Although he also made clear that he would be able to do little in the riding until the election, the executive had accepted his terms, and he was continued as the party's candidate in North York.[24]

The Rockefellers, both senior and junior, wished Mackenzie King to make his association permanent after the original study was completed,[25] and King, for his part, found his political ambitions occasionally weakening before his new and unique opportunities.[26] But on the whole, in spite of the manifold attractions of a life of study in the field of industrial relations—or, as an alternative, a career as confidential adviser to a Rockefeller—King's determination to make Canadian politics his life-work remained dominant. Leadership, as usual, was at the root of it. "I keep before me the idea of still serving my country as a leader" runs an entry in the diary on October 10, 1914. His heart's desire was still "to take a leading part" (actually, *the* leading part) in the shaping of Canada's destiny; and for such a purpose, politics knew no effective rival.

The liking which Mackenzie King and the young Rockefeller developed for each other was a vital condition in making their relationship successful. Rockefeller originally knew nothing of King; King's impressions of Rockefeller were slight and, such as they were, bound to be unfavourable because of his strongly ingrained dislike for men of great wealth. But the progress of understanding and affection between the two was rapid, and once begun, it never faltered. Macken-

231

zie King was soon to regard John D., Jr. as one of his greatest friends; Rockefeller's biographer, Raymond B. Fosdick, has stated that King was "the closest friend" John D., Jr. ever had.[27]

Points of contact had at first seemed few. They were within a few months of the same age. Simplicity in early home life had marked the upbringing of both, despite widely different economic and social backgrounds. Each had a strong religious bent, and they shared a desire to make their lives worth while in terms of human interests and happiness.[28] This was not a broad basis on which to found a friendship, yet it proved more than adequate, for in the last resort the major considerations were character and personality. "Seldom have I been so impressed by a man at first appearance," said John D., Jr.,[29] and King wrote as early as December, 1914:

I left him [John D., Jr.] with the feeling that of all men who have yet come into my life I have more to be grateful for for the friendship which has sprung up out of our association together than for any other like association yet formed. In the first place I know of no man living whose character I more admire and in the second place I can see wherein, with the purpose he has at heart, it is going to be possible for me to work out in a practical form ideas and ideals respecting industrial relations which I have long cherished and which it has been the first ambition of my life to have realized in a manner likely to prove of service to men.[30]

With this propitious beginning and owing in large measure to King's constant help, Rockefeller made substantial progress in reaching a new understanding of industrial relations. He had appeared as a witness in April, 1914, before a Congressional sub-committee on the Colorado strike, known as the Foster Committee. Here he had made a bad impression, especially in his reactionary opposition to trade unions and his insistence on the major responsibility of the local management (at the expense of the company's head office) for all labour policies.[31] As a result of the latter practice, moreover, he found himself trying to defend the activities of a company about which he had little information, and having to plead ignorance about many matters which the public considered should have been his especial interest. "The general reaction to his testimony, certainly in liberal circles," writes Fosdick, "was not favorable. . . . He gave the appearance of believing that by delegating authority to the operating officials of the company in Denver he had discharged his full responsibilities as director and stockholder."[32]

232

Two weeks later the "Ludlow massacre" occurred as a result of intervention by the State militia. Several strikers were killed, and eleven children and two women died as an indirect result. A most unhappy situation had thus suddenly become a tragic one. Popular criticism of the Rockefellers turned to resentment and hatred; the bitterness spread rapidly from Colorado over the nation. John D., Jr.'s failure, even at this moment, to go over the heads of the management in Colorado and negotiate with the union for a settlement was naturally interpreted as a refusal to try to stop the conflict. But the junior Rockefeller had nevertheless been greatly shaken. It was about this time[33] that his confidence in the local management and in the relation of the management to the company weakened, and he began to question many ideas which he had hitherto accepted as axiomatic. He could not escape the conclusion that the company's agents in the field had failed to grasp the important considerations which underlay much of the trouble in Colorado, and that he by his acquiescence in the company's policies had been made a party to them. He saw that somehow the company's attitude and policy would have to be scrutinized carefully before he could ever again rest easily about his own responsibility in this and kindred matters which he had hitherto considered to be beyond his province.

King had thus been brought to the scene at the opportune moment. Rockefeller was anxious to have the advice of one who favoured new methods and improved labour policies, and a great part of King's immediate work was to fill this need. But Rockefeller's sincere and eager desire to do the right thing was made partly ineffective by his own unsureness and the areas of opposition which appeared within the management itself. King tried to show him the way and to strengthen his arm, and in the process he was delighted to find confirmation of the qualities in Rockefeller which he had earlier discerned. In 1917 he wrote Violet Markham of Rockefeller's "humility, his sincerity, his fearlessness, his simple faith, his fidelity to principle—so far as he has horizon at all his one purpose is to serve his fellow men in the spirit of true Christian service. . . . If there be error in what I do, the fault will be mine not his—and I want you to believe that I knowingly will not further what is false or untrue."[34]

King soon began also to advise John D., Jr. on many things which had nothing to do with industrial relations: his excessive seriousness,

233

his method of living, his failure to see enough of his family, his aloofness, his inability to relax, and the need for him to get away from detail and to deal with major issues. "The truth is," King admitted to his diary, "I see in Mr. R. precisely the same mistakes which I have heard others complain of in myself."[35] In these personal affairs as in others Rockefeller was very appreciative of King's sympathy and help, and he has never hesitated to say so: "Loyal, able, high-minded, utterly to be trusted" was part of his description in 1953 of King as a colleague and friend; "virtually everything I know of industrial relations I learned from Mr. King."[36] Few of those close to Mackenzie King at any time have been so unreserved in their praise.

CHAPTER NINE

THE ROCKEFELLER FOUNDATION

MACKENZIE KING'S early work with the Rockefeller Foundation was devoted to a general survey of the questions which were likely to be involved in his research. It was tentative and not directly productive. He developed, for example, a passion for abstruse charts; some of the diagrams that were later published in *Industry and Humanity* were originally drafted at this time and form an interesting commentary on his approach to the problem. King also had a bibliography committed to some 10,000 cards of various colours, which after the first few months he does not appear to have used again. He was continually jotting down and revising the chief topics of his research in response to new ideas. However, all this was part of the inevitable process of trial and error associated with such projects, and his thoughts did begin to assume a more orderly shape. Eventually his plans became less ambitious than at first, and he discarded, at least for the moment, any idea of setting up a large staff and limited himself to the assistance of F. A. McGregor, his secretary.

King's mind worked to much better advantage on concrete problems. Here he was speedily confronted of course with the awkward situation that some of the Rockefeller industrial troubles impinged directly on his general subject. A scheme that proposed to spend Foundation funds on the task of devising improved labour policies yet ultimately derived some of its income from an industry the labour relations of which had become a national scandal, was inherently absurd. Interest in the Colorado strike was thus not only immediate and urgent, it had a direct relevance to King's work. He lost no time in coming to grips with the difficulty. He drove home to the Foundation and to John D. Rockefeller, Jr. the double proposition that they should never forget that they obtained a substantial revenue from the disaffected mines, and that ownership could never become divorced from a responsibility for the miners' welfare. The trials of the Colorado Fuel and Iron Company and the problems of industrial relations had many aspects in common. It therefore became a natural move for Mackenzie King to plan to follow up his conviction with a trip to Colorado in order to see what practical changes he could suggest to meet the discontent there and to turn the situation into an experiment, a demonstration of the validity of some of his theories of reform.[1]

Colorado also made its appearance in King's life through the activities of an outside organization. The United States Commission on Industrial Relations, composed of nine representatives of employers, employees, and the public (and known as the Walsh Commission), had been appointed by the President of the United States as early as 1912 to investigate the problem named in its title. King had appeared before the Commission in April, 1914, to give evidence dealing with the Canadian Industrial Disputes Investigation Act. As an aid to its inquiry, the Commission sent out an elaborate questionnaire to various organizations, among which were the Rockefeller Foundation and King's own Department of Industrial Relations. This came up for answering late in 1914. In August, the month of his appointment to the Foundation, King had won Rockefeller's early goodwill by preparing at the latter's request a rough scheme of reform designed to promote better labour relations in the mining camps.* Rockefeller had been much attracted by these suggestions (which included, as a major feature, industrial representation in industry) and he had sent King's proposals to Denver for consideration by company officials. The necessity, four months later, of preparing a reply to the Walsh Commission's questionnaire appeared to King to be "truly providential."[2] He and Rockefeller worked·over these answers together, and the two men were brought into prolonged intimacy for the first time. King was thereby able to examine critically with Rockefeller many labour problems, to help him formulate his revised and untried convictions, and to suggest certain policies which would be in accord with those which Rocke-

*See Raymond B. Fosdick, *John D. Rockefeller, Jr., a Portrait* (New York, 1956), pp. 154–5. John D. R., Jr. to W.L.M.K., Aug. 1, 1914; W.L.M.K. to John D. R., Jr., Aug. 6, 1914. The latter was written from Ottawa two days after war broke out, and King was for that reason very busy. He noted in his handwritten diary for August 6, 1914: "[The letter] was not all what [sic] I should like to have it, very cursory & incomplete, but the best I could manage with the situation as it is."

feller wished to see applied. The discussion proved to be extremely helpful in its effects on Rockefeller's ideas on labour questions, and both men experienced an enhanced appreciation of each other's views and character.[3]

John D. Rockefeller, Jr. was summoned in due course to give evidence before the Walsh Commission in January, 1915. King once more perceived the use which could be made of this opening. Rockefeller could place his altered position on the record and by this means counteract some of the bad effects of his evidence before the Foster Committee in 1914.[*] King therefore undertook to prepare Rockefeller for the coming ordeal. He advised, and even preached, improved labour relations in season and out of season, at meals, in the office, in walks along the New York streets, in the subway, and in the family car. The diary contains many references to such talks. He stressed the importance of Rockefeller's position in the industrial world, the need for exercising leadership among employers, and the desirability of allowing the public to gain an insight into Rockefeller's character and opinions:

I repeated . . . to him, that there appeared no alternative so far as he was concerned, to his being either the storm centre of a great revolution in this country or the man who by his fearless stand and position would transfuse a new spirit into industry. I advised him strongly to nail his colors firmly to the mast at the hearings of the Commission . . . we were living together in a different generation than the one in which his father had lived. . . . Today, there was a social spirit abroad, and it was absolutely necessary to take the public into one's confidence, to give publicity to many things, and especially to stand out for certain principles very boldly.[4]

Rockefeller was before the Commission for three days. Much of the examination was turned into a virtual prosecution, for some members of the Commission, notably Senator Frank P. Walsh, the chairman, could not resist the temptation to grill a witness whom they looked upon as the protagonist of selfish capitalism.[†] But despite many

---

[*]See supra, pp. 232–3.

[†]See, for example, Fosdick, John D. Rockefeller, Jr., pp. 156–9. King noted the opinion of many others as well as his own on this point. Typewritten Diary, Jan. 15–27, 1915, pp. 101–69, May 17–25, 1915, pp. 656–7. Also, Testimony of W.L.M.K. Given before the U.S. Commission on Industrial Relations (May 25, 1915), pp. 85–91.

In fairness to the Walsh Commission, it should be said that although the conduct of some of its members was often grossly biassed the results of its inquiry in the long run probably proved helpful. The investigation did much to expose the evils of

examples of prejudice against him, Rockefeller acquitted himself well. The general impression he conveyed was one of honesty and courtesy, a willingness to learn and to adopt a more liberal attitude towards labour. Indeed some of Rockefeller's advisers were extremely critical of the conciliatory attitude which he adopted towards the Commission.[5] King was on the whole satisfied with his protégé, though he privately noted several "weak spots" in his testimony.[6] Rockefeller was still ignorant of many conditions in the mines, but he had wisely announced (at King's suggestion) an intention to go to Colorado so that as soon as possible he could see things at first hand. King summed up the effects of his performance in his diary:

Not only has Mr. R. given himself a new start with the American public, and particularly with labour, but he has also helped to mark an epoch in the industrial history of this country itself. Students will go back to his evidence of to-day in indicating the period of transition from indifference on the part of directors to the assuming of obligation by them. . . . I look forward to seeing Mr. R. ultimately get a great reception from the working-men of Colorado.[7] *

King lost no time in preparing the way, even while the Commission was still holding its hearings. He was able to arrange meetings in New York immediately (January, 1915) between Rockefeller and a number of the labour representatives, and he was gratified to find a marked improvement in their attitude when they realized Rockefeller's genuine interest and friendliness. The most startling of these conver-

---

absentee capitalism and the injustices under which labour was suffering at the time, and it gave trade unionism a status which it had hitherto not been accorded in the United States. Selig Perlman, *A History of Trade Unionism in the United States* (New York, 1922), p. 228. The Commission's final report, submitted in August, 1915, reflected in large measure the divergence in the views of its members, and thus was made up of majority and minority reports, supplemental statements, and reports by its own staff. United States, Senate, *Final Report . . . by the Commission on Industrial Relations* (Washington, 1916).

*Rockefeller and King had yet another examination by the Commission in the early summer under much the same conditions and with similar results. Here King and Walsh came into heated conflict when Walsh attempted to make King admit that in giving his testimony he had boasted that "the will and conscience of John D. Rockefeller, Jr., were more potent in Colorado than all the public opinion of all of the people of the United States, and that the American people must look to that one man for an improvement of conditions, conceded by all to be un-American and intolerable." (Quoted in Typewritten Diary, May 17-25, 1915, pp. 662 (a)-(b).) King considered this a flagrant distortion of his words and naturally refused to make the admission to Walsh. See Fosdick, *John D. Rockefeller, Jr.*, pp. 158-9; *Testimony of W.L.M.K. Given before the U.S. Commission on Industrial Relations* (May 25, 1915), pp. 85-91.

sions was that of "Mother" Jones, a fire-eating agitator from Colorado. She had spent most of her eighty-three years fighting in the cause of labour, had served several months in jail, and had been one of Rockefeller's most uncompromising enemies. She was captivated now by his evident sincerity and good intentions, and he in turn took "quite a fancy" to her.* King recorded in his diary:

When a number of socialists were taking her to task for shaking hands with him, she had upbraided them, and said that he was really their friend though they did not know it. . . . [She admitted that] Mr. R. did not understand the conditions, but that if the working people and middle class folk had done half as well as he had, they would bring about decent conditions for the workers.[8]

Later "Mother" Jones and Rockefeller discussed the workers' grievances frankly in a talk which King described as "One of the most interesting I ever expect to witness."[9]

King's wish to go to Colorado himself soon after his appointment in August, 1914, in the confidence that he could clean up the situation there, had not yet been fulfilled. Rockefeller had also suggested in that same month the possibility of such a trip, in order that King might have an opportunity to consult with the officials. But King's presence had not been desired by the Colorado Fuel and Iron Company. The strike was still in progress, and the president, J. F. Welborn, and his assistants were in no mood to consider changes in labour relations at that or perhaps at any other time.[10] Eventually, the strike had ended in December in favour of the company, and the hope of something being done to effect a permanent improvement began to strengthen.

King was disposed to blame both sides for the strike and its excesses, and he considered that the western management was out of sympathy with the purposes and some of the plans for reform of those in the east.[11] The campaign to win over the officials in Colorado had already been opened in August, 1914, when Rockefeller had forwarded some of King's schemes to Denver,[12] and it was continued in New York where in February King had been able to hold long discussions with Welborn. Here King made (with Rockefeller's backing) substantial progress, and in the end he received an invitation from Welborn to go to Colorado. John D., Jr. had intended to accompany him, but his

*Rockefeller was later to describe her as the "marvelous, vigorous, courageous organizer of the United Mine Workers of America." Fosdick, *John D. Rockefeller, Jr.,* p. 148.

plans were changed by the death of his mother. King left for the west on March 16.*

Two major problems faced Mackenzie King in Colorado, both of which had to be met and at least partially solved before he could hope to make much progress with his plan of representation and co-operation. The company officials—managers, superintendents, pit bosses, and others—had to be converted to a new way of thinking and acting in their relations with labour; and the men had to be convinced that they had a right to a voice in their own working and living conditions and an obligation to exercise it. Moreover, although King had a scheme in his mind in broad outline, he knew nothing of local conditions. It was imperative for him to assure himself that the environment was favourable to his plan, and that if difficulties developed, it would be possible to make suitable alterations.

King's survey of the communities in Colorado and his contacts with the people at all levels were extensive. Rarely had his enthusiasm and charm of manner stood him in such good stead. Fred A. McGregor, who accompanied him, has given a witness's account of King's activities at this time:

He visited every community in which the Company had interests. It was not a "conducted" tour. He talked freely with everyone he came across from President to mule-drivers, and, outside the company, from Governor to merchants and school teachers. Most of them in turn talked freely with him. He had a knack of establishing friendly relations with and winning the confidence of the men and women he talked with. It was not long before he was on first-name terms with President Welborn and his wife. Their conversation was not confined by any means to problems of industrial relations. King was probably stronger on poetry and religion than either of them, but Mrs. Welborn could keep up her end when it came to art and music. Welborn's hobby was his farm, and King tells a delightful story of a week-end visit to the farm. Welborn pointed proudly to three young bulls he had recently added to his herd, and then broke it to King that the names he had given them were in honour of his brother, his secretary and himself: "Macdougall, McGregor and Mackenzie." "Some chance now," King commented gaily, "of descendants bearing my name." But even a social week-end was not merely social. "After dinner," he entered in his diary, "I finished drafting the memorandum on social and industrial betterment,

*King had diplomatically consulted the Foundation before his departure; W.L.M.K. to Jerome D. Greene, March 1, 1915. The trustees approved, at the same time making it clear that he was quite free to come to his own decisions in such matters; Typewritten Diary, March 2, 1915, p. 268.

and read through the whole of it to Mr. and Mrs. Welborn. We all three discussed very freely and fully the points raised in its several divisions. Welborn seemed particularly pleased to have this outline as a guide."[13] The evening was a nice example of one of Mackenzie King's techniques, an intermingling of seriousness and fun, of purposeful discussion and discursive talk. More was accomplished in that week-end of friendly intercourse than could have been in a week of board meetings.

In going about from camp to camp, King sought information about housing and rents, fencing and gardens, water supply, sanitation facilities, wash houses, industrial accidents and workmen's compensation, hospitals and doctors and nurses, recreation and social centres, social workers, churches, schools, company stores, saloons and the administration of justice. He went into the mines and steel mills, workers' homes and the schools, and into at least one saloon. Always he had in mind not so much recommendations to the Company for improvements it might finance (he did make some such suggestions) as ways and means whereby the employees themselves could participate in the shaping of policies affecting their interests and carrying them out. The whole emphasis was upon the human element; the whole objective was a framework within which ideas of joint control and partnership, a limited form of representative and responsible government, could be developed.[14]

After two months King was forced to return east to give further evidence before the Walsh Commission.[15] He had, however, gathered enough material to enable him to draw up the kind of "industrial constitution" he had had in mind, and he spent the early summer of 1915 in its preparation. Rockefeller was much taken with the "statesman-like, comprehensive carefully worked out plan" which King submitted;[16] but Welborn, while approving it in principle, was very doubtful if it was feasible.* After discussion, however, the top executive officials gave their ,approval. The decision was then made that John D., Jr. should go to Colorado and present the Plan—an assignment he could scarcely have welcomed, for memories of the strike were fresh and the attitude of the men was considered dangerous. King, however, had steadily pressed for Rockefeller's presence in Colorado to enable both sides to gain a more accurate idea of the people involved and to create an atmosphere of goodwill. John D., Sr. had

---

*Following the end of the strike in December, Welborn had set up a mild plan for representation in the industry which embodied King's suggestions "as far as seemed practicable"; J. F. Welborn to John D. R., Jr., Dec. 18, 1914. Both he and Rockefeller were pleased with it, although King regarded it as no more than a beginning, and not at all the plan he had had in mind; W.L.M.K. to John D. R., Jr., Feb. 12, 1915.

serious doubts of the wisdom of the trip and did not want his son to go. He even asked the junior Rockefeller's secretary to carry a revolver, but it was refused.

The basis of the Plan,* King wrote years later,

was to make of industry a partnership in which each of the contributing parties: Capital, Labour, Management and the Community would share in a knowledge and an understanding of the enterprise as a whole, of each other's rights and duties worked out on the principle of round table conference effected through some device of representation. . . . Its significant feature was the application of the principle of representation in the affairs of industry, as over the years, representation has come to be applied in the affairs of State.[17]

In more concrete terms the Plan dealt with such matters as the representation of employees (one elected for every 150 men) and the machinery to achieve it, conferences of labour with management, joint committees on various phases of industrial relations (such as health, recreation, and housing), and special procedure to secure the adjustment of disputes. Attached to the Plan were various undertakings regarding employment and living and working conditions. One feature which it gave Mackenzie King special satisfaction to obtain, was the provision that the company should show no discrimination against anyone because of membership in a union. Joining a union could not be a ground for dismissal, and union organizers were not to be excluded from the camps as had been the practice in the past.

Rockefeller arrived in Colorado late in September, 1915, and he at once set out to acquire some familiarity with local conditions. King, who had preceded him by several days, acted as his guide and interpreter. In such a capacity the politician was at his best, remembering names and incidents, and guiding Rockefeller towards the bad spots which some of the officials might be inclined to avoid. Rockefeller went down the mines, heard complaints, visited many miners' homes and families, joined in discussions, and talked to almost all the employees' representatives. When a dance was billed for the Cameron mine on the last day of the tour, King insisted that Rockefeller should be there. The "big boss," it was reported with some exaggeration, danced with every miner's wife and daughter on the floor. At the end

---

*It was known popularly as the "Rockefeller Plan" of Industrial Representation. Here, as with the Lemieux Act (*supra*, p. 136), it was King's ill fortune to have the authorship of his outstanding measure nominally vested in another.

Mackenzie King electioneering, 1908

Mackenzie King in Windsor uniform, 1910

of each day, Rockefeller and King went over their impressions and discussed the application of these impressions to various phases of the new Plan.

After a two weeks' stay in Colorado, Rockefeller presented and explained the Plan and the Memo of Agreement to a joint meeting of employees' representatives and company officers and superintendents. They gave their unanimous approval. The proposals were then voted on and accepted in a secret ballot by the miners and later by the steel workers and others. The Plan as affecting labourers in coal, coke, steel, and iron was put in operation in 1916; and contracts embodying agreements on wages, hours, and other vital matters were signed by the representatives of the company and of the employees.

The adoption of the Plan and the change in the general atmosphere of labour relations furnished a tribute both to the proposal and to the attractiveness and sincerity of Rockefeller. They also confirmed King's reliance on the power of personal factors to solve many of the problems of industry. Rockefeller himself had no doubt where the major credit belonged. He told his biographer years later,

I was merely King's mouthpiece. I needed education. No other man did so much for me. He had vast experience in industrial relations and I had none. I needed guidance. He had an intuitive sense of the right thing to do—whether it was a man who ought to be talked with or a situation that ought to be met.[18]

And in a contemporary letter to King he wrote:

For your untiring efforts in developing this plan, in assisting to bring about its adoption, for your wise and safe counsel throughout our tour of inspection, for the splendid spirit of service which animates your every action and which has made the association and co-operation with you a privilege; for all of these and many other things which you are and have done, I thank you in deepest sincerity.[19]

Once launched, the new scheme was fervently supported by the management who did their utmost to make it work in all its branches. The social welfare activities which had begun before the Plan had been adopted, made rapid progress, and company funds were spent generously on house improvements, wash houses, schools, and recreation centres. The policy of requiring workers to buy at company stores was abandoned. The employees, for their part, showed their appreciation. They used the new facilities for adjusting grievances, for example, though they were human enough to display little enthusiasm about attending meetings of committees, and were apathetic when they were called upon to vote for representatives. The State also assisted in establishing new relations by passing legislation in certain fields, one of its contributions being a plan of compulsory investigation along the lines of the Canadian Industrial Disputes Investigation Act. In general, both officials and men of the company showed an increased interest in and understanding of each other's problems, and co-operation between the two was both more common and in much better spirit than in the past.

The great drawback in the Plan was the strong paternalism which was implied, for the part of the workers was largely confined to the expression of opinions and the making of recommendations. Many amenities were introduced, but the expenses were paid by the company, which looked on the cost as justified because of the greater measure of industrial peace and contentment that resulted. The blame for this condition must be apportioned in several ways: to the Plan itself, which necessitated paternalism on a large scale; to the company, which was not eager to relinquish its functions as chief benefactor; and to the workers, whose unwillingness or incapacity or both often made greater participation on their part impossible. Yet although the new régime still used too much a paternalism directed by the company alone, it at least encouraged consultation with the men and acted as a bridge towards more self-government. The assumption of responsibility by employees could not fail to supply a little of the gradual training which was an indispensable preparation for any more ambitious scheme for participation by the workers in the decisions of industry.

One controversial issue raised by the Plan was its potentially competitive relation to trade unionism. It is difficult to attack King effectively as a contributor to this result except on the assumption that the unions should always be helped and defended, a doctrine to which King never agreed. His sympathies throughout his career had been strongly in favour of the unions, but he did not always give them undeviating support. He was their ally when they were fighting to remedy undesirable conditions, but he could never be worked up over a fight merely to achieve "union recognition." He told the Walsh Commission,

To carry a fight for four or five years simply on the question of recognition and leave the actual conditions out of account altogether, is losing the substance while you are chasing the shadow. . . . True unionism is not an end in itself, it is a means to an end. It is a means of obtaining and improving standards for the working classes.[20]

He thus developed little sympathy for the union in Colorado in 1914–15: he felt the United Mine Workers there had disqualified itself by bad leadership, bad because of its resort to arms, internal dissension, intimidation of non-union workers, and complete concentration on the goal of union recognition.* On the other side, however, the record of the companies was also bad. It was one of political intrigue, domination of State officials, disregard of the human rights of employees, failure to provide means for redress of grievances, and the establishment of a method of control akin to feudalism. Recognition of the union would have changed conditions—but with the kind of leadership which obtained in the union at that time in that area, the remedy would have been worse than the abuses. Management was almost always adamant against recognition but King was properly suspicious of this hostility. "While the managers talked a good deal about union recognition," he told President Eliot of Harvard, "they were doing so as a means of concealing their own methods of dealing with employees and of permitting themselves to persist in these methods."[21]

One of King's beliefs, as has been seen, was that the bringing of antagonistic persons together would often lead to the destruction of misunderstanding and hostility. Without the right kind of personalities in them, he contended, the finest organization and machinery could achieve little. Accordingly, he made frequent efforts to bring Rockefeller and prominent union leaders together, and the results often justified his belief. Thus Rockefeller got on very well with Garretson of the Railroad Conductors, and he found many points of agreement with John Mitchell, a former president of the U.M.W., and John P. White and William Green, contemporary president and secretary respectively of the same organization. At one of these meetings, for instance, the matter of unionism appeared and could be dis-

*The organization of the U.M.W. as a whole had generally a good report, but the western section had fallen under the influence of a lawless and irresponsible group. Typewritten Diary, Feb. 27, 1915; E. R. A. Seligman, quoted in G. P. West, *Report on the Colorado Strike* (1915), p. 40.

245

cussed amicably. In view of later criticism regarding the attitude of King and Rockefeller to "company unions," the following extract from King's diary showing the position of the union at the time is of unusual interest:

The third point to be developed was brought out by Green and also by White, who urged that Mr. R. should have the Company make an agreement for a term of years with its own employees. I noted particularly his emphasis of the words "its own employees," seeing thereby that clearly the head organization knew the matter of union recognition to be out of the question *at present*. They preceded this statement by saying that in labour unions much education was necessary and speaking of the difficulties they had in dealing with the masses of uneducated labour of which the mining classes were composed. . . . They did not try to put blame on one side or the other, but seemed entirely to take the point of view that they would help to further industrial peace and could be helpful in getting their men to agree to an agreement which might be made between the Company and its employees. . . .

Later, when we were about to say Good-bye, Mr. White said to me himself about the agreement that they would not expect anything in the way of an agreement with the union, that it was an agreement with the Company's own employees, leaving them free to join the union or not. *It would be sufficient at this time.* He and Green could go a long way, and their union could go a long way in helping to right Mr. R. with Labour and the people if this much were done.[22] * [Italics added]

Rockefeller, in truth, did not comprehend unionism and did not want union recognition; he dreaded it and welcomed the Plan as a possible alternative to the wider union. King, for his part, did not favour recognition with the union's existing leadership; but he looked forward with equanimity to the acceptance of the union in due course. The union leaders were mostly willing to take the Plan as being temporarily acceptable, but did not regard it as a permanent solution. Immediate recognition, they saw, was impossible, but representation foreshadowed unionism and could be utilized as a beginning of collective bargaining.† The first step taken through the Plan had been,

*Samuel Gompers, President of the American Federation of Labor, did not meet Rockefeller or King before the Colorado trip, and he denounced the Plan.

†Later, as company unions grew out of favour with the unions, the latter shifted their ground and accused the Rockefeller Plan of providing "a substitute for trade unionism." King did not believe this was necessarily so, and found in the Whitley Council movement in Great Britain, for example, an illustration of his contention. He prepared two long memoranda on the point for the Seth Low Commission in February, 1916, which he attached to a letter to John D. Rockefeller, Jr., dated Feb. 21, 1916. See also the Report of the Commission in United States, House of Representatives, *Letter from the President transmitting Report of the Colorado Coal Commission of the Labor Difficulties in the Coal Fields of Colorado . . . 1914 and 1915*, Feb. 23, 1916.

indeed, a very long one: a written contract in the nature of a bill of rights, a start at free election of the employees' representatives, freedom for the miners to join the union and for union organizers to campaign for membership, a protection against unfair dismissal, and collective bargaining to a degree unheard of in Colorado.[23] The freedom to organize was the greatest victory; and the union leaders believed that the resulting strength of unionism would in time have its reward. Industrial representation could scarcely be expected to provide a permanent solution: its conspicuous merit was a modified responsibility for the workers combined with a training in function, and these were likely to lead to a greater participation. But it enjoyed a limited success under the conditions it was designed to meet, and it was able to moderate the harshest side of an industrial warfare which had been waged for many years before its introduction. The scheme was used with profit in the Colorado Fuel and Iron Company for some twenty years, and it was adopted (in a number of instances as a result of King's recommendation) in hundreds of other industries. Dissolution came shortly after Congress in 1935 passed the Wagner Act, which prohibited "company unions" and in effect rendered the industrial representation plan obsolete.

Mackenzie King left the Foundation in 1918, but he kept an active interest in Rockefeller's affairs and his deep friendship for the man himself which never faltered made him feel called upon to intervene on those occasions when he thought Rockefeller was in danger of falling from grace and losing his grip on some of the basic doctrines of trade unionism.[24] One illustration may be given.

In 1919 E. H. Weitzel, General Manager of the Colorado company, urged Rockefeller to agree to a proposal that all their employees should enter into individual agreements with the company. Rockefeller passed it on to King with the comment: "What is the objection to this suggestion? Mr. Murphy and I can see none."[25] King was naturally horrified at such heresy, and he wrote Rockefeller a strong rebuke in these lines:

The fact that . . . neither Mr. Murphy nor yourself can see any objection in the suggestion, is conclusive evidence that, as respects the right of collective bargaining—which as Fosdick says, is now an established fact beyond all controversy—you have been drawn away, through lack of technical acquaintance with all-important features of the case, from a fundamental position, and are in grave danger of being drawn into the very

247

position which the opponents of the Colorado representation plan would like to see you drawn into.

I am utterly and irretrievably opposed to Weitzel's and Matheson's suggestion, for the reason that it lies at the opposite pole to what is meant by collective bargaining. It is a reversion back to all that Labor has been struggling against in seeking to prevent employment being made on the basis of a vast corporate interest, on one side, versus an isolated and helpless unit of Labor on the other. You may have no such thought in your own mind, and certainly have not, in approving of the suggestion; but it is the construction the whole world will place upon any attempt of the kind. To me it is truly heartbreaking to see your whole great position imperilled by such reactionary suggestions and possibilities. I implore you, in the interests of your own life and work, to be over-cautious in returning to any position from which you advanced years ago. For the sake of yourself and industry in America, hold at least to the ground you have already gained, and do not be forced back into a false position.[26]

Letters like this from King to Rockefeller were not infrequent and King apparently enjoyed expressing his views with frankness. Certainly John D., Jr. did not resent them. On an earlier occasion King had described another similar exchange in his diary:

Indeed I imagine that no such letter was ever written to a Rockefeller from any of the precincts of the Standard Oil, as this one which went out from the Board of Directors room of the Indiana company. . . . For a long while I have felt that Mr. Rockefeller, sooner or later, would be brought to face squarely the question of whether he is prepared to co-operate with organized Labor, or to face a conflict of unparalleled magnitude with organized Labor forces.[27]

A result of Mackenzie King's study of industrial relations was the publication of a book called *Industry and Humanity* in 1918. A substantial part was devoted to a discussion of the general organization of economic society and the principles and rules which should be followed there. Taking as his text a quotation from Pasteur (which Max had contributed some years before)* on the unending conflict of contrary laws in society King thought he saw this illustrated in the

---

*"Two contrary laws seem to be wrestling with each other nowadays: the one, a law of blood and death, ever imagining new means of destruction, and forcing nations to be constantly ready for the battlefield—the other, a law of peace, work, and health, ever evolving new means of delivering man from the scourges which beset him. The one seeks violent conquests, the other the relief of Humanity. The latter places one human life above any victory; while the former would sacrifice hundreds of thousands of lives to the ambition of one." Quoted in *Industry and Humanity*, pp. 4–5.

modern economic world—in a clash between the selfish interests in the economic world and the interest of the community as a whole. With this somewhat novel approach, he went on to discuss the forces which were likely to advance the life, peace, and health of industry and those which might work to its detriment (for which he used Pasteur's dramatic terms of "blood and death"). This contrast became the critical test which he brought to economic problems and he judged them accordingly. King had long acknowledged the existence of another party in industry besides the three generally accepted (labour, capital, and management), which he called the community. It provided the environment in which the other parties functioned, and the resources and powers which underlay production. All four parties were interdependent and essential, and trouble ensued when any one of them set out to neglect or dominate the others. Hence, King pointed out, the state must possess the right of intervention in an emergency to maintain the rights of the parties against one another and to represent the interests of the general public.

The book received a mixed reception, for its contents were very uneven in quality.[28] It dealt extensively in abstractions;* it was too ready to preach and to place reliance on moral concepts; it dwelt on human qualities and motives, on ethical canons and principles, on emotions and instincts carefully designated by capital letters. It was far too long. A lavish use of diagrams did little to help the reader who was already overcome by an excess of words. Judgments were frequently given on obvious things. King was by natural inclination prone to moralize, and this tendency was encouraged by the nature of the subject, which was, broadly, the restoration of personal relations to industry. His zeal as an uplifter, joined with his weakness for platitudes, often became very trying. A typical passage ran:

A solution of the problems of Industry is not to be looked for in forms, something more vital than forms is needed. A new spirit alone will suffice. This spirit must substitute Faith for Fear. It must breathe mutual confidence and constructive good-will. It must be founded on a belief in an underlying order which presupposes between individuals, not conflict, but community of interest in all that pertains to human well-being.[29]

*One reads with sympathy a comment of Starr J. Murphy on a report of King's to the Foundation: "I think I get the idea, but confess to a certain confusion of mind similar to that produced by attempting to read metaphysics, which always was too deep for me." Starr J. Murphy to W.L.M.K., Jan. 10, 1916.

There is nothing new or revealing in such a passage. These statements will be accepted by all: the great difficulty, of course, is to have the ideas implemented in practice.

The best element in the book was not its theoretical part, but the places where King drew freely on his extensive experiences in the industrial field to emphasize his points. The facts he had assembled cut through the excess verbiage and introduced a practical note which helped to bring the whole volume to life. "The truth is," he wrote in his diary in 1917, "I am not suited to theoretical work, but to practical and need the active touch with men and affairs to give vitality to what I write."[30] His publishers agreed; and they frequently advised him to insert more humour in the manuscript and not to hesitate to illustrate principles from his own life.[31] *Industry and Humanity* was really built on the author's past experience with the problems he had encountered as a civil servant; on the sweatshops of Toronto and Montreal; on the long hours in the telephone industry; on the conditions which he found in the manufacture of matches; on the labours of conciliation and on the Industrial Disputes Investigation Act. These contributions redeemed the book from obscurity. King could not do himself justice when he simply produced platitudes and wordy paragraphs: but when he wrote about events in which he had taken part, his special knowledge and his ardour as a student of social problems furnished the spark missing elsewhere.

King, the reformer, who from his college days had usually been on the side of the "humble and lowly" thus furnished the best part of the book. Moreover, King was even prepared, if traditional liberalism should appear to bar the path to action, to push it aside. The following sentences, for example, seem to contain some of the impatience of William Lyon Mackenzie mingled with the practical idealism of the investigator and the deputy minister, his grandson.

An awakened social conscience demands that conditions which make for ruin and decay in urban or rural communities must be eliminated, that the well-being of society as a whole may be conserved. I can think of no service possible to render Humanity greater than that of scientific research into occupational diseases, and the fatigues of Industry, and their effects upon the well-being of mankind. . . .

There is no private right, or law, or custom, so absolute or inflexible that it may not be cast to one side, if it can be clearly shown that it menaces personal health or stands in the way of community well-being. In the conflict between the temporary interests of selfish individuals and the permanent welfare of nations, the latter alone is entitled to consideration. Wherever, in social or industrial relations, the claims of Industry and Humanity are opposed, those of Industry must make way. . . .

By prohibition, by regulation, by inspection, the State in numberless ways has admitted the principle that the life and health of workers is not a matter which the workers themselves can be expected effectively to safeguard. Standards of living conditions and standards of working conditions are now definitely recognized as wholly essential to community well-being. . . .

Most effort to promote human welfare necessitates some interference with individual liberty. Where wisely applied and enforced, it is an immediate restriction, that a wider liberty in the end may be secured.[32]

There is no doubt that Mackenzie King was convinced of the truth of these statements: and Bruce Hutchison naturally raises the question why many Liberals who later supported King for the leadership of their party did so, knowing that his beliefs, as the book indicated, were far removed from ordinary Liberal doctrine as held in Canada at that time.[33] Hutchison is forced to the only possible answer that many of King's supporters did not comprehend the new leader's views or perhaps had not read *Industry and Humanity* to try to discover what King's views really were. It seems impossible to doubt the soundness of his conclusion that when the Liberal party came to choose Laurier's successor a few months later, it obtained an unorthodox leader, and eventually a welfare state, largely because it had not troubled to find out where that leader stood or anything beyond his political suitability as a young man with a promising record and a somewhat engaging personality.

Several people who were connected with the Rockefeller Foundation were inclined to be disappointed with *Industry and Humanity*. King's reputation, they felt, had rested on his practical work in industrial relations, and for this achievement they had nothing but praise. But why should he abandon this field in favour of one which was primarily theoretical, when his past gave no justification for the belief that he was especially qualified in it? Much to King's disappointment, even John D., Jr. was only lukewarm in praising the book, and said he found it "too philosophical" and somewhat long.[34] The Foundation was also not very enthusiastic, and eventually decided to drop the investigation of industrial relations as a major project. The public, thanks in large measure to the Walsh Commission, had become sus-

251

picious of and hostile to the work which was being undertaken, and consequently little good was likely to come from its continuance. Henceforth the Foundation resolved it would sponsor investigation of only special and restricted subjects.[35]

The writing of *Industry and Humanity* had been for a number of years a burden on the author until at last, on September 16, 1918, it was finished, just missing by a few days King's deadline of the anniversary of his father's birthday. This was a significant event in King's life and it was duly recorded in his diary:

I had concluded this part, which was the last of the book proper, and was reflecting that the book meant a dividing line in my life, that it was my life & work up to date so to speak, that hereafter I begin life anew under the conception of the presence of God in all things—when I looked up to the little clock on the cottage shelf & to my surprise saw both hands exactly over the hour twelve, I exclaimed aloud at the significance of the fact, then went to my little room & knelt by the side of the little bed in which dear mother suffered so patiently & so long, and prayed God that He would accept my life consecrated anew to His work, and give me strength to do and to reveal his work.*

It was some quaint fancy on King's part that moved him to "exclaim" when the hands of the clock came into certain positions (together, opposite, or at right angles) at the moment certain "facts" of importance made their appearance. The reference in the above paragraph is apparently the first entry in the diary in which attention is called to such a phenomenon. In later diaries, particularly in the thirties and forties, the frequency of these references suggests that the idiosyncrasy was becoming something in the nature of a fixed obsession. What significance he attached to the occurrences is difficult to determine; there is no key to his interpretation. The hands of the clock seem to have had as much importance in one position as in another. It may be that he interpreted such coincidences as confirmation of the rightness of the decision reached or the action taken at the particular moment. Or he may have taken them, for reasons which only he could understand and never explained, as a grand indication that he was in tune with the infinite. They comforted him. Certainly none of these

*That his ideas on superstitions had changed with time is suggested by comparison with the diary written only four years before the extract quoted above. "This was supposed by Geo. Duncan to be his unlucky day because of Friday & 13. What a tyranny superstition would become if one permitted it, one has to force oneself out of all such beliefs." Diary, Nov. 13, 1914.

outward manifestations ever conveyed messages of disapproval of his own conduct. One is impressed by the seriousness with which he records them: they were never treated in a spirit of fun; the religious overtones were always apparent.

King's relief at the finishing of the book was amply justified; for in addition to the usual barriers to literary accomplishment, he had encountered a number of interruptions, both personal and political. His family worries had been many, for both parents were reaching the time when they began to feel the effects of old age. In addition, his mother was in delicate health and his father had become almost blind. The eldest child naturally bore a large part of the load of responsibility for them. In the summer of 1916 he had taken both parents to Kingsmere and built an extension to his cottage to make them more comfortable. His father's death on August 30, 1916, had inevitably raised further problems. He had set his heart on having his mother live with him in Ottawa,* and he assumed the responsibility for her care in his own small apartment in the Roxborough. At one time her life was despaired of by her physician, but King took such strong exception to this verdict that he dismissed him in anger, thereby losing an intimate friend as well. His mother lived, saved, as he often proudly asserted, by faith and love. The dismissal of the physician in response to his gloomy diagnosis was typical: King always demanded that anyone with whom he was associated should remain in substantial agreement with him. In his eyes, this was an inescapable condition of his success and one which he applied to a wide variety of circumstances. His mother had died the day after the 1917 general election and his own defeat in North York.†

When King's connection with the Rockefeller Foundation ceased in February, 1918, he was forced to seek other employment. Politics was, for a time at least, closed to him by the decision of the electorate in 1917.‡ Once again, however, John D. Rockefeller, Jr. came to his rescue, and offered the suggestion that King should devote his energies to his specialty and set himself up as an industrial relations adviser. Eventually King decided to do so. *Industry and Humanity* was at this

---

*She had been living with her daughter, Jennie (who was now Mrs. H. M. Lay) at Walkerton, Ontario.

†Isabel King had died on April 4, 1915; Macdougall King was to die on March 18, 1922.

‡See *infra*, p. 259 *et seq.*

253

time some months from completion; and he therefore could work away at his book, keep a foothold in Ottawa to guard his possible political future, and yet accept retainers and special engagements from industrial firms to help them with their labour relations and allied problems. It was not a final solution; but, as King said, it would "allow time to disclose its opportunities," and it had the great merit of permitting him to keep his hands free for most eventualities. He wrote Violet Markham in May:

Perhaps I have been unwise in not taking advantage of this offer [to act as industrial relations adviser with residence in New York] at the present time; but, as you know, I have never abandoned my hope of a further opportunity in Canadian public affairs, and I told him [Rockefeller] quite frankly that, until at least this year was past and I saw what developments there might be in connection with the future of the Liberal party, I would not make any arrangement which would necessitate my going to live in the United States. I pointed out, . . . that, at least until the war was over, it would be unwise to sever my connection with Canada. The situation is a little different now that the United States is in the war, and inasmuch as my work has to do with Industrial Peace and is as such a service to humanity rather than to any particular country, there is, perhaps, no reason why the larger field of effort should not be preferred to one which offers practically nothing at all at the present time. Still I feel I should like to wait to see what develops.[36]

Rockefeller had promised to help King in his new venture. He did so. He recommended King in the right quarters, and he added to these good offices, part-time employment; with his experience and reputation, King soon secured the desired business. In 1918 this amounted to $1,000 a week and expenses. Over the next year or two King worked for a large number of American concerns, such as the Consolidation Coal Company, Bethlehem Steel, General Electric, and Standard Oil of New Jersey. In these engagements "labour relations" embraced a wide field, and King's ardour as a reformer and his concern for the working people frequently appeared. His diary, for example, contains the following remarks on conditions in the beet sugar industry:

I felt to-day that these workers were in a position of veritable servitude; a condition of slavery of as bad a kind as almost any conceivable. They have no home life whatever, spend the day amid excessive toil, no Sunday, no chance for reading, no opportunity for bringing up their families. All this is demoralizing to the nation's present and future. . . .

254

The working of three months at a stretch, with no holidays, is wrong. Working seven days in the week is wrong. Twelve hours a day is wrong; even eight hours without an hour for meals is wrong. Working amid humid atmosphere, without opportunities of bathing and cleaning before going out is wrong. . . . Men need hours to work, hours to rest, and hours for recreation, campaign or no campaign. Human nature cannot be expected to endure such conditions without degradation of the standards of life. . . .

The men at the top of this concern are mostly very wealthy men, living lives of social ease and amid luxurious surroundings. As I went through the factory, I felt, were I compelled to share the work of those I saw, I should certainly become an advocate of the Guild system of having Labor take over the entire industry.[37]

After reading these lines and considering the war-time circumstances under which they were written, one finds it difficult to sympathize with those critics who thought that Mackenzie King should have abandoned this type of work to become a volunteer in the army. Zeal (or political bias) may easily overcome common sense. To have taken such a step as this would simply have destroyed an exceptionally useful endeavour to promote industrial peace and hence to accelerate the war effort—in order to obtain the services of an unsuitable and, it must be feared, mechanically inefficient soldier of 44 years of age.

CHAPTER TEN

THE FIRST WORLD WAR AND ITS
POLITICAL CONSEQUENCES

IN THE EARLY YEARS of the First World War Mackenzie King's influence in Ottawa was naturally determined by his position in Canadian public life. No longer a member of the Government or of Parliament, and not even belonging to the party in power, he could not therefore affect the course of events directly. He was, it is true, the editor of the *Canadian Liberal Monthly* for a period, but his other work forced him to sever even this limited connection with his party. The only public office King held at this time was one on the national executive of the Canadian Patriotic Fund, a post which was far removed from active politics.

It was alleged in the election of 1911, and later in the election of 1917, that King was a pacifist and was even pro-German. Certainly he did not display enough enthusiasm for the war to satisfy many of his more belligerent countrymen. This was not, however, a new aspect of his character nor an odd quirk which had appeared as he became older, but an expression of liberal thought which was not uncommon at that time. King had been for years identified with several American peace movements and had taken a fairly prominent part in some of their activities.* He abhorred war; and like many other liberals he thought that the peoples of the world should be trying much more earnestly to develop better means to keep peace. Norman Angell had recently argued in *The Great Illusion* that no nation could ever win a war for in the long run all belligerents would become impoverished. Reformers were inclined to shift from ethics to self-interest as a ruling consideration in preserving peace, and they therefore tended to rely more than formerly on economic sanctions as the chief curbs on

*Cf. *supra*, p. 214.

aggressive nations. Modern wars, they believed, could not last long if the combatants had only a limited access to those immense financial resources without which no war could be successfully waged.

These ideas consorted easily with King's own experience in industrial disputes, and he was probably for that reason especially receptive to them. Human conflicts, he had found, were usually capable of settlement if people would agree to submit their differences to discussion and make an honest effort to appreciate one another's point of view. These methods admittedly had proved to be imperfect, but they were more apt to be effective and their results to last longer than could be hoped for with others.* Was there any reason why they should not be applied to the international field with much the same successful results that had been obtained elsewhere? King's attitude of mind was the same in all cases: an intense dislike for strife, coupled with the conviction that full discussion, personal contacts, compromise, and human understanding could alone in the end obtain general acquiescence in a decision.

This attitude is the chief clue to King's much publicized[1] message to William Jennings Bryan in 1914 which expressed the hope that the United States would control its loans to the existing belligerents, as "a part of that higher sense of obligation in international affairs," and thereby bring hostilities to a halt. It will be recalled that the Governor-General, Earl Grey, had earlier shared in this same belief, and in 1909 had tried to induce Laurier (through King) to take the lead in applying an Empire boycott on essential goods against an erring belligerent.† Is it within the bounds of possibility that King had learned his lesson in what was later alleged to be a lack of patriotism from no less a person than Grey, the representative of the Crown itself?

While Mackenzie King pursued his work largely outside the political life of Canada, the First World War progressed slowly towards the crisis that was to play such a vital role in the history of the Liberal party and to a lesser extent in the life of King himself. After its early mobile months, the war settled down into a set pattern. It became more static, based on long periods of trench fighting which were interrupted each year by the futile "push" designed to break the enemy line. On both sides, the wastage of manpower was enormous and it soon became evident that the war would be both long and costly.

*Cf. *supra*, p. 144.   †Cf. *supra*, p. 177.

Sir Robert Borden brought this impression back with him from a trip to Europe in 1915, and he immediately prepared for an extension of the Canadian war effort. This involved a substantial increase in the Canadian armed forces, and also confronted him with several political problems of great magnitude. Parliament would legally expire in the autumn of 1916 and an election would ensue, but Sir Robert considered that the national interest would be best served by stopping all political activity for the duration. He suggested, therefore, that the life of Parliament should be extended until one year after the end of hostilities, wih a moratorium for that period on by-elections and party controversy both in and out of Parliament. But Sir Wilfrid Laurier, a strong believer in the efficacy of an organized opposition as an aid to efficient government, thought Borden's proposal was both indefinite and premature. He rejected it, although he agreed to an extension of Parliament limited to one year.

At the end of 1915 Sir Robert Borden decided that further efforts were imperative; and he announced the immediate doubling of the Canadian armed forces, this time to 500,000 men. On January 17, 1916, he made it clear in the House that he did not propose conscription to fill this new quota, and the initial response of the country was such that it did not appear to be necessary. However, the competitive appeals of agriculture and war industry for the available men began to have their effect, and enlistments in the second half of 1916 rapidly fell behind even those needed for replacements at the front. A National Service Board was established to allocate manpower and in spite of protests by the Government to the contrary, conscription began to be considered by the public as a possibility.

The military crisis came to a head in the spring and summer of 1917. The Canadian Corps was heavily engaged in several major operations, and casualties were high. In no month in 1917 did enlistments match the requirement. Sir Robert Borden returned from a meeting of the Imperial War Cabinet with the determination that the Canadian war effort would be maintained and, if possible, intensified. There was some support in Canada even then in favour of conscription, but no one was in a position to know with certainty either the strength of this opinion or its extent. Parliament was again faced with the prospect of an election and with the further possibility that it might be fought on a far-reaching and divisive issue. The Prime Minister considered it imperative to avoid an election which might prove to be destructive to both national unity and the Canadian war effort, and he concluded that, however unpalatable it might be, the only way of avoiding it was a coalition Government—a coalition which would put the winning of the war above party animosities, would be able to extend the life of Parliament, and would also enact the necessary conscription bill.

Mackenzie King's political ambitions had not disappeared entirely during the early years of the war. It will be recalled that he had asked for Laurier's opinion before he accepted a position with the Rockefeller Foundation, and he maintained his candidacy in North York and his right to participate in Canadian politics whenever he should so wish. He became a member of the National Liberal Advisory Committee* in December, 1915, and attended several party conferences as an active partisan. At the same time he strongly resisted efforts on the part of his own riding executive to get him to play a more important part in his constituency. He pleaded pressure of his own work and used the excuse of a party truce to avoid any further commitment in politics. In the later years of the war he was also preoccupied with his father's death and other family troubles and his prolonged labours on *Industry and Humanity*.†

Absence from both Parliament and North York in 1917 gave King certain advantages since he was able for some months during a very critical period to avoid committing himself publicly on the dangerous issues which appeared in discussion. Yet he could live in Ottawa and maintain easy access to senior members of the Liberal party. He could of course communicate with his constituency also whenever it seemed to be necessary. He appeared there rarely in person, but frequent correspondence with his riding executive kept him informed of the feelings of at least one small part of the country, which he used as an index of the whole.‡

Late in 1916 King had heard from his riding and elsewhere of the complete lack of success of the last recruiting campaign, and the spring

*This was a committee of leading Liberals, set up by Laurier, to consider and report on various post-war problems; their report was to be used as a basis for future Liberal policy. A number of sub-committees were created, and the reports approved in July, 1916.

†See p. 253.

‡Throughout his candidacy King received an unusually informative flow of letters from his riding, and particularly from W. H. S. Cane and J. M. Walton.

of 1917 brought further indications that conscription was being favourably considered by many as the answer to the manpower problem. At the same time, the belief was growing that both a coalition Government and a further extension of the life of Parliament were desirable in the interest of winning the war. Such news from his constituents could not be anything but disquieting, for King knew that Sir Wilfrid Laurier was opposed to all three: conscription, coalition, and extension. His own assessment of the significance of these views brought him to the disturbing conclusion that conscription was doubtless necessary in principle, and that it should be widened to include all essential war services. King, by April, 1917, thus found himself in a most uncomfortable position for a man who possessed strong party feelings. He was at variance with the leadership of his party on the major questions at issue: he was opposed to an election, and in favour of an extension of the life of Parliament in combination with a coalition Government; above all, he desired to see conscription introduced as part of a comprehensive plan of national service. Mackenzie King could perceive at this time the danger to the party in Ontario should it follow any other line but this, and he therefore set to work to try to modify party opinion to bring it more into line with his own.

He lost no time in approaching Laurier and other Liberals, but the results were not encouraging. The leader of the Liberal party was firm in his opposition to any form of compulsory national service, even on the broad scale envisaged by King. The discussion continued in the parliamentary Liberal party for some days in May, 1917, but from this King, although invited to attend a meeting of members on May 17, was absent. He recorded in his diary that he thought that he would be in a minority of one at such a meeting in his support of conscription and the extension of the parliamentary term, and it must be assumed that he thought also that his presence there would do little good.

The next day Borden made his conscription announcement in the House, and the political crisis was upon the country. Conscription itself, however, was of little use without an effective means of bringing it into force and Borden shortly opened negotiations with the Opposition on a wider front. He offered Laurier a coalition Government with equal representation of both parties for the express purposes of carrying out conscription and any other measures necessary to win the war. Ten days later Laurier finally refused the offer and in his refusal made it plain that conscription was the main obstacle. He opposed the measure both in principle and as a matter of public policy. It was foreign to his instinct and conviction, and he believed that the necessity for the step and its probable efficacy could not be established.

The attitude of all members of the Liberal party on this matter was not nearly so clear cut. Laurier had consulted his colleagues and many political friends before he rejected Borden's offer, and he had found the party badly divided. Borden's terms had made it clear that coalition and conscription were indivisible. But, while conscription was a fatal objection to Laurier and to his Quebec supporters, it was, in the view of many English-speaking Liberals, the only thing which would commend a coalition. Laurier realized that there was no hope of holding the party together on the principle of conscription and he instinctively shifted his attention from the immediate problem of the coalition to the task of avoiding a split in the party on conscription when Parliament would be faced with the specific proposal. He therefore eagerly grasped at the idea of submitting the principle to the country in a referendum which would at least postpone the final step of enforcement of the measure and eventually might cause its abandonment for one reason or another.* Borden showed no willingness to accept the suggestions, but his attitude was unimportant in view of the reaction of the Liberals throughout the country. At last Laurier believed that he had found a principle around which all Liberals could rally.

King was among the Liberals consulted by Laurier on this proposal and he seems to have accepted it whole-heartedly. He at once began to sound out public opinion in Ontario, but the results were discouraging. A letter from J. E. Atkinson of the Toronto *Star* to King, for example, was a blunt acceptance of the necessity for conscription and an equally blunt refusal to delay its application by use of a referendum.

The lack of response in Ontario did not move Sir Wilfrid who remained antagonistic to all of Borden's proposals. If Borden had really wanted a coalition, he should have issued his invitation to the Liberals before committing the Government to a decided policy. Conscription itself was unacceptable and a "moribund Parliament" had no right to pass upon it. Laurier maintained his stand that if Borden would not

---

*The idea was not entirely new. Australia had held such a referendum and conscription had been rejected by the country as a whole and even by the military vote.

agree to a referendum, then he himself would take the responsibility of forcing a general election to give the Canadian people an opportunity to express themselves on the issue.

King made no further attempt at this time to influence Laurier on the subject of either conscription or coalition. He did, however, realize the problems attendant on an immediate general election. For many candidates, particularly in Ontario, an election would offer the disagreeable choice of defeat on the conscription issue on the one hand or the repudiation of Laurier's leadership on the other. King's proposal to avoid the dilemma was placed before Laurier on June 5. Let the Opposition grant an extension of the life of Parliament for one year if the Government, in return, would agree to submit conscription to a referendum. This, however, Laurier rejected on the grounds that any extension would be unacceptable to a large section of the party.

A split in the ranks of the Liberals was not long in coming. Within a week of Laurier's rejection of the offer of a coalition, Borden introduced conscription by way of his Military Service bill. One after another, the Liberals from the English-speaking provinces rose in the House to speak, and later to vote, in favour of the measure. Laurier moved an amendment providing for a referendum, but without effect. Even on this the Liberals could not unite. Some voted against the amendment and for the bill, while others voted for the amendment, and then, when it was lost, for the bill.

Borden took immediate advantage of this division in the Liberal party to advance his proposal for a Union Government. He made overtures to many of the leading conscriptionists on the Liberal benches, but was met with a blank refusal to co-operate. The debate in the House demonstrated that they could be detached from Laurier on the one issue, but not on others. Their determination became evident on July 17 when Borden introduced a resolution to extend the life of Parliament. The resolution passed, but the Liberals presented such a united front of opposition that Borden announced his decision to take no further action on it.

Throughout these developments King continued to be on the sidelines of politics. North York, however, made it impossible for him to remain in complete detachment from the events of the day. The riding executive pressed for a conference with him in the early part of June, and he as persistently tried to postpone the meeting. His letters to his friends in North York were masterpieces of evasion; while he assured them that their views were being advanced at every opportunity, he avoided any definite statement of his own opinions. He was not entirely satisfied with so passive a role, and he hoped to prevent a disastrous swing of Liberal opinion against Sir Wilfrid Laurier before it was too late. He by this time had begun to realize that Laurier was fighting a losing battle, but the day might yet be saved. Could not such people as the Liberals of North York be persuaded to abandon their interest in a strictly military conscription and exchange for this narrow form a more comprehensive one which would make it possible both to have conscription and to preserve national unity?

This approach to North York thus reveals the heart of King's general policy at this time. Unfortunately the wider form of compulsory national service made little appeal to Laurier, for he feared that the very word conscription was anathema in Quebec and if advocated in any form would merely leave that province in the hands of the extremists led by Bourassa and other nationalists. It was even possible that the change which King proposed would prove to be more divisive than the course the Liberals were already following.

King saw his worst fears realized while the Military Service bill was still under debate in the Commons. More and more the question was being narrowed down to a straight fight for or against conscription, and he could see from this only the most alarming consequences. If put to the public in this overly simplified form in a general election, the issue would be discussed as a simple moral question of right and wrong, and the finger of reproach would be directed at the number of recruits raised in Quebec as compared to numbers from other provinces. The ensuing racial fight would almost certainly destroy any hope of achieving national unity for at least a generation.

King was eventually drawn out of his seclusion by an invitation to Liberal members of Parliament and candidates from Ontario to attend a party meeting in Toronto on July 20. He went prepared to declare himself against the application of conscription until every other avenue was tried. The discussions were a surprise. The meeting was unmistakably opposed to conscription, coalition, and the extension of the present Parliament, and enthusiastic in its support of Laurier. The strength of the anti-conscription sentiment among the candidates from rural Ontario was encouraging, and there appeared to be a general

263

desire to bring about a speedy restoration of party unity in preparation for the coming election.

The satisfaction which King felt after this meeting was further increased when he proceeded to his constituency the following day. He found a few of the leading Liberals in the riding to be firmly conscriptionist, but others were far from enthusiastic. His conclusion was that pro-conscription feeling was not strong outside of a small, though influential, minority. "I find it is all due to a hatred of Quebec," he recorded in his diary. "A policy framed on a basis of hatred can work no good. cooperation & good will is the only basis of government. On this line I shall stand if I have to stand alone."[2]

But the optimism engendered by his brief visit to Toronto and North York was shortlived. On July 22 Mackenzie King reported to Sir Wilfrid Laurier on the Toronto meeting. He again urged Laurier to make national unity the main theme of any amendment to the conscription bill, and that night with Laurier's approval drafted a resolution on these lines which he thought might appeal to all Liberals. King showed the amendment to several party members and obtained their qualified assent to it, but his hopes were shattered when Sir Wilfrid refused to support it. With this last effort at compromise, King relinquished completely his role as a party strategist. He retired to Kingsmere to join his mother who was very ill, and to resume work on his unfinished book. For six weeks he devoted himself to these two interests and emerged from his seclusion only three times during the concluding days of the 1917 session and the appointment of the Union Government.

The formation of the Union Government was preceded by prolonged negotiations between Sir Robert Borden and the Liberal leaders in Western Canada. The Prime Minister had proposed a coalition early in the summer when the Liberal party had split on the conscription bill, only to be rebuffed by an unexpected re-forming of traditional party lines in the House. In the third week of August he opened negotiations with T. A. Crerar and H. W. Wood, the two leading figures in farmers' organizations in the West. The next day he interviewed Arthur Sifton and J. A. Calder, two prominent Western politicians. All were sympathetic, but refused to serve in a coalition under Borden. The setback was only temporary. He left his offer open to the Westerners, and reopened negotiations with representatives of central Canada.

In the meantime, Parliament had proceeded with preparations for the election. By the end of August the House had passed the Military Voters Act which conferred the franchise on every member of the Canadian armed forces and disfranchised conscientious objectors. This was followed closely by the War-time Elections Act, which was passed by the House under closure on September 14. The Act enfranchised close female relatives of members of the overseas forces, and removed the vote from those of enemy alien birth or mother tongue who had been naturalized after 1902. It became law on September 20, 1917, the day Parliament prorogued.*

Two days later Borden learned that four Western Liberals were willing to join his Government. Soon after, two Eastern Liberals, Hugh Guthrie and C. C. Ballantyne, were sworn in as Ministers. The remainder soon followed. Thus within a few days ten Liberals had been appointed to the Cabinet, and the coalition or Union Government was born.

King, throughout the period in which a Union Government was considered and finally brought to fruition, remained loyal to his leader. Sir Robert Borden's *Memoirs*, however, later quoted what purported to be an extract from Borden's own diary for August 7, 1919, referring to the election of King to the Liberal leadership:

Quebec and Mr. McKenzie have killed Mr. Fielding, whom the Quebec Members regard as having betrayed Laurier; but possibly Fielding may have been truer to Laurier than was King. I was told in the summer of 1917 by an intimate friend of King that he (King) was ready to join the proposed Union Government.[3]

This charge would indeed be a serious one, if substantiated. But an examination of Borden's diary for August 7, 1919, discloses an astonishing discrepancy between the diary and the printed *Memoirs*.† The entry in the existing Borden diary for this date concludes with the words "Quebec and Mr. McKenzie have killed Mr. Fielding." The remainder of the portion quoted in the *Memoirs* (and above) does not appear in the diary at all.[4] Moreover, a wider reading of the Borden diary is not more enlightening. Borden in 1917 recorded conversations

---

*King was of course absent from Ottawa, in seclusion, while the War-time Elections Act and Military Voters Act were passed. He had no part in shaping Liberal policy regarding these measures.

†Sole credit for this discovery must be given to Professor F. W. Gibson, who has examined the Borden diary with the kind permission of Mr. Henry Borden. No explanation of how the error occurred has been given.

with and about such leading Liberals as Carvell, A. K. Maclean, Pardee, Guthrie, Michael Clark, Rowell, Ballantyne, Calder, Crerar, and Mewburn. At no time is there any indication that he approached or considered approaching Mackenzie King. Further, there is no sign that King, even uninvited, was seeking a place in the Cabinet. To this evidence, or lack of it, must of course be added the unqualified denial that Mackenzie King himself made in the House of Commons in 1944, in referring to the statement in the Borden *Memoirs*:

> May I say, Mr. Speaker, that there is not a scintilla of truth in it. There is no mention made of who the intimate friend was who is mentioned by Sir Robert Borden, but I have no doubt that someone must have made some such statement to Sir Robert Borden, or he would not have included it in his memoirs. May I say that there was never a man in this country who was more constantly, steadily and unequivocally with Sir Wilfrid Laurier, and more opposed as he was to the Union Government than myself.[5]

The announcement of an election followed closely on the creation of the Union Government. On October 15, Sir Robert Borden issued a statement of the new Government's policy and on the last day of the month the date of the election was set at December 17.

Mackenzie King was, of course, not unprepared for a campaign and, as we have seen, had been planning his re-entry into federal politics for some years. His nomination in 1913 in the constituency of North York had been an essential part of the plan. The riding was traditionally Liberal, and although it had gone Conservative in 1911, it had done so by only a narrow majority, and was still considered to be excellent fighting ground for a Liberal candidate.

King's treatment of North York in the four years of his candidacy was nevertheless, in retrospect at least, nothing less than foolhardy. His nomination was the work of a small group of local leaders, and the riding as a whole knew little or nothing of him as a person. In the early months and in the summer of 1913, he did exert himself to become better known in the riding, and he spent most of July attending picnics and meeting party workers. Personal problems and his work on the *Canadian Liberal Monthly* interfered with a projected series of visits in the fall, and it was some months before he reappeared.

The next year he campaigned briefly for the local provincial candidate, but he did little more. His work entailed long absences from

Ottawa and even from Canada, and he observed the general wartime limit on party controversy. North York was not insensible to his absence, and the party executive kept up a steady pressure on King to return to the riding, if only for a few days. King's answer was a virtual ultimatum in which he offered to resign the nomination if the executive saw fit to have him do so. The decision to keep the candidate was unanimous.

In the year following King's attendance was little better. He carried on a steady correspondence with the riding in which the party officers urged him to pay more attention to his political fences and King retreated behind the party truce and the general expectation of another session before an election. He surrendered at last in the summer of 1915 and spent a holiday in North York. The visit was a distinct success and King left at the end of the period satisfied that his chances were good.

For the next two years the local association was left to shoulder the main burden of King's candidacy. Parliament had been extended for a year, and two provincial elections had given the federal Conservatives a serious set-back. King paid only one visit to his constituency in 1916, and only one in the first six months of 1917.

The latter part of 1917 produced greater activity on his part. Immediately after the Union Government was formed, he spent ten days in a state of indecision. There was an increasing certainty of disaster for the Liberal party on a national basis, and reports from North York were equally discouraging. The War-time Elections Act and the Military Voters Act were both certain to affect King in his riding, and this possibility of personal and party defeat even made King go so far as to re-examine his decision to continue in politics. At the same time he found that his old friends, Sir William Mulock—who had held North York for five elections—and J. E. Atkinson would offer him no support or encouragement. On October 23 King made his final decision to run in the election. Two events on that day swung the balance. King raised the question of a withdrawal from North York in conversation with Sir Wilfrid Laurier, and Laurier said flatly "you must run." According to King's diary this simple imperative settled the question. A letter from North York on the same day strengthened his decision by bringing to his attention unexpected support in his riding for Laurier and opposition to the Union Government.

With this decision finally made, King threw himself into the fight with great energy. He spent two weeks helping Laurier draft the Liberal manifesto, and then retired again to North York. In contrast to his conduct in the 1911 election, King in 1917 devoted all his efforts to his own constituency. He rejected invitations to speak from many candidates and even an invitation from Laurier himself. He made only two trips outside North York between November 5 and December 17, and both were to Ottawa on urgent family business.

The odds against King were heavy. He had generally neglected his riding, and he was faced with the necessity of making new friends quickly. In normal times this accomplishment would have been difficult enough, but in the atmosphere of the 1917 campaign it was nearly impossible. North York had been deeply affected by the war, and anti-French and anti-Catholic feeling was strong. Any representative, therefore, of Sir Wilfrid Laurier was bound to appear as a man fighting under the wrong leader and for the wrong principle.

The Liberal party organization in North York, moreover, as in many other parts of the country, was shattered by internal dissensions in this election. This was a split which was to trouble the party for many years to come. Some prominent Liberals in the riding stood by Mackenzie King, but others stood aside, and sometimes even openly supported the Union Government. Along with this, the normal sources of funds dried up and the local and Toronto newspapers turned against King.*

The campaign was short and vicious. King set out for himself a heavy series of meetings and interviews; he wrote his own literature and distributed it with Laurier's manifesto. Two points were emphasized in his speeches. He was opposed to the Union Government which was the creature of the "big interests," and lacked French-Canadian representation. He also attacked the War-time Elections Act as an example of the extreme and unwholesome methods which the Government was prepared to use to achieve its ends. With conscription he dealt on a specific basis. He was not opposed to conscription in principle, but he was unalterably opposed to the particular bill which brought it into effect. In this argument King fell back on the point of view he had formerly put forward to Laurier and to his

*Much of the money for King's campaign came from a personal friend P. C. Larkin, who had no connection with North York.

constituents: national unity was threatened, and the risk was disproportionate to the possible returns.

The Union Government forces were equally determined in their attack, and the worst fears of King were realized when the country abandoned itself to an orgy of vilification. The integrity, intelligence, and patriotism of the Opposition were denied in terms of unrestrained abuse. A persistent attempt was made to identify Laurier with Bourassa, and even with the Kaiser. King, in North York, was further identified with Rockefeller and Standard Oil. The nature of the attack may be judged by the following extract taken from the Newmarket *Express-Herald*:

> A vote for Armstrong is a vote for reinforcements for our boys on the firing line. A vote for King is a vote of betrayal to these same lads who bank on our immediate support.[6]

In a country in its fourth year of war, and in a constituency which had contributed heavily to the troops at the front, there could be only one result. King was defeated in North York by 1,078 votes—a remarkably good showing, however, when it is remembered that the Unionist majorities in six neighbouring Toronto constituencies ran from 5,104 to 18,237. The Laurier Liberals fared little better in the rest of the country. The Union Government was returned with 153 seats to Laurier's 82; of the Government's 153 members, 115 were Conservatives and 38 were Unionist Liberals. In the popular vote the split in the country was even more striking.* The Government was given a sweeping majority in Ontario and by the services. On the other hand, Quebec alone gave the Opposition an overwhelming four to one majority. Or to put the results in another way, the Government drew all its support from English Canada, sweeping in almost all the seats from Ontario and the West (127 out of 137), and the Opposition was driven back almost as completely on the support of French Canada (62 members out of 65 in Quebec; the three others were English-speaking, and the voters in these three ridings were predominantly so). The long-dreaded apparition of a sharp break between races on a national issue of great importance had at last made its appearance.

While the war moved on to its ending, King was engaged with his last few months' work for the Rockefeller Foundation, with the writing

*In popular votes, the Government polled 1,057,793, the Opposition 763,371.

of his book, and with his consultation work for various industrial firms. His residence was still in Ottawa, but his connection with political affairs was desultory.*

The armistice was followed by a period of grave economic and political uncertainty in Canada. The war had subjected the economy to unparalleled stresses and adjustments, and its abrupt cessation had begun to set in train a new series of forces no less disruptive than those which had previously moved in the opposite direction. The incentives to increase the production of wheat, to turn out munitions of war, to build ships, to expand manufacturing facilities, were suddenly removed by the armistice and although the wartime boom still moved ahead under its own momentum, some signs of faltering were evident. New capital investment was drying up; the farmer was beginning to think less of increasing his acreage and more of how he would carry his mortgage and pay for his equipment at inflated prices; the industrial labourer was trying with only limited success to keep his wages in step with the rising cost of living; shifts in population set in motion by war demands were slowing down; while the soldiers, returning home in tens of thousands, brought a host of problems of their own—employment, re-establishment, training, housing, etc. In May, 1919, the metalworkers in Winnipeg struck and thereby precipitated a general sympathetic strike which paralysed the city for almost six weeks. More moderate but related outbreaks occurred in Toronto, Vancouver, Calgary, Ottawa, and other cities, all symptomatic of a profound discontent which was general throughout the country.

The most potent single cause of unrest in Canada was the high cost of living, whether it took the form of a race between wages and daily expenses, or between the selling price of wheat and the outlay required to raise it, or between the revenues of the manufacturer and his costs of production. "I doubt," said T. A. Crerar at the time of the Winnipeg strike, "if there is a city of any magnitude in this country where there is not at the present time labour disturbance of some kind or another. Whenever the question is raised, the invariable answer is that the problem to be solved is the high cost of living—that there the remedy lies."†

*See *supra*, p. 254.
†*Can. H. of C. Debates*, June 11, 1919, p. 3333. The Lieutenant-Governor of British Columbia was so disturbed by the prospect of unrest and Bolshevik agitation on the West Coast that he urged Sir Robert Borden to have a British cruiser des-

An important factor contributing to the unrest was the common conviction that there would soon be a decided break in the prosperity of the war years, but no one knew how severe it would be or when it would occur. Thus to a considerable degree the anxieties of 1919 were anxieties of anticipation, which were made more acute by the uncertainties of the moment. So far as these worries centred on a drop in prices there was no immediate cause for alarm, for the movement of prices continued upward, although this unfortunately carried with it an increased cost of living with an accentuation of present discomforts and of more serious troubles to come. Nor did the employment situation show at this time any marked sign of distress, and even the returned soldiers, although giving rise to a number of problems, were absorbed into civilian life with only moderate difficulty. But uncertainty was everywhere; and each member of the community transferred his misgivings to his own special situation and endeavoured to protect himself for the future as best he could by immediate action. The returned soldier demanded speedy remedies for his real and fancied grievances; the working man struck for higher wages; the farmer demanded a market, higher prices for his crops, and a lowering in production costs; the employer, the manufacturer, and the commercial institutions—still operating for the most part at a satisfactory profit—were developing a wariness and timidity in their plans as they contemplated the doubtful days which lay ahead.

The general political situation, and especially the party situation, was also confused and unstable to a degree hitherto unknown in the Dominion's history. The outlook for the Union Government in 1919 was obscure and disquieting. It is true that the Government had seen the war to a successful conclusion, and now while the Prime Minister and some of his colleagues could be found in Paris helping to negotiate the treaty of peace, the Ministers at home were beginning to draft a substantial programme for the period of reconstruction. The term of Parliament had a long time yet to run, and the Government enjoyed a majority of from 65 to 70 votes. But behind this cheerful scene lay a party situation which was far from reassuring. The Union Government, as an entity, had virtually no corporate party membership in

patched there for protection. Borden scorned the suggestion in January, but by April had become much more sympathetic. Borden Papers, F. S. Barnard to Sir Robert Borden, Dec. 4, 1918; Sir Robert Borden to Sir Thomas White, Jan. 1, 1919, and April 29, 1919.

the Commons and not a single French-speaking Minister from Quebec. Although its nominal representation from Ontario and Western Canada was impressive, this was, by the very nature of the coalition on which it rested, impermanent. The Government had accomplished its essential purpose and its supporters, both Liberal and Conservative, could now feel free to revert to their old loyalties.

But successful parties are not apt to relinquish power readily, and many of the Unionist members (although this was not so evident among Unionist voters) were not at all anxious to break up the partnership. Reasons were easily found. The problems of war, it was urged, did not vanish with the end of hostilities, and the nation was expecting the Union Government to finish its task and remain in office until peacetime conditions were fully restored. The members of the Union Cabinet had got on excellently together and their happy association augured well for the future. Where would the country look for leadership? Where could it be found in the trying days ahead if not in the present Cabinet? These were plausible arguments and suggestive questions, although the rhetorical character of the latter was apparent when they were confronted with the facts. The truth was that with the notable exceptions of Arthur Meighen and N. W. Rowell the great bulk of the leading Ministers, from the Prime Minister down, were old, worn out from over-work, or in bad health, and they asked nothing better than a release from active political life as soon as it could be arranged.*

It was clear that if the Unionist party was to be preserved as an effective political body, firm and authoritative action was imperative. In truth, there was no *party* in the sense of an organization below the parliamentary level: workers had simply come together at the time of the 1917 election for a momentary co-operative effort on behalf of the Union Government which had left no permanent residue in the constituencies. A new platform should be drawn up, an organization of supporters of the Union Government created and placed on a permanent basis, and young vigorous men brought into the Cabinet to replace those who needed retirement. This rehabilitation, moreover, admitted of no delay: the golden moment must be seized before the

---

*Sir George Foster stated in his diary for December 11, 1919, that Borden, Ballantyne, Sifton, Reid, Burrell, Kemp, Doherty and himself were all *hors de combat* from one cause or another.

friendliness of war collaboration wore off and before the old loyalties and animosities of members and voters had an opportunity to assert themselves. Already the Laurier Liberals were trying by organization and argument to undermine the Union Government, and in this endeavour they had found an unexpected ally in Robert Rogers, a former Conservative Minister, who was conducting his own campaign to induce Conservative Unionists to abandon the coalition and openly re-assume control as Conservatives.[7] Every week increased the danger of disruption, as the old controversies, and especially those associated with the tariff, began to come to the surface. A number of the Ministers appreciated the danger as early as December, 1918,[8] and a Government caucus in February decided almost unanimously that a reconstruction of the party should be carried out "with proper organization, press, and platform."[9] Unfortunately, this was not possible, for the Prime Minister was in Europe, and even after his return to Canada in May his ill health caused further postponements. The consequences of this delay were set forth by the chief Government whip in a letter to the Prime Minister in June:

I should like to impress upon your attention . . . the absolute necessity for some immediate understanding as to the future status of the Unionist Party. If we are to continue as a party and go to the country as such we should, before we prorogue, have a definite understanding and a platform of some kind, as we are now more or less drifting while the Liberals are organizing on every hand, and [sic] which platform should be announced before the Liberal Convention so that we shall have the choice of planks. At the present time one cannot even call an annual or other meeting in his own Riding, because there is no regular Unionist Association, and one does not like to call a Conservative Association [meeting] for fear of offending those Liberal Unionists who supported us, and who might also support a regular Unionist Party, and so most of the Members have called no meeting.[10]

The outlook for the Liberal party was also darkened by many threatening uncertainties. The party had been in opposition for eight years, and it had suffered a disastrous defeat in 1917 which left it almost entirely dependent on Quebec with a little scattered support in Ontario and the Maritime Provinces. It is true that in Quebec the Liberals were in no danger of losing their supremacy, for the memory of conscription still rankled and remained the dominant issue,* and

*The Quebec provincial election of 1919 returned 74 Liberals out of 81 members.

support for them in the Maritime Provinces also showed no sign of weakening. But the prospects elsewhere were unpredictable and sombre, and if the Liberals were to regain their position as a national party they had to make very substantial gains in Ontario and the West. It became imperative, therefore, for them to persuade their former members to withdraw support from the Unionist Government and at the same time to induce them to rejoin the Liberals. The second step was not a necessary consequence of the first, for (as will appear below) a great many farmers in Ontario and the West were disposed to strike out for themselves and start a separate organization.

Sir Wilfrid Laurier lost no time in making the initial moves towards the rebuilding of the Liberal party. Eight days after the armistice he announced that a national convention would be held the following year to decide the Liberal post-war programme and policy. He stressed the need for reconciliation, and at a meeting in Ottawa two months later he gave an invitation:

We have differed in the past; but let the past be forgotten. Let us all be Liberals again, actuated only by conscience. If a Liberal who has been a Unionist comes to me, I shall not rebuke him. I will say, "Come, put your hand in mine, we must not look back, but ahead, not at the past, but to the future, for that is the only horizon for us.[11]

He also reaffirmed his faith in reciprocity and advocated a tariff for revenue rather than protection, a plain inducement to the dissatisfied farmers to co-operate with the Liberals.

Laurier died, however, on February 17, 1919, so that the difficult task of rehabilitating the party passed to other hands. It is difficult to estimate the effect of his death on the *ci-devant* Liberals. Inasmuch as he personified the opposition to conscription his presence could not help but serve as a barrier to reunion, and those who had displayed great courage in 1917 in forsaking him and following what they conceived to be their duty would need even greater courage to return while he still held the leadership. His very magnanimity would make him to some extent a living reproach to what was freely and bitterly described by many of his continuing supporters as infidelity. On the other hand, Laurier's hold on the affections of his followers was enduring, and his great career and personal warmth and charm still made a strong appeal to those who had turned against him politically.* All

*Sir Robert Borden's privately expressed opinion is not without significance for an assessment of Laurier's position: "On the whole I think there never has been a more

The woods at Kingsmere

Mackenzie King with John D. Rockefeller, Jr. (on the right), and a miner,
Archie Dennison, in Colorado, 1915

Leader and disciple: Mackenzie King and
Sir Wilfrid Laurier

Liberal Unionists received the news of his death with regret; but while to some it meant simply the severing of one more tie with Liberalism, others felt that the way back to the old party had thereby been rendered a little less difficult than it had been before. The extent to which this latter feeling could be utilized would depend in large measure upon Laurier's successor.

It is important to remember that the 1917 rupture was not restricted to the party strength as revealed in Parliament and in the popular vote. The continuing Liberals lost an influential section of their newspaper support, and their party organization in most English-speaking provinces was split at both the local and the higher levels. Several Liberal Unionist editors, such as J. W. Dafoe, had shown little restraint in their attitude to Laurier Liberals in 1917, and both sides might well feel some embarrassment at the thought of once again becoming friends and partners in a common enterprise. In the constituencies and party associations, too, many wounds were still fresh; and the defeated party workers (who, outside Quebec, usually formed the nucleus of the Liberal group) were still resentful and were determined to keep any of the rewards or offices in the giving of the party for themselves. Civil wars are as destructive for political parties as for nations, and in 1917 the Liberals had gone through a bitter civil war the crippling effects of which would take many years to overcome.

The course of the Labour and Farmer parties and the backing they were likely to receive from the more dissatisfied elements of the population were the most difficult factors to assess in the national political scene. The Labour party was by far the less important. It drew its support from the restive elements that were prevalent among the industrial urban population, and its organized strength was confined to those areas. As a party it did not cut much of a figure in national politics, but it made its influence felt indirectly on the Liberals and Conservatives through its not inconsiderable voting power. In several provincial legislatures, however, the Labour party was a force to be reckoned with, and before the year had ended it took twelve seats in the Ontario Assembly and became a partner in the provincial Government.

The Farmer or, as it was later called, the Progressive party drew its strength from rural Ontario and the Prairie Provinces. It was the out-

impressive figure in the affairs of our country." Borden Papers, Sir Robert Borden to Sir Thomas White, Feb. 24, 1919.

come of agrarian radicalism precipitated into a separate political existence by the shock of war and the temporary alliance with the Union Government. For many years the Prairie Provinces had been regarded as one of the main sources of Liberal strength; their views on many questions approximated more closely to those of the Liberals than of the Conservatives, and on election day they leaned as a rule decidedly in the Liberal direction. But the Prairie Provinces became ardent conscriptionists, and in 1917 they returned forty-one Unionists and only two Liberals.

The coming of peace revealed how unstable was this union, for almost immediately the farmers began to show signs of restlessness. They were by long experience distrustful of Conservative policies, and they had never ceased to resent two wartime acts of the federal Government: the disfranchisement of many foreign-born Canadians under the War-time Elections Act, and the drafting of farmers into the army after the Government had promised them exemption. The post-war movement of the farmers was therefore anti-Government without being necessarily pro-Liberal. Not only did most of them continue to resent the Liberal stand of 1917, but they tended to group the Liberals with the Conservatives and regard both as contaminated by their Eastern affiliations. It was a Western belief, prevalent before the war and now returned with all its early vehemence, that both the old parties had been captured by the industrial, transportation, and commercial interests of Eastern Canada, and that the two major parties therefore shaped their policies to the great detriment of the farmer.[12] Their suspicion was amply borne out, they alleged, by the record of the Conservatives, and although the Liberal professions were unexceptionable, the actual performance of that party differed little from that of its chief rival. Thus in the vital matter of the tariff, both the old parties had shown they favoured its continuance at a fairly high level, although the Liberals were conceded two creditable efforts in the establishment of the Imperial preference and the reciprocity proposals of 1911. It is evident, therefore, why the Western farmers, though not at all reluctant to leave the Unionist party, were loath to cast their lot once more with the Liberals, unless, of course, they could get concrete proof that the Liberals were really prepared to do what they, the farmers, wished. The Liberals, not being in power, were in no position to provide the proof, and the farmers were not willing to accept the past Liberal record as being adequate evidence of good intentions.

The Unionist Government was thus faced with an incipient revolt from its prairie supporters in the electorate, augmented by a substantial number from Ontario. These were confident and very much in earnest; they were filled with ideas, although most of them were far from new or revolutionary; they had one or two, but no more, able leaders, but they professed not to need leaders and on the whole they were inclined to distrust them. They were sure that a sectional party, held together by common economic ties, would be in a position to carry through their reform proposals with a singleness of purpose which the national parties, built on much wider and more diversified areas and interests, could not hope to emulate.

What, in concrete terms, did the farmers want? In November, 1918, the Canadian Council of Agriculture, representing the organized farmers from the Prairie Provinces and Ontario, drew up a platform which was later accepted by their separate organizations. It proposed the abolition of the tariff on many raw materials, on all foodstuffs, and on certain machinery; a reduction in the tariff generally; the acceptance of the old reciprocity agreement with the United States; an increase in the Imperial preference; direct graduated taxation on personal and corporation income; inheritance taxes; assisted land settlement for veterans; extended organization of co-operatives; public ownership of coal mines and public utilities; and a number of miscellaneous political reforms, such as the initiative, referendum, and recall, proportional representation, abolition of patronage, reform of the Senate, and the repeal of the War-time Elections Act.

The original purpose of drawing up the platform was to formulate the farmers' demands and to give strength and coherence to their agitation for greater consideration from the two major parties. In view of the well-known Conservative attitude on the tariff, however, it is likely that this influence was expected to be exerted on the Liberals, a supposition which receives partial confirmation from the Liberal antecedents of a large number of the leading farmers who helped to draft the resolution.[13] Some members of the Council, however, were prepared to go further and use the platform as a rallying point for a third party, although other similar platforms of earlier years[14] had had no such results. In any event, the farmers had defined their objectives; the platform was there for all to read and for any party to accept if it

277

so desired. Shrewd observers,* however, suspected that while some farmers might anticipate that this new agitation would eventually aid the Liberals, they might well prove to be wrong; for the movement was beginning to acquire so much drive that the local organizations were likely to take matters in their own hands and elect independent candidates of their own.[15]

The response of the Union Government to these conflicting economic and political demands was seen in the reconstruction measures placed before Parliament in the two sessions of 1919. Its programme was severely restricted by the limited funds available† and by its own desire to lower taxes and balance the budget. The magic era of systematic deficit financing had not yet arrived, and the Government was alarmed at a national debt which at the conclusion of demobilization would be in the vicinity of $2,000,000,000.‡ Annual charges on the debt would be about $115,000,000§ to which would be added each year about $35,000,000 to $40,000,000 for pensions. Fixed charges alone would therefore be approximately $150,000,000 annually out of a total revenue of less than $300,000,000.[16]

The specific programme of the Government was under the circumstances a creditable one. An effort was made to increase foreign trade, but negotiations were hampered by the necessity in most instances of loaning money to enable the purchase of Canadian goods to be effected. A number of such loans were authorized. The Government also embarked on a programme of public works to counteract an anticipated drop in business and employment. Expenditures on government-owned railways were increased, harbour improvements were undertaken, the building of ships to government order was continued for another year, loans were made to the provinces to promote better housing conditions, and highway construction was encouraged by a scheme of grants-in-aid to the provinces. The Immigration Act was amended to keep out enemy aliens and others considered undesirable. A new department of public health was established. Parliament created

*J. W. Dafoe, for example.
†The financial worries of the Government are clearly visible in the following letter from one of the Ministers: "We are arranging for a lot of work to be done in the several departments to employ the men let out of munition plants. We do not know where the money is coming from, but we can't stop now." Borden Papers, J. D. Reid to Sir Robert Borden, Dec. 1, 1918.
‡In 1914 the national debt had been $336,000,000.
§Under $13,000,000 in 1914.

a Board of Commerce to restrain combines and monopolies and prevent excessively high prices. The marketing of the 1919 wheat crop was entrusted to a Wheat Board and the farmer was given a guaranteed minimum price.

The Government was forced still further into the public ownership field by the inability of the Grand Trunk Railway to meet its obligations. Parliament passed an Act in the first session of 1919 to incorporate the Canadian National Railway Company which was to operate the Canadian Northern (acquired in 1917) and other government lines. In the second session another act authorized the acquisition of the Grand Trunk at a price to be determined later by arbitration.

The changes in the tariff were relatively minor. The Government's ingrained disinclination to introduce substantial reductions in the tariff coincided with its conviction that it could not afford to lose the revenue which the tariff produced and its desire to afford protection to new industries begun during the war. Speaking in general terms, the budget embodied a complete or partial removal of special war tariffs, a moderate reduction in the ordinary tariff, and an agreement with the railways to modify freight rates on agricultural implements shipped to Western Canada. On the other side, the loss in revenue was to be made up by the retention of the war tax on business profits, and increases in the corporation and personal income taxes. A new loan of $300,000,000 was floated to meet extraordinary expenditures (notably for demobilization) arising out of the war.

These proposals, so far as they went, were excellent, especially in view of the limited funds available; but they failed to check the mounting tide of disfavour which threatened to overwhelm the administration. Aside from the general dissatisfaction, there was no escaping the fact that the Government's present and future existence depended on its seats in Ontario and the West,* for there was no immediate prospect of securing any substantial foothold in Quebec or increasing its modest following on the Atlantic seaboard. The key to the situation in Ontario and the West was the farmers, and if the farmers could not be propitiated, the Union Government would break up and face certain defeat. The only effective approach to the farmers was through the tariff, and the action on the tariff had been unconvincing.

*The Government seats in Ontario numbered 74, in the West, 54; or 128 out of its 153 seats. A majority of the Commons was 118.

Some of the Cabinet were aware of the peril in which they stood, while others, perhaps misled by their comfortable majority in the House and the obvious disorganization of the Liberals both before and after Laurier's death, faced the future with confidence. Thus Sir Thomas White had written in January that the members of the Government were "working with fine co-operation and enthusiasm" and that the country was settling down nicely. "There is a good deal of pressure in the West upon Union Members there in connection with the tariff, but I am fairly confident that it will not give us undue trouble during the session."[17] The Minister of Railways had confirmed this for the most part. The public were inclined to be panicky, he said, but the Government could hold them; and he had reported in January that there was a marked swing to Union Government in the West.[18] A trip to the prairies by Mr. Arthur Meighen in January had produced substantially the same comforting news, with a reservation that something would have to be done about the tariff.[19]

The Ministers, however, were not at all agreed on the weight which should be attached to the tariff agitation of the farmers. One Minister referred impatiently in January to the "resolutions urging free agricultural implements, etc., etc., [as] the same old ones we have had for so many years"[20] and had earlier called the programme in the farmers' platform "so absurd [that] I cannot understand how such a body of men would agree to it. . . . I am sure no other Member of the Government [except Crerar] would consider it."[21] A parliamentary undersecretary, F. H. Keefer, wrote the Prime Minister in March that the need for revenue would probably bring a compromise which the farmers would be forced to accept.[22] On the other hand, J. A. Calder, a Minister from Saskatchewan, had no illusions and, following a caucus of Western members, warned Borden that "feeling [of] all Western members is good, but unless something material is done [concerning the tariff] we may have difficulty in holding followers. With few exceptions, if any, all Western members desire perpetuation of Union."[23]

The tariff was, indeed, the crux of the matter. It was all very well to plunge—or be pushed—into public ownership, to prop up temporarily the price of wheat, and to persuade the railways to lower the freight rates on agricultural machinery moving west: these the farmers wanted; but their outstanding grievance was the tariff. Efforts were made, of course, to avoid a break, and when the budget was being drafted the Prime Minister cabled from Paris to remind his Ministers of "the extreme importance of preserving so far as possible solidarity between our eastern and western members."[24] He eventually speeded up his return in order to arrive in Ottawa some days before the budget was introduced. But even his influence was insufficient to hold T. A. Crerar, the Minister of Agriculture, who resigned in protest.

> The present Budget [he said in the House] is a protectionist Budget. I think there is no disguising that fact. . . . It does not provide for reducing the costs of the necessary machinery to develop our natural resources in Canada. It does not do away with, and only very inadequately reduces, the duties on agricultural implements and other farm machinery, and does not make any real effort at solving the high cost of living by reducing the taxes on the necessaries of life that enter into the homes of all our people.[25]

The tariff had already been put to one test in the House when Andrew McMaster, a Liberal, had moved an amendment on supply in March. The Government forces had stood fast, supported by all the Western Unionists and even by three Liberals. In June McMaster offered a tariff amendment to the budget, and this time twelve Western Unionists voted against the Government. When, later in the month, the House divided on the budget itself, Crerar and eight other Western Unionists voted against it, and moved over to the cross benches between the Government and the official Opposition. The first major breach in the ranks of the Unionists had been made.

It was clear, however, that a large section of the Western Unionists were prepared for the moment to accept the Government's plea that it had reduced the tariff as far as the heavy demands on the treasury permitted. Even the rebellious nine, while continuing to sit apart in the House, gave a general support to Government measures. A Unionist caucus was held on June 26, eight days after the budget vote, and was attended by most of the Westerners, with the notable exception of Crerar. In response to Borden's plea for the maintenance of the coalition, the members of the caucus agreed to continue their support.[26]

A few of the Eastern Unionists, who had formerly been Liberals, were also beginning to feel uncomfortable. F. F. Pardee had withdrawn from the coalition in April,* and the chief Liberal Unionist,

---

*In 1918 Pardee had declined a position in the Cabinet. *Robert Laird Borden: His Memoirs*, II, 861–2.

W. S. Fielding, voted against the Government on the budget. Some months before Fielding had let it be known that he considered himself a Liberal, although he was prepared to vote for Government measures so far as they concerned the winding up of war activities. His old allegiance, however, became more and more pronounced during the early months of 1919.

Increasingly it was evident that a reorganization of the Unionist party and Cabinet was already overdue, but again Borden's ill health prevented any decisive action. In July he was compelled to leave Ottawa for a much needed rest. It is doubtful whether such a reorganization would have sufficed to retain the Westerners unless the Conservative wing had been prepared to make drastic tariff concessions which would have been quite at variance not only with its party's traditions and principles but also with Borden's stand against Crerar on the budget. One Unionist Minister, N. W. Rowell, did face the question squarely and was quite willing to make the necessary concessions. He, however, was a former Liberal, and his views cannot be considered to represent those of his colleagues, either Conservative or Liberal Unionist. Nevertheless a letter he wrote to Sir Robert Borden on July 4 contained a statement which cut right to the heart of the problem:

I believe that the establishment of a good understanding between East and West is of more vital importance to Canada than is the particular percentage of our tariff. I believe with our great natural resources, and the business ability and organizing capacity of our people as displayed in the war, Canada would prosper under any reasonable tariff so long as there is stability so that business can adjust itself to the conditions. I do not believe it is possible to secure this good understanding with the West without substantial reductions in our present tariff on a very large list of staple commodities. While I do not profess to speak with any intimate knowledge of the situation, it appears to me almost incredible that many of our most important industries could not carry on their business successfully on a substantially lower tariff than that which now prevails.[27]

It was the great misfortune of the Unionist party that it disregarded Rowell's advice. It was also the great misfortune of the Liberal party that it was not at this time broad-minded enough to forgive Rowell his past desertion and make a special effort to bring him back and utilize his exceptional ability in what was in its essentials a common cause.

The Liberal efforts in the first half of 1919 were naturally affected by the death of Laurier. The convention which had already been announced now became a virtual necessity, for to the original purpose of reuniting the party and formulating its new programme was added the even more important and urgent one of choosing a new leader. The task of marshalling the forces for the convention did much to help the party organization get back on its feet after the demoralizing split of 1917. In the East rehabilitation took the form of building anew on the old foundations and around the men who had remained loyal to Laurier. In the West, however, the Liberal federal organization was so completely broken up that it carried little weight, and the most valuable support came from the provincial organizations and governments which were, in name at least, still Liberal, although they were undecided on their future relations with the Liberals in the national field.

The parliamentary caucus chose D. D. McKenzie as the temporary leader of the Liberals in the House, and he was given twelve members as an advisory committee. Fielding was by far the ablest Liberal available, but he was still a bit of a Unionist and was not trusted by the inveterate anti-conscriptionists. McKenzie was an anti-conscriptionist from outside Quebec, and his choice was thus designed to placate both Quebec and the other provinces. Beyond this, he had few assets. He was cautious, unimaginative, parochial, and the contrast to his predecessor was painful even to his opponents. His attitude to the Unionist Liberals was mildly conciliatory, and early in the session he announced that in the old party home the light was in the window, the latchstring was outside, and all would be welcome. The effectiveness of the appeal was somewhat lessened, however, by Dr. Michael Clark, a former Liberal, who suggested that the invitation should have included a request to the wanderers to bring their own provisions, for the Liberal homestead appeared to contain no constructive ideas or policies which would make a return to it very attractive.[28]

This was a fair criticism, and it indicated the uncertain and vacillating course followed by the Liberals in Parliament during this period. On many issues they had no common policy, and they had no leader who could effectively direct their efforts in a consistent and united attack on the enemy. Fielding, who might have compensated for McKenzie's deficiencies, was still physically and mentally on the cross benches and no one could be sure whether he would support or attack the Government. Even when he attacked, his influence was not always helpful to the Liberals. He criticized, for example, separate Canadian representation at the Peace Conference and decried the increasing emphasis which was being placed on Canada as a nation in her own right, thereby driving one of the leading Quebec members, Rodolphe Lemieux, to reply that any one with such a colonial outlook had no right to call himself a Liberal.[29] Although the Liberals had before them a fairly comprehensive programme which had been drafted in 1916 by the National Liberal Advisory Committee[30] and a temporary platform announced by Laurier in January, 1919,[31] little or no use was made of them, presumably because the members were awaiting the approval of the coming national convention or because they considered new commitments to be undesirable under the existing conditions. They limited themselves largely to skirmishes and rearguard actions: against the War-time Elections Act, against government by order-in-council, against the high cost of living, against patronage, against government extravagance, etc. The chief exception was the tariff, and here, as already stated, their efforts were profitably directed towards emphasizing the divergence of views between the Western Unionists and their Eastern associates. They were also astute enough to defeat an effort by the Government which was designed to place them in opposition to the public ownership of railways, one of the few policies on which the Eastern and Western supporters of the Government were agreed. For the most part, however, the Liberals were content to criticize and mark time, realizing only too well their internal conflicts and the impossibility of making a successful bid for power until some of the old wounds had healed.

It is very probable that at this stage in the party's history these negative tactics were the best. The Liberals had little to gain by precipitancy, and their careful avoidance of anything which might give the Government an excuse for an election suggests that many of them at least were not unaware of this fact. The Government was unpopular and its hold on the country was steadily deteriorating. Dissatisfaction inevitably was focussed on those in office, and the wisest tactics were to allow it to do its work and to interpose no distracting issues, although here and there a pungent criticism or helpful suggestion might add somewhat to its virulence. It is true that the Liberals were leaderless and their numbers were still divided and unreconciled; but the plight of the Government, supported by an increasingly restless combination of diverse elements, was equally unsatisfactory. Above all, the future possibilities seemed likely to weaken the position of the Unionists and improve the lot of their opponents.

Time, the invaluable ally, appeared to be on the side of the Liberals, but only if they used their opportunity wisely. The great unsolved question was whether the Liberals could not only produce harmony within the party but also gain the co-operation and political support of many outside its ranks and especially the Western farmers. The success of this endeavour would depend primarily and almost immediately upon the party's ability to do two things: first, to reorient its policies to meet at least some of the political demands which were being vigorously put forward; second, to choose a leader who would be not only gifted, but acutely sensitive to the flow of opinion and sufficiently conciliatory to be able to bring together competing interests to their common satisfaction. Both these decisions rested with the national Liberal convention which was to meet in August.

CHAPTER ELEVEN

PARTY LEADER

"THIS IS TO BE A YEAR of momentous decisions so far as my own life is concerned." Such were the opening words of Mackenzie King's diary for 1919, and they in no way exaggerated the nature of the problem with which he was confronted. His life up to this time had been in general a preparation for public and social service, but the form which that service was to take was still unpredictable. He had been in turn a student in economics, politics, and law, a tutor, an editor, a civil servant, a Minister of the Crown, an author, and a consultant in labour relations; and although his present position as consultant was both interesting and profitable, he never regarded it as more than a stepping stone to something else. The greater his ability, the more necessary was it that his energies should seek some more permanent and continuous channels if it was to attain the maximum of effectiveness and if he was to achieve the maximum of satisfaction from it. This transient period was happily now drawing to a close. At the opening of the year three possible careers presented themselves, and it seemed certain that circumstances would force a decision about each within a few months.

The first alternative was substantially a continuation of the work on which King had hitherto been engaged for more than four years: the study of industrial relations which the Rockefeller Foundation had sponsored and the introduction of measures designed to provide more adequate representation of labour in the government of industry. He liked this type of work and his gifts as a conciliator and reformer were unquestioned. He had built up an international reputation as a consultant on industrial problems, and his intimacy with John D. Rockefeller, Jr. assured him not only employment but also the opportunity to excercise a profound influence on the labour policies of several of the leading corporations of the world. From these activities he could count on a minimum income of $30,000 a year.

The second opening was as the Director of the Carnegie Corporation where he would play the major role in overseeing the Carnegie benefactions and the disbursement of the income derived from an endowment of about $150,000,000. His salary would be at least $25,000 a year; and if he were willing in addition to his other duties to write the biography of Andrew Carnegie, there was a modest perquisite of $100,000 for this special endeavour. In all likelihood he would also become the adviser to Mr. and Mrs. Carnegie on all charitable matters: he would become their "philanthropic son" as Schwab was their "business son." The work with the Carnegie Corporation would be much less arduous than that as an industrial consultant. King described the advantages in his diary for the early weeks of January:

It would mean going to live in New York, being able to have a comfortable house & library there, to meet the best people of the world, to be in touch in a commanding way with the affairs of the world on the subjects which I have most at heart, industrial peace, international peace, social well-being. . . . Were I to go the world over, it is impossible to conceive anywhere on either side of the Ocean, where an opening more attractive could be presented.[1]

The third opportunity was a return to the parliamentary career which had been so abruptly terminated seven years before. King not unnaturally believed that here lay the largest field of usefulness for his peculiar talents. Industrial and economic problems were bound to be of increasing importance in the years ahead, and no one in Canadian politics could begin to equal his theoretical knowledge and practical experience in this area. Family traditions and interests were also strong; and the attraction of politics—once savoured, rarely, if ever, forgotten—lingered in his memory. The political outlook, moreover, was favourable. The life of the Union Government, now that it had done its part in "winning the war," was becoming daily more uncertain and a general election, though not imminent, could not be long postponed. Sir Wilfrid Laurier had announced his coming retirement, and if that occurred, the national party convention which had been already called would almost certainly choose a successor. The substantial record of the young Minister of Labour was still remembered, nor had the Laurier Liberals forgotten how he had stood loyally by the old man in the conscription election of 1917. King recognized that in any contest for the leadership, his chances were at least the equal of those of anyone else in the party.

His view of the first and second alternatives was by no means unfavourable. He could justifiably feel flattered at having two of the wealthiest families in the United States competing for his services. But there were, King conceived, serious drawbacks to both these proposals. He wanted to live in Canada, and while this might be possible for him as an industrial consultant, it would become increasingly difficult to maintain Canadian residence because of the frequent and growing demands for his services in the United States. He protested to himself, and sincerely, that he had no desire for money as an end in itself, and, less sincerely, that he took no pleasure in being brought into close association with great wealth. Such intimacy, indeed, could prove a heavy handicap in that it might easily destroy public confidence in any industrial, social, or political work he might attempt.* "I need action," he wrote further in his diary, "for [my nature's] highest expression. The primrose path does not make for greatness in any true sense. To be a benefactor with someone else's money is not as noble a part as giving one's own life in the service of others. It is life service that must be my part, to be true to myself & my traditions."[2]

Yet financial security appealed strongly to him as a necessary equipment for both marriage and public life, neither of which he felt able to undertake without some reserves on which he could fall back in the event of a reverse. A few years with Rockefeller or Carnegie would make him independent: he could then marry if he desired, and would be able to go into Parliament free to say or do what he wished. "It is freedom my nature craves, freedom to speak my mind anywhere & everywhere, without the restraints which capitalistic or other connection brings."[3] He was none too sure that even if he were to be chosen leader of the party, the salary would be sufficient to give him the full independence he sought. However, he was prepared to take that risk, and he drew comfort from the thought that if he ever became bankrupt in such a cause, he had many good and influential friends who would help him get on his feet again.[4]

*His brother (with a fine disregard of metaphors) described the Carnegie position as "a plutocratic *cul-de-sac* that would as effectually veto political aspirations in the democratic field as anything you could undertake." D. Macdougall King to W.L.M.K., Feb. 21, 1919.

The third alternative thus attracted him far more than the others. Indeed, even while he wrote of a "momentous decision," one can read between the lines of his discussion of the alternatives that the decision had already been made. His "swithering" was all on paper. His heart was set on a political career. The other possibilities could be but means to an end, to be used if necessary, but only until the larger opportunity presented itself. He felt the lure of politics, he had demonstrated his ability as a public servant, and his prospects of attaining the leadership were excellent. Success would mean the achievement of an ambition which doubtless meant more to him than he was consciously aware, a vindication of his grandfather and an opportunity, as he was fond of regarding it, to continue the work which his grandfather had begun. "It really looks," he wrote to his brother in February, "as though Destiny had intended me to continue to carry on the fight which Grandfather commenced so bravely on behalf of the common people in their struggle against autocratic power. His battle was against the political autocracy; mine must be against the industrial autocracy."[5] His diary for early January gives his views in greater detail:

There seems to be a call to me at this time, a call through the necessities [?] of the party, the need for leadership. It was never greater. The party's fortunes are at a low ebb, the lowest for many years. To build up a strong progressive party would be as noble & great a work as it would be possible to perform. There is the tradition of our family and the purpose of my life. These seem rooted in Liberalism. "Tell Willie I am glad he is speaking in grandfather's name." Those were Mother's last words sent to me. Surely there is significance in them. I have always wished to carry on grandfather's work, that is nearer my heart than all else. North York, Toronto, Canada, all these have associations which are as the very warp and woof of existence itself. I should rather serve my own country than any other land, tho' service for humanity would command me anywhere. . . . To live & die honoured & respected there is closer to my heart than any other ambition. . . . My desire, my inclination is all for politics.[6]

Within a week of the time he wrote these words his mind was made up. The further conversations he had had in the meantime with the Rockefellers and Carnegies in New York were less convincing than the renewal of family associations on a visit to Toronto in the middle of January. There he attended services at St. Andrew's Presbyterian Church, walked to the old home on Grange Road, and finally visited the graves of his father, mother, and sister at Mount Pleasant Cemetery. There he went, as he said, "to confess my wrong-doings, to pray forgiveness, to ask God's guidance and their tender watchfulness and care." He left feeling that his prayer, "What shall I do?" had been answered: "I came away to seek a new life of service with the assurance my heart needs most."[7]

The death of Sir Wilfrid Laurier on February 17 in his seventy-eighth year had important consequences for Mackenzie King. He felt Sir Wilfrid's death deeply, for he appreciated his leader's great qualities, and his own sense of loneliness and isolation, never long absent, was rendered all the more acute by the loss of one of the few men who had his affection and his confidence and to whom he could always go for sage counsel. Some reservations, however, had appeared in recent years in King's admiration for Laurier. His self-esteem and pride had suffered, for example, when Sir Wilfrid had been reluctant to make any decided effort to obtain a seat for him after his defeat in 1911, and again in 1917. King had a child-like desire to be appreciated, and this was accompanied by a pronounced sensitiveness to real or imagined slights. He was apt to become uneasy when Laurier bestowed any favour or word of commendation on a rival for the leadership, and he would brood over this imagined injury to his chances of success. His admiration for Laurier's generalship, moreover, had been severely shaken during the political crises of 1917, when he seemed strangely backward in accepting King's advice. The latter found difficulty in explaining Laurier's unwillingness or inability to anticipate the political menace which King so plainly perceived to be rising for the future. His own effort to make conscription more comprehensive in its scope and thereby to shift the issue of the election so that it plainly emphasized the necessity to preserve national unity was, King felt, much more far-sighted. He did not object to Laurier's referendum as such, but he thought it should be on a question sufficiently wide to call forth support from English and French Canada alike. Yet the old man had persisted in a course which was bound to split the Liberal party and to turn the electoral fight into one for or against military conscription alone. Surely, King thought, his proposal had been the wiser one and would have made more possible the task of holding the Liberal party together, and with it the nation itself. Did Laurier not seem to be developing rigidities which the party in King's opinion could ill afford at that time? Was not Laurier becoming too old and too tired to bear the weight of leadership? King's diary clearly suggests that as the months of 1917 went by he was beginning to think so.[8]

Laurier's attitude towards King, for its part, had been one of carefully guarded esteem. He entertained a higher regard for this young disciple than for many of his older and more experienced colleagues; but he was naturally cautious, and sometimes would show a slight preference for one, sometimes for another. In the interest of party unity, however, the balance had to be kept fairly even. Mackenzie King always liked to regard himself as the favoured candidate in Laurier's eyes and when his diary mentions Laurier's showing a preference for himself, the inclusion was not based on explicit statements but usually involved a deduction which was the result of wishful thinking on King's part. Laurier had, of course, been instrumental in bringing the young man to political maturity, and he therefore might be thought to have had somewhat of a prejudice in King's favour, but he does not appear to have shown it in any obvious way. One suspects, of course, that King was guilty of defeating his main purpose. His ambition was a little too blatant, his eagerness too pronounced, and Laurier may well have become weary of his aggressiveness and importunities, particularly when for a considerable time King was not even a member of Parliament. Laurier's generally favourable impression of King's many merits, however, remained strong, and there could be little doubt but that the young man's industry and capacity were exceptional.

Mackenzie King's awareness of Laurier's appreciation had thus always enabled him to contemplate his political future with some degree of assurance, knowing, as he did, that he would not be forgotten if fortune should again favour the Liberal party. At Laurier's funeral, to King's great regret, he was not asked to be a pall bearer, and he recorded that although he realized that those chosen had older claims of friendship or were to be preferred on other grounds, "there was a fitness and a justice in the situation which was being overlooked." Events were to provide ample justification for his statement.

Speculation on the Liberal leadership was naturally stimulated by Sir Wilfrid's death, and the politicians, the public, and the newspapers began to weigh the chances of the possible aspirants. In this review King received a moderate degree of support although it was conspicuously lacking in warmth and was based largely on his ability and his loyalty to Laurier. He and W. M. Martin, Premier of Saskatchewan, stood out as the only young men who warranted any serious consideration, and Martin's name was put forward chiefly because of a vague desire that the Liberal party should seek its new leader from the West. King's view was that his own chances were excellent. He fully believed that had Sir Wilfrid lived he would have guided the convention so as to secure his election, and even with Sir Wilfrid gone, he was convinced the convention would never choose anyone who had "betrayed" the leader in 1917. In mid-February he recorded this conviction in his diary:

All the Liberal members of the Union Government . . . failed in a moment of crisis, at a time of great need. They left their leader when the popular tide was rising against him. As Sir Wilfrid once said to me "it required a man of 'iron courage' to stand out in the last election." That stand will not be forgotten, and on it, and on Sir Wilfrid's known preference will turn the choice.[9]

When he reached Ottawa for the funeral, King found it as much concerned with securing a new leader as it was with paying its last respects to the old one. He was, indeed, waylaid by influential party members before he reached the capital, and the pace seems to have quickened during the few days he spent there. He was assured of the endorsement of the Toronto *Star*, and an encouraging number of people offered their support. Although King in no way neglected any of these informal exploratory conversations, he seems to have taken the Calvinistic attitude that the solution of the main problem was really predetermined and out of his hands. He quoted with approval in his diary: "For if this counsel or this work be of men, it will come to naught; but if it be of God, ye cannot overthrow it," and added: "[These words] express my attitude toward the possible leadership of the Liberal party. If it be of men, it will come to naught. If of God it cannot be overthrown—That makes it God's work, if it comes. God's work to be done in the world, that is all I meant it for."[10] One feels that in his heart he had little doubt of the final decision, and more so, perhaps, because he was, like most Calvinists, quite prepared to assist inevitable events to move in the right direction.

Yet despite his confidence in the result or, rather, perhaps, because of it, he was assailed during the next few weeks by many misgivings as to his capacity to do the work which his selection would make inevitable. He expressed some doubt whether he possessed the necessary moral, physical, and intellectual strength, but was consoled by the reflection that other contestants were no better qualified. He reproached himself because he had not studied more history and politics, and because he had not watched with sufficient care his "every thought and word." He realized that the Liberal party was torn with intrigues and discord, and that the leader's task of integration would make tremendous demands on his ability and patience. "It is essentially a venture of Faith, a belief that it will be the right thing in the end," he wrote in mid-March. Above all he was concerned about his lack of parliamentary experience, and he would have preferred to serve in the House as a private member for a few years before taking over the leadership. But once again he voiced the conviction that "there is a destiny in it,"[11] and resolved to go ahead. Characteristically, he does not admit that in confirming his decision he took any account of the substantial advantages of the political present over the political future. A leadership in the hand was worth incalculably more than one five years hence, when other contestants might appear and the entire outlook be very different and perhaps much less favourable.

At the same time that Mackenzie King was being troubled with these doubts and questionings he was endeavouring to make himself better known in the right places, since his obvious weakness as a candidate was his seven-year absence from Canadian public life, with the brief exception of his editorship of the *Canadian Liberal Monthly* and his unsuccessful attempt to be elected in 1917. In March he addressed the Empire Club, Toronto, the North York Reform Association at Newmarket, a citizens' meeting at Montreal, the Canadian Club, Young Liberals, and Trades and Labor Council at Quebec (two of these speeches were partly in French), and in April another labour group in Montreal. In most instances he spoke chiefly on the subject he knew best, the need for improving industrial relations, and his efforts met with appreciative audiences and a favourable press. He was thus able to remind French Canada of his fidelity to Laurier and Ontario of his more recent achievements, while suggesting to both his availability as a candidate for the leadership. He also managed to attend a number of informal party gatherings, to aid in forming party organization, and to meet party members whose support might later be useful.

An effort was made at this time to have the Liberal nomination for Quebec East (Sir Wilfrid's old seat) offered to Mackenzie King. At first he encouraged the idea: he realized that it would not only give him a seat which was reasonably safe, but one which would stand as a symbol of tolerance and racial goodwill and carry the implication that he might succeed Laurier in the leadership. Eventually, however, King put off making a decision until after the convention. He thereby was enabled to strengthen his position with the Quebec delegates while avoiding the very real danger of being considered by the rest of the country as entirely dependent on Quebec support and wholly identified with its interests.

King therefore walked softly among his French Canadian friends. He avoided any possibility of giving offence, and he was not above reminding them of his loyalty to Laurier in the gloomy days of 1917 when so many of his colleagues had gone over to the other side. The old bitterness over conscription he made no effort to accentuate or revive, although admittedly he did not shrink from the prospect of accepting substantial political support which sprang from a bitterness already existing. He realized, however, that past issues must be forgotten and a new start made, and this, translated into party terms, meant that as an initial move Liberals and Liberal Unionists must be reunited. "The War is over," he wrote in a private letter in May, 1919, "and for a long time to come it is going to take all that the energies of man can do to bridge the chasm and heal the wounds which the War has made in our social life."[12] This was his opinion as a candidate, and it furnished a clear indication of his purpose as party leader, and later as Prime Minister.

King had not actually refused a connection with Carnegie or Rockefeller but he had also decided to make no permanent commitment to either until after the convention had chosen the leader, for he realized that any such engagement would give the impression that he was no longer a contestant. This was agreeable to both corporations, but John D. Rockefeller, Jr. wished to continue to use his services, and King was able to make an arrangement whereby he would carry on temporarily with Rockefeller and with any others who might want to employ him in similar work, with Rockefeller furnishing a guaranteed minimum salary. This enabled him not only to reside in Canada, but to feel assured that if he failed to win the leadership he could still hope to enter Parliament and also be financially secure.

A pleasant interlude for King in the industrial relations projects he was engaged in was a trip abroad undertaken at Mr. Rockefeller's long-standing invitation and expense for the purpose of studying industrial problems in Great Britain. King was anxious to make this study, and to renew old acquaintances and to visit the battlefields on the continent. He needed the change, and the trip would freshen his mind and spirit for the strenuous days ahead. He would be out of Canada, however, from the end of May to the latter part of July, and the Liberal convention had been called for the first week of August. His absence at this time would appear at first glance to have been most inopportune; but in reality it furnished almost a literal demonstration of the truth of the French proverb: "She approaches by going away." His decision was the outcome of a mixture of pride, fatalism, and a shrewd appraisal of the way men's minds usually work. He also had discussed the trip abroad with Sir Wilfrid and Sydney Fisher; and though Fisher thought it a mistake to go, Laurier said it would make, in his opinion, very little difference to his possible success.[13] King was convinced that it would be well for him not to appear too anxious for the leadership, and he carried this restraint so far that he almost persuaded himself that he was genuinely indifferent to the outcome. Moreover, if the choice was predetermined, as he was inclined to believe, there was nothing to be gained by an undignified scramble for the prize. Most important of all, perhaps, he was too astute a politician not to realize that his absence would be an effective way to keep him out of a number of factional struggles, hampering commitments, and other difficulties and embarrassments. He had been sounded out in April by Sir Charles Fitzpatrick, Lieutenant-Governor of Quebec, who was anxious to act as a political broker between King and Sir Lomer Gouin, the Premier of Quebec. Fitzpatrick suggested a weekend at Quebec for "a tripartite chat" and in a later note ventured the opinion that "much good might be accomplished."[14] King, however, kept aloof. He wrote to Sydney Fisher:

I have hesitated accepting Sir Charles's invitation, not wishing to be drawn into a position which might prove embarrassing in any particular. I had a feeling, while in Quebec, that certain of our friends there were likely to be more concerned about keeping the tariff where it is than effecting any modifications of it. Under the circumstances, it has seemed to me the part of wisdom not to be involved in any discussion of this subject just at this time.*

It is likely that King also foresaw a possible danger in the development of a premature boom which might falter or collapse before the voting for the leadership took place. Indeed, any marked movement in his support or any real or supposed identification of his interests with those of any special group or area would almost certainly have led to an opposition or coalition being organized to block his candidacy. The most impressive part of Mackenzie King's decision was the thorough manner in which he adhered to it. He not only went abroad in person, he seemed also to withdraw in spirit and entertain no concern in the coming contest. No preliminary reconnaissance or preparation for the convention was made on his behalf during his absence, no person or committee was given the task of watching over his interests or sounding out delegates; no contact or communication with his friends was maintained during his trip on the one subject which lay nearest to his heart. However, he did time his return to Ottawa so as to give himself two weeks to "learn something of the lay of the land and possible developments before the convention is held."[15]

His European trip was a broadening experience, and he discovered with some dismay that his absence from public life had caused him to lose touch with many changes in contemporary ideas and institutions. He was surprised at the strong socialistic trend in English labour and found that it was inclined to look down on North American thinking on labour matters (including even the cherished Colorado Plan) as quite out of date. He renewed old acquaintances and met John Buchan, Sir Robert Morant, the Webbs, J. H. Whitley, and many others whose major interest was social reform. King's trip to the battlefields and his talks with such Canadians as Sir Arthur Currie and C. J. Doherty gave him a new appreciation of the achievement of the Canadian forces in the war. He came home with his Liberalism broadened and confirmed, with a more conscious awareness of his Canadianism, and with a strengthened conviction of the need for stressing the outward forms of Canadian autonomy.

*W.L.M.K. to Sydney Fisher, April 13, 1919. King later saw Fitzpatrick in Ottawa at the latter's request. He told Fitzpatrick frankly that one of his reasons for going away was to avoid entanglements with any faction or group.

The news which he received on his return to Canada was of a mixed character. A letter to Sydney Fisher in which he stated that, from what he could gather, matters in regard to the convention were "pretty much just where they were two or three months ago" brought a disturbing reply:

Glad to hear from you & to welcome you back *in time*. . . . Things are not at all as before. There is a strong movement of the financial protectionist interests for Fielding, & Gouin's Mont[real] Liberals are with it. Rural Quebec doesn't want Fielding but they don't want to propose anyone preferring that the names should come from other Provinces. . . . I know the old gang are quietly but insidiously pushing Graham. It was for that Pardee came over & Billy Moore wrote "The Clash"—to win Quebec for the Can. Northern gang.[16]

An old friend from Brockville, Arthur Hardy, wrote for some enlightenment on his plans, and said that he had heard that King would prefer to serve for a time under another leader before taking over the position himself. Would he favour Fielding as temporary leader? Mackenzie King's reply seemed to leave a fairly open field, but in its practical application reduced the rivals under whom he would serve to only one not very serious contender, Sydney Fisher:

If it were the feeling of the Convention that one of the elder statesmen should be put into the leadership at this time, I should not wish to stand in the way of any of our friends who had been loyal to Sir Wilfrid in the last political contest. I would be quite unwilling, however, to stand aside for anyone who helped to divide the Liberal Party at that time.

I leave it to your judgment to do what you think best in the matter; but you may go ahead with the assurance that whatever you and other of my friends wish me to do, either in the way of getting out of the running or staying in it, I shall be only too happy to do. In this matter, I must place myself wholly in the hands of those whom I know and am able to trust. Among the number, I recognize, of course, no better friend than yourself.[17]

Other letters in much the same non-committal vein were written to a few bewildered friends who, while anxious to help, wished to assure themselves that they really had a candidate. Even when the convention met there were no hotel headquarters, no campaign trappings, no meetings of prominent supporters, no organized bands of workers, but only a mild canvass here and a few interviews there which would have made any self-respecting convention worker in the United States withdraw in embarrassed exasperation. King wrote his brother after the contest:

I had no organization of any kind and did not seek the support of a single man. When spoken to, I told my friends it was a matter for them to consider and do as they might think best. I literally abstained in every direction from exerting any influence whatever. The trip to England was evidence of my desire not to intrigue, and my attitude since my return was not less visibly so.[18]

The national convention of the Liberal party which met in August was the first of its kind in Canadian history. The only earlier party gathering on a national scale was one held by the Liberals in 1893, but its purpose was simply to consolidate the party, arouse its enthusiasm, and have it discuss and approve a programme. The 1919 convention was designed to do not only these things, but also to provide for a permanent national organization and to choose a leader, a function which had heretofore been left to a parliamentary caucus. Although the choice of a leader, because of its importance, its novelty, and its dramatic possibilities, was regarded as the outstanding task of the convention, the peculiar circumstances of the time made the meeting itself and the platform it produced scarcely less significant. It was clear that the convention would determine in large measure how permanent was to be the disruption of the Liberals, to what degree the party could forget the animosities of the conscription election and reach out and meet some of the more recent movements which were breaking down traditional loyalties and threatening the stability of the old federal parties. Liberals, Conservatives, Farmers, and Unionists awaited the outcome of the assembly with mingled curiosity and misgiving.

The Liberals who called the convention together were determined that the control of it would be firmly vested in the staunch party members who had never wavered in their support of Laurier; but at the same time they were not unmindful of the need for conciliating the Liberal Unionists. The first purpose was accomplished by admitting all Liberal members of parliament and senators, all Liberal candidates defeated at the last federal election, and three delegates chosen locally from each federal constituency organization, which in almost every instance was still made up of Laurier Liberals. Liberal Unionists might qualify as members of the Senate or House of Commons "who desire to co-operate with the Liberal party," or they might be included in provincial delegations which were based on provincial party organizations and party candidates in the provincial constituencies. Inasmuch as every province except Ontario had a Government which was nominally Liberal, these delegations were apt to be of first-rate importance, although collectively they were greatly outnumbered by those who were there by virtue of Dominion affiliations. In the event, comparatively few federal Unionists appeared; the provincial delegations, however, contained a large number who had given support to the war policies of the Union Government but were now uncertain as to what course they should pursue. These Laodiceans were mostly from the West, where, it will be remembered, the support for Union Government had been overwhelming. Thus the Manitoba delegation, led by the Premier, came to the convention; but Premier Norris made it clear that the delegation was not necessarily bringing itself under the domination of the Liberal party and that if the convention adopted an undesirable platform or elected a leader not in accordance with a satisfactory platform the Manitoba delegation would consider that it was quite free to dissociate itself from any or all of the decisions made. The total number of delegates was approximately one thousand, and these were accompanied by a large number of alternate delegates.

The general political uncertainty in the nation and the need to conciliate and attract many wavering elements both within and without the Liberal party accentuated the importance of the convention's decisions on the platform. Special committees had been constituted before the meeting to receive and scrutinize material and give guidance to the resolutions committee of the convention. This committee submitted its proposals to the convention which discussed them and took such action as it considered necessary. The most important of these dealt with the tariff, Canadian autonomy, labour and industry.

The tariff resolution was aimed at lowering both the high cost of living and the production costs in industries based on Canadian natural resources. It proposed to admit free of duty the principal articles of food; farm implements; mining, flour-mill and lumber-mill machinery; gasoline; fishing equipment; fertilizers, etc. Tariffs on wearing apparel and general necessities, as well as on their constituent raw materials, were to be reduced, and the British preference was to be increased to 50 per cent of the general tariff. An allied resolution reaffirmed the reciprocity agreement which had been rejected in 1911, and expressed a desire to promote close economic relations with the United States.

The autonomy resolution strongly opposed any centralized Imperial control, and stated that no major organic change in Canadian and Imperial relations should come into effect until it was passed by Parliament and was ratified by a referendum.

The resolution on labour and industry accepted "in the spirit they have been framed and in so far as the special circumstances of the country will permit" the terms of the labour conventions set forth in the Peace Treaty, associated with the Versailles Treaty and the League of Nations, including the right of association, a living wage, an eight-hour day, a weekly day of rest, the abolition of child labour, and other reforms. The resolution also endorsed the introduction into industry of the principle of representation of labour, capital, and the community, and it stated that, "so far as may be practicable having regard for Canada's financial position," "an adequate system of insurance against unemployment, sickness, dependence in old age, and other disability, which would include old age pensions, widows' pensions, and maternity benefits, should be instituted by the Federal Government in conjunction with the Governments of the several provinces." Other proposals were also included, as well as two purely political reforms which wandered into this alien company, one advocating proportional representation, and the second "restoration of the control of the executive by Parliament, and of Parliament by the people through a discontinuance of Government by Order in Council and a just franchise and its exercise under free conditions."

Although these resolutions were considered in some circles to be rather radical, their Liberal provenance was unmistakable. The tariff and reciprocity resolutions embodied sound party doctrine going far back in Canadian history and restated in the earlier convention of 1893; the special mention of the Imperial preference and the reciprocity agreement referred to more recent manifestations of that policy. The emphasis on Canadian autonomy was in the best tradition of Blake and Laurier. The resolution on labour and industry had a much shorter history, for while some clauses derived their inspiration from the policies of the Laurier Government, the vital parts came from the proposals of the National Liberal Advisory Committee of 1916 which had favoured old age pensions, mothers' allowances, and insurance against sickness and unemployment.

It is, however, equally evident that these resolutions were also the product of the political conditions of their time. The resolutions on the tariff and reciprocity were directly aimed at inducing the prairies and rural Ontario to return to their earlier Liberal allegiance. The proposed tariff reductions, the 50 per cent preference, the list of commodities on the free list, and the endorsement of reciprocity were all to be found in the farmers' platform adopted by the Canadian Council of Agriculture in November, 1918; and although this source was never mentioned on the floor of the Liberal convention, the reappearance of these items in this explicit form at this particular moment was scarcely fortuitous. The resolution opposing any attempt to centralize Imperial control showed both Liberal uneasiness at the progress the Unionists had been making in asserting Canadian autonomy and a strong conviction that the Unionists must not be permitted to become more Liberal than the Liberals in this field. It, too, was a part of the farmers' stated programme, and the appended referendum clause was doubtless a mild concession to the same document which had advocated a system of direct legislation.

The rapid industrialization of Canada during the war and a general recognition of the growing importance of economic and social questions furnished the background for the labour and industry resolution. The great majority of the clauses embodied recommendations which had been put forward by the Mathers Royal Commission on Industrial Relations, a body appointed by the Dominion Government in March, 1919, to submit suggestions for the improvement of labour conditions. It had presented its report only five weeks before the Liberal meeting. The report of the Commission, no less than its appointment, was a symptom of the times, and it bore the marks of the industrial unrest, the Winnipeg strike, the mounting ability of labour to disturb profoundly the national economy. The war upheaval and the searching of heart that accompanied it had prepared the Canadian people for comprehensive changes, and reform in the labour and industrial field (which even before the war had been the subject of legislation in several other countries) seemed to be the next step towards the new Jerusalem. In short, Canada was for the time being, at least, in a reforming mood; and the Liberal party, compelled to look to its own rehabilitation and driven on by the need to attract Western agriculture and Eastern labour, was quite prepared to explore different and relatively untried paths.

Mackenzie King was naturally the chairman of the preliminary committee which worked over the material for the resolution on labour and industry before the convention met and he was also chairman of the convention sub-committee on the same subject which made a formal recommendation to the convention. This sub-committee was composed of delegates who were members of the House of Commons or of a provincial Assembly or past members of the House. No delegate on the sub-committee could be said to speak in any authoritative sense for capital or labour: exactly one-half were lawyers, and the balance came from agriculture, trade, and various other occupations. It is probably fair to assume that most of these had no special familiarity with the subjects before them; and while they might entertain some prejudices, they would be predisposed in most matters to follow the lead of a well-informed chairman. King's intimate association with labour problems and his activity on the Liberal Advisory Committee three years before gave him the knowledge to initiate a group of proposals and the necessary prestige to secure their acceptance. In this endeavour he could rely on the support of two other members of the sub-committee who had also served on the Advisory Committee in 1916 and whose views on this section of the party platform would be substantially the same as his own.

It is not surprising, therefore, that the hand of Mackenzie King may be discerned in almost every clause of the long resolution on labour and industry, although he had drawn freely from such sources as those noted above. King's original plan was apparently to present a report on labour and industrial relations to accompany the actual resolutions; but as draft succeeded draft in the committee the explanatory matter gradually disappeared and some of the resolutions were toned down or dropped. Thus up to the day before the presentation of the report it contained several paragraphs dealing with the removal of the causes of widespread national discontent: one recommended a capital levy on "wealth not usefully employed," and another demanded a forfeiture of all gains from war profiteering. Both of these were eventually struck out. Mackenzie King was responsible for placing some of the proposals as suggestions from the labour conventions of the Peace Treaty, a device which made it possible to avoid the awkward question of Dominion and provincial jurisdiction. The vital section on social insurance also came from him, although its real parent was the Liberal Committee of 1916. A number of relatively minor clauses were added on the initiative of labour representatives, both delegates and others outside the convention whom he consulted from time to time. The clause on proportional representation was the contribution of an Ottawa newspaper editor. The other anomalous postscript to the main labour resolution which dealt with responsible government was suggested by King himself, partly, no doubt, as a gesture to his grandfather, and also, perhaps, to enable the grandson, when moving the adoption of the general resolution, to switch to a subject which lent itself more readily to the kind of eloquent appeal he wished to make to his audience.

The resolution on labour and industry, like several others approved by the convention, was open to the criticism that it laid too little stress on general principles and was too detailed in many of the reforms it proposed. The tariff resolution was, indeed, attacked in the convention on that very ground, the obvious objection being that an enumeration of particular measures necessarily introduced an awkward rigidity into the programme. No party could hope to do all the things the Liberals promised except over a long period of years, and every specific proposal which was not immediately carried out when the party came into office was sure to become a weapon in the hands of the enemy.* But while the explicit wording may have been dangerous, it bore an air of reality and carried a conviction which a vague and ambiguous statement of principle would have lacked. "The people of Canada," as one speaker said at the convention, "want the truth, and the truth shall set them free." It was a noble if not a very accurate expression, and the convention welcomed it—and the disputed wording—with enthusiasm. But it was not without significance that after the new leader had been chosen, his speech of acceptance referred to the party's platform simply as a "chart on which is plotted the course desired by the people of the country." Seldom has a modest qualification been so aptly phrased and seldom has it proved so valuable an asset in later years.

The outcome of the contest for the leadership remained in doubt up to the final count. Even the actual candidates were not known with

*One of their opponents, at least, pounced on this the day after the tariff resolution was passed. "They have made the mistake of trying to arrange a tariff in detail instead of sticking to an expression of principle." Diary of Sir George E. Foster, August 7, 1919.

certainty until shortly before the voting began. Four eventually appeared in the lists: D. D. McKenzie and W. L. Mackenzie King were Laurier Liberals; George P. Graham was a Laurier Liberal whose record was a bit ambiguous inasmuch as he had voted for the Military Service Act; and W. S. Fielding was a Unionist.

McKenzie and Graham were not of the same quality as the other two contenders, although each had a fair following. McKenzie was a run-of-the-mill politician, and his temporary leadership of the House was his chief claim for consideration. Graham was an ex-Cabinet Minister of moderate ability, universally well-liked, but definitely not in the Prime Minister class. Both these men were sixty years of age.

W. S. Fielding was in a very different category. He had been Premier of Nova Scotia before 1896 and Canadian Minister of Finance for the entire fifteen years of the Laurier administration. He was Laurier's mainstay during that period, and on one occasion when Laurier wished to resign would undoubtedly have been indicated as his successor.* Fielding was an exceptionally able administrator, an excellent speaker and parliamentarian, and of such high character and capacity that he had the unquestioned respect of everyone, friend or foe. Two chief reasons were advanced against his election as leader: his age, which was seventy, and the fact that he had approved of conscription and had deserted Laurier and the Liberal party. His apostasy, however, had never been complete. He refused to take office under the Unionists, he sat on the cross benches to indicate the provisional nature of his approval, and some months before the convention he had largely withdrawn even the lukewarm support which he had hitherto accorded the Government. It was thus possible to turn the second reason against his candidacy into a strong one in his favour, for if the Laurier Liberals and the Unionist Liberals were to be re-united, Fielding's sterling character and his midway position would mark him as the ideal party catalyst for the next few years. This had apparently been Laurier's opinion; for while he was accustomed to look upon Mackenzie King as his successor (and in all likelihood never abandoned the idea of his eventually becoming the leader) he had during the last few months of his life spoken of Fielding as the one who could best make the Liberals forget their differences. Lady Laurier let it be known that this had been her husband's wish, and even appeared in

*This incident occurred in 1908. Halifax *Chronicle*, June 24, 1929.

the gallery of the convention in the hope of aiding the Fielding cause.

Although Fielding's prospects were encouraging, he was most reluctant to become a candidate. He believed that the anti-conscription feeling was still so bitter in Nova Scotia and Quebec that even if he were elected he would not be able to count on the united support of these provinces. He also disapproved of certain parts of the new platform, especially the resolution on the tariff. His advisers urged him to run because his election or even a substantial vote for him would furnish indisputable evidence that the convention was a genuine reunion of the party and that the Liberals who had been Unionists nevertheless retained the confidence and respect of the delegates. This appeal Fielding found it impossible to ignore, and on the day the voting took place he agreed to allow his name to go before the convention. He stipulated, however, that if elected he would demand, before accepting, a substantial modification in the platform.

The rules of the convention did not allow the candidates to address the delegates as such. The programme, however, was so arranged that on the evening before the poll (August 6) King moved the adoption of the resolution on labour and industry, and he was followed shortly by Graham and McKenzie, who nominally spoke to the same resolution but who actually wandered where they willed. On the following morning Fielding moved the adoption of the resolution on reciprocity.

In this preliminary contest of words Graham and McKenzie gave fair but uninspiring performances, and they were handicapped by coming after King and at the end of a long tiring day. Fielding spoke well and kept strictly to the resolution, but his lack of ardour for the contest apparently prevented him from reaching the top of his form. Mackenzie King, on the other hand, was both willing and enthusiastic, and good fortune had given him the best time in which to make his effort. He spoke quietly and effectively on his familiar theme of labour and industry, and then, using the "responsible government" clause of the resolution as a pretext, he turned to an allied topic. "It has been my desire, at the right time, and in the right place, to pay some slight tribute to the memory of our great and dearly beloved leader, Sir Wilfrid Laurier. This, I think, is the time, and this, I think, is the place, because the questions we are discussing here are bound up with the great principle to the maintenance of which he gave his life, for which he fought all his political battles—yes, and for which he died;

namely, the right of the people to control the Parliament of their country." There followed a brilliant attack on the record of the Borden Government and an eloquent panegyric on Laurier, and when he stopped, almost every delegate was on his feet in what the reporters called "a tumultuous demonstration." The time and place may or may not have been right for a tribute to Laurier, they could scarcely have been more so for Mackenzie King. King was always best when fighting with his back against the wall and on a subject in which he believed implicitly. Both these conditions were present, and both contributed to the result. "I spoke more to my own satisfaction than on most occasions," was King's own comment in his diary. "The audience were wonderfully receptive. It was the most difficult of all moments, and I felt I got over the last hurdle without a stumble."[19] The general impression seems to have been that up to this moment Fielding would probably have been the choice of the convention, but King's speech induced a large number of hesitant delegates to cast their votes for him.

Two other qualities which King possessed and which were plainly visible to all delegates were his age and his physical energy. "King's voice," wrote an enthusiastic admirer on the last day of the convention, "was clear as a bell and his face was bright as the morning sun."[20] These assets gave him a marked preference over his opponent: everyone may have been optimistic about the outcome of the next election, but there was no escaping the fact that they were choosing a Leader of the Opposition and not a Prime Minister. Youth and vigour were of tremendous advantage immediately, but they gained progressively in value as the delegates contemplated the party's uncertain future.

Little can be said here of the pull of the various forces at the convention, and any generalizations on matters of this kind can be only approximately accurate. The widely scattered areas from which the delegates came, the trials which the party had encountered during the preceding two years, and the uncertainty which surrounded some of the candidates made any comprehensive canvass of delegates very difficult and any accurate forecast impossible. The Graham forces were the most active, particularly in Ontario, where they had been at work for several months. McKenzie had little solid or permanent support; but he could count on a "courtesy" vote from the Maritime Provinces on the first ballot. Virtually no work could be done on Fielding's behalf until he had made up his mind, and when the decision

came, it was too late to do very much good. He had the support of
seven provincial Premiers, including Gouin of Quebec, although most
of the Quebec anti-conscriptionist vote opposed him. King's potential
strength depended in large measure on whether Sydney Fisher decided
to run, for they both appealed to much the same element. Fisher's
withdrawal early in the convention brought King not only his influence but also that of Sir Allen Aylesworth, who then became King's
chief spokesman and interviewer of delegates. Aylesworth carried
great weight among the Quebec delegates who remembered his un-
swerving devotion to Laurier. King's detached attitude to his candidacy
continued during the convention and he made very few direct efforts
to promote his cause. He even carried this to such lengths that he did
nothing to secure the names on his nomination paper: that responsibility rested on the North York delegation.

The first ballot on August 7 gave Mackenzie King a substantial
lead, Fielding was in second place, and McKenzie and Graham far
behind in a tie.* The second ballot, which was generally expected to
be the decisive one, proved to be so; but instead of Fielding forging
ahead, as had been predicted, he gained only 47 votes as against King's
67. Graham and McKenzie thereupon retired; and the third ballot
elected King with a majority of 38.

All the facts concerning these votes are not known, but it is generally agreed that the Maritime Provinces gave Fielding a small majority;
the West split fairly even, with Fielding getting most of the provincial
group and some others who were mindful of his 1911 stand on reciprocity; Ontario gave Fielding a substantial majority; four-fifths of the
Quebec delegates voted for King. The decisive factor in electing King
was the anti-conscription pro-Laurier vote in Quebec and the failure
of Nova Scotia to support Fielding, its own distinguished son. Quebec
could not forgive Fielding for deserting Laurier, and in Nova Scotia
both the defeated and the successful Liberal candidates were still
resentful because Fielding had used his exceptional influence against
them in the 1917 election. The piquant flavour of the convention, the
tactics which were employed to secure King's election, and a few of

*The voting was as follows:

	King	Fielding	Graham	McKenzie
First ballot	344	297	153	153
Second ballot	411	344	124	60
Third ballot	476	438		

the forces at work are brilliantly described by Sir Allen Aylesworth, in a letter written to his brother on August 8, the day following the election:

There was a big time this week in Ottawa. You can judge of it from the newspapers.

The big thing of course was the question of the new Leader. Fielding would have got it almost without opposition if he had not supported the present Government last year and this. It was a big contract to undertake to beat him out. Every one of the 8 Provincial Premiers with most of the Provincial Ministers were on hand working for Fielding. Gouin was in it too—as strong as any of them because of the Big Interest influence. Gouin stands in with the wealthy capitalists of Montreal—and talks of blue ruin to the country if the tariff is seriously interfered with at all. Dewart and his friends from here were for Graham but, failing Graham, were in the same boat with the others. It was just a rich-man against poor-man fight for who should get their man for next Premier of Canada. I went down intending of course to do my utmost for Fisher—on the lines of Laurier and anti-Laurier. And that element continued in the struggle of course all through. But on those lines we should have won *easily*. So the Fielding and Graham crowd talked Socialism against King—and argued that Fisher was a rich man and an aristocrat—to beat *him*. We found that these lines of talk were getting lots of our Laurier Liberals in the West and in the Maritime Provinces to agree to forgive and forget—and so to vote Fielding or Graham. Accordingly we had to consolidate the Fisher men and the King men—or lose. And that course being decided on Fisher and I turned in and nominated King. That did the business—though it was a tight squeeze in so big a Convention where hundreds of delegates were complete strangers to all of us Easterners. But the Frenchmen did the grand thing. They met in caucus—and actually turned Gouin down *cold*. They told him in plain English—that is to say in plain French—that he could run his own Local Legislature, but that *they* would run themselves in Dominion matters—and they voted—practically solid—to stand by Fisher and me *because* we were English and had stood by Laurier and the French Canadian.

That is the inwardness of the whole business. Fielding got 25 or 30 votes from Quebec—all of them Englishmen—and not more than 30 all told—whatever the poor old fool Globe may say.

You never saw such friends as those Frenchmen are to stick to a man they like. Dozens of them *hugged* me. They'd have kissed me if I would have let them—and they voted—every man Jack of them—just to stand by the men who had stood by Laurier. That is the whole story in a nutshell—let the newspapers prattle all they like.[21]

It is evident that the convention had a mind of its own, that many opinions and preferences remained fluid throughout the proceedings, and that a slight additional pressure in the opposite direction would have produced quite a different result. Wise heads had foretold that the convention, having drawn up a radical, Western, and young man's platform, would surely endeavour to redress the balance by placing the leadership in a conservative, Eastern, and old man's hands to carry out. But the delegates thought otherwise. They were consistent, rather than cautious; they decided to take the plunge, whole-heartedly and without reservation, and worry about ways and means later. There is reason to suppose that some of the delegates did not get exactly the type of leader they anticipated, but as the years elapsed few of them could be found who regretted the choice that had been made.

Mackenzie King had approached this great climacteric of his life first with doubt and apprehension, later with a calm certainty of victory and an assurance that he was the one destined to assume the momentous task. On the night before the convention made its choice he began to worry about the strain and animosities of public life and to question the wisdom of the step he was about to take. He was inclined to hope that Fielding would win, and that he himself could then enter upon a successful parliamentary career with the leadership as his final but not immediate goal. The next morning the picture had brightened, and he records in his diary how his zeal, his idealism, and his confidence returned as he read his *Daily Strength for Daily Needs*:

I thought: I shall see what is the little message for to-day. Here it is.—Look ye who doubt, and say whether or not ye believe there is a God who rules the world?

AUG. 7, *p.* 220.

"If thou canst believe, all things are
possible to him that believeth."

"Nothing shall be impossible unto you."

"So nigh is grandeur to our dust
So near is God to man
When Duty whispers low, *Thou must*
The youth replies, *I can*."

Emerson

Then dear old Carlyle:

"Know that 'impossible,' where truth & mercy & the everlasting voice of nature order, has no place in the brave man's dictionary. That when all men else have said 'impossible,' and tumbled noisily else-whither, and thou alone art left, then first thy time and possibility have come. It is for thee now: do thou that, and ask no man's counsel, but thy own only and God's. Brother, thou hast possibility in thee for much: the possibility of writing on the eternal skies the record of an heroic life."

T. Carlyle

"In the moral world there is nothing impossible, if we bring a thorough will to it. Man can do everything with himself; but he must not attempt to do too much with others."

[Wm. von Humboldt]

I wrote after the words, Aug. 7, the figures *1919*—I almost feared to write them, lest I should not be chosen & there might seem to be reflection upon my belief in God—That some voice of derision or mockery might be heard—but I said: I shall write. . . . Up to the reading of these verses, it was only my pride, not my inclination, which made me wish for victory. I felt now it was God's will that I should, & I asked Him to give me the needed strength. I believed to the extent that I carefully thought over during the morning what I should say in acknowledging the outcome. . . . I confess, but for the words of the little book, I doubt if I should have prepared any thing. All through the day they were in my thoughts. . . .

Just before the result of the last ballot was announced, I sat quietly waiting on the platform. . . . I thought of [Sir Wilfrid's] words that he wanted me to succeed him, and I felt—tho' still wishing I might be saved the choice, happy in the thought I had made an honorable run—I shall win or rather, I shall be chosen. There was no thought of winning in my mind. The majority was better than I had anticipated. I was too heavy of heart and soul to appreciate the tumult of applause, my thoughts were of dear mother & father & little Bell all of whom I felt to be very close to me, of grandfather & Sir Wilfrid also. I thought: it is right, it is the call of duty. I have sought nothing, it has come. It has come from God. The dear loved ones know and are about, they are alive and with me in this great everlasting Now and Here. It is to His work I am called, and to it I dedicate my life.[22]

CHAPTER TWELVE

LEADER OF THE OPPOSITION

MACKENZIE KING, though comparatively untried in politics, was in many ways particularly well fitted for the position of party leader. His political inheritance as a grandson of William Lyon Mackenzie and as Sir Wilfrid Laurier's bright young man recommended him to many Canadians. He had some administrative and political experience, and he had a record of successful accomplishment in all the tasks to which he had set his hand. He was young, vigorous, and exceptionally industrious. Above all, he had proved to be unusually adept in bringing about harmonious relations between conflicting interests by conciliatory methods. While this talent had been exercised in the sphere of labour and not of politics, it was the product of many qualities which were essentially political—an alert mind, a high degree of sensitivity in human relations, a bland and easy manner, an instinctive ability to find a common ground of agreement, and a gift for persuasive and mollifying statement which could minimize differences and make compromises more palatable.

These qualities Canada needed badly, and she needed them at once. The general post-war unrest and uncertainty were not to be quieted nor was any satisfactory solution of the many problems confronting the Canadian people to be found through the separate and exclusive groups and parties which were suddenly appearing and giving battle across the country. Only a party built on a Dominion-wide scale, sufficiently comprehensive to be able to integrate some of the existing groups and programmes and sufficiently well led to be able to make its appeal for unity and co-operation effective, could hope to carry Canada forward to the next stage in her development towards political and economic maturity. Although the Liberal party itself was not able at this critical time to meet the specifications, it was successful in choosing by accident or design the man who could in time evoke or bring about the desired conditions. Laurier's supreme purpose had been to maintain and strengthen the unity of the nation, and King also gave this first place in his endeavours. But the disciple faced a much more complex and troublesome problem than his master. Laurier's major effort had been directed at securing harmony between English and French elements in Canada; King was confronted not only with distrust and suspicion between the English and the French, but also with misunderstanding and antagonism between capital and labour, East and West, industry and agriculture. In their common endeavour to promote national unity both Laurier and King relied chiefly on the same powerful instrument, the Liberal party.

Mackenzie King's immediate problem was to secure a seat in Parliament, for his influence in public affairs could be most effectively exercised from the floor of the House of Commons. It so happened that no less than eight seats were vacant, and by-elections to fill them were to be held in October. The Liberal nomination for two of these seats—Glengarry-Stormont (Ontario) and Prince (Prince Edward Island)—had been offered to Mackenzie King as soon as he had been chosen as party leader, but he postponed making a decision for a few weeks until the general political situation became clear.

His difficulty lay in the fact that this choice of a constituency could not be considered apart from the broader question of Liberal strategy in the whole group of by-elections. The eight constituencies involved were distributed among six provinces, and the outcome of the elections would be regarded as forming a significant test of the relative strength of the Government and its opponents. The confused party situation, moreover, made such a group of contests unusually valuable, since they furnished a proving ground for the rising Farmers' movement to show its strength, for the Liberals to demonstrate their capacity to forget old differences among themselves, and for the Unionist party to prove that it could still resist the centrifugal forces which threatened to destroy it. Most important of all, perhaps, was the further question to which the elections might provide the answer. Was the third party to enter these contests as a separate organization without coming to terms with the Liberals or the Conservatives, or was it possible to find a common denominator which would make some compromise or understanding possible?

312

Some of these problems were presented in miniature in the constituency of Glengarry-Stormont where Unionists, Farmers, and Liberals were preparing to enter the fight. Mackenzie King was anxious to avoid an election in which a Liberal and a Farmer would be pitted against each other, for they would thereby split the anti-Government vote while advocating (in King's opinion) substantially the same things. His own candidacy in particular would place the Liberals dramatically in opposition to the agrarian movement and make any collaboration with the Farmers in the West, which was a vital requirement for a national Liberal party, virtually unattainable. When King discovered that the Farmers were determined to contest the seat and had not only chosen a former prominent Liberal for that purpose but had placed him early in the field, he declined to run. His views were stated in a letter to the local Liberal Association[1] and they give a key to what was for many years one of his major party endeavours:

The policy of the Liberal Party, as laid down at the National Convention just concluded, is so akin, in essentials, to the policy of the United Farmers, as set forth in their platform, that a contest at this time between a Liberal candidate and a Farmers' candidate could not, in my humble judgment, prove other than detrimental to the interests of both. Its only effect, so far as I am able to see, would be to create such a division in the forces which are naturally opposed to the reactionary policy of the Government in power, as to afford the Government just the opportunity it would like to have at the present moment.

As Leader of the Liberal Party, I should feel that I was placing both myself and the Party in a false position, were I to consider accepting any nomination which would have the effect at this time of placing me in an attitude of apparent antagonism to the Farmers of our own Province. Such a position would be as unjust to my own feelings as it would be unfair to the aim and purpose of the Liberal Party, as expressed in the platform adopted at the recent Convention.*

This did not mean that King did not approve of running a Liberal against a Farmer candidate under any conditions. He encouraged his followers to place men in the field before those from other parties were nominated, and, if it was a rural area, to endeavour to choose farmers as the Liberal nominees.[2] In this way he hoped to discourage Farmer

---

*The Liberals in Glengarry-Stormont did not contest the election, and the Farmer-Labour candidate defeated the Government candidate by 2,300 votes.

candidates, to emphasize the sympathy which he felt should exist between the Liberal and the Farmer parties, and to remove the responsibility for insisting on a contest from the shoulders of the Liberal organization. If, however, the Farmers showed no desire to co-operate in a joint attack on the Government or to promote policies which the two parties held in common, King was quite prepared to forget diplomacy for the time and do nothing to prevent a Liberal from entering the fight.[3]

He accordingly decided to accept the nomination from the Liberals of Prince, although it was understood that he would represent them only for the duration of the existing Parliament. He was elected by acclamation on October 20, 1919.

By taking a seat in Prince Edward Island King deliberately gave up any idea he may have entertained of running for Quebec East.[4] His own feelings and the advice of others warned him of the political inadvisability of allowing himself to be too closely associated with the province of Quebec. His early preferment by Laurier, his anti-conscription record, his unpopularity in Ontario (as illustrated by his showing at the convention and his defeats in 1911 and 1917), the marked support he had received from French-speaking delegates to the convention—all tended to identify him with Quebec and revealed the need for overcoming his political weakness in Ontario. An obvious but very useful move in this direction was to represent an Ontario constituency. So while he gladly welcomed the temporary hospitality of Prince, he once more accepted in September the nomination in his grandfather's old constituency of North York for the next general election. In the sentimental conflict between Laurier's seat and that of William Lyon Mackenzie, blood—with a strong dash of expediency—proved to be thicker than water.*

The story of the results in the eight by-elections is quickly told. The Liberals held two seats, the Unionists held two, and the Farmers won four, all of the last taken from the Unionists. Of the six seats which went to the Unionists and the Farmers, the Liberals had contested only one, Assiniboia, and this decision had sprung from a complicated and difficult situation in that constituency.

---

*King was therefore nominated on two occasions as the Liberal candidate for North York: on March 8, 1913 (*supra*, p. 227) and again on September 20, 1919, for the post-war election.

Mackenzie King had originally been anxious to run a Liberal candidate in Assiniboia, but he developed misgivings after some correspondence with W. M. Martin, the Premier of Saskatchewan. "It will never do," Martin wrote in August, "for the Liberal party in this province to get into conflict with the Grain Growers' Organization. . . . [It would] ruin the chances of the Liberal party in the province for several years to come."[5] And in another letter the following month he continued his point:

The whole situation in this Province with respect to the Grain Grower candidates is of such a serious character that we must proceed very slowly. If we proceed in such a way as to get the opposition of the Grain Growers Organization to my mind we will make a very serious mistake. It is true that a number of our strong Liberal friends in various portions of the Province insist upon this course being pursued but the majority of the men whom I consult feel that it would be far better ultimately to support the Grain Grower candidate in some of the constituencies rather than get the Liberals in active opposition to the Grain Growers. As a matter of fact, the main thing in Assiniboia is to see that someone is elected who is opposed to the present Government—whether he calls himself a Grain Grower or a Liberal makes very little difference.[6]

A group of Liberals in the constituency, however, became impatient with a policy of giving in to the Farmers and determined to run a man of their own even after the Farmers had nominated a candidate. King did his best to avert disaster by trying to make a bargain with the Farmers, and when that failed, by giving W. R. Motherwell, the Liberal candidate, much needed support. In the election Motherwell was so badly beaten that he lost his deposit.

Martin's advice on the political situation in the West was thus completely vindicated, and King was not the one to ignore the object lesson. The Liberals had not only been badly beaten, they had lost prestige and had been thrown into open opposition to the organized Farmers. To the general advisability of avoiding such contests was now added a further argument: in an election between a Liberal and a Farmer—at least in Western Canada—the Liberal stood an excellent chance of being defeated.

The radical tide in Ontario was rising as rapidly as in the West, and the Ontario provincial election, which was held in October within a few days of the federal by-elections, displayed the same broad tendencies. To the utter astonishment of everyone, and especially of the

315

Conservatives,[7] the Conservative Government suffered a crushing defeat. Its seats dropped from 77 to 25; the Liberals held their own at 30; those of the United Farmers of Ontario jumped from 2 to 43. Labour, which had had only one before, secured 11 seats. The result was a Farmer-Labour Government.

In this election King had tried to induce the Ontario Liberals to follow the same policy in regard to Farmer candidates which he had been urging on his federal followers, but his efforts were not always successful and there were a large number of three- and four-cornered contests.* The Liberals were nevertheless overjoyed at the punishment inflicted on the Conservatives in their strongest province. "All our men were jubilant," wrote King in his diary, "they see the handwriting on the wall, the overthrow of existing Toryism. It means as sure as I am writing that I shall be called on to form a government at [the] next general election if no serious mistakes [are] made in [the] interval."[8] He was, however, quick to appreciate the dangerous consequences which might follow this agrarian and labour revolt unless the Liberals were able to reach an understanding with the new parties. In this effort he clearly saw his opportunity to play the leading role:

The win of the Farmers [in the by-elections] . . . coming on top of the Ontario elections, creates a serious outlook for [the] Liberal party whilst it spells complete ruin to the old Tory party. The farmers' movement is a people's movement & as such the truest kind of Liberalism. The same is true of Labor, which has also shown its strength combined with Liberals, in B.C. against the present Government. One thing is certain, the Union Government is doomed completely. Whether the Liberal party will survive the Farmer-Labor combination depends on our conciliatory attitude. I fear Dewart [the Ontario Liberal leader] in this connection—He is not sympathetic with the farmers as he ought to be. Liberalism to hold its own must make clear that it stands for the essential reforms the Farmers and Labor are advocating. I have always done that & indeed as I see the situation, I am the one man who by natural sympathies & past record can bring these three groups into alliance & to a single front, should it come to the formation of a Ministry in Federal affairs later on. I welcome these new forces, as shewing our own men in the ranks of Liberalism that we are right in a progressive platform, also as shewing "the interests" that a wise conservative leadership of radical forces is better than reactionary Toryism. Time will have its effect on these "sectional" movements. Two parties in the end will be necessary & I shall win the Leadership of the Liberal and other radical forces, thru' being true to Liberal principles.[9]

*In 59 out of 111 constituencies more than two candidates ran.

This statement of King's party philosophy also occurs in his correspondence.[10] He believed that fundamentally there are two opposing forces in politics, one liberal and one conservative, and that the farmer and labour movements were simply manifestations of liberalism representing an indignant response to the autocratic reactionary policy of governments, federal and provincial, during the war.[11] The problem, as King saw it, was to induce these radical movements to accept liberalism as a common bond and join with the existing Liberal party to achieve in co-operation the purposes which they were unable to achieve separately. The Liberal policy, he said, was "sufficiently broad to reconcile secondary considerations, whilst maintaining with strength the main position."[12] If any of these movements persisted as class organizations, they would tend to arouse other class organizations in opposition and they would either destroy one another or would be driven back to their foster parent where they properly belonged. The present rivalry among liberal elements he therefore conceived as unnatural and transitory; it would defeat their common purposes by dissipating their resources and thereby prolonging the ascendancy of their enemies.

What was this "liberalism" which King thought would unite in one brotherhood the farmers, the trade unionists, the Laurier Liberals, and all men of goodwill? If one were to consult his speeches and his many references to "the rights of the people," "free and responsible government," and so forth, one might suppose that his was an orthodox *laissez-faire* liberalism or some mild modification of it. It would be closer to reality, however, to think of King's liberalism as being less theoretical and having a much more practical bent. Negatively, it was expressed as a hatred of entrenched privilege and special position, unless this was able to justify itself by good works and the willing assumption of responsibilities, and as a suspicion of great wealth unless, again, accompanied by a strong social conscience. Positively, his liberalism spoke for the essential worth, dignity, and importance of the common man. He was a genuine humanitarian, who believed that while the rights of the individual were extremely important, "the greatest good of the greatest number" must be preferred to that of the few. He was thus a sincere advocate of social reform and wished to bring about a greater degree of social equality. The traditional abstract rights and liberties of the citizen were excellent and must be preserved, but he wished also to secure many concrete benefits as well: an adequate reward for labour, shorter working hours, the representation of labour in industry, unemployment insurance, old age pensions, health insurance, and the like.[13]

Family tradition drew him irresistibly to the Liberal party, but he also thought he found there a more sincere concern for fundamental liberties, a wider tolerance, and an advocacy of those social and economic measures which were both necessary in themselves and the desire of the Canadian people. After the election of 1917 he wrote to Arthur Hardy:

> You are right in believing that this is the moment when we must begin, not to hew out a new party, but to reveal Liberalism in its true light, and to maintain its present position in accordance with past traditions. Our party had become overweighted with men who were Tories at heart, whose interest in politics was primarily that of furthering the ends of corporate interests and special privilege in one form and another. Such men, no matter by what name they are called, are not Liberals in any true sense of the word. Liberalism is a progressive, freeing force, and those who wish to advance its doctrines must be prepared to consider, first and foremost, the common people and their right to an enjoyment of a heritage here and now, not in some happy land in some hereafter. I believe there are enough of us to assist Sir Wilfrid in reconstituting the party on radical and progressive lines.[14]

Although King's words might not always suggest it, he was at heart a pragmatist who was primarily concerned with achieving concrete results: he frequently talked in vague generalities, but his aims could be extremely practical. His speeches abound in platitudes, abstract terms, and high sounding and often empty phrases, and these he found extremely useful since they helped him to evoke the appropriate stereotypes in widely different groups of people, and also enabled him to command a large measure of agreement without which all projects would necessarily fall to the ground. The same intangible quality of many of his pronouncements also had the solid advantage of leaving little for his enemies to seize upon and use against him. His programme was founded on his inner conviction of its social worthiness plus a shrewd appraisal of its timeliness, both as a political bond and as an issue likely to command popular support.

His enemies did not hesitate to label him an opportunist without principles. The accusation cannot be sustained. He was an opportunist, but with principles. The basic objectives were fixed, the steps towards those objectives and especially the advisability of taking those steps at a certain moment were variable. There were occasions, there were many occasions, when he would temporarily abandon a measure which he desired, simply because it was not expedient, that is, because more was to be lost than to be gained by persisting at the moment in that special undertaking. He preferred to sacrifice the lesser for the maintenance of the greater good; and although he may fairly be criticized for the way in which this worked itself out (inasmuch as every one is bound to have his own scale of values) his actions are quite defensible on his own appraisement. Over the years his progress towards realizing many of the reforms he desired may have appeared wavering and irregular, but he never lost sight of the main purpose towards which he had set his course.

This attitude of Mackenzie King to political questions cannot be fully understood until one has grasped his conception of the role which the political party should perform in a democracy, and particularly in the Canadian democracy. He considered that the parties in Canada had two major functions: the propagation and carrying out of ideas and policies, and the bringing together of diverse and even conflicting groups and interests so as to secure a working agreement and a measure of common action. The second function was in his eyes even more important than the first; indeed its operation might necessitate party principles being temporarily shelved or substantially modified in order to secure the necessary consent among the rival forces within the party —the highest common factor on which all could unite. Such a conciliatory and mollifying influence was indispensable in a country like Canada where the bonds of national unity were weak and the centrifugal forces of race, religion, geography, economic interests, etc. were unusually strong; these, if not held in some restraint, might quite conceivably disrupt the state itself.

King's belief in the party system and his conviction that the party was the necessary means for achieving popular consent thus led him at times to make enormous concessions to preserve the unity of the Liberal party. It seemed to him short-sighted indeed to push a much needed reform through Parliament and into the statute books at the price of a divided support and the virtual paralysis of that party for years to come. Gladstone had tried it, and had not only disrupted his party and been driven from office, but also failed to achieve the immediate objective, Home Rule. The danger of pursuing King's policy is, of course, obvious, for the party leader may well confuse the retention of office with the necessity of maintaining party unity, and jettison all principles in a frantic effort to stay in power at any cost. The discussion of this issue is better postponed until later events in King's life provide material for a judgment.

Once King's ideas on the essential liberalism of the Farmer and Labour movements were accepted as valid, the attitude which the Liberal party should adopt in the existing political situation was virtually determined. Liberals, King said, should not rest content with welcoming only their erring brothers who had temporarily thrown in their lot with the Unionists, they should also regard the new radical movements with sympathy and make it easy for the parties of protest to make common cause with them.[15] Expressed in concrete and realistic terms, the major problem was to find issues on which all could unite with the double purpose of strengthening the opposition to the Government and carrying out a common programme, although admittedly the need for compromise would severely restrict the area of effective action. Once the parties had developed confidence in each other through experience and association, they might well be prepared to make further advances which would lead ultimately to a permanent union. King's policy in dealing with the Farmers was to keep hammering away at the virtual identity of Liberal and Farmer policies, to persuade the Farmers, if possible, to work in immediate fellowship with the Liberals, and at all times to say and do nothing which would form a barrier to the union he was convinced would eventually prove to be inevitable.

Mackenzie King lost no time in applying this policy of reconciliation to all liberal-minded Canadians. The Liberal Unionists were the first in his mind, and following the lead of Laurier, he did his utmost to make it easy for them to rejoin the party. In a reply to J. E. Atkinson's warm letter of congratulation on the leadership, he wrote of this desire for reunion:

I am in most hearty accord with your suggestion that every effort should be made to emphasize the rapprochement which has already been effected in such large measure between Unionist and other Liberals. In this matter, there can be but one attitude from now on. The National Convention has laid down a platform of principles and policies. All who are in accord with views therein expressed, and who are willing to assist in making them prevail, must be recognized as members of a party whose past divisions and differences have faded from view in the larger single aim and purpose by which all true Liberals are now united. Only those are against us who are not for us; and this is a test which, in determining political allegiance, no man can apply to another, but each must apply to himself.[16]

Speaking in his by-election campaign in Prince Edward Island a few weeks later he again took up the theme:

Are we to believe that these men—men and women of Liberal convictions—numbering themselves by thousands, were not honest, were not conscientious, were not patriotic in the votes they cast, in the light of the knowledge they had at the time and the circumstances as represented to them? For my part, I decline to entertain any such belief. . . . Many of them suffered for conscience sake as they have seldom suffered in their lives. . . . It is not surprising that, having acted thus from motives of conscience and the highest patriotism, the issue of conscription being no longer a political issue in this country, these men and women are now but awaiting the opportunity to sweep from power a Government that has become a colorless affair, that is neither Liberal nor Conservative, and is Unionist in nothing save in name and the determination to hold on to office at any cost; and to join with their fellow-Liberals and the forces in this country that are making for progress, in placing in power a government that will be Liberal and progressive and have a policy it can call its own.[17]

King's conciliatory gestures were extended, of course, to the Liberal Unionists in Parliament, and in this move he drew some advantage from his absence from the House during the war years when political antagonisms were most acute and bitter. His relations with the continuing Liberal Unionists were on the whole friendly, and he and N. W. Rowell (who was anathema to most of the Laurier Liberals) regarded each other with mutual respect and esteem.[18] The ex-Unionists on the cross benches, led by Crerar, naturally received his special attention at all times, since they had already taken the first step towards what he hoped might prove to be the desired reunion.

King also took exceptional care to prevent his recent rivals for the leadership from nourishing any resentment. He insisted that D. D. McKenzie should continue during the autumn session of 1919 to lead the party in the House, even though King took his seat some weeks before prorogation. Fielding, who was reluctant to abandon his seat on the cross benches and his attitude of partial neutrality, was finally

321

persuaded to move to the Opposition front bench with McKenzie. When King took over the leadership, Fielding naturally became his chief colleague and supporter in the House and any reservations he may have had about supporting the Liberal party quietly faded.

This policy of reconciliation, while generally approved by the Liberals, had nevertheless its hostile critics who did not want to forgive or forget. Many staunch members of the party liked to dwell on the great betrayal of 1917 and professed a distrust for any who had been a party to it,[19] and there were those who feared that the returned Liberal Unionists might take over some of the higher positions in the party to which they themselves aspired. One of the irreconcilable old Liberals was Charles Murphy (Secretary of State in Laurier's Cabinet) who cherished a wide assortment of suspicions and hatreds, and who kept pushing gigantic memoranda at King and demanding immediate action against the alleged traitors.[20] Some Liberals reserved a special hatred for those who had been originally Liberals, then Unionists, and finally Farmers, inasmuch as they were considered to have been guilty of a double apostasy. Nor were the shortcomings and recriminations all on one side; for many Liberal Unionists were self-righteous and arrogant and looked down on their erstwhile colleagues as narrow-minded men who had in the crisis placed party interests above the common good.[21] Even the more charitable had their pride and were quick to show resentment if any doubts were cast on the integrity of their position in 1917. After so violent an eruption, it was not surprising that the lava cooled slowly.

A special aspect of the problem of reclaiming the former Liberal Unionists was presented by the prairie provincial Governments, which had strongly, though indirectly, supported the Unionist cause during the war. It will be recalled that these Governments were by the end of 1919 all nominally Liberal but although their Unionist sympathies had virtually disappeared, much of their antipathy towards the Laurier Liberals—based in large measure on Quebec's war record and a fear of domination by Quebec—remained vigorously alive. Little help, therefore, could be expected from this direction in the task of harmonizing the discordant elements in the national party. Moreover, the Farmer movement was already becoming so powerful and widespread on the prairies that no provincial Government, however kindly disposed, dared to come out and align itself publicly with the Liberals in the federal field. Even when these provincial Liberals had sent delegates to the national convention, they had shown an inclination to remain aloof, and some of them had been quite prepared to repudiate the decisions of the convention if they did not measure up to the prairie standard of enlightened agrarianism.[22] This attitude of being both in and out of the Liberal party continued for some years. Had the provincial Liberal leaders done otherwise they would have courted quick and certain destruction at the hands of both the Farmers and those Liberals who still cherished a grievance against the supporters of Laurier in 1917.

The prairie provincial Governments were thus compelled to insist that the parties in the provinces and in the Dominion should be regarded as operating in quite different spheres, and that despite the use of the same name, a Liberal in Regina might have very little in common with a Liberal in Ottawa. There was, of course, some truth in this idea, for a provincial administration, which was composed in the main of farmers and of those intimately connected with the farmers, was bound—whatever its name might be—to be primarily concerned with the farmers' interests, and it was entitled to be judged by its acts rather than its label. Why, it was suggested, upset a Liberal Government of farmers to put in a Farmers' Government? The argument gained force from the fact that at this time the Governments in all three Prairie Provinces were both honest and efficient. For all these reasons any association with the federal party could do the provincial Liberals little good and might well cause them substantial injury. A report from a Manitoba Liberal to Mackenzie King in September, 1919, indicated that the party unity as displayed at the recent national convention had hidden rifts, and that the Norris Government, about to face an election in Manitoba, did not count the federal Liberals as an asset in the provincial party's balance sheet:

I am afraid that our friends connected with the local Government are not as enthusiastic in standing behind the Convention as they should be. You are aware that they have a local election coming off here next Spring. They are not at all easy anyway and are openly of the opinion that close alliance between themselves and the Federal Liberals would injure them in their Provincial Campaign. I do not agree with them, of course, but that is the attitude they take. Consequently they are anxious that the Dominion Liberals should not become too active as they realize that standing aloof might also injure them.[23]

The same letter states that the provincial Liberals in Saskatchewan are equally "lethargic" in relation to federal politics. Seven months later (May 5, 1920) Premier Martin, who had hitherto been quietly co-operating with and advising Mackenzie King, found it necessary publicly to dissociate his Government from the Liberal party at Ottawa on the ground that close co-operation on both levels had proved harmful in the past. "I have, therefore, decided," he announced, "that as long as I remain a member of the Government I will devote my time and my best endeavours to the affairs of the Province. I will not be responsible for the organization nor for the policies of any Federal political party."[24] He qualified this statement, however, by adding that it did not apply to some issues, such as the tariff, in which the province was vitally concerned.

It is evident that the movement to bring the Farmers of the West and Ontario into the Liberal party was making very little progress at this time. The Farmers were, indeed, not in a co-operating mood. Their sense of grievance remained at white heat and their hostility was directed against both the old parties and the Union Government—with slight attempt at discrimination. "The farmers have temporarily gone mad," wrote one despondent Conservative after the Ontario election. "It is, one would think, another form of Sinn Feinism, as their whole cry is 'We for ourselves.'"[25] The Farmers would doubtless have replied that for the first time they were approaching a position where they might hope to receive a fair deal, and that in trying to gain power to protect their own interests they were simply following the example of other economic groups which had been doing the same thing for many years. To this end the Farmers laid about them with a will, and their immediate successes drove them on to greater efforts and a wider territory. Their goal, particularly in the early days of the movement, was not clearly defined. They were primarily concerned with repudiating the older parties and electing members of their own, and when, as in the Ontario election, they happened to be successful, they were not at all ready to take office as a Government. The more the Farmers prospered the more faith they developed in the integrity of their movement and the more confident they became of their ability to reach their objectives without the necessity of pooling their forces with any of the major parties.

Many of the farmers brought to the movement an emotional and almost religious fervour which raised their appeal to a much more lofty plane than that of their opponents. The old political parties, they asserted, were not only selfish and dominated by Eastern interests, they were bad and corrupt; indeed, a large section of the farmers believed that the party system itself was inherently harmful and should be abolished, and its place taken by a system of co-operating groups which in some rather obscure fashion were to conduct the government. This evangelical note was derived, in part at least, from the earlier progressive movement in the United States from which the Canadian farmers obtained many of their reform proposals, some of their vocabulary, and, eventually, even their name.[26] "We stand at Armageddon and we battle for the Lord" would have been as natural a slogan for them as it had been eight years earlier for Theodore Roosevelt.[27] This passionate earnestness had the merit of being simple and direct; it was also somewhat irritating, for the farmers' self-righteous way of talking and acting suggested that they recognized little competition in virtue. Thus the Secretary of the United Farmers of Ontario, J. J. Morrison, wrote in November, 1919, as follows:

Ours is not a class movement. Politically there is not a class plank in our platform. You admit in your letter that it is almost identical with the Liberal platform. Then why label us with a class endeavour any more than the Liberals? Is it not rather that the U.F.O. took the initiative in condemning our partizan mode of electing our legislatures? That we led in condemning the old machine politics that befogged issues and led nowhere except to political debauchery? We were following the shadow and ignoring the principle. . . . Labor has followed suit and has been endorsed at the polls although their platform is very much more class in its plank than ours. Still it repudiates party machine politics, which has tended to debar rather than to promote progress. Liberalism has been more progressive than Conservatism, but only in a degree. Both systems were bad and of late years were running mates identified only by name. . . . We have passed through an orgy of corruption that is a disgrace to true Canadians and was only made possible by the utter failure of machine party politics to defend the rights of the people. I followed partizan politics long enough and am disgusted. Something better must be found. I don't say that we have found it, but we have wrecked the machine and set people thinking. Now there is hope. We do not purpose to look back like Lot's wife in the days of old. We will not worship idols though they be Dewart or Hearst, King or Borden. "Progress" is our watchword, "Principle" our motto.[28]

There is here not the slightest suggestion that the Farmers' movement might be in part a reflection of their special economic interests; any imputation of class selfishness is brushed to one side, for anyone can see that they, and they only, are upholding the "rights of the people." Morrison is breathing a rarer air than his opponents, and his view from the mountain top happily overlooks the grosser elements in the political life on the plain below. But this attitude, which was by no means unusual in the movement, tended to make the Farmers almost unapproachable as a party organization and deaf to any suggestions of co-operation or compromise. Their motives were pure, their cause was just, their sword sharp, and victory sure. Why should they turn aside to negotiate? Why should they bargain or compromise?

It was quite clear by the autumn of 1919 that the time had passed when the Farmers' movement could be headed off, except possibly east of Ontario where the organization was spotty and relatively weak and where the traditions of the old two-party system were particularly tenacious. Throughout the rest of Canada the farming community had virtually repudiated the old parties and was pushing ahead with its own class organizations directed at political action. How did the old parties in the immediate post-war period propose to deal with this threat to their power, particularly in the decisive area of Western Canada? The answer of Borden, and later of Meighen, to the challenge of the Farmers was to fight them; the answer of Mackenzie King was to refuse to be drawn into a fight. Just as Laurier had responded to pressure from the farmers in 1910 by negotiating the reciprocity treaty, so King responded to a more violent agrarian revolt ten years later by a studied policy of immediate co-operation looking to ultimate absorption.

One of the resolutions passed by the national Liberal convention had recommended the formation of a national party committee with a head office and organizer at Ottawa. This and a number of related questions were considered in December at an organization meeting which was attended by representatives from all provinces. Andrew Haydon, an Ottawa lawyer, who had been the extremely competent secretary in charge of the national convention, was appointed national organizer, and John Lewis, a journalist, was placed in charge of the information branch. Provision was also made for raising money for the party needs, although, on King's insistence, it was expressly understood that he was to have nothing whatsoever to do with the party funds. Before the meeting broke up, King took care to secure its endorsement of his policy towards the Farmer and Labour parties.

The organization committee also decided that in the early part of the coming year, King should make a speaking tour in Eastern Canada and, if time permitted, in Western Canada also. He was little known outside Ontario and Quebec, and if an election should come soon, the Liberals would be badly crippled by a relatively unknown leader at the head of their shattered forces. The Eastern trip offered few difficulties, but a number of Westerners had written and advised caution in undertaking at this time a visit to the prairies. It was by no means certain that King would be welcome in an area which was still strongly resentful of the Laurier Liberals, and the result might well be a revival of strife within the party so that what was designed to serve as a rallying point might prove to be a humiliating failure.

The Liberals were slow in recovering the support of a party press, but in the latter part of 1919 a number of newspapers were beginning to make the shift. The Toronto *Star* and the Toronto *Globe*, for example, became increasingly critical of the Union Government and more in sympathy with the Liberal party. But the Western newspapers, led by the *Manitoba Free Press*, were still resentful of the Liberal stand in 1917 and remained almost uniformly hostile, although most of them were turning against the Union Government.[29] On the whole they led and were being led by the farmers' movement. The Liberal party therefore found it extremely difficult even to reach the Western farmer, who heard little but the virtues of the new movement compared with the vices of the old established parties or, in rarer instances, a plea for the continuance of the coalition.[30] When King was told of opportunities to acquire papers or found new ones which could be used to back the Liberal effort, he had to reply that there was no money in the party purse which could be used for this purpose. The alternative was simply to wait hopefully for the time when the Liberal cause would appear sufficiently attractive to win back its old support in the press and even, perhaps, make a few new converts.

The autumn session of Parliament saw the weight of debating skill in the House more evenly balanced. The Unionists had lost Borden through illness,* Crerar to the cross benches, and Fielding to the Liberals, while the worsening of the political situation dampened both

*Borden spoke on the second day of the session, and did not appear again.

their spirits and their confidence. The Liberals, on the other hand, had made substantial gains. Fielding was now on the front Opposition bench; King had come into the house eight weeks after the session began; Lapointe was becoming increasingly effective as a debater; and the morale had been stimulated by the national convention and the promise it held for the future.

The chief issues were the approval of the peace treaties with Germany and Austria, the agreement leading to the acquisition of the Grand Trunk Railway, and the soldiers' gratuities. The Liberal position was very much the same as in the year's first session. They were still not entirely united in their policy, they criticized freely but not consistently, and their chief endeavour was, while criticizing, not to allow the Cabinet to outmanoeuvre them and seize a profitable election issue from the proceedings. The Unionists were divided on the tariff, and they would have been only too pleased to be rescued from their predicament by a fighting issue on which they could unite and forget their differences. A refusal by the Opposition to approve the peace treaties might have given the Government an opportunity to raise the question of loyalty to the Imperial connection (which had proved so disastrous to the Liberals in 1911 and 1917), or outright opposition to the Grand Trunk purchase might have allowed the Government to dissolve on the question of government ownership.[31] This caution was probably necessary in the early part of the session,[32] though it became unnecessary after the federal by-elections and the Ontario provincial election had shaken the confidence of the Unionists.[33]

The debate on the approval of the peace treaties confirmed the disturbing indications of the first session that the Liberals were not agreed on the desirability of Canada's endeavouring to advance her status and powers as a self-governing nation in the Empire. Fielding and McKenzie took what might fairly be called a "colonial" attitude which stressed the impossibility of progressing beyond the strict legal position of subordination in external affairs. "Canada," said Fielding, "is not a nation, Canada cannot be a nation. . . . The pretence that we need this ratification or approval of the Treaty by Canada is arrant humbug. The ratification by Great Britain is beyond all question effective. . . . There is no need of a constitutional change in the status of Canada today."[34] On the other hand, Liberals like Lapointe and McMaster objected that Sir Robert Borden had not gone far enough in his assertion of Canadian autonomy. All the Liberals regarded with suspicion Article X of the Covenant of the League of Nations which guaranteed the territorial integrity of League members, for according to some interpretations it might automatically commit Canada to war. Mackenzie King was not a member of the House at the time of this debate. He was embarrassed, however, by the colonialism of Fielding and McKenzie, and the "liberal" speeches of Arthur Sifton and Rowell on the Government side did not make the views of his two chief supporters any easier to bear.[35] King was not only a strong nationalist by conviction, he realized that the Liberals would have to move to the left of Borden's policy or become reactionaries in Empire relationships. This emphasis on Canadian nationalism was later to play a vital part in his efforts to bring about a better understanding between Quebec and the West, and although he may not at this time have fully appreciated its possibilities as a bond, he was none the less sure of his stand. One of his supporters wrote to him about the desirability of a forward step:

We must not give the Conservatives any ground for classing us as reactionaries in the matter of constitutional development. I was quite prepared for them to take the stand they do. I think that I mentioned to you just before the convention that we should take advanced ground or they would take it. We did not go as far as we should have done, but we certainly can prevent them from outdistancing us. The weak point on their side appears to me to be the emptiness of their accomplishments. It is easy to call Canada a nation, but we shall want something more than names. . . . The idea of a declaratory resolution setting forth that no body or nation shall have the power to involve us in a war unless [our] Parliament consents seems to me excellent.[36]

With these views King said he was "in entire accord."[37]

While D. D. McKenzie, as mentioned above, was discharging the duties of official leader and spokesman for the Opposition in the House, King was endeavouring to fit into what had become an unfamiliar environment. Any parliamentary talent he had shown in his two years as a Minister had grown rusty from disuse and his long absence from politics had left him ignorant of many of the current issues. He was therefore quite content to allow McKenzie and Fielding to carry a large part of the load, although he was active in caucus and, after his election, assumed a progressively prominent position in the Commons. His lack of familiarity with some of the questions and his

329

disposition when he interposed in debate to commit the party to as little as possible combined to leave a poor impression, and the Government members were on the whole scornful of the capacity of the new Liberal leader. "He is not cut out for a leader, that is certain," wrote Sir George Foster in November.[38] "King is by no means a howling success," wrote another Minister. "He has left a distinctively weak impression on the House & the country."[39] A parliamentary undersecretary added his opinion that King had "made a very poor showing."[40] His opponents also seemed to think little of him as a tactician, and on one occasion an amendment he proposed is reported by the same commentator to have been "sufficient to consolidate the Government supporters," which up to that time had threatened to split on the issue.[41] Less than two weeks after King's parliamentary debut Mr. Arthur Meighen offered his tribute to the new leader in what it pleased him to call "the courtesies of debate":

The courtesies of debate require that an address in this House delivered by one occupying the conspicuous position [of] the leader of His Majesty's loyal Opposition shall receive at all events the attention of a reply even though that address be little more than a repetition, perhaps for the tenth time, of the same remarks uttered by himself as well as by many of his followers.

The congratulations of hon. gentlemen on this side of the House are due however to the leader of the Opposition by reason of the very manifest evidence of the determination on the part of his followers to show fidelity to his leadership—evidence that came frequently to our ears in the way of applause and which was all the more pronounced and impressive when we recall the long succession of demagogic platitudes that evoked that applause. He read a lecture which he has read, I think, every time he has stood upon his feet since he entered the House about duties to the people of members of the Government and members of this House, duties that I venture in all humility to suggest every hon. member of this House was thoroughly aware of, thoroughly conscious of, long before the House received this rather nauseating reminder from the hon. gentleman.

If I have one suggestion to offer to the fair rose of expectancy of His Majesty's loyal Opposition, it is that when we have a concrete subject before the House for debate he would be good enough to offer some remarks which really bear upon the merits of the issue and leave out of consideration, if he possibly can, these old, hackneyed phrases "democracy," "autocracy of executives," and all the rest of it which have no more relevancy to this discussion than were he to discuss the merits of the government of Japan.[42]

The lack of restraint in Mr. Meighen's language is so marked that one is tempted to suggest that subconsciously he must have recognized his Nemesis, who in future years was destined to bring about his defeat, his humiliation, and his retirement from public life. A more probable interpretation, however, is that he, himself a superb debater, was utterly exasperated at the fumbling efforts of his opponent and that he set out to reveal to the Liberals what a feeble threat was contained in the person of their new leader. Mr. Meighen was yet to learn that there was a great deal more to political leadership than making brilliant speeches in the House, and that he himself would prove capable of developing wider and more significant areas of ineptitude than King had ever dreamt of.

A pleasant incident at this stage of King's life was the conferring of the degree of Doctor of Laws, *honoris causa*, by Queen's University (Kingston) on October 16, 1919, on the occasion of the installation of a new principal and a new chancellor. It was the first of many such degrees which were to come to him in later years, but, being the first, it was the more esteemed. The reasons given were his "eminence as a citizen, as a thinker, and as a constructive statesman." He also represented Harvard at the installation ceremonies. Any special mark of distinction almost always evoked some family memories. In a letter to his brother he expressed the regret, stated many times before, that his father had not had such an honour conferred on him, and he mentioned fondly how his sister Isabel would have responded to this new recognition. "It used to be a source of great amusement to her to say to me: 'Yes, Willie is a great little man.' I can imagine how she would have chuckled over this combination of distinctions."[43]

Another event which gave him even greater pleasure was the gift by John D. Rockefeller of $5,000,000* to the Rockefeller Foundation which was to be devoted to medical education and research in Canada. Some months earlier King had made representations to John D. Rockefeller, Jr. on behalf of Canadian educational authorities, and when the announcement was made on Christmas Day he was gratified to receive a wire from the Rockefeller solicitor stating that "our regard for you was not without its influence in causing the gift to be made." This

*This was a minimum sum and formed a part of $100,000,000 given for the same purpose to institutions in the United States and Canada.

331

munificent gift, King said, gave him more delight than anything else within his memory, for he could not but feel that he had been instrumental in bringing it about.

A widespread rise in the tempo of party activity was evident throughout 1920. Early in the year the agrarian movement decided to enter federal politics formally and the parliamentary group began to regard itself as a third party. The decline in the reputation of the Union Government was partially checked, the Prime Minister retired, and the Government party was reorganized under a new and energetic leader. The Liberals, for their part, succeeded to some degree in closing their ranks and Mackenzie King undertook a transcontinental tour in order to make himself known to the country at large. Thus this political year, though somewhat colourless and lacking dramatic quality, provided the training ground and the preliminaries for the major engagement which was to follow.

On January 6, 1920, the Canadian Council of Agriculture held a conference in Winnipeg to discuss the political future of the organized farmers. Although they had hitherto been phenomenally successful at the polls, the virility of the movement had been derived largely from the enthusiasm of local groups with only a small degree of co-ordination furnished by the provincial farmers' organizations.* While all were united by a common distrust of Eastern interests and a desire to lower or abolish the tariff, the exceptional degree of local autonomy encouraged divergent views on other questions, the chief of which was the nature and purpose of the movement. Some of the members, particularly those from Alberta, who were inspired in large measure by H. W. Wood of that province, thought that the party should be avowedly a group or class movement. They developed a theory of representation and government based on conflicting economic and class groups, and this, whatever its merits, had little if anything in common with parliamentary democracy, which takes as one of its postulates representation in the general as opposed to the particular interest. Another section of the farmers, whose chief spokesman was T. A. Crerar, was strongly opposed to the group idea and desired to make its appeal to all classes in the community, though it was no less

*Approximate membership in the farmers' movement at the end of 1920 was distributed as follows: Alberta, 30,000; Saskatchewan, 40,000; Manitoba, 15,000; Ontario, 50,000; Maritime Provinces, 7,500.

concerned with the maintenance of the farmers' interests. The method of making their influence felt, however, was in some dispute within this section. Several of the leaders were sufficiently realistic to understand that if the Farmers were to command the necessary voting strength and consistent support in Parliament which they needed to achieve their ends they must form some kind of alliance with one of the major parties, preferably with the more congenial of these, the Liberals. In this view the political side of the farmers' movement was therefore primarily a device to enable it to put pressure on the Liberals to compel them to give to agriculture adequate recognition both in Cabinet membership and in the statute book. Most of the members of this farmer group, however, were not prepared to follow this policy of co-operation. They lacked the political experience and judgment which made such a conclusion inescapable, and their distrust of the old parties went so deep that they would entertain no arrangement which would in any way fetter their complete freedom of action in the constituencies and in Parliament. This excessive individualism and consequent political irresponsibility were, indeed, characteristic of the movement generally, and they were always present to weaken the farmers' influence, to make party co-operation difficult, if not impossible, and to introduce an element of uncertainty and impermanence into all political arrangements in which they might directly or indirectly become involved.

The conference of the Council of Agriculture reaffirmed with minor changes its 1919 platform, sustained the more orthodox position of the Crerar section, and, while leaving the movement essentially provincial as before, declared the intention of electing as many members as possible to the House of Commons. In February, eleven members of Parliament formally declared themselves as the representatives of the National Progressive party under Crerar's leadership. In the newly opened Commons chamber they occupied a block of seats to the left of the Speaker but apart from the Liberals.

In the uneventful session of 1920 it was evident that the Liberals were drawing more closely together as a united party, the outstanding exception being Fielding whose mind on Empire and international relations was still moving along the pre-war lines of legal subordination of Canada to Great Britain.[44] King, on the other hand, believed that in this field strict legal powers were of secondary importance, and he was thus quite prepared to accept the dictum of Rowell that "constitutional practice develops into and becomes constitutional right," and to judge current developments accordingly.[45] He admitted in the House that Canada under Borden's guidance had made very substantial advances during the war and the peace negotiations by securing a much wider and more explicit recognition of her special status, but he expressed a fear that in the future there might be a swing in the direction of a common Empire policy and centralized control which would impair Canadian autonomy.[46] The Liberals, Fielding notwithstanding, had thus caught up with their political opponents on the question of status, and a base had thereby been prepared from which new advances could be made into other controversial areas in Imperial and foreign relations. "I think," King wrote in his diary regarding the treaty debate, "I got our party out of the wrong lines of last session on this all important matter. . . . The debate was interesting throughout and helped, I think, to 'nail down' Canada's position to date."[47]

When the proposal was made in May to attach a Canadian Minister to the British Embassy in Washington who would deal with matters of purely Canadian concern, Mackenzie King gave it his guarded approval, though he emphatically stated that the Liberals were "unalterably opposed" to the proviso that the Canadian Minister would substitute for the British Ambassador in the latter's absence.[48] He believed that such an arrangement would divide responsibility and create unnecessary friction between the governments, and there can be no doubt that he also feared that it might prove to be one step towards the centralization of Empire policy.

In the course of debate on the proposal King clearly set forth his opinions of the Canadian position in international relations and the methods which he thought should mark the course of constitutional development. These words were unusually significant in view of the manner in which his later tactics followed the course which he here outlined.

There are two extreme views that may be taken in regard to a matter of this kind. One is that the affairs of Canada should be managed exclusively by the British Embassy; the other that the Canadian representative should manage the British Embassy for part of the time as is here proposed. What seems to be the more rational course is the middle one, that in matters between Canada and other countries Canada should manage her own affairs, and that in matters between Great Britain and other countries,

Great Britain should manage her own affairs, always when necessary with co-operation and conference between the two. . . .

I do not believe the Canadian people wish to launch too deep into experiments in foreign policy at the present time. All matters of government, and particularly matters affecting diplomatic relations, are matters of constitutional evolution. If we are going to advance, by all means let us proceed along the line of evolution; but let us take one step at a time. Do not let us begin with the extreme step that is being taken in this arrangement without any reference to the views of the representatives of the people. I submit to my right hon. friend [Sir Robert Borden] that at this of all times it would have been fitting and in accordance with the rights of this Parliament, as it was owing to the supremacy of parliament and its position as a great deliberative assembly, before concluding anything, to have brought before this House a resolution expressing the opinion of the Government that Canada should be represented at Washington by a Minister Plenipotentiary and to have given hon. members an opportunity of deciding upon that question here . . . but the Government has not done that; the Government has brought forward no resolution. It has done all of its own volition.[49]

A franchise act on which the parties were in substantial agreement, a temporizing naval appropriation, awaiting a permanent policy "to be formulated after the coming Imperial Conference," and a budget which imposed some new taxes, raised and modified others, and removed the remnants of the customs war duty, were the other legislative measures of importance in the 1920 session. The tariff was not materially changed, although the Government announced that the Department of Finance would hold an investigation with the purpose of deciding upon a later revision.

Mackenzie King, as already noted, had been accused on a number of occasions of not making any significant contribution to the war effort and of having resided in the United States when his services were badly needed at home.[50] He was very sensitive to the injustice of these and other rumours and accusations, and he had made his war service a major issue in the by-election in Prince Edward Island. Despite the efforts of some of his friends to dissuade him, he insisted on bringing the matter up in the House on April 20, when he gave a full account of his work during the war. He pointed out that he had never relinquished his Ottawa residence and that his absence from Canada had at no time been prolonged. He explained that his association with the Rockefeller Foundation was quite different from employment with any of the Rockefeller corporations, and that his

335

efforts in promoting better relations between labour and capital had materially aided the Allied cause by increasing the production of war materials in vital industries. To substantiate this statement he produced letters from high officials in such companies as Bethlehem Steel, Colorado Fuel and Iron, and General Electric, which spoke of his wartime activities in terms of highest praise. King concluded by saying that he was in his fortieth year when war broke out, and that his family responsibilities were such that he had never entertained any doubt where his duty lay.[51] Whether this defence of his war activities was necessary may well remain a matter of dispute, but it had the incidental advantage of enabling him to make more explicit the nature of his relationship with the Rockefeller Foundation which had often been misinterpreted. At all events, he experienced "a tremendous sense of relief" to have the matter laid to rest, for there would now be "no occasion for me to make further reference to the nature of either my services or my obligations during the war period."[52]

In this session Mackenzie King took over the Leadership of the Opposition for the first time, and while his effectiveness as a debater and critic seems to have shown some slight improvement over the previous year, it still left much to be desired. His private records abound in misgivings and expressions of self-reproach and of resolutions to do better. His mind, he says, is not nimble enough; he is weak in public finance; he has been lazy and has "wasted precious time and opportunity"; he is determined "to get down to hard work again and to make every moment count"; he is alarmed at his "ignorance of *everything*, especially procedure and knowledge of questions of the day." On one occasion when the Liberals got into difficulties in the House, he attributed the trouble in large measure to his own neglect in not checking up on the members beforehand. He found Meighen with his "legal and technical twisting" an exasperating opponent, and he developed a healthy respect for Sir George Foster, the acting leader. When for the first time he and Borden faced each other across the House, he felt on his mettle and struck out vigorously when he followed Borden in debate, although he said that he found Borden "child's play compared with Foster." This uncertainty and misgiving had appeared in a letter to his brother in December, 1919, when Borden's retirement was being discussed:*

*The retirement did not occur for another six months.

The change in leadership in the Conservative party is an advantage to me. I shall feel much freer in debate with a new Leader of the Government than in opposing Sir Robert, who was [sic] a much older man and has been longer in office. The change comes, too, at an opportune time because of the next session of Parliament being held in the new buildings. There being so much in the way of adjustments on all sides, my own limitations will perhaps be less apparent than otherwise might be inevitable.[53]

Despite the improvement the Government members were still convinced, however, that King would never make a good leader; indeed, they were prepared to go farther and count him a Government asset rather than a threat. "The Opposition," reported the optimistic Minister of Marine and Fisheries to Sir Robert in April, 1920, "are more disorganized under Mackenzie King than ever before."[54] The Minister of Customs also wrote: "I cannot believe King will ever make a big leader; a sort of immaturity & lack of political instinct are quite obvious, nor do I think he has a very united or enthusiastic following."[55] The Acting Prime Minister conceded to his leader that King was a good speaker—but he "does not carry weight somehow." "There is no pep in King's leadership—he doesn't impress people. He will not go far in my opinion."[56] The summary of the Minister of Justice on the general situation was cautious, and his comment on King to the Prime Minister was short and devastating:

In the House the position of the Government is I think decidedly stronger and better than it was during the course of the fall session and at the opening of this one. There seems to be more cohesion among the members who are counted as our supporters and a much more general disposition to get together.

In the country generally while the "grouch" continues widespread, and it certainly cannot be said that we have at the present moment behind us the serried ranks of enthusiastic cohorts impatient for the fray, still I think that the common sense of the country is at least convinced that there is nothing better in sight. Mackenzie King is—to us—a tower of strength.[57]

King's enemies were doubtless anxious to belittle his capacity, but their criticism contained a substantial amount of truth. The strongest debater in the Opposition ranks was Fielding. His long experience in Parliament, his mental agility and quickness to seize an advantage, his trenchant style and fluency made him a most formidable opponent and one who despite his seventy-two years could hold his own with the best speakers on the Government benches. "Fielding," wrote Sir

337

George Foster, "really gives the lead in the House from his side,"[58] and Mackenzie King was quite conscious of the fact that his leadership was under a cloud until he could at least equal the parliamentary performance of his lieutenant. Fielding's support in Parliament, the respect which he commanded from the Unionist Government, and the moral weight which his name and character gave to the party in the country made his reactionary views on some matters a relatively minor handicap. These views, like the free trade ideas of Andrew McMaster, another prominent Liberal, did not disqualify them from leadership in the Liberal party: the reconciliation of ideas translated into concrete terms could await the time when the party in Parliament became the Government.

Divisions in the House and by-elections in the country were both encouraging for the Opposition. In the first session of 1919 the division on the budget (when Crerar and his group first voted against the Government) had given the Unionists a majority of 50. In 1920 the majority on the Address in Reply to the Speech from the Throne was 34; on the budget, 26; on the Grand Trunk bill, 21; on the Canadian Minister at Washington (for the production of papers), 5—all of these being major divisions. In the four by-elections from December, 1919, to the following April, the Liberals retained two of the seats and the Unionists lost two to the Progressives.

The shrinking majorities and the vanishing seats were significant symptoms of the wasting disease which was threatening the continued existence of the Unionist party. All the difficulties which had been encountered a year earlier[59] were still actively present—the absence of any organization in the constituencies, the lack of a platform, the virtual certainty of a change in leadership, the fragility of the bond which held the Unionists together, the general detachment of the party from contact with public opinion, the isolation of the Government from the two great areas of Quebec and the prairies—and the neglect in coming to grips with these problems had served to accentuate them.[60] It was doubtless much too late to avert the catastrophe which threatened, but no effective measures could even be attempted until the Government was reorganized under a new leader. Sir Robert Borden was genuinely anxious to retire, but he was always willing to reconsider whenever conditions of health held out promise of recovery, and as few Unionists believed that any adequate successor could be found,[61] pressure was always forthcoming to induce him to remain. In June, 1920, after a further trial convalescence of six months, he finally decided to resign, and the party turned eagerly to the problem of reorganization and reluctantly to the choice of a new leader.

The Unionist caucus met on July 1, 1920. Dominated as it was by its Conservative membership, it nevertheless endeavoured to keep alive the fiction of a coalition, and to that end assumed the name of the National Liberal and Conservative party. It accepted Sir Robert Borden's resignation with genuine regret, and agreed on a method of choosing a successor. The platform accepted by the caucus was in complete accord with Union Government policy in its insistence on Canadian autonomy within the Empire and its approval of the unification of the nationally owned railways; it was unmistakably Conservative in its promises to revise the tariff both as a protective and as a revenue-producing instrument, though this revision was declared to be impossible until preceded by a thorough investigation; it was vague and hopeful in its endorsement of the labour clauses of the Treaty of Versailles, economy in the public services, the development of foreign trade, the adoption of progressive policies for the entire nation, and other highly praiseworthy measures. What deprived these promises of much of their appeal was that their execution was in the hands of a tottering Government and the phrasing was in many instances so ambiguous that that Government was free to move when and where it willed.

The choice of a leader was left to Sir Robert Borden, who was to make the decision after members of the caucus had communicated with him and after he had consulted with "prominent Canadians outside Parliament." Sir Thomas White was, by general consent, the favoured candidate and he had the endorsement of both Liberal and Conservative Unionists, but he could not be induced to consider the position. N. W. Rowell was not acceptable to the Conservatives; Sir George Foster was too old. The chief remaining contender was Arthur Meighen, but although he was strongly supported by the backbenchers of the party, a number of his colleagues in the Cabinet were opposed to his selection. One very serious objection arose from his close identification with the Military Service Act, the War-time Elections Act, and the acquisition of the Canadian Northern and Grand Trunk Railways, for these measures were extremely unpopular in Quebec and

339

he, as their putative parent, shared in the unpopularity. Would Meighen's great talents be able to overcome Quebec's antipathy, always bearing in mind that the future success of the Conservative party depended on securing at least moderate support in that province? J. A. Calder wrote Sir Robert Borden:

I am convinced Meighen is absolutely out of the question in so far as Quebec is concerned. In addition I know that several ministers will immediately retire should he be the choice. In case however it is decided to revert to the old order of things and reconstruct the Conservative party in the hope of success at the second general election it might be advisable to select Meighen as leader at this time. Personally however I doubt very much the wisdom of this course as I do not think Meighen possesses the necessary qualities to ensure his success as a leader at any time in the future.[62]

Sir Robert Borden nevertheless placed Meighen's name before the Governor-General, and on July 10, 1920, he succeeded Sir Robert as Prime Minister of Canada.

Mr. Meighen was 46 years of age, and his impressive intellectual powers were approaching their prime. His political rise had been rapid, and the Government had for some years relied heavily on his talents to give the leading exposition and defence of its policies. No one in Parliament was his equal as a debater: fluent, analytic, dispassionate, his effectiveness depended on logic and not on emotion, and it derived powerful aid from a wide vocabulary and biting phrases. His fighting instincts responded readily to the intellectual stimulus of debate, and his performance was accordingly always worthy of the occasion. He could be bitter and vituperative, and he never suffered lesser men, or those he regarded as lesser men, gladly, nor did he exert himself to conceal his contempt for them. Skill in presentation was reinforced by capacity for hard work, and he had the competent lawyer's facility for getting rapidly to the heart of a problem. An impressive background of information combined with his quick and orderly mind made his extemporaneous efforts almost as impressive as those to which he had given a great deal of preparation, and even the most skilful and courageous of his opponents hesitated before they exposed themselves to his devastating attacks.

The faults of Mr. Meighen as a party leader sprang in large measure from his personal qualities. Being the head of a party and possessed of exceptional ability he exaggerated the role of an élite in a democracy. The leaders in his opinion were to lay down policies on broad principles in which they believed, and these policies were to be referred to the people for their acceptance or rejection. There was little allowance for popular participation in the creation of the policies themselves; little appreciation of the need for a constant sympathy between Government and people; little patience with or understanding of any course of action which proceeded step by step as popular consent was forthcoming. In this his views differed radically from Mackenzie King's; instead of utilizing the party as a nation-wide council chamber for the reconciliation of differences and the implementation of the resulting product, Meighen expected the top level of authority to proclaim the policy and the party to accept it and carry it out. Few will quarrel with Meighen's dictum that "those in authority must lead," but many would question the kind of detached and dictatorial leadership that he was likely to provide. Moreover, Mr. Meighen's part in the passing of the War-time Elections Act would indicate that, if popular consent could not be secured, he was not above altering the franchise to secure acceptance of a measure if he thought the circumstances warranted it.

Mr. Meighen not only believed in firm leadership, he was at all times quite willing himself to point the way to his party supporters. His intellectual arrogance led him to trust too much to his own judgment and he showed a tendency to disregard the advice of colleagues who, while not his equal in some respects, possessed much more political experience and sagacity.* The same quality made him place too much confidence in rational processes which, as it often proved, were insufficient to win popular support. He seemed to overlook the essential complexity of political questions and the much greater complexity of the public response to them. The very clarity which existed in his own mind made him over-estimate his ability to win converts, who at best saw public issues in a glass darkly and not in the bright primary colours of the Conservative leader. They could not comprehend Mr. Meighen's inexorable conclusions drawn from his impeccable premises, nor were they attracted by the cold impassive figure

---

*Sir George Foster's judgment was not as harsh as this. He said that Meighen was "inclined to rigidity in opinion," but had "the spirit of reasonableness and fair compromise." Diary of Sir George E. Foster, July 4, 1920.

who was so sure that he was always right and who could be so fatally articulate in committing himself to unpopular causes. Mr. Meighen never learned that to win an argument was not to win an election, that reason by itself is at best an unconvincing pleader in politics, and that in a democracy he who reaches too obviously for power is likely to have it elude his grasp. A person who possesses well-defined principles is worthy of praise; but frequently it becomes necessary to make concessions and compromises, to be content with partial measures which are available rather than struggle unsuccessfully for the larger prize. Mr. Meighen preferred to go down fighting; and this privilege was accorded him on more than one occasion. It was assuredly no mere chance that led him in later life to give to his volume of speeches and essays the revealing title of *Unrevised and Unrepented*.

Mackenzie King's interest in the choice of a new Prime Minister was obvious, and he recorded his opinion on a number of occasions. The first extract is from the letter written to his brother when Borden's retirement was being discussed, which has been quoted from above (pp. 336–7); the second is from his diary six months later, when the selection had been made. He had no doubt of the advantage to him and the Liberals of the choice of Meighen for the leadership, and although the reasons he gave are not convincing, his conclusion was substantially accurate:

My impression is that Sir Thomas White will be chosen. If he is not, it will probably be Arthur Meighen. White is in every way a better stamp of man for Prime Minister. Meighen . . . lacks frankness in debate; he is a Tory of the Tories. Sir Thomas White . . . is a man of character and ability. He has a fine presence. For the country's sake, I should prefer to see Sir Thomas White chosen. Politically, it would be an advantage to our party were Meighen selected.[63]

I could not help exclaiming "Good for him" when I read of Meighen having won out, and achieved his ambition, immediately I added, walking up and down with feelings of satisfaction "It is too good to be true." Meighen is a Tory through and through, the very antithesis of myself in thought and feeling on political matters. I can fight him naturally, the issues will become clear and distinct. The hypocrisy of a false union in the Gov't will be more than ever disclosed. It is the beginning of a speedy end to the Unionist administration.[64]

Sir Robert Borden's farewell speech to the Unionist caucus had been a plea for unity and co-operation, and he later reported that the

Conservative and Liberal Unionists "were welded into a united, vigorous and aggressive party full of courage and determination."[65] These words, however, carry little conviction, for it was evident by this time that the party had no future as a coalition and that such co-operation as still remained was little more than the efforts of a desperate crew to keep their sinking ship afloat. The Conservatives were willing to be conciliatory because they were getting their own way in the Government councils and they needed all the support in the House that they could muster. The Liberal Unionists on the other hand were by this time occupying so precarious a position that they had no real alternative but to continue the wartime alliance. They not only had no party organization behind them in the constituencies, but the growing aggressiveness of the Liberals and Progressives destroyed any hopes of their securing popular support save from friendly Conservatives, who were in the nature of things none too numerous.

Those Liberal Unionists who were in the Cabinet were scarcely more fortunate; they might look back with melancholy satisfaction on their past achievements and services, but their political future was dark indeed. After the armistice they found themselves being forced into a position where they had either to abandon the Unionists entirely and trust to the cold charity of their former friends or remain where they were and share in the inevitable disaster which lay ahead. Moreover, they had now degenerated into a small group in the Cabinet and were compelled to merge their beliefs and identity with the Conservative members whose numbers and influence in the Government were steadily mounting. Crerar, Carvell, White, Mewburn, and Maclean left the Borden Cabinet for various reasons in 1919 and 1920, and only one Liberal, Guthrie, was among the replacements. When the Meighen Government was formed, Rowell, the ablest member outside the new Prime Minister, also withdrew, leaving only five Liberals (Sifton, Calder, Ballantyne, Guthrie, and Spinney) to justify the new Government's pretensions to be a coalition. Within fifteen months the first two of these had disappeared, and although Manion, an ex-Liberal, was added, even the most charitable observer could not discern by that time anything more than a vestige of the Liberal party in the Meighen Cabinet.

King's attitude to the Progressives in the House during the 1920 session had been uniformly conciliatory and designed to awake in them the twofold conviction that they had a strong sympathy with the Liberals and held nothing in common with the Tories.

Our men [he wrote] have been careful to avoid conflict, and where opportunity has presented, have gone far to co-operate with the Farmer group in some of the matters in which they are vitally interested. Thus far, they, in turn, have been equally helpful in a co-operative way.[66]

His hope was, of course, that this mutual respect and co-operation might spread from Parliament to the people, and one of his great aims during the session had been to secure "sufficient recognition from the public to command a respectful hearing once the opportunity is afforded to address the electors in open meeting."[67] His spare time in 1920 was thus devoted to the task of making himself better known to the Canadian people while at the same time he attempted to revive and reanimate the Liberal cause and pave the way for a Liberal-Progressive understanding. He had paid a brief visit to the Maritime Provinces in January, and he conducted a series of public meetings in Ontario in mid-summer. He was much encouraged by his reception in both areas; and in the autumn he undertook the major journey to Western Canada, accompanied by a small retinue of Liberal members chosen from the newer or younger members in the party.

He broke his tour, however, in order to pay two visits to his brother in Colorado. Macdougall King, having survived the onslaught of tuberculosis, was now suffering from progressive muscular atrophy, an incurable disease which was gradually to restrict his activity until it culminated in his death. The brothers were drawn close together during this period, and Will's thoughtfulness, sympathy, and gener-osity did much to help his brother and family face this new misfortune.

The degree of welcome and endorsement which King received from the four "Liberal" provincial Governments in the West depended in large measure upon the strength of the Farmers' movement in each province and the policy which its Government had adopted to cope with the threat of the new party. In British Columbia, although an election was pending, the Cabinet received King enthusiastically, and the Alberta Government, despite a very aggressive agrarianism in that province, also openly acknowledged a close blood relationship to the federal Liberal party. But the Governments of Manitoba and Sas-katchewan, though in private they remained friendly, were in public distant and undemonstrative, and their welcome to King resembled

344

one they might have extended to a distinguished and relatively unknown guest from a distant land. Norris had just come through an
election in Manitoba and needed Farmer support to maintain a majority; Martin in Saskatchewan was still endeavouring to persuade the
Farmer organization—not without success—that his Liberal administration was really agrarian and in no way stood for the federal brand
of Liberalism. Neither province was a sympathetic environment for
King's favourite gospel of Liberal goodwill and brotherhood, but he
preached it nevertheless. He was, indeed, willing to make allowances
for Norris's predicament, but his diary shows that he regarded Martin's
defection and capitulation to the Grain Growers' Association as little
short of treachery[68]—a change in attitude which may have been the
first sign that his sympathetic understanding of the Progressive movement was beginning to crack under the pressure of practical and immediate needs.

King enjoyed a good popular reception in all provinces, for they
were curious to see the new leader and were interested in hearing his
exposition of Liberal policies. "I should say," reported one shrewd
observer, J. W. Dafoe, "that he has improved his personal position
considerably because, whereas he was previously just a name, he is
now known personally to a very considerable number of Western
people who have heard him speak. I find no traces of any wild enthusiasm over his platform performances but he is regarded pretty
generally as a capable platform speaker with pretty liberal and progressive ideas."[69] King's references to the farmer in politics were
always amicable, but the farmers were not satisfied. They remained
only slightly less suspicious of the Liberals than of the Conservatives,
and King's protestations would have to be reinforced by acts before
the farmers would be convinced that their future could be confidently
entrusted to the Liberals. This scepticism was well expressed by a
Saskatchewan newspaper in its editorial comment on one of King's
meetings:

Mr. King was heard to advantage in Saskatoon last night. What impression does he create?
He is a purposeful man, is Mr. King; purposeful, forceful, direct, and
serious-minded. He believes what he is saying, and few public men in
Canada convey more strongly the impression of absolute sincerity in their
speeches.

345

At the same time Mr. King is not altogether convincing. . . . Inasmuch as the doubt of the prairie people is founded on uncertainty about the Liberal party of the present, on account of its past record, Mr. King is least definite about those matters on which they are looking for most accurate and detailed information. The thought voiced by Hon. George Langley when he said that under certain circumstances a victory for the Liberal party would be as great a disaster to Canada's national interests as a Unionist triumph, does not seem to have presented itself to Mr. King at all. Mr. Langley voiced the fear that influences which surrounded the Laurier government and made of it a strongly protectionist and rather reactionary administration would continue to direct the course of the Liberal party as a whole, a fear that is in many minds in the West. Mr. King makes no effort to dispel this fear. It is well enough to speak so eloquently of the traditional Liberal party as the protector of the common people and the standard-bearer of the masses against the forces of special privilege. In a broadly historical sense that is true, but what the people of the West are wondering is, is Mr. King satisfied to maintain the Laurier rather than the truly liberal tradition? Does he admit a flaw in the Laurier halo at all, and is he content to maintain, as Laurier did, liberalism in theory and reaction in practice? Mr. King is in a section of the country where the late Sir Wilfrid had as solid support as ever a political leader of Canada secured; but nevertheless these, crudely stated, are the thoughts in the minds of a great number of them, and they get no relief in their perplexity by hearing Mr. King.[70]

In Winnipeg King had a friendly talk with T. A. Crerar and A. B. Hudson, and although they do not appear to have promised anything very specific in the way of co-operation between Progressives and Liberals, King read into the conference much more. "We have concluded our trip," he wrote in his diary, "by the leaders of the progressive forces coming together & planning a joint campaign. What greater triumph or finer ending could there be to the Western trip—it is over now. It has been successful beyond all anticipations. . . . I have no regrets, see no political mistakes—policies of proceeding splendidly vindicated."[71] King should have known the Progressive movement well enough by this time to realize that its members would not consider for a moment supporting any "joint campaign" such as he fondly imagined. If this were the Progressive attitude, why would Crerar and Hudson make such empty promises and why, if they had (and it is not intended to suggest here that they had done so), should King suppose they could hope to execute them? The answer seems to be that King with his talent for self-deception was once more allowing his wishes to sway his judgment. Unpleasant events were soon to disclose how far from reality these optimistic hopes were.

The most helpful of all Progressive-Liberal arrangements, for example, would have been a division of constituencies so as to eliminate three-cornered contests at the next election. But such a move was certain to antagonize any Progressives who had formerly been Conservatives, while at the other extreme, wrote J. W. Dafoe, "there would arise a rebellious movement against the existing leadership, inspired by a class feeling which would probably take the form of non-partisan league candidates for office."[72] To these probabilities must be added the general reluctance of virtually all the Progressives to give any more than a nominal allegiance to their leaders, so that even the moderate or middle section could not be counted on to support any arrangement which their leaders might negotiate. The same difficulty arose in King's own prospective constituency of North York. When Crerar was approached by Andrew Haydon, the Liberal organizer, regarding a possible union of forces in some constituencies he suggested that the most convincing argument to gain Progressive support was for the Liberals to "put up good candidates." Despite the efforts of Crerar and others to discourage the move, R. W. E. Burnaby, President of the United Farmers of Ontario, was nominated by the Farmers to run against King in North York, a gesture which could scarcely be construed as friendly. Haydon's comment well expresses the feeling of futility and exasperation with which the Liberals were beginning to regard the general problem. "If the Leader of the Liberal Party," he wrote to King,[73] "is not a good enough candidate in the eyes of Farmers, then, I do not know how they could be satisfied in this respect. This sort of action militates strongly against getting together. We are in the field first in North York. What can we do but fight Burnaby?"* Steadily but reluctantly the Liberals were being drawn into a war on two fronts.

*Burnaby remained in the field and came at the bottom of the poll in the subsequent general election.

CHAPTER THIRTEEN

THE ELECTION OF 1921 AND
CABINET FORMATION

THE GENERAL ELECTION was called for December 6, 1921. It was not entirely unexpected; for the Meighen Government was badly in need of some popular pronouncement which would determine its right to govern. The problems of peace and reconstruction, the crumbling of the coalition element in the Cabinet, the unpopularity of the Government itself, the portentous agricultural revolt, and the choice of a new Prime Minister were all reasons for seeking a fresh mandate. By-elections, moreover, had been generally unfavourable, and the Government had found it safer to allow five vacancies to remain unfilled. The parliamentary session of 1921 had seen relatively little accomplished, but although the Government majorities were small (15 to 25), they were nevertheless adequate to carry the session to completion. The three major tendencies which had appeared in the previous year continued unchecked: the contraction in the Government's majority, the spread of the Progressive disaffection, and the healing of the divisions among the Liberals. What an election would produce through the regrouping of party forces was hidden in uncertainty, with the probabilities favouring the return of Liberals, Progressives, and Conservatives in that order, but no majority for any one of them.

The outlook for the Government was dark. Many of the recent Ministers had retired or were seeking retirement, and Meighen's attempt to rebuild and strengthen his Cabinet for the election merely showed in clearer outline the difficulty of his position. He was forced to take in no less than twelve new Ministers, a number of whom were of limited capacity, and the four French Canadians in the Cabinet lacked even a seat in Parliament. The administration had inherited the accumulated antagonisms towards the Conservative and Union Governments, to which it had added one or two towards itself, so that

348

it found opposed to it farmers, anti-conscriptionists, French Canadians, urban labour, and the transport interests centred about Montreal with whom were associated powerful groups of bankers and manufacturers. It was, of course, barely conceivable that these elements and the rival parties of protest might destroy their own effectiveness by fighting at cross purposes and that the Conservatives might as a result be able to remain in office. Unless the party were prepared to count on such a miracle, it would have to cast about for heavy reinforcements, and here its way was blocked, for there seemed little or no hope of gaining anything from the two areas where it was weakest—the prairies and Quebec. The post-war action of the Borden Government in maintaining the tariff, a policy inflexibly continued by Mr. Meighen, ruled out any support from the prairies; and although protection in itself would not necessarily have antagonized parts of Quebec, Meighen in the eyes of French Canada was so closely identified with conscription that any rapprochement under his leadership had become unthinkable.

If the Conservatives had little to gain from an election, the Progressives had much, and the party entered the ring with all the confidence of a challenger who has never been knocked out. The by-elections had swung heavily to their side and the last contest, in Medicine Hat, June 27, had transformed what had been a comfortable Union seat into one for the United Farmers with a majority of almost ten thousand. Two weeks later Alberta had held a provincial election which resulted in almost a two to one victory for the United Farmers. Ontario already had a Farmer-Labour Government, and the Liberal administrations in Manitoba and Saskatchewan were tireless in their efforts to avert disaster by placating the farmers at every opportunity. It was true that the Progressives had made little progress elsewhere, but they had not yet had an opportunity to show their full strength. They entered the fight without any past to rise up against them, under able federal leadership (if they would but follow it), and with the support of an influential section of the press. The latent threat to their success and to their solidarity as a united party has been already noted. Most of the Alberta and Ontario sections wished to keep the party a farmers' organization, refusing the responsibility of office but using their position in the legislature to wring concessions from the party in power; the Manitoba group were anxious to shake off the occupational limitation and broaden the basis of membership, and, if the opportunity occurred, form a new alliance with a reformed section of the

Liberals. For the moment, however, the Progressives could overlook these ominous differences, especially as they coincided for the most part with the geographical distribution of their members and therefore were not likely to cause embarrassment during the election.

The Liberals, too, entered the contest with a glad heart though not without some misgivings as to the size of their anticipated victory. They could capitalize on the popular dissatisfaction with the Government; they would also have to share the resulting electoral benefits with the Progressives. French Canada was solidly behind them, and in the Maritime Provinces and British Columbia weak competition from the Progressives would leave the Liberals with most of the dissatisfied anti-Government vote. Ontario was at least fair fighting ground. Even on the prairies the Liberals had hopes that they might derive some small advantage from the resentment against the Government, though they could not deny that the Liberals there were under much the same cloud of distrust as the Government itself. A major Liberal problem arose from the amorphous nature of the party's own membership. Even Liberal Quebec, solid though it might appear when it went to the polls, was divided into a radical and a reactionary wing, and the Liberals in other parts of Canada were at variance on many questions. The party had, in truth, not yet emerged completely from the shadow of the eclipse, and its rehabilitation, particularly in the sense of having accepted a common policy, was by no means complete and was not to become so for many years. The ostensible agreement contained in the 1919 platform had already proved to be in large measure illusory, and the degree of common action that could be achieved under these circumstances was undetermined. If the party could not be united on all major matters—and at this time that seemed visionary indeed—then it must be sufficiently united on some of them so that sacrifices and concessions would be possible within the areas of disagreement.

Many questions were discussed in the election campaign—railway policy, immigration, freight rates, grain marketing, and so forth—but the emphasis tended in large measure to be placed on two major issues, one stressed by the Conservatives, one by the Liberals. Meighen did his utmost to give first place to the protective tariff, while King kept bringing the argument back to what he contended was the main question, the record of the Conservative Government and its unfitness to continue in office. The Progressives were in the happy position of being able to fight the election on both counts, as well as to attack the old party system and to advocate economy, greater controls over big business, a nationally owned railway, and other reforms. The overwhelming preponderance of the Liberals in Quebec and of the Progressives on the prairies meant that these provinces did not receive nearly as much attention as other areas where the issue was doubtful. Ontario with the large number of eighty-two seats, closely contested by all three parties, was the key to the situation, for the result there would probably determine the next Government. Thus although neither King nor Crerar spent any time in Quebec and Meighen only a week, the three leaders devoted no less than 34, 18, and 31 days respectively to their campaign in Ontario, these periods representing over one-half of the total time spent by King and Meighen in their campaign and over one-third of that spent by Crerar.

The campaigns waged by Meighen and King were typical of the two contestants. Meighen was vigorous, bitter, fearless, contumelious, and uncompromising. His was the courage of impeccability, the conviction of unfailing logic. He went into anti-conscriptionist Quebec and defended in provocative terms his connection with the Military Service Act: "I never try to ride two horses. I favoured conscription. I introduced the Military Service Act. I spoke for it time and again in the House of Commons, and in every province in the Dominion. I did because I thought it was right."[1] He went also into free trade Manitoba and defended protection: "I stand for a protective tariff, and I have always done so. I stand for the measure of protection that I have applied."[2] Substantial reductions in the tariff, he asserted, would endanger Canadian independence, increase unemployment, jeopardize infant industries, destroy business confidence, and paralyse industry. If, he said, the Progressives' advocacy of free trade for Canada was a "blazing madness," King's advocacy of free food was little better, and his "tariff for revenue" was meaningless. "Those words are just the circular pomposity of a man who won't say what he means. He might as well say he favours a perambulating tariff, or an atmospheric tariff, or a dynamic tariff."[3] Attack in Mr. Meighen's book of rules was the only form of defence, and he spared neither words nor energy in an endeavour to bolster up a cause already marked for defeat.

Mackenzie King had no talent for invective and no desire to achieve lucidity. His was the far less spectacular and more adroit effort of picking his way carefully among a number of potentially dangerous issues, of holding fast to the Liberal support he already had while reaching out for any following which might be sympathetic and responsive, of cultivating friends rather than ridiculing enemies. His campaign, in short, was consistent with the policy he had followed since he had become leader. Party unity and with it national unity could never be achieved by harping on such a divisive issue as the tariff. To move too far towards protection would make any entente with the Progressives out of the question, to move too far towards free trade would drive the Liberal protectionists into alliance with the Conservatives. King tried to keep away from extremes and push into the background any issues which made co-operative endeavour difficult or impossible. The Liberal tariff thus became, for the moment at least, the Fielding tariff of the Laurier régime,[4] and was described by King as "a tariff for consumer and producer," "a tariff for revenue," or by some other equally non-committal phrase. Such ambiguous statements were not inspiring and might not satisfy completely either wing of the party, but they were not likely to rouse antagonisms and they could hold out quite genuine hopes for a later downward revision. Mr. Meighen could afford to be explicit simply because he had abandoned one of the primary functions of a party leader, namely, the discovery and maintenance of areas of common agreement which would enable him to build an effective party on a national scale.

Similarly, a firm pronouncement on railway policy at this juncture was also to be avoided, for a large part of Quebec was known to dislike nationalization while Ontario and Western Canada favoured it. There was everything to be lost and nothing to be gained by taking a premature stand. "I greatly doubt," wrote King during the campaign, "the wisdom of bringing the question of Government ownership and operation of railways into the present contest as an outstanding issue. We have nothing to lose in Quebec by limiting our discussion to the Government and its record, whereas it may cost us several seats in the other provinces to depart from this general course and lay down policies of our own on far-reaching questions such as the railway problem."[5]

The more these and other questions were examined the stronger became the case for continuing the Liberal parliamentary tactics and making the Government's record the dominant issue of the campaign. Public attention would thus be directed to the wide range of grievances which had accumulated during the past years, to the Government's retaining office with an outworn mandate, to its alleged arbitrary and autocratic tendencies, to its many exacerbating policies of which conscription was the outstanding example. This line of attack would have the effect of minimizing differences within the Liberal ranks, of recreating and vitalizing the party *esprit de corps*, of giving the Liberals and Progressives a greater sense of common interests and making easier, perhaps, some form of association between them when the election was over. As the election drew near Mackenzie King was able to write to his brother: "I have gone through the campaign without saying one unkind or harsh expression I am aware of, and without being irritated at any point except momentarily on a very few occasions. I don't think I have made enemies, and I know I have made hosts of friends."[6]

King's reluctance to make explicit commitments arose also from the insecurity of his position as head of the party. There were still Liberals who were doubtful of his ability and considered him to be on probation. His parliamentary performance had not been impressive; the by-elections had been only moderately successful; and his anxiety to conciliate the Progressives suggested some doubt of the orthodoxy of his opinions. Thus any pronounced swing to the left on such an issue as the tariff would be an invitation to trouble, especially with the group of protectionist Liberals in Quebec. This group, led by Sir Lomer Gouin and including Rodolphe Lemieux and Senators Dandurand and Béique, inherited much of the old *bleu* tradition in Quebec politics. They drew their support largely from the industrial areas of the province and held views on matters of public policy, especially the tariff, which were opposed to those of the Progressives and in large measure also to those of the other Quebec Liberal wing led by Ernest Lapointe.

Rumours had been current for some time past that the Gouin wing might not be averse to joining their fortunes with those of the Conservatives,* a move which would precipitate the realignment of party

*Sir Lomer Gouin's name had, for example, been mentioned as a possible Minister at the time of Sir Robert Borden's retirement; Montreal *Gazette*, July 2, 1920. See also, for some suggestion of the union of protectionist forces, the following: Borden Papers, J. A. Calder to Sir Robert Borden, March 11, 1920; National Liberal Federation File, Ernest Lapointe to Andrew Haydon, Feb. 11, 1920; Dafoe Papers, J. W. Dafoe to Sir Clifford Sifton, Feb. 14, 1921; A. K. Cameron Papers, A. K. Cameron to T. A. Crerar, Sept. 12, 1921.

forces desired by the Crerar Progressives, working from the other direction. How real this possibility was it is difficult to say, but certainly in these early years of his leadership King was by no means sure that he could count on the Quebec right wing and he did not hesitate on at least one occasion in 1921 to reproach Lemieux with his lack of loyalty.[7] A week before the election it was again rumoured that some Quebec Liberals were conspiring against King's leadership, and Lemieux wrote to assure him[8] that the rumour was quite unfounded: "In my name and in behalf of my Liberal candidates and colleagues of Quebec, I declare that we have but one leader and that he is Lyon Mackenzie-King."* King was sufficiently concerned about possible defection, however, to make an effort to procure a direct avowal of loyalty from Sir Lomer himself which could be used in the press, but apparently the best he was able to obtain was another indirect assurance from Gouin, delivered through S. W. Jacobs, that he endorsed the Lemieux message.[9] A further sign of Mackenzie King's uneasiness was the serious attention he gave to the suggestion that he should withdraw from the three-cornered contest in North York and remain as a candidate in Prince, P.E.I. In this way he would not only avoid the danger to the party inherent in his open opposition to a Progressive candidate and the personal danger of defeat, but he would also forestall any challenge to his leadership which such defeat might well encourage. Eventually, he decided to accept both risks and stay with North York.

Other aspects of the election received careful attention from King. Thus he kept Gouin and Lemieux out of Ontario because of their well-known hostility to a nationally owned railway and the danger that their presence on the platform might seem to confirm the charge that Quebec was too influential in the councils of the Liberal party.[10] Liberal-Progressive relations continued to be a source of worry and eventually of irritation. It was in the interests of both parties that in some constituencies mutual concessions should be made by the withdrawal of certain candidates, which would thus eliminate a number of three-cornered contests. King had tried long before the election to bring this about and had received some encouragement from Crerar and a few of his associates, but the exuberant optimism of the Progressives and their dislike of any control from outside their own ridings

*This was made public; cf. Montreal *Gazette*, Dec. 3, 1921, editorial.

made them deaf to all such suggestions. King therefore decided to have Liberal candidates run in as many constituencies as possible.* This would place the party in a better negotiating position if the Progressives later decided to co-operate; it would increase the total Liberal vote which King thought might be a factor in determining who should be Prime Minister if no party had a majority of seats; it would prevent the other parties from gaining prestige from acclamations; and it would, he hoped, furnish yet another answer to the cry of domination by Quebec.[11]

King's attitude to the Progressives became more openly critical as the election day drew near, a product, no doubt, of a growing confidence in the Liberal chances of victory and a growing exasperation at the persistent unfriendliness of the Progressives. It was fairly clear by mid-November that Quebec would return almost all Liberals and that the Maritime Provinces would not be far behind, so that moderate gains in the prairie West and Ontario would give the Liberals the vital over-all majority in the House. But the prairies and Ontario were the very areas where the Progressives were strongest, and hence a willingness to work with the Liberals in a few constituencies would have been of enormous value to the latter. It was frustrating indeed for Mackenzie King to see the opening door to all his ambitions about to be slammed in his face by the irresponsible actions of a group of naive reformers to whom he had in all sincerity extended the hand of sympathy and co-operation and for whom he was even then following a line of conduct which might well jeopardize his support within his own party. Twelve days before the election he sent to his brother a strongly worded comment:

This wretched Progressive movement will alone be responsible for the failure to secure a really effective democratic government in the next Parliament, should such prove to be a consequence of the divisions in the three-cornered contests. You will observe that I am beginning to deal a little more sharply with this aspect of affairs. I think the time has come to dwell somewhat on the class nature of the movement, and that heed will be given to my words, seeing that the public know that hitherto I have urged co-operation on the ground of our principles being much the same.[12]

King's speeches therefore dwelt increasingly on the class and sectional nature of the Progressive party and on its uncertain future in

*For the 235 seats the Government nominated 208 candidates, the Liberals 204, the Progressives 146.

355

Canadian politics, and lest its supporters should think they could run with both hare and hounds, he discouraged any thought of future coalition by stating that Canada wanted no more experiments of that kind. He closed his campaign on December 5 with an open letter to the electors in which he outlined in one involved sentence the type of government he desired—one representative in the widest sense, which would maintain policies sufficiently moderate and general to command the support of all the important elements in the national community:

Only by an administration which in all its policies is prepared to avoid the extremes of reaction and radicalism, and which in itself is broadly representative of all the constituent elements of our population—farmers and labour, the business and professional classes, the returned men and others—can we hope to secure, in matters of government, that co-operation between citizens of all occupations and callings which is necessary not less to a due consideration of particular needs than to the advancing of interests held in common, and which, moreover, is an absolute essential of national unity.

The election returns gave the Liberals 117 seats; Progressives 64; Conservatives 50; Independent Labour two; Labour-Liberal one; Independent Liberal one.* Meighen and nine of his Ministers were defeated;† Crerar was elected with over 5,500 majority, Mackenzie King carried North York in a three-cornered contest with a majority of 1,055.

The Liberals were thus one short of a majority of the House, although the Labour-Liberal and the Independent Liberal would give them the majority they needed. They had elected members from every province except Alberta and had carried three provinces—Quebec, Nova Scotia, and Prince Edward Island—without the loss of a seat. Ontario had given them 21 out of 82, but west of Ontario they had carried only six: three in British Columbia, two in Manitoba, one in Saskatchewan.‡ The Conservatives had ceased to exist as a national party in any representative sense, for they had failed to elect a single

*The evidence is most confused on the political affiliation of several members. They have been classified here primarily on performance in the House and secondarily on their announced affiliation which is often obscure in the *Parliamentary Guide.*

†Three others were safely ensconced in the Senate; thus only eight out of 21 former Ministers were elected.

‡King had written to his brother on election day that he expected over 20 seats in Ontario with 115 for the party total "which may even run to 120." W.L.M.K. to D. Macdougall King, Dec. 6, 1921.

member from six provinces.* All but 13 of their members came from Ontario, which had elected 37 Conservatives. The Progressives had captured 38 seats out of 43 on the prairies, 24 in Ontario, one from British Columbia, and one from New Brunswick.

The election yielded two unusual phenomena. There were no less than 143 three-cornered contests for the 235 seats—an unprecedented number in Canadian parliamentary history. Even more remarkable was the high concentration of the party strength in certain provinces: Liberal East, Progressive West, and a divided Ontario. Such an unbalanced distribution would obviously make it very difficult to select a Cabinet which would represent all the geographical areas in the nation. The election had settled decisively, however, one vital question: the next head of the Government would be Mackenzie King. He had passed triumphantly the first severe test as leader, and it now remained to see how he would acquit himself in the next and more crucial test as Prime Minister.

The election returns were barely in before King was confronted with one of the major problems of his new position, the selection of the members of his Cabinet. He addressed himself to this task very conscious of the two major objectives which he had kept constantly before him since his election as leader: the restoration of the Liberal party as an effective instrument in the government of Canada, and the maintenance and strengthening of his position as the head of that party. In the process of forming a Cabinet the first objective was to be fostered by giving careful recognition to both the Laurier and the Unionist Liberals, and also by endeavouring to make the Cabinet as inclusive as possible, representative of the many interests and areas which might be prepared to combine and work together under a somewhat vaguely defined and unifying Liberal philosophy. Inevitably, this conception of the omnibus character of the Liberal party (strongly reminiscent of the Liberal Conservatives under Macdonald and the Liberals under Laurier) raised the question of inviting Progressives to join the new Cabinet and the price King was prepared to pay to get them there. In a letter to Max of mid-December he outlined his hopes for the future:

*The Conservatives had, however, received a large popular vote in most provinces and had a national total of 972,000 against the Liberal vote of 1,297,000 and Progressive vote of 769,000. In the three Prairie Provinces they had actually received 16,000 more votes than the Liberals.

This is a moment for great generosity, and all the conciliation that is possible towards those who, believing in ideals which are strongly Liberal, have nevertheless been a powerful opposing force in the campaign just concluded. I want, if I can, to have the West feel that I am its friend. I also wish to begin at this moment to build up a strong Liberal Party for the years to come. I could easily form a government with the material I have, which would represent the big and powerful interests of the country. On the other hand, it is the people alone for whom I have concern, and I am thinking of their future chances through the years to come. Deliberately, therefore, I am seeking to bring about, not a coalition, but a coalescence of Liberal and Progressive forces whereby a new strong, vigorous, united, solid Liberal Party, representative of the will and the wish of the great body of the people [will be created?][13]

This statement was a marked change from King's earlier advocacy of coalition with the implied understanding that each party would keep its own identity, caucus, and leader, but he had abandoned that idea before the election. His hostility to coalition and his preference for what he called coalescence were based, as he said, on the solid virtues of union, though he was doubtless influenced also by the grim associations of the 1917 example, by the damage that venture had inflicted on the Liberal party, by the essential instability of any coalition, and by the latent challenge to him as Prime Minister presented by any separate group which owed its allegiance to another head.

But though the results of the election had, if anything, reinforced King's conviction on the desirability of getting Progressive members into the Cabinet, they had also made it clear, as King pointed out (above), that the Liberals could, if necessary, stand on their own feet. The new House had an impressive number of Liberals with Cabinet qualifications. Sixteen of them had already had federal or provincial ministerial experience, and twenty others were destined to hold office in Liberal administrations in the future. Gratifying though this wealth must have been, it was nevertheless only a partial answer to the problem of choosing, for while some provinces yielded an embarrassment of riches, others were virtually bankrupt. Thus only three of the thirty-six who might be regarded as Cabinet timber came from constituencies west of the Great Lakes, and two of these three came from Manitoba. Any Cabinet which was to be considered as truly national in character must give some recognition to the different interests and localities in the country. The potential role of the Progressives in meeting this problem was obvious. They had exactly the right distribution of members to make up for the Liberals' deficiencies in representation; at the same time their presence in the Cabinet would provide a visible demonstration of the ideological unity of their party and the Liberal party. Their assistance, however, would be much more certain and permanent if they could be induced to join as full-fledged colleagues of the Liberal Ministers without any of the mental reservations which would be implicit in a coalition.

King's second main objective, the personal one of strengthening his own position as the leader of a re-established Liberal party, also had its effect on the formation of the Cabinet. His relative youth and limited experience made him somewhat uneasy in a position where he would inevitably be compared with colleagues whose political reputation was more solidly established. He was therefore not willing to give all the choice positions in the Cabinet to the older men, "the left-overs of the Laurier administration," as Sir Clifford Sifton unkindly called them. Younger members would naturally be more sympathetic and grateful and almost certainly more amenable. But the old ones had claims which could not be denied. Thus King gave Fielding the top position in the Cabinet next to his own—the Ministry of Finance; yet his treatment of him during this period was both unkind and unfair. In the multitude of consultations which led up to the final selection for the Cabinet Fielding was almost completely ignored. King was inclined to be envious of Fielding's reputation, his general ability and experience, his superiority in debate, and he never entirely forgave the old rival who was still able, by contrast, to dim the lustre of King's leadership. There were others in this group whom King viewed coldly, and with much more justification. Rodolphe Lemieux's position as an ex-Minister and a leading Liberal orator in Quebec gave him powerful claims to a Cabinet appointment, and his vanity, ambition, and unpredictable temperament made him a dangerous man to neglect for preferment. King was suspicious of Graham because he was too favourable to the big interests and too closely associated with the machine gang in Ontario. Murphy, a fourth ex-Minister, was both fearless and honest; but his inveterate hatred of the Unionist Liberals marked him out as a potential troublemaker who was quite capable of carrying on his own little feuds against any colleague whom he disliked.

King's determination to make himself the acknowledged head of the party naturally led him to use his authority to entrench himself against possible intrigues designed to remove him from the leadership. The chief cause of his concern (as the election episode mentioned above showed) was Sir Lomer Gouin, whose fifteen years as Premier of Quebec, administrative ability of a high order, and recognized position among the big interests in Montreal, made him a formidable threat if circumstances should bring him forward as a rival. King accordingly set out to emphasize his primacy by keeping in addition to the Prime Ministership two of the most important positions in the Cabinet for himself—those of the President of the Privy Council and the Secretary of State for External Affairs. The most sedulous efforts were made in the period when the Cabinet was being formed to secure the Presidency of the Privy Council for Gouin, presumably with the idea of placing him in a position where he would be regarded as virtually the equal of the Prime Minister. King repeatedly refused to consider any such proposal. "I feel," he wrote in his diary, "I must keep that in my own hand, first to have greater control & prestige in Council and 2ndly to avoid emphasis of Quebec control."[14]

As King turned to the actual choice of a Cabinet, other aims and principles emerged. "A united Canada," in his opinion, demanded that the Cabinet Ministers should represent farmers, labour, soldiers, business men, and the professions. Although he expressed the pious wish that there should be no sectional feeling, he accepted the imperative necessity of maintaining a balance between Protestant and Roman Catholic and of giving representation on a basis of provinces. "There can be nothing more unfortunate for this Dominion," he said some months later, "than that any part of it should have cause to feel that it is not to have its voice in the councils of the country."[15] This representation, however, would not be based on the members the Liberal party had elected from each province but broadly on the total number of seats to which each province was entitled—a principle that was a severe disappointment to the three which had gone "solidly" Liberal in the election. He was also determined to reduce the Cabinet's size to sixteen members. Ontario was to be given four Ministers in addition to King himself, Quebec four and the Solicitor General (outside the Cabinet), the other provinces one each. A Minister without portfolio would speak for the Government in the Senate; but all other Ministers were to be in the Commons.

Two days after the election King went over with Andrew Haydon*
a tentative list of Cabinet possibilities. This list was to undergo changes
in both personnel and in departmental assignments, but it is not
without interest in showing King's intentions before he was subjected
to the demands and refusals which lay in the immediate future. The
list read: Fielding, Finance; Drury, Railways; Kennedy, Public Works;
Lapointe, Marine and Fisheries; Hudson (possibly), Justice; Crerar,
Interior; Murphy, Post Office; Gouin, Trade and Commerce; Sinclair,
Customs and Inland Revenue; Murdock, Labour; Motherwell or
Marshall, Agriculture; McMaster, Solicitor General; Béland, Secretary
of State; Dandurand, Leader in the Senate (without portfolio); Militia
and Defence, and Soldiers' Civil Re-establishment, undecided.[16]

It is not possible to trace the negotiations and manoeuvres of the
next three weeks, but their nature and complexity may be indicated.
The most important by far of these operations was the attempt to
induce the Progressives to enter the Cabinet and thus bring to fruition
King's consistent endeavour of over two years. He realized that this
might mean a break with some of the Quebec right wing, but if the
gains were large he was inclined to accept the risk, especially as his
natural sympathies were with the farmer and against big business.
Moreover, an offer at this time, when he could plainly get along without the Progressives' help, was likely to appear more generous and
disinterested than one made under more adverse circumstances, and
it might well produce the desired response. The tentative Cabinet
given above indicated the extent to which King was prepared to join
with the farmers. Crerar, Drury, and Hudson (nominally a Liberal,
but with strong Progressive affiliations) represented the farmers' movement, and with Motherwell, Marshall, and McMaster could be
counted as low tariff men. Lapointe and Béland could be relied on to
be in sympathy with the farmers' point of view on the tariff and on
other matters. Some balance, however, was achieved by the inclusion
of Gouin and Dandurand from the reactionary Quebec wing, and
these two with Fielding and Kennedy gave assurance that the protectionist interest in Quebec and Ontario would not be forgotten. The

---

*Andrew Haydon, the secretary of the national Liberal convention in 1919, served
as the secretary of the national Liberal organization from 1920 to 1922. He was a
most perceptive politician who combined to an unusual degree qualities of warmth
and intellectual objectivity. Mackenzie King placed full reliance on Haydon's discretion and personal loyalty.

names of some of the old guard, however—notably Graham and Le-mieux—do not appear on the initial list at all.

The meeting with Haydon was followed by another the next day, and a few slight revisions in the list were made. On the day after that (December 10) Ernest Lapointe arrived in Ottawa, the first member of Parliament to be invited by King to discuss the composition of the new Cabinet.

King had previously chosen Lapointe as his chief ally in Quebec; indeed early in September he had told him so and had also promised that if the Liberals won he could have his choice of portfolios.[17] Lapointe was now forty-five years of age and had been in Parliament over seventeen years. He was the leader and spokesman for those Quebec Liberals who were generally opposed to the reactionary wing led by Sir Lomer Gouin. Lapointe's followers included Henri Béland and Jacques Bureau, and the group as a whole drew most of its support from the agrarian interests of the province, being more responsive to the main objectives of the farmers' movement than Gouin and his associates.

King now renewed the assurances which he had given Lapointe in September, and he took further steps to consolidate a friendship which was to endure until Lapointe's death twenty years later:

> I told him I regarded him as nearest to me & wd. give him my confidence in full now & always. We would work out matters together. I regarded him as the real leader in Quebec, had sent for him first of all as promised. Asked which portfolio he wd. like & said he could have it—he said Justice—that he was not good at business administrat'n, that Justice gave chance of study. . . . He said Justice wd. give him the prestige he needed in his province. He is *worthy* of Justice, is just & honorable at heart—a beautiful Christian character—he shall have it.[18]

The Cabinet list was again scrutinized and various changes and contingencies considered. Lapointe expressed himself in full agreement with King's endeavour to bring the Progressives into the Cabinet. Haydon was therefore sent to Winnipeg to talk to Crerar and Hudson, while King undertook to see Drury, the leader of the Progressives in Ontario and the Premier of that province.

The negotiations in Winnipeg extended over five days, from December 12 to 16. Haydon kept in constant telegraphic communication with Mackenzie King, by code messages to and from King's secretary,

F. A. McGregor.* Haydon at once told Crerar and Hudson that King's desire was to form a genuinely representative Government "free from the domination by the Montreal interests & any reactionary influences in his own party," and he then placed before them the proposed Cabinet which was essentially the same as the initial list given above.† Crerar and Hudson were very favourably impressed and said "they thought the slate would be regarded in the West as an evidence of King's desire to create a really forward looking Government."[19] From this point the discussion turned at once to the policies of the new Government and to the possibility that the Prairie Provinces might obtain four Cabinet Ministers instead of the three offered. In the negotiations which followed King remained firm on the question of the number of Ministers, but met the Progressives more than half way on the measures which they wished to have included in the Government's future programme.‡

When Crerar and Hudson declined to accept the suggested compromise and reiterated their demands, King abandoned any attempt to negotiate on details and on December 15 urged the Progressives to enter the Cabinet "on same basis as representation from ranks of Liberals namely on policies as announced and faith in personnel of administration to do justly by all concerned. . . . Pressure is very great as to other alternatives and I must come to quick decision stop Each day's delay likely to prove prejudicial with respect to what we have been considering."[20] Lapointe also sent a telegram which asked for their confidence and urged a speedy agreement.[21] Crerar and Hudson nevertheless refused to commit themselves, and, though hopeful of a

---

*The records for these meetings are for the most part contained in these telegrams (in the King Papers) and in a memorandum, which also includes the same telegrams, kept by A. B. Hudson (this is part of the A. B. Hudson Papers, Public Archives of Canada).

†A. B. Hudson Papers, Hudson Memorandum, Dec. 12, 1921. The list contained three additional names: General Currie, Copp, and Bostock. Those of Dandurand and Hudson had been omitted, Hudson's because of the inadvisability of giving seats in the Cabinet to two members from Manitoba, Crerar and Hudson.

‡The Progressives demanded: (1) a tariff according to the Liberal platform; (2) immediate transfer to the three provincial governments of the natural resources of the Prairie Provinces (withheld by the Dominion when the provinces were created) with possible financial adjustment later; (3) restoration of lower freight rates; (4) willingness to consider reciprocity; (5) full fair trial for public ownership of railways. (A. Haydon to F. A. McGregor, Dec. 12, 1921.) King accepted completely (4) and (5); was non-committal on (3); and met a large part of (1) and (2). (F. A. McGregor to A. Haydon, Dec. 14, 1921.)

successful result, asked for time to consult a meeting of Progressive members which had been called to assemble in Saskatoon four days later.[22] For the moment, therefore, negotiations between Mackenzie King and Crerar were held in suspense awaiting the decision of this conference.

Several comments are suggested by this exchange of views. King and Lapointe not unnaturally had a much livelier appreciation of the alternative claims pressing in on King and of the little time which was available for discussion. Time was, indeed, working against the Progressives and against King's effort to re-establish the Liberals as a national party. Each day that passed exposed King to further pressure from the reactionary Quebec group and increased the odds that more members from or in harmony with that group would be taken into the Cabinet. There was a very real danger that the original "purity" of this body, which had seemed so attractive to Western eyes, would become gravely compromised, and the Progressive leaders would then find it increasingly difficult to enter the Cabinet themselves or to justify their entrance to their followers. It is also interesting to note that no one at the Winnipeg conference had mentioned the possibility of any coalition between the two parties. Inasmuch as King had publicly taken a firm stand against coalition both before and after the election and Crerar had been emphatically warned that no Progressive should enter the Cabinet on any other basis,[23] one must assume that the Progressive leader at this juncture had abandoned the idea or thought it of little importance compared to matters of policy and Cabinet personnel. It can also be observed that Mackenzie King does not seem to have made sufficient allowance for the Progressives' distrust of the old parties or for the reluctance of Progressive members to follow their leader. He evidently expected that Crerar could with little or no delay accept a Cabinet position on behalf of his party and presumably also bring his party members with him. Crerar was similarly confident that a meeting with his followers on the prairies and in Ontario would enable him to enter the Cabinet with the necessary assurances of support. He did appreciate, however, the imperative necessity of securing the approval of the Progressive members before taking the decisive step and he had clearly prolonged the higgling over better terms for that express purpose.

While Haydon was consulting the Western Progressives, other conversations were being held in the East. Two days after King had seen Lapointe, he had held interviews with Kennedy, Lemieux, Murphy, Béland, Low, Euler, Fielding, Gouin, and others. The long procession of well-wishers and potential Ministers had begun, each of them offering advice and applying what pressure he could to influence King's choice. Letters and telegrams began to pour in from all sides asking for the preferment of certain members, who in most cases quite obviously had appealed to certain religious, economic, or racial groups for their written support.

King was to meet Drury in Toronto on December 14. Before this meeting took place, he had sounded out a number of prominent Liberals, and he had discovered that contrary to the general belief held in the West, most of these Liberals, including Gouin and Lemieux, favoured inviting Progressives into the Cabinet.* King found Drury very willing to join the Cabinet if he could discover someone to take his place as head of the Ontario Government. He was the first Progressive in all these Cabinet negotiations to bring up the question of coalition at Ottawa, but King refused to consider it. Drury sided against Crerar in thinking that the latter was unreasonable in his insistence on explicit pledges from King; but he too asked for time to consult his followers before making any further commitments.[24]

In the midst of these grave counsels came a brief interlude of comic opera in Winnipeg. By a devious channel involving a talkative telegraph operator, a young admirer with a discriminating ear for gossip, a shrewd bit of reasoning on the part of the admirer's father who also happened to be a disgruntled Liberal, the presence of Andrew Haydon at the Fort Garry Hotel and the purpose of his visit to Winnipeg were discovered. To add dramatic interest to the story, the vital telegrams were stolen from the telegraph office. They were later recovered; nevertheless the secret—if secret, indeed, it had even been—was out. The Montreal *Star* of December 15 mentioned Haydon's "significant mission" to Winnipeg, and the "pourparlers with the agrarian party," neither of which was calculated to soothe those Liberals who were averse to having any dealings with the Progressives. Whether, as frequently alleged, the pressure on Mackenzie King from Eastern sources

*Diary, Dec. 12, 13, 1921. The records reveal only one expression from Quebec against conducting negotiations with Crerar: a message from Premier Taschereau received by King on December 23. It is interesting that throughout all the conferences with the Quebec right wing leaders their efforts were always concentrated on getting their "sound" men into the Cabinet rather than on trying to keep "unsound" men out.

was markedly increased as a result of this disclosure, is not established by the records,* partly because from the day of the election to the day the Cabinet took the oath the pressure on King was unceasing, and also because it is well nigh inconceivable that the entrance of some Progressives had not already been considered as a very active possibility. After all, Gouin and Lemieux (as stated above) had not only considered such an eventuality but had given it their approval.

The continuing pressure on King assumed two forms: an effort to maintain or increase the number of Ministers from a particular province, and an effort to secure a special or any portfolio for a particular person. The most urgent representations of the former type came from Quebec and Nova Scotia, which naturally stressed their impressive election results. Nova Scotia was especially aggrieved by the suggestion that for virtually the first time in her history she was to have only one Minister in the Cabinet. Quebec also struggled to secure the prized positions for some of its members. Gouin and Lapointe were in the Cabinet without dispute; Lemieux had in some way to be pacified; and the reactionary wing never relaxed its efforts to secure berths— and good berths at that—for such men as Senator Dandurand, J. A. Robb, and, above all, Walter Mitchell. Even Lapointe, who was none too sure at this time of his position in Quebec, was anxious to conciliate the rival group by making concessions to its members, and he eventually withdrew his claims to the Department of Justice in favour of Gouin and took the much less important portfolio of Marine and Fisheries. Thus although King was very anxious to favour the Lapointe following and although he distrusted Gouin and the whole protectionist coterie from Montreal, he was, at least in the absence of firm support from the Progressives, in no position to ignore them. He could only fight them off, hold down their representation in the Cabinet to the minimum possible, and uphold to the best of his ability the position of the Lapointe group. In all this he was only moderately successful. The final result showed that the Gouin and the Lapointe supporters had each secured three Ministers, and that Lemieux had also been recognized by being made Speaker of the House of Commons.

In the meantime consultations were proceeding in the West.

*Thus Senators Dandurand and Béique talked to King on December 15, the day the Montreal papers carried the news of the conferences in Winnipeg with Crerar and Hudson. There is no evidence that the senators even mentioned on this occasion the possibility of Progressives in the Cabinet.

Haydon left Winnipeg for Ottawa on December 17, and that same evening a number of Progressives met with Crerar to discuss the results of the Winnipeg conversations. They clearly thought Crerar and Hudson had shown a lack of firmness in resisting King's advances. "There was practically unanimity," wrote J. W. Dafoe, one of those present, "in the view that co-operation could only be possible on the basis of a formal coalition with public guarantees which would be a protection for Mr. Crerar against his own people"—an opinion which was apparently now shared by Drury who had telegraphed Crerar to the same general effect.[25] The meeting evidently succeeded in convincing Crerar that he should have raised the question of coalition with Haydon and that his chances of winning the support of his followers without it and without a formal agreement with the Liberals on specific measures were very remote.[26] This had been the view persistently advanced by Sifton and Dafoe, who were very suspicious of Mackenzie King's sincerity and of his susceptibility to sinister interests in the East.[27] That such demands as these two men proposed would not only keep the Progressives out of the Government but would allow the dreaded Eastern influence a proportionately greater scope does not appear to have worried them, or, if it did, was more than overbalanced in their minds by a desire to promote the interests of the farmer, to maintain the continued existence and vitality of the Progressive movement, and to smash or exorcise the reactionary section of the Liberal party. Following this latest expression of Progressive opinion, Hudson was sent post-haste to Ottawa to make the revised terms known to King.

Hudson arrived in Ottawa on December 20, a day after Haydon. He saw King and Haydon at once, and raised the possibility of coalition, now advanced by both Crerar and Drury.[28] King said that neither he nor his followers would think of it, and expressed some surprise that Drury had gone back on the assurances which he had given him only a few days before. Drury came to Ottawa the next day, and told King that his followers insisted that he should remain at the head of the Government of Ontario, but that he would like to see Crerar and Hudson in the Cabinet. He again proved fickle on the coalition issue:

He agreed that I was right in not conceding a coalition, he saw I could not, that Progressives wd. have to play a minor role in federal govt, just as Lib's wd have to in provincial field, he thought I might have to give some

367

visible evidence of meeting progressive ideas, go some length. I said not the length of coalition & he said no, but something that wd. enable them to see that their ideas were recognized to a degree. I said taking in Crerar, himself, & Hudson was pretty good visible evidence, they could leave the Ministry if not in sympathy as we worked out our policies. I imagined he had "free agric'l implements" in mind but he did not say.[29]

On the same day, December 21, King received through Hudson a report on Crerar's meeting with his Western parliamentary followers in Saskatoon. These members promised to give general support to the Liberal Government in enacting measures which the Progressives had advocated "while at the same time maintaining the complete identity and organization of the Progressive party." Nevertheless, they gave their tacit approval (a number of the Alberta members dissenting) to the entrance of Crerar or any other Progressive into the Cabinet as individuals providing the policy and personnel of the Government proved satisfactory.* This moderate attitude was considered by both King and Hudson to be definitely encouraging. "I feel now," King wrote in his diary, "the Rubicon has been crossed and that the gulf between East & West has been bridged."[30]

But the Progressives were not to relinquish thus easily their propensity for political coyness and unreliability, and all hopes of agreement were speedily shattered by the intransigent federal members from the Ontario wing of the party. At a conference with Crerar in Toronto they refused to approve of his entrance or that of any other Progressive into the King Government.[31] No report of this meeting exists, but the decision would seem to have arisen from the bitterness of the recent election contests, the presence of former Conservatives in the Progressive party, a growing class consciousness of the Ontario farmers, the declared policy of the Ontario Progressives not to participate in the federal Government, and the unrelenting propaganda of the *Farmers' Sun*.[32]

This meeting took place on the evening of December 23, the same day that saw the maximum pressure exerted on King by the Quebec leaders. It was on this morning that King persuaded Lapointe in the interests of harmony to exchange Justice for Marine and Fisheries.

*Hudson Papers, T. A. Crerar to A. B. Hudson, Dec. 21, 1921. There are several versions of what was done at this meeting but the above is the most authentic. See W. L. Morton, *The Progressive Party in Canada* (Toronto, 1950), pp. 131–6.

He also beat off again the claims of Walter Mitchell, had a talk with Andrew McMaster who, by contrast, was agreeably modest in his attitude, and another with D. D. McKenzie who followed the more usual practice of dwelling on his own virtues. He had a rather unpleasant scene with Gouin and Dandurand in which the offer of Justice to Gouin scarcely atoned for King's flat refusal to make Gouin President of the Privy Council. Other talks with Premier Martin of Saskatchewan, Kennedy, Low, Lapointe (a second time), Hudson, and Haydon, made a full day. Some of these interviews were exploratory and marked by a desire to be genuinely helpful; others were given over to argument and the airing of grievances; still others were characterized by bitterness and recrimination. King listened on the whole patiently to the multitude of representations placed before him. On him fell the burden of decision, the weighing of possible men and possible offices against other men and offices, the discounting and whittling down of pretensions and claims, the soothing of hurt feelings—all being related to the suitability of the candidate for the department and to the balance of provincial, sectional, and religious representation. Hudson, who naturally obtained most of his information second-hand, wrote in his memorandum: "Conference King-Lapointe, Haydon and Hudson. Montreal pressure great Situation tense."[33] King's summary was: "A very strenuous day, but felt I had fought a good fight. Stood my ground firm against handing over Canada's future to the financial magnates of Montreal."[34]

Crerar arrived in Ottawa on December 24. He had a long talk with King[35] who pointed out the great opportunity open to Crerar to promote national unity and goodwill. King urged him and others whom Crerar might name to enter the Cabinet on the same basis as other Ministers. King refused, however, to discuss coalition or "terms" beyond a general understanding on policy. Crerar said he would like to come in and had left the West with that in mind provided the general policy was satisfactory. In view of the decided and unanimous opposition he had encountered in Toronto, however, he now felt he could not do so at the present time. He nevertheless assured King that the Government would receive independent support from his party for "progressive" legislation, and that it would not become the official Opposition in the House. King "emphasized the possible loss to the

West thro' not having adequate representation in the Cabinet in the shaping of policies, the need for Western men. Crerar agreed but frankly confessed he felt his following (Espec. in Ontario) wd not support him."

Crerar then consented to look over a list of proposed members of the Cabinet and found that it now contained more of the reactionary element than the earlier one which he had seen in Winnipeg. This, of course, should have occasioned no surprise; it was a natural consequence of the wide and varied pressures to which King had been subjected in the long interval when the Progressives were higgling with the Liberals for concessions and reviewing the situation in their own party conferences. Crerar took exception to some of the names,* but King pointed out that the list was still tentative, that one or two were mutually exclusive, and that at least one other was temporary. "He asked me," King said, "if he & others didn't come in would I change my line of policy in any particular. I replied no, tho' it might be more difficult for me to go as far as I would like. He said he was glad to hear me say that." This virtually ended the negotiations, and some hours later Crerar informed King of his final decision to stay out. After a few days Hudson also refused, but for a time King still had hopes he would change his mind, and on the final slate the Manitoba representation was left vacant to provide for this contingency.

Neither King nor Crerar could properly be blamed for the collapse of what might well have been a mutually satisfactory arrangement. The offenders were the Progressives in conference in Toronto assisted, no doubt, by the kindred spirits in the Alberta minority who had dissented in Saskatoon. Crerar could lead his party only so far, and he could not be expected to go into the Cabinet a leader without most of his following. Nor is it at all likely that even a radical alteration in King's terms, if he had felt free to make one, would have changed the minds of the Alberta and Ontario Progressives. A slate different from that shown by King to Crerar on December 24, for example, would probably have had not the slightest effect on Crerar's decision,†

*He objected chiefly to Gouin, Graham, Lemieux, and D. D. McKenzie. Of these four, only Gouin's name had been on the list he had seen in Winnipeg.

†Crerar in later accounts was inclined to blame changes in policy and personnel for his refusal, rather than the stand of the Ontario Progressives. A. K. Cameron Papers, T. A. Crerar to A. K. Cameron, Jan. 19, 1922; Dafoe Papers, Sir C. Sifton to J. W. Dafoe, Dec. 30, 1921. But the King Diary and the Hudson Memorandum agree with the account given above.

nor would King's acquiescence in a coalition have fared any better.

There is no doubt in my mind [wrote J. W. Dafoe] that under no circumstances could Crerar have taken the whole strength of the Progressive movement with him if he had gone into the Government, even though he had had his due proportion of colleagues and there had been provision made for preserving the identity of the Progressives. Correspondence which I am in receipt of from farmers out in the country makes it clear to me that they regarded the whole movement as one of the old fashioned manoeuvres by which they were to be buncoed in the interests of the big corporations.[36]

So long as the Progressives took this attitude and continued to hold to their demand to "influence legislation and yet not be responsible for carrying on the government,"[37] Crerar could scarcely take any other course.

The outlook of the Progressives was narrow, and the minds behind it incredibly naive. The way to achieve their ends was not by sitting in the seats of the scornful, but by gaining a hold on the executive power and through their own Ministers inducing the Cabinet to foster the measures they desired. King's argument to Crerar that without adequate representation the West would lose out in the formulation of Cabinet policies was thus the simple and obvious truth.* The reactionaries from Quebec may have been low creatures in the eyes of the Progressives, but they could have given them valuable hints on how to turn election results to the protection of sectional interests. These men did not withdraw to their sanctuary in St. James Street and refuse to accept the offices tendered them. On the contrary, they took all the portfolios offered, and fought tooth and nail for as many more as possible. The Nova Scotians were no less active in their insistence on two Ministers from that province. These men well knew that those who were represented in the Cabinet were exerting their power at the point where it was certain to produce the maximum effect.

The way was now clear for King to make his final selection. He proceeded to fill the portfolios which he had been holding provisionally for the Progressives, he appointed a number of those who had been already approached, and he brought to a conclusion his efforts to

*Three days before Crerar's arrival in Ottawa, King had written in his diary in reference to a proposal from one of the Quebec right wing that the Grand Trunk should be returned to its shareholders: "Already 'getting busy'—here is stronger need for Progressives if they want to hold principles & policies not to bargain but to get into the Govt." Diary, Dec. 21, 1921.

satisfy or postpone the demands of the Gouin group in Quebec. To secure a member from Alberta, he took the recent premier of that province, Charles Stewart, whose Government had been defeated five months earlier, and found a seat for him in Quebec. Seats had to be found for two other Ministers, James Murdock and Dr. J. H. King, the former having been defeated in the election, the latter being brought in from the British Columbia Cabinet to strengthen the representation from that province. The total number in the Cabinet proved to be three more than originally planned, although this was two less than its predecessor under Meighen. Ontario and Quebec emerged with six members each, Nova Scotia with two, all the others, except Manitoba, with one apiece.

There were other adjustments and concessions made in the process of Cabinet making. The Gouin wing received greater recognition than King desired, and at least two other members, Murphy and Graham, whom he did not want, were given portfolios. Yet of the sixteen names on King's original list, eleven eventually made the Cabinet, which, considering that three of the missing ones were Progressives, was not a very great departure from what had never been intended to be a final selection. The striking difference was in the beliefs of the Ministers who had been added and substituted, for with the defection of the Progressives only three low-tariff men remained, Stewart, Motherwell, and the Prime Minister, although a number of others had low-tariff tendencies. King's original intention of keeping the protectionist group in second place was therefore not realized. King had also played with the idea of following the British example by introducing parliamentary under-secretaries, but he apparently found he had enough on his hands at this time without offering further hostages to fortune.

Nevertheless King did succeed in a number of his objectives. The Cabinet brought about some reconciliation of interests between East and West, between French speaking and English speaking areas, and between the different groups in Quebec. It also effected a union of Laurier and Unionist Liberals, for four of the Ministers, Fielding, Graham, Murdock, and Stewart, had supported conscription. King's three rivals for the leadership in 1919 were all recognized by Cabinet appointments, though King viewed the acquisition of these members of the old guard with little enthusiasm. "I see that these old men are going to be troublesome, & will require some handling," he wrote impatiently in his diary during the negotiations; and later he consoled himself with the reflection that they "will not last long . . . meanwhile gives time to look around and make plans."[38] Several men he took into the Cabinet unwillingly, but he was successful, despite severe pressure, in his endeavour to keep others out, notably Lemieux, Mitchell, and E. M. Macdonald. He had also taken the unusual step of extracting written undertakings from five Ministers (McKenzie, Robb, Copp, Graham, and Motherwell) that they would resign whenever he thought necessary, so that the Cabinet had a flexibility which would permit the addition of younger men—even, perhaps, Progressives—if any later changes should be desirable.

The first Mackenzie King administration took office on December 29, 1921. The Ministers were as follows:

W. L. Mackenzie King: Prime Minister, External Affairs, President of the Privy Council
W. S. Fielding: Finance
G. P. Graham: Militia and Defence, and Naval Service
Charles Murphy: Post Office
Raoul Dandurand: Minister without Portfolio
H. S. Béland: Soldiers' Civil Re-establishment and Health
Sir Lomer Gouin: Justice, and Attorney General
Jacques Bureau: Customs and Excise
Ernest Lapointe: Marine and Fisheries
D. D. McKenzie: Solicitor General
J. A. Robb: Trade and Commerce
T. A. Low: Minister without Portfolio
A. B. Copp: Secretary of State
W. C. Kennedy: Railways and Canals
Charles Stewart: Interior, Indian Affairs, and Mines
W. R. Motherwell: Agriculture
James Murdock: Labour
J. E. Sinclair: Minister without Portfolio
James H. King: Public Works*

Two days before the Cabinet assumed office a constitutional issue had arisen involving the functions of the Governor-General. It was interesting for itself alone, and also for its relevance to several other questions which were to arise later. The Governor-General, Lord Byng

*J. H. King succeeded Hewitt Bostock on Feb. 3, 1922. Senator Bostock was originally appointed to the Cabinet, but it was announced at the time that he was to become Speaker of the Senate and that the portfolio would revert to the House of Commons.

of Vimy, had come to Canada in the preceding August after a distinguished military career which included the command of the Canadian Corps in France in 1916–17. He was handsome, friendly, forthright, and high-minded, with not only the merits of the soldier but the mental limitations as well. He had had no experience of political life, and, indeed, if we are to believe his wife, both of them "always shunned and detested politics"[39]—an extraordinary frame of mind for one who had chosen to live in that milieu for four or five years. To him, as to many other soldiers, politics presented few problems if he followed the path of duty: things were white or black, and greys, despite what the politicians might pretend, simply did not exist for those who were honest and unselfish in purpose. Early in September Byng had had a talk with King at which he presented his views with an engaging simplicity:

> Mr. King, I want to put myself in your hands. I have only one object that is to be of what service I can, I have no axe to grind, only to do what I can where opportunity offers, I shall be glad to have you speak very freely. As to being a constitutional gov'r, I understand that, there will be little difficulty to keep on right lines. As to party politics they are easily understood. I suppose the old parties are here much as they are in Eng. The one wants a little more 'Liberty,' the other a little more law. There are Libs who are conservative and conservatives who are Liberal. With the Farmers one can understand it is the tariff.
>
> I sd. I shld welcome a chance to tell him a few things on this score,—give him the Lib'l point of view. . . . I told him I might speak too frankly, without tact, etc. He replied that was what he wanted.[40]

December gave the Governor-General his first real contact with the harsh facts of political life. Mr. Meighen had been personally defeated in the election. On December 27, just before his resignation as Prime Minister became effective, he advised Byng to appoint one of the recently elected Conservative members of Parliament to a position in the government service. To accept a salaried government office of this kind would automatically make the member ineligible under the existing law to sit in Parliament,* and a seat would thus be opened up for Meighen which he could contest in the subsequent by-election. After some hesitation Byng accepted the advice and made the appoint-

---

*A member of Parliament who accepted an "office of profit or emolument under the Crown" thereby vacated his seat in the House, unless the office were a portfolio when a special provision applied.

ment. The writ for the by-election was issued immediately, and Meighen was elected.

Canada and Great Britain could provide a number of precedents to support Meighen's advice as well as the Governor-General's acceptance of it, though under similar circumstances in 1896 the Governor, Lord Aberdeen, had refused to follow the recommendations made by Sir Charles Tupper, the head of the defeated Government. Aberdeen's action had moreover been upheld by the Colonial Office, which was apparently more concerned about the unfairness of Tupper's attempt than about its constitutionality,[41] and a new and conflicting precedent had thus been created.

Mackenzie King, who was in the position of awaiting office, not unnaturally favoured the Tupper-Aberdeen precedent, and, indeed, he had *before* the election committed himself to a somewhat broader application of its underlying principle. He had written Meighen on December 4 to the effect that as the country had obviously lost confidence in Meighen's Government, nothing should be done in the way of appointments or contracts for which there was not "the fullest legislative sanction." Any such acts, he said, would not be honoured by any Government of which he was the head.[42] When he later heard of Meighen's expedient to provide himself with a seat in Parliament he was most indignant, and denounced it in a public statement as "high handed," "unwarranted," and "morally indefensible."[43] His private opinion was that Byng should at least have consulted his Prime Minister-elect and secured his consent before making the appointment. He nevertheless accepted the *fait accompli*.

Lord Byng, for his part, was most unhappy at the role he had been compelled to play in this political legerdemain. Meighen had made him a participant in what he thought was a discreditable act: and Byng's sense of fair play was outraged by this last minute attempt to circumvent the wishes of those whom the people of Canada had chosen. He had protested—which was, of course, his right—but in the end he had acquiesced because he felt that he was bound to accept the advice of his constitutional advisers. A few minutes before King and the Cabinet were sworn, he told King his story:

His Ex. then asked me to be seated then spoke somewhat in the following manner and strain. 'Mr. King, I want to give you my entire confidence, to tell you everything. I shall keep nothing from you, if there are matters I want to speak about I shall do so quite frankly, then when you have decided I shall have nothing more to say. Now just because I want you to know everything and to conceal nothing I am going to tell you that during the last few days I have had matters placed before me which I did not like, of which I was unwilling to approve, at least 8 or 9 important matters or appointments. I have spoken very openly and said I do not think these matters should be pressed. Mr. King is the elect of the people and without his knowledge or consent I do not think you should ask me to sign.

I have told Mr. Meighen that, and I have told his Ministers sitting in that very chair that you are in, I have said You are my constitutional advisor [sic] and I must act on your advice but I do not think you should ask me to do this thing. I say that Mr. King—I tell you that because of this one exception in the case of Mr. Meighen, it has caused me a great deal of worry and I have felt I should tell you everything—otherwise it would be like telling tales out of school. When Mr. Meighen placed before me the order regarding the seat in Grenville I did not like it, I felt tho' that he was my constitutional adviser, that I was acting in a constitutional way in taking his advice, because it was a matter personal to himself I did not like to raise a further question. I tell you this Mr. King that you may know my whole mind.

I then said "I think it was most unfair to your Excellency for Mr. Meighen to have put you in that position." I added I think he has done himself an irreparable injury. His Excellency then said to me "You can afford to be generous toward him" I replied that I was prepared to be, that I wd. have facilitated his getting a seat in the H. of C. but that the method he had taken did violence to the whole spirit of the constitution.[44]

In four and a half years' time Byng was to find himself in another quandary which was not entirely alien to this one although in the interval the two rivals for office had changed places. But the general problem which he had to face was in many ways the same. He perceived in each dispute the same desire to gain a political advantage; he was shocked by the same appearance of what to him was unfairness and lack of generosity; he felt the same need to offer his protests and remonstrances; and he was tempted by the same impulse to substitute his own judgment for that of his constitutional advisers and in so doing raise his voice on behalf of the absent opponent who was unable to defend himself. The two cases presented, of course, a number of different and distinguishing features, and Lord Byng added yet another: in the first dispute he followed the advice of his Prime Minister, and in the second he rejected it.

CHAPTER FOURTEEN

FIRST ADMINISTRATION, 1921–1922

ALTHOUGH Mackenzie King had finally reached his goal as Prime Minister, his political future and that of his party were by no means assured. It is true that under his relatively brief leadership the Liberals had made a remarkable recovery: the schism of 1917 had been in large measure repaired and the results of the election had given clear confirmation of the restoration of party unity. But the victory, while impressive, was incomplete. Not only had the Liberals failed by a narrow margin to gain a majority of seats, they had been unable to establish an understanding with the farmers, and their representation in Parliament thus lacked the breadth and variety which was indispensable for a national party. King was fully conscious of this weakness, and he had done his utmost to overcome it both before and after the election. He had endeavoured by fair words and practical proposals of co-operation to forestall the clashes in the conventions and the constituencies, but he had been defeated by the hostile attitude of the Progressives, who were exhilarated by their provincial victories and their success in the federal by-elections. He had made further attempts in forming his Government but his proposals had again been rejected; for the Progressives, having played a lone hand with such happy results at the polls, were now determined to put their fortune to the test in the much more complicated game which was about to begin in Parliament.

King was disappointed and somewhat irritated by the failure of the Progressives to respond to his advances, but he was by no means discouraged. He could afford to wait. A number of forces were working for him and in the long run were likely to bring about the union he desired. His recent negotiations with the Progressive leaders were not to be counted a complete loss. He had demonstrated his desire to have them in his Cabinet; they had been very friendly and even appreciative; and there was good reason to believe that they had only been dissuaded from entering the Government by a growing conviction that their followers would not support them. Moreover, Crerar had given King two valuable assurances for the future. The Progressives, he had said, would not become the official Opposition, although as the second largest party in the House they were entitled to avail themselves of that privilege. He had also told King that his party was not anxious to defeat the Government but would assist it in carrying out any legislative programme with which the Progressives were in sympathy. Any direct collision between Liberals and Progressives was therefore unlikely. There would be no institutional emphasis on their differences, and even the most informal legislative co-operation would tend to promote closer party relations.

The collapse of negotiations over the composition of the Cabinet had also emphasized the continuing rift in the Progressive party membership which might well have interesting implications for the future. The Progressives, while united by a common distrust of the old parties, were still divided into two separate and antagonistic sections on other matters no less vital. The Manitoba and many of the Saskatchewan members, led by Crerar, were essentially reformers who were seeking "to recapture the historic Liberal party of rural democracy and low tariff from the protectionist elements of Quebec and Ontario, and reinvigorate it with the democratic force of the West."[1] The other group, composed of the Alberta and many of the Ontario Progressives, led in their respective provincial fields by H. W. Wood and J. J. Morrison, was much more radical. It wanted to rescue the nation from the burden of the two-party system and replace it with non-partisan group government based on the principles of constituency autonomy and occupational representation. This fundamental disagreement had from the beginning interfered with the solidarity of the Progressives. It had proved to be a factor when King's offer of representation in the Cabinet was being considered. It was no less certain to impair the effectiveness of the party in the House and make its course much more uncertain and difficult when exposed to the attacks or blandishments of the other parties. For although the purposes of the radical Progressives could not be brought into harmony with the aims and interests of the two old parties (who embodied the very system which they were determined to destroy), the purposes of the reforming Progressives

378

might well be merged with the aims and interests of the Liberals. Indeed, the great object of these reforming Progressives was to effect such an identification, to redeem the erring Liberals and bring to a successful conclusion the missionary effort which they had undertaken.

In this internal conflict of the Progressive party lay Mackenzie King's immediate hope for continuance in office and his future hope for a reconciliation between the reforming Progressives and the Liberals. A vote to defeat the Government would bring little benefit to any of the Progressives, since it would either put the Meighen Government back in power or precipitate a general election. Both alternatives were distasteful, though in their effort to discredit the whole mechanism of party government the radical Progressives might conceivably risk such a crisis. The reforming Progressives, however, would approach a decisive vote in the House with a much greater concern for the fate of the Liberal Government. They would give no support as a block, for their hesitation to make commitments or to follow their leaders made united action most unlikely; but in time of need—and certainly such occasions were apt to be frequent—some of this group would probably vote with the Liberals and avert what in their eyes also would be disaster. This was more than a vague hope. Long before the House met, King received indirect assurances that several Progressives were prepared to vote with the Government on any issue which might endanger its security,[2] and there were probably others who had not yet declared themselves. These few votes could spell the difference between victory and defeat.

In such an environment, Mackenzie King's course was clear. He must do nothing which would prevent at least some of the Progressives from supporting him. He must discover and develop those policies on which the Liberals and the more friendly Progressives were prepared to take a common stand, and he must limit his activity as far as possible to that area of agreement. He must take up and make his own whatever Progressive demands were most consistent with the Liberal 1919 platform and were at the same time least likely to alienate any substantial section of his own following. These tactics might be expected to develop habits of co-operation between the Liberals and the reforming Progressives and they would also serve to push the two Progressive sections still farther apart and perhaps accelerate that party's eventual disintegration. Moreover, King might hope at a more propitious time to repeat his overtures to the leaders of the reforming Progressives, and these, if accepted, would hasten the break with their more radical associates and promote their union with the Liberal party.

There were further considerations which would work towards the same end. The more the Liberals brought forward measures favoured by the Progressives, the more they struck at the heart of the whole third party movement and rendered its separate existence unnecessary. If the meeting of the complaints of the farmer could be accompanied by a general economic revival and the consequent removal of the over-riding grievance of hard times, the need for a party of protest became even more questionable. Here, however, King might encounter another difficulty—aside from the very evident one of a depression which refused to co-operate and play the Liberal game. He might find that after his efforts at conciliation had been successful, the Progressives might appropriate the lion's share of the credit for the reforms on the ground that they had been gained only through the constant pressure exerted by the minority on the Liberal Government. Instead of the Progressive movement losing vitality, it might thus emerge stronger than before. To avoid so disastrous an interpretation of events, King would have to move quickly and seize the initiative for the Government in presenting measures which were designed to meet the farmers' needs. Even then he might fail in his attempt, for much would depend on his ability to carry conviction and on his followers' willingness to acquiesce gracefully and with some enthusiasm in the proposed programme.

Beneath this attempt to find a common meeting ground in Parliament lay what was really the fundamental problem: the detachment of the voter's support from the third party movement and the restoration of confidence in the two party system. If these could be accomplished, the party struggle would resume its traditional form; and the future would then turn largely on the relative ability of King and Meighen to rebuild their strength in the areas which had recently shown so much antagonism to them. In a contest of this kind Meighen would be no match for his opponent. Meighen's trait of doggedly maintaining his views in the face of the strongest opposition, his lack of flexibility, and his unwillingness to make concessions to those who dissented from him were fatal barriers to any conciliatory effort. He had shown no signs whatever of trying to lead the Conservative party away from the high-tariff policies which were the root of the farmers' revolt, and in the election of 1921 he had committed the Conservatives even more deeply, if that were possible, to these policies. King, on the other hand, had lost no opportunity to soothe the opposition rather than irritate it, and he had never failed to insist that Liberals and Progressives thought alike on all important issues. If the Progressive party should fall apart—an event which King confidently expected—there would be little doubt where its members would find their most congenial home.

Although Mackenzie King had no dependable majority and would have to pick his steps carefully, he had little reason to dread the meeting of Parliament. A combination of all the Conservatives, Progressives, and Independents could defeat him, but these parties were naturally antipathetic and skilful management should reduce the danger of the Government's being placed in such a position that all the opposition would be forced to take the same side. If it kept away from the middle of the road when it became dangerous and held to a broadly progressive course, some members of the third party would naturally be drawn to the rescue. The really doubtful element was found nearer home in the protectionist right wing of the Liberals and there was a danger that their intrigue against his leadership might be revived. This group had not lost their suspicion of King's motives and were still afraid that he might make too many concessions to the Progressives, especially on the vital matter of the tariff. King might well feel that he could not afford, at this stage at least, to trade solid Liberal votes for the less reliable support of the Progressives.

The Prime Minister's hopes and plans for the political future, however, were temporarily pushed to one side by the news of the critical condition of his brother in Colorado. Max had never been absent from his thoughts in the strenuous days which had just passed, and although Max's health was rapidly failing his interest in the election had never flagged. No matter how crowded the schedule, Mackenzie King had rarely let a week go by without dictating four or five closely typed pages to his brother relating his experiences and tracing the developments of the campaign. Max's comments displayed a shrewd understanding of the changing political situation, and Mackenzie King repeatedly assured him that his interest and encouragement were very helpful in the contest. King's first telegram bearing the good news on the night of the election had been sent to Max, he had sent another after he was sworn in as Prime Minister, and he had made the characteristic gesture of writing him a brief note during the first meeting of the Cabinet.

Max was also useful in another way. As a brother he could be outspoken on many personal matters and was thus able to perform that invaluable critical function which is usually reserved to a wife as one of her most thankless prerogatives. He might also at times invoke an additional authority as a physician. Thus in the early days of the election campaign he wrote a very plain letter to Mackenzie King on his habit of excusing an indifferent speech on the grounds of fatigue:

Let me impress upon you again, my dear Will, the necessity for dissociating irrational auto-suggestion with regard to your own health from work toward the great purpose which you have in view. Your statement in your last letter that you "felt so run down physically" as a reason for not doing yourself justice in your speech before the Bar Association is the sort of thing I refer to. You could not find one well-informed and honest physician on this continent who would tell you that you are run down physically, and to suggest such ideas to yourself is simply to labour under the handicap of self-deception. To be sure the plea of body frailty offers a salve to negative self-feeling but you have neither need for negative self-feeling nor a salve. The truth can be faced quite fearlessly and is simply that you had so little time to prepare your speech that you did not do as well as you might have done otherwise. Why always drag in the matter of health? Such assertions may call forth acquiescence and sympathy from the vast majority of people but those who think for themselves will not fail to ridicule a weakness of this kind. I do not mean to imply that you do not at times feel pretty tired, but I think you will be the first to admit that habit rather than the character of your work is responsible for the great proportion of your tiredness. If you are to be the great man in the Dominion that we all hope and expect you to be, the thoughts that I have voiced in this letter and my last must be taken into unemotional consideration. Once you are convinced of the truth of what I say, there will be little difficulty, but some way your ideas of body infirmity seem to have taken a surprisingly deep hold in your mind. If you were in a more humble position, you would find that many people would combat your false notions about your health just as I do, but when a man becomes a national figure or institution all that he says must be politely listened to at least to his face. If you become Prime Minister and have not got me to bump you up good and hard on this score I fear that in your own uncontested opinion you will become incompetent from the health standpoint to hold on to the position. I take it that the Prime Minister's duties are considerably more onerous than those of the Leader of the Opposition.[3]

The days had assuredly changed since brother Willie had issued pontifical letters to young Max who was struggling to live up to the family's conception of its position in the world. It was Mackenzie King's great misfortune that this salutary influence was to be removed at just the moment in his life when he needed it the most. King was at the beginning of a long period in office when his high position tended to make him more unapproachable and less subject to criticism on personal matters, and once Max had gone there was no one who could take his place. Many of the habits and idiosyncrasies which Mackenzie King as a lonely bachelor would in time develop might well have perished at an early stage had Max's judgment and common sense been available to act as a corrective.

Four days after Mackenzie King became Prime Minister he left for Denver. He found Max very weak and partially paralysed, sustained by truly amazing courage and the ministrations of a devoted wife. His doctors gave him only a few weeks to live. The brothers had seen little of each other for years, but the bonds of sympathy and affection were unusually strong, and this meeting was a poignant one because each knew it would be the last. Mackenzie King spent several days with Max and his family, and returned to Ottawa. Max died on March 18; and Mackenzie King returned to Colorado. He brought his brother's body to Toronto, where it was buried with the other members of the family.

Mackenzie King's Cabinet had no sooner been formed than the friendly overtures to the Progressives were resumed: an assurance that even though close relations had not proved feasible, the Liberals had not forgotten their Western friends. Less than a fortnight after Fielding had become Minister of Finance, he wrote a letter to Crerar to ask what the Progressives had to suggest as possible items in the Government's programme:

When I agreed to accept the office of Minister of Finance in the new Government, it was my expectation that you would be among my colleagues and that in all matters, but particularly in matters relating to our western country, I might look to you for information, advice and co-operation. That you are not with us is a cause of much regret. But, while officially I have no right to ask your assistance, I wish to say that I am still anxious to be favoured with your help in coming to correct understanding as to what is needed from the Government, particularly in matters to which the western folk attach importance. How far you may be willing to go in the way of offering suggestions is, of course, a question which you alone can decide. . . .

Parliament must meet pretty soon. . . . I fear that we shall not, between now and the opening of the session, be able to devise a large legislative programme. As respects many things we shall probably have to take further time for consideration.

With regard to the important question of the tariff, there are some people who will think that we should not attempt to deal with it at all. That probably is too strong a view. . . . There may be some things in which early action is desired along the lines that we have all talked of. I do not suppose that we shall be able to go as far in these things as you and your associates will desire. But where there are matters to which western public opinion attaches importance, I should be glad indeed if I could have your suggestions as to what should be done. . . .

I need hardly say that anything which you may communicate to me on the subject will be deemed strictly confidential.[4]

Crerar replied later in January in a long letter reciting a number of the farmers' complaints, and naming some of the remedies they desired: reductions in the tariff and freight rates, reforms in the banking system, transfer of natural resources to the Prairie Provinces, reciprocity with the United States, economy, consolidation of the government-owned railways, and others.[5] Fielding's acknowledgment was non-committal on some of the problems raised and encouraging on others. However, as he said: "We have hardly yet got comfortably seated in our chairs"; "there is really not the time that we ought to have to give to the big things of the day."[6] It is impossible to say what precise effect this interchange of views had on Liberal policy, but the circumstances were significant. The fact that the correspondence had been initiated by the most senior and influential of King's colleagues was impressive evidence that a desire for co-operation was not confined to the Liberal leader: it also showed that this desire had not been advocated merely as an aid in the elections but had become a continuing element in Liberal policy.

King was much more conscious than Fielding of his unreadiness to meet Parliament, though with him the problem was a more personal one. The interval between the election and the opening in early March had been short and crowded with meetings, appointments, and decisions of all sorts; his brother's illness had been a constant worry; his trip to Colorado (soon to be followed by another) had made deep inroads on his time; and he had had a limited opportunity to study and discuss the many complex problems which were coming up for decision. He knew his general inadequacy and inexperience in such matters. "I have not the faculty of getting others to do my work, or even to prepare it," he wrote in February, shortly before the opening of Parliament, "the consequence is I am lost when it comes to the [last] moments unprepared."[7] Six days later he added: "The whole business is getting to where I feel completely swamped and wholly incapable of dealing with the mass of matters presenting themselves."[8] The difficulty, however, was not only a lack of time or of preparation: his long preoccupation with other questions before and during the war had left him out of touch with substantive contemporary problems and about many of these he was still quite at sea. On the day he spoke on the Address, March 13—his parliamentary début as Prime Minister —he wrote in his diary:

To-day is over, and I thank God for having enabled me to get through it as well as I have. . . . I did not feel nervous, neither did I feel at ease. I was conscious all through of lack of preparation or of having my thoughts carefully ordered. There were many times when I slipped a cog altogether. . . . To my great surprise the impression on the whole seems to have been good. . . . With a little less stage fright & one day's preparation I might have done very much better. Still I might have done very much worse. . . . It was my first debate as Prime Minister, one of the *very* few occasions in which I have followed at all in debate. Members & the public forget that in actual parliamentary experience & practice tho' Prime Minister I am really a novice of but two or three years' experience. I can hope to grow with practice   I shall gain confidence. The task is immensely easier than leading an Opposition. Oh I am so glad to be through the first few days, with their *multitude* of demands. Now I can get gradually seated solidly in the saddle.[9]

Parliament opened on March 8, 1922. The Conservatives, as the official Opposition, sat directly across from the Government; the Progressives also sat on the Speaker's left but farther down the chamber.* The seating arrangement gave a fair indication of the Progressives' political position: they did not wish to be considered as an opposition of the usual kind, but rather as a group which held the balance of power between rival parties. Yet they were not fitted to perform such a role. They lacked the discipline, the willingness to agree on and be

*It will be recalled that out of 235 seats the Liberals held 117; Progressives, 64; Conservatives, 50; Independent Labour, 2; Labour-Liberal, 1; Independent Liberal, 1.

bound by a common policy, the corporate acceptance of leadership, and many of them were also handicapped by their bias towards the Liberals. If the Progressives were to exploit their strategic position to the full, they could not afford the luxury of divided councils nor could they allow their cold assessment of benefits to be disturbed by any rational or emotional preference for one side as against the other.

The idea of holding the balance of power also meant for many of the Progressives the privilege of evading responsibility. They would not take over the duties of the official Opposition nor, in the event of their votes helping to defeat the Government, were they prepared to assume office. They formed a purely class party, limited in outlook, using the methods of an outraged, inexperienced, and somewhat confused pressure group. They had been elected to safeguard the interests of the farmers, and they felt their primary responsibility was to their constituents. They considered themselves superior to the orthodox parties in purpose and under no obligations to obey the conventions of the parliamentary system. Their immediate aim was not concerned with the business of government, but was directed to the enactment of legislation favourable to the agricultural interests, and they were willing to vote for either major party or for both if they thereby could gain the passage of measures they desired. This, at least, was their attitude at the outset of their parliamentary career, though the reforming wing was not so sure that it could limit its obligations, and it became less sure as time wore on. The Progressive leader took the earliest opportunity to describe the position of his party to the House:

We are here . . . as an independent party standing for the principles that we believe in and prepared to further those principles by every honest and legitimate means within our power. . . . We are here, not to oppose for the sake of opposing; we are here prepared to give the Government every assistance in carrying on the government of this country, when it gives the country the policies that we believe it should have. . . . We are equally prepared to oppose the Government and to criticise it when we think the Government is doing wrong or not adopting the policies that we think this country should have. That, to my mind, frankly and clearly states our position. My own hope, and I am bound to say that the words of my hon. friend the Prime Minister give some ground for that hope, is that the policy pursued by the Government in respect of the great vital questions before the country . . . will be such as to command our support. If their course is shaped in that direction so that we can support them, we shall do so, but if it is not, our duty then will lie in another direction. . . .

We are . . . prepared to give the Government every reasonable time to shape its course and decide upon its line of action.[10]

This attitude was no more than Mackenzie King had expected; he had written Sir Allen Aylesworth only a few weeks before that although it had not been possible "to effect co-operation with any of their members in the Cabinet, I have, I think, succeeded in getting a large measure of their good will toward us in the House of Commons."[11] The auspices, in short, were favourable, but a continuance of the Progressives' goodwill would depend on the actions of the Government, and, despite Crerar's assurances, patient forbearance was not a characteristic of the movement. The Progressives could not be expected to show any concern for King's constant problem of keeping peace with the right-wing Liberals; indeed, the reforming Progressives would have liked nothing better than to see a complete split in the Liberal party which would give them their chance to join hands with its radical members after the purge of the conservative Liberals had been accomplished.

The possible revolt in his own ranks was the other major challenge to King's ability as a leader, though the right wing did not want to risk its existing strong position by precipitating a crisis. King's attitude to the group was one of cautious friendliness with a strong dash of distrust. The movement against his leadership had temporarily subsided, and Gouin had gone out of his way early in the parliamentary session to issue a belated declaration (withheld during the election) that "the Liberal party has one chief and one chief only. . . . He has, and he can depend upon, the loyal support of all his colleagues, of everyone of the Liberal members of this House, and of every Liberal in Canada."[12] King found Gouin a very pleasant person, but he did not give him his confidence and he disliked Gouin's attitude and that of his associates towards public appointments which savoured too much of Tammany politics. On more than one occasion when it appeared that Gouin might not get his way he professed a desire not to embarrass the Prime Minister and intimated that he would be quite willing to resign. In view of Gouin's commanding position among the Quebec contingent, King could scarcely be blamed for declining to permit so noble an act of self-effacement. At first Gouin's prestige gave him the support of a majority of the Quebec members, but his following gradually declined until at the time of his retirement two years later they numbered only ten or twelve, chiefly from the Montreal area.

The younger and more liberal members from Quebec, such as Lapointe, Power, McMaster, and Cannon, were completely out of sympathy with Gouin on both personal and ideological grounds. They still resented his support of Fielding at the 1919 convention as a betrayal of Laurier, and they distrusted his autocratic tendencies and his St. James Street affiliations. It was McMaster who in April, 1922, introduced a motion to prevent Cabinet Ministers from holding directorships in business corporations, and though it was substantially the same as one he had sponsored a year earlier, the chief offender in the existing Cabinet was clearly Sir Lomer Gouin. The Government felt obliged to throw its weight against the motion—an unfortunate circumstance in that the Liberals not only had to reverse their stand of the previous year but also because they found themselves aligned with the Conservatives and against the Progressives, thus confirming the Progressives' suspicion that both old parties were subservient to the business interests. The next day Power and a few others from Quebec objected to the size of the militia estimates, and eventually forced the Government to accept a substantial reduction. It was only too apparent that if the Government could stay in office by gaining the support of a number of Progressives, it might with equal facility go out of office by losing the support of some of its own members.

Behind the Gouin coterie stood the wealthy interests of Montreal. King had no desire to antagonize these people more than he could help, although it is doubtful if he expected to turn them into allies. "I seem to have run counter to or offended the Montreal group at practically every turn," he wrote in February, 1922, "first one then another, the very men I must do my utmost to placate. I have little hope of being able to hold them, they do not *belong* to the Liberal Party, but I do not want to give them cause for complaint or offence."[13] Thus while he refused flatly to make Sir Charles Gordon (Vice-President of the Bank of Montreal) High Commissioner in London, he soothed Gordon's feelings by appointing him the chief Canadian delegate to the Genoa Conference. He made a special trip to Montreal to meet Sir Lomer's friends at a dinner given for that purpose, and he spoke to them on the need for conciliation and better understanding. "I felt," he wrote, "that I was true to my Liberalism, but let those assembled see that I was not narrow gauged, prejudiced, nor vindictive."[14]

In this atmosphere and with the existing distribution of party strength in the House, the Government's initial programme was bound to be both cautious and circumspect. It introduced legislation to set up a Wheat Marketing Agency to dispose of the wheat crop in co-operation with the Prairie Provinces. It reopened negotiations for the assignment of their natural resources to the Prairie Provinces, although no agreement was possible in the face of excessive and conflicting demands by the Western and the Maritime areas. It urged the United Kingdom to lift the cattle embargo. It proposed a cautious immigration policy, which was a reflection of the attitude of the West and at the same time a compromise between the enthusiasm of the railways and the hostility of the labour unions. All these measures affected the prairies and in most instances (the natural resources being the chief exception) the policy of the Government differed little from that of the Progressive party.

The three major issues, however, were the ownership and operation of the government railway lines, the tariff, and freight rates.

Railway problems in some form or another had been coming before Parliament for many years, but during the war the threatened bankruptcy of a number of lines had made these problems acute. The result was that the Canadian people had been virtually forced to take over some 19,600 miles of railway which, with the old Intercolonial, made them the owners of a grand total of over 22,000 miles. Legislation had been passed in 1919 authorizing the operation of these roads as one system; but two and a half years later, when the Meighen Government went out of office, nothing had been done. The long delay in settling the terms under which the Grand Trunk was to be acquired by the Government was one cause of inaction, but there is also little doubt that with an election in the offing the Meighen Government was not anxious to risk further antagonizing those who were opposed to public ownership. The chief private interest was naturally the Canadian Pacific, which feared the competition of a publicly owned rival backed by the country's credit, and so long as the roads remained as they were, nationalization could still be regarded as little more than an ambition. Further action in the direction of public ownership, however, was inevitable, for while here and there pockets of resistance could be found, chiefly in Quebec and the Maritime Provinces, public opinion generally favoured nationalization; all parties were in some degree committed to it and realized how fatal the political consequences would be if the experiment were discontinued.

During the election the Liberals had shown the same discretion on the railway question as had the Meighen Government, and for substantially the same reasons. Meighen, being openly pledged to public ownership, was apparently abandoned in the election by the Canadian Pacific, which placed its chief hope in the Quebec block, exemplified by Gouin and the right wing Liberals. But this hope, which could never have been very strong on this particular issue (whatever it might have been on other railway questions), was soon disappointed. When King took office he determined to give the venture the fair trial which the party had ambiguously promised in the platform of 1919—a composite decision, no doubt, made up of the party pledge, his own convictions, his fear of the dominance of the Canadian Pacific Railway, and his desire to promote better party relations with Ontario and the West. It was clear that if the lines in public ownership were to succeed and to pay their way, they must be welded into one large system under one management, which could compete effectively with its one great rival, the Canadian Pacific. King had chosen as Minister of Railways W. C. Kennedy, an unusually able man and one who possessed the additional advantages of coming from Ontario and being free from any past associations with private railway interests. King gave Kennedy's proposals every encouragement, and secured the approval of the Cabinet to proceed with the plans. That many of the Liberal members were acquiescent rather than enthusiastic was evident when the Minister brought down his proposals to the House, and their lukewarm response fully justified Meighen's taunt that there was more applause from the Opposition than from the Government's own supporters.

Parliament passed the desired legislation, and King and Kennedy began a long and painstaking search for a president for the road. It was a difficult task; the new head needed not only the technical and administrative ability to effect the physical consolidation of the different lines, but also the personal qualities which would be able to create and stimulate a new corporate pride and loyalty in all the employees. They found such a man in Sir Henry Thornton, an American with wide railway experience in Great Britain; and the choice met with general approval. The new Board of Directors, on the other hand, encountered a different reception, for a number of its members were clearly appointed for political reasons. With so much to King's credit on the main question, he could, perhaps, risk a minor debit of this kind—the Board had largely decorative functions and it was likely to prove useful in quieting some of the restive elements in the party. At all events, the great decision had been made, public ownership on a large scale was to be put to the test, and the old Intercolonial Railway, government owned and operated for half a century, had become a senior but minor partner in a vast transcontinental system.

The Liberal fiscal policy under Fielding's guidance moved along traditional lines, a continuation of that established by Fielding himself from 1896 to 1911. Sir Henry Drayton's two budgets of 1920 and 1921 had gently sounded a modern note by his acceptance of a moderate responsibility for the direction of the nation's economic future through the use of fiscal policies. He was not obsessed with the necessity for securing a balanced budget, and to a limited degree he was willing to adjust his taxes with an eye to their effect on purchasing power and general employment.[15] Fielding, on the other hand, was not susceptible to these new ideas: his advanced age and a confidence born of long and successful ministerial experience made him cling tenaciously to familiar principles. He stressed a balanced budget as his primary objective, and although he was not able to achieve it immediately, it underlay all his proposals and arguments.[16] To this end he did his utmost to cut down expenditures, he husbanded the income from the tariff by making only minor changes, and he increased his revenue by imposing new taxes.

The general trend of Fielding's trade proposals was unmistakably towards the loosening of some of the fetters which hampered international commerce. Before the budget was introduced he had already followed in his own footsteps, now twelve years old, and made a trip to Washington to sound out the possibilities of a new reciprocity agreement; but on this occasion he met with no encouragement. Later in the year he opened trade negotiations with a number of countries, and was able to conclude new conventions with France and Italy. But it was to the tariff that popular attention was primarily directed. Here the changes were relatively little, for although Fielding lowered the duties on a large number of commodities—both for the consumer and for the primary producer—the cuts were very small. Their effectiveness was notably enhanced, however, by many administrative reforms removing a number of restrictive regulations which had been imposed by the Conservative Government and which had operated to prevent the importation of foreign goods just as surely as a high tariff.[17]

These cautious changes were in the best Fielding tradition of diffused and piecemeal deductions within an essentially stable tariff, and they were designed to guard "against any interference of a serious character with the business of the country."[18] This was not an impressive demonstration by a party which had denounced protection and advocated a "tariff for revenue only," but it was a slow start in the right direction. "If the Budget," wrote Andrew McMaster, one of the free-trade Liberals, "is to be regarded as the final attitude on the trade question of the Liberal party, it is absolutely unsatisfactory. If it is to be regarded merely as the first movement towards lower tariffs, to be followed without undue delay by other movements in the same direction, it can be accepted and defended."[19] The tariff proposals represented, of course, a compromise of sorts. There was no doubt that the party was not united on the subject, but for the moment there was little demand for action from the low-tariff Liberals, while the prestige of the two senior protectionist members, Fielding and Gouin, carried much weight. "We must frankly recognize the fact," Fielding wrote the Prime Minister in April, "that in matters relating to the tariff there is much difference of opinion, I might even say conflict of opinion, within the ranks of our own friends. . . . A frank discussion in caucus would disclose the extent of these differences and enable our Members to realize the difficulty of the situation. My task, by no means an easy one, is to try to reconcile these differences and reach a common ground on which we all can stand."[20]

Inevitably the Conservatives in the House compared the 1919 platform to the 1922 performance, a comparison which was made all the more pointed by a recent speech of Sir Lomer Gouin's in which he advocated "a reasonable measure of protection." They were also pleased to hear a statement by Fielding that he had never approved of the tariff section of the 1919 platform,[21] and this declaration naturally led Meighen to ask how many other Government members were prepared to stand up and deny their adherence to the announced principles of the party. Had the Prime Minister, for example, approved of this resolution? For this King had an effective answer in the speech he had given to the national convention after his election as party leader:

I stated that I would regard that platform as a chart which indicated the direction that the Liberal representatives assembled expected the party to take if returned to power, but that I would be guided as to how far it was wise to go at any particular time by the collective wisdom and the judgment of the ablest men whom it might be possible to bring together to direct the affairs of this country. I made that statement, not at some remote gathering, but at the very convention which enacted the platform. . . . I contend that every Liberal who was present at that convention heard that statement and accepted it, and there is not a single Liberal throughout the country, so far as I am aware, who has taken exception to that interpretation.[22]

The divisive potentialities of the tariff were also seen in its effects on the Progressives, who tried unsuccessfully to have the House change its rules so that they could express their views as a unit through an alternative amendment on the budget. The move was not successful. The mere drafting of this abortive amendment dealing with the tariff, however, caused a caucus revolt by a number of Alberta members, and it was rumoured that only a demand for united support by the leader, backed by very plain language, quieted the insurgents.[23] When the vote on the budget took place, most of the Progressives voted against the Opposition amendment as well as against the Government motion, which was carried 119 to 101. Two Progressives (and two Labour) supported the amendment, and eight Progressives (seven from Ontario) with two Independents voted with the Liberals on the main motion. If the ten loose fish (to steal a term from earlier Canadian history) had voted the other way, the Government would have been defeated.

The other *bête noire* of the Western farmer was freight rates. This was by no means a new grievance, but it was more sharply felt at this time when the farmer was struggling against the effects of a world-wide over-production of wheat. Prices had turned abruptly downwards in the fall of 1920, and by the end of 1921 wheat was selling in Winnipeg for $1.11 a bushel instead of the 1919 average of $2.38.

The struggle over freight rates, however, spread far beyond the prairie horizon, and it was to make irresistible demands on the attention of Parliament for some years to come. Ideally, the objective was to bring about a more equitable rate structure across Canada without jeopardizing the financial position of the railways and without causing serious dislocations in the nation's economy. Translated into political terms, the problem became one of striking a balance between the pressures from the prairies, the Maritimes, and British Columbia, from the Canadian Pacific, from the taxpayer, from diverse commercial and industrial interests throughout the country; of evolving a compromise solution for each phase of the freight rates question, one which would preserve the Government from defeat in the House and also receive popular support in the country.

The urgency in the railway freight rate problem in 1922 arose from the need for a declared policy on the Crow's Nest Pass Agreement. To understand the nature of this rather complicated story it is necessary to go back to 1897 when the Canadian Pacific Railway entered into negotiations with the Canadian Government in order to obtain help in constructing a branch line through the Crow's Nest Pass. The outcome was that in return for a government subsidy the Company agreed to make substantial reductions in certain freight rates on its lines: on grain and flour, passing from Western Canada through Fort William eastward, and on a number of miscellaneous commodities in common use, passing from the eastern provinces through Fort William westward. This agreement was confirmed by the Crow's Nest Pass Act, 1897, and the rates thus became statutory, as contrasted with railway rates generally, which (after 1903) were usually determined by order of the Board of Railway Commissioners. In 1919 these special rates had been suspended for three years by authority of Parliament, and they would therefore automatically become operative once more on July 7, 1922, unless Parliament decided to intervene and make some other arrangement.

Any action taken on the Crow's Nest rates was bound to have political repercussions beyond the prairies. No matter what the outcome of the discussion might be, it would provide the occasion for airing other grievances on rates which had been held in restraint by the war. Moreover, the decision on western rates would undoubtedly affect the competitive position of British Columbia (which since 1914 had been greatly altered by the opening of the Panama Canal) and it would also tend to affect the rates in Eastern Canada, inasmuch as a loss of revenue by the railways in the West might prevent rate concessions elsewhere.

The Speech from the Throne barely mentioned the rate question and King's speech on the Address added nothing. It was doubtless one of the subjects with which King, as he admitted privately, was not familiar when the Speech was being drafted, and he had had no opportunity to give it the attention it deserved. Nor, one suspects, had the Cabinet any policy,* though from their background and affiliations some members would have been disposed to restore the Crow's Nest rates while others, generally regarded as sympathetic to the Canadian Pacific, would favour continued suspension. On April 8 the Cabinet decided to ask the House to refer the rates question to a Special Committee which could hear testimony from the railroad executives and other interested parties. Here again King seemed unaware of the nature of the controversy and the difficulties to which it might lead. He anticipated that the Committee would be almost unanimous in recommending a revival of the rates,[24] yet at the same time he allowed three or four Liberals to be placed on the Committee whose inclinations on railway matters would be certain to align them with the Conservative and against the Progressive members.

On the evening of April 8 King had a talk with Sir Clifford Sifton and as a result became convinced that the Crow's Nest rates should be restored. There is little doubt that one factor leading to this decision was Sifton's argument that a settlement of this question and the creation of a Wheat Marketing Board would destroy two of the major grievances of the Progressives and make the party's continued existence unnecessary. King later made a commitment in the House in favour of the Crow's Nest Agreement, "unless," he added, "good and sufficient reasons" could be adduced against it.[25] The onus, in short, was to rest with its opponents to show why the old rates should not be allowed to revive, and the responsibility for the decision was placed largely in the hands of the Special Committee.

The report of the Committee was the product of long and troubled sessions. The Progressive members had submitted a solution of their own which, while making some concessions to the railways, revived the low Crow's Nest rate on flour and grain; but this proposal was

*Fielding, for example, had none. Fielding Papers, W. S. Fielding to T. A. Crerar, Feb. 1, 1922.

rejected by the casting vote of the chairman. Another quite different report, favourable to the railways, was then approved, presumably by a combination of Conservatives and a number of right wing Liberals. But before the report was presented to the House, the battle had shifted to the caucuses. The Progressives, now thoroughly aroused, determined in their caucus to fight the issue to the last ditch in the House, thereby prolonging the session until well past the deadline of July 7 when the Crow's Nest Agreement would automatically be restored.[26] The Liberals also held a caucus where it became apparent that many of the party were opposed to the terms of the report accepted by the Committee. The more conservative wing, led by Sir Lomer Gouin, was thus pitted against a substantial section of the party who were not only antagonistic to the business interests but found themselves to an increasing degree in sympathy with the stand of the Progressives on railway rates as well as on other matters.[27] It was evident that, unless instructed otherwise, a significant number of Liberals might support the Progressive opposition to the report, and no matter what the outcome might be, the prestige of the Liberal party and its reputation in Western Canada would be immeasurably damaged.

A solution was found by calling the Committee together again on the pretext of receiving new evidence; and on this being heard, it reconsidered the former decision. After long discussion the Committee passed an amended report with only one dissenter, though by the time the final vote was taken all the Conservatives had walked out, and three of the right wing Liberals had decided not to appear at the last meeting. The Committee said it was "impressed" with the cases presented by the Maritime Provinces and British Columbia, but it did nothing for them; it did provide tangible help to the prairies. The operation of the Crow's Nest Agreement was to be suspended for another year with the exception of the section on grain and flour rates, which were to be allowed to revive in due course, and the suspension could be extended by the Governor-in-Council for yet one more year if thought desirable. Reductions on basic commodities "should have the earliest possible consideration by the Board of Railway Commissioners."

The report was submitted to the House, accepted (after a Conservative amendment had been defeated), and its recommendations on the Crow's Nest Agreement implemented by legislation. The Railway Commission in due course ordered a reduction in rates on a number of "basic commodities," and also gave some relief to both British Columbia and the Maritime Provinces.

King must have derived little satisfaction from these troubled manoeuvres, although admittedly one of the outstanding grievances of the Western farmers had been at least temporarily quieted. But there was no escaping the unfortunate truth that Liberal-Progressive co-operation had temporarily disappeared and had made a belated appearance only after threats of obstruction by the Progressives and strong protests from a part of the Liberal ranks. Forced co-operation of this type was not likely to enhance the West's confidence in the responsiveness of the Liberal party to its needs: on the contrary, it was likely to confirm the fears of December and make the Progressives more suspicious of the power which Montreal and the "interests" were likely to wield in the Liberal councils. This feeling would be counteracted to some degree by the knowledge that when the Progressives had been in genuine need of assistance they had found allies in the ranks of the more radical Liberals, who welcomed the opportunity to block the right wing group and to demonstrate their sympathy with the prairie farmer. Yet it was inevitable that the Progressives should regard the outcome as a vindication of their movement and its entrance into politics as a separate organization. When put to the test, the lack of Progressive representatives in the Cabinet had not proved fatal to the achievement of their purpose. Both wings of the party had worked together and had secured a victory which only too obviously would not have been won without their aggressive action at the decisive stage. Did not the protection of the farmers' interests therefore demand the continued existence of the Progressives as a separate party?

King concluded his first session as leader of the House with a feeling of moderate security engendered by his success in obtaining essential support whenever it was necessary to his survival. This in turn was in large measure the product of his careful weighing of the probabilities in each situation and the employment of compromise adjusted to each need as it arose. In the attainment of his primary purpose of a party majority he found three major alternatives open to him, and his choice depended upon the circumstances. He could follow the desires of his left wing and the Progressives, as he did with the centralization and management of the nationally owned railways; he could capitulate to the right wing, as he did on the tariff (with small reservations); or he could allow, as he did with the railway rates, the weight of events to convince the dissenters that nothing but a middle course would be acceptable and that any other alternative would be worse. The party majority was vital, and to maintain it he was forced to work with the party material at hand in a constant search for a mean which would produce acquiescence, if not approval. To say that had he been genuinely liberal and more courageous he could have exchanged the support of the reactionary element in his party for that of the Progressives is a very doubtful assertion indeed, and its validity depends on the extremely shaky proposition that in such an event a large block of the Progressives would have given him unwavering collective support. The Progressives, it is true, were prepared to vote for him when it was to their advantage, but there was no reason to believe that they would give him any more consistent backing than they were prepared to give to Crerar, their own leader. Selective support, unfortified by reliability in the party, does not give a Government the sense of security which it must have if it is to pursue its course with confidence. King was not inclined to try to rebuild the Liberal party or to create a majority by any bold strategy of relinquishing the solid bone of Liberal votes for the shadow of problematical Progressive co-operation. Indeed, if boldness was the key to the political situation, the Progressives themselves had shown singularly little of it when they had refused to join King's Government and thus come to close grips with the reactionary Liberals who at this time presented the chief obstacle to a realization of their plans. Boldness is always the right and obvious course for the leader on the other side; but few politicians are willing to stake their future on one confident fling of the dice.

Several matters of a personal nature engaged King's attention during the session and thereafter. Lady Laurier (who had died in November, 1921) willed the Laurier home in Ottawa to Mackenzie King by virtue of his position as Sir Wilfrid's successor and leader of the Liberal party. A number of wealthy Liberals, the chief being Peter C. Larkin (appointed in 1922 as Canadian High Commissioner in London), undertook to renovate the house completely before King took up his residence there, and Mr. Larkin himself made many contributions of pictures, china, silver, and furniture. Some years later, a group of friends, again headed by Larkin, presented the Prime Minister with

$225,000. This was not in any way attached to Laurier House but was given to King personally, the purpose being to ensure a degree of financial independence and to enable him to maintain his new residence without undue strain on his income.

The result of the alterations to Laurier House was most satisfactory; for although the outside still lacked any pretensions to distinction, the interior had been given dignity and charm, and it was now well adapted to the purpose which it was meant to serve. King had always been very susceptible to his environment and he derived uncommon satisfaction from the comfort and elegance of his new home. In the first letter he wrote Larkin from Laurier House[28] he described his library and the pleasure he was already deriving from it:

I am writing in the new library on the top floor. Its front casement windows, with their leaded panes, look out upon All Saints Cathedral just opposite. The cathedral note is carried into this study with its oak rafters overhead. The walls are lined with books on three sides. They present a wonderful appearance. They speak of and help to inspire what is best in thought. I am writing at the table which I secured some twenty-one or two years ago, when I was appointed Deputy Minister of Labor. My dear mother and father were with me when I purchased it from Jenkins, out of some of my early earnings. I am sitting with my back to the windows and with the view of the room before me. Directly in front, in the centre, is the old cloister table which you secured from Heaven alone knows where, but which looks as though it had been in this land and place for centuries. At one side of the table, and facing the fireplace is the sofa I had in my apartments. It may have to go elsewhere later on, but will probably have another in its place. The fireplace itself is not finished as yet, but will be most effective when it is. There is no room for pictures on the walls, but the books to the ceiling give a fine appearance. I shall probably arrange to have the oil portrait of my mother mounted on an easel, and I may even bring into this room a piano she had as a girl and which was in our Toronto home.*

Although King took both pride and pleasure in Laurier House, his heart was in Kingsmere. At the same time that Laurier House was being renovated, King was beginning to expand his property in the country, in part to protect his existing holdings against encroachment but also as time went on to create a beautiful estate of modest size. He added several acres in 1922, ten more in 1924, over 160 in 1926, and in the ensuing years 300 more—a total of about 500 acres in all, includ-

*Both the portrait and the piano were later placed in the library.

ing two houses and three cottages. As he acquired more property he began to develop it, building stone walls, laying out roads and paths, extending lawns, and so forth. He continued to do a fair amount of manual labour himself, though he relied on local workmen for any major operations. Whether his contribution was the direct one of cutting out underbrush or the less strenuous one of planning new developments and watching the progress of the work seems to have made little difference: he entered into everything with zest and intense pleasure. It was his one great hobby, and remained so to the end of his life.

The proximity of Kingsmere to Ottawa and the quiet seclusion it afforded were of incalculable value in helping King endure the anxiety and fatigue of public life, for he used it as a refuge and a place of relaxation, available only to his family and a few friends. But in another way Kingsmere proved a handicap to him. It became too much a monastic retreat, and it encouraged him to withdraw even deeper into himself and to erect more barriers between himself and his fellow men. It gave encouragement, in short, to a side of King's nature which was already over-developed and it made more difficult than ever the cultivation of those social contacts which would have added materially to his stature as a well-balanced human being.

On June 3, 1922, King was made a member of the British Privy Council, and was thenceforward entitled to be addressed as "Right Honourable." The event furnished him with another opportunity to indulge in his habit of reviewing the past in the light of his own achievement. He prized the honour, he wrote, especially "because of the historic sequence of events, the vindication of a great purpose & aim in the life of Grandfather and of his name in history."[29]

The effort to bring the Liberal and Progressive parties together did not cease with the breakdown in negotiations at the time of the formation of the Cabinet, but was revived on two occasions during the summer and fall of 1922. The first of these attempts collapsed because apparently neither side had undergone any real change of heart. King was unwilling to enter into commitments which would provoke a revolt from one wing of the Quebec Liberals or even put a strain on their loyalty. Crerar, for his part, was not prepared with his uncertain support to be drawn closer to a Government containing elements which would make it difficult to carry out some of the major aims of the Progressives. The second attempt at a rapprochement followed close on the heels of the first. It was brought about by an entirely new factor in the political situation: an emergency in foreign affairs known as the Chanak crisis.

Before becoming involved in this question, however, it is necessary to make a brief departure to indicate the general attitude of Canada to international and Imperial affairs at this time. The First World War had left a deep impression on the thinking of most Canadians, who were determined not to be drawn into another war, or, as they would have phrased it, another European war. They were extremely conscious of the wasted opportunities of the past few years and the accumulation of national problems which were demanding immediate action. The work of readjustment and reconstruction, the heavy debt, the unbalanced budget, the widespread discontent of which the agrarian political revolt was a symptom: these and other questions had to be settled without delay. The more their energies and attention were taken up with domestic affairs the more disinclined Canadians were to intervene in outside matters, which seemed by comparison far beyond the range of their legitimate interests and resources.

The fear of being involved in another war was one aspect of an isolationist sentiment which had made rapid strides in Canada since 1914. For while the First World War had simply confirmed a traditional attitude in the United States long entertained in regard to foreign affairs and "entangling alliances," it had worked a more profound change in Canada, which had been accustomed as a matter of course to very close relations with Great Britain. Isolationism—hitherto a relatively rare phenomenon in Canada outside Quebec—had now become an integral part of the opinions of a large section of English-speaking as well as French-speaking Canadians, though it was still neither so widely nor so intensely held as in the United States. Home pastures, contrary to the adage, not only looked the best, they also appeared to be incomparably safer.

Isolationism in North America rested primarily on a distrust of European politics, statesmen, and ambitions, and on a conviction (despite the lesson of 1914–18) that the continent was so fortunately placed geographically that it could remain aloof from any future struggle. "We think in terms of peace," said Senator Dandurand in a famous speech to the League of Nations in 1924, "while Europe, an armed camp, thinks in terms of war. . . . We live in a fire-proof house, far from inflammable materials."[30] This statement also illustrates another element in the isolationist state of mind: the feeling of moral superiority towards other nations, the assurance that North America moved on a higher plane and was not subject to the same hatreds and tensions that plagued the more unfortunate parts of the world. Herbert Hoover gave expression to the same idea when he wrote that the United States "had developed something new in a way of life of a people . . . out of the boiling social and economic caldron of Europe, with its hates and fears, rose miasmic infections which might greatly harm or even destroy what seemed to me to be the hope of the world."[31] Isolationism may have been a reflection of a naive and restricted outlook, but it was none the less a most influential factor in determining the post-war approach of North America to world affairs.

One obvious manifestation of isolationism was seen in the Canadian attitude to the League of Nations. The great majority of Canadians accepted in a vague sort of way the need for all countries to meet together for the common good and for the discussion of common problems, and they were willing to take part up to that point in the League's endeavours. "The great thing about the League of Nations," said Mackenzie King to Lord Robert Cecil in 1923, "[is that] it is teaching all countries a common language—using language in a broad sense, of like concepts & ideas."[32] Canada would, nevertheless, draw the line at any risk of involvement in Europe. On the western side of the Atlantic the League was regarded as primarily a European institution, which, indeed, it was to a very great degree. Its headquarters was situated in the heart of Europe, it was preoccupied largely with European problems, it was dominated by European statesmen who were operating in a sphere of which Canadians had no experience. The defection of the United States from the League of Nations drew the League even further away from Canadian interests and sympathies, and inevitably increased the distrust which Canadians felt for what they believed to be an alien body.

Yet another supplementary influence which increased Canadian reluctance to become involved in League activities was the belief that Canada's new national status might thereby be placed in jeopardy. It was an odd and somewhat unexpected turn of the wheel. Canada had desired membership in the League of Nations as a recognition of her nationhood, but the ink on the Covenant was scarcely dry before she began to dread the responsibilities which that membership might entail. To bow to the dictates of Geneva at the very moment of liberation from the dictates of London was a strange way to realize self-government. It might even turn out to be a retrograde step. Lucien Cannon, speaking in the Canadian House in 1919, declared:

I am not in favour of England ruling this country, but I would rather be ruled by England than by Geneva. English statesmanship has always been characterized by generosity and broadmindedness in most cases; but I have very poor confidence in Brazil and in Spain, very little also in Greece, and not very much in the Kingdom of the Hedjaz.[33]

Mackenzie King did little to discourage this attitude to the League, although he was the type of uplifter who might have been expected to give the League his full and enthusiastic support. His academic liberal background, his zeal for peace, his interest in social and humanitarian reform, his experience in labour problems should all have predisposed him in its favour and he had an exaggerated faith in the adequacy of institutions to check force and sublimate political power. "I am heart and soul for a League of Nations," he wrote to an American friend in 1919, "imperfect as the beginnings of its organization must necessarily be. Both your Federation and ours grew out of conditions which were far from perfect, but which have developed a fine unity between all the parts. Why, with this example, can't we hope for a like development between the nations of the world."[34]

But these were opinions without obligations. A few weeks before writing this letter he had been elected leader of the Liberal party, and as the Leader of the Opposition his attitude towards the League was one of studied neglect. He ignored the League in Parliament, and he failed to make anything of it in the election of 1921. Later when he became Prime Minister he did no more than give it the routine support which was due from Canada as one of its members. Inquiries were made in 1923 whether he would agree to be President of the next meeting of the International Labour Conference, but he declined;[35] and in spite of blandishments from Lord Robert Cecil, N. W. Rowell, Sir Herbert Ames, and others he refused to attend any of the early meetings of the Assembly.[36] His plea was overwork, and it was no doubt genuine; but it is equally certain that King did not desire to run counter to the Canadian suspicion of the League's activities and the probable criticism which would ensue if the Prime Minister left urgent business at home to wander off to attend League meetings in Geneva.

It is clear that whatever King the idealist may have thought, King the party leader and Prime Minister was eminently realistic. For one thing, he was convinced that the efforts of Canada at this time had best be directed to her own salvation rather than to the redemption of the world. Domestic problems in the post-war period were a full-time job for any Canadian Government and even moderate efforts outside Canadian borders could be undertaken only at the risk of neglecting more urgent duties at home. He was also impressed by the necessity for anticipating the public response to any more of these foreign undertakings. In February, 1920 (while still in opposition), he was asked for his opinion concerning the possibility of Canada's accepting a mandate for Armenia; his reply showed his awareness of this necessity:

The Government has given so much time and attention to matters outside Canada in the last few years, and seems so utterly devoid of any capacity to deal with Canadian needs and conditions, that I have no hesitation in saying that, were the Government to propose Canada's accepting a mandate for the Armenian state, even under the exceptional conditions mentioned in your letter, it would provoke general protest from one end of the Dominion to the other.[37]

King did not believe that it was his job as the leader of the party to become the passionate advocate of new causes, however admirable, but to bring together, consolidate, and make operative a common will on all public questions when such a result was possible. Bold and imaginative ventures were invaluable aids in the creation of opinion, but they were luxuries which the reformers and pioneers could best afford. The political leader was bound in his endeavour by what was generally acceptable at any particular time. If King believed that he was unable on certain questions to obtain the consensus he sought, he could see no virtue in trying to force people's ideas into a mould which they resisted. So long as the majority of Canadians remained strongly isolationist and opposed to the League of Nations King would not try to convert them. Indeed, he would go further and capitalize on their common isolationism. It constituted one of the few issues on which he could find agreement—Ontario as well as Quebec, West as well as East—and he seized the opportunity to turn it to good account and use it as a binder to encourage co-operation not on this alone but on other questions as well. Whatever his own views on the functions of the League might be, King was ready to sink them, temporarily or permanently, if by doing so, he could accomplish what he considered to be the larger purpose. What King perceived in his early days as leader and what succeeding years confirmed, was that the Canadian people wanted no more commitments to and for the League of Nations than the minimum which was consistent with the maintenance of national self-respect. King gave them that minimum or even, at times, a little less.

King's coolness towards the League was, in fact, shared by most of his contemporaries in Canadian public life. Thus Meighen's attitude, if judged by his participation in the debates in Parliament, was even more indifferent than King's, and the Progressive leaders were equally silent. J. S. Woodsworth, the leader of the Labour party, was on the other hand an outspoken friend of the League[38] and he repeatedly deplored the lack of attention which it received from both Government and Parliament.[39] It also was supported by a few men like Sir Robert Borden and N. W. Rowell, who had retired from public life and did not feel the same need for reticence as those who were still in politics. The truth was that most members of Parliament were not interested in what the League of Nations was doing, and there was consequently little demand for discussion in the House. The chief exception was the annual vote to cover Canada's contribution to the League's expenses, and even then a few minutes' debate was sufficient to set the members' minds at rest for another year.

The Canadian reluctance to become seriously involved in external affairs was a potent factor in determining not only the national attitude to such a body as the League of Nations, but also the nature of Canada's constitutional position in the Empire. This position was still obscure in 1922. Canada and the other Dominions had for some time been moving away from the old condition of dependence on the British Government in foreign affairs, and the pressures of war had greatly accelerated the process towards greater autonomy in this field. Thus the British Government had agreed in 1917 that henceforth the Dominions should be consulted on foreign policy, though no one was very sure how this consultation was to be carried out or how effective the voice of the Dominions would be if and when it took place.

405

Foreign powers had also given some recognition to the peculiar semi-independent position of the Dominions in world affairs by accepting their representatives at the Peace Conference, their signatures to the Peace Treaty, and their membership in the League of Nations. This progressive enhancement of the influence and prestige of the Dominions had been accomplished on the initiative and persistent exertions of Sir Robert Borden, who was strongly supported by Lloyd George and other Dominion leaders, such as Smuts and Hughes.

If the first great advance in this recent movement towards complete Canadian autonomy in foreign affairs owed much to the work of Sir Robert Borden, the second great advance owed fully as much to the work of Mackenzie King. In 1922 this lay, of course, in the future. Stated in its broadest terms, the objective of Borden and of King was the same—the emancipation of Canada from all external control in foreign affairs; but their conception of how this independence was to be exercised was quite different. Borden's idea was that Canada would use her new power to influence the foreign policy of the Empire so that there would be a merging of national and Empire policy which would be supported by the Empire as a unit. King's idea was that Canada's foreign policy would have to stand on its own feet like that of any other nation. If Canada's policy impinged on or concerned that of any other part of the Empire, then by all means let those affected get together and work out something in common. Borden thus stressed the co-operative side of the relationship and preserved the diplomatic unity of the Empire: King's emphasis was on Canadian individualism with optional co-operation, a concept which inevitably threw a diplomatic unity of the Empire into the discard.

In the summer of 1921 a conference of the British and Dominion Prime Ministers was held in London. It was a continuation of the Imperial War Cabinet meetings of 1917–18, and its members sat as equals to discuss the affairs of the Empire. This "Peace Cabinet," as it was sometimes called, was chiefly notable for its acceptance of the principle that there was to be one foreign policy for the whole Empire and that this would be determined and kept up to date by periodic meetings like the one then in session. The policy would necessarily have to be expressed and applied through the machinery of the British Foreign Office, which would have the additional duty of keeping the Dominions fully informed in the interval between meetings of any important developments in foreign affairs. Mr. Meighen, who was the Canadian Prime Minister at this time, suggested to the Conference that special weight should be attached in these foreign relations to the views of any member who had a particular interest in certain areas, and he gave as an illustration the exceptional importance to Canada of any Empire policy which affected the United States. The suggestion was attacked by Hughes of Australia; although when Canada at a later session opposed the continuation of the Anglo-Japanese alliance because of its effect on American relations, her protests were heeded and the treaty was not renewed. In addition to Anglo-Japanese-American relations the conference also discussed problems in Upper Silesia, the Ruhr, Turkey, Egypt, and other countries.

The chief purpose of using the Imperial Peace Cabinet in this way was to maintain the unity and strength of the Empire in foreign affairs by admitting the Dominions as active participants in the formulation of foreign policy. It was, of course, understood that in exchange for this privilege the Dominions would join with the United Kingdom in defence of the policy so determined. Various expedients were discussed which might add to the effectiveness of the Dominions' participation: more frequent meetings of the Prime Ministers, resident Ministers from the Dominions in London, and improved communications. Little was done, however, to carry out any of the ideas, but on the last of these problems the British Government was co-operative and reassuring. It suggested that London might send confidential information to the Dominions at short, regular intervals so that all might be informed of any changes in the current international situation.

The Prime Ministers, doubtful, but somewhat comforted, returned to their respective homes; and the Foreign Office continued to discharge its normal duties subject to the above understanding. In a little over a year the sudden appearance of the Chanak crisis dramatically challenged the practicability of the scheme when confronted with an unexpected emergency.

The treaty of peace with Turkey, known as the Treaty of Sèvres, though signed in 1920 by the Allied Powers and Turkey, had never become operative; it was not ratified by the United Kingdom and it was repudiated by the new Turkish Nationalist Government. By September, 1922, the situation around the Straits had become critical. The Turks had defeated the Greeks, and the French had withdrawn their military support from the British in that area. The British found themselves not only diplomatically estranged from their allies, but the chief and later the sole defenders of Constantinople, Chanak, and the neutralized zone about the Straits against the advances of a victorious Turkish army.

Here was clearly an opportunity for an effective display of the diplomatic unity of the Empire: the Foreign Office could now carry out the common Empire policy and call on the Dominions to give their verbal approval and, if necessary, their armed support. But unfortunately no such policy was in existence. No meeting of the Prime Ministers had been held since 1921; no Dominion Ministers had been posted to London for continuous consultation; and the flow of confidential information, promised by Lord Curzon, had omitted even to mention any critical situation in the Near East. Undeterred by the absence of these vital prerequisites to action, the British Prime Minister, Mr. Lloyd George, sent a message on September 15 to the Dominions which outlined the situation in the Near East, reminded them of the sacrifices at Gallipoli in the recent war, and said he would "be glad to know whether Dominion Government wish to associate themselves with the action we are taking and whether they would desire to be represented by a contingent." It concluded by stating that the announcement that all or any of the Dominions were prepared to send contingents even of moderate size would undoubtedly in itself exercise a most favourable influence on the situation and might conceivably be a potent factor in preventing actual hostilities.[40]

In view of the total ignorance of the Canadian Government regarding the circumstances which had led to the emergency,* this suggestion that it should participate in a possible war came as a complete surprise. It rapidly became a major blunder when a few hours later the British Government gave a much more provocative and emotional statement to the press. This also described the situation in the Near

---

*"This [despatch] was the first and only intimation which the government had received from the British government of a situation in the Near East which had reached a critical stage." W.L.M.K., *Can. H. of C. Debates*, Feb. 1, 1923, p. 31.

Investigation disclosed that a Foreign Office report (which was sent by post) always took at least three weeks, and usually a month, to get into the hands of the Canadian Government. On one day, August 28, 1922, eight despatches were received, dated in London from July 17 to August 8. No reports having any bearing on the Near East situation were received during the ten days immediately preceding Lloyd George's message. King Papers, Memorandum by L. C. Moyer, Dec. 16, 1922.

East, and said that a communication had been sent to the Dominions "inviting them to be represented by contingents in the defence of interests for which they have already made enormous sacrifices and of soil which is hallowed by immortal memories of the Anzacs."[41]

The order in which these two messages came to the attention of the Canadian Government made the situation infinitely worse. Mackenzie King was in North York on Saturday, September 16, and that afternoon he was asked by a newspaper reporter what response Canada proposed to give to the British invitation to send troops to the Near East. King, having heard nothing whatever of the message, was justifiably taken aback, but he replied cautiously that the question would have to be considered by the Cabinet. He returned to Ottawa early the next day (Sunday) and received the official message which had been delivered to his office *via* the Governor-General Saturday afternoon between two and three o'clock—several hours *after* the Canadian newspapers had carried the London press release as well as a precipitate reply from New Zealand stating that she was prepared to send troops. King wrote in his diary:

I confess it [the official message] annoyed me. It is drafted designedly to play the imperial game, to test out centralization vs. autonomy as regards European wars. . . . I have thought out my plans. . . . No contingent will go without parliament being summoned in first instance. . . . I shall not commit myself one way or the other, but keep the responsibility for prlt.— the executive regarding itself as the committee of prlt.—I do not believe prlt. would sanction the sending of a contingent. The French Canadians will be opposed. I believe most if not all our members in Ont. & the maritime provinces will be opposed. I am not so sure of B.C.—I feel confident the Progressives will be opposed almost to a man.—It is the time now to bring them into the Government. . . . to strengthen us in our attitude of refusing to send a contingent without sanction of prlt., . . . New Zealand has offered a contingent—naturally she looks to the Br. Navy for everything. Australia will probably follow her example. I doubt if S. Africa will. I feel sure she won't. I am sure the people of Canada are against participation in this european war.[42]

King immediately cabled a complaint to Lloyd George about the press manifesto and asked how much of the official message could be made public. Two replies were received the next day (September 18) from Winston Churchill, the Colonial Secretary. The one marked "for publication" was much the same as the statement already given to the press, but the appeal or invitation had been toned down to a

hope that Canada would associate herself with the proposed action.
The private despatch stated that the original message had been
directed primarily to Australia and New Zealand and gave King permission to disclose its substance. Anything that the Canadian Government could contribute "towards a sense of Empire solidarity would be
of utmost value." War and hence the need for troops was unlikely, and
a statement that Canada would associate herself with the position of
the Allies and was willing, if necessary, to send a contingent would
be sufficient. Churchill ended by expressing his regret that notice
could not have been given owing to the rapid development of the
crisis.[43] On the same day King also received word from the Canadian
High Commissioner's Office in London that the press there was on the
whole antagonistic to any measures which might lead to war.[44]

Three meetings of the Canadian Cabinet also took place on the
18th, though the replies from Churchill were not received until the
evening meeting. King wrote:

I found all present,* strongly against participation by Canada in sending
of a contingent & feeling of exasperation at message having been given to
press. D. D. McKenzie was for recognition of principle that when Britain
is at war we are at war,—which others agreed to, with premise that it is for
us to determine our part in the conflict. . . . We all agreed that to send a
contingent prlt. wd have first to be summoned, it was felt that if it were
necessary to summon prlt., we wd have to have a policy as to extent of
participation, in other words, not to summon prlt. unless we were decided
to ask prlt. to intervene. I kept out for an open mind, pending events,—we
are a minority govt. . . . We sat till 1.45 again from 3 to 6.30 & again 9 till
11.15. In the evening 2 cables came from Eng., one "explaining" situation &
apologizing in part for message sent as it was, other giving a message for
public purposes—a greatly modified affair leaving out jingo appeal. . . . We
debated long over question of giving "moral support" & approving attitude.
I felt that involved whole question of participation in European wars &
held back on it. Cabinet agreed in this . . . all were inclined to feel whole
business an "election scheme" of Lloyd George & Co.[45]

From this Cabinet meeting a reply was sent to the British Govern-

*On September 17 King had cabled to Fielding who was in Geneva with Lapointe
to ascertain their opinion and to report on the seriousness of the situation. These
two Ministers were at first in favour of Canada's indicating a readiness to participate
though they were reluctant to agree to a contingent without parliamentary authority.
They later fell in with the Cabinet policy, but Fielding still thought the Government
should be emphatic in its expression of support in the event of what he called
"actual war." W. S. Fielding to W.L.M.K., Sept. 18, 1922; E. Lapointe to W.L.M.K.,
Sept. 19, 1922; W. S. Fielding to W.L.M.K., Sept. 26, 1922.

ment "that public opinion in Canada would demand authorization on the part of Parliament as a necessary preliminary to the despatch of a contingent."[46] The despatch added that the Canadian Cabinet would welcome the fullest information to shed light on the advisability of summoning Parliament to consider the situation. This cold response was so far removed from what the invitation had anticipated, as to be an unmistakable rebuff, made all the more pointed by the fact that Australia had by this time joined New Zealand in offering to send troops.*

King also gave a statement to the press to the effect that the Cabinet had received only one despatch from the British Government and that it was marked "secret"; but that the Canadian Cabinet was sure the people would demand parliamentary authorization before any troops were sent to the Near East. The Cabinet was seeking more information before it decided whether a special session should be called.

Lloyd George stubbornly returned on the following day (September 19) to his earlier request, the third effort to secure a promise of Canadian support:

The attitude of Canada at this moment is of great importance. We do not ask for any immediate decision to send troops. Were large re-inforcements to prove necessary we should immediately summon Parliament here and should notify you of our decision to do so at once. It is presumably not necessary for you to summon Parliament till then and we hope that it may not be necessary at all. A definite statement however that Canada will stand by the Empire in the event of terms of Armistice being broken will do much to ensure maintenance of peace.[47]

Yet it was precisely this assurance that Mackenzie King was determined not to give. On September 20 he countered the request for a "definite statement that Canada will stand by the Empire" with the observation that "we have not thought it necessary to reassert the loyalty of Canada to the British Empire." The British Government, he continued, could "rest assured that, should it become necessary to summon Parliament, Canada, by decision of its Parliament, will so act as to carry out the full duty of the Canadian people."[48] There was not

*The consent of Australia, however, was accompanied by a protest concerning the British failure to consult the Dominions before making its decision. When the original message arrived in South Africa General Smuts was away and did not return for a week. He then replied that he would have to secure parliamentary approval before complying with the request.

much assurance to be derived from that promise, as Mackenzie King knew full well.

At this point Winston Churchill cabled (also on September 20) that a special staff was being organized in the Colonial Office to keep Canada in touch with political and military developments. The first of its reports arrived in Ottawa on the same day, although it proved to be composed of one-third information and two-thirds propaganda. Once again—and for the fourth time—a promise of a contingent was sought in order to provide a "quiet but decisive demonstration that the British Empire is not to be threatened or bluffed."[49] Once again the plea produced no results. Despatches from the Colonial Office dealing with the question continued for some time thereafter, but a new armistice with Turkey on September 29 removed the danger of further hostilities.

King's response to Lloyd George's invitation had been both emotional and rational. He recoiled from the threatened conflict which had suddenly and unaccountably appeared in the Near East and his reluctance to promise a contingent was that of any nationally conscious Canadian who instinctively objected to being dragged into a war of another's choosing. But King's response was based also on a set conviction that Canada was a nation and must be treated as such, and that a large element in the British Government desired to keep the Dominions in a position of actual if not nominal inferiority. "Surely," he wrote, "all that has been said about equality of status and sovereign nations within the Empire is all of no account if at any particular moment the self-governing Dominions are to be expected, without consideration of any kind, to assume the gravest responsibility which a nation can assume, solely and wholly upon an inspired despatch from Downing Street."[50] King was also convinced that the popular feeling would be under existing circumstances strongly against another war. He likewise appreciated the possibility of turning the crisis to a good account in the cause of Liberal-Progressive relations, and saw the advantage of using Western support to forestall the criticism that the Government's policy was solely a reflection of the isolationism and anti-Imperialism of Quebec.

The Canadian people did not disappoint him. At first they were somewhat uncertain of the reply which should be given to Mr. Lloyd George's appeal, although there were a number of church groups whose feelings on alleged Turkish atrocities against Armenian Christians outweighed all other considerations. These and an element with strong British sympathies clamoured for immediate action. But a very large proportion of the public soon began to swing towards and approve of the Liberal position of no commitments without parliamentary authority or, in view of the fact that there was no move by the Government to summon Parliament, of no commitments at the moment. The Liberal party showed a gratifying unanimity in support of the official policy; the urban labour unions strongly endorsed it;[51] and the Progressives appeared to be equally favourable.

The meeting of the Cabinet at which the ill-starred message was first considered had given its approval (Gouin dissenting) to King's suggestion that Crerar should be invited to Ottawa for consultation. The two leaders had several talks together on September 22 and 23. Crerar was in complete accord with the stand King had taken; he believed that the question of participation in European wars transcended all others in importance and that there was no difference of opinion on the subject between the Liberal East and the Progressive West. But Hudson and he both objected (as they had in the summer during the negotiations with the Liberals) to the retention of Gouin in the Cabinet; he remained a sinister figure in Progressive eyes and his presence in the Government made any union virtually impossible. This was not King's idea of co-operation and compromise and he refused to push Gouin out, nor was he willing at this time to make any offer of portfolios to the Progressives. The negotiations thus reached another deadlock, and in a week or two the passing of the Near East crisis deprived any Progressive-Liberal union of urgency. The experience, however, was not without value, for it revealed, clearly and unmistakably, a large and important area where the two parties held identical views. King wrote to a prominent Liberal in Alberta: "It [the crisis] has demonstrated . . . that in matters of real fundamental concern our interest is a common one, and that unity of action is essential to secure our common end in the face of our common foe, the jingo-tory-militarist. I believe we have found the basis on which the Progressives of Western Canada may be brought into real accord with the Liberals of the Province of Quebec and other parts of the Dominion."[52]

Proof that King's fear of jingo-Tory-militarists was by no means imaginary had come from several quarters. The Toronto *Globe*, for example, had been bitter in its attack on the Government's attitude towards "the butchers of Armenia," and it had praised Australia for her swift affirmative response to the call from Great Britain.[53] No official Conservative pronouncement appeared, however, until Mr. Meighen at last broke silence in a public address on September 21, six days after the receipt of Mr. Lloyd George's invitation and the same day that King and Crerar were conferring in Ottawa. He said in part:

Britain . . . sends a message to the Dominions, not a mere indifferent inquiry as to what was in the mind of Canada, but a message to see if the Dominions were solid behind the Motherland. The exact wording of the message we do not know, but judging from the evidence that was its purport. From Australia and New Zealand the British Government got messages of co-operation in defence of the Treaty of Sèvres. . . . We were a party to the Treaty of Sèvres and the trials and sacrifices that made it possible.

There is no suggestion at all that we should send armed forces across the sea. Britain merely sought a declaration of solidarity on the part of the Dominions (applause)—the existence of which the war has demonstrated once and for all. Let there be no dispute as to where I stand. When Britain's message came then Canada should have said: "Ready, aye ready; we stand by you." (Loud cheers) I hope the time has not gone by when that declaration can yet be made. If that declaration is made, then I will be at the back of the Government.[54]

Such an attitude could be explained, it would seem, only on the assumption that Mr. Meighen thought that in following the British lead he was complying with the understanding of the 1921 Conference. But public appeals for assistance were never contemplated then or at any other time, and the Canadian request for information should have warned him that little or no consultation had preceded the original message. He should also have known that there could be no obligation on Canada to uphold the terms of a still-born treaty. The only people in Canada who would be in complete sympathy with his speech were the case-hardened Imperialists, and even they would not relish the idea that Canada could announce that she would support Great Britain without thereby incurring any obligation to send troops if war developed.* The Conservative party had, indeed, established a precedent many years before when in 1885 the Canadian High Com-

---

*King repudiated this kind of assurance as one for which "Britain would hardly thank us," and said that any Government which would be prepared to give it "would be wholly unworthy of the trust that might be imposed in it." W.L.M.K. to Senator G. D. Robertson, Sept. 30, 1922.

missioner suggested to Sir John A. Macdonald that he might send troops to help the British in the Sudan. Macdonald's refusal to be led into what he called "this wretched business" was forthright and even violent. He was not willing, he said, to have Canadian men and money sacrificed "to get Gladstone and Co. out of the hole they have plunged themselves into by their own imbecility."[55]

It was soon disclosed that Mackenzie King had many defenders in Great Britain who also were dismayed by the Chanak appeal. Although the British Cabinet had approved the original message, only two or three Ministers had seen the press manifesto which was chiefly the work of Lloyd George and Churchill. Lord Curzon, the Foreign Secretary, read the manifesto "with consternation." Mr. Bonar Law said he was amazed at the recklessness of the appeal made without any previous consultation. Mr. Asquith described it as sounding "the double note of provocation and of panic."[56] The Turkish situation proved, in fact, to be the final disagreement which broke up the Lloyd George coalition, for it led to the defection of many Unionists and the resignation of Lloyd George on October 19, 1922. Four days later Mr. Bonar Law took office at the head of a Unionist Government.

The Chanak incident provided an interesting contrast in Canadian political leadership, though the decisions were made under somewhat different circumstances, inasmuch as King had to furnish an immediate answer while Meighen could take his time—as he did—in announcing his position. King's cautious approach satisfied Liberals of all persuasions; Meighen's jingoistic appeal antagonized and probably alienated some of his Conservative following. Where King's policy tended to bring Progressives and Labour closer to the Liberals, Meighen's announcement tended to widen the existing gap between those groups and the Conservatives. King's prestige was greatly enhanced, and the country began to realize that while the Prime Minister might lack colour, he possessed both courage and common sense and was not to be hurried into mistaken policies on the impulse of the moment. The alleged necessity of consulting Parliament was his way of gaining time—to await events in Europe, to ascertain public opinion, and to give that opinion at the same time an opportunity to take shape and become stabilized—but it was also a policy, which Meighen's reproaches and Lloyd George's repeated requests for assurances made abundantly clear. If it turned out that Parliament had to be summoned (which was always possible) the Cabinet would have to bring down a policy for parliamentary approval and it might then have to be of a more positive nature. For the moment, however, the Cabinet considered that no case had yet been made to justify any overt action. Some time later a Progressive member of Parliament put the matter succinctly when he suggested that the crisis demanded not so much a policy of "ready, aye, ready" as one of "steady, aye, steady"—certainly a fair epitome of King's policy at that time.[57]

Mature consideration did not seem to improve Mr. Meighen's sensitivity. In 1925 he went a step further and antagonized also the right-wing Conservatives by giving a speech at Hamilton on what he felt should be done if war again threatened. The Government, he said, should decide on its policy, and not only should Parliament be called promptly, but the Government's decisions "should be submitted to the judgement of the people at a general election before troops should leave our shores."[58] At the time he was getting ready to make this speech representative men in the Conservative party pleaded with him not to do so; but he persisted. It was followed by an immediate cry of protest, and all over the Dominion many Conservatives were incensed at his proposals. Two years later he rose in a Conservative national convention, and tried to justify what he had said; he was "as tenacious of his own opinions," wrote a commentator, "as he is indifferent to the protests of his party."[59] The natural result was to revive the disagreement which his Hamilton speech had already caused among many Conservatives.*

The difference between Meighen's approach to a political issue and that of Mackenzie King was drawn by Meighen himself over a decade later at a gathering of the Conservative party which was held to bid farewell to R. B. Bennett. In the course of his remarks Meighen touched on the subject of political leadership in terms which not only

---

*Thirty-one years passed; and Mr. Meighen was still to be found at Chanak. When the unhappy Suez crisis occurred in 1956 and Canada refused to follow the lead of the British Government, Mr. Meighen was reported as follows:

"Canada, Mr. Meighen said, should have sought without delay alignment unmistakably and strongly with Britain. 'Prime Minister Anthony Eden, for whom I have the highest regard and respect, merits the support of the Commonwealth in his endeavour to maintain Britain's honor and her place in world affairs,' Mr. Meighen said. . . . While he refrained from any allusion to Prime Minister St. Laurent or External Affairs Minister Pearson, Mr. Meighen said it was his opinion that Canada might well have taken an example from Australia in its early and outspoken support of the British position." Toronto Globe and Mail, Nov. 5, 1956.

provided a clue to his own ideas but also quite clearly indicated Mackenzie King as the villain of the Canadian scene:

In our Dominion where sections abound, a Dominion of races, of classes and of creeds, of many languages and many origins, there are times when no Prime Minister can be true to his trust to the nation he has sworn to serve, save at the temporary sacrifice of the party he is appointed to lead. . . . If anyone tells me that fidelity to party and fidelity to country are always compatible, or that the wisdom of mere numbers is the wisdom of heaven, then I tell him that he loves applause far more than he loves truth. Loyalty to the ballot box is not necessarily loyalty to the nation; it is not even loyalty to the multitude. Democracy has failed and fallen in many lands, and political captains in Canada must have courage to lead rather than servility to follow, if our institutions are going to survive. There must be something better than an ambition to be re-elected, or democracy will fall, even in this Dominion.[60]

It is interesting that King and Meighen each advanced the heterogeneity of the Canadian people as a major justification of his special form of leadership. To Meighen the challenge had to be met by the formulation of some broad concept of the national interest which would transcend this diversity and in large measure obliterate it. Having formulated this concept, Meighen then invoked all the arts of rational persuasion to secure its popular acceptance. His confidence in the product of his own judgment was so profound and his advocacy so determined that the policy was open to little or no discussion, still less could it be recast or toned down in any way to meet the demands or soothe the feelings of dissenting groups or interests.

Mackenzie King also perceived in this diversity of population a challenge but a different kind of opportunity. Opposing views, as he saw it, should not be expected to undergo any rapid conversion. Such a change would come through the slow influence of sympathetic association. The emphasis should always be placed on those things which people held in common and on which they could be induced to co-operate. Shared experiences would in time lead to increased tolerance, compromise, and understanding.

> First across the gulf we cast
> Kite-born threads, till lines are passed
> And habit builds the bridge at last!

Nevertheless any fair appraisal would have to recognize a certain degree of truth in Meighen's criticism, and concede that King's leadership would have been improved had he been more venturesome and more willing to offer forthright guidance to the nation. King's tactics enabled him to secure and retain office—the indispensable first step. But King, too frequently, stopped right there; and because he was reluctant to press on and try to realize some independent conception of the national interest, his policies slipped into the mire of pure expediency. King was always reluctant to venture into the unknown. He avoided taking risks, and he would postpone action, if by so doing he could ensure a greater degree of safety. He dreaded unnecessary discussion which might lead to disagreement and even threaten the existing party solidarity on which the whole security of his position rested. He was not prepared to use his own power extensively in an effort to modify the character and scope of those common elements on which he sought to base his policy. He was too willing at times to yield his own judgment when confronted with opposing opinion. He was slow to admit that he had a duty as leader to exert a moderate pressure in the direction in which he believed the country should move. Franklin Roosevelt, for example, was able to follow King's general course, but with a significant difference. He found it possible to maintain this precarious balance, this unending compromise and adjustment between the leader and the led. Thus in the field of foreign policy Roosevelt was usually able to keep in touch with and even follow American opinion, while at the same time his confident personality was guiding that opinion in the general direction he desired.

Meighen's excessive self-confidence inclined him to be somewhat contemptuous of and superior to public opinion. King's excessive caution and search for common ground tended to make him too acquiescent and too sensitive to that opinion. Yet King was able to accomplish infinitely more. His method was the necessary approach to office, although admittedly a stronger realization of his duty to take the initiative would have added to his effectiveness. It was, of course, King's sensitivity to existing conflicts of belief and his search for existing areas of agreement which led to Meighen's taunts of loyalty to the ballot box and servility to public opinion. King might well reply that the best hockey player in the world is no use off the ice; that a party leader who cannot get elected and stay elected cannot govern and in due course will destroy the party he is supposed to lead. A condition precedent to the exercise of power in a democracy as elsewhere is to gain a place in the seats of the mighty.

Political leadership, in short, must always meet two tests: the ability to gain and stay in power, and the ability to use power once it has been gained. King's technique in bringing conflicting groups together made him a master in passing the first ordeal, though he allowed the same talent to undermine his effectiveness after he was in office. Meighen's technique never got him over the first barrier. He showed some ability to meet the second of the requirements of democratic leadership, but he was given little opportunity to demonstrate this capacity. There is, moreover, no escaping the fact that the same difficulties which prevented him from obtaining office would have been equally operative in preventing his staying there. In point of fact, they did exactly that, for on the two occasions when Meighen attained the Prime Ministership, he was unable to secure confirmation from the electorate.

To return to Chanak and its implications. Mackenzie King must not be regarded as an extreme nationalist who desired to break off the connection with Great Britain and the rest of the Empire. He was most emphatically against centralization and in favour of Canadian self-government, but he was equally anxious to preserve Canadian membership in the Commonwealth. Immediately after Chanak he wrote to Violet Markham:

You know, I think, the views I entertain as to the basis upon which the nations comprising the British Empire can be held together. Anything like centralization in London, to say nothing of a direct or indirect attempt on the part of those in office at Downing Street to tell the people of the Dominions what they should or should not do, and to dictate their duty in matters of foreign policy, is certain to prove just as injurious to so-called 'imperial solidarity' as any attempt at interference in questions of purely domestic concern. If membership within the British Empire means participation by the Dominions in any and every war in which Great Britain becomes involved, without consultation, conference, or agreement of any kind in advance, I can see no hope for an enduring relationship. It is for this reason that my colleagues and myself have taken the position that Parliament must decide whether or not Canada is to take part in the present war in the Far East. Indeed, any other decision would be impossible, when one considers the complexion of our Parliament.[61]

The Chanak incident was considered at the time of its occurrence to be of vital importance, and later developments have increased rather than diminished its significance in Empire relations. The most obvious effect was the shattering blow it dealt to the conception of one common Empire foreign policy formulated through an interchange of views between Great Britain and the Dominions. The existing provisions to secure this interchange had proved to be quite ineffective in coping with a sudden international crisis and the doubts raised at the Conference of 1921 had been only too well justified by events. The system had been tried and found manifestly wanting.

It might, of course, be argued that the solution was simply to introduce the much needed improvements in communications so that consultation between the British and Dominion Governments could be made effective, and thereby remove the obstacles which lay in the way of a common Empire policy. That solution, thanks to Chanak, was no longer possible. Whatever the feasibility of a common policy, it had now become politically unacceptable. Canada, for one, had learned her lesson, and she was very much afraid that the next time she might not come out of a crisis without finding that she was more actively committed. If war over remote issues was to be the result of an Empire foreign policy, most Canadians were determined to have nothing to do with it. Indeed, many of those who had given much thought to the subject began to suspect that the consultation, no matter how perfectly organized, would not enlarge the influence and power of the Dominion, but actually diminish it. Dr. O. D. Skelton wrote in 1923:

A common foreign policy . . . offers a maximum of responsibility and a minimum of control. It commits a Dominion in advance to an endorsement of courses of action of which it knows little and of which it may not approve, or in which it may have little direct concern. The real way in which the Dominions may extend their power is the way in which such extension has come in the past—by reserving for their own peoples and their own parliaments the ultimate decision as to their course of action. . . . If the Dominions are committed to action by blank cheques given the Foreign secretary by their Prime Ministers they have sham control and real responsibility. If they are committed to action only by their own parliaments and peoples, they will have real influence and responsible control.[62]

Chanak therefore made Canadians more eager to push this argument to its conclusion: that Canada should draw up and apply its own foreign policy, that Great Britain should do the same, and that conferences between the two (and with other Dominions) should be held whenever necessary to iron out differences and, when advisable, to agree on common action. Mackenzie King had been feeling his way to that solution for many years; he had clearly stated his position in Parliament in 1920;[63] and he now found his views confirmed by the problem which was precipitated by the Near East crisis. From this proposition there flowed a corollary, that the Empire would speak on foreign affairs with a number of voices, even, perhaps, conflicting voices, a practice which, if allowed, would involve a breach in the diplomatic unity of the Crown. Many British political leaders, strongly backed by the Foreign Office, were prone to dismiss this as a suggestion so fanciful that it was not worthy of serious consideration. Events were later to prove that although this attitude might be legally correct, it was short-sighted and could not withstand for long the political pressure generated by the continuing demands of the Dominions for greater autonomy.

Moreover, the policy of allowing Parliament to decide the extent of Canadian commitments combined, as it was, with the legal principle that "when Britain is at war, Canada is at war" could lead to virtually the same result of destroying the dogma of the indivisibility of the Crown. Mackenzie King had put before the House the lesson of Chanak as follows:

We have felt, and feel very strongly that, if the relations between the different parts of the British Empire are to be made of an enduring character, this will only be through a full recognition of the supremacy of Parliament, and this particularly with regard to matters which may involve participation in war. It is for Parliament to decide whether or not we should participate in wars in different parts of the world, and it is neither right nor proper for any individual or for any group of individuals to take any step which in any way might limit the rights of Parliament in a matter which is of such great concern to all the people of our country.*

There was nothing new in this position, and precedents had been supplied by both the South African War and the First World War. It nevertheless had far reaching implications. Its purpose was, of course, to avoid the awkward possibilities which might result from too strict and logical an enforcement of the legal consequences of a British declaration of war. It acknowledged a distinction between a condition of "active belligerency," when a Dominion decided to take an active part in the war to which it was legally committed, and a condition of

*Can. H. of C. Debates, Feb. 1, 1923, p. 33. At the first opportunity in the House both R. Forke and J. S. Woodsworth, the leaders of the Progressive and Labour parties respectively, endorsed King's stand on the Chanak invitation. Ibid., pp. 40, 45.

"passive belligerency," when a Dominion accepted its legal status as a belligerent but took no steps to make its participation effective. In the latter instance it was not beyond the bounds of possibility that an enemy might consider that it would be well advised to accept and recognize such a Dominion's abstention. "Passive belligerency" thus bore a strong resemblance to neutrality, although it could lay no claim to international recognition. The existence of two kinds of belligerency was an admission that parts of the Empire held divergent views on a matter of international interest, and within their own circle at least had agreed on different policies. The further step to complete neutrality, with this condition recognized and accepted by all nations, was a natural development, but it could obviously not be taken so long as the British Empire continued to speak with only one formal voice in international affairs. Once the concept of the indivisible Crown was discarded and the comity of nations had accepted this, the full rights of a Dominion as a belligerent or a neutral in an Empire war would become possible. This change was to take some years to mature, but it was implicit in the issues which were raised by the Chanak crisis.

The crisis in the Near East and the repudiation of the Treaty of Sèvres made a new treaty of peace imperative. Already on September 27, 1922, Mackenzie King was beginning to worry about what Canada should do "in the event of an invitation to participate" and what would be "our position when parliament is summoned, sooner or later. I think we should not participate at Peace Conference, having had nothing to do with note of Allies sent Mustapha Kemal Pasha [the Turkish leader]."[64]

The Lausanne Conference was not called until a month later, and Canada was not invited. Yet there was every reason to expect an invitation. Representation for the Dominions, if the precedents of the Paris and Washington* Conferences were to be of any value, should have been accorded without difficulty, and they should also have shared in the preliminary consultations in order to observe the understandings of the 1921 Conference of Prime Ministers. The British Government knew this full well and evidently expected that the

---

*The Washington Conference on the Limitation of Armament was held just after Mackenzie King became Prime Minister. Canada was represented by Sir Robert Borden, who was a member of the British delegation, and the precedents established at Paris were closely followed. Report of Sir Robert Borden, *Can. Sessional Papers* (1922), No. 47.

arrangements which it had agreed to in such summary fashion for Lausanne would meet with reproaches and criticism. Thus when the Duke of Devonshire (the Colonial Secretary) at the end of October informed Canada of the meeting and stated that Great Britain was to be represented by two members, Lord Curzon and Sir Horace Rumbold, he also sent a confidential message saying that the British Government had tried to secure representation for the Dominions, but, owing to French objections, its effort had not been successful.* The Dominions, however, were "to be kept informed" as the negotiations proceeded, and would "of course" be invited to sign any treaty that might result and any "separate instrument regulating the status of the Straits."[65] Once again Canada had a constitutional issue thrown in her lap.

But Canada was not looking for an issue—at least not quite on the grounds the British Government expected. King knew that the questions confronting the Lausanne Conference were of no real interest to Canada, and he felt nothing but relief at being left out. He wrote in his diary:

No invitation has come to us and we have not been consulted as to procedure. Nor have other Dominions who are similarly treated. I take no exception to course adopted. It was inevitable, but it indicates how right we are in the position we have taken. Australia & N.Z. are placed in a very invidious light. It was all to save Australian graves when the appeal for contingents was made & now Australia is not so much as invited to be represented at Conference! I think our attitude has been justified beyond our dreams. I had expected an invitation & was dreading the refusal it might be necessary to send.[66]

Three days later (October 31) the Cabinet approved King's despatch in reply, and the comment of one Minister—"Thank God, we weren't [invited]"—seemed to be the sentiment of all present.[67]

It was in King's reply that the constitutional issue was raised: not on the representation itself, but on the way in which the choice and character of the representatives affected the Canadian obligations under the resulting Treaty. The position of Canada may have been novel but in essentials it was relatively simple. First, Canada was not represented at the Conference and did not want representation. Secondly, she did not ask to have the Treaty submitted to her for

*France had taken the position that if the Dominions were given representation she would demand seats for Tunis and Morocco.

approval. Thirdly, inasmuch as she was not a party to the Conference, she would be bound by the Treaty only to the extent that her Parliament might decide.*

This is moderately clear, but the communications to which it gave rise were long, involved, and confused. They cannot be given in detail. The original *idée fixe* of the British Government that Canada wanted to participate at all costs at some stage of the Lausanne Conference or Treaty was never shaken off and continued to muddle the minds at the Colonial and Foreign Offices throughout all the interchange which ensued. Thus the Colonial Secretary replied to King that the British Government had assumed that Canada would wish to follow the precedent of the Paris Conference and "include signatures on behalf of all the Dominions."[68] Patiently King pointed out in another despatch that it was utterly impossible to apply the Paris precedent here. At both Paris and Washington there had been "four separate, distinct and essential stages": representation of Canada at the conference with full powers, signing of the treaty by her representatives, approval of the treaty by the Canadian Parliament, and assent of the Government of Canada in the ratification of the treaty, so signed and approved. In so far as each stage in the procedure "is necessarily dependent upon the stage" before it, the precedents could not apply to Lausanne. In any question in which Canada had "a direct or immediate interest" the Canadian Government would wish to follow the Paris precedent, but Lausanne was not in that category.[69] Having drafted this despatch King wrote in his diary on December 30 a more concise summary of his position:

Only in matters in which we have a direct & immediate interest will we expect to thus participate & in all others in which treaties are signed by Br. plenipotentiary we will decide "on merits of the case" what it is wisest to do, our parliament not the gov't of the day being the deciding authority.

The British Government agreed almost a month later that the Lausanne Treaty should be signed by only the British plenipotentiaries.[70] There the matter rested.

But not for long. On August 20, 1923, the British Government sent a despatch expressing the hope that the Dominion Governments

*This correspondence was published as "Correspondence with the Canadian Government on the subject of the Peace Settlement with Turkey." Great Britain, *Parliamentary Papers* (1924), Cmd. 2146.

would be in a position to signify their concurrence in the ratification of the Treaty and other instruments signed at Lausanne.[71] This failure to understand King's views, despite a correspondence of almost a year's duration, is quite incomprehensible from the evidence supplied by the published documents. The information of the British Government, however, was not derived solely from its correspondence with the Canadian Prime Minister. Lord Byng had sent on December 31, 1922, a secret despatch to the Colonial Secretary, in which he attempted to interpret the Canadian position. In doing so, he completely distorted it. "He [King] is quite agreeable," he said, "that Lord Curzon should sign for Empire and that treaty should be presented to Canadian Parliament for ratification in usual way."[72] King never at any time agreed to such ratification, nor is there any reason to suppose that he had any suspicion that Byng had so completely, albeit innocently, misrepresented him to the Colonial Office. This despatch does, however, explain in some measure the British Government's continued inability to grasp Canada's wishes. Mackenzie King was admittedly assuming an unorthodox position in regard to the Lausanne Treaty, and his attempt to state what he wanted, which was in itself none too clear, had been further obscured by the contradictory version submitted by Lord Byng. If it is assumed that Byng's cable remained on the file in the Colonial Office, its erroneous statement may have continued to mislead the British Government when the question again arose a year or two later.

King, quite inexcusably, made no attempt to reply to the British despatch of August 20, 1923.* Whether he was merely exasperated at the British obtuseness, or whether he decided to await events and the resulting embarrassment of the British Government, or whether he preferred to hold his fire and make his explanation to the Imperial Conference in six weeks' time has not been disclosed. In any event, Canada made no further attempt to rectify the misunderstanding before the meeting of the Conference in 1923. The remainder of the story is best postponed to a later period.

The lukewarm attitude of Canada to the League of Nations has already been described, and it was pointed out that Canada was willing to participate with caution, if not with enthusiasm, in its activities.

---

*Later King apparently forgot that he had ever received this letter; see *Can. H. of C. Debates*, April 2, 1924, p. 947.

This meant, of course, selecting delegates to attend the meetings of the Assembly and joining the International Labour Organization and other bodies associated with the League. Canada normally sent her full quota of three members to the Assembly, the delegation being composed as a rule of Cabinet Ministers and the High Commissioner in London. The political implications of these appointments were not neglected. Thus King began the practice of always including a French-Canadian; and in 1924 when he wished to make a conciliatory gesture to the ex-Unionist Liberals in Manitoba, he invited A. B. Hudson to attend the Fifth Assembly as a member of the delegation.[73] Hudson declined "with very great regret" because of "personal business reasons."[74]

A controversial appointment of a minor nature which aroused criticism was that of Mrs. James Carruthers (Violet Markham) as an acting member of the Governing Body of the International Labour Conference. This body held meetings every three months, and as the Minister of Labour could not attend all of them, the practice had arisen before the Liberal Government took office of selecting someone, not necessarily a Canadian, to act as a substitute. Mrs. Carruthers sat on the Governing Body in this capacity in April and June, 1923. Undoubtedly Mackenzie King appointed her because of their long friendship; but her capacity, experience, and special knowledge of labour conditions in Canada and elsewhere gave her other qualifications of a high order.[75] Meighen's description of her as "an English woman politician, who forsooth had written a book" was a much greater reflection on him than on Mrs. Carruthers.[76] A private letter written by Mrs. Carruthers to Mackenzie King after her return from Geneva furnishes an interesting assessment of the value of the Labour Organization to Canada and would suggest that Canadian indifference to this and similar activities had at least some justification:

[Lucien] Pacaud* put a blunt question to me on Thursday "what good is it to Canada to form part of that Geneva show"? I wish I could give a clear reply to that question which sat at my elbow through the whole session of the Governing Body! For the sake of what we all hope will be a happier future I should be grieved if Canada broke away. I am sure for the sake of larger & more remote issues it's worth while to hang on. But it would be idle to pretend that here & now your interests are directly affected or that your membership of the G[overning] B[ody] is bringing

*Secretary to the Canadian High Commissioner in London.

in immediate material gains. If America were in the League your presence would be essential on Canadian grounds. As it is the *material* value to yourself is small, though the *abstract* value of Canada's co-operation is substantial to the cause of internationalism. I should fail in my duty to you if I didn't make this view clear. But it's because I appreciate the difficulties of Geneva that I am doubly anxious you should yourself have the practical experience of presiding over the Conference & judging the situation first hand.[77]

As long as the League remained little more than a debating society and an organization to promote international goodwill and bring about a measure of co-operation on peace-time problems it was not likely to cause any uneasiness in Canada. Provided, that is to say, that it would not attempt to do anything more. There was, however, in France and in some of the smaller countries a disposition to strengthen the sanctions in the Covenant and make the League a powerful weapon for maintaining by force the territorial and political conditions which had been recognized by the Peace Treaty. The extent to which this effort might be successful depended in large measure upon the interpretation and effectiveness of certain of the provisions of the Covenant. The chief of these was Article X which read:

The Members of the League undertake to respect and preserve as against external aggression the territorial integrity and existing political independence of all Members of the League. In case of any such aggression, or in case of any threat or danger of such aggression, the Council shall advise upon the means by which this obligation shall be fulfilled.

It is easy to understand how an isolationist Canada would regard an Article possessing such ominous possibilities of collective stability. At the Peace Conference Great Britain and the Dominions, and especially Canada, had been dissatisfied with the wording of the Article and had endeavoured to have it clarified and restricted in its operation.[78] Their efforts had been unsuccessful. When the Covenant was eventually submitted to the Canadian Parliament for approval, the Liberals took strong exception to Article X and to the implied menace to Canadian autonomy. Sir Robert Borden and C. J. Doherty, who had fought against the Article in Paris, now felt constrained to come to its defence, for any piecemeal amendments at this stage might have imperilled the adoption of the document in other countries as well. The Covenant was eventually accepted by Parliament without change.[79]

427

At the First Assembly of the League, however, the Canadian delegation renewed the war on Article X, and Doherty moved that it be struck from the Covenant. The Assembly referred the motion to a committee and the question was thereby deferred for a year. From that time on the Canadians, irrespective of the party in power at Ottawa, continued to attack the Article, the only difference being that the Liberal demand was one for an interpretation rather than for outright repeal. This shift in tactics was made by Fielding and Lapointe at the League meeting in 1922,[80] when it was obvious that there was no chance of the earlier Conservative proposal being accepted. It presumably had Mackenzie King's full approval though there does not appear to be any direct evidence on this point. Even the diary is silent, although this might be explained by the fact that the Chanak crisis was engaging most of King's attention at this time. An important indication of King's general attitude to the League, however, is furnished by the fact that the diary of the early twenties rarely refers to the League or its activities. The Prime Minister clearly regarded the League as a matter of quite secondary interest which was completely overshadowed by the many domestic and Imperial issues constantly crowding in upon him.

In 1923 the Canadian delegation, led by Sir Lomer Gouin, succeeded in having an interpretative resolution on Article X approved which ensured that the geographical position and special conditions of each member would be considered by the Council in making its recommendation under Article X, and that each member would have the right to decide the degree to which it was bound to employ its military forces in discharging its obligations under the Article. This interpretation emasculated Article X, and quieted the fears of a number of nations which had shared the uneasiness of Canada as to what might be implied by its ambiguous phrases.

Only a few weeks after the Chanak crisis Crerar gave up the leadership of the Progressive party. He wished to devote more time to his business activities, and was also influenced, perhaps, by his failure to persuade the party to widen its interests and discard its ideas of class representation.[81] Robert Forke was chosen as his successor. Forke was another Manitoban who belonged to the reforming wing of the party—a kindly honest man, but with too little toughness or determination to make a good politician. King's first thought was that the loss of Crerar's leadership would mean the disintegration of the Progressive party, and he welcomed the choice of another Progressive from the Manitoba group as an encouraging augury of what he called "complete co-operation."

Two other events of party interest occurred in the closing months of 1922. One was a large dinner for King in Toronto which was designed to have the die-hard Liberal Unionists meet the Prime Minister and bring them back into the Liberal party. "Many of the 'Laurier' Liberals," King observed, "will look on this with resentment, they fail to see that a political party needs all the friends it can have, that those who are not for us are against us, that Toronto's influence spreads over the Dominion & particularly over Ontario. I shall speak on the need for the return of the two party system . . . for a united Canada. . . . of the present position of being a minority government, & its limitations, . . . and end with an appeal for their support in the interests of Canada, the Party, Ont. & Toronto, themselves & myself."[82] The dinner, which had been arranged by Leighton McCarthy, himself a former Liberal Unionist, was a great success; and although a number had accepted the invitation on the understanding that they were not committing themselves to any future conduct, most of the guests seemed very responsive to the Prime Minister's plea for support. "It was a daring venture," King wrote later, "but carried off well."

The by-elections had made no change in the standing of any party in the House in 1922, but in the last two months of the year, W. J. Hammell and Joseph Binette, both Progressive members from Ontario, came over to the Liberal side. These with several other Progressives had been wavering for some months,[83] and their desertion of their party naturally suggested that others might soon follow. For the first time King had an undisputed majority in the House. This circumstance, added to his success in weathering the perils of his maiden session, gave King not only satisfaction, but confidence, so much so that he may well have thought that he could now afford to slacken his efforts to win over the Progressives. On the other hand the defeat of a Liberal Government in Manitoba in mid-summer by the Progressives indicated that the farmer movement was still in full cry, and that the continuing influence of the movement in federal politics was as unpredictable as ever.

CHAPTER FIFTEEN

FIRST ADMINISTRATION, 1923

MACKENZIE KING had seized with commendable speed the opportunity offered by the Chanak crisis and the Lausanne Conference to advance the cause of Canadian autonomy, and had thereby established two valuable precedents. Should this be the model for him to follow in any future extension of Canadian powers? Should he await the appearance of suitable issues, and so undermine the Imperialist position by innovation and precedent that it would become a legal anomaly impossible to defend? Or would a better policy be for him to accept the advice of the more impatient autonomists[1] and draft some simple but comprehensive formula, to be endorsed by Parliament, which would assert Canada's complete control over her external as well as her internal affairs?* At the time of the Chanak crisis he was "strongly tempted" to follow the latter alternative and make a declaration of policy on Canada's attitude in regard to participation in war, but "on reflection" he decided instead to wait and place a resolution on the subject before Parliament early the next session.[2] This resolution was never introduced. King was doubtless afraid to move too far in advance of public opinion. He knew that a large number of people in Ontario and the Maritime Provinces were strongly in favour of maintaining a close connection with the United Kingdom and that Quebec also might take alarm at a declaration of constitutional change without any indication of the constitutional procedures by which the change was to

---

*Sir Clifford Sifton suggested a declaration that "the governing powers of Canada as constituted by the British North America Act as amended and altered from time to time hereafter by the people of Canada, ought to possess under the British Crown the same powers with regard to Canada, its affairs and its people, as the Parliament of Great Britain possesses in regard to Great Britain, its affairs and its people"; Address given by Sir Clifford Sifton to the Canada First Club, Jan. 9, 1923. A motion in identical terms was moved (and later withdrawn) by J. S. Woodsworth in 1924 in the House; *Can. H. of C. Debates*, March 20, 1924, p. 508.

be effected.[3] Any explicit formula, moreover, was certain to encounter the formidable opposition of Fielding and perhaps others in the Cabinet. These objections added to King's own preference for a pragmatic approach to thorny problems were apparently decisive, and sweeping resolutions on autonomy were shelved in favour of a policy of steady encroachments on traditional practices.

This method by no means implied that the Canadian Government would be entirely the sport of circumstance and be compelled to await such opportunities as fate might happen to provide. If the rate of constitutional advance were to depend solely upon the propensity of the British Government to ignore or block Canadian national aspirations, its progress might be sure, but it would be uncertain; and the development could be materially accelerated by Canada's supplying a few additional issues on its own. Thus although Chanak was followed closely by Lausanne, the latter shared the limelight with another issue which owed its existence to a deliberate act of the Canadian Government. This was the Halibut Fisheries Treaty, and the dispute was centred on the right of Canada to conclude a commercial and political treaty with a foreign state without the intervention of the British Government.

An independent treaty-making power was one of the two prerequisites of Canada's control over her own foreign policy, for clearly any kind of interchange between nations must be supported by the ability of the countries concerned to enter into formal agreements with one another. The other prerequisite was the establishment of diplomatic representation in foreign capitals, so that all possible information would be readily available and access to foreign governments would be direct and speedy. Canada had already considered the advisability of opening a legation in Washington, but no Minister had yet been appointed. She was now to assert a greater authority in the making of treaties.

The right of the Dominions to conclude treaties with other countries had been steadily increasing for many years. By the time of the outbreak of the First World War they had won the right to negotiate their own commercial treaties; but their control over political treaties was slight, and hence their participation in the Peace Conference (albeit as part of a British Empire delegation) marked a notable advance on all past procedures. Even in regard to commercial treaties, however, the powers of the Dominions, though great in practice, had always been subject to at least three legal limitations. First, the Dominion negotiators were given their "full powers" by the King on the advice of the British Government, which in turn was requested to take such action by the Government of Canada. In the second place, although the Dominion representatives would conduct all the negotiations and would sign the treaty, the formal signature of a British representative was also required. Finally, when the treaty was ratified by the Crown, the King acted solely on the advice of his British Ministers, who again were following a recommendation of the Canadian Cabinet. It is true that the British participation at these three stages had reached the point where it was of little practical significance and interposed no real impediment; nevertheless it was constitutionally of some importance. Those Canadians who suffered from what Fielding unkindly called "status on the brain" wished to make clear that this British participation had become as a result of constitutional evolution purely nominal. The wishes of the Canadian Government, they argued, had become paramount, and the actual function which the British Cabinet now performed was simply to act as a channel of communication whereby the Canadian Cabinet made its wishes known to the Crown.

King, by making an issue of the Halibut Fisheries Treaty, endeavoured to establish new precedents at all the three points mentioned. Moreover, as the treaty was not purely commercial but had political implications, the precedents established would also become applicable to political treaties which affected Canada but had no direct interest for any other part of the Empire.

The Halibut Fisheries Treaty was signed at Washington on March 2, 1923, by Charles E. Hughes, the United States Secretary of State, and Ernest Lapointe, the Canadian Minister of Marine and Fisheries. It was, of course, the product of negotiations between Canadian and American officials. On the Canadian side its final stages had been preceded by a series of messages between the Canadian Government, the British Government, and Sir Auckland Geddes, the British Ambassador at Washington, dealing with the position of the Canadian signatory.

On January 16 the Canadian Government had asked the Colonial Office to have full powers issued to Lapointe to authorize him to sign the treaty on behalf of Canada. At the same time it endeavoured to have a change made in the title of the treaty, which read "a convention between the United States of America and Great Britain concerning the Halibut Fishery," by suggesting that the words "Dominion of Canada" should be substituted for "Great Britain." The full powers were issued in London without question; however, a compromise was offered, and accepted by the Canadian Cabinet, that the title should not name the contracting parties, but should simply state that the treaty was to regulate the halibut fishery on the Pacific Coast of Canada and the United States.

In view of later events, it is easy to see that the combination of these two Canadian requests to Great Britain was designed to allow Lapointe to stand as the only signatory, the sole representative of His Majesty acting on behalf of Canada, but this point was not brought out in the early correspondence. Such emphasis was the more necessary in that in two very recent Canadian treaties with France and Italy the old established procedure had been followed, and no indication had been given in either instance that any departure from the normal practices was intended.

As the time for signing the treaty approached, it became evident that neither the British Government nor its Ambassador at Washington was aware of the intention of the Canadian Government that Lapointe alone was to sign the treaty and that Geddes was to have nothing to do with it. In two messages to Geddes on February 20 and 28 and one to the British Government on the later date Mackenzie King cleared up the ambiguity for which he was to some degree at least responsible. Inasmuch as the proposed treaty, he said, was "of concern solely to Canada and the United States" and did not affect "in any particular any Imperial interest," the signature of the Canadian Minister "should be sufficient." The Canadian Cabinet therefore requested that the British Ambassador at Washington should be instructed accordingly.[4] The British Government acquiesced, at least to the extent of passing on the Canadian request to Sir Auckland Geddes with the understanding (apparently designed to save his feelings) that he might do as he pleased in the matter.* Geddes gave in to the

---

*Geddes' refusal was a real possibility, and had he refused, apparently the Canadian Government would have allowed the matter to drop. King wrote in his diary on March 1, 1923: "[Lord Byng] assumes it [the letter to Geddes] means Lapointe will

Canadian wishes with a bad grace, and Lapointe signed alone on behalf of Canada.

Lapointe and his deputy minister, Alexander Johnston, went to Washington the day before the treaty was to be signed. Hitherto the custom had been for a Canadian Minister always to be met at the train by some one from the British Embassy and for the British Ambassador to do his utmost to make the Canadian's brief stay in Washington pleasant. No one met Lapointe; no one communicated with him; and the next day he telephoned to the American Secretary of State, and he himself made the necessary arrangements. The treaty was signed by Hughes and Lapointe in a tense atmosphere. A noticeable lull ensued until Hughes remarked: "This may turn out to be a very significant day in the history of relations between Canada and the United States." Lapointe laughed, and with some relief replied: "I am glad that some one broke that long silence."†

King is probably open to some criticism for not being more frank with the British Government at an earlier stage. The Governor-General knew and informally agreed with the proposal at least as early as February 17, although he evidently did not appreciate the significance of the change until three days later when he asked King if it had been considered in all its aspects. King reassured him, and told him that the Cabinet had approved the change and that even Fielding, who had developed characteristic misgivings, had acquiesced.[5] King pointed out that if Canada could not sign directly through her own Minister, she would be compelled to press for her own legation in Washington, an argument which would seem to have had little to do with the immediate point at issue, but a good deal to do with quieting some of Byng's misgivings. The British Government remained in ignorance of King's purpose for another eight days, that is until only two days before the signing took place. King evidently wished to postpone raising the issue so as to give the British Government very little time in which to combat the Canadian proposal if the treaty was to be signed on the appointed day.

The treaty being signed, the success of King's plans was suddenly threatened from an unexpected quarter. When the United States

---

sign alone. I hope so, I hope he will be firm, tho' wd. not be surprised if he yielded to Geddes under pressure."

†Conversation with the late Dr. Alex. Johnston.

Senate ratified the treaty on March 4 it inserted an "understanding" that "none of the nationals, inhabitants, vessels or boats of any other part of Great Britain [sic] shall engage in the halibut fishery contrary to the provisions of the said Convention." The purpose of this clumsily worded clause was to bring in Great Britain and the rest of the Empire as parties to the treaty; and this would involve action by several Parliaments followed by ratification on the advice of the British Cabinet. The entire value of King's efforts would thus be destroyed, for his cherished precedent would have vanished and the old familiar procedures would be reaffirmed. The Canadian Parliament therefore refused to accept any changes, and on May 31, 1924, the American Senate ratified the original treaty without any "understanding" or condition.

King had apparently achieved his three aims: the appointment of the Canadian Minister on the advice of the Canadian Government; the signing of the treaty by that Minister acting alone; and the ratification by the King on the advice of the Canadian Government. But there were constitutional lawyers, among whom were Mr. Meighen and Sir Clifford Sifton,[6] who still insisted that this interpretation of events was erroneous, and that the powers of the Canadian Government in the making of treaties had not been advanced one iota. The crucial question was the identity of the authority who advised His Majesty and took the responsibility for his actions, and that authority, it was contended, was the British Government. How otherwise did the King receive the advice tendered by the Canadian Cabinet if not through a member of the British Cabinet? If this was the channel—and that was not open to question—then the British Government must have given its approval and taken the responsibility by virtue of its transmission of the advice to the King. Lapointe would then be regarded simply as a representative of the Imperial Government. That Government had really recommended his appointment; he had been its agent in signing the treaty, and the King, following the recommendation of his British advisers, had ratified the treaty Lapointe had signed. The question thus resolved itself into this: Was the British Government in this matter acting as a genuine adviser to the King or was it performing merely a mechanical function in passing on the advice of the Canadian Government? Was the nominal British power still the real power, or had the impalpable transfer of authority to the Canadian Cabinet been made, with the Halibut Fisheries precedent furnishing the visible sign of that change?

Mackenzie King naturally upheld the principle that the British Government had recognized "the right of His Majesty's Government in Canada to advise His Majesty on an international matter of concern primarily to Canada,"[7] and a few weeks later he told J. W. Dafoe that he considered the function of the British Government in relation to the treaty had been purely mechanical.[8] Yet in the House of Commons in June he blundered into an absurd contradiction which was quite inconsistent with his whole purpose. When Meighen was pressing his inquiry as to the exact nature of the transmission of advice to the Sovereign, King first accused Meighen of "hair-splitting" but later agreed with him that the Canadian recommendation was submitted to the King by the British Ministers "with their advice"—an admission which, if correct, would have completely destroyed the significance of King's whole accomplishment.[9] This may have been no more than a slip; but the most probable explanation is that at this time King wished to avoid stressing the full significance of the precedent with its bearing on the foreign policy of the Empire. Fielding's argument (which he developed a few weeks later in a letter to the Prime Minister[10]) that the old practice had occasioned no complaint and had given Canada all the power she needed, was more than the lamentation of a reactionary Minister. He spoke for a large number of Canadians who were much disturbed by Canada's post-war haste to become involved in international affairs without the reassuring backing of Great Britain. J. W. Dafoe wrote:

> There is undoubtedly quite a large number of Canadians who are chiefly concerned in seeing that nothing is done at all and they swing from one camp to the other and back again. They block the Imperialists when they try to commit Canada to schemes of organic union or to foreign adventures; and they also resist any attempt to advance along the only other road to the future. They are mentally lazy and timid.[11]

King had the stamp of authority placed on his precedents some months later in the relative obscurity of the Imperial Conference, where the topic appeared on the agenda as a direct result of the Halibut Fisheries issue. A memorandum was submitted by the Colonial Office regarding treaty procedure which was virtually a statement of the Canadian position. "Had I drafted the memorandum," King

436

wrote in his diary with gratification, "I could not have better expressed the views which were in my own mind."[12] A resolution to this effect on the Negotiation, Signature and Ratification of Treaties was approved by the Conference.[13] Furthermore, the Conference also agreed that at the time of the Halibut Fisheries Treaty the British Government had taken no responsibility in transmitting the advice of the Canadian Government to the King, and this opinion was fully supported by Sir Cecil J. B. Hurst, the legal adviser to the Foreign Office. King's diary records Sir Cecil's opinion:

> In his opinion the British Ministers were only the channel through which the advice of the Dominion Ministers reached the Sovereign, but... they themselves were His advisers with respect to all matters within their jurisdiction. He admitted that theoretically and to appearances it might be otherwise, but that in reality there could be no doubt that his point of view was right. . . . The King's Ministers in Great Britain [Sir Cecil added] could not be impeached for wrong advice given to the Crown or the Crown's representative by [a Dominion Government] . . . the test as to who was really advising the King lay in the liability to impeachment for a wrong done. . . . I regard this morning's meeting as most important and I asked Skelton to prepare a memorandum of what was said and took place; this he has done.[14]

In March, 1924, Mackenzie King alluded in the Canadian House to the stand adopted at the Conference, and in effect erased the qualification he had made in the previous session.[15] The precedents of the Halibut Fisheries Treaty had therefore become accepted without reservation, and from them followed the unquestioned right of a Dominion to exercise complete control in the making of all those commercial and political treaties which affected its interests alone. So marked an advance well merited J. W. Dafoe's description of the issue as "a superbly audacious stroke" on the part of King and his Government.

The right of each Dominion to make treaties independently of the British Government and the right of each to conduct its own separate foreign policy were almost indistinguishable, but King at this time was not prepared to assert—and perhaps not even prepared to accept or welcome—the second of these rights. His records contain some notes in his own handwriting on this subject, which were apparently jotted down as a guide for both the Halibut Fisheries and Lausanne Treaty issues (see below, paragraphs one and two respectively). These notes are dated January 1, 1923. A later endorsement on the page reads: "Material for Imperial Conference: Treaties," and the notes evidently were among the documents taken by him to the Conference in October and November, 1923.

The Treaties
January 1, 1923

Essence of Canada's
  relationship—immediate and direct interest
Where interest
immediate &
direct—

> We should be represented with full powers
> We should sign
> Parliament should be given opportunity to approve
> Assent to ratify if felt approval should be given by Govr Genl in Council.

Where interest
not immediate
or direct—

> We need not be represented
> If not represented should not be expected to sign
> Should approve or not become a party to "on merits of the case".
> Assent to ratification dependent on approval.

High Political
  treaties—re peace & war.

> Empire acts as one—British nations as against outside powers.
> Within Empire—Extent of obligation imposed a matter of arrangement—"merits of the case".

As to participation in wars.
  Procedure identical with that of Treaties
    If interest not immediate or direct—no participation
    "   "   immediate & direct—participation "on merits of case".

Advisable [that] Treaties should include clause "Not to bind Dominions save by their approval"
  Govt must take responsibility of recommending or declining to recommend approval.

From these notes it seems clear that Mackenzie King in following out the implications of the Halibut Treaty was not ready to interpret them as giving the Canadian Government the right to advise the King on all matters involving Canada, that is, the right to form a purely Canadian, as opposed to an Imperial, foreign policy. Such advice could be exercised legitimately only "where interest [was] immediate and direct"; on other occasions, such as the "High Political treaties re peace & war," the Empire was to act "as one . . . against outside powers," the extent of the Dominions' participation in prosecuting a war or making a peace being a matter for each Dominion Parliament to decide "on the merits of the case." King did not construe the Halibut Treaty as undermining the legal and constitutional validity of the proposition that "when Britain is at war, Canada is at war"; all parts of the Empire were as before technically committed by the British declaration. Yet the basic decision on the category to which a particular matter was assigned, whether the subject was to be considered one of immediate and direct interest or the reverse, could surely not be made except by each Dominion Government affected, and this decision in turn would necessarily set the bounds to the right of a Dominion to give direct advice to the Sovereign.

Mackenzie King at this juncture thus stopped short of accepting two principles which were later endorsed by the Commonwealth, and which might have been logically derived from the Halibut Treaty issue. The first was that each Dominion would pursue its own conception of its national interest in world affairs, and in so doing would rely upon its common political heritage with the other members of the Commonwealth to harmonize any conflicts and overlapping which might result. The second was the divisibility of the Crown: that a single monarch could as King of Great Britain accept advice from his British Ministers and also as King of Canada accept advice from his Canadian Ministers, even although this opened up the awkward possibility of different sets of Ministers proffering conflicting advice. Such inferences clearly went far beyond the situation of 1923. Neither Mackenzie King nor Canada was yet prepared for so radical an advance, but the Halibut Treaty issue helped to make that development possible and even, perhaps, over a period of time inescapable.

In the session of 1923 the pressure of the Progressives on the Government remained as persistent as in the previous year. The lot of the Western farmer, however, had improved, for while the price of wheat was slightly lower, the 1922 crop had been excellent. Dafoe reported that the farmers were nevertheless more disgruntled.[16] They had discovered that even a bountiful crop would not bring them prosperity, and the harvest had been followed by a plague of creditors most of whom were not disposed to help the farmers get back on their feet. The fact that Central Canada had begun to experience a small degree of recovery did nothing to check the vehemence of Western protests. Inasmuch as wheat prices were at the mercy of international forces, the farmers made little attempt to combat these conditions, and they turned their attention to the problem of reducing costs—costs of tariffs, of freight rates, of marketing, and of credit.

On the political side, the Progressive and Labour parties continued their efforts of earlier sessions to strengthen the parliamentary and electoral position of a third party. The amendments to the rules of procedure which they proposed* were again rejected by both Liberals and Conservatives, neither of whom wished to give the minor parties added institutional weight and recognition. The proposals to reform the electoral system fared a little better. A resolution was passed which approved the use of the alternative vote in single-member districts, but the proposal that proportional representation should be tried experimentally in one or more areas was voted down.† The two votes were not on party lines, and King favoured both reforms. His acceptance of the alternative vote is not surprising, for the system not only had genuine merit but was bound to work against the Conservatives, inasmuch as most Liberals and Progressives would give their second choice for the candidate of the other as representing the more friendly party. Liberals and Progressives would then have little to fear from three-cornered contests.

King's support of the more involved plan of proportional represen-

---

*They proposed: (1) that the Government should not resign on the defeat of a government measure except after the passage of an explicit vote of non-confidence; (2) that more than one amendment should be allowed to certain important motions. The first proposal would give the minor parties more freedom in expressing their opinions on specific issues and enable them to pick up support from the members of other parties; the second would allow them to take a clear-cut stand of their own as distinct from that of the official Opposition or the Government.

†In 1921 a committee of the House had endorsed the alternative vote, and had given a modified approval to proportional representation. In 1922 these proposals were debated, but were not voted on. The purpose of the alternative vote is to make it more probable that the successful candidate will secure over one-half of the total vote polled in his constituency. Proportional representation, which has many variations, tries to go much further. It creates a multiple member district, and endeavours to ensure that each minority of moderate size will be able to elect one or more representatives.

tation is incomprehensible on general grounds or on the terms of his own attempted explanation. There can be no serious doubt but that the system would have encouraged the formation and continuance of minor parties, which King abhorred in both theory and practice. It is possible that he may never have re-examined an early opinion formed under the influence of orthodox liberalism and the writings of John Stuart Mill, and fostered later by the ardent championship of Earl Grey. King had been for years a member of the Proportional Representation Society, which should have given him some clearer appreciation of the system, yet his speeches[17] indicate that his ideas on the subject were very hazy indeed. He seemed carried away by its superficial merit of giving an accurate temporary reflection of public opinion, but he failed to comprehend the splintering long-term effect it would have on two-party parliamentary government. In any event, he should have been warned by the enthusiastic support which proportional representation always evoked from the Progressive and Labour parties.

The star turn in the varied parliamentary performance of 1923 was the budget, although its significance lay not in its proposals but in its acceptance of the *status quo*. It left the tariff virtually untouched.* To do nothing on such a matter at this time was to the farmers convincing evidence of indifference, if not actual hostility, to their interests. This inaction, moreover, was made infinitely worse by Fielding's holding out little hope for future betterment. He intimated in his budget speech that the existing tariff was as fair and reasonable as circumstances would permit, and that if business men were to do their share in promoting the country's prosperity they must be able to rely on tariff stability. The wrath of the farmers at this incautious statement was not perceptibly assuaged by Fielding's accompanying proposal of a standing statutory offer of reciprocity with the United States in certain natural products. When the vote was taken, there were no waverers among the Progressives. Joined by two Liberals, McMaster and Hudson, they voted solidly for Forke's amendment, which in substance demanded an implementation of the Liberal and Progressive

*The chief tariff reductions were a 10 per cent discount off the British preferential duties on merchandise entering through Canadian ports, and reductions and increases on a few miscellaneous items. The general financial outlook was steadily improving; the deficit for the financial year was less than one-half that for the previous one; and a balanced budget was in sight.

441

platforms. The same members voted with the Conservatives against the main motion. On the latter vote the Government's majority fell to eight.

A policy of dead centre between protection in principle and tariff reduction in practice had brought the extremes together against the middle [writes W. L. Morton]. The Progressives for once had not allowed their fear of King James to overcome their dislike of King Charles. They had risked defeating the Liberal government. King had forfeited Progressive support by the standpatism of the Fielding budget, and would have to alter course westward if he were to avoid such narrow divisions in the future.[18]

Western Liberals as well as the Progressives were unanimous in deploring the Fielding budget, and they pointed out the fatal effect it would have on support for the Government in the West. The Speaker of the Saskatchewan Legislature sent the Prime Minister the following message on July 1:

Tell Mackenzie King from me that it is now all off in Saskatchewan. We proved we were ready to fight. He fell down, consequently he won't get a seat in Saskatchewan at all. Third parties are a d— nuisance, but, by heavens! we won't be trifled with. If we are going to have a high tariff, we will support Meighen at once and be done with it.[19]

Charles A. Dunning, the Liberal Premier of Saskatchewan, wrote King an equally frank letter later that month:

It would be folly for me to attempt to minimize the effect of Mr. Fielding's statement regarding stability contained in the Budget Speech. Lowering of the tariff has been the principal basis upon which Liberal organization has been built in Western Canada. The charge of the Progressives is that we have never been sincere in regard to the matter and now they point to the 1919 platform and to Mr. Fielding's statements regarding it on several occasions as proof of that insincerity. . . .
I am not one of those who believe that this country can get to a free-trade basis but I do believe that in order to remain a factor in Canada, and particularly in Western Canada with its growing electoral power, the Liberal party must demonstrate that it is sincerely a low-tariff party and give evidence of that by performance when in power.[20]

These were the natural responses of those far removed from the scene of action, and though the argument was indisputable, the reproaches were not wholly warranted. The chief reason for the Liberal party's timidity on tariff reform was the dominant position of the

442

protectionist element in the councils of the party. The budget was not representative of the prevailing balance of interests in the country. It represented much more closely the balance of interests within the Liberal party; but that party had not yet been restored to a genuinely national position, and it was still too heavily weighted towards that section of Canada which lay east of the Great Lakes. Mackenzie King was leading a mixed and ill-assorted team, and he was heavily handicapped by the absence from his Cabinet of those very people who now felt most aggrieved and whom he had tried to persuade to help him in December, 1921. The discussions in the Cabinet which had preceded the decisions on the tariff are most illuminating on this point.

The first of these discussions had been held on March 24 when a preliminary canvass of Cabinet opinion took place. It disclosed that more than half of those present were opposed to doing anything on the tariff in the current session. A suggestion that the British preference should be increased was at first supported by only five Ministers, Murdock, Lapointe, Motherwell, Stewart, and Copp. Murphy, Bureau, and probably Fielding, were absent. A number of others, including Gouin, Béland, Low, Robb, and J. H. King, were strongly protectionist. After some discussion Mackenzie King proposed a flat increase of 10 to 15 per cent* in the British preference on goods entering Canada through Canadian ports, and he enumerated the many advantages which would follow the adoption of the change. His views were accepted almost unanimously, and he concluded, rather prematurely as it proved, that this feature of the budget had been settled.[21]

In the weeks that followed, however, the protectionist Ministers showed that they were not satisfied, and they kept up a steady pressure against significant tariff reductions of any kind. Evidence was produced to support their contention. King himself had in his possession a letter from the late W. C. Kennedy, stating emphatically that western Ontario Liberals were opposed to any material change in the tariff in 1923.[22] Sir Lomer Gouin wrote on March 31 and stated bluntly that this "proposal to increase to 50% the preference in favour of British importations entering through Canadian ports is not advisable and is of a nature to cause a prejudice to some of our industries." Gouin also

---

*For example, if the existing preferential duty were 30 per cent, the proposal would have reduced it to 20 per cent, *not* 10 per cent of 30 per cent, i.e. 3 per cent. There seems to be no term which will serve to convey this idea without ambiguity.

reminded King that requests for greater protection for certain commodities had been received from the fishermen of Ontario, Quebec,
and the Maritime Provinces, from miners in British Columbia, from
Ontario farmers, and from silk, chemical, glass, and other manufacturers in the central provinces.[23] King replied with an assurance that
his proposal "did not go at all the length" that Gouin assumed;[24] but
he noted privately that the Minister evidently intended to make an
issue of the matter.[25]

Other Ministers, of course, came to the Prime Minister's assistance,[26]
and a number of Western Liberals, both in and out of the Cabinet,
suggested that immediate reductions in the tariff should be made.[27]
But King found that he could not rely on unflinching support from the
low-tariff Ministers, and such men as Motherwell and Stewart were
not prepared to make a determined stand for their beliefs. "I urged for
a discount of at least 20%" off existing preferential duties, he wrote
on April 4 when Fielding in Gouin's absence had tried to whittle
down King's proposal.

Mr. Stewart was not equal to backing up the suggestion with vigour,
Lapointe said practically nothing & Graham was silent. The others present
Dr. King, Robb were avowedly protectionist. D. D. McKenzie is regarded
as such but said little. It was difficult therefore to expect much. Murphy's
absence is unfortunate in this connection. I spoke out strongly against
increase of duties & need to introduce legis'n that wd. help people on the
land. It always comes back to where we receive our support.[28]

King returned to the attack two days later, but again he was able
to secure only a few supporters. He thus found himself out of tune
with most of his Cabinet, and unless he was prepared to assume an
extreme position and perhaps precipitate a crisis, he could do little
more. This was not, however, King's method of dealing with his
Cabinet nor was it his conception of the function of a Prime Minister;
and even if it had been, his position at this time was not strong enough
to justify his taking so grave a risk. The tariff came before the Liberal
caucus on April 12. Here again the general desire was clear: the party
wished to "stand pat."[29]

Emboldened by their success in blocking King's proposals, the protectionists in the third week of April took the offensive and pressed
for specified increases in the tariff. But King had now reached his
limit:

I spoke out strongly against considering any increases, unless Br. prefer-ence conceded. Sir Lomer fought against the latter, also Low, but I carried my point, tho' not for a large amount. Sir Lomer talked of resigning etc. Murdock was very outspoken about the big interests. I let the Cabinet see I was determined to head in the right direction—Some compromise will be necessary to keep the Cabinet a unit & that is most needed in govern-ment today.[30]

Five days later Fielding made an attempt to win support for a tax on food. King opposed this also very strongly and carried with him all his other colleagues except Gouin. By the end of April agreement was obtained: a "slight increase [in] Br. preference & no tax'n on food"; and King added in his diary: "I had to fight for that."[31]

While the Prime Minister appreciated the political necessity of making some concessions to the high-tariff element in his party,* he found his own ideas were undergoing change. He was beginning to appreciate more than ever before the great complexity of economic organization and the danger of trying to press any economic doctrine too far. In the midst of these Cabinet sessions he wrote his old friend, Rev. J. G. Inkster, about this change:

No one appreciates more keenly than I do the ills and evils of protection and the possible abuses of any banking system. I confess, however, that the more thought and study I give to these problems the less I find in the way of helpful constructive suggestion, despite all the criticism and denuncia-tion of conditions as they exist. The trouble with our whole economic order is that the minute one attempts to alter established institutions in some fundamental particular one discovers consequences wholly unfore-seen, and often more serious in their possible outcome than the evil it is being sought to remedy. Assume for a moment that we should lower our tariff walls against the United States just at this time when it is almost impossible even for our agriculturists to get admission of their products into the markets of the United States: what would the industrial and financial condition of Canada be in the course of a year?[32]

To give in any detail all the labours of the 1923 session is beyond the scope of this volume, but their political implications make some mention inescapable. The King Government's willingness to overlook the wishes of the farmers displayed when the tariff was considered was

*J. W. Dafoe wrote at this time of the "many groups and factions, with consider-able internal dissension" in the Liberal party, and that "King has his hands full." He found King "perceptibly older. He does not, I imagine, find his road very easy." Dafoe Papers, J. W. Dafoe to P. C. Larkin, April 20, 1923.

repeated at the time of the decennial revision of the Bank Act. The Progressives seized this opportunity to urge federal assistance in scaling down debts and obtaining easier credit. When the revision was referred to a Standing Committee, the Progressives brought forward theoretical monetary reformers (including Major C. H. Douglas, in person, the protagonist of "social credit") and members of the party advanced in both Committee and House a multitude of much more practical proposals. Virtually all their amendments were smothered indiscriminately by a combination of Liberals and Conservatives who took alarm at the novel ideas which had been put before the Banking Committee. Many of the Progressives, indeed, held views on these topics which were scarcely less orthodox than those of the other parties, with the result that the radical wing was left to fight the battle for monetary reform without receiving much aid from their more conservative colleagues—a circumstance which did nothing to promote mutual confidence between the two extremes within the party.

The Government tried to atone for its neglect on the tariff and credit policies by helping the farmer in other ways. It appointed a Royal Commission on the marketing of grain; it obtained a Select Committee of the House which, while studying agricultural conditions, also looked into the question of ocean freight rates; it continued to promote the consolidation of the national railways; it agreed to complete, when finances permitted, the Hudson Bay Railway; and it submitted, though the Senate turned its proposals down, a construction programme of branch railway lines. It had already (in 1922) appointed W. T. R. Preston to make an investigation of freight rates on the Great Lakes. Following Preston's report in January, 1923, it appointed a Royal Commission, with Preston as secretary, to pursue the same subject, and later, on the Commission's recommendation, endeavoured to strike at the Great Lakes shipping combine by setting up a mechanism for controlling rates by state action. The Government renewed its efforts to settle the natural resources question with the Prairie Provinces, and assisted them in an abortive effort to set up a wheat marketing organization. Finally, it put new life into Canada's immigration policy, although in view of the division among the Progressives on the subject it probably received but little credit for this endeavour.

The net benefits to the farmer, however, were not as impressive as this summary might suggest, for only a few of these efforts produced immediate and tangible results in legislation or administrative action. But the total was impressive enough to call forth protests from other parts of Canada which found themselves injured by these policies or, what was almost worse, forgotten or ignored. Thus although the prairies were fairly well satisfied with the partial restoration of the Crow's Nest rates in 1922, others were not. The action taken by Parliament had disturbed the precarious sectional equilibrium which Canadian Governments must always strive to achieve on this as on many other issues. British Columbia, although it too had received some concessions in 1922, asserted that it was still placed at a disadvantage,* and eventually in October, 1923, it secured a further reduction in rates. The Maritime Provinces also had their complaints about the freight rates, both because of the Government's solicitude for the West and because of its apparent indifference to the equally acute need of the East. They contended that all rates to and from the Maritime Provinces were too high, that the export grain rate should be reduced to help Eastern ports, and that they were being penalized because of the excessive mileage of the Intercolonial, which had been built with defence and not economy in mind. The Government did nothing to meet these complaints, though the railways made a few concessions. The sense of grievance was to find a very practical expression at the end of the year in the Halifax and Kent by-elections.

Other expressions of resentment at the preferential treatment meted out to the farmers could be heard. If the Hudson Bay Railway could evoke at this time little better from the prairies than a plea that it was an experiment worthy of a trial,† the Easterners could not be blamed for denouncing further expenditure on that romantic but extravagant project as simply throwing good money after bad. The Government's programme for the construction of branch lines was also received with varying degrees of asperity in the East, for 86 per cent of the new mileage was earmarked for Western Canada. Nor were signs wanting

---

*Chiefly through the "Mountain Differential," an extra freight charge which was imposed to defray the extra costs of construction and operation through the mountains. The high rail rate naturally affected the competitive position of Vancouver, and a reduction would divert to that port a larger proportion of goods (especially grain) moving out of the country.

†"Never will the western people be satisfied, until that railway has been completed and the question [of practicability] has been decided by actual experience. . . . The government should at least complete the railway to the bay and put us in a position to obtain more accurate information." Robert Forke, *Can. H. of C. Debates,* March 12, 1923, pp. 1048–9.

that the continual complaints of the Western farmers about their unhappy condition and their equally persistent demands for help were alienating Eastern sympathies. The Maritime Provinces, for example, were far from prosperous, and they found it difficult to restrain their impatience with statements which apparently assumed that hard times were a monopoly of the prairies. The policy of conciliating the Progressives was either being carried too far or not far enough: the Government's hold on the East was being loosened without there having been any commensurate gains in the West.

Another statute to the Government's credit which was incidentally to the benefit of the farmers was the Combines Investigation Act. This was the Prime Minister's bill in a very special sense, for it will be recalled that in 1910 he had as Minister of Labour sponsored another Act on the same subject. This had later been repealed, and its successor, owing to legal and constitutional difficulties, had become largely inoperative. The need for a statute to deal with combines was therefore apparent, and it had been felt by the Cabinet when casting about for some weapon with which to fight the freight rate combine on the Great Lakes. The primary purpose of the new Act was to provide "effective machinery of investigation which will disclose the existence of combines operating to the detriment of the public, and afford the information whereby proceedings under the Criminal Code can be made really effective."[33] The government would pay the cost of investigation, and the courts would impose the penalty after a normal prosecution had been undertaken.

King had no doubt that the public was being unfairly treated by a number of these combines, and he rather enjoyed meeting the delegations which appeared against his bill. With one such group, "a genuinely brute force gang," he lost his temper and "instead of saying nothing felt an innate repugnance at their looks which got me into an argument. It was a weakness & a mistake on my part—as all were friendly enough politically."[34] Although a few of the protectionist Liberals had criticized the bill, it passed with a large majority of 117. Everyone but the Conservatives supported it, and even one of them voted with the majority. "We forced the tories to take their medicine," King wrote happily in his diary, "put them in their true light before the country, and also gave a little wholesome discipline to one or two of our own members—Marler & Casgrain who at the instance of the big interests were unnecessarily critical of the measure & damned it by faint praise."[35]

The session also indicated that all was not well within the ranks of the Progressive party. The radical and reforming groups, as mentioned above, were not united on banking and monetary policy; and the Government's revivified immigration programme caused these two groups to enter into a public slogging match on the floor of the House which must have damaged both the party's reputation and its morale. But the most ominous action of the Progressives came late in the session when they divided three to one to prohibit the importation, manufacture, and sale of oleomargarine. This went much deeper than a split on the vote. The *laissez-faire* principles which they had with such conscious virtue advocated for the manufacturer vanished into thin air when the interests of the farmer were threatened. Several Progressives were very conscious of this inconsistency, and one of them, T. W. Bird, forecast the time (already reached, as he pointed out, in Great Britain and the United States) when the Canadian farmer, discouraged by the lack of support of free trade principles, would turn to the high protectionists for help for agricultural products.[36] The Progressives had, of course, been just as selfish as any other party in urging policies which would help the people they represented, but they had hitherto shown a commendable consistency in the application of their principles. This day was now over. When put to the test most of them had responded in the same way as the members of any other party: the decisive question was whose ox was gored, and they too had placed the immediate advantage ahead of their avowed beliefs. The Progressives might continue to be the sensitive and faithful representatives of agrarian and sectional interests, they could no longer assert that they were the uncompromising foes of privilege in all forms.

Mackenzie King could scarcely be blamed if at the end of the 1923 session he felt even more secure than at the beginning. He had survived all ordeals, and the signs of approaching disintegration in the Progressive party were unmistakable. Nevertheless he still hoped to induce a Progressive to enter the Cabinet. He had indirectly sounded out Crerar in March, and a few weeks later had offered Forke the portfolio of Immigration either for himself or for R. A. Hoey, another Manitoba Progressive. All of them refused. They still had little confidence in the Cabinet as it was constituted,* and a few months later they found their suspicions confirmed by a readjustment in portfolios and by the admission of E. M. Macdonald of Nova Scotia as a new member.† King was well aware that Macdonald's appointment would not be welcome in the West, but he apparently took him into the Cabinet as a conciliatory gesture to the Maritime Provinces. He was quickly reminded, however, that such moves were dangerous. In a characteristically tactful but candid letter Andrew Haydon wrote to him at the beginning of May:

> Circumstances are tending in the direction of putting you in a somewhat reactionary position. I know how much your own view is the other way. . . . The run of Cabinet changes is tending to give in the Country a further idea of reaction. The addition of E. M. McD[onald] brings in a capable man, but his bringing serves to divorce the West further than from where it is now.
>
> I have not had any talks with people; I have simply listened. . . . I am not saying anything against E. M. McD; on the contrary I think he is a real addition in the way of helping you, but I just want to add this that I personally feel . . . it is necessary for you to add someone to the Cabinet on the other side, who will counteract the impressions that are increasing daily in the way I have mentioned.[37]

Haydon strongly recommended that Hudson be appointed to meet this need, but King for some unknown reason did not follow the advice. After a long delay he filled the Manitoba vacancy by making E. J. McMurray Solicitor General. It was not a good appointment. McMurray's political ability was mediocre, he antagonized the Progressives, and he was one of an important Winnipeg group who persisted in keeping alive the old feud between the Laurier and Unionist Liberals in Manitoba.

Further warnings of trouble for the Liberals could be found in the election returns. The federal by-elections were not encouraging; though the Liberals held their seats, they made no gains, and the Progressive victory in one Western contest (Moose Jaw) was generally interpreted

---

*"[Crerar] thinks the government is falling more and more under the control of interests and influences which are hardly distinguishable from the interests and influences which could be expected to back and support a Tory government. He does not think the Government has any future." Dafoe Papers, J. W. Dafoe to Sir C. Sifton, March 12, 1923.

†W. C. Kennedy had died in January, and D. D. McKenzie was appointed to the Bench in April. This entailed a number of changes, and brought two new men into the Cabinet.

as a severe reverse for the Government. General elections in three provinces showed a more alarming trend. The Liberals were again returned in Quebec with a three to one majority, but this was more than offset by Conservative victories in Ontario and Prince Edward Island. Although the Ontario results* could be accounted for in many ways[38]—the general discredit into which the Farmer-Labour Government had fallen, the friction between the radical and moderate wings of the Farmer party, the struggles between Liberals and Farmers,† and so forth—the Conservative success had a significance which extended far beyond its immediate effect on provincial affairs. It made clear beyond all dispute that the Conservative party had passed its nadir and was once more a serious contender for federal power. Mackenzie King saw his favourite theme of the necessity for closer relations between Liberals and Progressives once more proved to the hilt. He wrote a private letter to J. F. Johnston, a Progressive member of Parliament, who had been from the beginning a strong advocate of a complete rapprochement with the Liberals:

I hope that one effect of the Ontario elections will be that both Liberals and Progressives will see not only the wisdom but the necessity of ending their differences and consolidating their ranks if the forces opposed to Toryism are not to be annihilated in Federal politics in a manner similar to that which has taken place in Ontario. Had Drury and Hay,‡ and their respective followings, gone to the country as a united party, they would be in power in Ontario today. . . . In the Federal arena, we have a chance to retain the ground that has been won from the Tories and to advance upon it, if our forces coalesce. I hope you will continue to emphasize this truth throughout the West in your own quiet and helpful way.[39]

Only nine months of 1923 had elapsed and the Imperial Conference was still to come, but King had already done a full year's work. The parliamentary session had not only run for five long months, it had been unusually difficult for the Government. The number and diversity of the issues, the unbalanced nature of the Cabinet's membership,

*The results were as follows (standing at dissolution is given in brackets): Conservatives (25) 77; United Farmers of Ontario (45) 17; Liberals (28) 14; Labour (9) 3; Independent and vacant (4).

†The federal Ministers felt compelled to hold aloof from the election lest they injure their friendship with the Progressives and "work an injury in a direction where healing is most needed." W.L.M.K. to W. Hay, July 9, 1923.

‡Wellington Hay was the Liberal leader in Ontario. One wag remarked that the trouble with Wellington Hay as a party leader was that he had not enough Wellington and too much Hay.

the necessity of maintaining agreement between radical and conservative Liberals, and the constant effort to conciliate the Progressives had all discouraged any attempt to do more than fall back on *ad hoc* solutions for most questions. All these demanded the Prime Minister's constant attention and made the most exacting demands on his adaptability, resourcefulness, and stamina. He had also many responsibilities as Secretary of State for External Affairs. Moreover, King was still very conscious of his lack of familiarity with many public questions. "I have been so little in Parliament," he wrote, "that most of the questions which come up for discussion there are entirely new to me. I have to master them in a rough and ready sort of way, and do the best I can to conceal my ignorance in debate."[40] He was experiencing the politician's never-failing problem, rendered more acute by long absence from political life: and the extra burden thus imposed curtailed still further his opportunities for study. He was himself largely to blame for his overcrowded calendar. Although he unhesitatingly delegated large and important questions to his colleagues, he was apt to take on too much for his own immediate attention, and he was not willing or able in this narrow sphere to organize his own work so as to turn the work of others to the best advantage. One friend, Violet Markham, who was no stranger to administrative work, did not hesitate to remonstrate in frank and refreshing terms:

If you hadn't been coming to England I should have taken ship to Canada! For it's clear that somebody ought to descend with a *very strong hand* on the Prime Minister & organise his work! I was really *aghast* when I read the account of all the various burthens & offices under which you are struggling. . . . No human being could carry such a load successfully; & even if it means appointing clerks to fill some of the posts better that, than that you should crack under an effort too great for human strength & endurance.

It seems to me really imperative that you should disentangle yourself at all costs & without delay. Delegation is the secret of all successful work. As Head of the Government it is essential that you should have some mental elbow room so that you can have a relative measure of peace in which to survey the scene. . . .

I have heard very little of you through friends but what has reached me is always an impression of your being terribly overworked & overdriven. This impression your letter has more than confirmed.[41]

To these purely Canadian labours were added those relating to Imperial affairs in which King was taking an increasing interest.

Chanak had been followed by Lausanne, Lausanne by the Halibut Fisheries, and he was now about to face what was the most trying ordeal of his political career up to that time, the Imperial Conference. As the representative of the senior Dominion, he would necessarily occupy a prominent position at that gathering, but his responsibility was much increased by the reputation he had recently gained as one who was seeking to bring about profound changes in the Imperial relationship. His part at the Conference was therefore bound to be arduous: it might well in the event prove to be decisive.

The Imperial Conference began to make demands on King some months before the meeting took place. One of his preparations was his attempt to ensure that the proceedings of the Conference would be fairly—and even perhaps favourably—reported in Canada. He believed that without someone to present the other side, Canadian public opinion would be at the mercy of "inspired despatches from Tory imperialist sources which are pretty certain to follow from the exclusive representation in London of Canadian Conservative journals. . . . Without the Liberal point of view being adequately presented we will be wholly at the mercy of our enemies."[42] * King accordingly wrote to several newspaper publishers who were not unsympathetic to the Liberals to suggest that special correspondents should be sent to England to cover the Conference. The chief result was that Sir Clifford Sifton selected J. W. Dafoe of the *Manitoba Free Press* to make the trip. Dafoe was at this time no great admirer of King and in a letter to Sifton he made it quite clear that he would go neither as an assistant to nor as a defender of the Prime Minister, although as it turned out his contact with the Conference was extremely close and he did in effect become an additional consultant in the delegation. He wrote Sir Clifford:

I must say that I have very little confidence in King. I am afraid his conceit in his ability to take care of himself is equalled only by his ignorance and I should not be surprised if he should find himself trapped.

I have no intention of becoming an unofficial member of a board of strategy to assist him while the Conference is on. . . .

There will be a concerted, carefully worked out, insidiously advocated and plausible plan to keep the question of status in suspension while committing us to policies as to foreign affairs which will hopelessly prejudice

---

*King was probably right. Part of the British press gave him on his arrival a somewhat hostile reception, and certain despatches to Canada were plainly prejudiced against him. See *The Scotsman*, Sept. 25, 26, 1923; *Daily News*, Sept. 25, 1923.

our claim to equality of status. Every attempt to bring up this question will be blocked or side-tracked by one ingenious excuse or another. King will certainly need all the help he can get if he is to be saved from the pitfalls which will be carefully and specially dug for him.[43]

King had already taken steps to guard against some of these pitfalls by engaging as his chief expert assistant one of the ablest men in Canada for the purpose, Professor O. D. Skelton of Queen's University.* Skelton spent two months before the Conference supervising the preparation of briefs and memoranda on foreign policy, defence, naturalization, and other kindred topics, and he later went with King to London as chief of his advisory staff.

It was fitting that these two, Skelton and Dafoe, should be at King's right hand in his first appearance at an Imperial Conference. King's nationalist ideas had been for some time strengthened and refined through contact with Skelton and with Dafoe's *alter ego*, Sir Clifford Sifton. In April, 1922, King had listened with great pleasure to a "splendid address" by Sifton on Canada's status, and the two men also discussed the same subject privately and found themselves in substantial agreement.[44] Three months earlier King had heard a lecture by Skelton which had left an even stronger impression:

An excellent address—pointing out that foreign policy was an extension of domestic policy & that as we had gained control of the one so we must gain control of the other as to matters affecting ourselves, & by conference & discussion co-operate with other parts of the league of Britannic Nations on the things we have in common. Skelton's address would make an excellent foundation for Canadian policy on External Affairs, and Skelton himself would make an excellent man for that department. At the luncheon I told him that he might be wanted there some day. . . . He certainly has the knowledge & the right point of view.[45]

*The staff of the Department of External Affairs had at this time a normal complement of only three administrative officers, and one of these had resigned. Mr. Meighen had left behind him an exceptionally able legal adviser, Loring C. Christie, who had served also under Sir Robert Borden. Christie's very close personal association with the two Conservative Prime Ministers and his part in helping to develop the Conservative Empire policy of greater Dominion autonomy combined with a system of representation at the centre, made him *persona non grata* to Mackenzie King. King believed he could not rely on Christie to give whole-hearted support to the Liberal policy, which ran directly contrary to that with which Christie had been identified. Christie was accordingly given little responsibility in the Department, and he resigned early in 1923. Shortly after this, however, Christie changed his views on Canada's Imperial and foreign relations and became a strong nationalist. He came back to the Department under the Bennett administration, and in 1939 King appointed him Canadian Minister to Washington.

These men, holding essentially the same views on Imperial and foreign relations, were now to come together at the Conference, and they would continue to agree on most of these questions in the future. Dafoe and Sifton differed from King on domestic matters, but this would not prevent their giving full support to his plans for extending Canadian autonomy in external affairs. Skelton became even more closely identified with King's policies. In a year's time he accepted the post of Counsellor in the Department of External Affairs, and in 1925 he became the deputy minister or Under-Secretary of State in the Department.

The Canadian ministerial delegation to the Conference consisted of the Prime Minister, Sir Lomer Gouin, and George P. Graham, each being attended by his own personal staff. The expert advisers consisted of Skelton and a number of officers and civil servants of high rank,* many of these being necessary because of a second group of meetings, the Imperial Economic Conference, at which matters relating to their specialized fields would be discussed. King did not accept the suggestion that he should take a Progressive with him to London, but he nevertheless made an arrangement with Forke that he would give advice if King should cable for it during the Conference. King was evidently determined to make himself the undisputed visible champion of Canadian nationalism.

A common Canadian attitude towards the Conference was one of uneasiness and even suspicion: the British Government was still reaping the harvest from Chanak. Dafoe's opinion of British wiles (already noted) was by no means exceptional, and a debate in the House revealed that a number of members were afraid that King might make incautious commitments which might limit the freedom of the Canadian Parliament.[46] "Goldwin Smith used to say," wrote W. D. Gregory to King in this vein, "that whenever Laurier got up to speak at an Imperial Conference he felt a French Canadian tugging at his coattails. You will, I expect, feel some 'tugs' at yours, but they will not be confined to the French Canadians."[47] Underlying much of this uneasiness was also the feeling expressed by Dafoe that the youth and inexperience of the Prime Minister made him exceptionally vulner-

*The chief of these were R. H. Coats, A. G. Doughty, J. H. Grisdale, Duncan Marshall, Charles Camsell, Graham Bell, Major-General J. H. MacBrian, and Commodore Walter Hose.

able to the influences, both direct and insidious, which might be brought to bear upon him. "He is a young Prime Minister," said a veteran Conservative member in the House, "and Shakespeare says something about the temptation of 'silken dalliance.' There is a silken dalliance in the drawing rooms of the duchesses of London, and a Prime Minister may come within, I will not say that temptation, but that presentation."[48] But one of King's past private secretaries writing to another of his private secretaries knew his chief much better. After enumerating the hidden schemes to entrap the Prime Minister, he concluded:

Extraordinary pressure will be brought upon him and from unsuspected directions too. Personally I rely upon his persistence and courage. Few of our friends know him as I do, and much concern is expressed as to the outcome of his trip. Passive resistance—*vis inertiae*—is the only arm necessary to ward off danger—as stubborn and relentless as the opposing forces. Opinion here [Montreal] is openly favorable to such action and no apprehension need be felt in this respect. Beware lest your knight be unhorsed; let him get a stranglehold on his principles, and never let go.[49]

King arrived in London on September 29. He was now almost forty-nine years of age, though his photographs suggest that he could easily have been taken to be five years younger. He carried himself well, though perhaps with too little assurance and too much self-consciousness. His face was full and unlined, his eyes unusually level and direct, and both eyes and mouth appeared ready to break with little provocation into a broad friendly smile. His frequent horseback riding had not prevented his putting on weight, but the chief sign of age was an increasing baldness, which was ill concealed even at this early stage by long locks brushed over towards the right side. His clothes were conservative in cut and material, and showed a tendency to fussiness with white piqué along the top edge of his waistcoat and the corner of a handkerchief peeping from his breast pocket. A part of his first week in London was devoted to the selection of a number of suits, a new silk hat, and several pairs of shoes, and, thus fortified, King was prepared to face whatever might lie ahead.*

The social fringe which surrounded the work of the Conference

---

*Several years before King had written: "Was disappointed in photos taken yesterday. . . . I have nothing in the way of looks, but I like to look at least intelligent, have a loathing for a face that looks flabby or heavy, fear mine is more so than it should be." Diary, March 9, 1920.

was in itself intimidating. King found some fifty invitations already awaiting him at his London hotel—demonstrations of British hospitality, whose sincerity was unquestioned, though tinged with the knowledge that overseas guests would to some degree yield to its subtle influence. "Sir John Macdonald arrived here," wrote Disraeli cynically in 1879, "too late for us to pay him those social attentions, which it was highly desirable he should experience."[50] King had originally decided to attend only the most important of these functions and to confine his attention chiefly to official business, but this austere resolve soon weakened. The reason for the change may have been the undoubted pleasure which he derived from these engagements or he may have wished to prove that even a Canadian politician could enter the silken drawing rooms of the much publicized duchesses, submit to the lionizing treatment with enjoyment, and yet emerge unscathed from the ordeal. The second week of his stay, October 8 to 15, will illustrate the encroachments which these unofficial and semi-official functions made on his time. In these seven days King's round of activities included luncheons or dinners at Buckingham Palace, at Lancaster House as a guest of the British Government, at Lord and Lady Astor's, at *The Times* office, and at the Savoy to meet the British Industrial Advisory Committee. On October 9 he had a long audience with the King. Two days later he was sworn as a member of the British Privy Council. He was given the freedom of the City of London at the Guildhall and this was followed by a luncheon at the Mansion House. He attended several receptions and called on a number of old friends. Somehow he was also able to dispose of his correspondence, to hold discussions with the members and staff of the Canadian delegation, and to prepare his own work. All this was done while two full days were being devoted to the Imperial Conference itself, and at one of these meetings King delivered what was probably his most important speech, that on foreign affairs. He was the week-end guest (with twenty others) of the Duke and Duchess of Devonshire at Chatsworth. On Monday, the 15th, he returned to London and the whirl began again: luncheon with the Austen Chamberlains, dinner at the Admiralty, with a Conference meeting in the afternoon. At a number of these semi-official functions King was expected to speak, and at some length, and his careful and time-consuming preparation is attested by the two and sometimes three drafts which are to be found in his papers. Rarely did he get to bed before one or one-thirty in the morning. It was a punishing grind, and only a strong constitution could have borne it. King resolved not to attempt it again.

Were I attending another Conference, I should refrain wholly from accepting any luncheon engagements and would make it a point to retire early in the evening. The irregularity of meals, lack of exercise and numerous engagements have made extremely difficult the thought and care which should have been given to the Conference itself. It has all been a matter of careful balancing of advantages in different directions, and on the whole, for purposes of this Conference, it was perhaps as well to take advantage of opportunities of meeting people and learning something of England and English life in many of its most interesting aspects.*

The Imperial Conference of 1923 was bound to be controversial, for it could not escape making at least a limited choice between the two alternatives which lay before it. Should the ties of Empire be drawn closer by formal devices in which the Dominions should participate as partners, or should they be loosened by increasing Dominion autonomy leaving Empire unity to be attained by voluntary co-operation on a more informal basis? The invitation to attend the Conference referred to the meeting as similar to that of 1921, and the agenda included a review of foreign policy, the consideration of future foreign policy, and a discussion of Empire defence.

Lord Curzon, the Foreign Secretary, in a speech in the summer of 1923 alluded to "a common policy in international matters so that the Foreign Minister of this country, when he speaks, may speak, not for Great Britain alone, but for the whole British Empire. . . . Think of the addition to his power and his strength that will result if, in speaking, he knows—and the world knows—that there lie behind him the sentiments and the might of the British Empire as a whole."[51] This was a fair statement of what many members of the British Government considered to be the primary purpose of the Conference. The chaotic conditions in Europe demanded firm leadership, backed by a show of strength, and the war had proved that the support of the Dominions could constitute an important element in any international marshalling of forces. The expedient of invoking younger nations to help redress the balance in Europe was to be tried once more, and the Conference was to provide the consolidating process which would

---

*Diary, Nov. 8, 1923. Six days later he added: "No words can describe the relief at being through with speech making for a time." Ibid., Nov. 14, 1923.

458

make the Empire's influence effective. Any Unionist Government in Britain would endorse this effort to strengthen Empire ties as commendable *per se*; but the existing state of Europe added necessity and urgency to any move towards centralization.

With this idea Canada had little sympathy. The people had no stomach for war, and felt they had no interest or responsibility in any of the manoeuvres of power politics. Significantly, perhaps, Canada had made a clean sweep of her war Government, while the Government of Great Britain still contained many members who had been active in the struggle and who tended to look on current problems as part of the war's inevitable aftermath. In Canada the war-time consciousness of Empire solidarity had diminished in force while the nationalism, also engendered by the war, had continued to flourish. The fear of becoming involved in further hostilities had become very real and politically significant, and the isolationism which had become so rampant in the United States was reflected to some degree across the border.

The Chanak crisis had supplied an unequivocal illustration of what could happen if the Dominions allowed themselves to be committed to an Empire foreign policy, and it had left a legacy of doubt and suspicion of Britain's motives in her relations with the Dominions. Mackenzie King's beliefs, his record since he became Prime Minister, and the knowledge that he represented at least an important element in Canadian opinion, marked him out as a leading antagonist to the policy of centralization. He was quite willing to accept the part. He wrote to Sir Clifford Sifton in August, 1923:

It is becoming increasingly apparent that at the forthcoming Conference . . . many questions involving far-reaching considerations with respect to foreign policy will be raised. . . . When to [other difficulties] is added the very apparent intention of those participating in the Conference to make it the occasion of fresh efforts at centralization in all matters of imperial concern, it seems to me that, unless our position is made very clear to both the British and Canadian public, consequences may be more far-reaching and serious than many at present imagine.[52]

King had no illusions, however, that his task would be light, and he was by no means confident that he was sufficiently equipped to do it well. "I am far from prepared to meet the different subjects that are likely to come up for discussion," he wrote P. C. Larkin in London, "and I shall probably require before every meeting, and certainly before every public function, to work to the last minute to have in readiness what I may wish to say."[53] He might well have developed misgivings on other grounds also: many members of the Conference were both distinguished and formidable, with an experience of Empire and world affairs far transcending his own.

The British Prime Minister, Stanley Baldwin, did little at the Conference save to act as the gracious host. The records suggest that he intervened decisively in the proceedings only when a motion to adjourn was being entertained, and then usually in its favour. He willingly left to his colleagues all the duties which involved preparation, knowledge, or even interest in Imperial and foreign affairs. "Nothing," wrote Lord Curzon, "can exceed the cheerfulness, good temper and courtesy of Baldwin, except his impotence. At the Imperial Conference he never opens his mouth and leaves the entire lead to me."[54]

Lord Curzon was undoubtedly the ablest man at the meeting, for he had no equal in international diplomacy at that time. His talents were many. He had an agile, brilliant, well-stored, and perceptive mind, and a genius for mastering a subject down to the most minute detail. His presentation of an argument was exhaustive and penetrating, and it gained much by the wit and pungent style with which he stated his case. Curzon's self-confidence and dominating character frequently led him to ride roughshod over all who disagreed with him and he would on occasion assume so cold and majestic a demeanour that opponents literally quailed before it.* His high sense of duty and almost fanatical belief in the British Empire as a world influence for good naturally made him the leader and chief advocate for the centralizing element at the Conference.

L. S. Amery, the First Lord of the Admiralty, probably came next to Curzon in effectiveness. Amery had been associated with Lord Milner in South Africa, and his ideas on the Empire had advanced through the Round Table federation stage to a belief in a future Commonwealth based in large measure on decentralization. He was an excellent product of Tory democracy: intelligent, aggressive, tole-

---

*Thus on one occasion Admiral Sir Roger Keyes, who had a well-earned reputation for exceptional bravery, became speechless and "lost the thread of his discourse" when Curzon looked at him with disapproval. H. Nicolson, *Curzon, the Last Phase, 1919–1925* (Boston and New York, 1934), pp. 320-1.

rant, and enterprising. Sir Philip Lloyd-Greame,* the President of the Board of Trade, was one of the promising younger men in the Unionist party, with most of his political career still before him. His weapons were personal charm combined with a fairly well developed talent for driving a shrewd bargain. He was supported and to some degree overshadowed at the 1923 Economic Conference by Neville Chamberlain, the Chancellor of the Exchequer. Chamberlain had not yet become a prominent figure, though he was fully conscious of his obligation to live up to the family reputation. "His father's name was always in mind, and constantly on his lips,"[55] and this obsession committed him by heredity as well as conviction to a policy of reciprocal tariff agreements within the Empire.

The delegates from the Dominions and India varied greatly in ability and importance. Those from the Irish Free State were John MacNeill and Desmond Fitzgerald, with W. T. Cosgrave and Kevin O'Higgins (the President and Vice-President of the Executive Council) hovering in the background. Historically the centre of dissent should have been Ireland, now making its appearance at an Imperial Conference for the first time, but on this occasion the Free State played a minor part. The unaccustomed environment, the recent hostilities against the British, and the trace of distrust that still remained,† made the Irish delegates ill at ease and diffident in pushing themselves forward. They preferred to have Mackenzie King take the initiative, and give their strong but not too emphatic support to his views with which they were usually in sympathy.

The Indian delegates, owing to India's peculiar status and the range of topics discussed, occupied a minor position throughout the proceedings, and the smallness and relative unimportance of Newfoundland kept its Premier, W. R. Warren, in the background. W. F. Massey, the Prime Minister of New Zealand, was very vocal and in all Empire matters more loyal than the King. But the general similarity of his approach and that of the Prime Minister of Australia combined with

---

*Not the least of his claims to fame were the mutations in his name. Born Lloyd-Greame, he later became Cunliffe-Lister, Viscount Swinton, and eventually Earl Swinton.

†Thus very confidential matters were discussed not at the Conference but at a meeting of "Prime Ministers," a device to exclude the Irish Free State and India, neither of whom had a Prime Minister. See also L. S. Amery, *My Political Life*, II, *War and Peace 1914–1929* (London, 1953), p. 274; Sir Harold Nicolson, *King George the Fifth* (London, 1952), p. 480.

his lesser ability and importance made him on most questions little more than Bruce's satellite.

General Jan Smuts of South Africa was by far the most notable of all the Empire visitors. His distinguished military bearing marked him out from his fellow members and served to some degree to conceal his warm sympathy, friendliness, and personal charm. His career had repeatedly showed that he possessed also magnanimity and an unusual breadth of view, notably in his efforts to bring about a genuine reconciliation between British and Dutch in South Africa, in the leading part he took in creating the League of Nations, and in his passionate espousal of the things for which the League stood. He had been a member of both the Imperial and the British War Cabinets, he had participated in the Imperial Conferences of 1917, 1918, and 1921, and he had represented South Africa at the Peace Conference. His mind and outlook had marched with this experience. He was now endowed with a perspective on human affairs more spacious and illuminating than that of any other Dominion Prime Minister. Thus in 1919 when Mackenzie King was contending with Fielding, McKenzie, and Graham for the leadership of the Liberal party Smuts was struggling at Paris with Lloyd George, Woodrow Wilson, Balfour, and Clemenceau to secure the peace of the world.

Although Smuts was compelled by circumstances to walk the slippery road of South African politics, he did not hesitate to support the British Government in what he conceived to be the over-riding responsibility of bringing peace and contentment to Europe. He thus gave his support in general to British policies, though he was by no means unsympathetic to King's demand for greater decentralization. On some occasions the latter sympathies would become paramount, for Smuts could never ignore the danger that his stand might be misinterpreted and used to his detriment in South Africa. Smuts thus had a foot in both camps, and he became the obvious intermediary between the centralizing demands of the United Kingdom and Australia and the blocking nationalist tactics of Canada.

It was Stanley Bruce, the Prime Minister of Australia, who furnished the natural foil for the personality and opinions of Mackenzie King. Bruce was only thirty-nine, tall, slender, and strikingly handsome. He had not only been educated in Great Britain, he possessed the ineluctable and weighty advantage of having been a Cambridge rowing blue. He had already proclaimed his faith in a united Empire, Imperial preference, and a common policy of Empire defence—all easily understood when examined in the light of Australia's isolation and the potential threat of Japan. The British Government rightly regarded him as its strongest and most reliable ally in its effort to bring about closer Empire relations.

Mackenzie King was bound to suffer by contrast on a number of counts. He lacked Bruce's good looks, and he had no quick way to British hearts through any record of athletic prowess. Nor was he very well known in Britain, and the few events which had brought him to the attention of the British Government and the British public were not apt to increase their regard for him. Unlike Bruce he seemed unmoved by Curzon's glowing conception of Empire unity and the effects it might have on British influence throughout the world. On a number of Imperial questions which had arisen since he became Prime Minister his attitude had been controversial and unco-operative, and he had been the author of cold and even censorious despatches. The British Government was inclined to regard him with reserve, not unmixed with an element of distrust. The play which was about to begin might indeed prove to have no villain; but if one should appear, there was no doubt in British minds who was the most likely one to carry the part.

It had been assumed by a number of Canadian nationalists (of whom Dafoe was one) that the British Government would wage a war of minor engagements on detailed proposals rather than risk a major battle on the question of the status of the Dominions, and Dafoe wanted to secure a general declaration on the main issue. The assumption proved to be correct, but King declined, as he had in his own Parliament, to put forward a general declaration as a counter-offensive. He preferred instead to fight the British Government on the ground it had chosen, and to uphold, resolutely and unequivocally, the nationalist view on every issue that arose for decision. These tactics demanded ceaseless vigilance and a refusal to commit himself or his Government to any statement which might imply acquiescence by Canada without first securing the approval of Parliament. It was a most unsatisfactory and exasperating answer to the plans of the British Government, but it was effective, and it doubtless accomplished more and caused less friction than a forced vote on status.

463

When King arrived in London he lost no time in placing his cards on the table. In his second and third days there he held private talks with Stanley Baldwin, L. S. Amery, Lord Peel, Sir Philip Lloyd-Greame, and the Marquess of Salisbury. The chief purpose of these conversations, which were held on British initiative, was obviously to sound King out and find what his stand was likely to be on such questions as defence, Imperial preference, and foreign policy. King did not hesitate to state his opinion and to point out politely but firmly why certain views would not be acceptable to Canada.[56] He also took especial care when the Conference was in session not only to state his own case, but to correct any wrong or misleading statements lest his silence be misconstrued and later used against him. Thus on no less than three occasions he intervened to make clear Canada's position in regard to Lausanne. Again, when Lord Curzon at an early meeting referred to the Conference as a Cabinet, King at once objected to the possible implications of the word. He admitted that so far as procedure and a few minor matters were concerned the meetings were not unlike those of a Cabinet, but he insisted that the term was quite unsuitable in all vital particulars. The gathering had neither the powers nor the significance of a Cabinet: it was a Conference of Governments, and the members represented no one but their own Governments and were responsible to their own Parliaments. King maintained this attitude throughout the proceedings. He was willing to meet, to discuss, to exchange points of view, to consider possible courses of action, but he would not enter into commitments without the consent of his Cabinet and Parliament. In short, King insisted that the old conception of the Imperial Conferences as purely consultative bodies be reaffirmed, and that the idea of an Imperial Cabinet, which had crept in during the war and was continued in 1921, should be abandoned as inconsistent with the full autonomy of the Dominions.

After the preliminaries of the Conference had been concluded, the British Government brought forward what it considered to be the subject of greatest importance, foreign relations. The situation was reviewed by Lord Curzon in a long speech which King described as "the finest intellectual treat I have ever witnessed." At the next meeting (on October 8) King, as the Prime Minister of the senior Dominion, delivered his statement. He dwelt for some time on Canada's special interest in all relations with the United States, and pointed out how in many instances, such as the Halibut Fisheries Treaty and the Rush-Bagot Agreement,* the problems were of no concern whatever to any other part of the Empire. Having touched on Canadian relations with several other countries, he turned to Lord Curzon's opening remark that the Conference was to assist in carrying on "the foreign policy which is not that of these islands alone, but that of the Empire." Such an understanding, King said, had never been sanctioned by the Canadian Parliament. His Government was emphatically against the Lloyd George–Curzon conception of Empire and the possibility of another Chanak affair. He pointed out that "given widely scattered communities within the British Empire growing steadily in numbers, in intercourse with the world, and in the habit of self-government . . . it is inevitable that each of these communities should seek to control those foreign affairs which concern it primarily." Each had its own sphere, though "at certain points the arcs cut, the interests become common." It was with these issues of fundamental concern to all parts of the Empire that the Imperial Conference should deal. "The Governments of the Empire must confer; the Parliaments of the Empire, if need be, must decide." The Conference would not act in any executive capacity, but simply as a means of exchanging points of view and information. He did not wish to promise the Imperial Conference that Canada would do certain things, and then find on his return home that he could not make his promises good.

Canada is not putting forward any new principles. . . . Canada stands on the old principle of responsible democracy. . . . For seventy years our most honoured leaders have done what they could to develop the basic principle of responsible government, and to apply it in steadily increasing measure to the whole range of domestic and foreign affairs. . . . Canada desires no special privilege. We believe that the decision of Great Britain on any important public issue, domestic or foreign, should be made by the people of Britain, their representatives in Parliament, and the Government responsible to that Parliament. So the decision of Canada on any important issue, domestic or foreign, we believe should be made by the people of Canada, their representatives in Parliament, and the Government responsible to that Parliament.[57]

King was followed by Stanley Bruce who, as was expected, opposed

*An agreement made between Great Britain and the United States in 1817 severely limiting the naval vessels to be maintained on the Great Lakes. Negotiations looking towards the revision of the agreement had been initiated by Mackenzie King in 1922, but they were eventually abandoned.

the idea that each part of the Empire should strike out on a foreign policy of its own, and who added that in the event of war no enemy power would respect the neutrality of a Dominion for a moment. Imperial unity in all aspects of foreign affairs might not be possible or necessary, but "on important questions and on the broadest lines" a united policy was essential. Other Dominion Ministers spoke. Massey supported Bruce; the Irish Free State, King; Smuts displayed more of a European outlook than the others, and neither accepted nor rejected King's position.

The two opposing conceptions of Empire relations were thus laid before the Conference. The next few weeks were to disclose a gradual repudiation of Bruce's conception and the acceptance, albeit reluctantly, of the principles enunciated by King as the only realistic foundation upon which permanent future relations could be constructed. The doctrine of centralized control was to appear in several guises, but each was essentially little more than an example of the main proposition.

Imperial defence, which from the point of view of the Dominions meant primarily naval defence, was perhaps the most obvious of these examples of the doctrine of centralization. Each of the three British services made a special plea to the Conference for support. To all appearances their plans had met the basic demand of the Dominions that the defence forces should be decentralized; but King thought—and closer examination disclosed that there was much to substantiate his belief—that what had been kept out of the front door had sometimes gained an inconspicuous entrance through the rear. Thus though the Admiralty memorandum came out flatly for separate Dominion navies (a reversal of its plans of 1921), these navies were to be designed in large measure to fit into a scheme of Empire defence: in organization, training, type of ship, design, and so forth. "The Admiralty," wrote Skelton, "is to be a central controlling authority, outlining policy and fitting the various local units into a mosaic."[58] King chose to pass over this side of the proposals without comment, and emphasized the basic factors in the situation. He could not resist expressing his gratification at the belated conversion of the Admiralty to the Dominions' idea of local navies which Canada had long advocated. Co-operation rather than centralization, the national note rather than the Imperial note, he said, must be the policy of the future, for each part was bound to take its own situation into account in determining its policy. Those who opposed centralization were no less the friends of a permanent Imperial relationship than those who in high sounding phrases demanded that the bonds of Empire be drawn more tightly. King took strong exception to a suggestion of the Admiralty that it might publish throughout the Empire a memorandum on the subject of defence and thus, in effect, appeal over the head of the Dominion Governments to their people. This, King asserted, could not be allowed: it would be as objectionable as a memorandum from the War Office on the Canadian militia or one from the Treasury on Canadian fiscal policy.

A week later in a private talk Amery tried to induce King to begin at once on a modest naval programme. King replied that he could not do so, nor could he commit the Government to any naval or military expenditure, especially in view of the hostility in Canada against any increased demands for defence. He said he was willing to present the need for Canada's doing more towards her own defence, but the present was certainly not the time to raise the question.[59]

King's suspicions were also evident when the War Office proposals of co-operation were being discussed. He was sure that Canada would approve of similar training methods and general standards so that in the event of an emergency common action could be speedy and effective, and he assured the War Office that Canadian officers would be glad to confer with British officers and receive suggestions. But he wished to make very clear that this policy did not mean that specified Canadian forces would be available at a given moment for war. Any participation in war must be decided by the Canadian Parliament. The Secretary for Air also made a submission to the Conference. His proposals, however, were so innocuous and showed so careful a regard for Dominion autonomy that even King could find little fault with them, though he suggested, and the Conference accepted, some minor changes.

When the time came for King to give his formal review of defence policies, he felt it necessary to be more outspoken. Briefly his position was this: that while Canada was not opposed to all co-operative defence measures in themselves, and would perhaps be willing to take an active part in a war, she was signing no blank cheques for any situation which might arise in the future.

Lord Derby . . . rather tried to force my hand in the matter of how far the Dominions might be expected to go with respect to the Empire being attacked at any point. I felt obliged to interrupt him and to point out that Canada's co-operation could not be taken for granted. I stated that had war arisen last year against the Turks it is extremely doubtful if Canada would have supplied any troops.

It was an unpleasant and somewhat trying experience. . . . However, it constitutes to my mind the most important of all the statements made at the present Conference. It can leave no doubt or give rise to no false security as regards Canada's position, and may prove a steadying factor in international relations.[60]

Over a week later Bruce came to King with a draft resolution on defence for which he and apparently Amery were responsible. It purported to have been written to meet King's objections, and to some degree it did so, but it also implied Canadian approval of the Singapore naval base scheme, the defence of the Suez Canal, and other projects in which Canada had virtually no interest. King refused to accept it. Canada, he asserted, would not be bound by any defence policies laid down by an Imperial Council: "to attempt to commit us by resolution in any way was simply to make impossible any subsequent approval by parliament of anything the Conference had done in this direction."[61] King then suggested a number of revisions which rendered the resolution innocuous and these were later accepted.

Several other matters of interest to Canada came before the Conference and its sub-committees. One of them, the procedure to be used in the negotiation, signature, and ratification of treaties, has already been discussed.[62] Another one related to the publication of intergovernmental correspondence, a problem which for over a year had been causing King a great deal of trouble by preventing him from giving Parliament a full explanation of his position in several controversial issues with the British Government.* This difficulty was eventually settled quite in accordance with King's wishes by the concession that the Dominions should have the same right to decide questions of publication as the United Kingdom. Yet another topic involved the

---

*The question of publication was somewhat complicated owing to the different degrees of secrecy attaching to despatches. The most preposterous of the claims put forward by the Governor-General's secretariat at Ottawa was that even "public" (i.e., not secret, etc.) despatches sent by the Canadian Government to the Colonial Office could not be tabled in the Canadian Parliament until released by the Governor-General, on the ground that they were not sent direct but through the Governor-General, and hence were *his* despatches to the Colonial Office. At the Imperial Conference this contention was described as "mediaeval" by one of the British Ministers.

status of the Dominion High Commissioners in London. King's effort to have their status approximate that of the members of the diplomatic corps received little support from other Dominions, and he agreed not to press his proposal.

The bulk of the Canadian load at the Imperial Economic Conference (the meetings of which usually alternated with those of the Imperial Conference) was carried by Sir Lomer Gouin and George P. Graham, though Mackenzie King attended a number of sessions. The major issue* to come before this body was the British proposal for the extension of Imperial preference. Some of the British Ministers were opposed to any increase in the British tariff which would necessarily follow the acceptance of such a proposal, but Amery, Lloyd-Greame, Neville Chamberlain, and others were keen on providing economic bonds which, they thought, would safeguard British industries, strengthen inter-Imperial sentiment, and make the Empire impregnable in war. It was even hinted that Amery wished to use the preference proposals to induce the Dominions to make tariff demands on the British Government which in turn would force the hands of his reluctant colleagues.

The Canadian attitude to Imperial preference had been set out when the Laurier Government initiated the system in 1897. The preference had always been regarded by the Liberals as a free act unaccompanied by any request for a *quid pro quo*, a position which enabled them to approach any future negotiations without hampering commitments. Some of the Canadian Conservatives, on the other hand, desired to use all tariffs as bargaining instruments with which to gain additional concessions. "Preference," said Mackenzie King at the opening of the Economic Conference on October 2, "has been based on goodwill; bargaining has not been the basis of it. We have done what we have done believing it would be to our advantage, but believing also that it would be helpful to the countries to which the preference was extended and especially to the Mother Country."[63]

*Other items on the agenda which had some interest for Canada but which are not discussed here were: settlement within the Empire, preference for Empire products in public contracts, Empire patents and statistics, communications, grants for Empire development schemes, and the British embargo on livestock. The Canadian Government after years of agitation had only recently been successful in securing the removal of the livestock embargo, but this had been rendered partly ineffective by further restrictive regulations.

The subject was placed before the Conference by Bruce, who advocated specially favourable treatment and facilities for the produce and manufactures of other parts of the Empire. Australia had already made new concessions to Great Britain in its tariff; the next step, he implied, rested with the British Parliament. Bruce wanted, above all, markets for agricultural products and raw materials, and he proposed an involved arrangement which included a British protective tariff for agricultural products with tariff preferences, a sliding-scale tariff, a subsidy, a licence system, and a stabilization policy.[64] When Lloyd-Greame replied he stated that the British Government was prepared to make a special preferential rate on dried and preserved fruits, sugar, and tobacco, and would like the Conference to discuss any other proposal or aspect of the question.[65]

The representatives from Australia, New Zealand, and South Africa expressed their gratification at this advance, and though all speakers disclaimed any thought of haggling, they hinted that some preference on Australian and South African wine and New Zealand meat would also be warmly received. Canada was prepared to accept the proposals without any discussion whatever. "It is dangerous ground," Graham said on October 9, "it is your business. We are willing to accept what you give us, and, so far as you wish to go, we will not stop you. But to attempt to drive you along faster than you feel it is in the interests of your own people to go, I think would be altogether out of place so far as we are concerned."[66] These speakers were followed by Neville Chamberlain, the Chancellor of the Exchequer, who intimated that more concessions might be forthcoming, and invited the Dominions to submit additional proposals for the consideration of the British Government.

Following this offer, informal meetings were apparently held behind the scenes. King at any rate had a long interview on tariff matters with Lloyd-Greame on October 20, and another with Baldwin that evening. Lloyd-Greame asked King bluntly whether Canada would give Britain a 50 per cent preference on everything if Britain would do the same for Canada, but King said he was not prepared to bargain though he was quite willing to indicate what tariff concessions would be most useful to Canada. He could, of course, scarcely do less without exposing himself to the accusation in Canada that he had neglected a unique opportunity to secure valuable concessions in the British market. King wrote Lloyd-Greame three days later giving him a list of Canadian food stuffs on which a preference would be most welcome.[67]

On October 26, Baldwin in a public speech made a personal declaration in favour of protection, and it was speedily adopted as the official Conservative programme. A general election was announced for December so that a popular mandate might be secured on this violent break with the party's traditional policy.

At a meeting of the Economic Conference on November 7 a number of the proposals which had been submitted by Bruce were pronounced impracticable, but the essential one on preference received further endorsement of a substantial kind from Great Britain. Lloyd-Greame offered preferences on a number of other commodities: wine, raw apples, honey, fruit juice, barley, etc. All the Dominions welcomed these additions to the list, and each speaker, taking advantage of Chamberlain's earlier invitation, named other commodities on which further preferences might be considered. The Canadian Minister's contribution to the discussion was a virtual repetition of King's letter, noted above, to Lloyd-Greame.[68]

The British Government had set great store upon the establishment of some central organization to give assistance in the formulation of tariffs and trade policies. Lloyd-Greame had broached the scheme to Mackenzie King in their initial talk on October 1, but King was wary.[69] The following extract, from a memorandum by Skelton, dated the following day, indicated the Canadian suspicion of all plans which contemplated the creation of centralized machinery:

This proposal is simply another variant of the endless schemes for establishing a central government here [London]. Parliament or council or secretariat, it matters not, so long as the machinery of control can somehow be established in London. It would be a complete reversal of our long established policy. It may be that the "permanent organization" will be pictured as a mere statistical and fact-finding body, but on such wide questions, questions of policy, it could not be merely this even to start, and would soon develop into something much more active and executive. It would commit us to central review of every important economic activity of our government, and would for example give good ground for intervention if we proposed a reciprocity arrangement with the U.S. It is superfluous, because each Government has access to all the material facts and can collect and judge them; if then common action is desired, that can be effected by negotiation between the governments concerned.[70]

471

When on November 8 the Economic Conference decided to set up an Imperial Economic Committee to consider and advise upon matters of an economic character, Canada dissented on the grounds that no such body was needed and that it might grow into a permanent organization with a tendency to interfere in Dominion economic affairs.*

The sequel to this endeavour to extend the Imperial preference by making tentative agreements in the Conference was not without its moral. The Conference ended in November and the British general election came in December, 1923. That election upset the Baldwin Government on the issue of protection (an integral part of the Empire preference) and the succeeding Labour Government, together with the supporting Liberal party, was therefore irrevocably committed to free trade. The preference arrangements of the Conference of course stood in direct antagonism to the new Government's domestic pledges. The British Cabinet was soon able to forget any embarrassment, however, after it had been exposed to the irritating and unwarranted attacks of Bruce, Massey, and Smuts, all of whom insisted that Britain was bound to honour the Conference agreements.† They had, of course, not a vestige of a case, as The Times[71] pointed out on December 23:

These speeches obviously imply that the Imperial Conference has power to impose taxes upon the people of Great Britain. No Conference has any such power. . . . It is satisfactory to see that no such false conception of the power of the Imperial Conference has entered into the mind of Mr. Mackenzie King. . . . These considerations seem so obvious . . . that one can only assume that General Smuts and Mr. Massey are thinking less of Imperial considerations than of political influences in their own countries.‡

This prompt vindication of King's reluctance to bargain or enter into binding commitments at the Conference inevitably enhanced his

---

*The proposal to create the Imperial Economic Committee was badly buffeted by British political changes in the following months. Eventually the second Baldwin Government set it up in the early part of 1925, and Canada, after receiving an assurance that the Committee was of an *ad hoc* character, agreed to be represented on it. See W.L.M.K.–P. C. Larkin correspondence for December, 1924.

†King also was embarrassed, however, by a letter to The Times (Jan. 16, 1924) from F. C. Wade, Agent-General for British Columbia, urging the MacDonald Government to honour Baldwin's preference proposals. King complained to John Oliver, Premier of British Columbia, at this attempt to influence British policy, and Wade was instructed to desist. W.L.M.K. to J. Oliver, Feb. 9, 1924; J. Oliver to W.L.M.K., Feb. 21, 1924.

‡Following another election in Great Britain late in October, 1924, the Baldwin Government was again in office pledged to support Imperial preference. But in the

472

reputation for perspicacity. Violet Markham wrote on December 18:

What impresses me more than anything else is the extraordinary acumen of *your* judgment about the causes which have led to this upheaval. Not only recently but for years past you have declared that sooner or later the Imperial Conference would wreck one of the component governments—though I hardly imagine you foresaw in old days that the first government to perish at its hands would be the British Government. People are only slowly waking up to the fact that the Conference led to the Election. The second point is that owing to your admirable discretion & wisdom you are the only Prime Minister to extricate yourself from the collapse with dignity. You alone are on velvet because you asked for nothing & wanted nothing & repeated steadily we here in England must manage our own fiscal affairs in our own way.

What is going to happen to all the Preference proposals so laboriously noted? This new House of Commons will have none of them—it's Wilson & his Senate over again—Smuts Massey & Bruce are all sending up cries of distress. The whole situation is a real triumph for yourself & the policy you laid down. I hope that fact is properly appreciated in Canada.[72]

The concluding sessions of the Imperial Conference were devoted to the consideration of resolutions. This in King's opinion was the most dangerous period and he was very uneasy about its outcome. To some of the resolutions proposed, such as those on treaty powers, he took no objection, for they gave a formal approval to a notable advance in Dominion self-government; but others, especially those dealing with defence and foreign policy, he regarded as traps to inveigle the Dominions into matters in which they had no direct interest or responsibility. There could be no advantage in his exercising the utmost care during the Conference to avoid awkward commitments on what he regarded as essentially British ventures, and then relinquishing all the ground he had gained by agreeing in the last few days to a mass of resolutions which implied that these ventures had his approval. Resolutions were only too likely to be the cause of misunderstandings. They could not properly bind any part of the Empire represented at the Conference, yet they might create a semblance of an obligation

campaign Baldwin had made "some loose remarks . . . in one of his election speeches which were held, by the Cabinet, to preclude even the most modest additional preferences on anything that was edible or potable" (L. S. Amery, *My Political Life*, II, 346; see also pp. 273–8). So the preference was scrapped by the same party and virtually the same Government which had sponsored it. In notifying the Dominions that the preference had been abandoned, the British Government said it proposed to spend annually the equivalent advantage of the preference in Britain (about £1,000,000) to promote the marketing of Empire products there.

and raise possible hopes which would not be gratified. King did not want Canada to be on record as approving policies over which she had no control or in which she had no direct or immediate interest nor as agreeing to a course of action which had never been accepted by the Canadian Cabinet and Parliament. Why should he be asked to approve of the fortification of Singapore or endorse British policy in Egypt? On the other hand, how far was he justified in carrying his opposition in the teeth of a large part of the Conference? His struggle over the resolutions on foreign relations was severe and is best told in his own words:

November 5, 1923

. . . At three o'clock there was a secret session of what purported to be the Prime Ministers. There were present the Prime Minister, Lord Curzon, the Duke of Devonshire, Sir Maurice Hankey on one side of the table, Massey, Bruce myself and Smuts on the other. Lord Curzon explained that the conference was for the purpose of considering the statement to be placed in the report of the conference on foreign policy; he outlined further developments of the last few days and sketched the grounds on which he had prepared a statement which was subsequently handed to us and discussed paragraph by paragraph. It was really an effort to commit the conference to a common foreign policy and I had a most difficult and unpleasant hour or two strongly opposing many of the paragraphs that were inserted. I protested against our assuming the rights of a cabinet in the determination of foreign policy and maintained that at most we could give advice on matters on which we were fully informed and concerning which we were prepared to accept responsibility. I pointed out that we had, in a communication to the Foreign Office, refused to recognise the telegraph despatches which were sent to us as giving us any real opportunity of discussion or shaping foreign policy and that we had refused to regard their acceptance as more than for purposes of information. I pointed out that the course they were pursuing would certainly lead to a re-action in Canada and possibly to resolutions in our Parliament which would make the situation more difficult than it had been.

I protested against expressing approval of the present Government's foreign policy, maintaining that the only information we had was the one side given us by the Government itself, and that we had no authority from our Parliaments to assume any such power. I also protested strongly against trying to shape the affairs of Europe, beyond very general statements as to matters arising out of the Peace Treaty. All the other Premiers were more or less keen on shaping foreign policy and contended that the information with which we had been supplied was equal to that which the British Government itself had received. Lord Curzon, in fact, made this as a statement.

474

I pointed out that it might be necessary for the Government to consider whether it would accept an invitation to subsequent conferences if their purpose was to have the Dominions committed in matters over which their Parliaments had no control and insisted on any statement being safe-guarded by having it contingent upon the approval of our parliament. I succeeded by absolutely refusing to sanction certain of the clauses as they appeared in the draft. I still have fears that the general impression left will be one for which I shall be more or less criticized. However, one can carry objection to the point where further modification will not be conceded without absolute threat of withdrawal, and I do not think it wise to go that length at this time, especially as I have succeeded in getting most of the points that I have fought for restated in a manner which I think will have an important influence on the future trend of development.

I was very outspoken, and perhaps too much so, but I know I have saved a very serious situation developing so far as Canada is concerned.[73]

November 6, 1923
. . . I had a talk with Skelton and [Dafoe]* about the report on foreign affairs. [Dafoe] thought I ought to consign it to the waste basket. I pointed out this would be a mistake and would not be wise for me to refuse to participate with others in assuming a general responsibility so long as I safe-guarded the supremacy of our parliament in the shaping of and execution of matters of foreign policy. I pointed out to [Dafoe] that it was more important to get a specific statement of a position for which we were striving included in the general statement of policy than to lose the chance of the latter by avoiding acceptance altogether of the former. I outlined what I thought advisable in this connection and it was generally approved by [Dafoe] and also by Skelton. . . .

When I reached Downing Street I learned that Lord Curzon had not found it possible to accept some of the suggestions I had made and had decided, in order to avoid a full-dress debate, not to bring up the foreign policy report for consideration to-day. . . .

After the conference adjourned I took up with Sir Maurice Hankey,† at his request, the differences between Lord Curzon and myself with a view to seeing if they could be met by a further conference which Hankey was to have with Curzon. I held firmly to all the essential features that I had fought for and at 6.15 o'clock left for the Ritz.[74]

---

*The diary reads "Doughty" (the Canadian Archivist) instead of "Dafoe" in four places in this paragraph. It is unquestionably a slip because there would be no reason whatever to consult Doughty on such a matter; and also because Dafoe, in his own private record, describes this same conversation in detail even to the point of his making the "waste basket" recommendation.

†Sir Maurice (now Lord) Hankey was one of the most distinguished British civil servants of his generation. He was Secretary of the Committee of Imperial Defence, 1912–38, Secretary of the Cabinet, 1919–38, and head of the Secretariat of the Imperial Conferences of 1923 and 1926.

475

November 7, 1923

. . . Sir Maurice Hankey came to my rooms about eleven o'clock and showed me the one or two minor changes which Lord Curzon had been prepared to accept in the wording. He said he was insistent on the report including what had been written with reference to Turkey and Egypt; the former related to the recommendation to assist Turkey in her economic development and establishment of her Government along the right lines; the latter was a reference to maintaining an obligation on the part of the Empire to retain a certain position which would secure the Suez Canal for British commerce.

I held out in the strongest possible fashion against committing our Parliament to any obligation of the kind, and told Hankey that if Lord Curzon held to the position he did I must add a reservation so far as Canada was concerned along lines I had drafted and which I handed to him; this simply stated that nothing in the report could bind Canada without the express endorsation in the first instance by her Government of what it contained, and secondly approval by her Parliament; putting forth in so many words that we could not permit an obligation in matters of foreign policy beyond those things which we regarded as of immediate and direct interest, also, from our point of view, that the proceedings of the Conference were to be regarded merely as those of a conference and not of a cabinet. I told Hankey that I must be absolutely firm in this. We tried modification of some of the paragraphs. Hankey himself suggested that probably the one regarding Turkey would be better out altogether; I told him I thought it certainly would. Finally, he said that he did not think it would be much good his going to Curzon, but that he would go and see General Smuts and have Smuts see Curzon and ascertain what could be done in this way.

An hour later Smuts came with Hankey to my apartment at the Ritz Hotel, greeting me as follows: "Mackenzie King, you are a very terrible person; you are giving an awful lot of trouble." This was said in a very good natured way. He then went on to say that while he agreed with what I was proposing as a reservation, he would find it very difficult to get his parliament to act upon, or approve, the report with a reservation of the kind; that he could do more in the way of getting approval of certain policies by having them in the form of recommendations of the Conference, or rather statements of policy, drawn up by it. I told him that that was just where there lay a fundamental difference between us; that I would only be inviting opposition to the report of the Conference before I reached Canada were I to agree to what it contained without reservation as suggested.

After considerable discussion, Smuts asked if I would be willing to cut down my reservation into a brief concluding paragraph indicating that the proceedings of the Conference were all subject to the approval of parliament if the paragraphs regarding Egypt and Turkey were eliminated altogether. I told him I would, and we could work together on the final draft. He then said he did not know how Lord Curzon would view this last proposal; I replied that it was a matter of indifference to me which of the two he took; that I must insist on Canada's position being frankly stated, and I thought if I did so the other Dominions would find it necessary to join with me. This, he replied, was quite certain.

I told him, what he knew, that the Irish members were also thinking of inserting certain paragraphs in the report or introducing formal resolutions with reference thereto, and I would have to support them in these resolutions unless changes were made as I desired. I did not wish to embarrass the situation by so doing, and thought it in the interests of all that whatever went out from the Conference should be unanimous. Smuts cordially agreed. He left about four o'clock, and an hour later telephoned to say that Lord Curzon had accepted my last proposals to Smuts and that the report would be revised accordingly.[75]

Curzon's comments on these discussions were not flattering to Mackenzie King; but he gave King full marks for tenacity and exhibited (as might be expected) a complete lack of understanding of the Canadian viewpoint and of the Canadian political situation. He wrote to his wife on November 8:

The last two days have been a whirlwind of negotiation and trouble in order to get the Imperial Conference to agree to a report (written by myself) on Foreign Affairs. The obstacle has been Mackenzie King, the Canadian, who is both obstinate, tiresome and stupid, and is nervously afraid of being turned out of his own Parliament when he gets back. Smuts has been a tower of strength in these pourparlers, and has been running in and out of this house with Hankey 2 or 3 times a day.[76]

The report of the Imperial Conference on these issues made no commitments of any consequence: the Conference, as Dafoe said, "may be accounted a success by virtue of the things it declined to do."[77] The report contained no explicit repudiation of the single Empire policy of 1921, but, on the other hand, it made no recommendations for improving the system of consultation on that policy. The significance of the latter omission, in view of Chanak, was inescapable. Moreover, the vague terms in which so-called decisions were phrased and the reservations which were frequently made also pointed to the abandonment of any common policy on many topics. The saving clause appended to the section on Foreign Relations at King's insistence may be taken as an example. It reads:

This Conference is a conference of representatives of the several Governments of the Empire; its views and conclusions on Foreign Policy, as

477

recorded above, are necessarily subject to the action of the Governments and Parliaments of the various portions of the Empire, and it trusts that the results of its deliberations will meet with their approval.[78]

These words accepted the departure of the Imperial Cabinet from the scene, and at the same time let it be inferred that the earlier Imperial Conference with its non-committal conversations had quietly taken its place.

There is no reasonable doubt that the British Government made a concerted effort to mould the Conference to its purposes and that King beat off the attack almost single-handed. In these engagements, it will be noticed, Stanley Baldwin as Prime Minister took little more than a formal part; the real burden was carried by his colleagues. The frontal attack was led by Curzon, and was backed by Bruce, Massey, and to some degree by Smuts. It had as its goal the re-establishment of the unity of the Empire, embodied in the single Empire foreign policy. This was aided by two flanking movements of no less importance. The first was on common defence, with Amery at its head, and the Secretaries for War and Air in support. Here generous concessions were made in the direction of local autonomy, but it was expected that the ground so yielded would be fully recovered by methods of indirect control and a pooling of forces when danger threatened. The other encircling movement was economic: the means, the Imperial Economic Conference; the directors of the attack, Lloyd-Greame and Neville Chamberlain. None of these manoeuvres was successful, though it was the British electorate who took the final responsibility for defeating the move to extend the Imperial preference.

The British Government was clearly not interested at this juncture in the status of the Dominions except as it might affect British prestige and authority in international affairs. The inescapable and almost superhuman task which gave them no respite was the restoration of an unsettled Europe to a condition of peace and tranquillity. Lord Curzon had made this very plain in his masterly speech at the opening of the Conference when he dwelt at great length on the distrust and turmoil throughout the world. "Although it is now nearly five years," he said, "since the Armistice was signed . . . the tramp of armed men is still heard upon the Continent, and you have only to pick up your daily paper to hear the rumble of almost chronic revolution in your ears."[79] The British Government was pre-eminently concerned to bring

478

the concerted influence of the Empire to bear on these recurring crises, and Mackenzie King's concentration on Dominion powers showed in their minds a complete lack of perspective. Moreover, the fact that King on a number of issues received little if any encouragement from some of the other Dominion Prime Ministers doubtless led the British Government to regard King's attitude as distinctively and narrowly Canadian, while his shaky parliamentary majority may well have raised the further question as to whether his views were really those of the Canadian people. "Mackenzie King," wrote Amery many years later, "was chiefly concerned [at the Conference] to avoid committing himself to anything."[80]

Yet this judgment did not do justice to King. Obtuseness was not all on the Canadian side. Admittedly King did not share the British conviction that the Empire should intervene in Europe, for the Atlantic Ocean had given him like other North Americans a feeling of security which sapped a sense of responsibility for the well-being of other nations. Nor was King merely an obstructionist. He had his own concept of what Empire relations should be and it was soon to prove more realistic and more flexible than its British rival. King's scheme grew out of his profound awareness of the new vitality of Canadian nationalism and it demanded from the British Government that that Government should give full recognition to this fact as a basic principle of the Empire of the future. In his conduct at the Conference King was bent on proving to the British representatives that there was nothing half-hearted in Canada's pursuit of autonomy. Whatever other Dominions might want or believe, Canada at least was no longer willing to accept an unreal participation in British policies in exchange for a very real and costly support in emergencies. By his single-minded blocking of all centralizing proposals throughout the Conference King undoubtedly left the erroneous impression that he was little more than a destructive critic, although he did in fact affirm his belief that the Empire should be a partnership of equal nations which would combine for common purposes wherever common interests could be discerned. Constructive plans along these lines, however, could make little progress until all hopes of centralization had been completely annihilated.

The Imperial Conference of 1923 gave Mackenzie King one of the great personal triumphs of his career. This Conference was the decisive one in Empire relations: the turning point where the Empire reversed

479

its tendency of the war and post-war period and moved towards a more stable condition based on the nationalism and independence of the Dominions. The Conference of 1926 was of undoubted importance, but it was most concerned with confirming the change in constitutional development, the lines of which had been broadly determined by the Canadian stand three years earlier.

Although Mackenzie King was personally acceptable to the members of the British Government, he could scarcely have gained their affection in view of the annoyance and frustration which his pertinacity so often had produced. Yet before the meetings were over he had probably earned the Ministers' respect. Before King left for Canada he paid a farewell call on Lord Curzon, who at least appeared to hold no grudges. "I remarked that possibly I had been too persistent in putting forward my point of view. To this Lord Curzon said I was over critical of myself; that I had displayed great candour and great courtesy and was most helpful. I said I was sure I had saved trouble in the long run and that it was all-important that Governments to-day should feel that Parliaments and peoples were behind them in any policies they were framing."* At the final session of the Conference, it was reported, Smuts turned to King and remarked: "You ought to be satisfied. Canada has had her way in everything." It was a remarkable tribute to a remarkable performance.

*Diary, Nov. 18, 1923. Lord Curzon's version of the incident was much the same as King's, though each participant was inclined to dwell on the complimentary remarks made by the other:

"Nov. 18, 1923. . . . This afternoon Mackenzie King the Canadian Premier came in to say good-bye. He said that he had come to the Conference with a violent prejudice against me based on the newspaper pictures of the superior person. He said that he and the whole of his colleagues had been profoundly impressed by my courtesy and affability, knowledge of the subject and eloquence. He declared that in all their opinions this was the main souvenir of the Conference, and that in future he would follow everything that I did and said with intense interest and regard.

"I nearly sank into the ground with surprise and confusion."

Lord Curzon to his wife; see Marchioness Curzon of Kedleston, *Reminiscences*, pp. 192–3.

NOTES

CHAPTER ONE: EARLY LIFE

1. This is Mackenzie's own account. Charles Lindsey, *The Life and Times of Wm. Lyon Mackenzie* (Toronto, 1862), I, 18–19.
2. A. R. M. Lower, *Colony to Nation: A History of Canada* (Toronto, 1946), pp. 242–3.
3. Harriet MacNicol to Donald MacNicol, Dec. 14, 1935.
4. Marchioness of Aberdeen, "A Prime Minister in Quest of the Homes of His Ancestors," *Deeside Field*, No. 8, 1938.
5. W.L.M.K. to Robert English, May 10, 1948.
6. Willie to John King, May 1, 1888.
7. W.L.M.K., Memorandum, April 25, 1949.
8. Address at the Rideau Club, Ottawa, Dec. 9, 1946.
9. Willie to Mr. and Mrs. King, Aug. 6, 1888.
10. Max to Willie, Feb. 21, 1897.
11. Jennie to Willie, June 12, 1899.
12. Jennie to Willie, Oct. 23, 1899.
13. Jennie to Willie, Nov. 29, 1896.
14. Jennie to Willie, Dec. 6, 1896.
15. Diary, July 26, 1897.
16. John King to Willie, Oct. 8, 1896.
17. "Our English Shakspere," *Canadian Monthly*, July, 1876.
18. T. M. Mulligan to W.L.M.K., Dec. 17, 1940.
19. W.L.M.K., Memorandum, April 25, 1949.
20. John King to Willie, Dec. 27, 1899.
21. *Ibid.*
22. John King to Willie, May 1, 1898.
23. J. W. L. Forster, *Under the Studio Light* (Toronto, 1928), p. 94.
24. Mrs. King to Willie, March 31, 1899.
25. Jennie to Willie, June 8, 1898.
26. John King to Willie, May 17, 1898.
27. Willie to Mrs. King, Feb. 4, 1898.
28. Mrs. King to Willie, March 10, 1898.

CHAPTER TWO: UNIVERSITY OF TORONTO

1. T. A. Reed, ed., *A History of the University of Trinity College, Toronto, 1852–1952* (Toronto, 1952), pp. 92–5.
2. *Varsity*, Oct. 20, 1891.
3. W.L.M.K. to Mr. and Mrs. King, Nov. 1, 1891.
4. "The Varsity and the Students," by Justice, *Varsity*, Dec. 6, 1893. "Greek Letter Societies," by ΓΛΣ, *ibid.*, Oct. 17, 1894. "Hallowe'en," by Rex, *ibid.*, Nov. 7, 1894.
5. *Ibid.*, March 20, 1931.

6. Hector Charlesworth, *More Candid Chronicles* (Toronto, 1928), pp. 57–92; Edwin C. Guillet, "Student Rebellion," vol. 18 in the unpublished manuscript of "Famous Canadian Trials."

7. Toronto *World*, Jan. 23, 1895.

8. Diary, Feb. 15, 1895.

9. Toronto *Mail*, Feb. 16, 1895.

10. Toronto *Globe*, April 18, 1895.

11. Ontario, Royal Commission on the Discipline in the University of Toronto, *Report* (1895).

12. Diary, Dec. 3, 1893.

13. *Ibid.*, July 8, 1894.

14. W.L.M.K. to H. A. Harper, June 7, 1896.

15. Diary, Sept. 13, 1896.

16. *Ibid.*, Feb. 16, 1894.

17. *Ibid.*, Aug. 15, 1896.

18. W.L.M.K. to Mr. and Mrs. King, Oct. 18, 1891.

19. Diary, Dec. 31, 1893; Jan. 15, 1894.

20. W.L.M.K. to Mr. and Mrs. King, Oct. 18, 1891.

21. Diary, Jan. 16, 1894.

22. *Ibid.*, Jan. 27, 1894.

23. *Ibid.*, April 27, 1894.

24. Beatrice Webb, *My Apprenticeship* (London, 1926), p. 174.

25. B. Jowett, "Memoir," in Arnold Toynbee, *Lectures on the Industrial Revolution in England: Popular Addresses, Notes and Other Fragments* (London, 1884), p. xvii. See also F. C. Montague, *Arnold Toynbee* (Baltimore, 1889).

26. Diary, Dec. 2, 1939.

27. *Ibid.*, Dec. 9, 1895.

28. *Ibid.*, Dec. 7, 1895.

29. *Ibid.*, July 20, 21, 1895.

30. Charles Lindsey, *The Life and Times of Wm. Lyon Mackenzie* (Toronto, 1862), I, 20.

31. Diary, June 17, 1895.

32. *Ibid.*, June 19, 1895.

33. *Ibid.*, June 22, 1895.

34. *Ibid.*, July 18, 1895.

35. *Ibid.*, Aug. 27, 1895.

36. *Financial Post*, Feb. 7, 1953.

37. Diary, March 13, 1896.

38. *Ibid.*, Nov. 5, 1895.

39. *Ibid.*, Nov. 14, 1895.

40. W.L.M.K. to H. A. Harper, July 24, 1895.

41. W.L.M.K., Memorandum, June 14, 1896.

42. Diary, July 11, 1896.

43. *Ibid.*, July 25, 1896.

CHAPTER THREE
UNIVERSITIES OF CHICAGO AND HARVARD

1. W.L.M.K. to Jennie King, Oct. 18, 1896.

2. W.L.M.K. to H. A. Harper, Dec. 25, 1896.

3. W.L.M.K. to Mr. and Mrs. King, Nov. 8, 1896.

4. W.L.M.K. to Mr. and Mrs. King, Nov. 1, 1896.

5. John King to W.L.M.K., Nov. 25, 1896.

6. W.L.M.K. to Mr. and Mrs. King, Nov. 29, 1896.

7. Diary, Dec. 31, 1896.
8. *Ibid.*, Oct. 24, 1896.
9. *Ibid.*, Dec. 4, 1896.
10. *Ibid.*, Dec. 12, 1896.
11. W.L.M.K. to Mr. and Mrs. King, Jan. 10, 1897.
12. *Ibid.*
13. W.L.M.K. to H. A. Harper, June 7, 1896.
14. W.L.M.K., Memorandum, Oct. 6, 1897.
15. Diary, April 28, 1897.
16. W.L.M.K. to Mr. and Mrs. King, May 1, 1897.
17. Diary, Aug. 22, 1897.
18. Chicago *Record*, Jan. 14, 1897.
19. Diary, Dec. 3, 1896.
20. "In Chicago Slums," *Globe*, Jan. 16, 1897.
21. *Journal of Political Economy*, March, 1897; Sept., 1897.
22. Diary, May 6, 1897.
23. *Ibid.*, June 22, 1897.
24. *Ibid.*, July 12, 1897.
25. "Crowded Housing, Its Evil Effects," *Daily Mail and Empire*, Sept. 18, 1897; "Foreigners Who Live in Toronto," *ibid.*, Sept. 25, Oct. 2, 1897; "Toronto and the Sweating System," *ibid.*, Oct. 9, 1897.
26. Diary, Sept. 15–17, 1897.
27. *Ibid.*, Sept. 18, 1897.
28. *Ibid.*, Sept. 19, 1897.
29. Canada, *Report of the Royal Commission on the Relations of Labor and Capital in Canada* (1889); Canada, Department of Secretary of State, *Report upon the Sweating System in Canada*, Alexander Whyte Wright, Commissioner (1896).
30. Toronto *Globe*, Sept. 30, 1897.
31. *Ibid.*, Oct. 7, 1897.
32. W.L.M.K. to Mr. and Mrs. King, Nov. 28, 1897.
33. W.L.M.K., *Report to the Honourable the Postmaster General of the Methods Adopted in Canada in the Carrying out of Government Clothing Contracts* (1898).
34. "Sweating System in Montreal," Montreal *Herald*, April 16, 1898; "Sweating System in Montreal City," *ibid.*, April 23, 1898.
35. "The Sweating System in Canada," Toronto *Globe*, Nov. 19, 1898.
36. Consumers' League of Massachusetts, *Report No. 2* (1898), Appendix by W. L. Mackenzie King, "Report on Hours and Other Conditions in the Smaller Mercantile Establishments of Boston and Vicinity."
37. *Can. H. of C. Debates*, July 17, 1900, pp. 10495–502.
38. W.L.M.K. to Mr. and Mrs. King, April 7, 1900.
39. W.L.M.K. to John King, Sept. 29, 30, 1897.
40. W.L.M.K. to Mr. and Mrs. King, Oct. 3, 1897.
41. John King to W.L.M.K., Oct. 2, 1897.
42. W.L.M.K. to Mr. and Mrs. King, Oct. 3, 1897.
43. W.L.M.K. to Max King, Nov. 14, 1897.
44. W.L.M.K. to Mr. and Mrs. King, Feb. 27, 1898.
45. Diary, Dec. 13, 1897.
46. *Ibid.*, Nov. 15, 1897.
47. *Ibid.*, June 11, 1898.
48. "Charles Eliot Norton" by W. R. Thayer, *The Nation*, Oct. 29, 1908.
49. W.L.M.K. to Mr. and Mrs. King, June 28, 1898.
50. W.L.M.K. to Mr. and Mrs. King, Oct. 10, 1897.
51. W.L.M.K. to Mr. and Mrs. King, Nov. 28, 1897.
52. John King to W.L.M.K., Nov. 18, 1897.
53. W. J. Ashley to Mr. and Mrs. King, Oct. 5, 1897.

54. Diary, Nov. 10, 1899.
55. W.L.M.K. to Max King, Oct. 16, 1898.
56. Diary, Feb. 28, 1899.
57. *Ibid.*, Feb. 26, 1898.
58. Jennie King to W.L.M.K., April 6, 1898.
59. John King to W.L.M.K., April 9, 1898.
60. Mrs. King to W.L.M.K., [April 6] 1898.
61. Mrs. King to W.L.M.K., January ?, 1899.
62. Diary, Sept. 22, 1898.
63. *Ibid.*, Jan. 2, 1899.
64. *Ibid.*, July 29, 1899.
65. W.L.M.K. to Mrs. King, Jan. 26, 1900.
66. Diary, Sept. 4, 1900.
67. W.L.M.K. to Mr. and Mrs. King, Sept. 24, 1899.
68. W.L.M.K. to Mr. and Mrs. King, Nov. 1, 1899.
69. W.L.M.K. to Jennie King, Dec. 6, 1899.
70. Diary, Oct. 9, 11–13, 18, 19, 26, etc., 1899.
71. *Ibid.*, July 5, 1899.
72. *Ibid.*, July 11, 1899.
73. *Ibid.*, Jan. 23, 1900.
74. *Ibid.*, Feb. 15, 1900.
75. *Ibid.*, Jan. 25, 30, 1900.
76. *Ibid.*, Feb. 22, 1900.
77. *Ibid.*, Jan. 2, 3, 1900.
78. *Ibid.*, Jan. 8, 1900.
79. *Ibid.*, Jan. 3, 1900.
80. *Ibid.*, Jan. 26, 1900.
81. *Ibid.*, Jan. 27, 1900.
82. W.L.M.K., Memorandum on Visit to Cambridge, Nov. 4–8, 1899.
83. Isabel King to W.L.M.K., Dec. 5, 1899.
84. Diary, March 4, 1900.
85. W.L.M.K. to Mr. and Mrs. King, Nov. 1, 1899.
86. *Ibid.*
87. Diary, Oct. 26, 1899.
88. *Ibid.*, May 25, 1900.
89. *Ibid.*, June 26, 1900.
90. *Ibid.*
91. W.L.M.K. to Mr. and Mrs. King, June 23, 1900. (The diary shows that this date should read June 26.)
92. Diary, June 29, 1900.
93. John King to F. W. Taussig, June 25, 1900.
94. F. W. Taussig to John King, June 27, 1900.
95. Diary, July 5, 1900.

CHAPTER FOUR: CIVIL SERVANT

1. Diary, Aug. 11, 1900.
2. Canada, *Report of the Royal Commission on the Relations of Labor and Capital in Canada* (1889), p. 89.
3. *Ibid.*, pp. 8, 87, 88, 91, 100.
4. Ottawa *Free Press*, July 25, 1900.
5. *Can. Statutes*, 63–64 Vic., c. 24.
6. *Report of the Royal Commission on the Relations of Labor and Capital in Canada* (1889), pp. 11, 14.

7. *Can. Statutes*, 53 Vic., c. 15.
8. *Can. H. of C. Debates*, July 6, 1900, p. 9395.
9. Diary, July 24, 1900.
10. *Ibid.*, July 24, 1900.
11. *Ibid.*, July 26, 1900.
12. *Ibid.*, Aug. 3, 1900.
13. *Ibid.*, Aug. 5, 1900.
14. *Ibid.*, Aug. 6, 1900.
15. *Ibid.*, Aug. 9, 1900.
16. *Ibid.*, Aug. 14, 1900.
17. *Ibid.*, Aug. 17, 1900.
18. *Ibid.*, Aug. 17, 1900.
19. *Ibid.*, Sept. 11, 1900.
20. *Ibid.*, Oct. 19, 1900.
21. *Ibid.*, Nov. 19, 1900.
22. *Ibid.*, Jan. 11, 12, 1901.
23. W.L.M.K. to Mr. and Mrs. King, Nov. 4, 1900.
24. Fred L. Fowke to William Mulock, Dec. 13, 1900.
25. *Labour Gazette*, Sept., 1900, p. 29.
26. *Can. H. of C. Debates*, April 3, 1901, p. 2590. See *ibid.*, April 25, May 7, 1901, pp. 3754–67, 4536–83.
27. W.L.M.K. to John King, Nov. 8, 1900.
28. W.L.M.K. to Mr. and Mrs. King, May 13, 1901.
29. Diary, Feb. 8, 1901.
30. *Ibid.*, Sept. 2, 1901.
31. *Ibid.*, Jan. 10, 1902.
32. W.L.M.K. to John King, Nov. 23, 1901.
33. Deputy Minister of Labour, "Annual Report," *Can. Sessional Papers* (1903), No. 36, p. 39.
34. Diary, April 6, 1901.
35. *Ibid.*, April 8, 1901.
36. *Ibid.*, Nov. 23, 1900.
37. W.L.M.K., Memorandum on Kingsmere.
38. W.L.M.K., *The Secret of Heroism* (New York, 1906), p. 57.
39. Jennie King to Isabel King, Aug. 8, 1904.
40. Diary, Aug. 24, 1901.
41. *Ibid.*, Aug. 26, 1900; March 5, 1901.
42. Deputy Minister of Labour, "Annual Report," *Can. Sessional Papers* (1903), No. 36, pp. 33–4.
43. Diary, June 3, 1902.
44. Toronto *Globe*, July 23, 1904.
45. Diary, Aug. 9, 1901.
46. *Ibid.*, Sept. 3, 1901.
47. *Ibid.*, Aug. 8, 1901.
48. *Ibid.*, Aug. 9, 1901.
49. *Ibid.*, Jan. 24, 1902.
50. *Ibid.*, Feb. 10, 1902.
51. John King to W.L.M.K., May 7, 1902.
52. John King to W.L.M.K., Dec. 6, 1900.
53. John King to W.L.M.K., Aug. 28, 1902.
54. Mrs. King to John King and Jennie King, Dec. 2, 1903.
55. Mrs. King to W.L.M.K., Aug. 12, 1902; John King to W.L.M.K., Aug. 28, 1902.
56. Mrs. King to W.L.M.K., Nov. 15, 1902. See also Mrs. King to W.L.M.K., June 1, 5, 1906.
57. John King to W.L.M.K., June 10, 1903.

58. W.L.M.K. to Mrs. King, March 1, 1901; Jennie King to W.L.M.K., March 3, 1901.
59. John King to W.L.M.K., April 24, 1901.
60. W.L.M.K. to Mr. and Mrs. King, April 28, 1901.
61. Diary, Sept. 23, 1902.
62. Isabel King to W.L.M.K., Sept. 10, 1902.
63. Diary of H. A. Harper, Feb. 18, 1901.
64. Diary, Feb. 18, 1901.
65. John King to W.L.M.K., Feb. 28, 1901.
66. W.L.M.K. to Mr. and Mrs. King, March 9, 1901.
67. W.L.M.K. to Mr. and Mrs. King, Feb. 1, 1903.
68. *The Secret of Heroism*, p. 145.
69. W.L.M.K. to Mr. and Mrs. King, Dec. 15, 1901.
70. W.L.M.K. to B. K. Sandwell, Aug. 22, 1919.

CHAPTER FIVE: DEPUTY MINISTER

1. "Report of the Department of Labour," 1906–7, *Can. Sessional Papers* (1907–8), No. 36, p. 33.
2. L. Dexter Jr. to William Mulock, April 10, 1903.
3. Frederic A. Morrison to William Mulock, April 18, 1903; see also Frederic A. Morrison to W.L.M.K., April 20, 1903.
4. "Report of the Department of Labour," 1906–7, *Can. Sessional Papers* (1907–8), No. 36, pp. 49–50.
5. W.L.M.K., *Industry and Humanity* (1st ed., Boston and New York: Houghton Mifflin, 1918), p. 511.
6. *Can. Statutes*, 3 Edw. VII, c. 55.
7. *Can. H. of C. Debates*, May 6, 1903, p. 2540.
8. Diary, Jan. 3, 5, 9, 1907.
9. *Can. H. of C. Debates*, Jan. 9, 1907, pp. 1166–71.
10. W.L.M.K., *Industry and Humanity* (1st ed.), pp. 210–11.
11. *Toronto Electric Commissioners v. Snider* [1925] A.C. 396.
12. *Can. Statutes*, 11–12 Geo. VI, c. 54.
13. Diary, Jan. 3, 1907.
14. W.L.M.K., *Industrial Peace*, a speech to the "Representative Business and Labor Men of Cincinnati," Sept. 18, 1913 (Cincinnati, 1913).
15. See extract, *supra*, pp. 114–15.
16. W.L.M.K. to J. P. Reynolds, Sept. 16, 1903.
17. Diary, May 13, 1903.
18. *Ibid.*, May 14, 1903.
19. *Ibid.*, May 15, 1903; cf. also *ibid.*, Dec. 9, 1906.
20. *Can. H. of C. Debates*, Feb. 14, 1907, pp. 3023–6.
21. C. F. Adams, address to the American Civic Federation in New York, Dec. 8, 1902. Published in the *Bulletin* of the United States Department of Labor, May, 1903, pp. 669–77. See also Charles Eliot Norton to W.L.M.K., Jan. 26, 1903.
22. E. P. Wheeler, "Compulsory Investigation of Labor Disputes," *Outlook* (New York), June 2, 1906, p. 273.
23. See W.L.M.K. to Charles W. Eliot, Oct. 23, 1916.
24. *Can. H. of C. Debates*, Jan. 9, 1907, p. 1175.
25. W.L.M.K. to Charles W. Eliot, Oct. 23, 1916.
26. Canada, Department of Labour, *Report of the Royal Commission on Industrial Disputes in the Province of British Columbia* (1903), p. 63.
27. Diary, Jan. 2, 1903.
28. *Ibid.*, Jan. 3, 1903.

29. *Supra,* p. 133.

30. From transcript of shorthand notes of address by W.L.M.K. on February 17, 1914, to the Board of Commerce of Detroit.

31. Canada, Department of Labour, *Report of the Royal Commission on a Dispute respecting Hours of Employment between the Bell Telephone Company of Canada, Ltd. and Operators at Toronto, Ont.* (1907), p. 95.

32. *Ibid.,* p. 97. See also W.L.M.K., *Industry and Humanity* (1st ed.), pp. 316–21.

33. *Report of the Royal Commission on . . . the Hours of Employment . . .* (1907), p. 97.

34. W.L.M.K. to John King, Sept. 15, 1907.

35. Diary, Sept. 13, 1907.

36. *Ibid.,* Sept. 11, 1907.

37. *Can. Sessional Papers* (1907–8), No. 36, pp. 58–61.

38. *Report of the Royal Commission Appointed to Inquire into the Methods by which Oriental Labourers have been Induced to Come to Canada* (1908), pp. 13, 30–1.

39. *Report of the Royal Commission to Inquire into Industrial Disputes in the Cotton Factories of the Province of Quebec* (1909).

40. *Can. Statutes,* 4–5 Edw. VII, c. 16.

41. *Can. Sessional Papers* (1906), No. 36, 88–90; (1906–7), No. 36, 69–76.

42. Canada, Department of Labour, *Report by W. L. Mackenzie King, C.M.G., Deputy Minister of Labour, on the Need for the Suppression of the Opium Traffic in Canada* (1908).

43. *Infra,* pp. 151 ff.

44. *Infra,* p. 176.

45. Laurier Papers, Sir Wilfrid Laurier to W.L.M.K., Nov. 20, 1908.

46. Diary, Oct. 1, 1906.

47. *Ibid.,* Oct. 2, 1906.

48. Lord Elgin to Rodolphe Lemieux, Nov. 1, 1906, *Can. Sessional Papers* (1907–8), No. 36, p. 104.

49. *Brit. Statutes,* 6 Edw. VII, c. 48.

50. Diary, Sept. 19, 1907.

51. Grey Papers, Earl Grey to Lord Elgin, March 3, 1908.

52. Theodore Roosevelt to Arthur Lee (later Lord Lee of Fareham), Feb. 2, 1908; *The Letters of Theodore Roosevelt,* ed. E. E. Morison, *et al.* (Cambridge, Mass., 1951–4), VI, 918–21.

53. John James McCook (1845–1911) was a corporation lawyer in New York. He had been invited to join McKinley's Cabinet, and was a friend of Theodore Roosevelt.

54. J. J. McCook to W.L.M.K., Jan. 9, 1908.

55. Diary, Jan. 25, 1908.

56. *Ibid.*

57. *Ibid.,* Jan. 31, 1908.

58. *Ibid.,* Jan. 25, 1908.

59. *Ibid.,* Jan. 28, 1908.

60. Grey Papers, Earl Grey to James Bryce, Jan. 31, 1908.

61. Laurier Papers, Theodore Roosevelt to Sir W. Laurier, Feb. 1, 1908.

62. Diary, Feb. 7, 1908.

63. Laurier Papers, Sir W. Laurier to Theodore Roosevelt, Feb. 20, 1908.

64. Diary, Feb. 17, 1908.

65. Theodore Roosevelt to Whitelaw Reid, March 30, 1908; *The Letters of Theodore Roosevelt,* ed. E. E. Morison, *et al.,* VI, 985.

66. Grey Papers, Earl Grey to Lord Elgin, Feb. 17, 1908.

67. Diary, Feb. 22, 1908.

68. *Ibid.,* Feb. 25, 1908.

69. *Ibid.*, Feb. 24, 1908.
70. *Ibid.*, Feb. 27, 1908.
71. *Ibid.*, Feb. 7, 1908.
72. *Ibid.*, Feb. 17, 1908.
73. *Ibid.*
74. *Ibid.*, Feb. 3, 1908.
75. *Ibid.*, Feb. 1, 1908.
76. *Ibid.*, Feb. 27, 1908.
77. *Ibid.*, April 7, 1908.
78. *Ibid.*, March 28, 1908.
79. *Ibid.*, April 9, 1908.
80. *Ibid.*, March 20, 1908.
81. Charles Lyell, Parliamentary Private Secretary to Sir Edward Grey; Diary, March 28, 1908. Sir Charles Hardinge, Permanent Under-Secretary to the Foreign Office; *ibid.*, April 8, 1908.
82. *Ibid.*, Feb. 1, 1908.
83. *Ibid.*, March 26, April 9, 1908.
84. P. C. Jessup, *Elihu Root* (New York, 1938), II, 32.
85. *Ibid.*, II, 30.
86. T. A. Bailey, *A Diplomatic History of the American People* (New York, 1950), p. 573.
87. *Ibid.*, p. 574. See also S. F. Bemis, *A Diplomatic History of the United States* (New York, 1950), pp. 671–5.
88. Diary, April 9, 1908.
89. *Ibid.*, April 1, 1908.
90. *Ibid.*
91. *Ibid.*, April 3, 1908.

CHAPTER SIX: THE SHIFT TO POLITICS

1. Diary, Oct. 12, 1904.
2. Violet Markham, *Return Passage* (Oxford University Press, 1953), p. 82.
3. Ottawa *Citizen*, Jan. 28, 1904.
4. W.L.M.K. to John King, Feb. 2, 1905.
5. W.L.M.K. to Mrs. King, Sept. 9, 1907; Mrs. King to W.L.M.K., Sept. 11, 1907.
6. W.L.M.K. to Mrs. King, May 5, 1910.
7. Diary, Jan. 29, 1908.
8. Harold Begbie, *Albert, Fourth Earl Grey: A Last Word* (London, 1917), pp. 46–7.
9. Diary, Dec. 12, 1909.
10. Moreton Frewen, quoted in Harold Begbie, *Albert, Fourth Earl Grey*, p. 114.
11. Diary, Feb. 5, 1906.
12. *Ibid.*, Sept. 9, Dec. 2, 3, 1908.
13. *Ibid.*, Sept. 23, 1907.
14. Laurier Papers, Earl Grey to Sir Wilfrid Laurier, Feb. 5, 1908.
15. Diary, Nov. 9, 1909.
16. *Ibid.*, Nov. 10–26, 1909.
17. *Ibid.*, Dec. 12, 1909.
18. Grey Papers, Earl Grey to Lord Crewe, March 3, 1910.
19. Earl of Stanhope to W.L.M.K., June 10, 1943.
20. Diary, Nov. 4, 1905.
21. W.L.M.K. to Mr. and Mrs. King, Nov. 4, 1905.
22. John King to W.L.M.K., Nov. 6, 1905.
23. Mrs. King to W.L.M.K., Nov. 6, 1905.

24. Diary, Jan. 2, 1906.
25. *Ibid.*, Feb. 3, 1906.
26. *Supra*, p. 172.
27. Diary, Nov. 4, 1905.
28. *Ibid.*, Aug. 27, 1907.
29. *Ibid.*, Aug. 28, 1907.
30. *Ibid.*, Oct. 8, 1907.
31. Toronto *News*, June 24, 1907.
32. W.L.M.K. to Sir Wilfrid Laurier, June 4, 1907.
33. C. F. Hamilton to W.L.M.K., June 24, 1907.
34. Diary, June 24, 1907.
35. W.L.M.K. to Sir Wilfrid Laurier, June 27, 1907; Sir Wilfrid Laurier to W.L.M.K., July 11, 1907.
36. Diary, June 29–July 3, 1907. See also, A. B. Aylesworth to W.L.M.K., Oct. 29, 1908.
37. Diary, July 25, 1907.
38. Sir Wilfrid Laurier to W.L.M.K., July 11, 1907.
39. Diary, July 25, 1907.
40. *Ibid.*, Sept. 6, 1908.
41. *Ibid.*, May 4, 1908.
42. *Ibid.*, Aug. 29, 1908.
43. *Ibid.*, Sept. 9, 1908.
44. *Ibid.*, Sept. 10–21, 1908.
45. *Ibid.*, Sept. 9, 1908.
46. Grey Papers, Esme Howard, Councillor of the Embassy, Washington, to Earl Grey, Aug. 26, 1908.
47. See *supra*, p. 176.
48. Grey Papers, Earl Grey to Lord Crewe, Dec. 8, 1908.
49. Diary, Jan. 31, 1908.
50. W.L.M.K., Memorandum re Emigration from India to Canada, Feb. 5, 1909.
51. Diary, Dec. 7–13, 1908.
52. *Can. Sessional Papers* (1910), No. 36, pp. 11–12.
53. W.L.M.K. to Earl Grey, Jan. 1, 1909.
54. W.L.M.K. to Earl Grey, Jan. 31, 1909; W.L.M.K. to Sir Wilfrid Laurier, Jan. 31, 1909; Laurier Papers, Earl Minto to Sir Wilfrid Laurier, March 1, 1909.
55. Diary, Jan. 25, 1909.
56. *Ibid.*, Feb. 26, 1909.
57. J. Clementi Smith to W.L.M.K., June 7, 1909.
58. Diary, Feb. 26, 1909.
59. Sir J. N. Jordan to Sir Edward Grey, April 1, 1909. See also Sir J. N. Jordan to Sir Edward Grey, March 17, 1909; Laurier Papers, W.L.M.K. to Sir Wilfrid Laurier, March 22, 1909.
60. Diary, Dec. 6, 1908.
61. *Ibid.*, May 10–23, 1909.
62. *Ibid.*
63. W.L.M.K. to Charles W. Eliot, Jan. 15, 1909.
64. Montreal *Herald*, Nov. 12, 1909.
65. Mrs. King to W.L.M.K., Nov. 18, 1909.
66. Diary, Nov. 10–26, 1909.

CHAPTER SEVEN: MINISTER OF LABOUR

1. *Can. H. of C. Debates*, Jan. 19, 1911, p. 2041.
2. J. F. Mackay to W.L.M.K., Feb. 1, 1908; W.L.M.K. to J. F. Mackay, Feb. 6, 1908.

3. Diary, Nov. 10–26, 1909.

4. *Ibid.*, Dec. 6, 1909.

5. Canada, Royal Commission on Industrial Training and Technical Education, *Report of the Commissioners* (1913).

6. *Can. H. of C. Debates*, Dec. 9, 1909, pp. 1230–1, re "An Act respecting the hours of labour on public works."

7. G. H. Brown to W.L.M.K., Jan. 25, 1911.

8. W.L.M.K. to Stewart Lyon, Feb. 21, 1911. See also the letter to the editor of the Toronto *Star*, W.L.M.K. (probably F. A. Acland) to J. E. Atkinson, Feb. 25, 1911.

9. Stewart Lyon to W.L.M.K., Feb. 23, 1911; W.L.M.K. to Stewart Lyon, Feb. 24, 1911.

10. An Act to Prohibit the Manufacture, Importation and Sale of Matches made with White Phosphorus, *Can. Statutes*, 4–5 Geo. V, c. 12.

11. An Act to Prohibit the Improper Use of Opium and Other Drugs, *Can. Statutes*, 1–2 Geo. V, c. 17.

12. Diary, Nov. 1, 1909.

13. *Can. H. of C. Debates*, April 12, 1910, pp. 6831–6.

14. *Can. Statutes*, 9–10 Edw. VII, c. 9.

15. See D. Gordon Blair, "Combines Law in Canada" in *Anti-Trust Laws*, ed. W. Friedmann (Toronto, 1956).

16. *Can. Statutes*, 13–14 Geo. V, c. 9.

17. Toronto *Globe*, Feb. 5, 1910.

18. W.L.M.K. to George P. Graham, Nov. 10, 1910.

19. W.L.M.K. to A. M. Patterson, July 20, 1911.

20. W.L.M.K. to Hamar Greenwood, March 22, 1910.

21. *Can. H. of C. Debates*, Dec. 6, 1909, p. 1066.

22. *Ibid.*, Dec. 9, 1909, p. 1231.

23. *Ibid.*, Dec. 15, 1910, p. 1416.

24. A. B. Garretson (International President, Order of Railway Conductors) to W.L.M.K., Aug. 10, 1910; S. N. Berry to W.L.M.K., Jan. 28, 1911; *Railroad Trainman*, Sept., 1910, p. 797; *Railway Conductor*, Sept., 1910, p. 718.

25. W.L.M.K. to R. A. Daly, Aug. 8, 1910.

26. The correspondence is voluminous, for there were other unfulfilled promises as well. C. M. Hays to W.L.M.K., Nov. 10, 1910; S. N. Berry to W.L.M.K., Jan. 28, 1911; W.L.M.K. to Judge J. A. Barron, June 12, 1911; S. N. Berry and J. Murdock to W.L.M.K., Aug. 30, 1911.

27. Memorandum of F. W. Giddens (King's secretary) re telephone conversation, W.L.M.K. to W. Wainwright (Vice-President, Grand Trunk), Nov. 4, 1910. *Can. H. of C. Debates*, April 16, 1920, pp. 1347–9.

28. *Can. H. of C. Debates*, March 21, 1911, p. 5774.

29. *Ibid.*, April 12, 1920, pp. 1126–7.

30. W. D. Robb to W.L.M.K., Oct. 12, 1922; Ottawa *Citizen*, Oct. 14, 1922.

31. Toronto *Mail and Empire*, Nov. 1, 1909.

32. W.L.M.K. to Rodolphe Lemieux, May 26, 1909.

33. Toronto *Globe*, July 1, 1909.

34. See *infra*, p. 256.

35. W.L.M.K. to Earl of Stanhope, July 23, 1909.

36. Earl of Stanhope to W.L.M.K., April 14, 1909.

37. *Canadian Annual Review*, 1909, pp. 60–1, 100–9.

38. Quoted by Sir Wilfrid Laurier, *Can. H. of C. Debates*, Feb. 3, 1910, pp. 2963–4.

39. W.L.M.K. to Earl of Stanhope, Jan. 8, 1911.

40. Hamilton *Evening Times*, April 2, 1910.

41. W.L.M.K. to L. S. Amery, July 16, 1910.

42. Laurier Papers, James McMullen to Sir Wilfrid Laurier, Jan. 6, 1911; J. P. Rankin to W. S. Fielding, Nov. 1, 1910 (copy in King papers); J. Sims to W.L.M.K., Jan. 29, 1911.

43. Laurier Papers, J. F. Mackay to Sir W. Laurier, March 6, 1911.

44. Diary, Sept. 26, 1911.

45. *Ibid.*, Oct. 6, 1911.

CHAPTER EIGHT: CASUAL EMPLOYMENT

1. Diary, Sept. 25, Oct. 23, 1911, Jan. 9, 1912; W.L.M.K. to Mr. and Mrs. King, March 3, 1912.

2. Berlin *Telegraph*, Oct. 20, 1911.

3. Diary, Oct. 31, 1911.

4. *Ibid.*, Feb. 29, 1912.

5. W.L.M.K. to Violet Markham, June 27, 1913.

6. W.L.M.K. to James Bonar, Sept. 28, 1911.

7. Diary, Sept. 25 (*sic*), 1911.

8. *Ibid.*

9. W.L.M.K. to Violet Markham, Dec. 15, 1911.

10. W.L.M.K. to Violet Markham, Nov. 29, 1912.

11. J. D. Greene to W.L.M.K., June 1, 1914.

12. C. W. Eliot to W.L.M.K., June 1, 1914.

13. Jerome D. Greene to W.L.M.K., June 3, 1914.

14. Allan Nevins, *John D. Rockefeller: The Heroic Age of American Enterprise* (New York, 1940), vol. II, Part II, p. 673.

15. Jerome D. Greene to W.L.M.K., June 9, 1914.

16. Typewritten Diary, June 1–Dec. 31, 1914, p. 23.

17. *Ibid.*, pp. 24–5.

18. *Ibid.*, pp. 16–17.

19. Violet Markham to W.L.M.K., June 11, 1914; Max King to W.L.M.K., July 21, 1914.

20. Typewritten Diary, June 1–Dec. 31, 1914, pp. 16–17; cf. p. 23. Diary, Dec. 4, 1914.

21. Typewritten Diary, June 1–Dec. 31, 1914, p. 37. Diary, Oct. 10, 1914.

22. Typewritten Diary, June 1–Dec. 31, 1914, pp. 34–6, 46–7.

23. Diary, Nov. 27, 1914.

24. *Ibid.*, Oct. 18, 1914.

25. John D. R., Jr., to W.L.M.K., June 23, 1914. Typewritten Diary, June 1–Dec. 31, 1914, pp. 48–9.

26. Typewritten Diary, Jan. 16, 1915, pp. 118–19.

27. Raymond B. Fosdick, *John D. Rockefeller, Jr., a Portrait* (New York, 1956), p. 421; cf. p. 171.

28. See Alexander MacNeill [Fred A. McGregor], "Is Mackenzie King Responsible for a New Note in Rockefeller Jr.'s Relations with Labour?" Toronto *Star Weekly*, Jan. 29, 1916.

29. Fosdick, *John D. Rockefeller, Jr.*, p. 154.

30. Typewritten Diary, June 1–Dec. 31, 1914, p. 74.

31. Fosdick, *John D. Rockefeller, Jr.*, pp. 148–50.

32. *Ibid.*, p. 149.

33. *Ibid.*, p. 153.

34. W.L.M.K. to Violet Markham, Feb. or March (undated), 1917.

35. Typewritten Diary, March 4, 1915, p. 304.

36. In a conversation with the author.

CHAPTER NINE
THE ROCKEFELLER FOUNDATION

1. Diary, Nov. 30, 1914.
2. Diary, Dec. 5, 1914.
3. *Ibid.*, Dec. 3, 4, 17, 1914. W.L.M.K. to John D. R., Jr., Dec. 13, 1914.
4. Typewritten Diary, Jan. 12, 1915, pp. 89–90.
5. Raymond B. Fosdick, *John D. Rockefeller, Jr., a Portrait* (New York, 1956), pp. 157–9.
6. Typewritten Diary, Jan. 25, 1915, pp. 146–51.
7. *Ibid.*, p. 151.
8. Typewritten Diary, Jan. 25, 1915, pp. 152–3.
9. *Ibid.*, Jan. 27, 1915, p. 169.
10. J. F. Welborn to John D. R., Jr., Aug. 20, 1914.
11. Typewritten Diary, Jan. 16, 1915, pp. 121–2.
12. *Supra*, p. 236.
13. Typewritten Diary, May 8, 1915, p. 641.
14. Fred A. McGregor, Memorandum, June, 1957.
15. *Supra*, p. 238, n.
16. John D. R., Jr., to W.L.M.K., Aug. 9, 1915.
17. W.L.M.K. to John D. R., Jr., Sept. 27, 1949. See also W.L.M.K., *Industry and Humanity* (Boston and New York: Houghton Mifflin, 1918), pp. 435–48; Report of Seth Low Commission in United States, House of Representatives, *Letter from the President . . . transmitting Report of the Colorado Coal Commission of the Labor Difficulties in the Coal Fields of Colorado . . . 1914 and 1915*, Feb. 23, 1916; Fosdick, *John D. Rockefeller, Jr.*, pp. 162–4.
18. Fosdick, *John D. Rockefeller, Jr.*, p. 161.
19. John D. R., Jr. to W.L.M.K., Oct. 7, 1915.
20. *Testimony of W.L.M.K. Given before the U.S. Commission on Industrial Relations* (May 25, 1915), pp. 108–9.
21. Typewritten Diary, Jan. 27, 1915, p. 167.
22. Typewritten Diary, Sept. 8–11, 1915, pp. 716–18.
23. Ben M. Selekman and Mary Van Kleeck, *Employees' Representation in Coal Mines: A Study of the Industrial Representation Plan of the Colorado Fuel and Iron Company* (New York, 1924), pp. 286–7.
24. See also Fosdick, *John D. Rockefeller, Jr.*, pp. 164–5.
25. John D. R., Jr., to W.L.M.K., Oct. 3, 1919.
26. W.L.M.K. to John D. R., Jr., Oct. 6, 1919.
27. Diary, Jan. 25, 1919.
28. For example, *American Economic Review*, Sept., 1919, p. 582; *North American Review*, March, 1919, p. 423; *The Nation*, Aug. 16, 1919, p. 229.
29. W.L.M.K., *Industry and Humanity*, p. 148.
30. Diary, Jan. 9, 1917.
31. Typewritten Diary, May 7, 1918, p. 50.
32. *Industry and Humanity*, pp. 331, 334, 335–6.
33. Bruce Hutchison, *The Incredible Canadian* (Toronto, 1952), pp. 39–40.
34. John D., Jr. to W.L.M.K., Oct. 14, 1918.
35. See Allan Nevins, *John D. Rockefeller: The Heroic Age of American Enterprise* (New York, 1949), vol. II, Part II, p. 661.
36. W.L.M.K. to Violet Markham, May 24, 1918.
37. Typewritten Diary, Nov. 4, 1918, pp. 233–5.

CHAPTER TEN: FIRST WORLD WAR

1. See H. S. Ferns and B. Ostry, *The Age of Mackenzie King: The Rise of the Leader* (London, 1955), pp. 180–1.

2. Diary, July 21, 1917.
3. *Robert Laird Borden: His Memoirs* (Toronto, 1938), II, 995–6.
4. Borden Diary, Aug. 7, 1919.
5. *Can. H. of C. Debates*, Dec. 7, 1944, p. 6901.
6. Newmarket *Express-Herald*, Nov. 23, 1917.
7. *Robert Laird Borden: His Memoirs*, II, 968–9.
8. *Ibid.*, II, p. 969.
9. Borden Papers, Sir Thomas White (Acting Prime Minister) to Sir Robert Borden, Feb. 28, 1919.
10. Borden Papers, W. S. Middlebro to Sir Robert Borden, June 20, 1919; see also Sir Thomas White to Sir Robert Borden, April 5, 1919.
11. Ottawa *Journal-Press*, Jan. 15, 1919.
12. W. L. Morton, *The Progressive Party in Canada* (Toronto, 1950), pp. 8–9, 24–6, 43–5.
13. *Ibid.*, pp. 43, 62–7.
14. *Ibid.*, pp. 23–4, 45–6.
15. *Ibid.*, p. 66.
16. *Can. H. of C. Debates*, June 5, 1919, pp. 3143–7.
17. Borden Papers, Sir Thomas White to Sir Robert Borden, Jan. 14, 1919.
18. Borden Papers, J. D. Reid to Sir Robert Borden, Dec. 18, 1918; Jan. 20, 1919.
19. Borden Papers, J. D. Reid to Sir Robert Borden, Jan. 28, 1919.
20. *Ibid.*
21. Borden Papers, J. D. Reid to Sir Robert Borden, Dec. 1, 1918.
22. Borden Papers, F. H. Keefer to Sir Robert Borden, March 15, 1919.
23. Borden Papers, J. A. Calder to Sir Robert Borden, April 26, 1919.
24. Borden Papers, Sir Robert Borden to Sir Thomas White, May 5, 1919.
25. *Can. H. of C. Debates*, June 11, 1919, pp. 3330, 3337.
26. Morton, *The Progressive Party*, pp. 78–9; *Robert Laird Borden: His Memoirs*, II, 980–1.
27. Borden Papers, N. W. Rowell to Sir Robert Borden, July 4, 1919.
28. *Can. H. of C. Debates*, Feb. 25, March 6, 1919, pp. 27, 234.
29. *Ibid.*, March 14, 18, 1919, pp. 476–82, 570.
30. See p. 259.
31. Ottawa *Journal-Press*, Jan. 15, 1919.

CHAPTER ELEVEN: PARTY LEADER

1. Diary, Jan. 1–14, 1919.
2. *Ibid.*
3. *Ibid.*
4. W.L.M.K. to D. Macdougall King, Feb. 10, 1919.
5. *Ibid.*
6. Diary, Jan. 1–14, 1919.
7. Diary, Jan. 14–21, 1919.
8. Diary, June 5, July 22, 23, Oct. 27, 1917.
9. Diary, Feb. 18–22, 1919.
10. *Ibid.*
11. Diary, March 15–27, 1919. See also W.L.M.K. to D. Macdougall King, March 4, April 2, 13, 1919.
12. W.L.M.K. to John Lewis, May 5, 1919.
13. Diary, Dec. 17, 1918.
14. Sir Charles Fitzpatrick to W.L.M.K., April 8, 1919; April 19, 1919.
15. Diary, June 21, 1919.
16. Sydney Fisher to W.L.M.K., July 25, 1919.

17. W.L.M.K. to A. C. Hardy, August 1, 1919.
18. W.L.M.K. to D. Macdougall King, Aug. 11, 1919.
19. Diary, Aug. 5–9, 1919.
20. H. F. Gadsby in Toronto *Saturday Night*, Aug. 16, 1919.
21. Sir Allen Aylesworth to George A. Aylesworth, Aug. 8, 1919.
22. Diary, Aug. 5–9, 1919.

CHAPTER TWELVE: LEADER OF THE OPPOSITION

1. W.L.M.K. to C. H. Cline, Aug. 18, 1919.
2. W.L.M.K. to A. W. McIntyre, Sept. 22, 1919; W.L.M.K. to N. T. MacMillan, Sept. 25, 1919.
3. W.L.M.K. to W. R. Motherwell, Sept. 23, 1919.
4. *Supra*, p. 294.
5. W. M. Martin to W.L.M.K., Aug. 16, 1919.
6. W. M. Martin to W.L.M.K., Sept. 8, 1919.
7. Borden Papers, Sir George Foster to Sir Robert Borden, Oct. 23, 1919; Sir William Hearst to Sir Robert Borden, Oct. 27, 1919.
8. Diary, Oct. 20, 1919.
9. *Ibid.*, Oct. 27–Nov. 1, 1919.
10. W.L.M.K. to Thomas McMillan, Nov. 26, 1919.
11. W.L.M.K. to C. D. Allin, Nov. 25, 1919.
12. W.L.M.K. to O. D. Skelton, Nov. 28, 1919.
13. See *Industry and Humanity*; *supra*, p. 250.
14. W.L.M.K. to A. C. Hardy, Jan. 9, 1918.
15. W.L.M.K. to Thomas McMillan, Aug. 16, 1919; to G. A. Brodie, Dec. 24, 1919; to James Pearson, Jan. 21, 1920.
16. W.L.M.K. to J. E. Atkinson, Aug. 14, 1919.
17. Charlottetown *Island Patriot*, Oct. 4, 1919.
18. N. W. Rowell to W.L.M.K., Aug. 13, 1919; Diary, Sept. 3, 9, 1919.
19. Sir A. Aylesworth to W.L.M.K., Oct. 21, 1919.
20. C. Murphy to W.L.M.K., Aug. 19, 30, Nov. 10, 1919.
21. J. E. Adamson to W.L.M.K., Sept. 24, 1919.
22. See above, p. 299.
23. J. E. Adamson to W.L.M.K., Sept. 24, 1919.
24. *Canadian Annual Review*, 1920, p. 755. Cf. W. R. Motherwell to W.L.M.K., June 3, 1920.
25. Borden Papers, Frank H. Keefer to Sir Robert Borden, Oct. 22, 1919.
26. W. L. Morton, *The Progressive Party in Canada* (Toronto, 1950), pp. 30, 120.
27. Theodore Roosevelt at Chicago, June 17, 1912.
28. King Papers, J. J. Morrison to V. A. Clarke, Nov. 18, 1919.
29. J. E. Adamson to W.L.M.K., Sept. 24, 1919; Dafoe Papers, J. W. Dafoe to N. W. Rowell, Dec. 13, 1919.
30. A. E. Hill to W.L.M.K., Nov. 18, 1919; A. McLeod to W.L.M.K., Nov. 28, 1919.
31. See R. T. Harding to W.L.M.K., Sept. 5, 1919; W.L.M.K. to R. T. Harding, Sept. 11, 1919.
32. Sir Robert Borden in *Can. H. of C. Debates*, Sept. 2, 1919, pp. 22–3.
33. Diary of Sir George E. Foster, Oct. 28, 1919; Borden Papers, J. D. Reid to Sir Robert Borden, Oct. 23, 1919.
34. *Can. H. of C. Debates*, Sept. 11, 1919, pp. 185–9.
35. Diary, Sept. 8, 9, 1919.
36. W. D. Gregory to W.L.M.K., Sept. 11, 1919.
37. W.L.M.K. to W. D. Gregory, Sept. 13, 1919.

38. Diary of Sir George E. Foster, Nov. 7, 1919.
39. Borden Papers, J. A. Calder to Sir Robert Borden, Oct. 28, 1919.
40. Borden Papers, F. H. Keefer to Sir Robert Borden, Oct. 22, 1919.
41. Borden Papers, F. H. Keefer to Sir Robert Borden, Nov. 12, 1919.
42. *Can. H. of C. Debates*, Nov. 4, 1919, pp. 1711–12.
43. W.L.M.K. to D. Macdougall King, Oct. 8, 1919.
44. *Can. H. of C. Debates*, March 16, 1920, pp. 493–8.
45. *Ibid.*, March 11, 1920, p. 360.
46. *Ibid.*, March 16, 1920, pp. 468–74.
47. Diary, March 16, 1920.
48. *Can. H. of C. Debates*, June 30, 1920, p. 4543.
49. *Ibid.*, May 17, 1920, p. 2458. Cf. *supra*, pp. 217–19.
50. See, for example, *Can. H. of C. Debates*, March 1, 2, 3, 1920, pp. 36, 56, 99.
51. *Can. H. of C. Debates*, April 20, 1920, pp. 1405–16; cf. *supra*, pp. 254–5.
52. W.L.M.K. to D. Macdougall King, April 26, 1920.
53. W.L.M.K. to D. Macdougall King, Dec. 15, 1919.
54. Borden Papers, C. C. Ballantyne to Sir Robert Borden, April 12, 1920.
55. Borden Papers, Martin Burrell to Sir Robert Borden, April 13, 1920.
56. Borden Papers, Sir George Foster to Sir Robert Borden, April 23, 1920.
57. Borden Papers, C. J. Doherty to Sir Robert Borden, April 16, 1920.
58. Diary of Sir George E. Foster, April 25, 1920.
59. *Supra*, pp. 278–82.
60. Borden Papers, Sir George Foster to Sir Robert Borden, March 4, 1920.
61. Borden Papers, Sir George Foster to Sir Robert Borden, Dec. 15, 1919; J. E. Armstrong to Sir Robert Borden, Dec. 16, 1919; Sir Robert Borden to Sir Thomas White, Dec. 17, 1919; Sir Thomas White to Sir Robert Borden, June 22, 1920.
62. Borden Papers, J. A. Calder to Sir Robert Borden, June 27, 1920.
63. W.L.M.K. to D. Macdougall King, Dec. 15, 1919.
64. Diary, July 8, 1920.
65. Borden Papers, Sir Robert Borden to Lord Beaverbrook, July 14, 1920.
66. W.L.M.K. to W. R. Motherwell, May 15, 1920.
67. *Ibid.*
68. Diary, Feb. 28, April 23, Oct. 22, 1920.
69. Dafoe Papers, J. W. Dafoe to the proprietor of the *Manitoba Free Press*, Sir C. Sifton, Nov. 10, 1920.
70. Saskatoon *Daily Star*, Oct. 28, 1920.
71. Diary, Nov. 9, 1920.
72. Dafoe Papers, J. W. Dafoe to Sir C. Sifton, Nov. 10, 1920.
73. A. Haydon to W.L.M.K., April 26, 1920.

CHAPTER THIRTEEN: THE ELECTION OF 1921

1. Toronto *Globe*, Nov. 8, 1921.
2. Montreal *Gazette*, Nov. 15, 1921.
3. Halifax *Morning Chronicle*, Oct. 10, 1921.
4. Rodolphe Lemieux to W.L.M.K., Sept. 7, 1921; W.L.M.K. to Rodolphe Lemieux, Sept. 9, 1921.
5. W.L.M.K. to J. A. Robb, Oct. 8, 1921.
6. W.L.M.K. to D. Macdougall King, Dec. 1, 1921.
7. Diary, Oct. 19, 1921.
8. Rodolphe Lemieux to W.L.M.K., Nov. 30, 1921.
9. S. W. Jacobs to W.L.M.K., Dec. 3, 1921.
10. W.L.M.K. to J. W. Domville, Nov. 14, 1921.
11. W.L.M.K. to Andrew Haydon, Nov. 9, 1921.

12. W.L.M.K. to D. Macdougall King, Nov. 24, 1921; see also W.L.M.K. to D. Macdougall King, Dec. 1, 1921.
13. W.L.M.K. to D. Macdougall King, Dec. 17, 1921.
14. Diary, Dec. 22, 1921.
15. *Can. H. of C. Debates*, March 13, 1922, p. 48.
16. Diary, Dec. 8, 1921.
17. *Ibid.*, Sept. 4, 1921.
18. *Ibid.*, Dec. 10, 1921.
19. A. B. Hudson Papers, Hudson Memorandum, Dec. 12, 1921.
20. F. A. McGregor to A. Haydon, Dec. 15, 1921.
21. E. Lapointe to A. Haydon, Dec. 15, 1921.
22. A. Haydon to F. A. McGregor, Dec. 16, 1921.
23. Sir Clifford Sifton Papers, Sir Clifford Sifton to J. W. Dafoe, Dec. 8, 1921; Sir Clifford Sifton to T. A. Crerar, Dec. 12, 1921.
24. Diary, Dec. 14, 1921.
25. Dafoe Papers, J. W. Dafoe to Sir C. Sifton, Dec. 19, 1921.
26. A. K. Cameron Papers, T. A. Crerar to A. K. Cameron, Dec. 18, 1921.
27. Dafoe Papers, Sir C. Sifton to J. W. Dafoe, Dec. 8, 12, 14, 1921; J. W. Dafoe to Sir C. Sifton, Dec. 19, 1921.
28. Hudson Papers, T. A. Crerar to A. B. Hudson, Dec. 19 (or 20), 1921.
29. Diary, Dec. 21, 1921.
30. Diary, Dec. 21, 1921.
31. Hudson Papers, Hudson Memorandum, Dec. 23, 24.
32. W. L. Morton, *The Progressive Party in Canada* (Toronto, 1950), pp. 136–7.
33. Hudson Papers, Hudson Memorandum, Dec. 23, 1921.
34. Diary, Dec. 23, 1921.
35. The following account is taken from the King Diary, Dec. 24, 1921.
36. Dafoe Papers, J. W. Dafoe to Sir C. Sifton, Dec. 31, 1921.
37. *Farmers' Sun*, Dec. 24, 1921. Quoted by Morton, *The Progressive Party in Canada*, p. 137.
38. Diary, Dec. 24, 28, 1921.
39. Viscountess Byng, *Up the Stream of Time* (Toronto, 1945), p. 171.
40. Diary, Sept. 2, 1921.
41. *Can. Sessional Papers* (1896), 2nd Session, No. 7.
42. W.L.M.K. to Arthur Meighen, Dec. 4, 1921.
43. Montreal *Gazette*, Dec. 29, 1921.
44. Diary, Dec. 29, 1921.

CHAPTER FOURTEEN
FIRST ADMINISTRATION, 1921–2

1. W. L. Morton, *The Progressive Party in Canada* (Toronto, 1950), p. 149.
2. G. Boyer to W.L.M.K., Jan. 14, 1922; D. Buckles to Andrew Haydon, Jan. 27, 1922; G. N. Gordon to W.L.M.K., Feb. 15, 1922.
3. D. Macdougall King to W.L.M.K., Sept. 22, 1921.
4. Fielding Papers, W. S. Fielding to T. A. Crerar, Jan. 11, 1922.
5. Fielding Papers, T. A. Crerar to W. S. Fielding, Jan. 25, 1922.
6. Fielding Papers, W. S. Fielding to T. A. Crerar, Feb. 1, 1922.
7. Diary, Feb. 19, 1922.
8. *Ibid.*, Feb. 25, 1922.
9. *Ibid.*, March 13, 1922.
10. *Can. H. of C. Debates*, March 14, 1922, pp. 51–2.
11. W.L.M.K. to Sir Allen Aylesworth, Jan. 31, 1922.
12. *Can. H. of C. Debates*, March 16, 1922, p. 142.

13. Diary, Feb. 5, 1922.

14. *Ibid.*, Feb. 27, 1922.

15. B. H. Higgins, *Sequence and Timing of Economic Events in the Last War and Postwar Period, 1914–1923* (mimeographed).

16. *Can. H. of C. Debates*, May 23, 1922, pp. 2104–27.

17. *Ibid.*, pp. 2113–14.

18. *Ibid.*, p. 2111.

19. A. McMaster to W.L.M.K., June 8, 1922.

20. W. S. Fielding to W.L.M.K., April 29, 1922.

21. *Supra*, p. 305.

22. *Can. H. of C. Debates*, June 6, 1922, p. 2541.

23. Dafoe Papers, J. W. Dafoe to Sir Clifford Sifton, June 8, 1922.

24. Diary, April 8, 1922.

25. *Can. H. of C. Debates*, May 4, 1922, p. 1436.

26. *Manitoba Free Press*, June 25, 1922.

27. A. E. MacLean to W.L.M.K., June 23, 1922; Dafoe Papers, J. W. Dafoe to Sir Clifford Sifton, July 11, 1922.

28. W.L.M.K. to P. C. Larkin, Jan. 14, 1923.

29. Diary, June 4, 1922.

30. League of Nations, *Records of the Fifth Assembly* (1924), pp. 221–2.

31. *The Memoirs of Herbert Hoover: The Cabinet and the Presidency, 1920–1933* (New York, 1951), p. v.

32. Diary, April 9, 1923.

33. *Can. H. of C. Debates*, Sept. 9, 1919, p. 140.

34. W.L.M.K. to Dr. R. C. James, Oct. 13, 1919.

35. E. J. Phelan to Violet Markham, April 20, 1923(?).

36. Sir Herbert Ames to W.L.M.K., March 27, 1922; Sir R. Cecil to W.L.M.K., April 10, 1923; N. W. Rowell to W.L.M.K., June 13, 1924.

37. W.L.M.K. to A. Williams, Feb. 18, 1920.

38. *Can. H. of C. Debates*, June 15, 1923, pp. 3992–7; *ibid.*, June 26, 1925, pp. 5045–8.

39. See also speeches of A. K. Maclean, Ernest Lapointe, *ibid.*, June 15, 1923, pp. 3997–8; March 14, 1924, p. 317.

40. Sec. of State for Colonies to Gov.-General, Sept. 15, 1922.

41. Sept. 16, 1922; see *The Times*, Sept. 18, 1922.

42. Diary, Sept. 17, 1922.

43. Sec. of State for Colonies to Gov.-General, Sept. 18, 1922.

44. W. L. Griffith to W.L.M.K., Sept. 18, 1922.

45. Diary, Sept. 18, 1922.

46. Gov.-General to Sec. of State for Colonies, Sept. 18, 1922.

47. Sec. of State for Colonies to Gov.-General, Sept. 19, 1922.

48. Gov.-General to Sec. of State for Colonies, Sept. 20, 1922.

49. Sec. of State for Colonies to Gov.-General, Sept. 20, 1922.

50. W.L.M.K. to Sir Campbell Stuart, Sept. 22, 1922.

51. James Watt to W.L.M.K., Sept. 28, 1922; Emerson Campbell to W.L.M.K., Oct. 9, 1922.

52. W.L.M.K. to J. R. Boyle, Oct. 3, 1922.

53. Toronto *Globe*, Sept. 19, 1922, editorial.

54. Toronto *Daily Mail and Empire*, Sept. 23, 1922.

55. Sir J. Pope, *Correspondence of Sir John Macdonald* (Toronto, n.d.), pp. 337–8.

56. See R. MacG. Dawson, *The Development of Dominion Status* (1937), pp. 60–1.

57. J. T. Shaw, *Can. H. of C. Debates*, March 20, 1924, p. 531.

58. Quoted in R. MacG. Dawson, *Constitutional Issues in Canada* (1933), p. 412.

59. *Willison's Monthly*, Nov., 1927, pp. 203–5. Quoted in Dawson, *Constitutional Issues*, p. 413.

60. Arthur Meighen, *Unrevised and Unrepented: Debating Speeches and Others* (Toronto, 1949), p. 319.

61. W.L.M.K. to Violet Markham, Sept. 29, 1922.

62. O. D. Skelton, Memorandum, "Canada and the Control of Foreign Policy" (1923).

63. *Supra*, pp. 334–5.

64. Diary, Sept. 27, 1922.

65. Sec. of State for Colonies to Gov.-General, Oct. 27, 1922.

66. Diary, Oct. 28, 1922.

67. *Ibid.*, Oct. 31, 1922.

68. Sec. of State for Colonies to Gov.-General, Dec. 8, 1922.

69. Gov.-General to Sec. of State for Colonies, Dec. 31, 1922.

70. Sec. of State for Colonies to Gov.-General, Jan. 27, 1923.

71. Sec. of State for Colonies to Gov.-General, Aug. 20, 1923.

72. Gov.-General to Sec. of State for Colonies, Dec. 31, 1922.

73. W.L.M.K. to A. B. Hudson, Aug. 6, 7, 1924.

74. Hudson Papers, A. B. Hudson to O. D. Skelton, Aug. 13, 1924.

75. *Can. H. of C. Debates*, March 24, 1923, pp. 1647–9.

76. *Ibid.*, p. 1649. See Ottawa *Journal*, March 24, 1923, editorial; *New Statesman*, April 28, May 12, 1923.

77. Violet Markham to W.L.M.K., May 6, 1923.

78. G. P. deT. Glazebrook, *Canada at the Paris Peace Conference* (London and Toronto, 1942), pp. 70–1.

79. *Can. H. of C. Debates*, Sept. 2, 4, 9, 11, 1919, pp. 2–240.

80. W. S. Fielding to W.L.M.K., Sept. 15, 1922.

81. W. L. Morton, *The Progressive Party in Canada*, pp. 161–5; Dafoe Papers, J. W. Dafoe to Sir C. Sifton, Nov. 2, 1922.

82. Diary, Nov. 9, 1922.

83. G. W. Kyte to W.L.M.K., June 16, 1922.

CHAPTER FIFTEEN
FIRST ADMINISTRATION, 1923

1. See W. D. Gregory to W.L.M.K., Sept. 20, 1922, Jan. 26, 1923; J. W. Dafoe to Sir C. Sifton, Jan. 29, 1923.

2. W.L.M.K. to W. D. Gregory, Sept. 26, 1922.

3. See J. W. Dafoe to Sir C. Sifton, Jan. 29, 1923.

4. Gov.-General to Sec. of State for Colonies, Feb. 28, 1923.

5. Diary, Feb. 17, 20, 1923.

6. Dafoe Papers, Sir C. Sifton to J. W. Dafoe, March 26, 1923; see also, A. B. Keith in *The Scotsman*, March 16, 1923.

7. W.L.M.K. to Lord Byng, March 1, 1923.

8. Dafoe Papers, J. W. Dafoe to Sir C. Sifton, March 30, 1923.

9. *Can. H. of C. Debates*, June 27, 1923, pp. 4477–8.

10. W. S. Fielding to W.L.M.K., July 31, 1923.

11. Dafoe Papers, J. W. Dafoe to Sir C. Sifton, Feb. 12, 1923.

12. Diary, Oct. 25, 1923.

13. Imperial Conference (1923), Summary of Proceedings; Great Britain, *Parliamentary Papers* (1923), Cmd. 1987, pp. 13–15.

14. Diary, Oct. 25, 1923.

15. *Can. H. of C. Debates*, March 21, 1924, pp. 550–1.

16. Dafoe Papers, J. W. Dafoe to Sir C. Sifton, Jan. 2, 1923; J. W. Dafoe to P. C. Larkin, April 20, 1923.

17. *Can. H. of C. Debates*, May 10, 1922, pp. 1655–6; Feb. 19, 1923, pp. 417, 421–3.

18. W. L. Morton, *The Progressive Party in Canada* (Toronto, 1950), p. 185.

19. G. A. Scott in J. F. Johnston to W.L.M.K., July 1, 1923.

20. C. A. Dunning to W.L.M.K., July 27, 1923.

21. Diary, March 24, 1923.

22. W. C. Kennedy to W.L.M.K., Dec. 30, 1922.

23. Sir L. Gouin to W.L.M.K., March 31, 1923.

24. W.L.M.K. to Sir L. Gouin, April 5, 1923.

25. Diary, April 4, 1923.

26. C. Murphy to W.L.M.K., March 12, 1923; W. R. Motherwell to W.L.M.K., March 29, 1923.

27. R. F. McWilliams to W.L.M.K., April 2, 1923; J. G. Gardiner to W.L.M.K., April 27, 1923.

28. Diary, April 4, 1923.

29. *Ibid.*, April 12, 1923.

30. *Ibid.*, April 21, 1923.

31. *Ibid.*, April 28, 1923.

32. W.L.M.K. to J. G. Inkster, April 5, 1923.

33. W.L.M.K., *Can. H. of C. Debates*, March 9, 1923, p. 988.

34. Diary, April 13, 1923.

35. *Ibid.*, May 8, 1923.

36. *Can. H. of C. Debates*, June 6, 1923, pp. 3567–9.

37. A. Haydon to W.L.M.K., May 5, 1923.

38. See A. K. Cameron Papers, A. K. Cameron to T. A. Crerar, June 26, 1923; T. A. Crerar to A. K. Cameron, June 26, 1923.

39. W.L.M.K. to J. F. Johnston, July 3, 1923.

40. W.L.M.K. to Violet Markham, July 19, 1923.

41. Violet Markham to W.L.M.K., Aug. 8, 1923.

42. W.L.M.K. to A. C. Hardy, Aug. 17, 1923.

43. Dafoe Papers, J. W. Dafoe to Sir C. Sifton, Sept. 12, 1923.

44. Diary, April 8, 1922. See also Dafoe Papers, Sir C. Sifton to J. W. Dafoe, Dec. 14, 1922.

45. Diary, Jan. 21, 1922.

46. *Can. H. of C. Debates*, June 29, 1923, pp. 4638–66.

47. W. D. Gregory to W.L.M.K., Sept. 7, 1923. See also Raoul Dandurand to W.L.M.K., Sept. 12, 1923; Archer Martin to W.L.M.K., Sept. 14, 1923.

48. W. F. MacLean, *Can. H. of C. Debates*, May 29, 1923, p. 3223.

49. Lucien Giguère to F. A. McGregor, Sept. 21, 1923.

50. Lord Beaconsfield to Lord Lorne, Aug. 13, 1879; see W. S. MacNutt, *Days of Lorne* (Fredericton, 1955), p. 230.

51. *The Times*, May 5, 1923.

52. W.L.M.K. to Sir C. Sifton, Aug. 17, 1923.

53. W.L.M.K. to P. C. Larkin, Aug. 17, 1923.

54. Marchioness Curzon of Kedleston, *Reminiscences* (London, 1955), p. 183.

55. K. Feiling, *The Life of Neville Chamberlain* (London, 1946), p. 120.

56. Diary, Sept. 30, Oct. 1, 1923.

57. The King Papers contain the MS of this speech.

58. O. D. Skelton, Memorandum, "Naval Defence," 1923.

59. Diary, Oct. 24, 1923.

60. *Ibid.*, Oct. 22, 1923.

61. *Ibid.*, Oct. 31, 1923.

62. See *supra*, pp. 436–7.
63. Imperial Economic Conference (1923), Record of Proceedings and Documents; Great Britain, *Parliamentary Papers* (1924), Cmd. 2009, p. 37.
64. Imperial Economic Conference (1923), Proceedings, pp. 57–83.
65. *Ibid.*, pp. 174–9.
66. *Ibid.*, p. 184.
67. W.L.M.K. to P. Lloyd-Greame, Oct. 23, 1923; *Can. Sessional Papers* (1924), No. 111.
68. Imperial Economic Conference (1923), Proceedings, pp. 199–243.
69. Diary, Oct. 1, 1923.
70. O. D. Skelton, Memorandum, Oct. 2, 1923.
71. *The Sunday Times*, Dec. 23, 1923.
72. Violet Markham to W.L.M.K., Dec. 18, 1923.
73. Diary, Nov. 5, 1923.
74. *Ibid.*, Nov. 6, 1923.
75. *Ibid.*, Nov. 7, 1923.
76. Lord Curzon to his wife; see Marchioness Curzon of Kedleston, *Reminiscences*, pp. 181–2.
77. J. W. Dafoe, "Did the Imperial Conference Fail?" *Maclean's Magazine*, Jan. 15, 1924.
78. Imperial Conference (1923) Summary of Proceedings, p. 13.
79. Lord Ronaldshay, *The Life of Lord Curzon* (1928), III, 243.
80. L. S. Amery, *My Political Life*, II (London, 1953), 273.

INDEX

INDEX

503

504

Carlyle, Thomas, 309
Carnegie, Andrew, 175, 287, 288, 289
Carnegie, Mrs. Andrew, 287
Carnegie Corporation, and W.L.M.K.,
286, 288, 289, 294
Carruthers, Mrs. James; see Markham,
Violet
Cartwright, Sir Richard J., 180
Carvell, F. B., 266, 343
Casgrain, P. F., 448
Cecil, Lord Robert, 402, 403
Chamberlain, Austen, 161, 457
Chamberlain, Mrs. Austen, 457
Chamberlain, Joseph, 166
Chamberlain, Neville, at Imperial Eco-
nomic Conference (1923), 461, 469,
470, 471, 478
Chanak crisis, 401, 407–16, 419–22,
428, 430, 431, 453, 455, 459, 465,
468, 477
Charity Organization Society, 44
Charlesworth, Hector, 33 n6, 37
Chicago, 53; see also Hull House; Uni-
versity of Chicago
China: immigration from, 146, 192,
193–4, 196–7; opium traffic, 195;
Canadian representation in, 195
Christie, Loring C., 454
Churchill, Winston, 99, 149, 161–2;
Chanak crisis, 409–10, 412, 415
Cincinnati, W.L.M.K. speaks at, 137
Clark, Michael, 266, 283
Clark, William, 30
Clemenceau, Georges, 462
Cline, C. H., 313 n1
Coats, R. H., 37, 102, 133, 455
Cohoe, W. P., 77
Colonial Advocate, 4
Colorado Coal Commission; see Seth
Low Commission
Colorado Fuel and Iron Company, 336;
strike against (1913) and aftermath,
227–8, 229, 232–3, 236, 238–48
Colorado Plan; see Rockefeller Plan of
Industrial Representation
Combines Investigation Act (Canada),
(1910) 204–6, 448–9; (1923) 206,
448–9
Commission on Industrial Relations
(U.S.) (Walsh Commission), 140,
236–8, 241, 244, 251
Conciliation Act (Canada) (1900),
97–8, 104, 105–6, 108, 109;
W.L.M.K.'s work under, 106–12,
114–15, 118–19, 132–3
Connor, J. W., 12

Conservative party, federal: naval policy
(1909), 216; reciprocity, 219–20;
post-1919 role, 273, 276, 282, 316,
339, 343, 349, 353 (see also Union
Government); 1921 election, 356–7;
position in 1921 House, 381, 385, 388;
tariff, 392, 469; freight rates, 396;
Chanak crisis, 414–15; League of Nations, 428; House activities (1923),
440, 443, 448; party strength (1923),
451
Conservative party, provincial: Ont.,
316, 324, 451; P.E.I., 451
Consolidation Coal Company, 254
Constantinople, 408
Consumers' League of Massachusetts, 70,
78
Copp, A. B.: Cabinet of 1921, 363, 373;
tariff, 443
Cosgrave, W. T., 461
Coulter, R. M., 99, 102, 104
Crerar, T. A., 270, 451 n38; Union
Government, 264, 266, 280, 281, 282,
343; cross benches, 281, 321, 327;
Progressive House leader (1920–1),
332–3, 338, 346–7; 1921 election,
351, 354, 356; Cabinet of 1921, 361,
362–71; Progressive leader (1921–2),
378, 383–4, 386–7, 393, 398, 400–1,
413, 414, 428–9; Cabinet post (1923),
449–50
Crewe, R. O. A. Crewe-Milnes, 1st Mar-
quess of, 177 n18, 193 n48
Cromer, E. Baring, 1st Earl, 161
Cross, Charles W., 37, 51
Crow's Nest Pass Agreement, 394–7, 447
Cummings, Edward, 73
Cunningham, William, 74, 76, 88, 93
Currie, Sir Arthur, 296, 363
Curtis, Smith, 106
Curzon, G. N., 1st Marquis Curzon of
Kedleston: Imperial Peace Cabinet,
408; Chanak crisis, 415; Lausanne
Conference, 423, 425; Imperial Con-
ference (1923), 459, 460, 463–5,
474–8, 480
Curzon, Marchioness, of Kedleston, 460
n54, 477 n76, 480
Customs Tariff Act (Canada), 204

DAFOE, J. W., 353, 364 n23, 370, 435
n6, 454 n44; Liberal Unionists, 275,
327 n29; Farmers' movement, 278,
347, 393 n23, 396 n27, 428 n81,
439; W.L.M.K. as leader, 345, 445,
453; Cabinet, (1921) 367, 371,

505

Date Due